BUSINESS-TO-BUSINESS MARKETING: ANALYSIS AND PRACTICE

Business-to-Business Marketing: Analysis and Practice

Robert P. Vitale

San Jose State University

Joseph Giglierano

San Jose State University

Waldemar Pfoertsch

China Europe International Business School

Prentice Hall

Boston   Columbus   Indianapolis   New York   San Francisco   Upper Saddle River
Amsterdam   Cape Town   Dubai   London   Madrid   Milan   Munich   Paris   Montreal   Toronto
Delhi   Mexico City   Sao Paulo   Sydney   Hong Kong   Seoul   Singapore   Taipei   Tokyo

Editorial Director: Sally Yagan
Editor-in-Chief: Eric Svendsen
Acquisitions Editor: Melissa Sabella
Editorial Project Manager: Kierra Bloom
Editorial Assistant: Karin Williams
Director of Marketing: Patrice Jones
Marketing Manager: Anne Fahlgren
Marketing Assistant: Melinda Jensen
Senior Managing Editor: Judy Leale

Production Manager: Meghan DeMaio
Creative Director: Jayne Conte
Art Director: Suzanne Behnke
Cover Art: Shutterstock
Full-Service Project Management/Composition:
   Hemalatha/Integra Software Services, Ltd.
Printer/Binder: Edwards Brothers
Cover Printer: Lehigh-Phoenix Color
Text Font: 10/12 Times

Credits and acknowledgments borrowed from other sources and reproduced, with permission, in this textbook appear on appropriate page within text.

Library of Congress Cataloging-in-Publication Data
Vitale, Robert P.
   Business-to-Business Marketing : Analysis and Practice / Robert Vitale, Joseph Giglierano, Waldemar Pfoertsch.
      p. cm.
   Includes bibliographical references and index.
   ISBN-13: 978-0-13-605828-1
   ISBN-10: 0-13-605828-0
   1. Industrial marketing.   I. Giglierano, Joseph J.   II. Pfoertsch, Waldemar.   III. Title.
HF5415.1263.V582 2011
658.8'04—dc22

                                          2010004856

10 9 8 7 6 5 4 3 2 1

Prentice Hall
is an imprint of

www.pearsonhighered.com

ISBN 10:   0-13-605828-0
ISBN 13: 978-0-13-605828-1

To our families,
who have tolerated this effort

BRIEF CONTENTS

CONTENTS

Cases

FOREWORD

In recent years, the importance of marketing in the business-to-business sector has grown. Many companies operate now in a more volatile and changing market and have to deal with fierce competition in an increasingly global market. To remain viable and competitive, business-to-business marketers are increasingly adopting marketing strategies that go beyond previous "price and ship" tactics.

Business-to-Business Marketing: Analysis and Practice provides a learning platform for the next generation of managers in industrial companies. In this practitioner oriented and international B2B marketing textbook, managers can find concepts and examples that help to take a more analytical and disciplined approach to sales and marketing of industrial goods.

While all companies claim to deliver superior value, companies particularly serving business-to-business (B2B) markets must be able to prove such claims. In the increasingly global world, it is more important than ever to be able to demonstrate in an objective and data-driven fashion that products, platforms, systems, and services will yield economic benefit to customers, collaborators, and stakeholders. Companies can deliver this value creation either by reducing costs or by providing broad-based, solution-oriented offerings. Industrial conglomerates, as well as small and medium-sized B2B companies, are constantly being challenged, and it is now not enough to offer "the most scalable, reliable, secure solution available today."

Many companies, from heavy construction equipment to microprocessor chips, have moved from technology-assisted selling concepts to marketing concepts offering proven value to their customers and business partners. The stakes are high and the need for professional knowledge and advice is predominant. The structured approach and up-to-date case studies of *Business-to-Business Marketing: Analysis and Practice* will fulfill the need for more in-depth understanding of marketing in the twenty-first century. This book explains situations, effects, and trends and also presents concepts, frameworks, and models in a very comprehensive way. It offers, for students and professionals alike, an easy way of learning what is needed to be marketers in the current B2B environment.

The art and science of marketing has evolved well beyond early concepts. The differences between business-to-business markets and consumer markets have grown such that many generalizations of one market are not applicable to the other. Yet, the basic precepts, the product life cycle, the marketing mix and the promotion mix, to name a few, still apply. Concepts of customer value, market ownership, and total offering management add new dimensions to business-to-business marketing. When these ideas are integrated and combined, they provide a richness and depth to market understanding. However, this integration has not always come about in a way that is manageable for students. This textbook, *Business-to-Business Marketing*, starts with a basic review of concepts and then differentiates the differences between business and consumer markets. In a down-to-earth fashion, these basics are then integrated in a way that each supports the other, providing an anchor for the student.

The combined experiences of the authors, Vitale, Giglierano, and Pfoertsch, represent expertise from academics, consulting, public agencies, and large and small industries, as both customers and marketers. They deliver an approach that is understandable yet comprehensive, logical yet enlightening, to both students and professionals of business-to-business marketing. Real companies in real situations, combined with believable academic exercises, demonstrate the experience and depth of the authors. Their effort provides an opportunity to understand the complexities of these markets where others have been vague and somewhat arcane. This book gets to the heart of business-to-business marketing—it's a good read for students with just the right nurturing of the subject while it is also a good read for professionals, with just the right touch of insight to provide "Aha!" for both groups.

In my recent books about marketing principles and the marketing management books, examination of B2B has claimed an increasingly important position beyond the customary one chapter of B2B selling and channels. This book covers all subjects and areas of the industrial business environment and thus is a comprehensive B2B marketing textbook. I wish the authors and the readers much success.

Evanston, July 2009

Philip Kotler
S.C. Johnson & Son Professor of International Marketing
Kellogg School of Management
Northwestern University

PREFACE

When we began our first business-to-business book, *Business to Business Marketing: Analysis and Practice in a Dynamic Environment*, the "parent" edition of this textbook, we felt that our perspectives as business-to-business practitioners, consultants, and academics over many years and with different industries, from the high-tech firms of Silicon Valley to the "old economy" of the automotive industry, created a foundation to develop a text that reflected our experiences while also being understandable to students whose preparation might be limited to an introductory course in marketing (and of course experience as consumers!). We emphasized the dynamic realities of the marketplace while reinforcing the most important principles that one will need to be effective, competent professionals in the real world. Based on feedback from many adopters around the world, we succeeded in many ways. Additionally, our continuing effort to improve both our research in the field and through classroom testing of concepts led us to understand the areas where we could make improvements.

One of the additions to this textbook is Waldemar Pfoertsch, originally from Pforzheim University in Germany, now at CEIBS Shanghai (China Europe International Business School). Waldemar, as an international adopter of our book, provided heartening feedback and critical suggestions. Waldemar was so enthusiastic about our efforts that he came to California to meet with us. Waldemar's book with Philip Kotler, *B2B Brand Management*, was new, and his work in brand management was an excellent verification of the brand concepts we espoused. His contributions include the new Chapter 13, as well as classroom-tested case studies.

Several principles that guided the development of our previous book continue here. Porter's Value Chain provides the underpinning for the Marketing Concept, and its application and implementation. The Product Life Cycle and Moore's Technology Adoption Life Cycle form the basis for considering the dynamics of market evolution. Hamel and Prahalad's ideas on business strategy and Dickson's thoughts on competitive market behavior form the basis for our discussion of marketing strategy formulation. The Societal Marketing Concept is a key element of ethical marketing behavior. In each of these areas, we build on common threads that hold the whole together.

Each chapter benefits from observations made in real-world situations. We rely again on our academic and consulting research to contribute ideas and examples in each chapter as well. Each chapter benefits from the multiple dialogues we have conducted with executives and managers since we began work on this project. Of particular note is the addition of Chapter 11, focused on Business Development. Forecasting has been shifted from Chapter 6 into this new Chapter 11, acknowledging its importance to business development efforts and based on the feedback that Chapter 6 in our first effort was overcrowded.

Other changes in response to feedback include the expansion of Chapters 4 and 16 (originally Chapter 14). During the review of our original edition, adopters had mixed opinions about the need for a separate chapter on the legal environment and our business ethics approach as well. We believe these to be critical issues too often overlooked in business marketing and included the chapters anyway. Preliminary reviews for this book demonstrated significantly increased interest in these topics. In response, a discussion of Sarbanes–Oxley and its global offspring and the Foreign Corrupt Practices Act have been added. Licensing, cross-licensing, and joint ventures, which are often key to the concept of Value Networks, are also discussed. Chapter 16, "Business Ethics and Crisis Management," gives increased coverage of crisis management and examples of ethical decision making in business. Ironically, the opening vignette of the chapter in the previous book concerned the recommendations that resulted from the investigation of the crash of TWA 800. We pointed to the incomplete implementation of the recommendations provided by the investigating task force in 2001. Now, TWA 800 is back as the opening vignette for this chapter, as seven years after the original task force recommendation, the Department of Transportation has adopted more stringent rules (see the vignette for details!).

We continue our departure from traditional approaches to textbooks. Our experience has shown us that a person's assumptions about business-to-business marketing are often based on his or her familiarity with consumer marketing. Throughout the text we have compared and contrasted between the two fields to bring out their most important differences and to give weight to the distinguishing characteristics of business-to-business principles and practices. Whenever possible, we have attempted to use examples from corporations and organizations that are familiar. A notable example of this occurs in the discussion of "Integrated versus Networked Supply" in Chapter 1. The changing environment of outsourcing versus vertical integration in the automotive industry provides an excellent groundwork to demonstrate to students that while the consumer brand is on the outside, many corporations' expertise contribute to the total offering. It may surprise many students to learn that the auto entertainment system in Ford, Honda, and BMW might all be manufactured by the same company—but with different consumer identities.

Planning, strategy design, and decision making are important skills that are common to all current areas of business; we have continued to introduce the basics while quickly showing real-world connections. A practical and real-world approach is enlivened through interesting scenarios and sidebars and emphasizes changes brought about by technology, entrepreneurship, relationships, and globalization.

Robert P. Vitale
San Jose State University

Joseph Giglierano
San Jose State University

Waldemar Pfoertsch
China Europe International Business School

ACKNOWLEDGMENTS

We would like to thank the following reviewers for their helpful feedback during the development of this book:

Peter Reday, *Youngstown State University*

Robert Green, *Lynn University*

Jonathan Hibbard, *Boston University*

Gary Bridi, *Bloomsburg University*

Kellie McGilvray, *Tiffin University*

Chickery Kasouf, *Worcester Polytechnic Institute*

D. Eric Boyd, *James Madison University*

In addition, the following individuals remain good friends, have contributed valuable feedback, and serve as important sounding boards for our thoughts: Buford Barr, Connie Zumhagen, Peter Dickson, Mike Adams, Chuck Erickson, Jeff Kallis, Susan Bayerd, and Allison Giglierano.

BUSINESS-TO-BUSINESS MARKETING: ANALYSIS AND PRACTICE

Chapter *1*

Introduction to Business-to-Business Marketing

OVERVIEW

In this chapter, we will introduce you to business-to-business marketing, provide you with an overview of the differences and similarities between business-to-business and consumer marketing, and, finally, provide you with an approach for studying this field that is built around the concept of value for customers. Value includes both customer benefits and customer costs incurred in realizing these benefits. We close the chapter by introducing several trends currently changing the face of business-to-business marketing. These trends, which are important for you to keep in mind as you progress throughout the book, raise the question of whether we need to change our ideas about what works in business-to-business marketing.

In the opening example, two transportation companies—UPS and FedEx—take their partnerships with office services companies to a new competitive level. UPS's acquisition of Mail Boxes Etc. and FedEx's acquisition of Kinko's, Inc., created new bundles of services creating differentiated value for their small business clients. In so doing, they illustrate several of the core concepts that will be examined in later chapters.

Example: FedEx Kinko's versus The UPS Stores[1]

In 2001, United Parcel Service (UPS) bought the company Mail Boxes Etc. This gave UPS much greater presence in urban areas, neighborhoods, and shopping districts. While much of the business UPS acquired was retail (consumers), visibility and services were also extended to small businesses. Offered services went beyond shipping: the former Mail Boxes Etc. stores also gave small businesses mail drop locations and "suite" business addresses, which lent credibility to their images. The big increase in value came from offering shipping locations closer to the locations of many more small businesses since the old UPS locations were typically in industrial or commercial areas.

Mail Boxes Etc. was a franchise operation with over 4,000 franchised locations. In the acquisition, UPS became the owner of the central Mail Boxes franchisor operation. Shortly after the acquisition, UPS worked with a small number of franchisees to test some operational changes and new alternatives for rebranding the stores. The results favored renaming the chain as The UPS Store.

In 2003, the Mail Boxes Etc. franchisees were offered the chance to sign new franchise contracts that adopted the new name and some changed operating policies, which included new pricing 20 percent below the existing Mail Boxes price schedule. The franchisees who participated in the test became advocates for the changes because they had seen the financial impacts to their own operations—in some cases almost double the sales, with an increase in profitability. Over 90 percent of the franchisees switched over. Those who held out will operate under the old Mail Boxes Etc. name until their franchise agreements expire. A lawsuit was filed by some of the franchisees.[2] These franchisees principally have locations in high cost areas and they do not believe the new pricing will allow them to remain profitable. This suit is still pending.

Three years after the UPS acquisition of Mail Boxes Etc., FedEx responded to this competitive move by acquiring Kinko's, Inc., Unlike UPS, FedEx acquired all 1,200 stores outright, thus FedEx had more control of the stores and their operations (this also cost FedEx a great deal more—FedEx paid $2.2 billion, while UPS paid only $190 million for Mail Boxes Etc.). FedEx also tested new names for the Kinko's stores. They settled on the new name FedEx Kinko's.

The FedEx Kinko's stores are targeted toward small businesses that need office and graphics services combined with shipping. This move was considered by analysts to be a "leapfrog" competitive move, offering more service and value than UPS's earlier move with Mail Boxes Etc. Initially, UPS Stores had a sizable advantage simply in the number of locations they offered. However, even with fewer stores, FedEx Kinko's tends to offer more in the way of copying, printing, and graphics—UPS Stores have added similar services, but FedEx Kinko's has more capability on-site. Plus, these services were Kinko's bread-and-butter. FedEx saw Kinko's as an attractive purchase target in part because Kinko's was good at what it did!

By the fall of 2004, FedEx Kinko's, through FedEx's partnership with Microsoft, launched a new service that gave it even more of a service edge.[3] FedEx Kinko's launched its File, Print FedEx Kinko's (FPFK) service, in which a customer can send FedEx Kinko's a document via the Internet. FedEx Kinko's will print it, copy it, bind it, and do whatever else to it the client requests. The client can then pick up the order at any specified FedEx Kinko's location or have it shipped elsewhere.

Both companies are offering convenience to small businesses. But they offer different kinds of convenience. Both will have to innovate to stay in the race. And the competition is not just between the two of them—Staples, Inc., upgraded its in-store copying/printing services.[4] Staples, Inc., of course, offers office supplies, so this represents a third value bundle now in the competitive mix, and DHL acquired the ground stations of Airborne Express to get a nationwide access points.

LEARNING OBJECTIVES

By reading this chapter, you will

- Remember the basic marketing principles.
- Gain an appreciation for the main differences between consumer marketing and business-to-business marketing.
- Understand the marketing concept and its implications for business-to-business marketing.
- Understand the meaning of value.
- Gain a sense of how the value chain is structured and how it is related to the concept of a supply chain.
- Gain an understanding of the implications of the value chain for business-to-business marketing.
- Obtain a sense of the changing nature of the business environment.

INTRODUCTION

Business markets present different types of challenges and opportunities than those presented by consumer markets. The concepts of *relationships*, *value*, and *buyer decision making* function in very different ways than would be expected in consumer markets. The example of the acquisitions of Mail Boxes Etc. and Kinko's, Inc., by UPS and FedEx, respectively, illustrates all of these and more. First, FedEx's combination of shipping with copying and other office and graphics services creates a different kind of value for small businesses than does the combination of UPS and Mail Boxes Etc. Both combinations of services have the potential to create lasting relationships with their customers. In this case, the customers will engage in extended decision making that continues well after the initial usage of the service. Both FedEx Kinko's and The UPS Stores must understand this and adapt their post-sale service to focus on maintaining customer satisfaction and reselling the service.

Entrepreneurial marketing is a major emphasis of this text. Entrepreneurial marketing can be practiced by established companies as well as by startups. It involves innovation, acting proactively, and controlled risk taking.[5] In the opening vignette, both UPS and FedEx have marketed entrepreneurially. UPS initially saw an opportunity by offering a combination of services, with Mail Boxes Etc., aimed at a segment of small businesses. FedEx saw a somewhat

Entrepreneurial marketing is conducting marketing in a way that involves innovation, acting proactively, and taking calculated risks.

different opportunity, a different segment, and addressed it with a different offering. In both cases, the company had to interpret an existing market condition and see needs that were not fully addressed. They proactively addressed the market opportunities they thought were there, but they took risks because they did not know for certain whether their interpretations of the market were correct. What should the competitors do to deal with this new situation and create a high chance of turning it into a profitable business activity? As an organization, how should each modify its behavior to suit these new and different market opportunities? This chapter sets the stage for answering these questions.

To fully appreciate the differences and similarities between business-to-business and consumer marketing we need an understanding of marketing basics and how these basics apply in business-to-business marketing. For those of you who have already taken a marketing principles course, this will be a review of what you have already learned. These basic marketing concepts presented in a business-to-business context will ensure that everyone reading this book starts with approximately the same background—a level playing field.

MARKETING FUNDAMENTALS IN BUSINESS-TO-BUSINESS MARKETS

To see how marketing principles apply in business-to-business markets, an understanding of what business-to-business markets are and how marketing principles apply in business markets is required. These definitions and the context in which they are presented are part of the foundations that should be kept in mind throughout the following chapters. **Business markets consist of** all organizations that purchase goods and services to use in the creation of their own goods and services. Their own goods and services are then offered to their customers. Notice that this does not include transactions for resale. These are considered to be within the purview of managing transactions within channels. Generally, business markets consist of fewer but larger customers than consumer markets and are involved in purchases of significantly large value having complex economic, technical, and financial considerations.

Business marketing, then, is the process of matching and combining the capabilities of the supplier with the desired outcomes of the business customer. Business marketing is the creation of value for business customers. The business marketer must understand that business customers create value for their own customers. Thus the business marketer must define the "value" he provides in terms of helping the customer provide value for the "customer's customer." The companies in the entire chain, from those that accumulate and process basic raw materials through those that modify, refine, manufacture, and assemble final consumer products, do not rely only on the next customer in the chain for their business. Each participant in the chain must recognize that the value added by its operations has a major impact on its customers' ability to satisfy the needs of all downstream participants throughout the chain to the final consumer. The many facets of the business buying decision process and the needs of many stakeholders in the buying organization create a behavioral situation usually far more complex than in the consumer market.

Many students of marketing face difficulties in the study of business-to-business marketing because they come into it from their existing viewpoint as consumers. Students, as do most consumers, often feel inundated by promotional messages from what seems to be an unlimited number of sources. The volume of these messages can lead consumers to believe that these messages are all there is to the entire marketing effort. In a business marketing course, students can begin the process of separating their marketing analysis from their perspectives as consumers. This is not a suggestion, however, that students abandon their understanding of consumer behavior. Quite the contrary—decision makers in business-to-business marketing situations often behave similarly to consumers in buying situations, albeit with different and often more complex motivations.

The Marketing Mix

Recall the **four Ps** of the marketing mix: product, price, place, and promotion. These are still the four Ps of marketing whether operating in a consumer or a business market. There are, however, some differences that require explanation.

PRODUCT   In general marketing theory, the term *product* refers to a core product (or service) that can be augmented by additional features and options that will appeal to different buyers. In a consumer product such as a new car, buyers can add many options to the core vehicle, such as a premium sound system or a sports suspension package. Beyond those options made available by the vehicle manufacturer, the dealer may provide options to assist in the ownership process, such as financing, acceptance of a trade-in, or insurance. Taken together, these options, those that modify the performance of the vehicle and those that facilitate purchase and ownership, create the augmented product. Buyers have the choice to customize—to design—their vehicle to their own tastes and needs.

In contrast, consider the product when an automobile company, such as General Motors (GM), markets a fleet of new cars to a car rental company, such as Avis Rent-a-car. The core product is still the cars, but now the quantity and assortment of many different models in the product line become important as well. The magnitude of the assortment and quantity available are major concerns for Avis. An arrangement by which GM creates a no-hassle payment plan is also desirable. In addition, Avis prefers a schedule of deliveries over a manageable period of time, with an assortment that will provide its customers with several choices. Avis will also have a need for regular and routine spare parts delivery and training for its service personnel. Avis may also have previously rented cars it wishes to dispose of—a trade-in deal with GM would be an attractive part of the offer. Avis isn't buying just cars; it is interested in a total value package from GM that includes

- Assorted cars, in large quantities
- Financing terms
- Convenient schedule of deliveries
- Routine and reliable source for parts
- Training for Avis service personnel
- Disposal of old models.

From the viewpoint of GM, each of the above attributes is a necessary part of "the product" to be competitive in the car rental market. Reluctance on the part of GM to provide all elements of value sought by Avis would leave an opening for another car manufacturer to capture the business. In this text, we define the augmented business-to-business product as the **total offering** that will provide a complete solution to the buyer's needs. This may encompass features such as financing terms and delivery options or, based on the buyer's preference, be simply the core product. The desirability of the augmented portions of the offering will vary among different business-to-business buying organizations, requiring flexibility of the marketer and the marketing organization.[6]

Total offering is the offering that provides a complete solution to the buyer's needs. This may include financing, delivery, service, or based on the buyer's preference, only the core product.

There are often fundamental differences between core product characteristics in business-to-business and consumer markets. Because business-to-business products are often incorporated into the buying organization's offering to its own customers, the products are often defined and developed to specifically match the buying organization's requirements. Whether the supplier regards this as a minor modification to an existing offering to meet a particular customer requirement or a major new offering development, the result is an offering created by a partnership between the buying organization and the marketing organization. This process produces a product that is specific to the buying organization's needs while maximizing the value creation capabilities of the marketer. Because the specifically tailored product is often more technical in nature, it is often defined by a written specification whose purpose is to maintain a given level of performance. The outcome is not just a component manufactured in quantity for volume sales to a business customer, but a total offering that matches the capabilities of the supplier with the needs of the buyer, facilitated by the relationship between the two organizations.

PRICE   As in any transaction, price is the mutually agreed-upon amount (of money or something else of worth) that satisfies both sides in the exchange. Both the buyer and the seller realize an increase in the value they hold as a result of the transaction. Price, the measure of value exchanged, is determined by the market—not by the costs associated with the creation of the offering. In business-to-business markets, price determination can be the final step in a complex design, development, and negotiation, particularly when the product is the result of a collaborative effort. For less complex or standardized products, price may be the result of a competitive bidding process. Only for the most generic of products, or when sold in small quantities through industrial distribution, will price in business-to-business markets be based on a "list" price as in consumer markets.

Continuing with the automotive example, the price for the new car is a fixed price based on the manufacturer's suggested retail price (MSRP). Each of the options has a list price as well, and several options may be bundled together and priced as a single package. Automobiles are relatively unique as consumer products in that price negotiation is acceptable and expected. Most consumers—in the United States, at least—do not expect to negotiate on price for most other products that they buy.

Prices for consumers are often fixed and discounted, with some financing provided for high-cost purchases. Pricing for business customers often varies from fixed price, includes far more special discounts and allowances, and involves complex financing. Business-to-business pricing may also involve forms other than a one-time price payment or fee, such as commissions or profit sharing. Pricing internationally may also be more complex, particularly if the customer company is multinational.

PLACE   In consumer markets, place is about getting the product to the customer in the right **form** (size package, quantity, etc.) at a useful **time** (availability of extended retail hours, short waiting periods for special orders, etc.) with minimum inconvenience associated with the **place** of purchase, and with **possession** ease (transfer of ownership, such as cash, credit, acceptance of personal checks). Form, time, place, and possession comprise the four types of economic utility and are a major part of the value delivered to the customer. In consumer markets, providing **economic utility** often appears as satisfaction of consumer preferences in locational convenience, required purchase quantities/sizes, temporal convenience, and acquisition convenience. In the automobile example, the car company provides economic utility to consumers by locating dealerships near population centers or heavily trafficked shopping routes (usually clustered with other dealers—why is this?). The dealerships are set up to routinely process single car purchases in which the car is available immediately or can be quickly ordered. All the activities that facilitate purchasing the car (credit check, financing, registration, etc.) make it possible for the buyer to start the transaction and drive off with the car in a few hours.

Economic utility is a necessary (though not sufficient), pivotal part of the concept of *value* in business-to-business markets which often takes on the form of supply chain management, inventory services, and material resource planning. Businesses design their marketing channels to provide maximum value to their customers while minimizing costs associated with the creation of economic utility. This is true for both consumer and business-to-business channels. The major differences lie in the length and concentration of the channel. The quantities purchased in business-to-business marketing are substantially larger than consumer purchases with timing of delivery a critical factor, leading to direct relationships between manufacturer and customer and eliminating channel intermediaries.

Supply chain management is the planning, coordination, and delivery of the place part of the marketing mix. Overall, supply chain management works to deliver the economic utility of form, time, place, and possession as a minimized cost and at a maximized value—value as determined by the customer. This effort usually involves many companies at different stages of the supply chain.

In the example of GM marketing to Avis to add to its fleet, the car manufacturer offers cars in appropriate quantities and assortment in the appropriate time interval. The right cars are shipped to the right locations, perhaps throughout the nation. Spare parts are made available in appropriate quantities as well. They also are shipped to the right locations at the right times. This is no easy accomplishment when car companies have production schedules to match with delivery schedules and the assembly plants are not all located near the myriad of rental company outlets. The process of coordinating the flow of value and components that make up the total offering—for example, from the iron ore mine through the steel fabricators, from the rubber tree plantation through the installation of tires on the vehicles—is referred to as **supply chain management**. This effort involves many companies, operating as both buyers and sellers, creating value that is ultimately acceptable in the eyes of the consumer. Seldom is a company fully vertically integrated to own and manage the entire supply chain.

PROMOTION   Business-to-business marketing places different emphasis on the parts of the promotion mix (advertising, sales promotion, personal selling, and public relations) than is commonly found in consumer marketing. Consumers are inundated with advertising as manufacturers attempt to create awareness of and interest in their products. In consumer markets, advertising plays the largest role in the promotion mix.

In business-to-business markets, the capabilities of advertising can seldom be leveraged. Generally, we know advertising as a monologue—a one-way communication.[7] Feedback from the customer is not always encouraged and is not automatic. Advertisers must make a separate and purposeful effort to know how their customers have responded to promotion campaigns (or wait for sales results). In the new car example, the carmaker advertises heavily in television, radio, print, and the Internet to build brand awareness and beliefs. Dealers also advertise in television, radio, and newspapers to provide information and incentives to buy (sales promotion). Dealerships have salespeople who work with consumers to help them through the buying process. The relationship formed is usually a temporary one, focused on completing the transaction and getting the consumer happily through the first few weeks after acquiring the new car.

In business-to-business markets, personal selling is the most used and effective type of promotion. Personal selling, as a dialogue, allows rapid and accurate feedback to the marketer. As noted earlier, products in business-to-business marketing are often the result of collaboration between the supplier and the customer. This collaboration requires the building of relationships between individuals in their respective organizations, necessitating a strong personal selling (dialogue) effort. The carmaker in the example (GM) may have a sales team that manages the account with the car rental company (Avis). The efforts of the sales team focus on providing information and personal service to the executives and employees of the car rental company involved in purchasing, managing, and maintaining the rental car fleet.

Two of the major differences, then, between consumer and business-to-business promotion are the closeness and the duration of the relationship. In business-to-business marketing the relationship is often closer and longer lasting than in consumer marketing, with the individuals having developed personal ties. For many consumer products, contact between the consumer and the marketer is confined to advertising, the relatively short-lived transaction period, and maybe a consumer response to a follow-up survey.

Marketing Philosophy and Culture

In the preceding section, we have discussed the traditional four Ps of the marketing mix, highlighting the differences between the four Ps in consumer marketing and the four Ps in business-to-business marketing. Configuration of the four Ps, whether in consumer marketing or business-to-business marketing, should be driven by the **marketing concept**.

The marketing concept has been the philosophy at the forefront in the field of marketing over the last fifty years. It says that, to be successful, a company should understand customers' needs, meet those needs with a coordinated set of activities, and do so in a way that meets organizational goals.[8] A firm that operates under the culture of the marketing concept focuses all of its efforts and resources toward satisfying the needs of its customers. This is distinctly different from organizations that operate in a production, sales, or marketing department culture.[9] In each of these cultures, marketing is a distinct yet dependent part of the organization, often viewed as an expense rather than as a generator of margin.

*The **marketing concept** states that, to be successful, the firm should be contextually market sensitive, understand customer needs, meet those needs in a coordinated way that provides value to the customer, and do so in a way that meets organizational goals. A firm that is (or claims to be) a market-driven/customer-driven firm is applying the marketing concept, recognizing that every employee of the firm contributes to the marketing effort.*

The marketing concept implies that marketing is the driving force in the organization, defining the roles of other functions in meeting the needs of customers.[10]

FURTHER DIFFERENCES BETWEEN BUSINESS MARKETING AND CONSUMER MARKETING

Exhibit 1-1 summarizes several potential differences between business marketing and consumer marketing. Depending on specific circumstances, all these factors may or may not be present in any given business situation. While all of these differences are discussed in the following chapters, a few are crucial for understanding the context of business-to-business marketing and are highlighted in the immediate discussion. The first is the nature of demand; of particular note is the difference between **consumer demand** and **derived demand**.

Consumer demand is the quantity of goods or services desired to be bought, given market conditions (usually expressed as a function of market price).

Derived demand is the demand experienced by the chain of suppliers and producers that contribute to the creation of a total offering. Without initial consumer demand, there will not be any demand on the chain of suppliers.

Supply chain is the chain of entities and activities that results in products provided to end-users. It starts with raw materials and traces the flow of materials and sub-assemblies through suppliers, manufacturers, and channel inter-mediaries to the final customer. In the eyes of most organizations, supply chains are stable, yet flexible enough to meet varying market demands. (Compare this concept to the value network, introduced in a later chapter.)

Derived Demand and Business-to-Business Supply Chains

The demand for nylon fibers by consumers does not exist. Nylon is, however, demanded to spin yarn because yarn is demanded to weave fabric because fabric is demanded to make clothes; all of these demands are *derived demands*—a result of the ultimate *consumer demand* for nylon clothing items. Demand in business markets is derived from consumer demand. As we mentioned previously, the chain of organizations, operations, and transactions traceable back to raw materials extracted from the earth has come to be known as the **supply chain**. Supply chains have become very important to business competition over the last twenty to thirty years. Manufacturers' and service companies' internal operations received the most attention in the 1980s in order to meet global competition. Through concerted efforts aimed at process improvement, global companies squeezed a great deal of cost out of their internal operations, and at the same time realized improved product and service quality. With these improvements in place, the cost of materials, components, and supplies rose to account for well over half the selling price of products, on average.[11] At the same time, variation in supply timing and vagaries of supply quality accounted for a sizable share of product quality problems. So in the late 1980s and early 1990s attention focused on improving and integrating supply processes.

The derived nature of demand has several consequences that characterize business-to-business markets. Among these are the bullwhip effect and volatility of demand. Supply chain management is intended to mitigate the problems caused by these effects and so make the whole supply chain more competitive.

THE BULLWHIP EFFECT   Because of the derived nature, demand in business markets is leveraged—greater swings occur than in consumer markets—thus the term *volatile* in Exhibit 1-1. A small percentage change in consumer markets leads to much greater changes in business markets.

The volatility of derived demand is partially explained by the **bullwhip effect**.[12] As consumer demand varies, either as a result of seasonality or other market factors, "upstream" suppliers of services and components that contributed to the total offering experience a leveraged impact. This leveraging can cause wide swings in upstream demand as inventory levels, order

Business-to-Business	Consumer

Market Structure

• Geographically concentrated	• Geographically dispersed
• Relatively fewer buyers	• Mass markets, many buyers
• Oligopolistic competition	• Monopolistic competition

Products

• Can be technically complex	• Standardized
• Customized to user preference	• Service, delivery, and availability only some
• Service, delivery, and availability very important	what important
• Purchased for other than personal use	• Purchased for personal use

Buyer Behavior

• Professionally trained purchasing personnel	• Individual purchasing
• Functional involvement at many levels	• Family involvement, influence
• Task motives predominate	• Social/psychological motives predominate

Buyer–Seller Relationship Expectations

• Technical expertise an asset	• Less technical expertise
• Interpersonal relationships between buyers and sellers	• Nonpersonal relationships
• Significant info exchanged between participants on a personal level	• Little information exchanged between participants on a personal level
• Stable, long-term relationships encourage	• Changing, short-term relationships encourage switching loyalty

Channels

• Shorter, more direct	• Indirect, multiple relationships
• Organization involvement as part	• Little/no customer supply chain involvement

Promotion

• Emphasis on personal selling, dialogue Most communications invisible to the consumer	• Emphasis on advertising, monologue
• Consumer seldom aware of business-to-business brands and companies	• Companies compete for visibility and awareness by consumer market

Price

• Complex purchasing process or competitive bidding, depending on purchase type	• Usually list or predetermined prices

Demand

• Derived	• Direct
• Inelastic (short run)	• Elastic
• Volatile (leveraged)	• Less volatile
• Discontinuous	

EXHIBIT 1-1   Business-to-Business versus Consumer Marketing *Summarizing the Differences*

timing, and order quantities adjust to the new level of end-use demand. The initial correction is usually greater than the difference between the old and new demand levels. This is not solely a result of human overreaction. The ordering and inventory systems throughout the supply chain must make rapid adjustments and work through inventories that are too high or add extra product to inventories that are too low for the new demand conditions.[13]

A good example of the bullwhip effect can be seen in the story in Exhibit 1-2, a story about Ford and Firestone. Because of the recall of tires, Ford stopped production in its assembly plants. This had a ripple effect back through the supply system feeding the assembly plants. Ford "sneezed," and the industry "caught a cold."

In response to the tremendous need to find replacements for 6.5 million tires recalled by Firestone in August of 2000, Ford Motor Company halted production of its popular Explorer sport utility vehicles (SUV) and Ranger pickup trucks at three facilities in August, 2000. (Ford recalled an additional 13 million Firestone tires on its own, without Firestone cooperation, in May 2001.) The tires, originally intended for use in approximately 3 percent of annual production of these vehicles, were redirected to the replacement market. Most of the recalled tires had been used as original equipment on Ford SUVs and were also the primary tire installed on current production models. The production shutdown was estimated to cost Ford $100 million in profits for the quarter. Overall, the Firestone tire recall was expected to reduce Ford 2000 profits by $500 million. (The added 13 million tires recalled in 2001 pushed the total expense to Ford for the tire problem to near $3 billion.)

Ford and Firestone are not the only companies whose profits suffered from the production shutdown. Ford builds the largest selling SUVs in their market. Each vehicle is comprised of many components and systems provided by several major automotive suppliers. Though not common house-hold names as they are not major participants in consumer markets, companies such as Dana, Eaton, ArvinMeritor, TRW, Lear, and Visteon are major suppliers to Ford SUVs, many of the items specifically designed and built for these vehicles and not used by other manufacturers. In a dramatic example of the volatility of demand in business-to-business markets, all of these suppliers announced reduced earnings, either partly or substantially a result of the Ford production halt.

Eaton Corporation reported a 49 percent drop in third-quarter net, partly because of the Ford production cuts (previous reports set the reduction attributable to Ford at 10 percent of quarterly results), and Dana Corporation said its third-quarter results were 82 percent below the prior year's results. While not entirely attributable to the Ford production halt (Dana is a supplier to the heavy truck market, also in a slump), Dana announced it would cut 2000 jobs from its work force of 80,000 in an effort to boost fourth-quarter earnings.

The impact of the production shutdown does not end with components and systems. The International Natural Rubber Organization (INRO) reported that rubber producers who sold rubber to INRO as buffer stock are now enthusiastic bidders to put the inventory back on the market. The now defunct INRO had been seeking bidders for its 138,000 metric tons of buffer stock. Heavy rains in Indonesia had cut raw material supplies at the same time there was an increased demand from tire makers to replace the recalled tires. Of course, there were additional complications. While rubber producers were interested in buying back the stock they sold to INRO, they were also concerned about possible product degradation due to less than ideal storage conditions. The Firestone tire recall had generated concern about using old rubber to manufacture tires. As a result, any firm that purchased the material was told that it was INRO buffer stock. One rubber trader related the feeling that INRO rubber may be old but it could still be used in low-demand applications, such as bicycle tires, canvas shoes, tires for vehicles used in China (low-speed applications), or on agricultural vehicles.

EXHIBIT 1-2 Assembly Lines (and Tires) Stop Rolling   *Sources: The Wall Street Journal*, various articles (September–December 2001); *Business Week* (September 18, 2000).

More recently, a slowdown in orders for U.S. companies' automobiles has resulted in bullwhip effects in the auto parts supply chain. Reduced demand and competitive pressures pushed U.S. automakers to slow down their payments to parts suppliers creating an even tighter cash situation in the supply chain. Coupled with rising energy costs, many parts suppliers, such as Collins & Aikman and Metaldyne, sought debt financing at elevated interest rates to survive the cash crunch. Others, such as Tower Automotive Inc., and Intermet Corp., sought protection from creditors through Chapter 11 bankruptcy.[14] Even Alcoa, Inc., a supplier of aluminum to the automakers, faced financial pressure, even though Alcoa's markets are diversified. This diversification gives Alcoa the ability to balance poor performance in one sector with better performance in other industries. It also gives Alcoa more leverage in setting prices, since it is not completely dependent on one industry. Still, reduced demand from automakers and rising energy prices combined to weaken Alcoa's performance in early 2005.[15]

Another factor in the leveraged, **discontinuous demand** of business markets is the issue of capacity throughout the supply chain resulting from the desire of manufacturers to closely monitor capacity utilization. When a consumer goods manufacturer experiences an increase in demand, additional raw materials and supplies are consumed. Suppliers of these items experience greater demand and are required to increase production capacity. When the demand on suppliers reaches a level that is the maximum that existing facilities can efficiently produce, the capitalization of new production capability is required, resulting in a discontinuity in supply capability. If the supplier elects to invest in additional capacity, the addition not only provides increased capacity to the marketplace of the supplier but also creates demand in the markets of producers of manufacturing equipment and other production and infrastructure-related products. In this scenario, the increased demand for manufacturing capability in the first supply chain impacts the supply chains for several other markets. Multiply this scenario by all manufacturers who experience an increase in business and thus increase the supply requirements of all their suppliers, and the power of the leverage of consumer demand is obvious. A small change in consumer behavior can impact an entire economic structure, that is, "a rising tide raises all ships."[16]

Discontinuous demand is the condition in which quantity demanded in the market makes large changes up or down in response to changes in market conditions. The transition from one market state to another occurs in large increments rather than small incremental changes in demand.

While demand fluctuates more in business markets, it is also **inelastic** in the short term. Your customer, a manufacturer who has incorporated your product into the design of its own offering to customers may not be able to substitute another component for that item, particularly if, as a business marketer, you have managed to maintain a significant differentiation from your competitors. If the item's cost is driven up by unforeseen factors, the manufacturer has the choice of continuing production by paying the higher price or ceasing the manufacturing process, alienating its own customers who may be expecting delivery. Your customer's reluctance to alienate its customers is a major source of *inelasticity*. If the change in the supply situation that caused the price increase is expected to continue, the manufacturer eliminates use of the component *by design* in the next generation of its product offering.

Elasticity of demand refers to the percentage change in quantity demanded relative to the percentage change in price. If a price change produces a change in demand that is less in percentage than the percentage price change, then demand is said to be inelastic.

VOLATILITY The bullwhip effect, or leveraging, described here can help us understand logistics-oriented supply chain effects on business-to-business demand. The bullwhip effect, however, is only part of the cause of volatility in business-to-business markets. Because of the volatility in business-to-business demand, small changes in consumer buying attitudes are closely watched as potential indicators of changes in our economy. The inelastic nature of derived demand may lead the uninitiated business marketer to a false sense of security, believing that the short-term persistence of demand translates into long-term stability.

We have seen many examples in history in which sudden environmental changes have destabilized entire markets. Rapid changes in the economy can have medium-term—or faster—impacts on derived demand. The almost 30 percent drop in consumer purchases of large automobiles in 1974 and again in 1979, coincident with each oil crisis, is an example of a fast-acting economic event. Many suppliers to the automotive industry found orders stopping immediately, not to return until it was financially too late for the supplier to recover. Again, in the Ford and Firestone example discussed in Exhibit 1-2, the situation in which Ford ceased production of a very profitable, high-volume vehicle was caused by a combination of events. The resulting lower earnings reported by suppliers of components for the Ford Explorer could not have been anticipated.

A relatively slow-acting event was the "dot.com bust" that occurred in 2001–2002. What started as some disappointing earnings reports for publicly traded e-commerce companies turned into a full-scale recession whose impacts lasted several years. When stock prices initially began falling in the spring of 2001, many analysts felt that this "correction" was necessary and the "dip" would turn around by year's end. It didn't. Other factors and events—the terrorist attacks of September 2001, scandals at Worldcom and Enron, for instance—exacerbated the worsening economy. The effects of the downturn spread to other sectors, as well as globally. The effects were slowed and mitigated within the United States due to lower interest rates and tax cuts, which kept consumers consuming. Eventually, in 2004, businesses increased their capital spending and began slowly hiring back workers.

Complexity—A Rationale for Relationship Marketing

One of the major implications of derived demand is that business marketers must understand their customers' customers. Only if marketers are customer focused are they able to fully understand their customers' network of derived demand. The business marketer can design products and services to fully benefit customers and, hopefully, anticipate changes in levels of demand instigated by the customers' market. The impact of the discontinuous nature of demand can be lessened by business marketers' participation in the relationship with the customer on a continuing, ongoing basis. If, as a result of its complacency, a business marketer allows a competitor to take advantage of its inattention by offering a lower price or better product, the loss of short-term business could translate into lost opportunities to be the supplier of the customer's next generation needs. Consequently, business marketers must be diligent in their efforts to continually reinforce buying decisions and create more value for their existing customers.

Outsourcing is the purchasing of part of the company's continuing operations, such as recruiting or manufacturing, rather than investing in the infrastructure to accomplish the task internally.

Another factor that separates business-to-business markets from consumer markets is the complexity created by the various attributes that make up the total business offering. Partly in response to this complexity is the complex nature of the buying decision process. Complexity on both sides is obvious when one studies the **outsourcing** of product research and development, the acquisition of such things as computer information systems, manufacturing facilities or equipment, or a new power plant. However, on the other end of the spectrum lie products that are not very complex, such as office supplies. While the products themselves are not particularly complex, attributes of the offering such as quantity discounts, complementary products, and delivery schedules create complexity. All in all, this pervasive complexity reinforces the differences between business-to-business and consumer marketing. The differences that we have discussed do not stand alone but combine to create unique difficulties and opportunities.

OPPORTUNITIES THROUGH RELATIONSHIPS   In business-to-business markets, additional product design effort is often needed to ensure that a product's complexity will enhance customer value rather than detract from it. The dialogue between customer and marketer must quickly convey complex concepts that are generally more difficult to understand than those required in consumer marketing. As already noted, communications in business marketing must often focus more on personal selling than in consumer marketing. The sales force becomes the focal point for developing the relationships that will enhance the position of the selling organization in its attempt to address the complex and diffused buyers' decision processes. Marketing based on building close relationships with customers becomes the glue that holds all the other pieces together to create value by ensuring that the customers' uniqueness is accommodated. In contrast, relationships in consumer marketing are often part of "customer service" and are often treated as sources of costs rather than enhancement to interaction with customers.

One effect of the necessity for close relationships is that **switching costs**—the costs of switching suppliers—become very high for both the customer and the supplier. In consumer markets, switching costs usually are not nearly so constraining. High switching costs in business-to-business markets can result from the investment that the partners make in matching buying, ordering, inbound logistics, and delivery systems to each other—the creation of an efficient, specialized supply chain. High switching costs can also come from the working relationships established on a personal level, which may be less tangible than the logistical linkages. However, such personal linkages can be just as close and binding and just as difficult to break. Because business-to-business customers realize that commitment to a supplier creates such high switching costs, they become very careful about whom they choose as suppliers and often establish back-up, second-source relationships with other suppliers. Meanwhile, suppliers seek out other customers so that they are not so reliant on a single large customer. Once all these primary and secondary relationships are established, the high switching costs make the supplier–customer relationships difficult to split, making it difficult for new partners to enter the picture. Partners need to realize, though, that they cannot abuse these locked-in relationships with poor quality or service or untenable demands. Durable partnerships break at times and the aggrieved partner makes it difficult for the penitent party to re-establish the relationship.

Market Structure

Another major difference between business-to-business and consumer markets is that, usually, business marketers face markets with a much smaller number of customers than consumer marketers face. The reasons for this are quite simple. First, there are simply fewer organizations in existence than there are consumers. Second, organizations differ greatly in what they do and how they do it. Hence, their needs for products and services differ greatly. This means that many market segments (discussed in Chapter 7) have relatively few organizations populating them.

Having many market segments with differing needs implies that mass marketing approaches will not be particularly useful. Our natural instincts as consumers, conditioned to mass marketing approaches, are often contrary to effective business-to-business marketing logic. Mass promotion is not particularly efficient or effective as a tool to communicate with the business-to-business market. In consumer markets, the high cost of mass media is spread out over a large audience such that cost *per contact* is low. If mass media do not or cannot reach enough prospective customers, due to small populations in target segments, then cost per contact remains high and more efficient means of communications must be sought. This high-cost business model analogy extends to other aspects of marketing as well. Since business segments often have a small population of buyers (see the discussion of oligopolistic markets in Chapter 2) and it is likely that each buyer, from the perspective of one's organization, has a different idea of what product provides the best value, marketers tailor offerings to specific buyer value definitions. At first, it may seem that the proliferation of product variables would lead to high product costs. However, the large quantities usually purchased by a single buying organization often allow manufacturing economies of scale to be reached. Without the volume of large purchases, business-to-business offerings must have significant value built in, such that the resulting price is accepted by buyers.

Integrated versus Networked Supply, Brand Identity

In consumer markets, consumers believe brands that they know and trust provide more value than brands that they do not know. Brand identification is important in business-to-business markets as well. Individuals in business-to-business markets will have knowledge of the reputation and track record of brands and their suppliers. Just as consumer markets have "go to" brands that are known as reliable and dependable, so too do business-to-business markets.

What contributes to quality and reliability in consumer markets versus business-to-business markets can be significantly different, and the well-known brands and companies in business-to-business markets usually do not have a strong consumer presence. All the parts, materials, sub-assemblies, and so on that comprise a consumer product are seldom manufactured by the company whose brand appears on the product. Manufacturers often find it more appropriate to purchase components of their products from other companies rather than integrate into the manufacture of those components. While there are many brands of refrigerators in the market place, an examination would likely reveal that there are only two or three prominent brands of motors for the compressors in the refrigerator. It is also likely that the brands are not well known in consumer markets.[17] The suppliers of motors, for instance, are specialists in the design, development, and manufacturing of motors. To support that specialization, they will have invested in technologies and competencies that make them a better, more competitive motor supplier. The refrigerator company is not interested in an investment in motor technology, but is interested in using motors that incorporate new technologies and techniques. The practical outcome is that the many refrigerator manufacturers will purchase motors from one of a few motor producers, likely an oligopoly.

The degree to which a company networks, on the supply side, to other companies (e.g., outsources motors) depends on many factors including

- How long the company has been in business
- The desirability of diversifying, through vertical integration, into another business
- The availability of quality supply choices in the market
- The speed at which technology is changing the market
- The degree of uniqueness or specialization of the supplied or manufactured component.

Historically, many large companies, well known today, are more vertically integrated than younger companies. This is often out of necessity—early manufacturers were required to vertically integrate into diverse businesses, as there was not an existing industrial infrastructure to rely on for supply. In today's market, newer companies view formal integration as a potential impediment to flexibility and thus often partner or network ("outsource") with other similarly sized companies to complete their offerings.

Exhibit 1-3, Networked versus Integrated Supply, shows several recently introduced car models and the suppliers for several components. Notice how few of the component suppliers are household names, and how many of them supply the same or similar components to customers that compete with each other. Note also that the supplier list for the 1990 Ford Crown Victoria, a car that has undergone only minor changes since its introduction, is heavily dominated by vertically integrated Ford supply operations. In the past fifteen years there has been a trend to reduce dependency on vertically integrated supply chains, lowering fixed costs and increasing flexibility. The 2005 Ford Escape has a more diverse supply base.

Sourcing decisions like those noted in Exhibit 1-3 demonstrate that the choice of supplier for any given situation depends on many factors not necessarily related to the material or component to be sourced. A heavily integrated customer will seek to maintain profitable volumes in its supply divisions, while a smaller, younger, and more flexible company will be more open to outside sources. These considerations have put many older American industries at a disadvantage as they face newly structured, recently developed foreign competition.[18]

Some International Considerations

There are international implications that are part of the differences between business-to-business and consumer markets. In part because of international standards-setting organizations, the complexity of doing business beyond one's own borders is less for business-to-business markets than for consumer markets. International consumer markets are subject to many more cultural, language, regulatory, and individual value differences than business-to-business markets. An exporter of a packaged food product must be concerned not only with packaging, promotion, and language differences but also with cultural beliefs and values about ingredients, colors, and style as well as buying habits. Additionally, international standards in foods and packaging of consumer products vary greatly. Conversely, business-to-business products have fewer hurdles to clear.

While business-to-business products are subject to the same politics of tariffs and other trade barriers, many materials, supplies, and components meet standards that are agreed to and consistent across international borders. Plastic materials have been nearly standardized through the voluntary effort of the Society of Plastic Engineers (SPE); and the transportation industry, through the Society of Automotive Engineers (SAE), has created performance standards for vehicle systems. These are but two examples. Steel, plastic, pulp and paper

---

Consumer Brands Aren't Always What They Seem

Examine a consumer product that you purchased recently. Did the brand of this product play an important role in your selection process? Note the different components and elements that make up the product. Did the producer of the consumer product manufacture all of the components or have some parts been purchased from other producers? What considerations did the producer of the consumer product have when selecting the manufacturer of the various components and parts that make up the final product? What values did the producer look for (cost, reliability, durability, power consumption, etc.)? Review Exhibit 1-3, Networked versus Integrated Supply. Note that the same company often supplies similar components of different vehicle brands. Note also that the suppliers are seldom recognizable by consumers—they are not familiar brands. As you make your examination, the number of different manufacturers who contributed to the final product may surprise you.

Component	1990 Ford Crown Victoria	2008 Ford Taurus	2008 Toyota Corolla	2007 Saturn Sky	2009 BMW X6	2007 Volvo S80	2008 Honda Accord	2007 Lincoln Navigator
Airbags-Various		Autoliv/ TRW, Key Safety	Takata				Takata, TRW	TRW
Brakes/Calipers, Components, etc	Ford (1)	TI, PBR	TI, Honeywell	Continental	Honeywell, ITT	Honeywell	Honeywell, Hitachi	Federal-Mogul
Bumpers/Fascias	Ford			Omnium	Omnium	Plastal	Decoma	
Engine Management	Ford	Visteon		Bosch, Delphi		Bosch, Denso		Visteon
Glass	Ford (1)		Pilkington, AGC			Sekurit		
Half Shafts/ Drive Shafts		Haldex AWD	NTN	GKN		Haldex AWD		NTN
Headlamps					Hella	Zizala	Stanley	
HVAC	Ford (1)	Visteon		Air Intern'l	Preh	Behr		
Steering System	Ford, TRW	Continental			ZF Lenksys.	Visteon, ZF		
Premium Audio Components	Ford (1)	Panasonic, Harada, etc.	Harman/ Becker	Delphi (2)	Alpine	Alpine/ Mitsubishi	Clarion	
Seats	Ford			Lear	Faurecia	Lear		
Seat Belts				Takata			Takata	

EXHIBIT 1-3 Networked versus Integrated Supply

Component	1990 Ford Crown Victoria	2008 Ford Taurus	2008 Toyota Corolla	2007 Saturn Sky	2009 BMW X6	2007 Volvo S80	2008 Honda Accord	2007 Lincoln Navigator
Shock Absorbers/Struts, Chassis Components	Ford	ZF, Cosma Intn'l, Sachs	ArvinMeritor, Mubea	Thyssen-Krupp	Mubea, Dana	Tenneco		SKD, NHK
Steering wheel	Ford (1)	Autoliv		Autoliv	Takata			
Taillamps	Ford	Visteon			Hella		Stanley	Auto Lighting Visteon
Transmission/Transaxle	Ford							ZF
Camshafts	Ford (1)	Thyssen-Krupp				Mahle	Thyssen-Krupp	
Wiring	Yazaki	Yazaki	Yazaki		Draeximaier		Yazaki	Yazaki

EXHIBIT 1-3 (continued)

Notes: (1) The Ford divisions that supplied these components have been spun off into Visteon, an independent company.

(2) Delphi is the name of the supply organization created when General Motors spun off its various supply divisions.

Source: Automotive News Car Cutaways, Secondary Research, Author conversations.

products, chemicals, and electronics industries have technical standards that are applied worldwide. Organizations such as the International Standards Organization (ISO) have created a common language to define and specify the technical performance of manufacturing and quality systems. Compliance by suppliers with many of these standards has become a requirement of many global firms.

AN EXAMINATION OF VALUE

Throughout this chapter, as well as the rest of this text, a recurring theme is the customer's perception of value and that perception's impact on buying decisions. The notions of value, the value chain, the networks that build value, and the nature of competition are very powerful in giving depth to business marketers' decisions. For example, the role and management of marketing channels and business logistics become much clearer when value for the final customer is understood as the necessary outcome of an extended value chain. Value and the value chain deserve a close look, then, in some detail. In this chapter, we elaborate on the value chain as described by Porter;[19] in Chapter 2 we expand the discussion to better reflect changes implied by new and emerging business styles and formats.

This brings us to the point where we must make explicit the concept of value. The adage, consumers who purchase a quarter-inch drill bit do not want a quarter-inch drill bit—they want a quarter-inch hole—is quite appropriate. As consumers, we do not purchase music compact discs (CDs) because we like the shiny plastic discs; we buy them because we are interested in the entertainment value of the music. The disc is merely a container for the value.[20] Customers do not purchase products; they purchase offerings that create solutions and satisfaction. Consumer and business markets are alike in the exchange process. All parties who are part of an exchange must leave the transaction believing they acquired more than they gave up. The value of an offering is determined not by the cost to create it but, rather, by the net value of satisfaction delivered to the customer.

So what is value? Treacy and Wiersema[21] define **value** as the sum of all of the benefits that a customer receives in the process of buying and using a product or service *less* the costs involved.[22]

The concept is quite simple, but quickly complicated because lots of things contribute to benefits and lots of things contribute to costs. All of the customer's benefits from buying and using a product or service are not measured in the same units. The same is true for costs incurred by the customer. There are certainly costs involved in the search for, purchase, and maintenance of products, but there are also time costs and aggravation costs in the purchasing process, as well. Purchasers encounter hidden costs associated with usage, such as learning time and the cost of mistakes made while learning how to use the product. The sum of these costs, the total cost of owning and using a product, is referred to as the **evaluated price**. Additionally, purchasers' definitions of what comprises the best value changes with time, experience, technology, and competitive positioning. Accordingly, value—which is complex and variable, depending on the view of what contributes to it—is often hard to quantify. However, this does not mean that the concept is not a useful one. Explored in a theoretical sense, the concept of value provides excellent insight about how business marketing works.

Evaluated price is the total cost of owning and using the product. This may include transportation, inventory carrying costs, financing costs, potential obsolescence, installation, flexibility to upgrade, cost of failure, and obsolescence of existing products or equipment, plus the price paid to the vendor.

The Value Chain

In the mid-1980s, Harvard business professor Michael Porter put forth the idea of a **value chain**.[23] When the *value chain* is understood and applied wisely, it is a powerful concept that can help a company create competitive advantages that competitors often do not even know exist. As with any management tool however, if misunderstood and misapplied, the results can sometimes be disastrous. Let us examine the fundamentals and propose an adaptation.

The basic idea is that companies compete with each other to be selected by buyers. Buyers select from among competitors' offerings based on the buyers' perceptions of where they will receive the most value (subject to the realities of budgets). Each vendor who is competing, then, tries to do so by offering more value, *as perceived by the customer*, than is offered by the other vendors. The value chain, then, is the chain of activities that creates something of value for the targeted customers. The "something of value" is an offering (which was implied by Porter but not made explicit). The offering is everything that the customer or prospect perceives as contributing to benefits *and* costs. This includes the product and the service but goes much further. The offering also includes brand image, the economic utility provided by distribution such as availability and appropriate quantity, and, as noted earlier, evaluated price. *Evaluated price* includes all the costs that are subtracted from benefits to produce value—the "cost of doing business" with a supplier. Exhibit 1-4, Direct and Support Activities Contribute to Value shows the support and direct—or value enabling and value creating—activities that usually occur within the firm. The left side of Exhibit 1-5, Value Chain and Offering, represents the value chain in relation to customers who will perceive the value offered.

The center of Exhibit 1-5, "the puzzle," shows the created offering as a combination of product, service, image, availability, and quantity—all part of the factors that make up the evaluated price. Note that these factors are created by the supplier's direct and support activities; yet their market value is determined as a result of the perception of the target customer. This customer perception also considers the offering in the context of the business environment. For instance, the customer may also see the offering as consistent with standards promulgated by international standards organizations. Or an industry commentator, in his blog, may recommend the product. Thus the customer's perception includes more factors than just the offering created by the supplier. This distinction between the offering and what the customer perceives is important. The decision to select a particular supplier will be based on the customer's perception of the created value, not the creator's perception.

- Support Activities: "Value Enabling"
  - Infrastructure
  - People management
  - Technology development & management
  - Resource acquisition

- Direct Activities: "Value Creating"
  - Input logistics
  - Operations
  - Delivery logistics
  - Service

Other contributions to value include adoption by channels, adoption by Original equipment manufacturers (OEMs) or upstream suppliers, affiliation with industry trade organizations, cultural acceptance of end-use products, etc.

EXHIBIT 1-4   Direct and Support Activities Contribute to Value

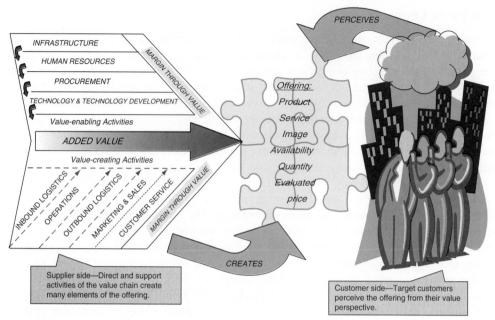

EXHIBIT 1-5   The Value Chain and Offering

Direct versus Support Activities

This conceptualization of the specifics of a value chain, internal to an organization, includes both direct and support activities. The direct activities contribute directly to the offering. The support activities make it possible to perform the direct activities. For instance, marketing creates brand image, which is valuable to customers because it provides assurances of quality, upgradability, and the like. Marketing is then a direct activity. Human resources management defines positions and recruits, hires, trains, and motivates the people who are necessary to do the marketing and other activities. Therefore, human resources management is a support activity.

The implications of all of this are fairly simple and familiar, but they are also quite powerful. The first implication is that the organization should start by really understanding its prospective customers. The organization should fully understand what those prospective customers would perceive as valuable. Further, the organization should understand how customers might be persuaded to change their minds about what is valuable. This is not manipulation but customer education. It is focused on getting the customer to better appreciate all of the value that it is possible to obtain from the attributes of the offering. The market-driven organization, focused on providing more value, not on giving less value and then convincing customers it is the best that they can expect, will be able to demonstrate superior value in its offering, enabling improved margin through customer recognition of that value. The organization must itself recognize all of the factors that provide value to its offering.

The second implication is that not all prospective customers are alike. Segments exist based on what value the prospective customers seek and what they can afford. Once this is understood, it becomes apparent that our traditional means of determining segments—demographically or by industry—are perhaps misguided.

The third implication is that both direct and support activities are equally important in the creation of value. Without critical links, the whole chain falls apart and the customer's value is

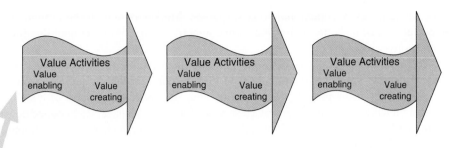

From Exhibit 1-5: Value-enabling activities include infrastructure, human resources, procurement, and technology and technology development. Value-creating activities include inbound and outbound logistics, operations, marketing and sales, and customer service.

EXHIBIT 1-6 Supply Chain Orientation of Value Chain

degraded. One of the misuses of the value chain concept during the recession in the early 2000s was to see value creation only in activities that produced or sold products. Significant cuts were made in "non-value producing" activities, as perceived by suppliers, without realizing the impact these cuts would have on value perceived by customers.

The fourth implication is that the creation of value extends from the customer back through distribution channels, through manufacturers, through component suppliers, finally to raw material providers (Exhibit 1-6). Each organization in the chain successively adds value to the offering to accommodate the next organization. This representation is not unlike the more logistics-oriented notion of a *supply chain*. Because of the nature of derived demand, business buyers define what is valuable to them in terms of what value they are providing to their own customers. Each purchase by a business contributes to the value it provides to its customers.

The value chain concept gives a powerful argument for following the marketing concept. Market-driven organizations recognize marketing not as a single departmental function but as the defining function (i.e., understanding and satisfying customer needs) in the organization. The marketing concept says that to do well, the organization should know its customers, meet their needs, and do so in a way that meets organization goals. The value chain concept provides a framework for pursuing the marketing concept—that everyone contributes to the success of the organization.[24]

MISUNDERSTANDING OF THE VALUE AND VALUE CHAIN CONCEPTS

The concepts of value and the value chain are so basic that marketers can lose sight of their implications. It appears that this happens in three principal ways.

First, marketing managers can get so caught up in trying to create profits for their companies that they lose sight of what customer value really means. They forget that customers will not choose to buy a total offering unless it provides superior value to the customers. To create profits, managers sometimes think that they can forgo some customer value to reduce costs by taking shortcuts on quality, service, or availability; or they lose sight of customer value altogether and wind up creating me-too or inferior products or offerings whose value is easily copied and soon surpassed. Marketers need to be reminded that perceived value must be better than value from competitors' offerings. Without this fundamental driver, profits do not happen.

Second, managers often lose sight of what creates value for the customer. As already noted, customers get value from more than just the core product or service. Some products provide prestige, some provide upgradability, and some have the support of a stellar service organization while others may never need service. Too often, managers get bogged down getting the product (or service) features right and they forget that communications, positioning, distribution, and pricing also create value.

Third, there are often so many different kinds of businesses that want a product or service and derive value from it in so many different ways that it is difficult to pin down exactly what combination of features in an offering is valued by the most important customers. When this occurs, it indicates that a poor job has been done in defining segments and/or choosing target markets. If segments have been defined well, they are practically homogeneous when it comes to benefits sought. If there is a great deal of heterogeneity within the target segments, then the segmentation needs to be rethought (see Chapter 7).

In all of the preceding situations, marketers lose sight of the fact that they need to be truly customer value driven. This means that they have to maintain the discipline of focusing on customers and finding a way to provide superior value for them. Time and again, when companies lose sight of this, they get into trouble.

TRENDS AND CHANGES IN BUSINESS MARKETING

To this point we have suggested that it is important to study business-to-business marketing separately from consumer marketing. We have also discussed the concepts of value and the value chain as the bases for thinking about business marketing. The retrenchment of the economy in the early 2000s and the subsequent recovery have borne out that these core concepts are as germane as they were in the past: understanding customers and building relationships with them, understanding segmentation, applying branding concepts, and careful management of the marketing channels and business logistics, just to name a few. However, the business-to-business marketing environment is changing rapidly, and adaptation to this change may require some new ways of thinking and acting.

Throughout this book we elaborate on trends that, at this time, appear to require attention from business-to-business marketers. While these changes are mostly obvious, how to address them may not be so obvious. Several of these trends are interrelated: they cause each other. Together they produce second- and third-level effects that become trends in and of themselves.

HYPERCOMPETITION   Several factors have combined, seemingly in the short term, to create many smart, fast competitors across many industries. New companies that emerge quickly or create new markets and industries almost overnight challenge established companies. In the face of this new, rapidly appearing **hypercompetition**, existing companies are rapidly embracing new methods and techniques. As companies learn to do more with fewer people, at least some of these companies downsize. This leaves many skilled people who are looking for work; some start companies, and more go to work for new companies, often with a well-established network of relationships in place.

The rapidly changing competitive landscape means that business marketers must anticipate a hypercompetitive environment even though they are unable to anticipate who tomorrow's competitors will be. This, in turn, means that competitive analysis techniques and competitive actions, which once focused on addressing competition from specific competitors, must be adapted to accommodate this heightened uncertainty. Techniques that can be used in such an environment are discussed in Chapter 6.

FORMATION OF PARTNER NETWORKS   Products, projects, and systems have become so complex and interrelated that no company can provide a "whole product" by itself. (The implications of this for many industrialized businesses have been noted and are demonstrated in Exhibit 1-3.) For instance, software providers need to partner with hardware vendors, other software vendors, and systems integrators to provide enterprise-level software systems (such as enterprise resource planning—ERP systems). What was once a sales channel—the software company to the systems integrators——has become a sales, service, and distribution cluster. Similar partnering occurs for new product development and filling product lines. Larger companies are recognizing that, often, other companies have crucial pieces of technology or complementary products. These trends are not just occurring in the computer industry and related industries. The same kinds of partner networks are occurring in industries as diverse as construction, energy production and distribution, consulting, and employment services.

This seems straightforward, and the solutions for addressing this trend seem to look a lot like extensions of channel management. However, the business marketer realizes that things are different when the marketer is approached by an arch-rival competitor with the offer of partnering on a new venture or in a new market. This is not collusion, because the competitor remains a competitor in other markets; and the competitor may break the partnership—probably *will* break the partnership—in the future and compete in this market that the two partners have pioneered together. The implications of this trend in partnering are examined more closely in later chapters.

ADOPTION OF INFORMATION TECHNOLOGY AND THE INTERNET   Another trend changing the face of business marketing is the increased pace of adoption of information technology. Internet technology, of which the Web is a subset, offers enhanced communication, enhanced customer service, and reduced costs. The concepts of total offering and evaluated price combine to demonstrate that these benefits accrue to buyers as well as sellers. Channel members and other intermediaries obtain all these benefits as well, as they act as buyers, sellers, and *facilitators*.

Channel facilitators are those service providers to the channel that are not necessarily part of channel design but who make possible the efficient operation of the channel. Channel facilitators are financial institutions, transportation and logistics companies, third-party service providers, etc. These organizations provide outsourced services to facilitate the effective operation of the channel.

SUPPLY CHAIN MANAGEMENT   Supply chains extend from raw material and component suppliers, through the manufacturer, and through the distribution channel to the final buyer.

The Web has and will continue to impact the dynamics of supply chain management. Theoretically, the participants do not have to have compatible equipment, just Internet access and an up-to-date browser (it is actually more complicated, but the compatibility issue is much more tractable using the Internet). A single supplier or distributor can participate in multiple channels, even though the channel leaders use different platforms. The supplier or distributor must still reconcile different tracking and accounting systems, and confidentiality between participants can be a problem, but such efforts can cost less than creating and maintaining several different information technology systems.

Online ordering, inventory and delivery tracking, coordination of marketing programs, and automated sharing of market information have always been available to the largest companies. The potential to squeeze a great deal of the costs out of the supply chain, while making the supply chain faster and more effective is now a capability of many smaller organizations. Market-driven pricing methods are challenged as well. Auctioning software allows excess inventory to be sold over the Web, allocating the inventory to the channel outlets where it will be valued the most. Using the auctioning concept from the other direction, manufacturers or distributors can run online bidding for supply contracts. In a very short time frame, they can get better prices and more effective delivery contracts. Auctioning can make existing suppliers, whose offerings do not provide good value, subject to quick termination of their contracts for nonperformance, because the transaction costs of switching have been minimized (other switching costs still exist, of course, and may give the incumbent supplier some breathing room).

Many products now are digital, including, of course, software; but a product such as an insurance policy or a consulting report can be a document, which can be transmitted in digital form. Drawings, photographs, videos, or combinations of these may constitute part or even all of a product. These, of course, can be delivered via the Internet or Web. Many software products that were once sold as "shrink-wrapped" products, or as major installations, now are sold as Web-enabled services. Customers do not have to install the application on their own systems. All they have to do is access the software on a central site and input their own data by completing forms on a Web site, and the central site runs the application. The output is returned to the customer through a custom-generated Web page. Selling such services via the Web provides a great deal of value to business buyers in that installation time is small and the overhead costs of installation and maintenance are shared with other users of the centralized service. The implication is that many more business customers now have access to the software, presumably making their business operations more efficient and effective. At the same time, the business model of the software company has changed from a software product manufacturer to that of a service provider. Many software companies, such as Oracle and IBM, are developing this model for addressing smaller company markets. All this changes the business environment for the companies that used to provide installation, training, and maintenance services for customers installing new software and hardware. A great deal of the business that used to be generated is now potentially going away. On the other side of the coin, the security, installation, training, and maintenance business that is left tends to be high value and high margin.

TIME COMPRESSION   Several factors combine to create **time compression**—an increase in the "speed" of doing business. How organizations react to this acceleration has both short-term and long-term effects on their survivability and performance. With hypercompetition, competitive pressures cause companies to attempt to get new products out faster and to replace these products with succeeding generations of products even more rapidly.

Discussions we have had with executives and managers have yielded disquieting results. For the question, "How are you dealing with time compression?" the responses range from well thought out, seemingly effective methods to some version of "work harder and faster." There seem to be too many of the latter.

THOUGHTS TO TAKE WITH YOU INTO THE NEXT CHAPTER

With all the change occurring in the business marketer's world, some ideas, such as the value chain and its implications, continue to have validity and can provide guidance. The best way to be successful and profitable is to focus on creating superior value for prospective customers. Do this first, and prospective customers will be willing to pay, commensurate with perceived value. The focus can then turn to managing costs in such a way that value is not diminished. With proper management, companies will be creating enough cash flow to pay for the value that is provided to them by their own upstream suppliers.

In the FedEx versus UPS example, the key to success is how much value can be created for business customers. Both companies, through acquisitions, changed the competitive landscape by creating differentiated offerings. To succeed, both companies will need to continue to learn about customers and innovate to offer more value. Meanwhile, technology will be changing, new competitors will enter the market, and customers' needs and behavior will evolve.

Chapter 2 concerns other key ideas that describe how business-to-business markets operate and how marketing implications are drawn from these concepts. Keep in mind, though, that providing value is still at the foundation of these concepts. Customers' perceptions of value change over time, and the way that value is created through organizations changes as well. Throughout this book, and indeed throughout your career as a marketer, the search for creative ways to provide new value to current and future customers must continue.

Key Terms

bullwhip effect *8*	entrepreneurial marketing *3*	possession *6*
business marketing *4*	evaluated price *18*	supply chain *8*
business markets *3*	form *6*	supply chain management *6*
channel facilitators *23*	four Ps *4*	switching costs *13*
consumer demand *8*	hypercompetition *22*	time *6*
derived demand *8*	inelastic [demand] *11*	time compression *24*
discontinuous demand *11*	marketing concept *7*	total offering *5*
economic utility *6*	outsourcing *12*	value *18*
elasticity *11*	place *6*	value chain *19*

Questions for Review and Discussion

1. Describe the differences between business-to-business and consumer marketing for the following market elements:
   products   buyer behavior   decision making

2. Describe the differences between business-to-business and consumer marketing for the following market elements:
   market structure   channels   promotion

3. Describe the difference between derived demand and consumer demand. How does the leveraging phenomenon occur?

4. What is the difference between value as perceived by the customer and value as perceived by the supplier?

5. We learned in economics the difference between elasticity and inelasticity. What is meant when we say that business-to-business demand is inelastic in the short term and discontinuous in the long term?

6. Ultimately, who is the long-term benefactor of application of the value chain? Explain your answer.

7. Considering all of the elements of evaluated price, would value to the customer's customer be a major consideration? Why, or why not?

8. How is value created in the transaction process?

9. As consumers, how do our "shopping instincts" make it difficult to understand business-to-business marketing philosophy?

10. What factors can contribute to a customer remaining with a particular supplier even though lower-cost substitutes may be available?
11. What factors contribute to the decision to outsource versus vertically integrate? How does proprietary technology affect this decision?
12. Discuss the bullwhip effect. How can management of the supply chain reduce the volatility produced by the bullwhip effect?
13. Discuss the relationship between evaluated price and value and the importance of that relationship to both suppliers and buyers.
14. How can a company gain competitive advantage through supply chain management?

Endnotes

1. Based on Dave Hirschman, "FedEx, UPS Tactics Diverge: Retail Shippers a Top Priority," *The Atlanta Journal—Constitution* (July 13, 2004), p. D.1; James F. Peltz, "FedEx, UPS Hope to Spark Chain Reactions in Battle For Customers; The Owners of the Old Kinko's and Mail Boxes Etc. Stores See Retail as a Key to Sustained Growth," *Los Angeles Times* (October 17, 2004), p. C.1.
2. Dawn Wotapka, "Feeling Blue about Going Brown; Some Mail Boxes Owners Fighting UPS over Control," *Chicago Tribune* (July 8, 2004), p. 1.
3. Ted Samson, "FedEx Kinko's Delivers Remote Printing," *InfoWorld*, 26(46) (November 15, 2004), p. 52.
4. Naomi Aoki, "Staples Tries to Make Copies Easy for Customers," *Oakland Tribune* (July 11, 2004), p. 1.
5. Minet Schindehutte, Michael H. Morris, and Leyland F. Pitt, *Rethinking Marketing: The Entrepreneurial Imperative* (Upper Saddle River, N.J.: Pearson Prentice-Hall, 2009).
6. A note about terminology is important here. In the previous paragraph, we introduced the term *total offering* to describe the augmented product. This is an intentional avoidance of the word *product* as we want to reinforce, throughout the text, that the value provided to customers often goes far beyond "just the product."
7. Regis McKenna, "Marketing Is Everything," *Harvard Business Review* (January–February 1991).
8. Kotler has introduced a societal element to the marketing concept. This is further discussed in Chapter 16. See also Philip Kotler and Kevin Keller, *Marketing Management*, 12th ed. (Upper Saddle River, N.J.: Prentice-Hall, 2006), p. 22.
9. William D. Perreault Jr. and E. Jerome McCarthy, *Basic Marketing*, 13th ed. (New York, McGraw Hill, 1999), pp. 33–35.
10. For a complete treatment of the concept of marketing as the defining parameter in the organization, readers are directed to Regis McKenna, "Marketing Is Everything," *Harvard Business Review* (January–February 1991).
11. David N. Burt, Donald W. Dobler, and Stephen L. Starling, *World Class Supply Management*, 7th ed. (Boston: McGraw-Hill Irwin, 2003).
12. Philippe-Pierre Dornier, Ricardo Ernst, Michel Fender, and Panos Kouvelis, *Global Operations and Logistics* (New York: John Wiley & Sons, 1998). Chapter 7 provides a complete discussion of the bullwhip effect and its relationship to supply chain management.
13. Hau L. Lee, V. Padmanabhan, and Seungjin Whang, "The Bullwhip Effect in Supply Chains," *Sloan Management Review* (Spring 1997), p. 96.
14. Mitchell Pacelle, "Detroit Woes Keep Suppliers in a Pinch," *Wall Street Journal* (April 12, 2005), p. C1.
15. Erik Ahlberg, "Alcoa Sees Pressure from Lower Auto Production Levels," *Wall Street Journal* (April 6, 2005), http://online.wsj.com/article/0., BT_CO_20050406_008025,00.html.
16. Some large business customers often provide suppliers with several forecast levels. Worst, likely, and best-case forecasts are often part of business-to-business arrangements. These forecasts are only as good as the business-to-business customer's forecast of its market and is subject to the same frailties of all forecasts. It is in the best interest of the business-to-business supplier to "know its customers' customers" and develop its

own forecast of the market. (See later chapters regarding forecasts and understanding markets.) When it is not customary for a business-to-business customer to provide best/likely/worst case forecasts, it is critical for the business-to-business supplier to obtain, either internally or through outside assistance, good market forecasts.

17. In the case of a fully integrated manufacturer such as General Electric, the motor brand is likely to also be GE. GE is also likely to be a supplier of motors to other refrigerator manufacturers.

18. Not very long ago, Ford Motor Company was integrated into its own iron ore mines, steel manufacturing, tires, fabrics and plastics, and glass. When the company began operations, there just were not any other sources for these materials and components.

19. Michael E. Porter, *Competitive Advantage: Creating and Sustaining Superior Performance* (New York: Free Press, 1985).

20. In fact, the recent shifts in the industry toward MP3 file transfers bear this out. As consumers, we want the music in whatever form and format is the easiest to handle, particularly if we can obtain it cheaply or for free.

21. Michael Treacy and Frederick Wiersema, *The Discipline of Market Leaders* (Reading, Mass.: Addison-Wesley, 1995).

22. We prefer the expression of value as a remainder of benefits minus costs rather than as a ratio of benefits to costs, as presented by Kotler and others. Something with relatively low benefits can have a high ratio value if the costs are low. In most cases, a minimum benefit level must be reached before an offering is attractive. Consequently, we feel it better to represent value as an amount subject to a maximum budget constraint. For the ratio expression see Philip Kotler, *Marketing Management: The Millennium Edition*, 10th ed. (Upper Saddle River, N.J.: Prentice Hall, 2000), p. 11.

23. Porter, *Competitive Advantage.*

24. Another way to consider this is to recognize that marketing is the only part of the organization that creates margin, not costs!

Chapter 2

Business-to-Business Environment: Customers, Organizations, and Markets

OVERVIEW

In this chapter, several key ideas are introduced that are used throughout this book. Categorizing business customers helps the marketer begin to understand the business environment in which she operates, while categorizing suppliers helps the understanding of the competitive environment. Looking inward, the marketer can also begin to understand the constraints faced by her own company as a member of a supplier category. Building on the value chain idea introduced in Chapter 1, the concept of value networks aids in a marketer's understanding of relationships that currently exist and that need to be built to create superior value for customers. Two models of business evolution are provided to give a framework for understanding how business environments change: the product life cycle concept and the technology adoption life cycle. These concepts provide frameworks for understanding the business-to-business marketer's environment from a large-scale viewpoint as well as help frame the problems and opportunities that need to be addressed.

The opening example shows how TRW operates in multiple categories, how its customers operate in multiple categories, and how TRW's business and marketing strategies are affected. The example also points out how operating in multiple modes creates management challenges.

Example: TRW Automotive Operates in Multiple Categories

Though the brands are not well known to consumers, TRW products contribute value to practically every car and truck produced. In 2007, TRW sales to the automotive segment totaled over $14 billion.[1] Does your car or truck have antilock brakes? TRW, including the Kelsey Hayes brand, has provided a greater number of antilock brake systems to the automobile manufacturers market than any other company, beginning in 1969 with the first electronically controlled antilock brake system (ABS) launched on the Lincoln Mark IV. Does your car or truck have an air bag? You have an even chance that TRW manufactured the sensors that detect the severity of an accident and trigger the air bag—also provided by TRW. It does not stop with these products. Lucas electrical components, sodium-cooled engine valves, vehicle suspension systems, and engine management systems are all part of the TRW basket of offerings. Of course, should you require service or replacement of any of these components, the repair technician can pinpoint the problem with TRW diagnostic service equipment and install TRW aftermarket parts. Not bad for a company that started in 1901 as a fastener manufacturer in Cleveland, Ohio (specialty fasteners are **still** one of TRW's product lines).

How does an organization continuously provide value to such diverse markets over a long period? By understanding the market, anticipating future value, and partnering with other market participants to create that value. TRW has recently gone through a process that has split apart TRW's two historic business lines—automotive and aerospace. Northrop Grumman acquired TRW in 2002. Northrop immediately spun off the automotive business to an investment group—Blackstone—who in 2003 relaunched TRW Automotive as an independent company, now solely focused on its automotive business.[2]

TRW Automotive is organized to address two major customer types, original equipment manufacturers and aftermarket customers. This initial segmentation might imply that customers within each segment have similar buying habits. This is, however, not likely. For instance, Volkswagen's purchase habits for braking systems are quite different from an individual repair technician's purchase habits for the same products in the aftermarket. While providing the same core product (e.g., brakes) to both customers, TRW recognizes that the value sought by each customer goes beyond a well-designed braking system that will safely stop the vehicle.

The Volkswagen perception of this value includes engineering design and development collaboration, durable components and reliable supply, and interaction with production planning to ensure effective supply logistics (the right quantity at the right time and place for this customer)—all at a competitive price. In this instance, the brakes are components specified and purchased by Volkswagen for incorporation into a Volkswagen product; Volkswagen becomes the **end user** of the components. There is little if any recognition of TRW parts by the purchaser of a new Volkswagen.

In the aftermarket, TRW recognizes that the customer wants quick diagnosis of the vehicle problem and immediate availability of replacement components. In this case, the end user is the repair technician or the vehicle owner whose primary interest is getting the vehicle roadworthy. While the core product is the same, the offerings are not alike. Volkswagen purchases millions of identical brake components directly from TRW. The repair technician buys brake components individually, as needed, and of many different designs and variations to match the different vehicles being serviced. TRW recognizes these fundamental differences in value sought and treats these markets as completely different segments.

The aftermarket organization at TRW represents all TRW products in the automotive sector. TRW Automotive Aftermarket operates as a separate business unit with a global service network covering more than 120 countries. Original equipment manufacturer markets are managed from a headquarters operation in Livonia, Michigan, with support centers for vehicle manufacturers in seventeen countries. While this may appear as logistics management, it is much more than that.

TRW partners with its customers and its suppliers. As a supplier, TRW must know the methods and culture of customers as well as the immediate supply needs. TRW must examine customers not just as buyers of components but also as participants in their own demanding markets. TRW's awareness of these demands, the needs of its customers' customers, helps TRW anticipate customer needs.

TRW manages its supply chain by requiring its suppliers to meet rigorous quality standards and share substantial information with TRW and other suppliers. In this way, TRW maintains product quality and assures on-time delivery. TRW continues to look to improve its supply chain systems. For instance, TRW participates as a member of the China Auto Suppliers Group, a consortium of automotive suppliers and manufacturers that cooperates to enhance supply chains involving Chinese auto systems and components manufacturers. In 2004, the China Auto Suppliers Group began offering a mobile, wireless electronic system for tracking and routing products moving through the supply system.[3] Such a system reduces time and cost of supply, value that is passed on to TRW's customers.

> Complete braking and traction control systems or complete suspension systems are designed and developed in conjunction with major customers. The performance of the system impacts the reputation of the customer. The customer seeks suppliers who demonstrate not just product or technology competence but an understanding of their markets and how the supplier can contribute value to the customer's offering. How does an organization continuously provide value to markets over a long period? It is by knowing its customers and their organizations and the markets in which they make decisions.

LEARNING OBJECTIVES

By reading this chapter, you will

- Understand the different kinds of business customers.
- Understand the different categories of business marketers.
- Gain an appreciation of the different kinds of competitive market structures and their effects on buying behavior.
- Understand how the value chain concept is extended by the value network concept and by the special case of integrated supply chains.
- Reinforce and extend your understanding of the product life cycle (PLC) and its impacts on business-to-business markets.
- Gain an initial introduction to the technology adoption life cycle (TALC) and its implications for targeting and positioning.

INTRODUCTION

Customer organizations and markets evolve over time just as products and technologies do. What at first may seem like a natural combination of two organizations in today's fast-changing market, the combination of FedEx and Kinko's described at the opening of Chapter 1, actually redefines the competitive positioning of the companies. No single element (i.e., the Internet or the increase in online purchasing—particularly by consumers) is the sole contributor to changes in the market environment. A combination of factors coincides to create change in the market, and companies often must respond with a new combined value of their offering. Similarly, the TRW example also illustrates how a company can operate in multiple value networks and form partnerships to enhance its positioning within those networks.

In this chapter, we examine traditional business patterns and see how organizations and markets have evolved as the value needs of customers react to an ever-changing environment. The concept of evolving business patterns and value as seen by the customer is not a new notion to industry; rather, it is just one that seems to have a large number of convenient exceptions. Firms engaged in fast-paced markets often claim that they usually do not have time to "study" their customers. More adept competition uses this as an opportunity to move ahead with new offerings better geared to meet customer desires.

PRACTICAL APPLICATION OF MARKET GENERALIZATIONS

The concepts discussed in this chapter are the foundation of a marketing manager's thinking process. In and of themselves, the concepts hold no prescriptions for specific actions that a business-to-business marketing manager can take. The practical aspect of categorizing products, analyzing the nature of competition in the market, tracking PLCs, and understanding the TALC is the framework provided for perceiving the business environment. All of these concepts provide insight into how the other actors in the marketer's environment will generally act and react. They also give some clues as to how the environment is likely to change in time—though not specific changes and when they will occur.

There are several forms of product, competition, and market combinations that make up the business environment. Common configurations often have sets of marketing activities that tend to be associated with them. An understanding of these generalizations can assist the marketer to better understand how customers in certain environments will behave, how they will perceive value, and how competitors will try to create superior value.

TYPES OF ORGANIZATIONAL CUSTOMERS

Many business-to-business marketers have established their own systems for classifying customers, suited to their own specific needs. What these systems are and how they are applied depend on the marketer's company's particular situation. Understanding different customer groups and why they are clustered together can provide insight into how and why customers in those markets view value. This section presents a standard way of thinking about categories of businesses. These categories represent a beginning for the marketer in trying to understand segmentation in her market and give a first clue concerning what strategies the customers will pursue and how they will be constrained. The categories are presented in no particular order.

Commercial Enterprises

The classification of commercial enterprises reflects a segmentation of for-profit organizations based on how the products or services in question are going to be used. This group includes industrial distributors and dealers, resellers, original equipment manufacturers, and users or end users.

INDUSTRIAL DISTRIBUTORS   Also known as industrial wholesalers, these organizations act as middlemen providing the economic utilities of form, time, place, and possession to the manufacturers of the products they distribute and segments of customers of those manufacturers that they serve. The creation of assortments of products from many manufacturers to closely match the needs of customer segments is a major added value of middlemen. Business marketers often elect to use middlemen to reach customers whose purchase volumes do not justify direct sales efforts. Chapter 14 contains a complete discussion of marketing channels, including appropriate products for this type of representation and the value provided by these middlemen. For now, note that these intermediaries take ownership of goods from manufacturers and provide their customers timely access to these goods.

VALUE ADDED RESELLERS   The addition of **value added resellers** (VARs) to the marketplace has broadened traditional intermediary concepts. More than distributors or wholesalers, VARs provide an offering with unique enhancements to manufacturers' products. Typically, a VAR provides systems to its customers (computer software and hardware integration, communications systems, etc.) tailored to a particular customer's needs. The VAR draws on goods and services from many manufacturers to create these custom systems, often developing unique expertise in the integration of many different products. The combined offering may include portions of products and services from different organizations that, without the VAR, would normally be competitors. Thus, the VAR's integration of offerings from many sources is, in effect, the creation of a **value network** at the user level. Later in this chapter we look at value networks, coalitions to satisfy specific segment needs, as a rapidly developing competitive form.

ORIGINAL EQUIPMENT MANUFACTURERS   **Original equipment manufacturers** (OEMs) purchase goods to incorporate them into goods they produce and sell to their customers. Business-to-business marketers spend the major part of their resources approaching, learning about, developing, and satisfying these customers. OEMs are usually the largest-volume users of goods and services, particularly in oligopolistic markets, as we discuss later in this chapter.

For example, General Motors (GM) purchases tires from Goodyear; Hewlett-Packard (HP) purchases computer processors from Intel. GM and HP use tires and computer processors, respectively, as an original part of the products they offer to their customers. Note that Goodyear and Intel, both OEM suppliers in this scenario, offer their products to customers in the replacement market through distributors as well. While the total offer is significantly different (tires through distribution are aimed at local dealers with lower volumes and greater geographic diversity than vehicle manufacturers), the core products, tires and computer processors, remain unchanged.

USERS OR END USERS   Manufacturers that purchase goods and services for consumption, either as supplies, capital goods, or materials for incorporation into their products such that the identity of the purchased product is lost are known as **users** or **end users**. When providing tires to GM, Goodyear is an OEM in the preceding example. When purchasing steel for fabrication into steel tire belts, Goodyear is an end user. Goodyear has specified the properties of and type of steel as part of its tire design process. The steel supplier views Goodyear as its end user because the steel, produced to the Goodyear specification, becomes an integral part of the tires and loses its separate identity.

Business marketers find that this traditional relationship is changing as end users attempt to differentiate their products by communicating the quality of their raw materials or components obtained from their suppliers. Recognizing this trend, suppliers have begun to brand their products and communicate the value of their brands downstream to the end users' customers.[4] Successfully branding business-to-business products allows the supplier or brand owner the opportunity to capture some of the margin that the end user obtains by charging higher prices to its own customers. This also places responsibility for the performance of the product with the supplier as well as the specifier.

TRW brands several of its product lines, principally because it does so much activity in the automotive parts aftermarket. TRW brands include *Kelsey-Hayes* braking products, *TRW* steering and suspension systems, *Autospecialty* brake and clutch components, *Power Stop Extreme Performance* rotors, and *9-1-1 Extreme Performance* heavy duty brake pads.[5] Using the same branding across the OEM and aftermarket lines of business actually increases the value that TRW provides to both OEM and aftermarket (end user) customers. OEM customers gain assurance that their products will be supported and can be easily maintained by service and repair technicians. Further, the inclusion of TRW's premium brands in the manufacturer's cars can be communicated to consumers to assure them that the cars are well built, using high-quality components. Value is provided to aftermarket customers—repair technicians and consumers—by offering to them the same brands of parts that were originally installed on the car. This assures end users that the replacement parts meet original equipment specifications and will work just as well as the original parts.

Government Units

Purchases by more than 85,000 local, state, and federal government units make up about one-third of the U.S. gross national product (GNP). Government is the largest consuming group in the United States. Widely dispersed with large numbers of players, government markets are influenced by specifying agencies, legislators, and evaluators, as well as, hopefully, the eventual users. Government purchasing can also be the subject of significant public scrutiny. What business marketers have come to appreciate as value in the private sector can take on a completely different meaning in the public sector.

Complicated procurement laws and regulations often have social goals and policies as the driving force. Preference to certain types of suppliers, socially motivated general contract provisions, and the potential impact of quotas and other regulations that seemingly have nothing to do with the product can be frustrating to business marketers. In these situations, the buyer's view of value will be quite different from a buyer in the private sector. For instance, the federal government, most state governments, and many municipalities have requirements that a certain percentage of contracts be awarded to small businesses, minority-owned businesses, or businesses owned by women. In many foreign countries, suppliers to government agencies are often required to be domestic (to that country) suppliers or have a domestic company as a partner. The social goals and policies of government purchasing can impact the entire supply chain of an offering. In theory, this is little different from the private sector, provided the marketer is focused on customer needs rather than the product. It is necessary to examine what value is expected by the government customer and who or what the influencing factors will be.

The specialized role that government activities play in our society (national defense, disaster relief, education, social and political agenda, etc.) leads to nonstandard products. This complexity and the lack of standardization are often the result of significant negotiation by a diverse group of stakeholders. While competitive bidding is often required to avoid demonstrating any favoritism or undo influence, negotiated contracts are also possible, particularly where research and development is necessary or there is no competition to the value provider in question. When the marketer understands the value chain of the customer organization, as well as the complexity of the government agency's buying center influences (see Chapter 3), the marketer can perform very effectively and profitably doing business with government.

Nonprofit and Not-for-Profit Organizations

Institutional customers such as hospitals, churches, colleges, nursing homes, and so on are part of this customer category. At first glance, it may appear that the major part of the marketing mix used to appeal to this customer base is price. As with any customer group, however, the best value recognized in the exchange is important. Many of these organizations are also subject to significant public scrutiny. As a result, their buying habits may become similar to those of government units, particularly if there is a strong social agenda associated with the organization.

Producer Types

The goods they produce may also serve to classify business-to-business organizations. As previously stated, these classifications may provide initial bases that a marketing manager can use for segmenting markets.

RAW MATERIALS PRODUCERS   Depending on the goods or materials position in its life cycle and the product degree of uniqueness or distinction from competition, producers of materials may find markets more sensitive to price. Raw materials suppliers, particularly those that have significant competition from generic types, will seek added value positions unrelated to the core product. A supplier of sugar to a large bakery may find that the texture or granule size of its product or how well it dissolves may be a distinctive advantage. Raw materials (such as steel, plastics, and glass) are usually supplied by a few very large producers who sell their products directly to large end users, relying on industrial distributors to serve smaller customers.

Often, raw materials lose their "identity" when combined into a customer's product. As an example, consider a metal fabricator whose customers are computer manufacturers. The fabricator purchases sheets of steel from its steel supplier of choice. The fabricator forms the steel into a computer cabinet, as defined by its customer's specification. The customer knows the sheet steel purchased by the fabricator as a sturdy cabinet for a computer housing, not as a branded material supplied by a particular steel company. The commodity nature of the steel has been replaced by the added value, created by the fabricator, of the form and function of the cabinet.

COMPONENT PARTS AND MANUFACTURED MATERIALS PRODUCERS   Components and manufactured materials (e.g., upholstery fabric for furniture, touchpads for notebook computers) usually retain their identity even when fully incorporated into the customer's product. These goods have a continuous identity and are more easily differentiated from their direct competition. Producers of these goods have added value to the materials and components they have purchased to create value for their customers. Component parts such as the small motors used in computer disk drives are incorporated by disk drive manufacturers in essentially the same form as provided by the motor manufacturer. The component producer's core product contribution is still recognizable after its inclusion in the customer's offering. In this instance, the small motor manufacturer is an OEM supplier to the disk drive manufacturer that incorporates the motors into the disk drives it sells to its customers.

Industry standards are parameters that describe the functionality, interface, and design practices in an industry. These standards can be developed by industry committees, professional groups within an industry, or established by government. Often, an industry standard will result from many players in a market embracing a particular way of doing something even though that method has not been formally agreed on. These "defacto standards" are often one of the goals of market owners. Market ownership is discussed in greater detail in later chapters.

CAPITAL GOODS MANUFACTURERS   Capital goods—those goods used to produce output—are usually purchased with input from many parts of the organization. These are "big ticket" purchases, such as machinery specifically designed for an automated assembly line or real estate for a new building, with considerable risk involved for the customer. The process is lengthy and usually includes the development of a rather sophisticated specification to ensure that the needs of the organization are met and that the organization gets what it has been promised. When customers invest in a capital item, they must place a tremendous amount of trust in the supplier—and write a good specification.

Customers of capital goods expect an offering that includes installation, equipment, accessories, employee training, and often, financing. Often, trials or evaluation installations are required. As a substitute, suppliers may provide testimonials of successful installation and application for other customers, provided confidentiality concerns of both the current and previous customers can be accommodated.

If a company is providing accessory equipment—or providing an accessory service, such as cleaning uniforms or moving trade show equipment—the key to providing value is to be compatible with the **industry standards** for the primary offering. For instance, keyboard manufacturers for computers must conform to standards for data input and connection to the computer. Makers of add-on gadgets for personal digital assistants (PDAs), such as the Palm Pilot, must conform to the physical connection requirements of the devices and to the PalmOS software operating system. To ensure high financial performance, the accessory equipment supplier must pick the right standard. Once a standard has been set, the surviving accessory suppliers need to focus on driving their costs down and, if possible, branding. Good branding strategy and execution earn a price premium (see Chapter 13), but this, too, is limited by the relative value and price of the primary offering.

CUSTOMER SPECIFICATIONS   Suppliers should realize that, from the customer's viewpoint, the specification is a device used to level the playing field among all potential suppliers. By demanding strict adherence to the terms of a specification, the customer reduces opportunities for differentiation between competing suppliers. Obviously, this is exactly the opposite of what the marketer or supplier strives for. The supplier searches for any possible way to make its offering distinctive— better and different—from the competition. This buying behavior is discussed in Chapter 3.

Customer Needs Influenced by Classification of Markets

The proliferation of so many classification systems can lead to questioning their usefulness. By now, you may be asking yourself why these classifications are important. As the classifications stand alone, they are of little value other than for creating data. No single classification method serves all marketing needs. In fact, rigid organizational classification systems can get in the way of effective benefit-based segmentation; but they can also be a significant factor in development of strategies.

Each of these different types of products and organizations, however, has different levels of involvement by the many individuals involved in the customer's purchase decision. Purchases of capital items used to produce output are often the endgame of a major investment decision by the customer, involving many people within the customer organization who play varying roles in the purchase (see the discussion concerning the buying center in Chapter 3). A routine purchase of materials and parts has a smaller group of interested parties; the supplier who recognizes and assists these participants to maximize the value of the offering for the particular situation can have a substantial advantage.

CLASSIFYING THE BUSINESS-TO-BUSINESS MARKET ENVIRONMENT

The discussion so far has dealt with classifying individual companies based on the kind of offering they provide. The marketer can use these classifications to get a sense of what kinds of needs the customer organization has, what sorts of motives and constraints drive the competitors in the classified market, and what constraints the marketer faces in designing marketing strategy.

We now shift our viewpoint to classifying the market environments in which business-to-business marketers must operate. As part of this, we briefly examine the effects of different economic market structures and how these structures impact the relationships between market participants.

Publics

Recall from your marketing principles course the factors that make up the market environment. These generally apply as well to business markets as to consumer markets. They include the various publics, or communities of interested parties who are not customers, channel members, suppliers, or competitors—not direct participants in a market. These publics have interests because of economic or societal effects of activity in the market or because they provide financing to the direct participants.

FINANCIAL PUBLICS   Financial publics include banks and other lending institutions, investors, investment banks, venture capital firms and investors, stock exchanges, brokerage houses and financial analysts, and investment institutions such as retirement funds and mutual funds investment houses. The members of this community seek to maximize their own financial performance by investing in companies and investment instruments they think will perform best. They develop and share a great deal of information about companies and industries. Very often, they attempt to impact corporate action with their ability to influence how the company is perceived by the financial community. Financial publics can be large employee retirement plans responsible for investing their funds for specific growth goals. (For example, the California Public Employees' Retirement System (CalPERS), has significant funds to invest and can influence the companies in which they choose to invest.) Or, financial publics can be the fund managers at major investment banks and firms (e.g., Fidelity Investments). Many independent (as well as institutional) investors are sensitive to the views and directions taken by the financial publics.

Business-to-business marketers need to understand the role played by these entities in making resources available. Much marketing effort is spent in communicating with the members of the financial public and working to meet their particular needs. Most medium- to large-sized companies now have specialists in investor relations devoted to maintaining relationships with the financial community. These specialists usually are part of corporate marketing or corporate finance within the organization. While these specialists handle most of the communication with the financial community, higher-level marketing managers are sometimes called upon to make presentations to venture capitalists, bankers, or brokerage house analysts to explain the company's marketing vision and strategy.

As is shown in Chapter 15, one of the most difficult tasks for corporate marketing communications specialists is to ensure that all outgoing communications have compatible and cross-reinforcing messages. The financial public must be considered another audience that perceives communications. They are not isolated from communications intended for customer groups, and vice versa. Accordingly, marketers must be careful to consider the financial public in efforts to keep consistency in all marketing messages.

INDEPENDENT PRESS   The media can publish news that can enhance or destroy a market position. On the positive side, it is important for companies to maintain good relationships with the news media that serves their particular industry so that good news about a company can receive the most notice. When negative things concerning the company arise, media attention can be devastating. We have sometimes referred to this as "the 60 minutes syndrome," named after the CBS long-running news magazine program. As is discussed later in Chapters 15 and 16, the best defense for a company in this type of situation is a proactive public relations effort that "inoculates" against a single incident causing serious damage.

PUBLIC INTEREST GROUPS   Many public interest groups, though comprising a minority in the population, are often able to get the attention of the media or opinion leaders and thus focus "popular" attention on their issues. In some instances, this effort can succeed in attracting the attention of the financial publics, leading to an impact on investors. Again, a good public relations effort combined with an effective inoculation strategy can minimize the negative impact of these groups. A market-driven organization, however, should recognize its societal role and that public interest groups may be an early indication of shifts in the mainstream market.

As an example of a firm's societal role and the attention interest groups can bring to bear, consider how the soaring gasoline prices during the first six months of 2000, and again during 2006, invigorated environmentalists efforts regarding fuel consumption. These efforts were focused particularly on large SUVs, also a target of vehicle safety groups. The largest and most profitable producer of these vehicles, Ford Motor Company, reacted by adding safety features to its larger SUVs and making a commitment to improve the fuel economy of its entire line of SUVs by 25 percent.[6] Were these actions recognition of societal responsibility, good marketing, or a clever public relations position? Whatever the answer, the result is the same.

INTERNAL PUBLICS   Every employee is a representative of the organization to the general public, and every employee is a representative of her part of the organization to the other components of the organization. The reputation and the image of a firm or its parts are greatly impacted by the attitude of its employees. Firms are known as "good to work for" primarily based on the word of mouth from current and past employees, just as different parts of a firm are impacted by conversation among employees. A major aim of internal marketing programs is to promote belonging and ownership among employees that will be reflected in their attitudes when away from as well as on the job.

The Macroenvironment

Also included in the market environment are existing trends and other macroenvironment factors. The seven macroenvironment factors generally addressed in marketing texts are the demographic, economic, sociocultural, natural, technological, competitive, and legal and political environments. In this chapter, we focus on the first six factors in this list, with emphasis on how they influence value creation. The legal and political environment is fully discussed in Chapter 4.

THE DEMOGRAPHIC ENVIRONMENT   Demographics are the vital statistics that describe a population. The demographic environment includes the characteristics of the population in the geographic regions in which the company does business. Demographic variables include the distribution of ages, incomes, wealth, mobility, education, family composition, religion, ethnic background, and living conditions. All of these variables have an influence on consumer consumption, which translates into business consumption in the effort to meet consumer needs.

Businesses themselves have demographic characteristics, including the type and size of industries that exist, the size and location of companies, the ages of the businesses, and the size of the functional areas within the companies. Many of these characteristics will be the basis of, as discussed earlier, a determination of how the business is classified. Demographic characteristics may be associated with particular needs and buying behaviors. Part of developing a relationship with customers is knowing the characteristics of the customer's organization. The demographic characteristics of a firm and its products can impact this. Older firms or products will behave differently than new firms with new products. Multiproduct firms will have several products at various points in the PLC. The multiproduct firm may design its marketing and sales operations around the point in the life cycle of the product and associated customer behavior. Marketers should thus be aware of the relevant demographics of the populations and businesses that comprise their environments.

THE ECONOMIC ENVIRONMENT   The macroeconomies of regions in which the company does business also influence how business-to-business customers buy and consume. The **macroeconomy** of a region or jurisdiction is the sum total of all economic activity in the area and certain economic characteristics of note. These characteristics include how fast the economy is growing (or declining) in size, the level of employment, the rate of unemployment, interest rates, and exchange rates of currency between different economies.

The state of the economy affects customers' willingness and ability to buy, principally by affecting personal income (which influences derived demand in business-to-business markets), interest rates, and company profits. The economy similarly influences channel members. Competitors may have lowered ability to respond to perceived threats and/or undertake new initiatives in an unfavorable economy, leading to an opportunity for other players in the same market, assuming the other player recognizes the environmental factors at play and takes advantage of the opportunity. On the other side of the coin, competitors may be more desperate and willing to attack when the economy has hurt them. Public policy may also be influenced by the state of the economy. Finally, the internal environment of a company will probably be affected by the economy: Individual employees may be more cautious when the economy is not favorable, and it is likely that fewer resources will be available for new initiatives. A grasp of the trends in the economy will help a marketer to anticipate how all of these participants within the marketer's environment will tend to behave.

THE SOCIOCULTURAL ENVIRONMENT   Just as in consumer marketing, the culture of the society in which the business operates has an impact on what people buy, why they buy it and use it, how they buy, and how they react to marketing stimuli. A **culture** is all the symbols and themes that reflect a society's norms and values. In any large society, multiple cultures and subcultures may be relevant. Social trends within a culture define the topics of interest to people in a society and further define what is acceptable and unacceptable in the way of products, services, communications, and even prices. Similarities in behavior—the cultural norms—of a market or group of businesses in that market can often be inferred by how they are classified. The business marketer must be aware of the cultural norms and social trends affecting customers, competitors, partners, and employees.

THE NATURAL ENVIRONMENT   The natural environment includes natural resources, raw materials, the ecology, the weather, and, on occasion, geologic activity. Much of the effect of the natural environment comes from raw materials, water, and energy resources, which of course are needed in some degree by almost every company. Marketers perceive the impacts of the natural environment principally as constraints on the products that they can offer. The constraints are imposed by the availability and quality of raw materials for products and water and energy for operations. For most marketers, the impacts of availability and quality are an interaction between the natural resources themselves and the companies involved in the supply chain. Suppliers of capital goods that require energy, cooling water, or even real estate can develop differentiation from their competition by maximizing the efficiency of the capital goods they market.

In the last several decades, the environment has taken on another set of influences as societal preferences and public interest groups have taken to the cause of environmental protection and conservation of natural resources. The effects of this movement are influenced as much by consumer perceptions as by reality in the natural environment. The leveraging of public attitudes, as expressed through the actions taken by business-to-business customers, can have a dramatic impact on a business.

A good example is the McDonald's switch from plastic foam packaging to wax-coated paper packaging for most of its menu items.[7] Consumers perceived foam packaging as unfriendly to the environment and paper as biodegradable and a good environmental choice. (In fact, foam packaging techniques no longer used chlorofluorocarbons—CFCs—in the manufacturing process and polystyrene foam is generally recyclable.) The wax-coated paper would not biodegrade. McDonald's made the change because of consumer perceptions, not reality. Consider the loss to their foam packaging supplier.

The lesson for business-to-business marketers is to pay attention to trends in the perceptions of consumers and try to anticipate how this will affect the behavior of businesses attempting to provide value to consumers.

THE TECHNOLOGICAL ENVIRONMENT   Advanced technology is developed and housed in companies; universities; research institutes; government agencies and laboratories; and sometimes in industry consortiums, such as the semiconductor industry's Sematech and the U.S. automotive industry's Advanced Battery Consortium. Technological developments can dramatically change business-to-business markets. This may include changes in a competitor's product or process technology, competition arising from outside the industry because a new technology meets customers' needs, changes in channel members' technology that alter their competitive position, or changes in customers' technology that change their needs or buying behavior. News of technology developments can surface in several forums.

The technological environment has been both a blessing and a curse for business-to-business marketers: a blessing as technology can open new markets and create new ways to satisfy customer needs; a curse if a firm has not kept pace with technology and finds itself with an obsolete product line. Through technology, customer service can be improved and more information is readily available to marketers. Technology, however, is changing at an ever-increasing pace. Still, this is no excuse for not being prepared. Technology was ultimately a major contributor to the demise of vacuum tube electronics powerhouses such as Sylvania, TungSol, GE, and RCA; and the railroads were victims of changing technology in business logistics and passenger travel. More recently, unwillingness and inability to adapt to technology trends—the dominance of networked workstations and personal computers over mini-computers—spelled the fall of Digital Equipment Corporation (DEC), and digital imaging has all but eliminated consumer demand for Polaroid instant imaging products. Today's technology has changed much more rapidly than the changes faced by RCA or DEC. This emphasizes the need for marketers to be even more vigilant in today's environment.

The warning that rapid technological change brings to business-to-business marketers is really very simple: *Product technology should not play a major role in your customer's decision to buy your product.* Technological advantage is fleeting. If you do not replace your technology with the next generation, your competitor will—and it's likely to be a competitor that you did not even know you had! Not anticipating a technological change that affects customer buying behavior offers another way for competitors to gain an advantage.

THE COMPETITIVE ENVIRONMENT   From Levitt's "Marketing Myopia"[8] to McKenna's "Marketing Is Everything,"[9] significant effort has been made to improve business marketers' recognition of the full dimensions of possible competitors. The IBM Selectric typewriter was not replaced in the market by another typewriter (not even the next-generation IBM typewriter that was the intended IBM replacement), but it was replaced by a new technology. Similarly,

---

Pure Competition

- Many buyers and sellers exist with no single entity having much effect on the price—no leverage positions. The market is significantly larger than any one entity (buyer or seller).
- Generally exists in commodities, such as raw materials and agricultural products
- Price is a major component of the marketing mix and products are not differentiable, thus sellers seldom deviate from the market-clearing price.

Monopolistic Competition

- Many buyers and sellers exist, but product is differentiable such that a range of prices is possible.
- Products can vary in terms of quality, features, style, and so on, such as in specialty steel fabrication or in advertising services.
- Branding, advertising, personal selling, and so on, important to differentiate branding

Oligopolistic Competition

- Market consists of a few sellers who are highly sensitive to each other's strategies.
- Products can be uniform or nonuniform. Typical examples include autos, airlines, and steel industries.
- Few sellers exist because of barriers to entry.
- Price has often been aimed at maintaining stability (note chaos in airline industry).

Pure Monopoly

- Consists of one seller
- Examples are Postal Service; utilities; and, before government action, Standard Oil.
- "New" competitors to the products and services provided by this group (such as windmill power companies) are generally small, niche players indistinguishable (or barely visible) in the market.

EXHIBIT 2-1 Competitive Forms in Business-to-Business Markets

---

dedicated word processor manufacturers (e.g., Lanier, NBI) should have seen that electronics technology and third-party software would lead to full-function desktop computers.

Exhibit 2-1 describes four common types of competitive markets (you may recognize these from your economics principles course). Although all of these forms can be found in business-to-business markets, as indicated in the examples for each of the four types, **oligopolies** have traditionally dominated the industrial competitive arena. For example, the small number of major automobile producers in the United States (GM, Ford, Chrysler, Toyota, Honda, etc.) purchase the large majority of all synthetic rubber, lead, and glass produced in the United States. A similar situation exists in the grain markets, with companies like Kellogg's, General Mills, and a few others purchasing most of the grains produced. Even when there are smaller players in the market, evolutionary trends are often established by the competitive positioning of the major players. Three major players and a host of smaller niche players seem a natural state of competition in an oligopoly. Fewer than three major players tend to drive market players to collusion.[10]

If a marketer competes in an oligopolistic market, strategy depends on the marketer's current position within the oligopoly. If the company is one of the leaders in the market, strategies should be pursued to differentiate from the other leaders while building volume. If the company is a smaller player, then its marketers should be looking for smaller, defensible niches in which the company can dominate. As you would expect, oligopolies are natural examples of the *80/20 rule*—80 percent of a supplier's sales volume is likely to come from 20 percent of its customers. It is imperative to build strong, collaborative relationships with those large-volume customers.

In many other business-to-business markets, monopolistic competition or pure competition exists. The key in either market is to look for ways to differentiate the offering, creating superior value compared to competitors' offerings. Even after differentiation has been established, the offering must be constantly updated to create more value.

Commodity markets might seem resistant to differentiation, but it can be done with some creativity. Consider a sugar processor who differentiated its offering to a cereal manufacturer. The company worked with the manufacturer to alter the texture for the sugar so that the sugar would adhere to the cereal better when doused in milk. The change in the composition of the sugar was only part of the differentiation, however. The value to the cereal company also resided to a great deal in the supplier's willingness to collaborate in the relationship built between the two companies.

Usefulness of Classification

The act of classifying the market and its actors will not provide all the information necessary for choosing target segments and designing strategy. However, classification helps marketers to frame the issues, threats, and opportunities they face. These characterizations provide a good starting place for understanding the business environment. This should be an ongoing effort, adding to the information base as new pieces of information surface, as new trends emerge, and as new interpretations are developed.

VALUE NETWORKS AND SUPPLY CHAINS

The next two sections of this chapter concern ideas that further frame an understanding of the business environment. The classifications that have been described so far help the marketer see patterns in the business environment. However, the classifications are static and do not reflect the complexity or dynamics of the market. The concepts in this section and the next present a more dynamic view.

The first idea extends the concept of the value chain introduced in the previous chapter. The idea of the extended value chain (Exhibit 2-2) has more than a coincidental similarity to the concept of a supply chain. We see a supply chain as a network of relationships that produces and facilitates a physical flow of materials and goods from raw materials producers through to final customers. A value chain includes these relationships, plus the relationships that create or enhance added value from raw materials to final customers. Thus a value network would include, for instance, a patent holder licensing her technology to a component manufacturer. The component manufacturer would be considered to be within both the supply chain and the value chain; the patent holder would only be part of the value chain. Some other examples of

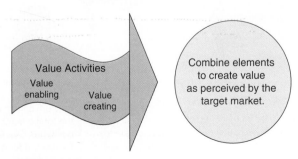

EXHIBIT 2-2   The Value Chain

value chain partners that would not be supply chain partners might include market research firms, research and development (R&D) laboratories, product design firms, security consultants, and so on.

The ebb and flow of market relationships that exist in today's complex markets, however, are not as straightforward as the flows of a supply chain or a value chain. From a marketing perspective, the implications of partnerships and alliances can create a multidimensional network of relationships that change frequently. In fast-paced markets, organizations are finding that the most productive way to create an offering with maximum value in the shortest time for a particular market or customer contains elements of offerings from several parties. These parties, or collaborators, can either be companies that the organization has previously allied with or may be a competitor in another market. Thus the chain expands into a multidimensional network. This network of collaborators includes nontraditional partners in a way that all partners in the network "win" as part of the team that provides the offering of greatest value.

For another customer or in another market, the network of partners may be completely different. When a marketer looks to enter a new market, a new network may be formed. This new network may include some or all of the members of the previous network. A firm's value network, depending on the variety of added value through collaboration, may be different for every major customer. Exhibit 2-3 represents the complexity of the network when multiple value chains are combined. Imagine how this network would look if more partners are added.

Companies that elect to operate through value networks must be well aware of the markets of their customers and their network partners. The network alliance will create opportunities to disclose, willingly or inadvertently, many facets of each partner's operations, creating challenges to many traditional organizational schemes and confidentiality (ethical) procedures. Proper barriers are needed to prevent undesired information exchange and can be developed to encourage the alliance while protecting other business interests.

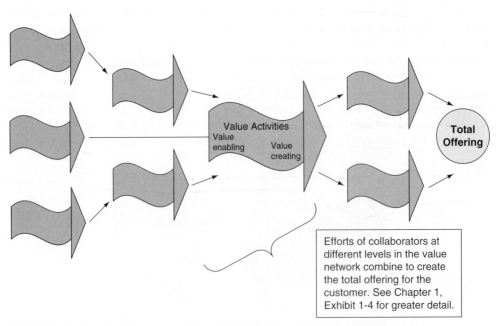

Value Activities
Value enabling   Value creating

Total Offering

Efforts of collaborators at different levels in the value network combine to create the total offering for the customer. See Chapter 1, Exhibit 1-4 for greater detail.

EXHIBIT 2-3   The Multidimensional Value Network

Supply Chain Management as a Form of Value Network Management

A supply chain can be seen as an integrated network of suppliers that provide inputs into the creation of an offering marketed to some segment of targeted customers. A lead collaborator usually integrates the supply chain and manages the relationships between suppliers within the chain. Often the lead collaborator will outsource the role of integration to an organization that specializes in supply chain management, such as United Parcel Service (UPS). In supply chains that are highly integrated—in which the lead collaborator sets strict terms for inclusion, enforces strict adherence to quality and timeliness requirements, and enforces the extensive sharing of information among supply chain members—we observe that lead collaborators are most often a very large customer for the supply chain.

The object of managing an integrated supply chain is to create value for the targeted customer(s) through a combination of availability, assured supply, customization, quality control, and cost control. Supply chain management thus results in higher sales quantities and more profitable pricing, consequently higher profits for the supply chain members. Exhibit 2-4 shows a depiction of an integrated supply chain. Company A is the lead collaborator. It specifies and manages the supply activities of Companies B through I, who provide inputs to Company A's internal value chain. Company A then offers the recombined inputs to its customers in target Segment X.

Using the Value Network and Supply Chain Concepts

What does this mean for the business marketer? Four sets of implications will be examined more closely in later chapters, because they concern specific analyses that must be done and specific actions to be taken.

1. When a business markets its products or services to a customer within an integrated supply chain, the marketer needs to understand the motives and behavior of the supply chain and the dominant company within the supply chain (see Chapters 3 and 14).
2. In analyzing competition, the marketer needs to look at competitive clusters of partnered companies rather than stand-alone single-company competitors (see Chapter 6).

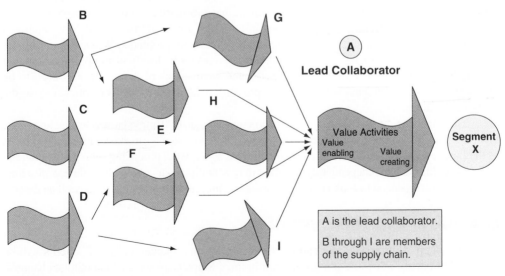

EXHIBIT 2-4 Supply Chain as a Value Network

3. In designing offerings, the marketer must decide on what pieces to outsource to partners, which to provide from the company's internal resources, and which to develop jointly with customer or supplier partners (see Chapters 8 and 9).
4. In building relationships, partners have to be sought, screened, contracted with, managed, and—in many cases—dropped (see Chapter 14).

The value network perspective is introduced here as an element of the market environment. While it is difficult enough to try to anticipate the effects of the business environment on several layers of customers and competitors, the marketer facing real-world situations must deal with an added layer of complexity in trying to understand the effects on a network of partners. In the context of this chapter, though, the question becomes, "How is a marketer's analysis of the marketer's own industry affected by consideration of partnership relationships?"

VALUE NETWORKS AND COMPETITION   One principal concern arises when a marketer considers the nature of competition in the market or industry. Monopolies, monopsonies (a **monopsony** is a market with one dominant buyer, much as a **monopoly** has a dominant supplier), and oligopolies tend to have some staying power, since the actors in such markets and the market forces themselves (such as high-entry barriers) can prevent substantial competition from arising. This is why we have antimonopoly laws (see Chapter 4). However, when a market is dominated by a partnership, instead of a single-company powerhouse, the partnership's dominance would seem to be more precarious. Partnerships can break apart or run into internal decision-making problems more easily than can a self-contained company. Thus, the competitive forms in which some players clearly dominate are in danger of transitioning rapidly into monopolistic competition due to shifting competitive forces. Also, partnerships can quickly produce sizable new competition that quickly changes the competitive landscape. For example, Microsoft, in its infamous U.S. antitrust case, made the argument that the partnerships between Netscape, Sun Microsystems, America Online, and others rapidly changed the nature of competition in many of the markets that were under scrutiny in the case.

Another concern arises in the technological environment. One of the key kinds of partnerships that has evolved over the last fifteen to twenty years is the joint development partnership. Very few companies have the resources to pursue basic research or comprehensive technical development of new products in complex technical areas. Joint ventures for such research and development can overcome many of the resource limitations problems. When examining the technical environment, then, a business marketer should look closely at the partnerships that exist to address new technology. The strengths and weaknesses of these alliances need to be examined to fully understand what technical progress is likely to occur—or not occur—in the foreseeable future.

The impact on the assessment of the macroenvironment, of the trend toward value networks, then, is a need to examine the partnership relationships that exist and can exist within the elements of the business environment. These networks may be synergistic, producing more value than the partners could produce independently; or, they may actually produce less value than is possible. Business marketers need to look at value networks as presenting opportunities as well as threats.

CHANGES IN MARKETS OVER TIME

It is not enough to understand the nature of competition in a market and what benefits will be perceived as having value just at a given point in time. Markets evolve as competitors, channels, customers, and technologies change. In this section, two ideas are introduced that help the marketer think about how her situation will change and how these changes might be successfully addressed.

It is important to have a sense of how a market has developed and how it is likely to change in the future. For instance, oligopolistic markets are generally not oligopolies from the very beginning. Usually they start out as a temporary monopoly when a company introduces a product with a radically new technology or business idea. As the product or business is improved and as prospective customers learn more about the value of the products and services, the market becomes more competitive as it draws more entrants. If the product easily becomes a commodity and there are minimal barriers to entry, the market often moves quickly toward pure competition with many players and slim margins. More complex offerings and markets will evolve more slowly. In either case, over time, a few competitors emerge that create brand identity and operating efficiency. As competitors who cannot match costs or differentiation drop out, the market evolves to an oligopoly

An oligopoly may also emerge after the market has gone through a period of monopolistic competition. After the introductory period, new entrants enter the market and are able to differentiate their offerings along several dimensions. They continue to develop the product technology but also make improvements on costs, business configurations, and the other three Ps of marketing. The market undergoes rapid or hypergrowth until the rate of new adoptions falls off. With the reduction in the growth rate, the inefficient competitors drop out and a slower-growing oligopolistic market emerges. A few companies dominate the mainstream market and smaller companies serve relatively small market niches.

Over the years, marketers, strategists, and academics have noticed patterns in how markets change over time. The following two ideas, namely the PLC and the TALC provide some generalizations about these patterns and what they mean. Of these two, the PLC is more generally usable. The TALC has particular applicability in the case of breakthrough innovations.

The Product Life Cycle

Marketing students will recognize characteristics of the PLC from prior discussion. The concept of the **product life cycle** is that product categories go through several "life" stages, as shown below in Exhibit 2-5.

Note that not all products follow the PLC as it is shown in the exhibit. Divergence from the classic bell-shaped PLC is partly dependent on the level of abstraction. The PLC for a single incarnation of a given technology (e.g., "Version 2" or "Release 3a") may deviate substantially

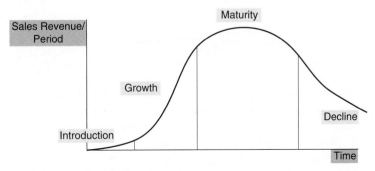

EXHIBIT 2-5   The Product Life Cycle

from the shape of the PLC and is really only a contributing element to the total sales curve for the product category as a whole.

The level at which the PLC has the most relevance is at the "category" level. Product category is still a nebulous concept and can create some ambiguity. For instance, one might ask whether Pentium-type microprocessors are a relevant category. The question arises when the marketer is trying to understand competitive dynamics for, say, laptop microprocessors from Intel and competitive offerings from Advanced Micro Devices (AMD). Should the marketer consider the "Duo Core" processor to be part of the overall Pentium life cycle, or does it deserve to have its own life cycle analyzed?

The answer lies in the purpose for which PLC analysis is chosen. The principal reasons why a marketer wants to understand the PLC for her offering or market is *to anticipate the general behavior of customers and the general nature of competition* that will be faced in the near future. Accordingly, the most useful level of abstraction for the Pentium or Duo Core example is probably at the level of the Pentium, overall. The nature of competition in the processor industry reflects a mature industry more so than it does an introductory market. Customers, such as Dell Computers, HP, and Gateway, know their needs and what they must do to meet them. Competition exists and is well entrenched. The market is oligopolistic, with Intel a dominant player and AMD a smaller but competitive second company. The next round of microprocessor innovations may upset this stable—though not static—environment. The new technology may be so advanced that the product-market behaves in a way that is consistent with the introductory stage of the PLC, in which the innovator has a temporary monopoly. Under these circumstances, members of the oligopoly must recognize that the business they are in is the value they create for customers—not the products they supply.[11]

As the use of any tool requires an understanding of its capabilities, the assumptions behind the PLC concept should be understood. First, the PLC, without the inclusion of significant additional information (such as those tools discussed later in Chapter 5), gives only general guidance on what to expect. It *does not specifically provide a means for predicting changes* from one stage to the next. Similarly, it *does not provide prescriptions for strategies or actions* that a firm should take during the current PLC stage or some future stage.

Concerning the first assumption (the inability to predict when the shape of the sales curve will change), realize that markets change as the various factors driving their nature change. Predicting when changes will occur is like predicting when the weather will change. Oftentimes a forecaster will get close, particularly when the prediction is for the very near future and historic patterns are well known. However, inflection points in the PLC curve occur because several factors interact concurrently that lead to these changes in trends in total sales. For instance, in the latter half of the 1980s, pundits predicted at the beginning of each year that year would be the "Year of the LAN," i.e., local area network. Finally, at the end of the decade, when Novell had a stable operating system available and when customers were ready to buy new equipment and software, LAN system sales rocketed. Several pundits were correct in predicting this growth period. However, they had been inaccurate in the prior two or three years for having predicted the same thing.

Concerning the second assumption (the inability to derive specific strategies from the PLC), the same difficulties arise. Any individual company faces a unique combination of multifaceted factors. The PLC provides a framework for organizing these in the marketer's mind. The marketer must assess the opportunities and threats that are posed at any given time and construct strategy based on matching the firm's strengths and weaknesses to these opportunities and threats. The PLC, then, can suggest some general directions in which the market may go, but the marketer's job is to find a unique strategy that provides superior value to targeted customers.

The PLC can be an aid in market situational analysis. Understanding the general theory that several factors interact concurrently, leading to changes in trends in total sales, marketers should be aware of and examine these factors (competitive actions, major price changes in the market, withdrawal of a major competitor, a major competitor adds new capacity, a major player introduces a new technology, and so on). An important ingredient in a strategic view of the market can result if there is recognition that a combination of events has taken place.

Understanding of the tenets of the PLC can be a major learning tool for students. Many strategic management tools (discussed in Chapter 5) relate to the stages of the PLC and have overlapping "rules." An understanding of this relationship can simplify the understanding of various tools and aid in the understanding of the interrelationship of the concurrent factors impacting a market situation.

The Technology Adoption Life Cycle

While the PLC has uses and limitations, it still provides a reminder to the marketer that things will change and the marketer must adapt. In the case of breakthrough innovation, additional insight may be gained by examining another life cycle that can be superimposed on the PLC, the **technology adoption life cycle**. The TALC focuses more on the kinds of customers and how they come to adopt the new technology.

BRIDGING A CHASM The TALC describes how a breakthrough innovation becomes adopted in a market. Geoffrey Moore[12] has taken the innovation diffusion model described by Everett Rogers[13] and extended it. Rogers divided adopters of a new innovation into groupings he called *innovators, early adopters, early majority, late majority, and laggards.* Moore updated these groupings based on his own research on high-tech, business-to-business products. He called the groupings *technophiles, visionaries, pragmatists, conservatives,* and *skeptics.*

Moore did not just change the names of the groups, though. He uses the TALC as a framework for explaining two principal observations about how technology markets evolve. The first observation is the existence of a **chasm**, a break in the sales growth curve for a new technology. The second observation is the chaos that occurs in a period of rapid growth that Moore calls the **tornado**. The tornado eventually produces the emergence of a dominant supplier. These two observations and the implications of the TALC have potential for providing useful guidance to the business marketer in technology markets.

Moore suggested that there were natural breaks in the TALC that occurred between each group or segment. Note on Exhibit 2-6 that a relatively large break—the chasm—occurs in the TALC between visionaries and pragmatists.[14] Moore claims this occurs because pragmatists will not treat visionaries as credible references when it comes to adoption. Pragmatists want proven solutions, with little trauma in their adoption. Pragmatists will not buy until other pragmatists buy and provide references. It is difficult, though, to find the pragmatists who buy first and then provide references for other pragmatists. Visionaries, on the other hand, try to make quantum jumps in the way they compete. Hence, they adopt an innovation before all the pieces are in place to make the product work well, that is, before a "whole product" exists. The visionary users then create or buy customized pieces of the system to make the whole thing work. The trial-and-error process of sculpting such a customized solution can create a state of chaos within the adopting organization. Thus, visionaries tend to obtain a reputation for wreaking havoc and pragmatists will not trust them.

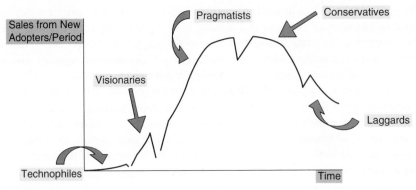

EXHIBIT 2-6   The Technology Adoption Life Cycle

To cross this chasm, Moore claims that the supplier of an innovation must pass through the first two segments—the technophiles and the visionaries. These are necessary because the whole product cannot be defined and then developed until enough experience has been gained. Then the supplier must find a "beachhead," or foothold, niche among pragmatists on the other side of the chasm. This niche must have a need for the product that is so compelling that pragmatist buyers will take the risk of buying without the assurance of references from other pragmatists who have already adopted. The supplier must find such a niche, create a whole product to meet the compelling need of these buyers, and offer the whole product to these buyers through proper positioning, translating a "specialty" product to a more mainstream and higher-volume offering. The proper positioning means that the one or two most compelling benefits of the whole product are clearly communicated and delivered.

The chasm, or **market development gap**,[15] marks a major change in the way an organization does business. Externally, the customer segment changes from visionaries to pragmatists. Accordingly, the main benefits sought by customers will change and the marketer's offering will have to change to meet this need. Internally, the company's production capability, size, and culture will change. None of this change is automatic.

ACROSS THE CHASM AND INTO THE TORNADO   Once this first beachhead is addressed, pragmatist buyers talk to other pragmatists and a chain reaction spreads across many niches within the market. Naturally, if an organization successfully capitalizes on a new technology, either its own or that of a supplier, competitors for that market segment with similar value offerings will gravitate to the new technology. Instead of customer acceptance of the technology, the *market* begins to accept the technology. Eventually, this acceptance can lead to standardization within a segment or an industry.

If the market is large enough, a groundswell of demand can develop. The market goes into a period of rapid sales growth, the tornado.[16] This portion of the TALC superimposes directly onto the growth period of the PLC. Moore claims that in a tornado, the market wants to support the market leader. This occurs because the buyers, pragmatists that they are, face the least internal chaos if the systems they are buying are a recognized standard.[17] There will be plenty of peripherals and software that will work easily with the leader's product. There will be plenty of consultant expertise available to help them through problem periods. As upgrades become available, adoption of these upgrades causes the least internal upheaval if they are backward compatible with the leader's product that was purchased earlier in the tornado.

The market-chosen leader, then, has the opportunity to become the "gorilla," as Moore dubs it. The gorilla can do what it wants as long as it does not deviate too far too often from what the pragmatist buyers desire. In return, the gorilla receives the "gorilla's share" of the sales and obtains a healthy margin on these sales. This, of course, allows the gorilla to invest in new technology to reinforce its leadership position in the market.

Moore suggests that the way to become the gorilla in a tornado involves a certain amount of luck combined with smart coordination of several factors. The gorilla must have assembled the "whole product" and this product must be standardized so that the members of the main-stream market can all obtain roughly the same product (with minor customized features).

Readers should compare Moore's viewpoint, at least through this portion of the TALC, with the concept of market ownership expressed by Regis McKenna.[18] A major difference is that Moore's concept of the gorilla concerns market dominance starting in the tornado and lasting through the remainder of the TALC for a given technology platform. McKenna's concept of and path to market ownership implies that an organization needs to continue to "push the envelope" within its market niche to maintain a growth market. This implies that the market owner will continue to innovate to dominate from one TALC to the next, and so on. The ownership focus is on continuously innovating the value presented to the market rather than focusing only on innovating the technology itself.

Another logical comparison is the TALC and the PLC. To make this comparison, note that the vertical axis on Exhibit 2-5 for the PLC is "Sales Revenue per Period" while on the Exhibit 2-6 for the TALC, the vertical axis is "Sales from *New* Adopters per Period." Also, realize that the TALC represents sales from all products based on a particular technology. To be comparable, the PLC and TALC have to both represent sales from a product category based on a particular technology. Consider as an example the technology or product category of "Wireless Local Area Networks." Exhibit 2-7 shows the TALC superimposed onto the PLC for this product category.

Notice that the TALC reaches its apex well before the apex of the PLC. The difference is that the PLC tracks total sales—repeat sales to customers who have already adopted—not just sales to new users. A clear implication of this diagram is that the marketers must enlarge their targeting efforts to include repeat and long-term users sometime during the growth period (during hypergrowth in the tornado). In Chapter 11, the character of different adopter groups and the acceptance of offerings along the PLC is further discussed.

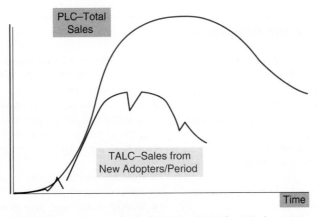

EXHIBIT 2-7   A Hypothetical TALC and PLC for Wireless LANs

THOUGHTS TO TAKE WITH YOU INTO THE NEXT CHAPTER

The concepts described in this chapter—classifying products, defining different types of competition, emerging value networks and supply chains, the PLC, and the TALC—help marketers to begin to frame their business environments. Differences in products help marketers understand how differing kinds of value may be desired by differing kinds of customers. The PLC and the TALC help marketers characterize how value desired by customers and competition will change over time. The nature of competition helps marketers think about how to develop and maintain competitive advantage.

Good marketing strategy cannot be based solely on these "mental models." Now marketers must delve deeper into the specifics of their markets. In Chapter 3, you will get more of a sense of how individual business customers attempt to obtain value from their suppliers. If you keep in mind the concepts we have discussed in this chapter, you can then begin to understand how value is pursued differently under differing market conditions, by different types of organizations, and even by different types of individuals within those organizations. Beyond Chapter 3, subsequent chapters help build an understanding of legal constraints (Chapter 4) and the context of company strategy (Chapter 5). Chapters 6 and 7 provide guidance on obtaining and utilizing information about the market. Together, these chapters provide the detail necessary to create strategy and tactics that provide superior value to target customers, thus making it possible to beat the competition.

Key Terms

capital goods *34*
chasm *47*
culture *38*
demographics *37*
end user *32*
industry standard *34*
macroeconomy *38*

market development gap *48*
monopoly *44*
monopsony *44*
oligopoly *40*
original equipment
   manufacturer (OEM) *32*
product life cycle (PLC) *45*

publics *35*
technology adoption life
   cycle (TALC) *47*
tornado *47*
user *32*
value added resellers (VARs) *31*
value networks *32*

Questions for Review and Discussion

1. What are some of the differences between marketing to typical commercial enterprises and marketing to government agencies?
2. Classify the following businesses as VARs, users, component producers, or raw material producers.
   a. A supplier of copper to a wire manufacturer
   b. A supplier of rear axle assemblies to a heavy truck manufacturer
   c. A distributor of private telephone exchange equipment (PBX) and installation services
   d. A supplier of pigments to a paint manufacturer

   e. A maker of automated assembly equipment
   f. A supplier of small motors to disk drive manufacturers
3. How can the agenda and focus of financial publics and public interest groups create seemingly opposite goals for business-to-business marketing managers?
4. Defend the validity and importance of internal publics.
5. How can market-sensitive internal publics improve a firm's competitiveness?
6. Should technology play a major role in your approach to your customers? Why or why not?

7. How do oligopolies support the 80/20 rule?

8. Describe the areas of validity and fallacy associated with the study of the PLC.

9. What market characteristics make it unlikely that pragmatists will easily follow the role model of visionaries?

10. Relate the PLC and the chasm with particular emphasis on the market factors that undergo change from introduction to rapid growth of an offering.

Endnotes

1. TRW Automotive Corporate Web page, "Who We Are."

2. Anonymous, "Product Innovation for Today's Aftermarket," *Aftermarket Business*, Vol. 113 (January 2003), p. 60.

3. "GlobalAutoIndustry.com's China Auto Suppliers Group Expands Product Line by Offering Low Cost, High-Tech Telematics *Solution* from China," *Business Wire* (September 15, 2004), p. 1.

4. Gerry Kobe, "The Demise of Brand X," *Automotive Industries* (May 1999), p. 53.

5. Matthew Beecham, "TRW Automotive: Company Profile—2004 edition," *Just—Auto* (June 2004), p. 4.

6. The timeframe of the commitment, made in 2000, was later modified by the dramatic change in the market environment—including the Firestone tire crisis and shifts in vehicle preferences by the market.

7. Robert Grace, "McD's & Politics of Perception," *Plastics News* (November 12, 1990), p. 6.

8. Theodore Levitt, "Marketing Myopia," *Harvard Business Review* (July–August 1960).

9. Regis McKenna, "Marketing Is Everything," *Harvard Business Review* (January–February 1991).

10. Jagdish N. Sheth and Rajendra Sisodia, "Only the Big Three Will Thrive," *The Wall Street Journal* (May 11, 1998).

11. Levitt, "Marketing Myopia," is the classic discussion of this situation.

12. Geoffrey Moore, *Crossing The Chasm, Marketing and Selling Technology Products to Mainstream Customers* (New York: Harper Business, 1991).

13. Everett M. Rogers, *Diffusion of Innovations*, 4th ed. (New York: The Free Press, 1995).

14. A similar approach to customer adoption and market development can be found in Roger J. Best, *Market-Based Management*, 2nd ed. (Upper Saddle River, N.J.: Prentice Hall, 2000), Ch. 3.

15. Ibid., p. 64.

16. Geoffrey Moore, *Inside the Tornado* (New York: Harper Business, 1995).

17. This standard may be an industry standard or a defacto standard arrived at by the momentum of the market.

18. McKenna, "Marketing Is Everything."

Chapter *3*

Organizational Buying and Buyer Behavior

OVERVIEW

Chapter 1 introduced business-to-business marketing and Chapter 2 established the nature of the many types of participants in business-to-business markets. Successful business-to-business marketing involves understanding how organizations buy and how individuals are likely to behave in the roles of decision makers within the organization. This chapter examines the nature of buying and individual behaviors associated with the buyer's decision process.

Organizations "buy" to satisfy rational needs that result from their desire to be successful in their markets; however, it is individuals within organizations who make the buying decisions. In this chapter, we demonstrate that the need of the organization may be quantifiable but that behavior in organizations has many qualitative elements that influence the buying decision. It is in the qualitative elements of decision making that the importance of the customer–supplier relationship becomes a critical factor in the success of the marketing effort.

The complexity of the business buying process varies. Routine purchases are automatic, repeated with an almost mechanical approach. More complex needs require greater involvement by a larger number of stakeholders in the organization. We examine the levels of buying complexity and how a marketer's relationship and approach are impacted by this complexity.

Covisint: Illustrating the Importance of Adapting to Customers' Buying Behavior

Late 1999 could arguably be the beginning of the end of the dotcom explosion. General Motors Corporation and Ford Motor Company had each started their own Internet marketplace exchange and the two long-time rivals were battling to get the upper hand with suppliers. The Internet exchanges were supposed to streamline communications, inventory, and logistics management for all major suppliers to the companies.

Of course, each exchange was tailored to the specific methods and technologies of its specific creator—General Motors (GM) or Ford. Ford had chosen Oracle to develop and supply the software that would run its exchange, while GM had chosen the latecomer Commerce One as its supplier. Within weeks, suppliers that served both companies were complaining that the new exchanges were incompatible with each other and usually incompatible with their own in-house systems Suppliers were threatening to band together and form their own exchange to develop a common platform of operation.

Early in 2000, Morgan Stanley Dean Witter (MSDW), financial advisors and consultants, proposed a unique solution. By combining the two rival exchanges, the resulting exchange would have tremendous purchasing power. The forecast purchases through the exchanges by Ford and GM, combined, hovered around $600 billion, making it the largest business-to-business operation. MSDW argued that the combined exchange could strip out millions in costs for both customers and suppliers. An independent exchange could invite additional automotive companies to join. Profits would be generated by the transaction fees the exchange would charge users.[1] There were immediate comparisons to Sabre, the reservation system of American Airlines that, as an independent operation, became worth more than the airline. MSDW argued that such an operation could be worth $10 billion in five years as a separate company on the stock market.

By February 25, 2000, GM, Ford, Oracle, Commerce One, and the newest member of the team, DaimlerChrysler (DC) announced the plan: build the biggest-yet industrial Web exchange. Industry analysts estimated that a successful common exchange could shave as much as 6 percent off of the cost of building a car.[2] The mood was euphoric—the United States' biggest "rust belt" companies were entering the e-commerce business.

Soon, other automotive businesses joined. Toyota would become an exchange participant, but not an investor. Nissan, Peugeot, and Renault joined. Johnson Controls, Delphi Automotive, Visteon, Magna International, Lear, and about twenty-five other supplier companies soon joined the exchange. Membership was forecast to rocket to more than 30,000 companies.

Covisint had its own board of directors comprised of the Who's Who of automotive executives. Since each automotive manufacturer had previously required its suppliers to conform to its own standard, many suppliers maintained a connection to an Internet portal for each company. Covisint set its sights on simplifying this to one common portal/exchange for all. It would be simple, really. The auto companies would all use a common system; suppliers would adopt that system; efficiency would lead to significant cost savings. Could this really happen between companies known for their intense rivalries? Nope.

Decisions had to be made fast, but the corporate egos involved didn't always make that easy. Selecting a corporate name took three months. Oracle, Commerce One, and DC's supplier SAP all wanted to be the lead supplier for the exchange technology Whichever technology was selected, two out of three of the U.S. auto companies would have systems throughout their operations become obsolete. Though the technologies were supposed to be able to work together, the final execution, requiring cooperation of all three of the technology companies, never quite seemed to be complete.[3]

While the executives of Covisint might have been euphoric, many of their potential customers were not. Four issues would prove to be practically insurmountable. First, industry leaders estimated that over 80 percent of all purchases by the auto companies involved "intellectual capital collaboration and sharing of proprietary content."[4] These were not routine repurchases of nuts and bolts or copy machine paper. Second, Covisint required all tier one suppliers to add their own exchange systems to Covisint. This would provide transparency to the supplier supply chain. Suppliers balked—they feared that the auto companies would use this information to justify lower prices. The tier one suppliers coveted the relationship that they had built with their own suppliers. Third, the potential cost savings appeared as a very large inducement to proceed with the project, so time was of the essence. Suppliers were not willing to wait as those savings were slipping away. Fourth, and possibly the biggest problem, Covisint required all participants to give up their own systems ("the way they buy") and adopt the system that Covisint was developing.

By mid-2000, Dana Corporation, who had already set up its own internal e-commerce system with Ariba, Incorporated (competitor to Oracle and Commerce One), brought five suppliers together to set up their own exchange. Indeed, suppliers were sold on the attractiveness of the efficiencies and cost savings. Also, Volkswagen announced it would not join Covisint but would instead develop its own exchange. The critical mass that would make Covisint work wasn't coming together.

By the year 2002, GM, Ford, and DC had invested $200 million in Covisint, the automotive e-commerce marketplace. Covisint had become a battleground for control of supply chain information. Ford and DC, while theoretically participants in Covisint, had continued development of their own exchanges, requiring suppliers to join. By the end of 2003, Covisint had been through four CEOs, the third of which had served for just one month. Suppliers had continued to hesitate to join, instead developing their own systems or adopting to the systems of their various individual customers. Covisint had sold its auction services business to FreeMarkets (which would eventually be purchased by Ariba) and would now focus on its supplier management portals and data messaging services.[5] In 2004, the remaining businesses of Covisint were sold to Compuware for $7 million.[6] At its peak, Covisint had posted $50 billion of auction activity annually—a far cry from the MSDW five-year forecast of $600 billion. For fiscal 2004, Covisint is on track to meet its expectation of $25 million in revenue.[7]

As a postscript to this story, Commerce One announced in the fall of 2004 that it would wind down its operations and probably file for bankruptcy.[8]

LEARNING OBJECTIVES

By reading this chapter, you will

- Develop an understanding of the difference between quantifiable organizational needs and the often qualitative process used to fulfill those needs.

- Understand how organizations develop and satisfy the requirements for selecting and maintaining relationships with suppliers.

- Understand how individuals within organizations develop and satisfy the requirements of their professional responsibilities as dictated by their organizations and, within that framework, their own individual needs.

- See how the supplier–customer relationship is the principal defining factor in the success of business-to-business marketing efforts.

- Gain an initial sense of the concepts of trust and commitment in effective relationship development.

- Gain an appreciation for the different levels of complexity of decisions made in the buying process and how a business-to-business marketer can influence the process.

INTRODUCTION

The scenario described in the opening example took place over a period of approximately four years. At the start of that period, it was thought that technology, as demonstrated by online exchanges, could significantly reduce transaction costs in business-to-business sales. In the development of Covisint, there was also the goal of standardizing the specifications of routinely purchased components and materials, thus reducing costs. At the end of the four-year period, however, the market witnessed the demise of Covisint as well as several of the technology companies that had been considered the business models of the future.

The Internet is a great communications tool in the information transfer and transaction process, but what happens to the relationships between supplier and customer that have in the past been considered so important? This chapter examines the often-taught classical buying process and its value as well the interpersonal dynamics and relationship aspects of how organizations and individuals make buying decisions—whether at the pace of the Internet or more conventional means.

THE NATURE OF BUYING

Many consumer purchases (i.e., buying decisions) are spur-of-the-moment decisions, often associated with the availability of funds to make the purchase. While consumers seldom conduct a conscious value evaluation, the act of making the purchase indicates that they have decided that the value they are about to receive is greater than the value they are giving up (i.e., their costs). If this were not the case, the exchange would not take place. The value assigned by the customer is influenced by many factors beyond the serviceability of the core product or service. The nature of the buyer decision process in a business-to-business environment is not unlike the consumer process, though the steps are often thought to be more visible and theoretically more quantifiable. Let us further compare the processes.

The Consumer Buying Decision Process

Our purchases as consumers are influenced by the roles we play in our daily lives. As parents, teachers, students, children, managers, and individuals, we are influenced to "do what's right" within the framework of the role we are playing. Sometimes that is a responsible decision with a broad range of beneficiaries; at other times, what is right is an impulsive, self-satisfying choice (e.g., "I bought it because I liked the color"). In any event, though we are influenced by many factors, we make the buying decision as individuals and are usually accountable to only ourselves for the outcome. What we have just described is part of the need-recognition stage in the classical five-stage consumer buyer decision process:

1. Need recognition
2. Information search
3. Evaluation of alternatives
4. Purchase decision
5. Post-purchase behavior

   This process, or a similar representation, is familiar to every student who has completed a marketing principles course. As presented, these five stages imply that the process consists of five discrete, sequential events. Depending on whether the purchase is a repeat of an earlier purchase or an entirely new task (or is low involvement or high involvement), some parts of the process may be de-emphasized or extended. As consumers, our experience tells us that this process is more of a simultaneous process rather than a sequential process. Consumer beliefs about legitimacy of information sources, brand reputations, and the influences of others combine into a final purchase decision by the individual consumer or family group. Afterward, the consumer evaluates the purchase relative to either individual or family expectations.

Organizational Buying

How do organizations "buy" compared to how we, as consumers, "buy" in the retail market? The initial response from an inexperienced observer might be that organizations purchase whatever is cheapest, that is, that organizations must make the most rational, lowest-cost, most-profitable decision. While the ultimate profitability of the buying organization (or minimized cost for the nonprofit organization) plays a major role, price is only a part of the delivered value.

   Organizational purchases involve inputs from many of the professional specialties in the organization. The organization relies on decision makers and influencers at many levels and from

Stakeholders are the individuals and organizations that have an interest—a "stake"— in the company, its operation, and its performance. The interest may or may not be financial.

different disciplines to contribute their expertise to satisfy a diverse set of needs. The inputs from these **stakeholders** aim to ensure that the best possible buying decisions are made for the organization. Individual stakeholders may contribute their expertise to influence the decision process without full knowledge or appreciation for the requirements of other stakeholders. Seldom is any one individual entirely responsible for an organizational purchase decision.

This decision process requires communication among stakeholders within the buying organization. It is necessary for the supplying organization to *simultaneously* approach all influencers in the decision process with a message tailored to the needs of each individual influencer. When effective and trusted, it is not unusual for the supplying firm's communications with different stakeholders to substitute for, or instigate, greater communication among stakeholders.

The Buying Center

The **buying center** is a collection of individuals with a stake in the buying decision, individuals who contribute to the final purchase decision. Members of the buying center determine, within their own professional responsibilities, the organization's needs and the methods the organization uses to satisfy them. Buying center complexity changes depending on the complexity of the need. Contrary to what the term implies, a *buying center* is not one central location where buying decisions are made. The term simply refers to the representatives of the various independently operating portions of an organization (finance, production, purchasing, engineering, etc.) that influence the selection of the overall best solution for the organization's needs. Depending on the size and complexity of the organization, influencers (stakeholders) in the decision may be physically located a great distance (across the hall, locally, nationally, internationally, etc.) from each other. One of the major tasks of the business marketer is to simultaneously but individually influence all stakeholders by satisfying their individual professional *and* personal needs.

The needs of the organization are determined by the organization's customer needs, the organization's internal goals and objectives, and by external environmental factors. Stakeholders are accountable for the development of buying requirements that satisfy all of these influences. Depending on the intended market and customers of the organization, influences may include government agencies and independent standards-setting organizations and publics, as well as the quantifiable and relationship needs of the supplier and the customer. Exhibit 3-1 shows the various professional disciplines and organizations that may contribute to or influence the buying center.

The professional needs of engineering or technical specialists in the buying center are related to the physical performance of the product that is being supplied. Their concerns center on how well the component will meet design requirements and reliably perform in their application. Production or manufacturing specialists in the buying center are concerned with how well the component will integrate into their manufacturing process. Personnel responsible for the service and support of the product when it is in use by their customers will be concerned about how and what service the component will require when the product is in the field. If the purchase is a significantly large investment, the customer's finance organization is concerned with alternatives to fund the purchase. Each member of the buying center has a concern unique to his responsibilities and presents an opportunity for the business marketer to demonstrate a unique value of the offering his company seeks to provide.

Internal Factors	Typical Concerns
• Technology/engineering • Management • Finance • Accounting • Legal • Production/manufacturing • Purchasing/supply management • Marketing • Service	• Physical performance of product • Monitor organizational needs being met • Ability to pay for large capital investments • Verify/track associated cash flows • Clarity of long-term agreements • Integration into existing facilities; throughput to meet production volumes-Inventory costs; quality and assurance of supply • Input to customer trends/desire for flexibility • Reliability and ease of replacement
External Factors	
• Customer needs and buying behavior • Government agencies • Independent standards-setting organizations • Various publics	• Stakeholders in each discipline within the organization contribute their expertise to the decision such that both internal and external factors are accommodated

EXHIBIT 3-1   Many Disciplines Can Contribute to the Buying Center

For instance, consider a buying organization that is building a new fabrication or manufacturing facility. Included in this facility will be new fabrication tools used to manufacture the organization's product. Such assembly equipment is costly, should have a long life, meet the production volume forecasts of marketing, be reliable, and be easily and quickly repaired when problems do occur. Since this is a capital investment, the organization's finance department will be interested in the best purchase terms. Manufacturing and production personnel will want assurances that the equipment is reliable and easy to operate, and will likely want some kind of guarantee of access to rapid repair if problems do occur. Operations personnel will be concerned with the utility consumption (water, electricity, etc.) of the new equipment. Facilities planning will have requirements related to the physical space the new equipment will occupy. Human resources may be concerned with employee training. Because of the complexity of the purchase, the number of stakeholders—the size of the buying center—is large.

At this point, it should be noted that in many organizations the buying center has undergone a makeover in the last decade or so. As companies have moved toward more integration of supply chains, buying centers have evolved into more formalized cross-functional teams that take a more strategic approach to supply issues.[9] This has resulted in tighter and more predictable buying processes. The good news for suppliers is that customers are more willing to entertain long-term collaborative relationships with suppliers. The outcome of the selection process is a long-term commitment to buy products or service from the supplier. The challenge (bad news?) for suppliers is that the requirements are more difficult to meet than before and suppliers may be forced to spend more effort sharing information and adapting their logistics systems to customer requirements than they had in the past. On the whole, though, well-run supply chains foster an attitude aimed toward win–win relationships rather than the traditional battles to see which side—buyer or seller—can keep most of the profitability.

Summarizing the differences between consumer and business-to-business buying discussed so far,

- Organizational buying involves more buyers—more decision makers or contributors to portions of the decisions.
- Committees (the buying center) are involved, with professionals in each discipline (stakeholders) making decisions that are driven by their particular needs.
- Different types of decisions are often occurring simultaneously in the process, spread throughout the buying organization.

ORGANIZATIONAL BUYERS' DECISION PROCESS: A STEPWISE MODEL

Exhibit 3-2 shows the business buyers' decision process as it is usually presented. We believe this model can be misleading. Let us discuss what is important to understand about the buying decision process before examining some of the potentially misleading elements.

Intricacies of the Buying Decision Process

Successful business marketers understand the buying processes of their customers and work with these processes to provide value to customers and win their business. Several key concepts lead to successful interaction with customers' decision processes.

INDIVIDUAL ROLES AND PERSONAL NEEDS   Several people in the buying center are involved in any stage or step of the process. Each of them has individual needs related to his role in the buying center. Each of them has personal needs as well. Included in these personal needs will be needs related to the political interactions within the buying center. As occurs in most group interactions, the group will have power relationships among the members of the group. Individuals will want to maintain or alter these relationships and the buying decision may become the focal point of political relationships or tensions. If individuals try to maintain the power relationships within the group, the process might play out with very little contention. On the other hand, the process may become very contentious if individuals are trying to change relationships or improve their power position within the organization.

THE BUYING PROCESS IS SIMULTANEOUS, NOT SEQUENTIAL   The buying decision process progresses only loosely as a stepwise process. In the previous example of an organization

1. Problem recognition
2. General need description
3. Product specification
4. Supplier/source search
5. Proposal solicitation
6. Selection
7. Make the transaction routine
8. Evaluate performance

EXHIBIT 3-2   Steps in the Buying Decision Process

purchasing new fabrication equipment, many members of the buying center are simultaneously involved in the decision process. Particularly in new task situations (which is explained later in the chapter), a grouping of the steps into stages better represents the process. The steps within each stage may overlap, occur simultaneously, recycle, and/or change their character in midstream.

RELATIONSHIPS AND LOYALTY The quality of the relationships between organizations and individuals of the organizations is a key influence. If the buying center members have confidence in a supplier and the supplier's representatives—and if the supplier has an ongoing consultative relationship with the buying center's members—the buying center tends to use the supplier's information, take advice from the supplier, and buy its products. A key factor affecting the degree of influence exerted by the relationship is the track record of previous successes and the loyalty those successes have created between the participants.

THREE KINDS OF NEEDS The members of the buying center try to meet three kinds of needs as they participate in the buying decision process. The first type of need is the organization's needs for benefits from the product or service once it is finally purchased and used. The second type of need is the buying center individual's need stemming from his role in the buying center. The third type of need is the buying center member's personal need. These three kinds of needs are explained as follows:

- Organization's needs for benefits from the product or service once it is finally purchased and used: This "need" usually includes the technical specifications, performance requirements, and other elements, quantitative and qualitative, of the total offering that ensure both an immediate success and sustain long-term objectives.
- Individual's need stemming from his role in the buying center: Each professional is expected to perform the functions of his job in a way that supports the organization's needs. This may be obtaining the best designed component part, the most favorable contract terms, the highest quality materials, and so on.
- The buying center member's personal needs: Often overlooked, an individual's personal needs for career success, recognition, and quality of life factors will influence his decision.

CLUSTER OF STAKEHOLDERS' VALUES All of this adds up to the fact that a supplier's successful offering is really a cluster of values, each aimed at individuals in the buying center at given points in the process. The core product or service is only part of this cluster and really does not directly meet the organization's needs until after the product has been purchased and put into use. Needless to say, this makes business-to-business offerings very complex.

ORGANIZATIONAL BUYERS DECISION PROCESS: A PROCESS FLOW MODEL

Based on the previous discussion, the stepwise model can present some problems. Recognizing the value of relationships in the decision process and that the value offering is a cluster of values, we prefer a model that moves through a series of clustered stages. The "formal," step-by-step process implies a beginning and an end to each step, as well as the notion that each step must be completed before starting the next. For simple, familiar, or low-involvement decisions, this may be the case. Our experience of how buying decisions are really made, particularly for new task purchases, strongly suggests a process flow with significant overlap and feedback

Process Flow Stages	Buying Decision Process—Steps
Definition Stage	
• Problem definition	• Problem recognition
• Solution definition	• General need description
• Product specification	• Product specification
Selection Stage	
• Solution provider search	• Supplier/source search
• Acquire solution provider(s)	• Proposal solicitation
	• Contract for supplier(s)
Deliver Solution Stage	
• Customize as needed	• Make the transaction routine
• Install/test/train	
Endgame Stage	
• Operate solution	• Evaluate performance
• Reach end result	• Resell the job
• Evaluate outcomes	
• Determine next set of needs	

EXHIBIT 3-3   Stages in the Process Flow Model of the Buying Decision Process

loops and without borders between steps. We have presented the flow as a series of stages because, even in the most free-form decision process situations, there generally are milestones or transitions that occur between the stages. Within the stages, actions generally include the previously discussed steps, but they flow in a loose progression from start to transition point and then on to the next stage. Exhibit 3-3 shows the buying decision process as a **process flow model** rather than as a step model, as was shown in Exhibit 3-2. It also shows the correlation between the two models.

Notice that in Exhibit 3-3 we show almost all the classical decision steps in the definition and selection stages. We then expand the steps "Make the transaction routine" and "Resell the job." We do this because there is so much activity—especially marketing activity—that occurs in these last steps, particularly when the purchase is complex. These two stages become an integral part of the relationship that forms between buyer and supplier organizations and become the precursor activities for the next buying decision process undertaken by the buying organization.

To better understand how business marketers can address buying center needs, let us examine each stage in greater detail.

Stage 1: Definition

In this first stage of the process, the buying center attempts to learn more about what their organization needs and about what options are available to address those needs. In Exhibit 3-3, this stage is shown as having the following kinds of activities: recognizing and defining the organization's problem, defining the broad outlines of a solution, and specifying the product or service features sought. The stage ends with a first quantification of what is specifically sought by the organization. This specification may be revised later, but it sets the organization's buying center on a path with a specific direction.

A key thing to understand about the definition stage is that it includes "problem recognition," which determines how the buying center carries out the rest of the decision process. Problem recognition is analogous to consumer need awareness, albeit at an organizational level. The way that the buying center defines the problem and the general nature of the solution determines whether they approach the buying decision as a familiar or an unfamiliar task. At one extreme, the problem and its likely solution may be defined as a completely **new task**. The rest of the buying decision process then tends to be more rigorous, and time consuming as a result. At the other extreme is determination that the organization simply needs the same thing it obtained last time it had this particular problem. This results in a **straight rebuy** situation. A straight rebuy involves abbreviated steps in the process, fewer people in the buying center, and less time to completion. In the middle lie **modified rebuy** situations in which the buying center determines that the problem or solution is somewhat similar to past problems or solutions. Such a determination results in a buying decision process that examines alternatives but within a limited scope. As one would expect, it involves fewer people than the new task situation and more than the straight rebuy. It takes less time than a new task and more time than a straight rebuy.

An astute supplier benefits greatly from involvement with its customer in this early process stage. An understanding of the buying center's needs, both organizational and individual, during this stage allows the supplier to create value for the buying center by helping the buying center through the process. The supplier also has the opportunity to adapt its product or service through the process of helping the buying center define its problems and solution set.

As the decision moves through the stages, a general need and solution is defined. The buying organization's technical team fully details the need and solution through the development of a product specification. It is at this point that the technical team members of the buying center determine the extent of the product's intricacy. Prototypes are built and reviewed for how well the original need is satisfied. Component technology and appropriate alternatives from a cost and performance viewpoint are examined. The technical value assessment is made, and the product specification is created. The development of the specification should be the result of extensive collaboration between supplier and customer. It is in this process that technology alternatives are narrowed and designs begin to rely on the specific nature of the remaining alternatives.

This description can lead one to believe that this is the end of the defining process and that after this point the product design is frozen. In reality, this is too narrow a view. As was noted in the *value chain* discussion, concluding that all possible customer value can be quantitatively specified is a major misstep in the application of the value chain concept.

*A **new task** is a need that hasn't been faced by the organization previously. An entirely new offering, the incorporation of a new technology, development of new facilities, or a combination of factors can create this level of task. The organization has a significantly steep learning curve in a new task buying situation and will initially seek many sources of information and assistance, utilizing the complete buying process to investigate alternatives.*

*A **straight rebuy** is a buying situation that is routine and has established solutions. Straight rebuys are "more of the same" and often involve simply the reorder of a previous product. A marketer should strive to derive straight or **modified rebuy** situations from new task situations to limit established business to exposure from competitive forces.*

THE MEANING OF A SPECIFICATION   What purpose does a product specification serve? The obvious answer is that a specification is what a customer gives to a potential supplier that completely describes what the product must be and how it performs. Following this logic, it is then the responsibility of the supplier, if it wants the business, to quote the lowest possible per unit price on the product. Perhaps this is an accurate analysis in a straight rebuy situation and is true for most Web-based transactions. Not only does the specification give the customer a method to say what the product must be should there be any future disagreement, but also it provides the supplier with a very clear indication of what the product does not need to be—also useful in future disagreements.

The functions performed by the specification, however, are not limited to resolving conflicts between the buyer and the seller. Specifications are an attempt by the buyer to generalize the need description, regardless of its complexity. The specification seeks to reduce differences between different potential suppliers of the product, making it easier to choose from among competing proposals. Internally to the buying center, the specification serves as an assurance that when a supplied component meets the specification all of the requirements of the organization have been met. In this regard, the specification serves as an **internal brand** much the same way a national consumer brand reassures buyers about quality, function, and value in the consumer market. Thus, the buyer views a well-written specification as an enabling factor that virtually eliminates differences between competing suppliers.

The development of a product specification is a step where a business marketer can have significant input, particularly if the value provided by the marketer goes beyond easily quantifiable needs. Successful suppliers will have worked with the buying organization such that the specification utilizes attributes of the supplier's own total offering while minimizing the impact of the differentiating attributes of competitors' offerings. The development of early prototypes as noted earlier, the selection of component technology, and appropriate alternatives from a cost and performance viewpoint are all areas where suppliers can meet the buying organization's needs that exist during this phase of the process. Concurrently, such assistance provides assurance to the buying center that the supplier can provide superior value when the final solution is delivered at the end of the decision process.

Beyond this point in the process, it is much more difficult for a potential supplier who has not yet been involved in the definition stage to be truly competitive. The new supplier finds the buying center already predisposed to a particular form of solution.

THE SPECIAL CASE OF AN INTEGRATED SUPPLY CHAIN   Today most large companies and many medium-sized companies attempt to integrate their supply chains back to the point of raw materials extraction from the earth. As has been discussed in Chapters 1 and 2, integrating supply management through the supply chain can provide competitive advantages in terms of cost, quality, and flexibility. Entering into a relationship with an integrated supply chain can give the supplier advantages and benefits as well, once it becomes certified and integrated into the chain. The supply chain poses a special case of customer requirements that, notwithstanding a complete and competitive core offering, may exclude a supplier from further consideration.

The case of the integrated supply chain will occur mostly in industries where technologies and products are maturing or have matured. Some companies in markets or industries that are emerging will attempt to integrate their supply chains, but supply dynamics are so fluid at these early stages that little advantage can be gained from integrating supply management.

Many larger companies form a supply management committee or team to make supply policy decisions and manage the supply network's activities.[10] The supply management team will pursue inbound purchasing and logistics as strategic design decisions and tend to manage these activities as business processes. The team will emphasize strict quality tolerances for the purchase of materials, parts, and services. These requirements are specific for all links in the chain back to raw materials producers. In a further broadening of the supply chain management concept, the team will develop, or incorporate from an independent source, specifications for the processes that suppliers must adhere to. Many of these processes, including but not limited to quality manufacturing, inventory management, purchasing, and quality control, are defined under standards set by the International Organization for Standardization (ISO) and the Institute of Supply Management (ISM). The prospective supplier must show that they have incorporated these standards. The suppliers will also be required to share information about demand and supply levels both upstream and downstream. The supplier may be required to follow policies and procedures in ordering and inventory tracking. In return, the supplier can often expect special assistance in meeting these requirements, such as training, equipment, and financing.

Obtaining standard certification from ISO can qualify a supplier to participate in supply chains for many large customers. The initial qualifying effort will be of value at many customers. Because an independent standards organization is used, the requirements are readily determined and consistent. In this way the supplier gains legitimacy in an efficient manner. On the other hand, the strict requirements to enter the supply chain take away many sources of differentiation. This suggests that a prospective supplier can differentiate itself by learning to manage and improve its own internal operations so that it can exceed the stringent requirements of the supply chain. By creating a core competency of process improvement and maintaining an ongoing relationship with the standard-setting organizations, the supplier can rise to the level of a preferred supplier for one or more supply chains.

Some suppliers that have achieved this level of sophistication in process management and continuous process improvement have gone on to build new distinctive competencies in managing processes for creating innovations.[11]

Stage 2: Selection

Once the buying center knows what it wants to acquire, it seeks, during the selection stage, a supplier to provide it. The choice of supplier may be a foregone conclusion, particularly if, as noted earlier, the supplier has collaborated with the buyer throughout the specification process. The buying center may go through the steps of the selection stage, though, just the same. As shown in Exhibit 3-3, the activities performed in this stage include development and issuance of a **request for proposal (RFP)** or **request for quotation (RFQ)**, evaluation of offers, initial selection of a supplier, negotiation of terms, and specification of an order or contract. While the steps can occur simultaneously and in varying order, the stage ends and transitions to the next stage with the contract or order.

RFQ and RFP are acronyms for the common business practices of asking a supplier to quote a piece of business. RFQ is a Request for Quotation, usually associated with an offering that can be thoroughly and quantitatively defined. An RFP is a Request for Proposal, usually defined by a set of needs, specification, or outcomes that have greater leeway with regard to the final form or technology of the offering.

As already discussed, if the supplier organization can help the buying center through the process, the supplier stands a greater chance of becoming the supplier chosen. If a supplier has a good relationship with the people in the buying center, then the RFP often can be influenced to ask for proposals to do exactly what the supplier intends to do. Obviously, the proposal then will match very well with the buyer's requirements and will at least stand a good chance of being picked for a final round of proposal presentations.

After the RFP or the RFQ is issued, proposals or quotes are received and evaluated by members of the buying center. Depending on the complexity of the need, the competing suppliers' marketers are called on to marshal their writing and presentation skills as well as their knowledge of their own and their customers' markets. Straight rebuys of somewhat generic items, such as those that could be successfully purchased as described in the Covisint opening vignette, may require only a brief (perhaps only online, if suppliers are adequately prequalified) response to an RFQ that stresses price as the dominant part of the marketing mix. For new tasks and, to a certain degree, modified rebuy situations, however, successful and profitable responses to RFQs require a combination of elements well beyond price (and are not likely to be successfully purchased through online exchanges).

DISTINCTION FROM PUBLIC SECTOR PURCHASING   This process of issuing an RFP or an RFQ often runs a little differently in the case of government purchasing. Fairness or equal opportunity is often a legislatively mandated goal in structuring the proposal or quote and selection process. The RFP or quote often has to be published in specified newspapers or other outlets. Prospective suppliers have to meet a set of rigid criteria that are often much less flexible than criteria in private sector purchasing. This does not mean that suppliers' marketers are ignored in the design process for the RFP or the RFQ. In these situations it is critical to fully understand what degree of assistance is acceptable to the government agency and its oversight authorities. Government purchases are often subject to far more scrutiny than private sector purchases. What is considered normal design or development assistance in the private sector may be interpreted as undue influence when addressing public sector markets.

Marketers addressing governmental markets can still establish relationships with government buying centers and assist in designing and specifying the solution. They may face more competition, though, in the selection process. Indeed, they may also face fewer straight rebuy situations due to legislatively mandated rebidding on purchase contracts over time.

BUYERS SEEK SELLERS WITH BEST TOTAL OFFERING AND CAPABILITIES   In evaluating proposals, buying organizations seek to protect themselves from single-source and inflexible price situations by seeking additional or alternate suppliers. The search for qualified, acceptable suppliers leads to a list of those suppliers who, *in the view of the buying organization*, can meet the needs of the buying center. Depending on the stature of the buying organization, their reputation as a customer, and the nature of the supply opportunity, they may attract proposals from all or a few of the available qualified suppliers. If the buying organization is hindered by previous difficulties with suppliers or is experiencing other environmental situations (e.g., severe financial difficulties, etc.) the RFQ or proposal solicitation may require a marketing effort to appear attractive to potential suppliers.

As was discussed in Chapter 2, business markets are often oligopolies, with only a few companies having capabilities in any particular area. Many organizations may be capable of making exceptional one-of-a-kind items (that special cake that resulted from customization of the general recipe), but this capability does not automatically transfer to an ability to supply several thousand items each month (how big is that kitchen?). Organizations, because they have many concerns they are trying to address in acquiring a product or service, seldom have the luxury of many choices. Yet the supplier is an integral part of the success or failure of the efforts of the buying organization. So, business buyers must screen supplier organizations with regard to their capabilities beyond the creation of one component. Years in business, size and reputation, manufacturing capacity, ISO certification, and customer service commitment are among the screening factors, in addition to the supplier's product quality and ability to meet the technical specification. These screening factors can be the most difficult for a supplier to satisfy, especially for the small, technology-oriented young company without a track record of large volume production—such as a firm "before the chasm."

The classical process of supplier selection implies that the buying center weighs all factors as defined by the specification and selects the supplier that best meets those specified needs.

If there is an outstanding provider, the selection among potential suppliers can be obvious. However, all facets of the offer come into play, those quantifiable as well as those value chain features that are not as easily measured.

Assuming that all potential suppliers are qualified and that all have met the minimum performance requirements specified, the buying center selects from a group of providers who have worked very hard to meet the specification. The problem with this, from the suppliers' viewpoint, is that in all their hard work to create an offering as described by the specification they have probably accomplished exactly the worst outcome—to be just like each other, with no differentiation. Under such circumstances, the customer selects the supplier with the lowest price. From this result comes the entrenched myth that the successful supplier is the one that offers the lowest price. This does not follow good marketing logic.

Why would suppliers want to work to be just like each other? Smart suppliers work very hard to distinguish their offerings from each other. Market-driven suppliers do not use price as a marketing tool but will look to the buying center's broad and diverse needs to assemble an added-value approach that demonstrates qualitatively the advantages of their offer. This does not mean to imply that price is not important; it is, but competitive offerings need to be distinguished in other ways as well.

The buying center eventually arrives at a decision on which supplier it chooses. The final selection may be contingent on negotiations on some of the solution's features, on terms of the contract, or even on the final price. The selection stage reaches completion when the contract is signed.

Stage 3: Solution Delivery

Once chosen, the supplier begins the process of delivering on its promises. This portion of the overall process may take a longer period of time than the first two stages combined. When the product is complex and involves a high degree of customization and even technical development, this stage is an extended set of activities. The solution delivery stage ends when the "delivery" is complete and approved by the buying organization. An astute supplier already involved in the definition and selection stages already has, in many cases, had its offering approved or is proceeding through the approval process.

Activities that can be included in this stage include all solution development that remains to be done, customization of the product or service based on a diagnosis process, testing of early versions of the solution, delivery of prototypes and incorporation into manufacturing trials, installation and testing of the full-scale solution, training of the buyer's employees who will operate the solution or interact with the service provider, resolution of any supply chain or logistics management issues, and perhaps other readiness activities.

The process of merging the supplying logistics of the supplier with the consumption logistics of the customer occurs during this stage. It is incumbent on the supplier to match the operational buying needs of the customer. Suppliers must recognize "how their customers buy" and meet that pattern. The transaction process should be routinized in a way that it is invisible to the buying organization. The customer will want such things as materials planning, shipping quantities, inventory location, delivery times, and invoice routines (i.e., the utilities of business logistics—form, time, place, and possession) to match their existing methods.

How the supplier delivers on its promises up to this point is watched closely by the buying organization. All through this delivery stage, the buying organization evaluates how good the supplier is and what the likelihood is of a good working relationship in the future. If the supplier can provide this value during the delivery stage, it stands a good chance of making a successful transition into future buying decisions.

SUPPLY CHAIN IMPLICATIONS   Return briefly to the Covisint opening example and recall the fourth of the four major issues that proved insurmountable—Covisint required all participants to give up their own systems (the way they buy) and adopt the system that Covisint developed. Customers of Covisint included both downstream clients (the major automobile companies) and upstream clients (suppliers to the major automobile companies) in the supply chain. Covisint was not a customer of any member of the supply chain. As a result, Covisint had very little if any leverage to persuade its clients to follow the rules it established, particularly those that required clients to accept Covisint technology and systems as their system. Covisint made no effort to match the "way their customers buy."

Stage 4: Endgame

All of the prior activity has a purpose—to provide the buying organization with the products, materials, or capabilities necessary for the buying organization to reach its goals. Often, buying organizations formally evaluate purchase outcomes and these are the criteria by which the outcomes are judged. Many firms will have standardized supplier audits or "scorecards" that compare all suppliers on the same criteria. Individual members of the buying center also evaluate the purchase, the process, and the supplier after the purchase is in use. The needs at this point are the benefits that were anticipated to begin with. Along with this is a need for reasonable (and usually predictable) costs.

The supplier should use every opportunity to reinforce the validity of the buying center decision. Suppliers that continue to show an interest in the changing needs of a buying center after the supplier has been selected are preparing for the next RFQ from the customer as well as making it far more difficult for a competitor to encroach on the business. The quality with which the supplier meets the logistics needs described in the discussion of the delivery stage should be a positive influence in the business relationship, and suppliers should solicit feedback regarding these processes. The manner in which the supplier "resells the job" can be tangible evidence of otherwise unquantifiable factors that can make price less of an issue.

The endgame of a specific supply situation should also be the definition stage of the next— a natural flow in the involvement of the customer and supplier organizations. The degree to which this happens automatically is an indicator of the degree of success of the relationship viewed from either organization.

TWO EXAMPLES OF BUYING DECISION PROCESSES

Let us look at two hypothetical situations (based on real situations) to illustrate what happens in the buying process. The two examples represent the two ends of the spectrum: a straight rebuy on the one hand, shown in Exhibits 3-4 and 3-5, and a new task on the other, shown in Exhibits 3-6 and 3-7.

> For the straight rebuy, let us examine the purchase of office supplies by a small advertising agency. The need for the supplies is triggered when the office manager notices that some inventory levels are low. Maybe, though, they are a little more organized and the office manager places a monthly order. In either case, a *problem is recognized* (office supplies need to be replenished) and the process starts (see Exhibit 3-3). The next step involves checking the inventory to see if some items have sufficient inventory or need an extra large order. The office manager may also ask someone in each department (e.g., from the creative, media, traffic, account management, and administration departments) whether they have any special supply needs coming up soon. The order comes together and is typical of previous orders, except that one item is needed in larger than usual quantities. The office manager then makes out his list

EXHIBIT 3-4   Straight Rebuy Example—Buying Office Supplies

of things to order. This represents the *definition of need* and *definition of solution* steps, and this stage is complete (refer to Exhibit 3-3). The definition stage took all of maybe an hour to complete.

The next step is for the office manager's assistant to place the order. The assistant prepares a purchase order that is faxed to the agency's regular office supply dealer. The assistant follows up with an email message to the dealer's customer service rep that handles the ad agency account. The message verifies the unusual quantity of the particular item, as the supplier is likely to notice something out of the ordinary routine. That's the extent of the *selection* stage.

Let us say that the dealer makes its own deliveries. Three days after the order was placed, the delivery van shows up and drops off the supplies. The driver, along with the office manager's assistant, checks the packing list against the purchase order. The assistant signs off and the delivery stage is complete.

In the endgame, the invoice from the dealer is received and the agency's accountant pays the bill. Perhaps the dealer's customer service rep e-mails the office manager's assistant and checks to see whether the order was received with no problems. Perhaps the service rep also checks quickly to verify that no changes in procedure are expected for the next month's order.

The office manager may make a cursory evaluation of the process to verify that the value received was satisfactory. If a problem has occurred during this process, the office manager will pay more attention to the evaluation. Some problems that might occur include an increase in prices, a slow delivery, the delivery of the wrong items, the back ordering of some crucial items on the order, or a churlish attitude from the service people. Any one of these may cause the office manager to try to rectify the situation or to reopen the search for a new supplier.

EXHIBIT 3-4 (continued)

Discussion of Examples

A few key points need to be highlighted in the straight rebuy example. Notice that the ad agency did not actually need the supplies at the time when the office manager determined an order needed to be placed. Their need was for information on what supplies they were going to need in the coming month.

Notice, too, that a selection of supplier was made very quickly: The office manager determined, almost unconsciously, that the agency would use its regular dealer. Again, at that point, the agency does not actually need the supplies; it needed only to have a reliable supplier chosen and an order easily placed by the end of this stage. In a straight rebuy, this part of the process is almost trivial, unless something has happened to cause the office manager to re-evaluate whether the choice of supplier should be reopened.

At the point in the process where the order was delivered, the agency still had not reached a point where it actually needed the supplies; rather its needs at this stage were on-time delivery, the right products received, and the convenience of the transaction. After the order has been received,

Stage	Result
Definition	Recognized problem—supply inventory was low; departments specified what supplies they would need in the next month
Selection	Order placed with usual supplier
Deliver solution	Order delivered by supplies dealer; order checked by driver and office manager
Endgame	Supplies used; next month's order set up.

EXHIBIT 3-5 Summary of the Straight Rebuy Example

Consider a value-added reseller (VAR) of computer systems. It comes to the realization that it wants to improve its own sales and presale service operations. It finds that it is losing some customers to competitors because the competitors provide better presale service. To complicate this problem, the competitors seem to have controlled their costs to the point that they can offer superior service while charging lower prices. Competitors are finding customers, qualifying them, and "getting in the door" before the VAR even knows that an opportunity exists. At this point, the VAR has not determined what sort of solution to seek.

The next step for the VAR involves undertaking an analysis of its current sales and customer service processes. With the help of a consultant, the VAR and the consultant arrive at the conclusion that several processes would be improved with the installation of an automated sales and customer management system. As part of his solution development services, the consultant has brought in a business development person from a reputable supplier of software for automated sales and customer management. A discussion with the business development person from the software supplier launches the VAR into a new-task buying process to acquire such a system.

They begin this process by writing general specifications of the kind of system they are looking for. The consultant and a missionary salesperson from the software supplier help them write this specification. The consultant suggests several other companies that would also be good alternatives as suppliers. These companies are contacted and asked to make proposals based on the specifications that have been written. All potential suppliers ask the questions they feel are necessary for them to fully assess the VAR's situation. Three of the potential suppliers prepare detailed proposals and make presentations to the VAR's executives and several other managers within the organization.

The executives and the VAR's information technology (IT) manager confer to select a supplier. In their discussions, they discover that new selection criteria have arisen from some of the supplier presentations. They revise their criteria and determine that they need more information from a couple of the suppliers. After additional discussions with the suppliers, they finally select one supplier. It happens to be the first supplier, who helped them write the specifications and request for proposal. After negotiating the work and the terms, a deal is signed by executives for both the supplier and the VAR. The technical team for the supplier begins talking at length with the future users of the system and begins designing the system. Early versions of the system are tested with users and demonstrated for the VAR's executives. Modifications are made; some renegotiation of features and price results. First modules of the new system are installed, and the first batch of users is trained. They begin using the system, with mixed results. The supplier fixes some bugs and provides some additional training. Meanwhile, the users are becoming more proficient—some of the problems take care of themselves.

Over the next six months, the VAR's IT manager and the sales vice president begin to discuss how well the system is working. A sales assistant collects some evaluative information on system performance. The vice president and the IT manager generally conclude that they like the system, that they would have done a few things differently, and that they need more modules. Meanwhile the system supplier's sales team has been helping the VAR evaluate the system. They suggest some improvements and introduce the vice president and the IT manager to new modules that have been developed in the time during which the system was installed. It is some of these new modules that the vice president and the IT manager suggest to the VAR's CEO for improving the automated system.

EXHIBIT 3-6   New Task Example: Acquiring Automated Sales and Customer Management System

all the actions in the endgame reinforced the *routinization of the transaction* and even progressed to *reselling the job.* The needs of the organization during this stage were the availability and usefulness of the office supplies, as well as reassurance that the same thing will happen in the future. Note that it was during this stage that the actual need for the products was realized. It was at this stage, too, that the price of the order was actually realized.

A summary of the process for the straight rebuy is shown in Exhibit 3-5.

Let us contrast the preceding process with the second example, shown in Exhibit 3-6. The example is of a VAR acquiring a new computer system, representative of how the process might flow in a new task buying situation. The buying center took more time and effort throughout the whole process than was taken for the straight rebuy. In fact, the buying center itself was larger and involved people higher in the organization than were involved in the straight rebuy. The individual stages and steps did not occur in a stepwise fashion. While there was a general flow, the steps tended to recycle and repeat to a certain extent. For instance, the analysis of sales and service processes that occurred in the *solution definition* step probably further refined the definition of the organization's problem. When the selection team entered its initial deliberations on the selection of the supplier, they discovered new criteria to consider, which sent them back to the solution definition step and took them through more information search on the suppliers.

One feature of this process that stands out is the amount of time and effort that transpire between the time a contract is signed and the delivery of the "final" product (Exhibit 3-3). It might be argued that there is no final delivery as such; the endgame stage overlaps and flows into the early process stage of the next buying process. Another feature that stands out is the amount of uncertainty at each step. The recycling that occurs does so in part because so much uncertainty remains when the organization progresses from step to step. The organization uses much more information in the whole process to try to combat the uncertainty. The organization also makes use of a consultant in an attempt to help handle the complexity, newness, and uncertainty.

As occurred in the straight rebuy process, the VAR's needs differ from step to step. The organization does not need an actual product until it is well into the solution delivery activities. In the problem definition step, the VAR needs a good definition of the problem it is trying to solve. In the next step, it needs a good description of the parameters of a solution to its problem. It needs assistance in defining those parameters. It needs further help in designating prospective vendors. In the selection process itself, it needs good information, not only of the vendors' capabilities but also other characteristics such as their flexibility, their reliability, and the ease of working with them. The underlying need is the need for assurance that the vendor chosen will be able to deliver the value desired.

In the step in which the solution is defined, the needs include a need for increasing detail on how the new system will work and how it will help the VAR provide new value. This helps the VAR start to redesign its processes to take advantage of the system and to begin to plan to adapt and adopt. The VAR also needs further reassurance that it will get the desired value boost. As the system gets closer to implementation, the VAR needs the system to perform to specifications.

Stage	Result
Definition	Recognized problem; analyzed with help of consultant; supplier helps write specifications and RFP; suppliers submit proposals
Selection	Discussions and negotiations with suppliers; supplier selected (the one who helped initially); contract negotiated and signed
Deliver Solution	System delivered in modules; tested; users trained; system modified, redefined as needed
Endgame	System operated; results observed and analyzed; discussions begin with supplier for acquisition of new modules and upgrades

EXHIBIT 3-7 Summary of the New Task Example

Steps in Flow	Organizational Needs	Individual Needs
Define problem	Clear, concise, tractable	Information and time
Define solution	Appropriate, affordable	Design assistance
Acquire provider	Choice, speed	Information, assurance
Develop solution	Speed, easy use	Execution help
Install, test, train	Ease of integration, speed	Knowledge, comfort
Operate solution	User-friendly	Easy to maintain
End result	Effective, low cost	Recognition
Evaluate outcomes	Information	Communication, reward

EXHIBIT 3-8 Examples of Organizational and Individual Needs in the Buying Decision Process

Further, the VAR needs ease of use, ease of adoption, training of its employees, and merging with processes in place.

Exhibit 3-8 shows how needs progress through the stages of the buying decision process. Notice that we have distinguished between the buying organization's needs and the individual needs of the members of the buying center. Notice, as well, that individual needs can be classified as personal needs or needs related to the individual's role within the organization. In general, the needs of the organization tend to be addressed by the product and service portions of the supplier's offering. The individual needs, both personal and role related, of the buying center members are addressed mostly by the supplier's efforts to build a relationship with the customer.

Transition of Buying Decision Process—New Task Becomes Rebuy

If the supplier's marketing efforts are done well and have the desired effect, the new-task buying situation for a particular customer will transition into some form of rebuy situation in the next round, as illustrated in Exhibit 3-9. If the marketing effort fails for some reason—a

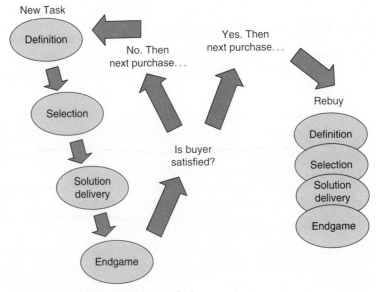

EXHIBIT 3-9 Buying Decision Evolution

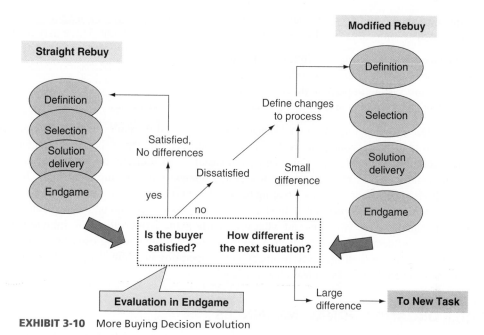

EXHIBIT 3-10   More Buying Decision Evolution

mistake is made, a competitor performs better, or the customer's situation changes drastically, for instance—the decision process may revert to an earlier stage or the customer may decide to choose an alternative supplier. Exhibit 3-10 shows such contingencies as having a recycling effect in the process. The supplier then has to change its approach, determining what stage the decision process is now in, and looking for ways to provide value to the customer at that stage.

Influences that Shape the Buying Decision Process

The preceding discussion described the effect of familiarity on the nature of the process. Also emphasized was the effect of the supplier's marketing efforts, particularly in the early stages of the buying process. Other factors that similarly affect the nature and flow of the decision process are the complexity of the problem and solution, the risk aversion of the decision makers and influencers, the importance of the decision (related to the importance of the problem), and the speed with which the solution needs to be in place. Complexity tends to lengthen the process. Importance and risk aversion tend to make the process proceed with more rigor or care and tend to involve people higher in the organizational hierarchy. A requirement for speed, of course, tends to work against rigor and care and tends to reduce the scope of investigation.

As has been noted, a business marketer must fully recognize the impact of joint decision making in the buying center. The ability of the supplier to influence each of these decision makers requires recognition not only of the rational facets of the process but also of the complexity of center members' simultaneous but individual influence in the process. Just as different ingredients in a recipe interact with each other throughout the baking process, the interaction among members of the buying center is a continuous process.

As individual members of the buying center influence the decision, they are guided not by the classical decision process but by conventions related to the organization. These may include

- the characteristics/corporate culture of the firm,
- the degree of risk aversion present in the culture,
- the reward system in place at the time of the decision, and
- the amount of vertical and horizontal management involvement.

In addition to these organizational conventions, the social dynamics of the situation will play a large role in the decision process. Missionary sellers can find themselves in the center of a conflict internal to the customer. This can be a disaster or an opportunity for the seller. The missionary seller can play roles as a communicator, a boundary person, diplomat, and a liaison between different customer interests. Treating these roles with respect can gain the trust and confidence of the various customer stakeholders. All require a marketer who understands the interpersonal dynamics of the situation and what each participant defines as a win. Individuals in these roles are influenced by several factors. Individuals within the buying center may be politicking as they plan for their own advancement and/or operating in a framework neither entirely rational nor beneficial to the organization as a whole.

OTHER ORGANIZATIONAL INFLUENCES

The mission, goals, and objectives of an organization determine its attitude toward many projects. Policies and procedures are created to reinforce those goals and objectives and impact the organizational structure. The degree to which an organization is innovative or bureaucratic, dynamic or static, risk accepting or risk averse impacts business decisions. If the marketer's goal is to enlist a customer as partner in a new development, the customer organization should be one that rewards innovation and leadership. Certainly this should be one of the considerations, and a possible segmentation variable (Chapter 7), in selecting which customer in an oligopolistic market would be the best candidate to approach with new ways of doing things.

OTHER INTERPERSONAL AND INDIVIDUAL INFLUENCES

Individuals in organizations react to situations with the same belief systems as in their private lives. Though in different roles, personality types and individual preferences will influence decision making. Customer reactions to authority and status, though not "rational," may be perfectly human. Understanding aspects of social styles and human relationships can significantly contribute to the persuasiveness of a marketer's position.

An individual's age, income, education, and job position all contribute to attitude. Personal assessments regarding risk and beliefs about how things are supposed to be done can overshadow the most logical and rational decision process. The personal assessment by the participants in the decision process, both the buyers and the sellers, have a greater influence on the decision than product and price.

IMPLICATIONS FOR BUSINESS MARKETING

Recognizing the concurrent nature of the decision process, the business marketer can influence each step to enhance the supplier's position relative to the competition. The continuous relationship between the supplier and the customer should contribute to the supplier's knowledge of where the customer's market is going and, within that market, where the customer sees its role. This provides insight into possible new product development efforts by the customer. This "need recognition" by the customer is an opportunity for the supplier to place information about its new products and technologies into the decision mix. As buying center individuals develop the initial general need description, they usually are not aligned with one type of solution or technology. The business marketer should participate with the buying center to influence the process. The added-value features and attributes of the marketer's offering and its suitability for the buyer's needs should be presented to individuals in the buying center in a way tailored to their individual focus. If customers are considering a major investment in a new facility, they may have concerns about financing the project and, as with any major facilities investment, be concerned about obsolescence. The finance professionals in the buying center should be approached with offering attributes that appeal to their needs, while manufacturing management should be counseled about the long-term flexibility of the facilities.

The business marketer must simultaneously appeal to all levels and disciplines in the buying center. It is not unusual for suppliers to jointly develop product specifications with customers. This is advantageous to both the customer and the supplier. The customer gets a component or service that is specifically tailored to its needs, often unique in the market and quite possibly a competitive advantage. The supplier gains from the development of the tailored product, both technically and through the enhanced relationship with the customer. The enhanced relationship can demonstrate not only a financial investment by the supplier in the business of the customer but also an emotional one. Competition is locked out, at least initially, from the business opportunity. If the supplier has a distinctive competence that is prominent in the offering, the competition may decide to not even pursue the business.

THE VARIABILITY OF RATIONAL BUYING DECISIONS

Many texts and training sources have proposed that business selling is primarily technical selling. A business presents logical benefits of its product relative to the competition's; and, provided its product is better, its product is selected. This is simplistic—nice in theory. In reality, as can be seen from this discussion so far, the business buying decision process has many elements of consumer decision making in it. Humans still make the decisions, so the decisions are still subject to many of the factors that are involved in consumer buying decisions.

Human Factors in Business Decisions

When human factors are involved, an entirely objective decision may not be possible. With this in mind, what can be said about the traditional stepwise process?

- Objective means are used to narrow choices. In many instances, several suppliers will be completely capable of providing the basic need of the organization. There will be a select group of suppliers, however, that match the cultural, interpersonal, value, and relationship needs of the organization.
- Suppliers that recognize the cultural, interpersonal, value, and relationship needs of the organization are more likely to be the "in" suppliers, favored by more members of the buying center, than those who rely merely on the capabilities and features of their core product. Members of the buying center will be more comfortable and receptive to a supplying organization they believe has their best interests (their organization's and their own) in mind, as well as selling a product.

- A review of the facts is often done because the cultural process says it is supposed to be done. There is safety in having made a decision in a conventional way. Members of the buying center can always say, "But I did it the way I was supposed to."
- Facts are arranged to justify the decision that individuals in the buying center want to make. As decision makers, they are influenced by many intangible factors. Why do we think they can make a decision without regard to those influences? Why should they?
- People seek reinforcement for their beliefs in every factor that is presented to them. It is human nature to want to be right. Individuals want what they already believe to be true. In consumer buying, this is acceptable. In business buying, there is a need for rational justification to narrow choices and serve as a backup to decisions.

Mutual Dependence and Customer Loyalty

While not completely irrational—the needs of the organization must be satisfied—business buying decisions also must satisfy the members of the buying center. Marketers can work hand in hand with a customer. Ideally, the goal is to create a mutually rewarding relationship in which the customer becomes dependent on the solution or system rather than on just the core product. The focus is to create customer loyalty. This can make it expensive for the customer to change to another supplier. This investment is mutual and visible in a number of ways:

- *Long-term contracts.* As in any relationship, long-term commitments increase both the risk and the reward for the parties involved. The reduced uncertainty of long-term commitments makes it possible to better utilize resources for both organizations.
- *Financial and emotional investment by both the selling organization and the buying organization in the success of the effort.* When the supplier and the customer have mutual financial interests that favor the success of their cooperation (not to be confused with any arrangements that may be termed illegal—see Chapter 4), there is more motivation to continue the relationship through the difficult times. In addition, the relationships among individuals in each organization develop an emotional investment in the success of "members of the team."
- *Organizational relationships are built on commitment; personal relationships are built on trust.*[12] Involvement with the customer in research and development effort contributes to the organizational display of commitment. Trust in the process is built by the individual interpersonal relationships. The relationship aspects of selling are further examined in Chapter 12.

A Brief Psychology of this Process

Like any managerial decision, decisions made in the supplier selection process are made with a degree of uncertainty. They must be. For a decision to be made with absolute certainty, all rational details and rational outcomes must be known. If these factors are known, the decision can be made by a series of binomial choices—a computer program—thus not requiring attention of management judgment or intuition.[13] Simon made the observation that decisions are made by "bounded rationality."[14] This model states that decision makers do not know all possible outcomes or payoffs and have limited motivation to search for additional alternatives, opting for the first alternative that meets the minimum standard of performance. This can lead to satisfactory, but not necessarily optimum decisions. Simon called this "satisficing" behavior.

In the buying center, behavior that reflects this thinking would lead the marketer to believe that being the first supplier with a plausible offering may be sufficient to win the business. Satisficing can be seen as the first step beyond core product offerings, but experienced marketers know this often is not enough to capture business, let alone create a lasting relationship. While being first to market is often cited as a good positioning strategy, marketers interested in maximizing the value offering should look for optimal rather than sufficient positioning.

Sherlock states that customers form a **value image** associated with supplier alternatives.[15] This image is the sum total of all impressions and experiences that the buyer has of the supplier, whether or not pertinent to the current buying situation. These impressions act at the individual, organizational, and personal levels. This value imaging is not unlike conscious product or market positioning in that it is entirely in the customer's mind. The value image is formed by the customer and may have little to do with the actual product or service. Marketers should actively seek to maximize (not satisfice!) positive value image in the "mind" of the customer.

Value image is the total of all impressions that a customer has of the firm. It is a very powerful motivator—perhaps because so much of an individual's beliefs about a firm, situation, or occurrence are based on forgotten experiences. While the concept of value image is more obvious in consumer markets, it has application in business-to-business markets as well.

APPLICATION IN BUSINESS RELATIONSHIPS   So how do we apply this in business marketing? Individuals have attitudes and beliefs about a number of things. Images and symbols are associated in memories with values and experiences: a pink bunny beating a drum—batteries;[16] a red circle with white script writing—a soft drink; a gecko in a heated conversation—auto insurance. These symbols represent whatever value, positive or negative, customers associate with those images and the type of outcomes they expect from those values. People relate to the roles that others play in the same way. Customers, the members of the buying center, have associations with the company, products, and marketing and sales professionals—all aspects the supplier brings to the table in the process of marketing. These associations create powerful expectations of behavior. In some instances, these are positive associations that aid the marketing effort; while in others, they may unknowingly work against the marketer. Unfortunately, they are difficult to generalize. We cannot make a table of five things to do, in typical business book style, to be successful. This cake has no recipe.[17]

As an example of rationalized decision making that seeks to satisfy more than core needs, say that you are a junior in college about to purchase your first new car. You have saved a long time, working two part-time jobs to get through school and still be able to afford this new car. You can purchase a small, economical (boring) car that, financially, is the logical choice for a student with at least one year of college remaining; or you can purchase that GT Convertible (exciting) that you would, "logically," keep beyond your graduation, eliminating the need to sell the economical car and buy another as a step up when you graduate. Which choice will you make? Either can be made to sound logical and rational.

This same type of rationalized decision making occurs in business buying decisions. In a business context, suppose you are the information systems manager for a start-up company. You must decide between Lenovo desktop computers for your employees or lower-cost clones assembled by a local reseller. Depending on your attitude toward risk and your need for quality assurance, after-purchase support, and ability to upgrade, you could, logically, select either supplier.

Lenovo rationale: Lenovo has been in business for a long time and will continue to be able to support us. Their product may not be the latest, hottest computer for the best price, but their quality and reliability make them the right choice. They better fit the image of the type of company we want to do business with, and we cannot get hurt choosing Lenovo. Besides, upgrading is not important since technology changes so fast we will not want to bother to upgrade old computers but will purchase new ones when necessary.

Local reseller rationale: Fast Freddie Computers (FFC) is a local business on the cutting edge of new systems integration. FFC can pick the best components from many suppliers to assemble a system tailored to our individual needs. They are local, in our community, and more able to understand the needs of a small start-up company. Reliability and service will not be an issue because they are nearby and will be on-site immediately if there are any problems. We will be a big customer to FFC, while Lenovo will not know we exist. Besides, they will be able to upgrade our computers with the latest technology at a lower cost than purchasing new units.

How do marketers reconcile this view of decision making with what is supposed to be a logical business approach? First, recognize that a good marketing plan and a good business marketer assist the buying center through the decision process. The marketer should recognize the steps previously discussed as components of the decision that can be influenced. The marketer that fully understands the nature of the customer's business, his own organization's supply capabilities, and the role he can play will seek opportunities to enhance his image with respect to the needs of the customer at every possible opportunity. All of these factors combine to create "the way the customer buys." It is impossible to standardize these factors into an eight-step routine decision process.

THOUGHTS TO TAKE WITH YOU INTO THE NEXT CHAPTER

The process by which organizations select suppliers is difficult to generalize. As a result, learning the way a particular customer buys is critical to the business marketer. The differences in consumer and business buying models have been discussed, with emphasis on the broad array of different types of decisions occurring simultaneously in the buying center. The marketer should address the different aspects of value sought by the different members of the buying center. Only in this way can the marketer provide superior value to the customer's entire organization.

Perhaps the most important observation to come out of this chapter is the importance for the business marketer's organization to be involved in the early portion of the customer's buying decision process. As the customer develops the general statement of need, the business marketer should be of assistance in offering alternatives and pointing out the supplier's unique values. The development of a specification should be a joint effort of the supplier and the buying center. When complete, the supplier's offering should be a natural fit with the specification and the organization's needs.

The development of a specification by the customer is often a method used by the customer to reduce differences between potential suppliers. The ability of the supplier to influence the specification is attributable in many ways to the expected value that the customer believes will be provided by the supplying firm. These expectations are the result of images and beliefs formed about potential suppliers long before this actual business episode.

Customers rely on suppliers for assistance throughout their design, development, and specification process. Particularly with new technologies, customers need coaching as to how to get maximum value from the supplier's products. A strong alliance with major suppliers to ensure that their best interests are protected is of value to customers. Suppliers do not become significant to the customer without forging these alliances. As we hope to demonstrate throughout this book, mutual trust, respect, and professionalism are essential to the business-to-business relationship.

This chapter has shown that understanding the buying center and the buying decision process is key to building customer relationships. In the chapters that follow, we discuss how to learn about customers and the business environment and how to turn this knowledge into executable strategy. A key component of this strategy focuses on meeting customer needs through the development of relationships with customers.

Key Terms

buying center *56*
internal brand *62*
modified rebuy *61*
new task *61*

process flow model *60*
request for proposal (RFP) *63*
request for quotation
    (RFQ) *63*

stakeholders *56*
straight rebuy *61*
value image *75*

Questions for Review and Discussion

1. Contrast the consumer buying decision process with the organizational buying process.
2. What is a buying center?
3. What organizations or departments are usually considered to be in a buying center?
4. How does the buying center change for different types of purchases (straight rebuy, modified rebuy, new task)?
5. Relate the value chain discussed in Chapter 2 with the buying center. How can they be intertwined to provide value for the customer?
6. Discuss how an internal culture within a buying center could work against rational, quantifiable decision making but results in satisfying decision outcomes.
7. Compare two or three internal cultures that you have read about (or experienced) and their impact in consumer decision making and business decision making.
8. Why is it difficult to generalize the process of business buying behavior?
9. Relate the buying process model to organizational and individual needs. How do they change through the process?
10. Under what type of purchase decision is an existing supplier at the greatest risk—new task; modified rebuy; or routine purchase?

11. What types of purchases are likely to experience extensive activity occurring in the following portions of the buying decision process model?
    a. definition stage
    b. selection stage
    c. solution delivery stage
    d. endgame stage
12. What types of purchases and purchase decisions lend themselves to the Internet or other Web-based decision strategies?
13. An influential member of the buying center has confided to a supplier's representative that she is anxious to "show her stuff" and move up in her organization. Into what part of the individual needs description does the statement seem to fit? When is such a request likely to occur?
14. Your company has been a reliable and trusted supplier of somewhat generic, frequently purchased hardware items. One of your largest regular customers has announced that all purchases of hardware and supplies will be subject to an online bidding service. Your company has a choice of either submitting to the bidding system or lowering your current prices by 5 percent (thus avoiding exposure to the online process). How would you respond?

Endnotes

1. David Welch, "E-Marketplace: Covisint," *Business Week Online* (June 5, 2000).

2. Christopher Koch, "Motor City Shakeup—The Future of E-Commerce," *Darwin Magazine* (January 2002), http://www.darwinmag.com/read/010102/shakeup.html.

3. Welch, "E-Marketplace."

4. John Waranuiak, Johnson Controls, as quoted in Motor City Shakeup – The Future of E-Commerce, http://www.darwinmag.com/read/010102/shakeup.html.

5. Dawn Kawamoto, "Covisint to Sell Auction Business (sic)," *CNET News.Com* (December 2003, 31), http://news.com.com/2102-1017_3-5134296.html.

6. Jim Ericson, "Compuware Buys Last of Covisint," *Line56 E-Business Executive Daily* (February 6, 2004), http://www.line56.com ArticleID=5357.

7. Jewel Gopwani, "Compuware renews (sic) Covisint," *Detroit Free Press* (September 3, 2004).

8. Anonymous, "Commerce One Inc.: Software Concern Tells SEC It Expects Its Business to Close," *Wall Street Journal* (Eastern Edition) (September 24, 2004), p. B.7.

9. David N. Burt, Donald W. Dobler, and Stephen L. Startling, *World Class Supply Management: The Key to Supply Chain Management*, 7th ed. (New York: McGraw-Hill/Irwin, 2003), pp. 29–30.

10. Ibid., Chapter 6.

11. Pete Engardio and Bruce Einhorn, "Outsourcing Innovation," *Business Week* (March 21, 2005), pp. 84–94.

12. Das Narayandas and V. Kasturi Rangan, "Building and Sustaining Buyer-Seller Relationships in Mature Industrial Markets," *Journal of Marketing*, 68(3) (2004 July), p. 63.

13. Richard R. Ritte and Ray G. Funkhouser, *The Ropes to Skip and the Ropes to Know*, 3rd ed. (New York: John Wiley & Sons, 1987), p. 66.

14. Herbert A. Simon, "Rational Decision Making in Business Organizations," *American Economic Review* (September 1979), pp. 493–512.

15. Paul Sherlock, *Rethinking Business to Business Marketing* (New York, The Free Press, 1991), p. 24.

16. The "Eveready Energizer Bunny" advertising campaign was named as one of the top ten commercials in 1990 by Video Storyboard Tests Inc. Ironically, a full 40 percent of those who selected the ad as an outstanding commercial thought it was for Duracell—Eveready's strongest competitor. Duracell's previous positioning (value image?) was able to negate the commercial's popularity! [As cited by Regis McKenna, "Marketing Is Everything," *Harvard Business Review* (January–February 1991)]

17. In Rethinking Business-to-Business Marketing, Sherlock applies the principles of Carl Jung to the decision process. Sherlock observes that the conscious mind (the area where we think we function); combined with the personal unconscious (forgotten personal experience); and of the collective unconscious (where our inherent nature combines with archetypical roles—mother, child, hero, seller, etc.) with its power and drive are the three regions of the mind responsible for decision making. Sherlock emphasizes that this unconscious-driven decision process is justified by an after-the-fact rationalization through the use of the classical decision model.

   For example, our conscious mind is where we think we make willful decisions, where we have willpower in decisions such as dieting, studying rather than partying, saving rather than spending. With willpower, we are not utilizing all of our capabilities and resources, which is why we are often unsuccessful in these pursuits. Our belief systems, created by our experiences and stored in less-than-conscious parts of our minds, exert tremendous influence on our decision process. To deny this would be to deny many of the motivational aspects of buyer behavior.

Chapter 4

The Legal and Regulatory Environment

OVERVIEW

The impact of law and politics on business is usually greater than imagined by students and consumers. Regulations impact many business decisions and can define the nature and positioning of competition. Patents and intellectual property laws are major considerations in many business models and a factor to consider in the formation of partnerships and value networks. Beyond short-term price decisions that impact the supplier–customer relationship, business regulation defines the extent of many activities between supply chain members.

In this chapter, we examine the logic of legal restraints applied to business-to-business activities in a market-driven economic system and introduce the primary legislative controls on business-to-business markets. Many of these regulations overlap, support, or clarify prior regulations. To assist you in understanding the regulatory environment, we discuss the combined focus of these regulations with a review of the activities they regulate.

One of the most complicated and easily misunderstood issues in marketing is the legal environment. Contributing to this confusion is that, like many pieces of legislation, the laws and acts are subject to interpretation. The discussion that follows does not attempt to legally interpret legislation beyond that which has already been done in marketing and legal literature. The focus of this chapter is to define the parameters of the legal environment that business-to-business marketers face each day. We believe that it is more important to understand when a business practice can be considered illegal rather than to be able to state specifically which act(s) the practice is governed by. Within this context, we demonstrate the legal issues and offer some insight into antitrust and price discrimination law enforcement. While most of this chapter references U.S. law, the principles of business legislation are quite common in most post-industrialized nations.

Example: Your Plight as Owner of Pacific Drives

Suppose that you are the owner of Pacific Drives, a small computer hard drive company in a Northwestern state. Your potential customers are major producers of laptop computers. Your two largest competitors, DynaDrive Peripherals and Spin Technologies, are large companies with extensive product lines, established customers, and well-developed and efficient market access. When you attempt to contract the shipping of your products to your customers, you find that the major logistics provider with the best service in your area will not ship your products because its nationwide contract with DynaDrive Peripherals awards it 100 percent of the DynaDrive shipping business but only if it does not ship any products of DynaDrive competitors. As a result, you are forced to use a piece-meal collection of regional shippers with neither the reputation nor the market reach to completely satisfy your needs. Your business faces slow and costly delivery service, putting you at a competitive disadvantage in the market-place. As e-commerce grows, however, you find an alternative to your present way of doing business. You begin to offer your products directly to customers over the Internet. In cooperation with several other small technology firms whose products complement yours, you start an Internet-based trading site. Your customers and the customers of your cooperating partners can access the site once a business relationship is established with one of the primary partners.[1] You make arrangements with a worldwide parcel service to handle all of your deliveries and other logistics needs. It looks like your problems are solved, until your Internet service provider (ISP) refuses to provide secure transmission capabilities for your ordering system. It seems that your ISP is a division of a conglomerate that is also the parent company of Spin Technologies. The parent company thinks the Internet operations are a good idea and wants to use it, so they are going to use their leverage to keep you out of the market.

LEARNING OBJECTIVES

By reading this chapter, you will

- Understand the primary goals and objectives of business legislation and its implications in a market economy.
- Understand the basic U.S. antitrust and business regulatory legislative acts.
- Gain a sense of the interaction of legislation and the activities it restricts or prohibits.
- Recognize the business-to-business marketing implications and nuances of those restrictions.
- Recognize the defining role that legislation can have with regards to intricate and multiple supply chain roles.
- Understand the methods and variability in enforcement of the acts.
- Understand the substantiality test in enforcement decisions.
- Understand specific market issues related to price discrimination.
- Be introduced to intellectual property protection, licensing, and the relationship to antitrust laws.

INTRODUCTION

Does the treatment of Pacific Drives in this opening case sound like a fair scenario? No? Why not? The logistics provider, by giving a quantity discount to DynaDrive, is legally providing a quantity discount to one of its larger customers, and the ISP cannot be expected to provide service features to a customer that competes with its parent company. In fact, this fictitious example contains two restraints of trade that are violations of antitrust law. First, while the logistics provider can give quantity discounts to large customers, the discounts must be justified by the cost savings associated with the economies of scale and the contract cannot shut out the customer's competitors from using the same logistics provider. The second violation is exclusive dealing, committed by the ISP. Companies cannot selectively restrict access to products and services in a way that lessens competition in the market.

In most situations, it is not likely that management with intentional harm or malice as a goal violates business legislation. Good marketers want to make the best deals for their employers and customers. Marketing managers, who daily make decisions regarding price and other components of total offerings to customers, must have a working knowledge of the potential pitfalls, traps, and nuances of antitrust and price discrimination laws. Application of this working knowledge not only avoids embarrassing situations with customers but, through the use of a proactive approach to avoid legal entanglements, can enhance the customer relationship.

BUSINESS REGULATION IN A FREE MARKET

Though the United States has what is called a "free market" economy, there are some necessary restrictions that must be placed on business to *assure equal access to the market* by all competitors and protect consumers in the market. As a result, business-related legislation has been focused in three areas:

1. *Protect companies from each other.* While competition is one of the fundamental strengths of a free market system, some organizations are much more able to compete than others. Smaller companies are often at risk of being overpowered by large companies attempting to dominate markets. By using its size and market presence, a large organization, acting as a predator, can leverage its impact in the market to make it very difficult for a smaller company to compete. Laws that prevent unfair pricing or restricted access to markets are often aimed at just such predatory situations.

2. *Protect consumers.* Without business legislation, some firms would misrepresent their products, lie or bait in their advertising, deceive in their packaging, or provide unsafe products. Unfair consumer practices, often highly visible to consumers and thus enforcers that answer to them, have been a major area of enforcement. Generally, business laws attempt to maximize choice to the consumer while providing all businesses with maximum access to markets.

3. *Protect the Interests of Society.* A market-driven economy works most effectively for its citizens when all businesses are on a level playing field. Equal opportunity for businesses, regardless of their size, enhances consumer choice in the market. Additionally, most new legislation has focused on holding businesses responsible for the social and environmental cost associated with their processes or products. Thus, environmental legislation has significant impact on the conduct of business.

ENFORCEMENT RESPONSIBILITIES

At the federal level, enforcement of business law is usually the responsibility of a federal administrative agency or of the Justice Department in the executive branch of the U.S. government. Though many state-level agencies exist, their diversity puts them beyond the scope of this book. Administrative agencies are neither legislative nor judicial bodies.[2] While some agencies reside in the executive office of the president of the United States (e.g., the Department of Health and Human Services and the Department of Agriculture), most are independent agencies like the Consumer Product Safety Commission (CPSC) and the Federal Trade Commission (FTC). The president can exercise a degree of control through his authority to appoint agency administrators, though a major difference between executive agencies and independent agencies is the term over which administrators serve. Independent agency administrators serve for a fixed term whose period is staggered with the president's term, reducing the influence of any one presidential term and thus reducing executive branch influence.[3]

It is very difficult to generalize about enforcement of business legislation because enforcement is often the *choice* of an agency or the Justice Department. Though traditional patterns have blurred in recent years, enforcement priorities can change with the change of a presidential administration or political party in power in Congress. As different candidates are elected to office and use the appointment powers of the office, current officials are replaced. The agenda and priorities of the new officials may place emphasis on different political and social issues. Thus, the successful and astute marketer has an up-to-date working knowledge of the legal aspects of marketing and the current attitude of enforcement agencies.

Injunctions are agreements—"equitable remedies"—that can be imposed by the courts to prevent, delay, or enjoin a particular activity.

Treble damages are three times the actual loss incurred by the injured party as a result of a violation of antitrust law. Damages are awarded as compensation to the injured party. The injured party must prevail in a civil court.

THE LEGISLATIVE ACTS THAT AFFECT MARKETING

This section summarizes major legislation in the United States related to business-to-business marketing situations. The acts themselves and their primary focus are summarized in Exhibit 4-1. Because of the interrelationship of these laws, this summary is followed by a discussion of legal issues that do not always fall clearly within any one act.

Sherman Antitrust Act (1890)

The Sherman Antitrust Act was the first to prohibit "monopolies or attempts to monopolize" and "contracts, combinations, or conspiracies in restraint of trade" in interstate or foreign commerce. The Sherman Act provides for **injunctions** to restrain activities found to be in violation and allows anyone injured to recover, in a civil action, **treble damages**. Sherman Act jurisdiction is not strictly limited to

Statute	Focus
Sherman Antitrust Act (1890)	Monopolies, attempts to monopolize. Provided for both civil and criminal penalties. Broad coverage was base for later legislation.
Clayton Act (1914)	Tying agreements, interlocking directorates, intercorporate stockholding. Provides for civil penalties only.
Federal Trade Commission Act (1914)	Broadly defined unfair competition or competitive situations.
Robinson-Patman Act (1936)	Often known as "the price discrimination act," provided penalties for both buyers as well as sellers. Requires proportionally equal terms to buyers in common markets.
Celler-Kefauver Act (1950)	The "Antimerger Act." Broadened power to prevent acquisitions where they may substantially impact competition.
Consumer Goods Pricing Act (1975)	Repealed Miller-Tydings Act (1937) which had allowed "fair trade," a form of price maintenance.

EXHIBIT 4-1 Summary of Antitrust Acts and Their Focus

interstate commerce but includes intrastate activities that have a substantial impact on interstate commerce.

The Sherman Act provides for criminal felony penalties for both individuals and corporations. Corporations are subject to substantial fines and potential prohibitions on certain market activities and individuals may be fined as well as imprisoned for up to three years.[4]

Clayton Act (1914)

The Clayton Act, passed in 1914, supplemented the Sherman Act by prohibiting certain specific practices before they advance to the definition of a restraint of trade as held by the Sherman Act. Clayton includes limitations on **tying contracts**, **exclusive dealing**, **intercorporate stockholding**, **interlocking directorates**, and mergers in which competition may be substantially reduced. The Clayton Act also provides that corporate officers and officials may be held *individually responsible* for violations. The Clayton Act, however, can be applied only to transactions and persons *engaged* in interstate commerce, rather than the more broadly defined jurisdiction of *affecting* interstate commerce as under the Sherman Act.

While the Clayton Act added teeth to Sherman, it specifically exempted labor and agricultural organizations from antitrust legislation.[5] Though the Clayton Act has no criminal penalties specified, intentional price discrimination carries criminal penalties under other acts.

Federal Trade Commission Act (1914)

The Federal Trade Commission was initially established by this Act to prevent unfair methods of competition and deceptive practices. The FTC has powers to investigate and enforce the federal legislation already mentioned. Its powers were broadened by the *Wheeler-Lea Act (1938),* which granted the FTC the power to regulate unfair or deceptive practices *whenever* the public is being deceived, *regardless* of the competitive environment. Thus, the commission is charged with the duty of preventing "unfair methods of competition in commerce and unfair or deceptive acts or practices in commerce." In 1953, the U.S. Supreme Court further broadened and strengthened the power of the FTC *(FTC v. Motion Picture Advertising Service Co.)* as follows:

> The unfair methods of competition which are condemned by. . . . the Act are not confined to those that were illegal at common law or that were condemned by the Sherman Act. . . . It is also clear that the FTC Act was designed to supplement and bolster the Sherman Act and the Clayton Act to stop *in their incipiency acts and practices which, when full blown, would violate those Acts.* (Italics added for emphasis).[6]

The real impact of this upon business marketers is to let the FTC address any kind of restraint of trade, not just those that fall under the Sherman Act or Clayton Act. This allows the FTC to keep up with the innovativeness of companies seeking new ways to restrain trade.

Tying contracts are contracts that require the purchase of unnecessary or ancillary goods or services "in a bundle" to get the offering really desired. Example: A manufacturer of office copiers leases the copier for a below market-value rate, but the customer must purchase all paper and supplies from the manufacturer at inflated prices.

Exclusive dealing occurs when a seller sells to only one buyer in a region or territory such that competition is lessened. Example: A manufacturer restricts access to its products via only one distributor and prevents the distributor from carrying competitive offerings. Both exclusive dealing and tying contracts are attempts to restrict buyers' access to competitive products. In specific circumstances, judgments about the legality of these situations often depends on the size and market power of the firm attempting to limit choice in the market. Chapter 14 includes further discussion of exclusive distribution.

Intercorporate stockholding occurs when one company controls the stock of another company and through that ownership exercises control such that trade is restrained.

A common pattern of enforcement by the FTC is to enter into consent orders with potential violators to minimize the possibility of future violations. Exhibit 4-2 provides an example of how consent orders are used to limit the anticompetitive nature of mergers and acquisitions.

Companies faced with legal challenges from the FTC have an alternative to a court battle not unlike a plea bargain between a prosecuting attorney and a defendant. This alternative, called a **consent decree**, is a written agreement between the agency and the company. When this type of negotiated settlement is possible, significant time and expense can be saved. These agreements are often used to alleviate FTC concerns that arise when mergers and acquisitions might limit access to markets. By reaching an agreement, the company involved can proceed with the intended acquisition in a timely manner. Consider the following examples.

Silicon Graphics and the FTC

Silicon Graphics, Inc. (SGI), provides 90 percent of the software used to produce three-dimensional high-resolution graphics. This software has made possible the images for movies such as *Jurassic Park*, *Terminator 2*, and similar high image-oriented movies. SGI acquired two of the three leading entertainment graphics software firms. The FTC became concerned that, as a result of the acquisitions, SGI would no longer support independent graphics software producers and might deny competitors access to the software of the firms it was acquiring. Such actions by SGI could limit choices in the graphics software market as well as make it more difficult for hardware suppliers to provide compatible equipment for the software market. Without resolution of these concerns, the FTC would likely have challenged the acquisition. Under the consent order, SGI agreed to maintain an open architecture for independent software developers and publish an application interface to give other graphics software producers the capability to write software for SGI workstations. SGI also agreed to assure that the acquired software could be run on hardware other than that provided by SGI.

Boston Scientific and the FTC

Boston Scientific Corporation (BSC), a principal player in the market for intravascular ultrasound imaging catheters (IVUS), intended to acquire its main competitor. The combination would give BSC 90 percent of the IVUS catheter market. In addition to this acquisition, BSC was acquiring another firm that was considered to be the only new competition in that market. To assuage FTC concerns, BSC proposed the licensing of a package of its patents and technologies and those of the acquired firms to Hewlett-Packard (now known as Agilent Technologies) or another FTC-designated firm to help launch a strong competitor. The FTC added two requirements: (1) BSC must provide the licensee, for three years, with IVUS catheters and technical assistance to obtain Food and Drug Administration approval of their own catheters, and (2) BSC cannot enter into any exclusive contracts with manufacturers of IVUS imaging consoles (consoles necessary to use the catheters). In other words, BSC was prevented from excluding any competitors from the market for other necessary equipment and was required to help their licensee successfully enter the market.

    As you can see, the FTC has the authority to act *before* a violation of law or restraint of trade actually occurs. This power acts as an incentive to bring firms desiring mergers or acquisitions to communicate with the FTC prior to actual acquisition or merger. The agency and the firm(s) agree to create a mutually acceptable set of circumstances that will maintain a competitive marketplace.

EXHIBIT 4-2   Alternatives to Court-Imposed Remedies   *Source*: "Antitrust Policy, an On-line Resource Linking Economic Research, Policy and Cases," Owen Graduate School of Management, Vanderbilt University, http://www.antitrust.org

Robinson-Patman Act (1936)

The Robinson-Patman Act amended and strengthened portions of the Clayton Act and also made it unlawful for a buyer to knowingly "induce or receive" a discriminatory price.[7] *Buyers* as well as sellers could now be held liable for actions that violate antitrust laws. Particularly for large firms engaged in interstate commerce, Robinson-Patman has been known as "the" price discrimination act. It specifically defines price discrimination as unlawful, subject to certain clearly defined exceptions. Robinson-Patman also provides enforcing agencies with the right to limit quantity discounts, prohibit brokerage allowances except to independent brokers, and prohibit promotional allowances or furnished services or facilities except when made available equally to all participants. This equality can be defined as **proportionately equal terms** and can be based on several factors.

Equality/proportionately equal terms means that a seller must provide substantially equal offers to buyers in horizontal competition with each other. The offers may differ in specific attributes, but must be relatively equal in value. The volume of business received from each buyer may proportion the offers.

Through the concept of proportionately equal terms as held by the Robinson-Patman Act, price alone does not determine equality. The total offering, which may include financing, inventory and delivery services, marketing assistance, and other factors, is considered in determining the total value in question.

Celler-Kefauver Act (1950)

Often referred to as the *Antimerger Act*, the Celler-Kefauver Act amended the Clayton Act and broadened the power to prevent the acquisition of one company by another where the combination may substantially impact competition.[8] Even with this legislation, many business combinations have occurred in recent years, such as BP-Amoco, Exxon-Mobil, and the Boeing acquisition of McDonald Douglas. In each of these mergers, enforcement agencies ordered that certain portions of one or both parties' activities and holdings in specific markets be ceased or divested to avoid any opportunity to monopolize the market.

Consumer Goods Pricing Act (1975)

The Consumer Goods Pricing Act (CGPA) repealed the Miller-Tydings Act, which had allowed *fair trade* pricing of consumer goods. Fair trade was intended to protect small retailers (what we might know today as small specialty boutiques) from the discounting by other retailers in the same area as well as from the buying power of large chains. Independent retailers could feel confident that they would not face price competition for the fair traded items. Many manufacturers were content with this arrangement as it made it easier to control retail prices. This control was considered necessary in positioning products as well as managing marketing channel margins. Fair trade evolved into a form of resale price maintenance, which is further described later. While the CGPA prohibits manufacturers from setting prices through their channels, a recent decision by the U.S. Supreme Court allows manufacturers, in some circumstances, to set a minimum price for their products.[9] Not unlike the "free rider" provisions discussed later in this chapter, manufacturers are expected to welcome this change. The ruling allows an opportunity to more quickly recover costs of the development and training related to sophisticated products. This is desirable to manufacturers that participate in markets with short life cycles. The ruling does not, however, allow for retail price maintenance where pricing policies have the effect of reducing competition.

Securities Laws

Complicated federal and state securities laws, beyond the scope of this book, are designed to protect the investing public, not business competitors and customers. Nevertheless, the effect of securities laws on the way we conduct business is enormous. In brief, business people in companies that have issued stock to outsiders cannot defraud the investing public and must "disclose" important information about the company and its business.

*The **Silent period** is a period of several weeks before a company IPO that blacks out any extraneous or private information about the company that may impact the initial value of the stock. The company assembles its pertinent and relevant data into a prospectus that is made available to interested investors. The silent period is another example of regulatory efforts to maintain a level playing field; this time among investors in newly listed stocks.*

From a marketer's perspective, probably one of the most important provisions of securities laws is what is known as the **silent period**. When a company is engaged in an **initial public offering** (IPO) there is a period of several weeks prior to the offering when the company and its executives cannot comment about the financial status of the organization nor its prospects for the future beyond that which is stated in the investors' prospectus. The goal of the silent period is to ensure that all potential investors have access to the same information, via the prospectus, about the company. "Inside" information about the company and its prospects is prohibited. Marketers must use caution in discussions with customers that they do not inadvertently violate this provision.

If you are involved with your company in an IPO or any issue of stock to "the public," you absolutely need the guidance of securities law professionals.

*An **initial public offering** is a company's first issue of stock to the general public. Prior to this point, the company has usually relied on private investors and operational funding. An IPO is usually a sign of success for a small company. Prospects for the firm are usually described in a prospectus that is available to the general public—the segment of investors the firm wants to attract.*

Sarbanes-Oxley Act and Its Offspring

In 2002, The Sarbanes-Oxley Act introduced major changes in financial regulation, mostly as a reaction to a number of major corporate accounting scandals, including but not limited to Enron, Tyco International, and Worldcom (now part of Verizon). Also known as the Public Company Accounting Reform and Investor Protection Act of 2002,[10] and commonly called "SOX," the Act established the *Public Company Accounting Oversight Board* to oversee wide-ranging new standards for all public company's boards, management, and public accounting firms.

The advent of SOX inspired regulatory activity in several other industrialized nations. In Canada, "Bill 198," known as the "Canadian Sarbanes-Oxley Act" (C-SOX), was passed in 2003; Australia has implemented "Corporate Law Economic Reform Program"[11] (CLERP) in 2004; and the "Financial Instruments and Exchange Law" (J-SOX) was implemented in Japan in 2006. All of these bills seek to re-establish public confidence in the financial activities of public corporations. Though not immediately apparent, the marketing impact of a lack of public trust can be a serious positioning problem (Chapter 16 discusses Business Ethics and Crisis Management).

Common law really is a method of interpreting law. Judges interpret any law based upon all case decisions already made about the same issue. This accumulation of decisions, called precedence, was developed in England.

The Uniform Commercial Code

Some form of written document defines most business transactions. These documents may be as simple as the terms of sale of an individual purchase or may comprise many pages of conditions of the sale and rights and remedies of the parties involved. The law that governs these contracts is either **common law** or the Uniform Commercial Code (UCC). The UCC is a standard set of laws that govern the contracts and associated case law. For clarity and uniformity, most portions of the UCC have been adopted by all states except Louisiana. Business contracts, particularly those concerning the sale of goods (UCC Article 2) across state lines, are assisted by the consistent provisions of the UCC.

It has been our experience that most students will have only limited need for extensive knowledge of contract law and, when necessary, will consult with legal professionals. Further coverage of the UCC and contract law, beyond topical discussions in other portions of this text (e.g., pricing and sales, Chapters 10 and 12), is left to business law courses.

BUSINESS LEGISLATION ISSUES

Marketers need a working knowledge of the combined nature and effect of business regulations. Since the regulatory powers of the acts overlap and amend each other, the best way for business marketers to approach this is with a discussion of the issues rather than the individual acts.

Intercorporate Stockholding

As already noted, intercorporate stockholding occurs when a company owns another company in the same market or own shares of another company in the same market in an attempt to control that company such that competition in the marketplace is reduced. It is important to emphasize that ownership of more than one company that participates in a marketplace by a parent firm is not, in and of itself, illegal. However, manipulating that ownership in a manner that reduces choice and competition in the marketplace is considered a violation. Consider a manufacturer of chemicals and plastics that has significantly large stock holdings in an automotive manufacturer such that the purchases of chemicals and plastics by the automotive manufacturer can be influenced. Applying this influence so that it is very difficult for any other chemical and plastics company to be considered as a supplier would be a restraint of trade.

Interlocking Directorates

A company may attempt control of another firm by having members of its board of directors serve as directors of the other company, a practice referred to as interlocking directorates. Companies that participate (ostensibly, compete) in the same market cannot have common directors such that actions could be influenced that would lessen competition between the companies or in the markets in which they participate, either as buyer or seller. Important to the particular situation is how enforcers define "the market." "Market" may be region, market segment, product line, or any factor in the competitive arena. Exhibit 4-3 provides an enforcement example.

Price Maintenance

A manufacturer's attempt to dictate the resale price of an item is called price maintenance and it is specifically illegal. The problem usually arises in marketing channels, either at the wholesale or at the retail level. Once an intermediary (wholesaler, retailer, etc.) purchases a product, it can sell it at any price it wishes. Obviously, price is a part of the marketing mix and manufacturers would like to control it. Oddly enough, this practice was legal at the retail level under the Miller-Tydings Act (1937) until 1975 and was actually called *fair trade*! The CGPA discussed previously eliminated this practice. In today's market, suppliers may suggest or recommend pricing, but this must not be interpreted as having coerced the reseller into maintaining that price. While

In the view of the Justice Department, whether mergers and acquisitions create a restraint of trade often depends on the definition of the impacted market. Here are two examples in which the market definition has significant impact on the proposed acquisitions.

Kraft General Foods, Incorporated, versus the State of New York

Kraft General Foods, Inc. (KGF), acquired the breakfast cereal business of Nabisco (Shredded Wheat, etc.). At the time of the acquisition, KGF's breakfast cereal line included *Post*-brand cereals. The state contended that the acquisition would have adverse effects in the ready-to-eat (RTE) adult breakfast cereal market. By defining the market as *adult RTE*, the state hoped to show that the two popular cereals, Post Grape-Nuts and Nabisco Shredded Wheat, would dominate the "market."

The court found evidence of both supply-side and demand-side substitutability. The "kid" and "adult" RTE cereal markets overlapped, with the dominant selection characteristic being variety. Thus, the "market" was expanded to include more than 200 RTE cereals. From a supply-side perspective, the court determined that the RTE cereal industry manufacturing processes were flexible enough that if, as a result of the Post-Nabisco combination, adult cereals experienced a significant increase in market price, additional competitive substitutes would become available.

Community Publishers, Incorporated, versus Donrey Corporation

In this example, we can see the potential restraint of trade implied by **interlocking directorates** as well as the impact of market definitions. Community Publishers, Inc. (CPI), publisher of the *Daily Record*, a newspaper in Northwest Arkansas, challenged the acquisition of the *Times*, a competing local newspaper, by an organization indirectly controlled by the same family that owned another Arkansas newspaper, the *Morning News*. In defense of the acquisition, the defendant argued that the market for news was served by a broad array of providers, including radio, television, and national- and state-level newspapers. Additionally, the defendant claimed that the market of each newspaper was different because the papers did not compete directly for advertisers nor was there significant switching of subscriptions between the papers. The court, however, defined the market narrowly as local daily newspapers in the northwest Arkansas geographic area. Under this definition, the combined newspapers had an 84 percent market share; the geographic area was integrated "socially, politically, and economically," and everyone involved with each of the newspapers considered the other to be a competitor. The need of advertisers to promote in a "dominant newspaper" could, through an increase in advertising rates, "soak up" advertising revenue from other newspapers. The court found that the combined newspapers could, through regional expansion, create an entity that would have little competition for subscribers or advertisers.

As corrective action, the court rejected the idea of divestiture by the defendant, as this would allow the defendant to still have significant say as to the fate of the divested newspaper. The court therefore ordered rescission of the acquisition, restoring the market to its condition prior to the acquisition.

EXHIBIT 4-3   Legally Defined Markets   *Source*: Antitrust Policy, an Online Resource Linking Economic Research, Policy and Cases, Owen Graduate School of Management, Vanderbilt University, www.antitrust.org.

manufacturers' suggested retail prices (MSRPs) are often used as tools to position the offering in the market and a retailer may often elect to follow the suggested price as part of an overall promotional plan, the retailer cannot be coerced to sell at that price. If a retailer elects to discount the items below the MSRP, the manufacturer cannot use other means (e.g., refusal to deal, which follows) to force the seller to maintain a specified price.

There are circumstances in which a manufacturer is allowed to exert some control over the resale price of an offering. When suppliers are contributing to the value of the offering (e.g., providing financing for inventory, selling through a consignment agreement, providing support services, etc.), they are allowed more influence on the final price. This, ostensibly, is allowed to reduce the impact of **free riders**—retailers who provide a reduced-service package to customers, enabling profitability at a lower sales price than full-service retailers. Full-service retailers who provide a full package that may include such items as product demonstrations, installation advice, and local parts availability incur costs associated with these services. Manufacturers can protect full-service retailers by limiting the discounts that limited-service retailers can provide. Without such an accommodation, customers would seek information and education from the full-service retailer and make purchases at the lower-cost alternative.

> *Free riders are those retailers who, either through mail order, e-commerce, or other means, provide a reduced service package to customers, enabling a lower sales price. This reduced package usually lacks purchase assistance, product information, and customer education—many of the services provided by full-service "brick & mortar" retailers.*

Refusal to Deal

When used as a method to enforce or encourage one of the preceding issues, such as price maintenance, **refusal to deal** is illegal. This may take the form of not restocking or not providing associated services to dealers that have not followed suggested pricing. The courts have, however, recognized the right of a seller to sell (or not sell) to whomever it wants, provided the motivation is not to restrain trade or fix prices.

Resale Restrictions

The courts have not come down firmly on either side of the issue of **resale restrictions**, which usually refers to suppliers maintaining house accounts (customers that, while they are located within a reseller's market area, remain a direct customer of the manufacturer) or limiting resellers to certain territories.

Price Discrimination

Price discrimination is one of the most difficult areas about which to generalize because court interpretations have been somewhat inconsistent. Essentially, **price discrimination** occurs when a supplier sells the same product to the "same class" of buyers at different prices such that the price differentials lessen competition in the marketplace *served by the buyers*. Prices for products that would be considered discriminatory but are sold to customers who are not in competition with each other are not illegal. Confused? Let us consider a sample scenario.

> *A sample scenario*   Your company, Pacific Drives (Pacific), manufactures hard drives for personal computers. Among Pacific customers are two large computer manufacturers, NBM and PaloAlto Computers (PaloAlto). NBM and PaloAlto are rivals, each competing for the desktop computer market. Both companies purchase Pacific Model 1000 hard drives in large quantities, 5,000 units per month, for their products. Since Pacific is selling the same product, in similar quantities, within the same time frame (so that obsolescence or seasonal

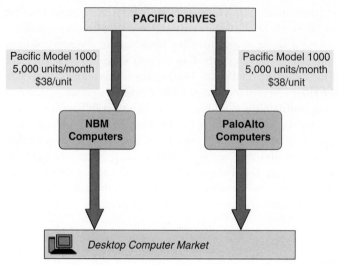

EXHIBIT 4-4   Pacific Drives Supplies the Same Product to Two Customers Who Compete in the Same Market

pricing is not a factor) to customers who compete with each other, Pacific is required to sell at the same price, $38, to both. In this scenario, illustrated in Exhibit 4-4, Pacific provides quantity discounts based on the size of the purchases.

This is a simple example that assumes comparable logistical considerations (e.g., shipping costs). Basically, neither PaloAlto nor NBM has an advantage in the marketplace as a result of any pricing irregularities on the part of Pacific Drives; but, wouldn't each customer strive for an advantage? Wouldn't Pacific be seeking opportunities to adjust pricing, up or down, as part of its value offering to its customers? The answer to both questions is yes. Let us add another factor to this scenario.

A competitive offer   One of Pacific's competitors, United Memories (UniMem), has become very aggressive. It is attempting to increase its market share by targeted price reductions at major customers in Pacific's market. UniMem approaches NBM with a special price on its Model UniMem300 drive, which is comparable to Pacific Model 1000. The Pacific selling price to NBM has been $38 per unit in quantities of 5,000 drives per month. UniMem offers the UniMem300, at the same quantities and service logistics as Pacific, for $32 per unit. This is a significant enough savings for NBM that it decides to take advantage of the offer and informs Pacific of its decision to change suppliers.[12] Of course you (Pacific) are interested in retaining the business and offer to meet the UniMem price of $32 per unit. (see Exhibit 4-5)

Wait a minute. Is this fair (or legal)? What about the Pacific price of $38 to PaloAlto? Doesn't this lower price to NBM give it an advantage over PaloAlto in their competitive battles?

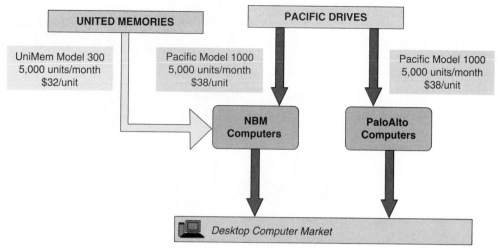

EXHIBIT 4-5 United Memories Aggressive Price at NBM Computers

In fact, pricing regulations allow a defending supplier (the one with the business—in this case, Pacific) to match the price of a competitor attempting to take away the business. Pacific Drives is not *required* to lower its price to any other customers. In fact, an across-the-board price reduction on the part of Pacific could be interpreted as a **predatory pricing**.

Predatory pricing occurs when a firm with a dominant position in a market, threatened by a new or smaller firm, changes its pricing structure such that the new firm cannot operate profitably.

The most serious marketing considerations here are not related to price. While pricing to different customers is considered confidential and customers theoretically do not tell each other what they are paying for components, Pacific Drives should be concerned about PaloAlto finding out that NBM is now getting a better deal. It is likely that UniMem will approach PaloAlto with its Model UniMem300, using the new pricing at NBM as supporting evidence of why PaloAlto should consider UniMem as a supplier, replacing the Pacific Drives product. The business relationship between Pacific Drives and PaloAlto may be tested as it could look like Pacific has been overcharging PaloAlto.

Marketing professionals at Pacific should be asking themselves how UniMem could surprise them in the marketplace like this. Pacific's knowledge of its competitors and the dynamics of the market seem to be wanting. As we discuss in Chapter 10, price is a very dynamic part of the marketing mix. Pacific needs to be aware of product life cycles and the leading edge of technologies that could impact demand and price for their product.

So far, our discussion has been relatively easy to follow within the guidelines of the Robinson-Patman Act. We now consider a situation in which price discrimination can occur notwithstanding adherence to the guidelines.

A new customer enters the market The desktop computer market is attractive to the entrepreneurial spirit and is a relatively easy market to enter. A small start-up company, Spartan Computers, contacts Pacific about supplying its hard drive needs. Spartan will manufacture desktop computers locally. Among its competitors will be PaloAlto and

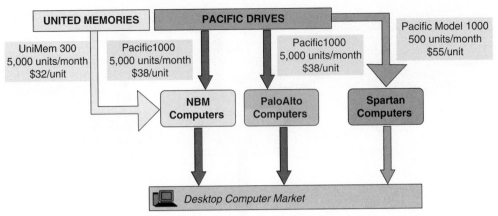

EXHIBIT 4-6   Spartan Computers Enters the Market

NBM. Spartan anticipates its volume will be approximately 500 units per month, but it will experience "significant growth" and would like Pacific to consider this in its offer. Of course, Spartan has also asked UniMem to quote the business. The Pacific response to the Spartan request for quote (RFQ) is $55 per unit, the standard "list" price for the anticipated volume of 500 units per month. Competitive information and the historic reaction patterns of UniMem convince Pacific marketers that this is what UniMem is likely to quote. Since discounts for large-quantity purchases are legal, Pacific does not anticipate any conflicts with its lower unit prices for higher volumes at NBM and PaloAlto. The addition of Spartan as a potential customer is shown in Exhibit 4-6.

It is not unusual for start-up companies to attract the employees of their larger competitors, and this has happened at Spartan. It does not take long for Spartan to realize that the Pacific offer of $55 per unit is significantly higher than the Pacific price to its larger competitors. Spartan's concern, beyond its cost of the hard drive, is that higher component prices in general will make it difficult, if not impossible, to compete in the market with NBM and PaloAlto. Spartan asks Pacific to reconsider the offer, notwithstanding the established list prices.

Pacific's initial reaction to Spartan is to stand by the standard prices. However, Spartan has pointed out that these prices will make it difficult for its products to compete in the market and that could be interpreted as a restraint of trade. It may be time for Pacific to re-examine discount policies for quantity purchases.

Quantity Discounts

Quantity discounts for volume purchases are normal business practice and entirely legal provided the discounts are cost justified. In other words, lower costs to serve high-volume customers may be passed on to the customer.[13] However, artificially low volume discounts can be (they are not always but can be) interpreted as discriminatory if they substantially impact the ability of the customer to compete in its marketplace. Thus, Spartan is justified in asking for a lower price *if* Pacific's quantity-scaled discounts cannot be justified by Pacific's cost to serve at those volumes.

In the foregoing examples, what happens if a purchasing agent from NBM told Pacific that NBM had an offer of a lower price than Pacific's current price and asked Pacific to match the competitive offer, but the competitive offer does not really exist? Well, the Robinson-Patman Act also makes it illegal for the purchasing organization to knowingly create a discriminatory pricing situation. Generally, any action that will create an imbalance in the marketplace or restrict competitors from equal access to the market can invite regulatory oversight.

Let's summarize the major tenets of price discrimination regulation.
Offerings sold

> for different uses,
> to separate markets,
> at different times,
> that are not identical,
> to government agencies, or
> at prices to meet a competitive threat

are generally not a violation of price regulations.

While this scenario is simplified and exaggerated, it nonetheless depicts real possibilities. Good marketing programs avoid possible regulatory problems. This summary provides some insight into how this is done. Most notably, offerings that are the result of a collaboration between customer and supplier, created through the process of partnering, or the result of customization for a particular customer's needs are not identical to any other offering but are unique to that specific customer. The degree of this difference is determined by the extent of new technology, specialization, and customization that was created in the process of satisfying the customer's needs. Standardized products sold by industrial distributors that specialize in particular market segments usually satisfy the market needs of small-volume customers that have not engaged in a custom development with suppliers. (This is further developed in Chapter 14.) Exhibit 4-7 provides a real-world example of a price-fixing conspiracy and Department of Justice enforcement.

On January 19, 2000, Mitsubishi Corporation, a distributor of graphite electrodes, and a former executive of UCAR International (a 50 percent owned joint venture of Mitsubishi during the period 1991–1995 and the world's largest manufacturer of graphite electrodes) were indicted in an international graphite electrode price-fixing conspiracy. Shortly thereafter, on March 13, 2000, the president and chief executive officer of Carbone of America Industries Corporation and the corporation pleaded guilty and agreed to pay more than $7 million in fines for participating in an international cartel to fix the price of isostatic graphite.

Graphite electrodes, made of fine grain carbon with great strength and chemical resistance are largely known as isostatic graphite and are used in, among other things, electric arc furnaces in steel-making mini mills, the fastest growing method of making steel in the United States. The electrodes generate the heat necessary to melt and refine steel. The total sales of graphite electrodes during a four-year period in the early 1990s were more than $1.7 billion. Steel makers, as a result of the conspiracy, paid higher noncompetitive prices for the electrodes used in steel manufacturing.

As of March 2000, several corporations *and individuals* had been charged and criminal fines assessed as a result of the Justice Department's investigation. In the two years leading up to these actions, the following companies and individuals pled guilty to participating in the conspiracy:

EXHIBIT 4-7 The International Graphite Electrode Price-Fixing Conspiracy

UCAR sentenced to pay a $110 million fine;

- UCAR's former CEO sentenced to serve seventeen months in jail and assessed a $1.25 million fine;
- UCAR's former COO, through a plea agreement, agreed to serve nine months in jail and pay a $1 million fine;
- SGL Carbon AG (a German corporation) sentenced to pay a $135 million fine;
- SGL's CEO sentenced to pay a $10 million fine (to this date, the largest ever antitrust fine imposed on an individual);
- Showa Denko Carbon Inc. (U.S. subsidiary of a Japanese firm) sentenced to pay a $32.5 million fine;
- Tokai Carbon Co. Ltd. (a Japanese corporation) sentenced to pay a $6 million fine;
- SEC Corporation (a Japanese corporation) sentenced to pay a $4.8 million fine;
- Nippon Carbon Co. Ltd. (a Japanese corporation) sentenced to pay a $2.5 million fine.

Other participants in the conspiracy were accepted into the Justice Department's Corporate Leniency Program.

In the matter of Carbone of America Industries Corporation, the guilty pleas were to charges that the company and its executive participated in meetings and conversations with cartel members to discuss prices, agreed to certain price scenarios, agreed to market share maintenance, and participated in several other anticompetitive actions.

At first, antitrust enforcement against makers of carbon electrodes used in steel manufacture may seem far removed from the consumer markets where business regulation aims to maximize choice and keep a level playing field. Steel, however, is an essential material in many consumer goods, medical devices, appliances, transportation, and construction, impacting practically every element of business and consumer consumption. As you read the list of enforcement actions, note the penalties levied against individuals who took part in the conspiracies. Review also the "Substantiality Test" as described in this chapter.

EXHIBIT 4-7 (continued)

Source: U.S. Department of Justice, press releases for January 19, 2000, *Mitsubishi Corporation and Former UCAR Executive Indicted in International Graphite Electrode Price-Fixing Conspiracy*; and March 13, 2000, *New Jersey Company and Chief Executive Officer Agree to Plead Guilty to International Price Fixing Conspiracy*, www.usdoj.gov/atr

SUBSTANTIALITY TEST

Contributing to the lack of precision in business regulation is that enforcement is at the discretion of the executive branch of government or administrative agencies. Enforcement is discretionary, just as a police officer may overlook a speeder doing 50 in a 45 mph zone but will ticket a vehicle traveling at 60 mph in the same zone. Agencies responsible for enforcing business legislation prefer to prosecute infractions with a high likelihood of successful prosecution and conviction. With limited resources available for investigation and prosecution, violations are often subject to a **substantiality test** to determine the extent of the discriminatory practice. The substantiality test, arising out of a court decision regarding exclusive dealing, serves as an excellent tool for the marketer to judge the intensity of a situation. Three considerations make up this test:

The size of the organizations involved: ("Size" may be sales volume, financial resources, market power, etc.) Is a large company attempting to coerce the behavior or business practices of a smaller company?

The volume of business involved: Is the dollar amount large relative to the size of the market? Does the offending company have a significant share of the market?

Market preemption: Does the questionable business practice or arrangement prevent competitive products from access to a substantial portion of the market?

Company Size

Business practices that are overlooked by regulators as not substantial when the company is small may receive much greater attention as the company grows and develops marketplace leverage. In 2001, a federal appeals court upheld Judge Thomas Penfield Jackson's ruling that Microsoft violated U.S. antitrust laws but sent back to the district court the proposed remedy to split up Microsoft, directing the lower court to develop an alternative.[14] Eventually, Microsoft and the Justice Department reached a settlement intended to impact Microsoft behavior in its many markets. Microsoft business practices that may have been acceptable or at least overlooked when they were small became questionable as the company and its market strength grew

Some International Implications

Market domination attracts scrutiny. Organizations must recognize the risks associated with business practices that will attract attention, be regarded as predatory, or construed as limiting competition or choice in the marketplace, regardless of the intent. The European Union (EU) has demonstrated the rising importance of regional economic communities and their competitive regulations. The EU has interpreted market practices and potential acquisitions that have passed the scrutiny of U.S. regulators differently. Operating with many of the same goals and principles, the EU naturally places a priority on the European market. Though seemingly settled in the United States, Microsoft continues to face challenges to its marketing practices by the EU. The EU also blocked, as anticompetitive, the General Electric (U.S.) acquisition of Honeywell Corporation, previously approved by U.S. regulators.

FOREIGN CORRUPT PRACTICES ACT (FCPA)   Passed in 1977, the U.S. Foreign Corrupt Practices Act was the result of a Securities and Exchange Commission (SEC) investigation of questionable payments made to foreign officials by over 400 U.S. companies.[15] The most common type of payment was made to foreign government officials with the intent of favorably influencing a business outcome. To be a violation of FCPA, payment[16] must be made to a foreign government official, political candidate for foreign office, a foreign political party, or any person that may serve as a third party or intermediary in the facilitation of such activities.[17]

After passage of the FCPA, there was concern among U.S. business as well as the Congress that American companies would be operating at a competitive disadvantage in international markets, particularly where legal and cultural norms routinely permitted bribery (including the ability to deduct the bribe as a business expense on their taxes!). In 1988, the executive branch began negotiations with major U.S. trading partners to enact legislation with the same intent as the FCPA. In 1997, the United States was one of thirty-four countries that signed the Organization of Economic Cooperation and Development (OECD) Convention on Combating Bribery of Foreign Public Officials in International Business Transactions.

The FCPA antibribery provisions make it unlawful to make a corrupt payment to a foreign official, and, since 1998, also applies to any foreign firms and individuals that take any such action while in the United States.

BASIC PROVISIONS OF THE FCPA   Several factors must be present to constitute a violation of the Act.[18]

- Who: The FCPA applies to "any individual, firm, officer, director, employee, or agent of a firm and any stockholder acting on behalf of the firm."[19] The FCPA may be applied to individuals as well as firms, and may lead to civil and/or criminal penalties.
- Corrupt Intent: The individual(s) making or authorizing the payment must have intended the payment to corrupt or induce the recipient to misuse his official position to direct business to the payer.
- Payment: Money, offerings, promises of payment or offering, or anything of value constitutes payment.
- Recipient: The FCPA applies to any public official regardless of rank, title, or position.
- Exception: Payments made to expedite or facilitate performance of a "routine government action," such as obtaining permits, licenses, or other official documents; processing of governmental papers such as visas and work permits; providing police protection, phone service, power, and water, and so on, are not a violation of the FCPA.

SUPPLY CHAIN IMPLICATIONS

A firm participates in multiple supply chains—assuming the firm has more than one customer. Competitive circumstances and customer requirements as well as effective market segmentation and a successful long-term business relationship will result in the supplying firm participating in many different supply chain designs. Customers that are part of highly competitive industries (e.g., oligopolies) will strive for every competitive advantage. Efforts will not only focus on obtaining the best value from suppliers but also extend to the design of both the inbound and outbound logistics systems. Suppliers will often be required to match the customer's materials handling process and inventory system.

INTELLECTUAL PROPERTY

Intellectual property law provides creators or owners of intellectual property the right to benefit from its creation, use, and dissemination. Intellectual property is regarded, for legal purposes, as essentially comparable to any other form of property. We focus on issues related to intellectual

---

Antitrust Guidelines

Go to http://www.antitrust.org for a review of antitrust policy. Particularly useful is the extended list of recommended practices "Common Sense Guidelines" excerpted from *The Antitrust Laws*, A Primer, by John H. Stenefeld and Irwin M. Stelzer. Students will also find an "Executive Summary of Antitrust Laws" written by R.M. Steuer at http://profs.lp.findlaw.com/antitrust/index.html. www.findlaw.com provides a friendly, "yahoo-like" interface to many business law issues and examples.

property in technology transfer and innovation, such as **patents**, **copyrights**, and **trade secrets**. This distinction removes trademarks, usually considered as symbols of identity and goodwill, from consideration.[20] From an antitrust enforcement view, trademarks are considered product or organization differentiating devices and are treated differently, though many of the same legal principles apply.[21,22]

Patents are protection or ownership rights granted by the U.S. government to inventors for their original products, processes, or composition of matter. The patent owner may exclude the use, sales, or manufacture of the invention for a period that depends on the type of patent. Functional patents that cover machines, processes, and devices have a protection period of twenty years. Design patents, applying to the features of a product, are granted protection periods of fourteen years. Patent owners may sell, license, or trade patents just as they would any tangible property.[23]

Copyrights apply to original works of, among others, authors, musicians, and photographers. Copyrights protect the expression of ideas, not the underlying ideas themselves. Copyrights are granted to individuals for their lifetime plus fifty years and, since 1989, automatically apply to all work. Signing nations of the Berne Convention also recognize international status for U.S. copyrights.[24] While registration of original works is not necessary, it is always recommended, particularly if ownership is intended to produce income. Like patent owners, copyright owners may sell, license, or grant permission for use of the copyrighted material.

Trade secrets are unusual in that their value is dependent on their secrecy. A trade secret is a process, technique, or competitive advantage whose owner has chosen not to seek additional legal protection, either in an effort to maintain the secret by avoiding disclosure or because the secret does not meet legal tests for originality. Protection has no definite term and is conditioned on efforts to keep the secret a secret. Trade secrets are an unusual category. By their very nature, owners are not able to license, sell, or trade them with the same degree of protection as patents and copyrights. Notwithstanding this, however, trade secrets can be the subject of use agreements between organizations.

Antitrust Implications of Intellectual Property

At first glance, intellectual property laws, which grant rights of exclusive use, and antitrust laws, which are aimed at maintaining an open market, may seem to be in total opposition to each other. This is, however, not the case. Intellectual property protection aims to protect creators and inventors of novel and useful inventions from copying, bootlegging, plagiarism, and other forms of theft. Without such protection, there would be significantly less incentive to innovate, as the market value of intellectual property would be significantly reduced. Innovation is a primary motivator in competition and market growth. Businesses spend millions of dollars of research and development programs to create a competitive advantage.

Intellectual property is but one tool in the creation of an offering for the customer. Just as the use of other tools (e.g., production, distribution, market dominance) may or may not be in compliance with business legislation, intellectual property can be used or abused in the marketplace. In business-to-business markets, competitors often **license** or **cross license** each other's intellectual property. Businesses do this because they recognize that the target market(s) for a particular offering will adopt a new product, feature, or technology faster if

*A **license** is permission to use an asset as one's own without any right of ownership, granted by the owner of the asset. Licenses can be for specific time periods, regions, or countries. All forms of intellectual property may be licensed.*

*A **cross license** occurs when two businesses each have patents or other intellectual property that is of value to the other. The cross license may be structured to allow both firms a greater advantage in the same market or the agreement may be related to separate markets. At times, firms will establish a jointly owned third firm to operate in a particular market with licenses of both firms' properties.*

both organizations are participating in its market development. (The relationship between innovation and competition is discussed in Chapter 9.)

Just as would occur with any restraint of trade, antitrust concerns arise when the leverage provided by the intellectual properties is used to limit access to or competition in the market. For example, firms may not use cross licensing to prevent new competitors from entering a market, to divide the existing market between themselves, or to create tying agreements to move unwanted merchandise.

Cross Licensing

Companies will find that, *within legal limits*, circumstances encourage licensing or cross licensing. Suppose that the R&D of a chemical company develops a new solvent for treatment of metal parts before the finish is applied. The company applies for and receives a patent on the composition of the solvent. Another chemical company, interested in the same market, has developed a unique cost-effective manufacturing process that makes it possible to produce the new solvent at approximately the same cost as older, less-effective products. The company applies for and receives a process patent on the manufacturing method. Both companies are blocked from effectively pursuing the market segment—one by the composition patent and the other by the process patent. The two companies cross license the patents, enabling each to effectively approach the market. Without the agreement, the market would not have the new solvent available at a viable value.

Consider an example often experienced by high-technology companies whose major investment has been in their research efforts. The high-tech company receives a patent for its efforts. While the company has successfully invested its resources in the development of this technology, it has neither market presence nor relationships among potential users. The company now must invest in building a sales and marketing team to approach users. However, the rapidly changing nature of new technology markets makes this approach risky at best. The time required to establish a market presence may allow other companies to enter the market and establish a foothold before our high-tech can get started.

As an alternative solution to the previous example, the company that holds the technology patent could license the technology to a company that already has a strong presence in the target market. This combination provides the technology with access to an established customer base and relationships.

When an organization considers a license of its technology to another firm, there are several precautions that must be taken. Licensing is legally tricky. Several factors must be considered in a licensing arrangement.

- Time period: the length of time that the license is valid must be specified.
- Market coverage: the technology owner may want to restrict the licensee to certain regions—an important consideration in international markets. These provisions are particularly important if the technology owner plans to also market an offering that includes the technology. Market coverage restrictions may also limit the licensee to use of the technology to certain products, offerings, or market segments.
- Technology coverage: the agreement must describe the specific technology to be licensed. The goal on the part of the technology owner is to avoid creation of a competitor as the licensee acquires experience with the licensed technology. The successful technology owner will likely continue to evolve the technology through subsequent research and development efforts. The license is not likely to include these improvements and should state the extent of coverage.

An industry adage says that a company should never license its latest technology—only that technology that it is about to make obsolete. While this may not always be a viable position, the technology owner must continue to "push the envelope" of innovation in the impacted market to maintain its leadership position. Well-defined organization goals and goals specific to the technology (as well as a good attorney) can create an agreement that works for both parties.

Joint Ventures

Another alternative might be for a company with technology and another company with a presence in the target market to come together and form a third company, transferring specific assets to the new entity. Many **joint ventures** are started in this way. A joint venture has some advantages over a simple license arrangement. The small technology company will be concerned that the large company could act in a predatory manner, particularly with access to the small company's technology. Assignment of the technology to a separate, new venture creates a barrier that allows the small company to continue its own research and development distinct from any efforts that arise out of the larger company knowledge of the technology. The license is limited to the venture—not available to the large company. The large company invests capital and access to its established customers. The mission of the joint venture is part of the agreement, as well as a definition of markets and technology licensed. Each company in the joint venture is protected from any potential dilution of its investment that may result from the other company's aggressive use of the knowledge and position gained through the

*A **joint venture** is an organization where two firms combine to approach a particular market or share a particular technology. The risk of sharing technology and lost investment is limited to assets assigned to the venture. The venture operates as an independent business. The two firms benefit according to their share of the venture—usually 50:50.*

license. The two parties can continue their business development independent of the venture yet still benefit from the success of the venture. The venture is allowed to use the knowledge and experience gained to continue technology and market development. The potential for disagreement over developments is lessened because they are owned by the venture, and thus, by both parties as determined by their share of the venture.

CONFIDENTIALITY AGREEMENTS

Marketers that work with customers in the development of new offerings, where the capabilities of both the supplier and the customer are brought together to create a new offering, will have access to future product plans of their customers. To protect both organizations, confidentiality or nondisclosure agreements are often used. While specific details will vary (and are beyond the scope of this discussion), most of these agreements contain elements of one or all of the following.

- Customers that rely on suppliers as design and development resources expect that the information revealed by the supplier to the customer (whether technical- or business-oriented) is, in the absence of any other agreement, in the public domain. In other words, the customer without fear of any intellectual property disputes can use whatever the supplier reveals to the customer. Marketers from supplying firms will be asked to sign a nondisclosure agreement that states that they are aware that anything they disclose will be considered in the public domain.
- Suppliers that partner with customers to assist in the development of the customer's future products will have access to the customer's product plans. Suppliers will be asked to sign confidentiality agreements that bind the supplier from discussions about the customer's products

or business. These are particularly sensitive agreements that require careful management to insure compliance. Suppliers that have many customers in the same market that compete with each other may find it necessary to manage many contacts between members of their value chain and the various customers' buying center members. The goal of the supplier is to protect the customer's confidentiality while also working with more than one customer in any given market.

• Customers that rely on partnerships with suppliers to assist in the development of the customer's future products will have knowledge of the supplier's developing technology and research and development directions. Customers must regard this information as confidential, and often be asked to sign appropriate agreements. The situation can become exacerbated when the customer is working with more than one supplier who is applying its latest technology to the customer's product.

POLITICAL FRAMEWORK OF ENFORCEMENT

Marketing professionals cannot ignore the politics of business regulation. Different viewpoints and philosophies are represented by different presidential administrations in our government.

*The **Department of Justice** Web site at http:// www.usdoj.gov provides a thorough though somewhat legalistic Web site with many reviews of the implications and intricacies of U.S. Code and case examples.*

Though some recent examples have blurred the generalization, historically, the political affiliation of an administration in power has been an indicator of the aggressiveness of regulatory enforcement. Regardless of political affiliation or beliefs about regulation versus the free market, there have been times when government intervention was appropriate as well as times when intervention was either insufficient or overzealous. The marketer should recognize that different views of the markets as well as historical precedent could impact the marketing environment.

PACIFIC DRIVES REVISITED

Recall the opening of this chapter and the difficulties Pacific Drives was having getting its offering to its customers. With consideration for the legal factors we have discussed, what do you now think of this situation? Should the obstacles faced by Pacific Drives be accepted as aggressive competition or be considered as illegal activities? Would your opinion change if you were the marketing manager for Pacific Drives? In the opening situation, what recourse does Pacific Drives have?

Well, if you were the marketing manager for Pacific Drives, you might first discuss the situation with your firm's attorneys. Your next step might be to contact the organizations (possibly with your attorney—avoid the appearance of collusion!) that you believe are engaged in illegal activities impacting Pacific Drives and see if a negotiated resolution is possible. Certainly all parties will have an incentive to avoid litigation. If that strategy is not successful, you have the option of civil litigation. Who knows? You may not be the only victim of DynaDrive and Spin Technologies. You might even find that the Justice Department or the FTC taking up your cause.

THOUGHTS TO TAKE WITH YOU INTO THE NEXT CHAPTER

As with most any illegal activity, ignorance of the law is not an adequate defense. Marketing managers cannot successfully plead a lack of understanding should their organization become the target of an antitrust or price discrimination investigation. Unfortunately, without a sufficient understanding of the "ins and outs" of business laws, managers may, when operating in a small organization or market that is not likely to draw attention, establish practices that become habit or increase in intensity as the organization or market grows. Certain business practices may seem like "just aggressive competition" or "finding an edge." If they infringe on any of the three areas described in the beginning of this chapter—protecting companies from each other, protecting consumers, and protecting the interests of society—*and* meet the substantiality test, they are likely to draw enforcement attention.

Successful market-driven strategy can help avoid many legal entanglements. As you progress to Chapter 5 and your understanding of business-to-business marketing continues to grow, we hope you will see that one of the best ways to avoid difficult legal situations is an ethical, market-driven approach from the start. In later chapters, pricing, channels, and personal selling are discussed. These activities are particularly vulnerable to the imprecise nature of the legal environment. Understanding the legal issues discussed in this chapter will greatly assist in the development and practice of market programs that provide long-term value to your customers.

Key Terms

common law *86*	injunctions *82*	price maintenance *87*
consent decree *84*	intercorporate stockholding *83*	refusal to deal *89*
copyrights *97*	interlocking directorates *83*	resale restrictions *89*
cross license *97*	joint venture *99*	silent period *86*
proportionately equal terms *85*	license *97*	subtantiality test *94*
exclusive dealing *83*	patents *97*	trade secrets *97*
free rider *89*	predatory pricing *91*	treble damages *82*
initial public offering (IPO) *86*	price discrimination *89*	tying contracts *83*

Questions for Review and Discussion

1. How can intercorporate stockholding exist without raising FTC or Justice Department concerns?
2. What market factors must be present under Robinson-Patman that require a supplier to offer the same product to two (or more) different customers?
3. What market factors must be present for a manufacturer to legally refuse to continue to offer its products through a particular channel (what are the circumstances when a "free rider" condition can exist)?
4. Describe the practical importance of good market intelligence in addressing potential competitive pricing situations under the Robinson-Patman Act.
5. When a marketing manager questions whether an action may or may not be interpreted as a violation of a competitive legislative act, what consumer-level factors can ultimately be used as guidelines?
6. Overall, it can be said that the unified goal of business legislation is to maximize choice in the marketplace. Of the philosophies of marketing (production, product, sales, marketing, and societal marketing), which has as its goal to maximize choice in the marketplace?
7. What extenuating circumstances must usually be present for a business practice to be scrutinized by the Justice Department? What limits the Justice Department from investigating all potential violations?
8. When there is significant disparity in size of competitors seeking the same customers, how do Clayton and Robinson-Patman fail to maintain the fabled "level playing field"?
9. How can continuous innovation and close partnerships with customers reduce the likelihood that market managers will be concerned with price discrimination issues?

10. Rather than the "letter" of the law as related to specific acts and legislation, understanding business regulation has often been described as understanding the intent of the law and the temperament of the enforcers. Explain.

11. How are the myriad of state and federal legislative acts and commissions consistent with a free market philosophy?

12. What protections does a joint venture offer to the two companies that have partnered together? What limitations must be agreed upon at the start of the venture? Why is a willingness to participate in a confidential agreement with a customer an important factor in the "resell the job" or endgame portion of the buyer decision process (Chapter 3)?

13. Discuss the ways in which use of industrial distributors can assist small companies to overcome uncompetitive price situations that develop in their small volume purchases. (This may be more easily understood if you return to this question after completion of Chapter 14.)

Endnotes

1. A real "Internet Marketplace Exchange," Covisint, is discussed in the opening example of Chapter 2.

2. Marianne Jennings, *Business: Its Legal, Ethical, and Global Environment* (Cincinnati: South-Western College, 2000), p. 172.

3. Richard A. Mann and Barry S. Roberts, *Smith and Roberson's Business Law*, 11th ed. (Cincinnatti, South-Western College, 2000), p. 83–89.

4. Jennings, *Business: Its Legal, Ethical, and Global Environment*, p. 524.

5. Mann and Roberts, *Smith and Roberson's Business Law*, p. 876.

6. Ibid., p. 880.

7. Ibid., p. 878.

8. Philip Kotler and Gary Armstrong, *Principles of Marketing*, 6th ed. (Upper Saddle River, Prentice Hall, 1994), p. 83.

9. Gary McWilliams, Joseph B. White and Jess Bravin, "Price-Floor Ruling May Have Small Effect," *The Wall Street Journal,* June 29, 2007, p. A2.

10. The Sarbanes-Oxly Act of 2002, http://www.soxlaw.com

11. Corporate Law Economic Reform Program, Australian Securities and Investment Commission, www.asic.gov.au.

12. The method and timing of notification to change suppliers can be indicative of the quality of the relationship between the supplier and the customer. Many businesses will not easily change suppliers unless there is a substantial incentive, particularly when everything is going well.

13. Chapter 10 discusses the importance of different costing methods. A thorough understanding of costs related to different channels, volumes, and customers is essential as a good justification for pricing decisions.

14. "Living in Microsoft's Shadow," *The Wall Street Journal*, July 2, 2001.

15. Lay-Person's Guide to FCPA, Antibribery Provisions, U.S. Department of Justice, www.usdoj.gov/criminal/fraud/docs/dojdocb.html

16. In this context, "payment" means something of value (money, property, and so on).

17. Jennings, *Business: Its Legal, Ethical, and Global Environment*, p. 253.

18. Lay-Person's Guide, Antibribery Provisions.

19. Ibid.

20. Business-to-Business branding and "branding as a standard" is discussed in Chapter 13.

21. Readers interested in a broader discussion of trademark law, particularly as it relates to the Internet, are encouraged to reference by Gerald Ferrera, et al., *CyberLaw, Text and Cases* (Cincinnati, West/Thompson Learning, 2001).

22. U.S. Department of justice and the Federal Trade Commission, Antitrust Guidelines for the Licensing of Intellectual Property, issued April 6, 1995.

23. Jennings, *Business: Its Legal, Ethical, and Global Environment*, p. 489.

24. Ibid., p. 490.

Chapter 5

Concepts and Context of Business Strategy

OVERVIEW

This chapter presents introductory material on the nature of strategy and strategic planning. While corporate executives are usually responsible for creating corporate and business unit strategies, marketers at many levels are called upon to contribute to the planning process. Accordingly, this chapter presents material to help marketers think strategically and make a substantial contribution to the process.

The opening example is a presentation of strategy management concepts and processes at work in an organization. Corporate strategy chooses the businesses to be in and the performance levels that will be achieved. Analytic tools are presented in the chapter to aid in determining which businesses should be pursued. Business unit strategy concerns a translation of corporate goals into business unit goals and objectives. It also includes the configuration of the functions of the business to achieve the business unit's goals and objectives.

This chapter concludes with a discussion of the strategy management process. This process can be used, with minor modifications, at any level of the organization. Understanding the basic process, as well as its limitations, will help a business-to-business marketer take an effective approach whenever the need arises.

The opening example shows how Siemens ties together internal operations and choice of external markets to boost its performance.

Siemens Changes Its Strategy[1]

In 1998, Siemens of Germany was making progress in productivity improvements in most of its lines of business. However, it seemed that all its efforts were working well but were simply five years too late. The problems Siemens addressed—those of quality and costs—were the problems of the late 1980s and early 1990s. Meanwhile, its competitors, such as GE, Cisco, and Nokia, were adapting products and marketing efforts to adjust to new and changing markets. Net income at Siemens was slim and falling. Not surprisingly, Siemens' stock price was headed in the same direction.

CEO Heinrich von Pierer created a ten-point plan to revamp Siemens. The plan placed emphasis on growing areas of business, such as telecommunications and automotive electronics. Acquisitions were made to bolster these areas. Existing businesses such as medical engineering and semiconductors received attention to increase innovation and customer focus while improving operating efficiency. Nonperforming business lines were sold off. Organizational structure and working relationships were reshaped. Management positions were trimmed, and top executive positions were filled by key hires.

Not all the old lines of business were divested, though. Siemens held on to and invested in its electric power business, even while competitors like ABB were divesting power generation lines. Siemens restructured its rail locomotive business supply chain, acquiring suppliers, and shifting assembly upstream. At the peak of the technology boom, Siemens sold off its semiconductor and components businesses and received a premium price.

CEO von Pierer produced encouraging results. Going into the worldwide slowdown, profits and share prices were up. Technology development has taken on a customer focus as marketers and engineers collaborate in the design of new products. Even though Siemens's new strategy focused on telecommunications and was thus hard-hit with the technology industry bust that occurred in 2001 and beyond, Siemens came out of the recession intact—with a good balance sheet and leadership in several key industries, such as medical technology.

Siemens' CEO, von Pierer, managed to weather the economic downturn by offsetting the risk of high-growth businesses with maintenance and investment in Siemens' core, "stodgy" businesses. Over time, von Pierer was able to bring a stronger customer focus and innovative culture to an old conglomerate that had a reputation for slow-moving bureaucracy. Coming out of the recession, Siemens was in a strong competitive position, supported by a healthy resource base.

Later in the decade, Siemens became embroiled in a scandal involving bribes paid to foreign governments. CEO von Pierer took responsibility, even though there was no evidence of his involvement, and resigned.

LEARNING OBJECTIVES

By reading this chapter, you will:

- Understand the value of strategy and its role in a complex organization.
- Understand the planning process for defining and executing business strategy.
- Relate mission, goals, and objectives of an organization to the process of developing strategy.
- Develop an understanding of how an entrepreneurial approach to marketing is not limited to small, start-up organizations.
- Identify ways in which a marketing organization can be made more entrepreneurially oriented.
- Demonstrate an understanding of different strategy tools (growth-share and business-attractiveness matrices and balanced scorecards).
- Recognize what it means to create a strategy that "changes the rules" for a market or for an industry.
- Understand the importance of agility, adaptability, and alignment in pursing integrated value network or supply chain strategies.

INTRODUCTION

The Siemens example illustrates the importance of two key strategy ideas. First, Siemens performed better than competitors during and after the recession because of its portfolio of businesses. Siemens pursued some high-growth businesses, such as telecommunications equipment, and suffered the consequences when these industries were severely hit by the recession. However, its poor performance in these industries was buffered by strong performance in several lines of business in which it had core strengths, such as power generation equipment, even though these were not high-growth businesses. Second, part of von Pierer's strategy focused on changing the culture of the company—changing the ways that Siemens does business. The CEO drove the company to be more innovative and at the same time to be more focused on customers. Coupled with Siemens' traditional strength in engineering, these new cultural elements created strong products across Siemens's lines of business and greatly improved its competitive strength.

While the Siemens example illustrates these concepts at the corporate level, the same ideas apply at the business unit level and the marketing program level. The concept of corporate portfolio management helps managers manage risk. But strategy does not stop with the corporate portfolio decision. The strategies of individual businesses, product lines, or products should align with corporate strategy to make their own piece of the company as competitive as possible. This is what Siemens has done—it has focused attention on every business in its portfolio to upgrade the competitive strength of each.

Within the framework of corporate level strategy, the marketer has to create and implement his own marketing strategy aligned with and in service to the company strategy. This strategy generally defines the marketer's direction, that is, the parameters the marketer has to live within on a day-to-day basis. Daily efforts by all members of the organization must be consistent with the **mission**, **goals**, **objectives**, and **strategies** of the firm. Knowing what strategies do and how they work will make the business marketing manager's decision making more informed and more closely tied to the intent of the company's strategy.

In addition to the discussion of strategic concepts, this chapter examines how strategies are created and managed. Too often, popularized strategy methods overlook useful ideas and tools because they are not "fashionable." In this chapter, some useful ideas and tools are provided that, while updated, have their roots in the past and, when fully understood, are as useful today as when they were the "in" tools.

WHAT IS STRATEGY?

Strategy is, literally, the "art of the general." Strategic thinking has been around in military matters for thousands of years. At its most basic, strategy is the determination of goals or objectives and the general means for reaching them.

For the corporate executive, strategy means the choice of businesses for the corporation to pursue and what will be emphasized in the running of each business to reach corporate goals and objectives. From the point of view of the person running the copier room in one of the company's division headquarters, corporate strategy is the context in which he works—if he even knows what the corporate strategy is at all. His strategy focuses on how to get documents done on time and with high quality. In either case, strategy helps keep the people involved working toward a desired outcome and approaching this goal (or goals) in ways that do not violate any constraints that may be relevant. Exhibit 5-1 shows how strategy in an organization is arranged hierarchically, from the top level to the functional level.

*The **mission** of an organization is the contextual definition of what the organization is and what it expects to accomplish. Usually a qualitative description, it is further defined by goals and objectives. A good mission statement should be useful to all members of the organization as a guide to proper decision making and direction.*

***Goals** are usually the first quantification of a business mission statement. Goals are a general statement of desirable outcomes, directly supportive of and aligned with the mission.*

***Objectives** are specific measurable expressions of the stated goals, with specific targets and time periods.*

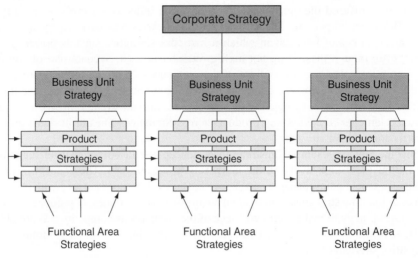

EXHIBIT 5-1   Hierarchy of Strategy

Developing effective strategy—strategy that leads to higher performance—requires several elements. First, strategy involves setting goals or objectives. Strategists usually think of a goal as being a general notion of a desired end-state. Goals are not time limited. Objectives, on the other hand, are specific targets that can be expressed in quantifiable terms, specifying a specific time frame in which these targets are to be met. Exhibit 5-2 shows how each succeeding step in strategy development adds more specificity.

A second element of strategy is gaining an understanding of the environment in which the business unit operates. A strategist seeks strategies that "fit" this environment or he may, when in alignment with capabilities, seek strategies that substantially change the environment. Either way, the strategist will want to obtain an understanding of what he has to work with, or

Mission	Goals	Objectives	Strategy	Tactics
Contextual definition of what the organization expects to accomplish.	General statement of desirable outcomes, supportive of and aligned with the mission.	Specific measurable expressions of the stated goals, with specific targets and time periods.	The plan by which the measurable objectives will be obtained.	Implementation of the strategic plan.
To become a leader in the data storage services market.	To become the leader in the data storage services market.	To have a 50 percent market share in data storage integration services sales within two years.	The marketing plan specifies target markets for data storage services and develops those markets to achieve the specified objectives.	

EXHIBIT 5-2   Increasing Specificity in the Layers of Strategy Development

against. The effort to understand the environment is to provide enough information upon which to make reasoned judgments of what directions to pursue and how to pursue them.

A third critical element is learning from experience. Good strategic management systems, no matter how formal the process, collect information on the impact of the strategies that are being executed. In a traditional strategic management process, performance is monitored and compared to expected performance. In less formal processes, informal interviewing of customers, channel members, and others may be performed to obtain feedback sufficient to diagnose problems and suggest strategy modifications.

The fourth critical element is thinking. Strategy development is *not* a mechanical process in which a model of the environment is developed, populated with data, the handle is cranked, and an optimal solution pops out. Rather it involves processes that are much more creative, interpretive, and learning oriented. Designing strategy is a creative act where decisions are made based on an interpretation of what is known about the environment and informed "guess-timates" of how customers, competitors, and other actors in the environment will act and react in the future.

Accordingly, strategy development and management is best considered as a dynamic, complex process. Indeed, there is no one best process that is usable and effective in all situations. Processes must be designed and evolved with the company's situation in mind, which is what is discussed in the next section.

STRATEGY-MAKING AND STRATEGY MANAGEMENT PROCESSES

The business environment, the competitors' potential actions and reactions in the market, and the companies' internal organization structures make the process of developing and managing strategy necessarily complex. Over the last half century, when strategic management has received direct attention from management and academics, different approaches have been tried and tested. The next section presents some of the key concepts that have emerged as useful in managing strategic processes.

One idea that has survived over time is a stepwise progression of actions to conceive, implement, and adjust strategy. Stages in this **strategic management process** are shown in Exhibit 5-3.

Performing Strategic Management in the Business-to-Business Company

We, the authors, have talked with executives, managers, employees, and consultants over the last several years asking whether the changing business environment has required the complete abandonment of the strategic management model presented in Exhibit 5-2. The answer we get is

1. Setting goals and objectives
2. Analysis of the current situation
3. SWOT analysis: Strengths, Weaknesses, Opportunities, and Threats
4. Strategy design and choice of the best strategy
5. Implementation plan design
6. Strategy implementation
7. Monitoring of environment and performance results
8. Analysis of variance from desired performance levels
9. Adjustments based on analysis of variance

EXHIBIT 5-3   Strategic Management Process

"not really," though some adaptation is necessary. We present it here as a template for application, but we add some caveats and adaptations.

Step 1 Develop Goals and Objectives First, distinguish between goals and objectives. As noted before, this is the distinction between the general and the specific. Goals are general, qualitative descriptions of some desired state of affairs. For a business, one might say, for example, that it is desirable for the firm to achieve superior profitability and leadership in its industry. Objectives, then, are specific expressions of these goals, with specific targets in specific time periods. Given the example of goals set by the hypothetical data storage company mentioned above, executive management might say they want to pursue these goals by achieving a return on investment of 20 percent, after taxes, on a sustainable basis, by the end of fiscal year 2011. In that same time period, they might want to achieve at least 35 percent market share in their principal lines of business. Further, they might want to achieve recognition by at least 75 percent of purchasing managers in their markets in which their offerings set the standards for product and service quality. These targets are specific in ways that allow measurement of performance against them.

When goals and objectives are set at the corporate level, corporate management must take care that the goals and objectives are "healthy" or "good" for the company to pursue. The relevant criteria are that performance must be in line with the expectations of the relevant stakeholders, such as investors, management, employees, and the community in which the firm is located. The objectives must also be reachable, challenging, and internally consistent (not contradictory, so that reaching one objective makes it impossible to reach one of the others). At lower levels in the hierarchy, goals and objectives become expressions of the corporate goals and objectives (see Exhibit 5-4). The strategy planners must decide what objectives will accurately measure the contributions of their business unit, product line, or program.

	Corporate Level	Lower Level
Goals	Performance must be in line with the expectations of the relevant stakeholders, such as investors, management, employees, and the community in which the firm is located.	Expressions of corporate goals but specific to the portion of the organization within the reach, control, and responsibility of lower management, not contradictory, so that reaching one objective makes it impossible for other units reach one of the others.
Objectives	Reachable, challenging, and internally consistent.	Accurately measure the contributions of the business unit, product line, or program in alignment with the corporate objectives.

EXHIBIT 5-4 Understanding Level of Goals and Objectives in the Corporate Hierarchy

Step 2 Environmental Analysis In this step, the current situation and future possibilities are explored. At any level, the environment includes the following elements:

Markets, segments, and customers
Competition
Channels of distribution

Internal company environment
Effects of the economy
Effects of technology change
Public policy

At the corporate level, the environment also includes other stakeholders such as the financial and investment communities, as well as supplier markets.

The analysis is usually arranged in the form of an analysis of the current situation and a SWOT—strengths, weaknesses, opportunities, and threats—analysis that is more future oriented. In Chapter 6, we present a more thorough approach to understanding two key elements—customers and competitors.

Step 3 Strategy Design   Strategy design is the step in which strategy planners decide how to meet or exceed the objectives that have been set, given the realities of the business environment. The tools discussed later in this chapter can aid in the determination of what businesses to pursue and how to pursue them.

The preferred method espoused by strategic management authors has been to create alternative strategies and choose the best from among the alternatives. In reality, strategy planners begin formulating strategies as they perform the SWOT analysis. Very often, a single best strategy is already in mind when they complete the analysis. When this occurs, little is gained from creating an alternative or two. These tend to be strategies purposely designed to be inferior to the original strategy, thus reinforcing the "intuitive" strategy developed concurrent with the SWOT analysis.

If we are designing corporation-level strategy, such a strategy should include:
• A vision of the business and its industry in the future
• The choice of goals and objectives (which may be revised or refinements of goals and objectives established in Step 1)
• The choice of which businesses to pursue
• The determination of allocation of resources across businesses
• Determination of which strategic competencies to emphasize and build in the future
• Allocation of resources to invest in building strategic competencies.

Business unit strategy involves these same elements, scaled down to the business unit level and adapted to fit within the corporate strategy. The content of marketing or product strategy is addressed in Chapters 7 and 8.

Step 4 Implementation Plan Design   After the strategy is designed, the planners must decide what actions need to be completed to accomplish this strategy. In this step, planners or managers decide who will do what, when, with whom, and at what cost.

At this stage resources must be allocated to measure results, analyze the measures, and make adjustments. Too often, strategy plans—at any level—do not include a specific allotment to accomplish the post hoc data collection and analysis. Without this monitoring effort, the organization does not learn much about what worked and what did not, reducing the value of the experience. Often, organizations attribute success to themselves and failure to outside forces. In this mode of operation, it is difficult to really know what worked and repeat it, and what did not work and avoid it.

Once the implementation plan is laid out, the costs, personnel resources, skills needed, and time required are determined. If the implementation plan requires more than the organization can afford, revisions in the strategy, or even in the objectives, need to be made.

Step 5 Strategy Implementation   Actions need to be taken and supervised, as required in the implementation plan. Systems should be in place to check that actions are started and completed per plan. If actions are not being taken or accomplished as scheduled, remedies need to be sought.

Step 6 Monitoring of Environment and Performance Results   As noted in Step 4, part of the implementation activities should be designated for collecting and analyzing data. These data should track progress toward the objectives determined in Step 1. In the implementation plan, subobjectives may have been set to track progress toward meeting some higher-level performance target. Data need to be collected relative to these subobjectives as well.

Step 7 Analysis of Performance   Any significant variance from desired performance levels needs to be examined. Both under- and over-achievement need to be assessed. The purpose of the analysis is to determine why the variance occurred. This may require interviews with participants, collection and assessment of satisfaction surveys, or other market research.

Step 8 Adjustments   Based on the analysis of performance, adjustments may need to be made to strategy, implementation, environmental knowledge, or any other planning element, including the original goals and objectives. Small adjustments can probably wait until the next planning cycle. Big adjustments may require an entirely new plan to be produced. Most organizations close the strategic management loop by starting from scratch once a year; though in rapidly changing markets this timing may not be sufficient.

A Critique of the Model

The implementation of this strategic-planning model is a long, drawn-out process, no matter at what level it is performed. It takes commitment to both undertake the planning process and tolerate the extended time it takes to create a good strategy. The process can be fast-tracked to a certain extent by running some activities in parallel and by making assumptions rather than collecting data. With the advent of collaborative software, either using the Web or running internally on a company's network, much work can be done "together." This also helps reduce time or makes the plan better.

To reduce the "time to strategy," planners may want to use software from reputable software vendors that helps the planner organize and analyze data about the business environment. The drawback to using template software is that the software does calculations that are invisible to the user and may imply a certain direction not entirely consistent with the unique situation at hand. The planner then does not get the feel for the operation of the market model or the company's profit model—the planner misses some of the "hands-on" implications of the plan. Perhaps a better approach is the use of off-line templates[2] that take the user through analysis quickly but rely on the user to understand the data and to do the calculations.

In the end, it is better to take the time to go through the analysis and planning steps rather than to give in to the temptation to not do the planning and rely on the company's ability to adjust "on the fly." The insight gained from taking some time to collect data and think about it seems to outweigh any advantage of being fast, but uninformed. In too many instances companies try to be first to seize an opportunity, only to fumble the attempt because they didn't understand it.

Another problem that this planning process will encounter is the tendency to drain the life out of a strategy. Related to this problem is the tendency to miss opportunities to innovate or change the rules of the market or industry, both potential outcomes from stifling the creative process. This problem stems from a tendency to get stuck in the analytic portion of the planning process. When it comes to designing strategy, time needs to be taken for a creative exercise. The difficulty here is to recognize that planners may have already created most of their preferred strategy while they were in the analysis phase, which may or may not have been done with a close understanding of the market and its participants. This suggests that a creative exercise may have to be done during the analysis phase rather than waiting for the strategy design phase to do it.

In summary, the process laid out here is based on the "old way" of designing strategy. We believe the drawbacks of doing this process, particularly in light of the time compression forced by today's fast-moving markets, can be overcome. The benefits from taking a little time to do this will pay off in most cases.

KEY STRATEGY CONCEPTS

Philosophies and approaches to strategy have evolved over time. Key ideas that have survived to form the basis for traditional strategic management are:

1. Business strategy designers should seek to establish a **fit** between the business environment and the strategy.
2. The key element of *fit* in business strategy revolves around providing superior value for customers.
3. Superior value means that the offering of a company must be differentiated from the offerings of competitors in the minds of the targeted customers.
4. Differentiation is produced by using core competencies to advantage; the more distinct a company's core competencies, the higher the customer value that can be achieved and the better the profit margins that can be produced.
5. Quality improvement and process improvement are fundamental to providing superior value.
6. Measuring and tracking results creates learning and sets the stage for later improvements.

Fit between the business strategy and the business environment means that the organization pursues purposes and takes actions that are consistent with the needs, perceptions, and behaviors of the other actors within the environment.

Modern strategy has become focused on *driving change* rather than on adapting to it. Hamel and Prahalad[3] espouse the idea of changing the rules, both internally within a company and externally within the industry. In light of the terms outlined above, the company attempts to drive change in the environment toward a configuration in which the company better fits the environment than does its competition. The company is able to provide more value to a set of customers that has been created than its competition can provide. The company identifies its **core competencies** that give it **differentiation**. It builds a vision of how the industry will change over the next two to five years. Then it builds a vision of how the company can influence change to create a favorable situation for itself. Core competencies to drive that change and to differentiate its offering in the future are identified, and methods for building those competencies are laid out. Learning objectives, opportunities, and methods are also spelled out and implemented. This proactive approach is somewhat different from the traditional model of adapting to change.

Core Competencies are a company's skills, capabilities, and knowledge assets that are necessary to compete in its markets. They may be competencies that the company currently has or ones that it will need to obtain.

New views of competitive dynamics have emerged recently, as well. The notion of "co-opetition"[4] says that companies operate in a business ecosystem, where their efforts involve cooperation as well as competition. Partnerships and alliances form to create combination offerings; the combinations may be driven by customers seeking to obtain whole products that no one company has produced or even coordinated. Value creation occurs through the kinds of value networks and integrated supply chains described in Chapter 2.

These recent ideas on strategy can be summed up as follows:

- Change in customers, channels, and competitors interact to create discontinuities in the evolution of industries or markets; these are somewhat predictable, with a high level of imprecision.
- While companies can have an influence on *how* markets change, they can seldom appreciably impact the pace of change.
- Companies need to look for ways to "change the rules" of the markets they compete in; this means proactively creating conditions for success that favor their own **business model** instead of those of the competitors.

Business model is a configuration of the elements of a business, how they work together, and how they produce profits.

- Such changes in the rules are still subject to the constraints of the business environment; constraints may have some flexibility and this flexibility must be recognized.
- Strategists need to identify the core competencies that will translate into advantages in the future when the rules have changed.
- Advantages are not sustainable for long, so the company must continue to innovate, changing the rules on an ongoing basis, to stay ahead of the competition.[5] (See box on page 115 for a definition of "market ownership.")

Strategic Resource Allocation

Organizational resources, be they infrastructure, personnel, finances, or technologies, are not limitless. A major outcome of the strategic planning process is to allocate finite resources to the opportunities that will have the greatest benefit to the organization. This requires knowledge of current distinctive competencies and an anticipation of future core competencies that the organization may develop or acquire. All of this is structured to address the organization's "strategic intent."[6] This is the vision of the future that gives the organization direction and a plan to have a role in the future.

Strategic Business Unit Management

Determination of *corporate* strategy creates the "strategic architecture" that will guide the organization over the next five to ten years. Business unit strategy is strategy at the next level down in the hierarchy and is guided by the corporate strategic architecture. In single product or single division firms, this is relatively straightforward. However, in firms that are engaged in multiple businesses that span a wide range of markets, alignment with the strategic architecture is not always obvious. A plan for a division of a large firm that operates in a long-cycle, mature technology market would not be suitable for another division of the same firm that operates in a short-cycle, fast-growth market. Additionally, the existing customer base of a division or firm, its size and behavior, contributes in the determination of what the best plan may be. Since these factors can vary between the divisions of a large firm (and in fact should such that a balance of business opportunities exists), a methodology that provides for incorporation of the firm's strategic direction while allowing a strategy at the division level appropriately tailored to the environment in which the division operates is desirable.

Many large, multidivision/multimarket companies (e.g., GE, Siemens) separate businesses into individually measurable pieces called **strategic business units**. A strategic business unit (SBU) is a business, department, organization, or possibly even a product line within the larger organization that has separate goals and objectives. These business units must be capable of being planned and measured separately from the rest of the organization. Note that separate planning and measurement do not mean complete independence from the larger organization or other SBUs within the larger organization. Firms that use SBU management view the different SBUs of the firm as comprising a portfolio of businesses. A significant management effort is committed to maximizing the productive allocation of resources to these units. Thus, this **business portfolio** is a collection of SBUs that serve various needs in the corporate structure. An ongoing firm will need sources of cash to fund investment in growing markets and new possibilities emerging from research and development that may be valuable business opportunities in the future. This balance should be consistent with the culture of the organization. This is not unlike the combination of investments individuals have in their personal portfolios—resources that are consistent with goals and culture of the individual. Strategy at these levels of the organization involves the following:

- a choice of the market segment or segments to target;
- a structure of a portfolio of products (including services) to address the targeted segments;
- positioning of the offering(s) for that segment or segments;
- product and service features to include and emphasize in the offering;
- communications and selling methods to address the targeted segment(s) and implement the chosen positioning;
- a design for managing distribution;
- design of a pricing structure;
- an approach for developing key capabilities and competencies; and
- a design for innovating in the elements of marketing in the future.

*A **strategic business unit** is a business, department, organization, or possibly even a product line within the larger organization that has separate goals and objectives. These business units must be capable of being planned and measured separately from the rest of the organization. Note that separate planning and measurement do not mean complete independence from the larger organization or other strategic business units within the larger organization.*

*A **business portfolio** is a collection of strategic business units that serve various needs in the corporate structure. An ongoing firm will need sources of cash to fund investment in growing markets and new possibilities emerging from research and development that may be valuable business opportunities in the future. This balance should be consistent with the culture of the organization. This is not unlike the combination of investments individuals have in their personal portfolios—resources that are consistent with goals and culture of the individual.*

TOOLS FOR DESIGNING STRATEGY

So far, we have discussed what strategy is, a strategy management model that can be used at any level of the hierarchy of a firm, and the key ideas for structuring strategy, no matter at what level of the organization. Our focus has been on the business marketing manager who makes strategy for an individual product, for a product line, or for the marketing function of an SBU. The rest of this chapter concerns the structuring of the portfolio of products and creating an entrepreneurial approach to marketing strategy. The prior discussion should give the future business marketing manager some idea of what will be asked of him concerning strategy and strategy development. The question then arises regarding what tools are available for strategy planners to use. In the next section, we discuss three tools. The first, the growth share matrix, may have its most relevance as a tool for students to understand some of what business strategists attempt to do with corporate strategy. The second, the multifactor matrix or attractiveness-strength matrix is used more often in the real world. The third is the balanced scorecard, which attempts to help the manager see the relationship between strategy and performance.

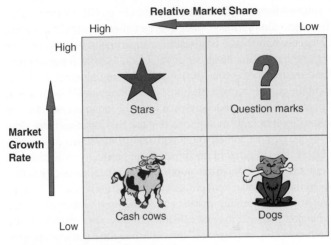

EXHIBIT 5-5 Growth-Share Matrix

The Growth-Share Matrix

Exhibit 5-5 shows the growth-share matrix, which was developed by the Boston Consulting Group over thirty years ago. Students may recognize this resource allocation tool and its categorizations of SBUs as stars, cash cows, dogs, and question marks. This tool is probably best used to illustrate the construction of business portfolios to create a company that will evolve and remain profitable over time. The idea underlying the growth-share matrix is that organizations seek to develop and nourish those business opportunities with the greatest potential for growth; maintain those that are self-sustaining producers of resources; and "harvest"—exit, while reaping as much benefit as possible—those that are no longer able to function productively within the organization. This is not unlike an individual seeking the greatest return from his or her personal investment portfolio.

Application of the matrix requires the user to identify those businesses—or products, if used at the level of the business marketing manager, —that generate resources for the parent organization (cash cows); those that need resources from the parent organization to keep pace with a fast-growing market and provide substantial returns in the future (stars); and those that may never be significant contributors to the corporation in the future (dogs and question marks). Without a thorough understanding of the tool and its nuances, the complexities of today's business environment will not be well reflected in its use. However, the matrix provides a useful starting point to discuss and illustrate portfolio strategy issues. This discussion also sets up a nice transition to the attractiveness-strength matrix, which can be more useful in light of today's business environment.

The definitions of the four elements of the matrix follow. Note the addition of the analogy to the product life cycle (PLC). Just as an offering can move through the stages of the PLC, a business unit, product line, or product will often evolve from question mark to star, star to cash cow, and cash cow perhaps to dog, counterclockwise around the grid:

- *Stars*: High-growth markets and large market share. The organization must invest heavily to maintain position in the growing market. A star could likely be a business unit with a prominent position in a product/market that is in the growth stage of the PLC. Stars should be managed with market ownership as an objective.

- *Cash cows*: Relatively slower-growth markets where the business unit has prominent market share and may be the market owner, albeit in a slower market. As the name implies, these business units generate cash that fuels other parts of the organization. Business units identified as cash cows are often in the late-growth, mature, or even decline stages of the PLC.
- *Dogs*: Slow or negative growth relative to the goals of the organization, with a less than prominent market share. While a direct analogy to the PLC places dogs in the decline stage, dogs can occur at any stage of the PLC except growth. Organizations must choose to either divest the business or continue to harvest it for short-term cash. In some instances, a dominant market share is not sufficient to make these SBUs attractive, particularly when the resources to maintain the business can be more effectively applied elsewhere.
- *Question marks*: Significantly attractive market potential, though the business unit does not have a significant share. Question marks are appropriately named. The business may require significant investment, may not be directly associated with the competencies of the firm, and may never grow to be a prosperous business. This situation could exist when an organization discovers a technology or business opportunity not aligned with corporate goals and/or in a new and unfamiliar market or not consistent with the company's core lines of business. Question marks raise the question, "Should the organization diversify (new product/new market) or divest?" Question marks can be viewed as in the introductory or early-growth stages of the PLC.

RETHINKING THE MATRIX   The growth-share matrix has several characteristics that can limit its usefulness in today's business environment. First, one of the key assumptions is questionable: the relationship between market share and profitability is suspect. This tends to undermine the validity of the analysis and its implications, depending on the organizational measurement of success. A myopic market view can be an implication of market share as a principal measure of success. (Later in this chapter, "**market ownership**" is discussed as a more dynamic, market focused measure of success. Market ownership is summarized in the box below.)

Market Share Is Not Market Ownership

In "Marketing Is Everything,"[1] McKenna discusses owning a market. From his discussion, we can form three indicators of market ownership:

1. Market owners define a market niche as theirs and work toward dominating it. Their brand is immediately identified as the standard in that market. Examples are Hewlett-Packard LaserJet printers and GE Lexan Polycarbonate Resin. These branded products are defacto standards in their industries. Competitors to both products note their equivalence to those offerings.
2. Market owners continue to evolve their offerings with the next generation as defined by the value presented to the customer.
3. Market owners benefit from other organizations developing ancillary products and markets that serve the owners' customer base. Third parties define their products as compatible with market owner. In this ancillary product development process, the market owner may be consulted by the developer to ensure compatibility with future products. The owner thus gains insight to other points of view about its market.

Market share is not a defining parameter that leads to market ownership, as is often mistakenly implied. Market share is more likely a result of, not a cause of, ownership.

[1] Regis McKenna, "Marketing Is Everything," *Harvard Business Review* (January–February 1991).

The second characteristic is that the distinctions between the categories of star, cash cow, question mark, and dogs tend to be circumstantially defined. Organizations must place business units in the matrix based on internal standards and perceptions of the relative market positions and growth opportunities of the business. Thus there is an inherent subjectivity in the analysis that makes it less likely that a business will be viewed the same way by two different organizations (e.g., one organization's dog could be another organization's star—see the example on page 117). Since there are no universal rules, an SBU's position in the matrix is meaningful only when compared to SBUs within the same corporate organization. Because of the subjectivity of the measurements, the investment implications of the categories are not consistent. Stars may not provide the investment return suggested by the model when compared to opportunities not on the matrix but available if the organization were to look outside its own portfolio; cash cows may not throw off as much cash as would be expected; dogs and question marks may be very viable businesses when freed from the restraints placed on them through the relationship to the other SBUs in the portfolio.

Perhaps the most telling problem is that the matrix is a snapshot in time. Current market growth may have little to do with future market growth and, indeed, that future market growth may be very unpredictable. Such unpredictability is one of the key reasons that Hamel and Prahalad advocate trying to change the rules of the market or industry. Notwithstanding these considerations, growth-share analysis still illustrates for the student the ideas underlying consideration of the portfolio, whether it's a portfolio of businesses within a corporation or a portfolio of products within a product line.

Multifactor Portfolio Matrix

Our experience is that most companies do not use the 2 × 2 growth-share matrix to allocate resources across business units. Rather they use a similar, but more sophisticated tool, the GE **market attractiveness—business strength matrix**, shown in Exhibit 5-6, or something

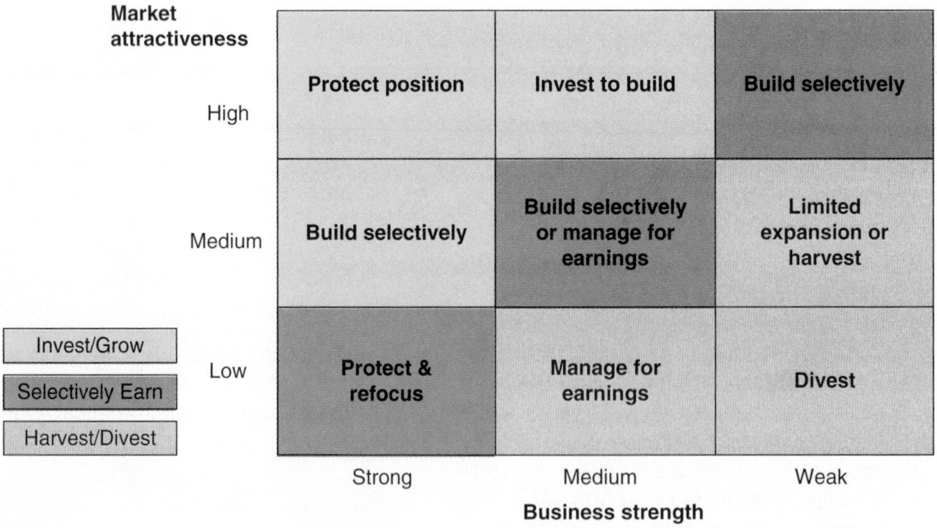

Market attractiveness	Protect position	Invest to build	Build selectively
High	Protect position	Invest to build	Build selectively
Medium	Build selectively	Build selectively or manage for earnings	Limited expansion or harvest
Low	Protect & refocus	Manage for earnings	Divest
	Strong	**Medium**	**Weak**

Invest/Grow
Selectively Earn
Harvest/Divest

Business strength

EXHIBIT 5-6   Attractiveness—Strength Matrix

similar to it. This model assumes that, at lower levels of abstraction, no new competencies will be built and gives preference to those businesses or products in which the company already has competencies in place.

This tool also does not directly consider synergies between businesses or products. Unlike the growth-share matrix, though, future business strength can be defined in such a way to give a higher score to a business or product that makes better use of available resources. Thus this tool offers more sophistication than the growth-share matrix.

Even though the idea of building a business portfolio is not new, it still has relevance today. It makes sense to have businesses that create resources that can be used in other businesses that require investment. Then, augmenting the portfolio idea with today's strategy concepts, a company may stick to businesses in which it has special competencies.

INCOMPATIBILITY OF CULTURES WITHIN ORGANIZATIONS Companies whose cultures feed on rapid change and "pushing the envelope" of new markets and technologies find that they must quickly abandon established, older offerings—their dogs. Alternately, they may become multi-offering companies with several businesses at different stages of the PLC.

This evolution to a large, multioffering (read "bureaucratic") company is not natural to many technology-oriented or entrepreneurially oriented companies—in fact, it may be considered an aberration! Thus, portfolio analysis creation may be naturally resisted. Older products are often discontinued rather than harvested. When two lines of business operate differently, such as cash cows versus stars, a rivalry for resources will likely arise. The corporation that does not handle this situation will see its cash cows stifle its future stars.

PORTFOLIOS AND VALUE Another factor that must be considered in this discussion of portfolio strategy is the relationship to customer value and the value network. As noted in Chapter 2, the most productive way to create an offering with maximum value for a particular market or customer is often to include several elements from other organizations. As designed, the matrix tools provide little assistance in partnership and network development. The internally defined rules do not provide effective evaluation of businesses across organization borders, and, as is often the case with internal metrics, a market perspective of value for customers is ignored.

General Electric Leaves the Small Appliance Business

An example of "one organization's dog could be another organization's star," albeit a consumer example, is the departure of GE from the small appliance ("countertop") market.

Under CEO Jack Welch, GE established guidelines to create a more dynamic organization. These guidelines said essentially that a GE SBU must be #1 or #2 in its market, fit with the vision and goals of the "new" GE, and meet certain levels of profitability. The small appliance SBU, while the major market player, was faced with a changing yet slow-growing market and poor (by GE standards) profitability. If placed on the growth-share matrix and compared to other SBUs, this business would likely be a "dog" by its internal measurements.

Black & Decker, the tool manufacturer, was interested in establishing a presence beyond the garage. The GE Small Appliance business was an ideal opportunity to obtain a major market presence. By Black & Decker measures, the return was more than acceptable and the technology fit very well into existing competencies. When Black & Decker acquired the SBU from GE, it is unlikely they considered it a dog.

The shortsightedness of not fully considering customer value can be problematic whether the company is engaged in a value network or not. The organization engaged in a value network to create unified solutions for customers may lose the possible synergies between internally generated businesses. At the same time, the conglomerate that uses portfolio analysis without recognizing synergies across businesses may find that different business units are qualitatively supportive of each other in the marketplace. Consider the example of Siemens acquisition of UGS Inc. in 2007. UGS contributed its product lifecycle management (PLM) software to Siemens' Automation and Drives group that offers automated production equipment. This move adds a line of business that allows Siemens to offer software for design and control that integrates Siemens manufacturing equipment more fully into a customer's supply chain.[7]

In summary, then, portfolios are a useful way to think about corporate strategy, business strategy, or product line strategy, but they are not, by themselves, sufficient. Strategy requires consideration of other important factors.

The Balanced Scorecard

Another tool—one that can integrate the steps of the strategic management process—has received a great deal of attention over the last ten years or so. The **balanced scorecard**[8] is as much a process itself as a tool for strategy content. It focuses on the goals of the organization and quantifies these into specific performance targets. The idea is to get away from sole reliance on measures that are rooted in the past—such as return on investment (ROI), sales growth, and market share—and concentrate also on measures that are forward looking, given the company's particular situation. Goals and measures are specified in four core areas: financial performance perspective, customer perspective, internal business perspective, and stakeholder (for instance upper-level management, partners, and channels) value perspective. Linkages between these perspectives are defined, and a limited number of measures are sought.

The process pursued in developing the scorecard starts with managers discussing their vision of the future and what will contribute to it. A facilitator draws a list of potential scorecard criteria from these discussions and presents it to the strategy-making participants. They discuss these and come to some agreement on strategy and a shorter list of measures. Further discussions set the vision, objectives, and measures. A set of activities to address the performance targets is designed and implementation plans instituted. Data are collected and compared to the targets. Performance is then the driver for strategy and strategy changes. Note that this approach is consistent with the strategic management model.

TAKING AN ENTREPRENEURIAL APPROACH TO MARKETING STRATEGY

Strategy often includes elements for shaping the internal workings of the company. It has become evident that building an entrepreneurial culture within a company helps the company adapt to environmental changes. In the last decade, entrepreneurial companies have also proven that they can create change as well.

Creation of an entrepreneurial culture and approach to strategy is presented here, as well as in Chapter 9, because the approach can be instituted at any level. If the business marketing manager is involved in setting strategy at the corporate or business unit level, he may want to address the reward system and organizational structure for creating a flourishing entrepreneurial orientation company-wide. If the manager is working on strategy at the business unit or the functional level, an entrepreneurial orientation can also be created with rewards and structure. However, the constraints of the overall company organization must then be accommodated while doing so.

As a first step in creating an entrepreneurial culture, companies begin by setting a mission for the company that sets the tone or context. In the new strategic planning environment, company executives are likely to ask business marketers to participate in these efforts, either directly in a planning group or indirectly through a representative participating in such a planning group. To assist the business marketing manager to think in these terms, it is useful to discuss what goes into a good mission statement, which can be developed for any level of the organization. The discussion then recasts this with the spirit and dream of the entrepreneur, which enlivens an otherwise static mission.

The Organization Mission

The mission for the organization must be an informed mission. In preparation for creating or reviewing/revising the mission, information should be developed on the future scenarios that the company is likely to face. This task should be done by the person in the organization who is responsible for tracking industry trends. If no one is responsible, then outside consultants can be utilized for this purpose. The information needs to be digested and disseminated to planning participants. Participants then work toward envisioning how the company will help create its future, as is discussed in the first section of this chapter. From this vision, the mission and broad goals are derived.

So how do you know that you have an enlivened mission and a good set of useful goals? The principal criterion is a sense of "ownership." If individuals at all levels of the organization have a sense that they are working toward something that they feel is significant to them—that the goal is their own—they will be motivated to pursue it. If they feel that this is the goal of the "company's executives," something separate from themselves, and they are pursuing it because they are being paid to do so, then the goal will take second position to the individuals' own agenda items. Similarly, if they feel the goal comes from the company's internal cultural code, they will have less sense of motivation.[9] Cultural codes generally do not produce a vision or goal that is particularly challenging. This is particularly true in large organizations.

FOSTERING OWNERSHIP How is ownership created? It is done best by involving individuals in determining vision and goals. A particularly entrepreneurial person may arrive at a unique vision for the organization. To get others on board, the executives need to provide support for such individuals and help them in persuading the other employees in taking ownership of the entrepreneur's vision and goals. Innovation should be rewarded with both monetary and organizational compensation. Innovators should be given freedom from traditional organizational constraints in the pursuit of their ideas. Management needs to be cognizant of the social effects of their reactions to the innovators. Management creates the context in which innovation can grow by its role model and attitudes toward innovation and should help create an environment in which the "whole is greater than the parts." Management can foster this by ensuring that all participants reap rewards from the new venture, commensurate with their contribution. Efforts to enhance the dream and the design of the product, project, or new venture should be encouraged and reinforced, as well.

Changing the Rules

The ultimate way for a company to act entrepreneurially is to change the rules of the market, as was discussed in the early part of this chapter. However risky it is to attempt to change the rules, if the new rules come to be adopted by the market, the action may have the effect of upsetting the current competitive balance and starting the process of establishing a new market owner.

Research in Motion Ltd. (RIM) launched its BlackBerry smartphone in the late 1990s with a concept that changed the rules of the game. The key differentiating feature of the BlackBerry was the wireless service, run by RIM, that allowed the user to send and receive e-mail. The primary customers were businesses that enabled their company e-mail systems to connect through the RIM service. The e-mail access that this produced for companies' employees, particularly professionals, managers, and executives, upset the competitive rules of the game in PDA and smartphone markets that existed at the time.[10]

We will return to developing an entrepreneurial approach to business marketing when we discuss innovation in Chapter 9. For now, it is important to note that developing a culture that facilitates entrepreneurship and pursuing strategy that changes the rules of the marketplace are integral to producing superior results from strategy.

SPECIAL ISSUES IN BUSINESS STRATEGY

This chapter provides an introduction to the nature of strategy and the process for developing and managing strategy. In this final section we explore the implications of the principal issues and themes we have raised in this text.

Strategy Implications of Value Networks and Integrated Supply Chains

In this volatile environment, winning strategies will hinge on developing a portfolio of core competencies. One of these competencies must be flexibility to change strategies and operating models rapidly. The value network concept, discussed in Chapter 2, provides a model for businesses to rapidly forge new offerings through a combination of both internal and external resources. This process can be viewed as analogous to a "fast vertical integration."

The idea of building in flexibility through "fast virtual vertical integration" stands diametrically opposed to the current trend toward integrated supply chain management. Most efforts to integrate supply chains have tended toward a reduced number of suppliers, lean inventory structures, and supply chains serving the primary interests of one large customer. These supply chains have been structured for efficiency and cost minimization. Supply chains have achieved lower costs at the expense of being able to adjust to changing supply economies and changing customer needs.[11]

The dynamic nature of competitive markets must be accommodated in strategy design. Flexibility is also required to cope with sudden contingencies, such as natural disasters, manmade disasters, or terrorism.

Strategy Development and the Internet

A special consideration is what happens to strategy management with the increased use of the Internet. As with most dramatic improvements in communications ability, markets can change more rapidly and with potentially different patterns. The Internet is thus a tool that can improve value to both suppliers and customers. In many business markets, new intermediaries have created market exchanges of one sort or another. Competitive dynamics, customer requirements, and the nature of relationships have all changed as a result.

The Internet can be used to do several things that ought to factor into the strategist's thinking:

- It can increase the speed with which the environment changes.
- It can reduce transaction costs, shipping costs, information costs, and inventory costs.
- It can increase the level of information available to customers and competitors.
- It can increase the capability to create an offering that is seamlessly pieced together from several partners' offerings, particularly when a Web site is a principal delivery mechanism for the offering.

Strategic Implications of Market Ownership

The portfolio of strategic competencies—either internal, the result of diversification or integration, or external, the result of relationships developed through a network of value providers—is key to pursuing market ownership. If the company chooses competencies to develop that are important in multiple businesses, the company can hope to produce value for customers across a range of possible futures. By taking a proactive approach and "pushing the envelope" within a market, the company can shape that market and the nature of its participants. The process to produce this strategy does not have to differ much from the process described earlier. While traditional strategic-planning processes are not geared for the uncertainty or speed of change engendered by the Internet, the process can be adapted to focus on monitoring the environment and performance, updating knowledge of the environment, and adjusting strategy accordingly.

Strategy Development in New Businesses

Strategy development in new business-to-business organizations is a particularly relevant topic in light of the activity in business-to-business Internet start-ups over the past decade or so. One advantage of starting a business-to-business operation is that often one customer can be the principal reason for going into business. That customer can provide all the financing, in whatever form, that the new business needs. The danger is that the new venture's business will become completely dependent on the one customer and will ignore any opportunities elsewhere. This may leave the new company in the unenviable position of having "all its eggs in the same basket"—being too dependent on the one customer.

Even though problems persist, executives in new companies should not forgo the strategy-planning process. New ventures that plan tend to do better than new ventures that do not, even if their plans rapidly become works of fiction as the environment changes. This is why venture capitalists require a business plan before they will consider funding a new venture. The planning process for a start-up is not so onerous—other than the founders' loss of sleep—than the process in an established company. Fewer people are involved; hence, fewer arguments occur over interpretation of trends and courses of action. The business is usually not as complex as that of an established company. Also, the people involved are routinely energized and enthusiastic. The important factor, though, is that the founders know the market and the business better after having done the planning. The pieces of the business tend to fit together much better as a result.

THOUGHTS TO TAKE WITH YOU INTO THE NEXT CHAPTER

Much of the last forty years' thinking on business strategy and strategy development processes still has relevance today. Businesses develop goals and objectives and then find ways to try to reach those goals. Businesses try to reach those goals by providing superior value to targeted customers. The strategy must fit the requirements of the business environment, including the requirements of all the relevant stakeholders. A portfolio of businesses is chosen that allows the business to grow and create profit into the future. The process for creating and managing strategy starts with developing goals, then uses knowledge of the environment to create strategy that can be implemented and adjusted.

Newer thinking on strategy and processes changes the nature of strategy to include a vision of the future and core competencies required to create that future. The process today is often more encompassing, involving more people throughout the organization. Very often it is driven by close attention to performance measurement that is customized for the company's particular situation. Measures are set and performance tracked. Performance against the measures is the basis for making adjustments.

The business-to-business marketing manager has to live with the strategy that is developed at the corporate level and may have to participate in its development. Knowing what is being done and why helps the manager to be a full participant and guides the manager's attempts to implement the strategy.

The Siemens vignette introduced at the beginning of this chapter illustrates several of the points made in this chapter. It shows Siemens altering its portfolio to improve its performance. It shows Siemens changing its core competencies to improve its performance in current and future lines of business. It shows Siemens attempting to alter its internal environment, making the company more customer focused and entrepreneurially oriented. One thing it does not show is a company that has changed its strategy through a drawn out strategic planning process. Rather, the CEO, Heinrich von Pierer, initiated the changeover. Think about the advantages and disadvantages of this approach. Would the outcome have been better or worse if von Pierer had involved hundreds of people within the organization to rethink Siemens's strategy?

Now that the discussion has examined strategy at the corporate and business unit level, it can move on to the development of marketing strategy within this strategic context. Chapter 6 presents the specifics of gathering and analyzing data concerning the relevant business environment. Chapters 7 and 8 discuss using this data to develop the specifics of the marketing strategy.

Key Terms

balanced scorecard *118*	goals *105*	objectives *105*
business model *112*	growth-share matrix *114*	strategic business unit *113*
business portfolio *113*	market attractiveness—business	strategy *105*
core competencies *111*	strength matrix *116*	strategic management process *107*
differentiation *111*	market ownership *115*	
fit *111*	mission *105*	

Questions for Review and Discussion

1. What is the difference between corporate strategy and marketing strategy? What are the similarities?
2. What is the process by which marketing strategy ought to be formulated?

3. How can a company mission statement be made to provide motivation and guidance for a company, rather just giving lip service to a set of unrealistic values and goals?

4. Suppose you are working on constructing a portfolio of businesses for your company to pursue in the next three to five years. What makes for a good portfolio of businesses? What makes for a good portfolio of products?

5. Is the balanced scorecard consistent with the strategic management process outlined in Exhibit 5-3? Explain any inconsistencies.

6. Suppose you are involved in starting a new business in a fast-changing environment, such as radio frequency identification (RFID) products. To what extent would the strategic management process be useful in planning strategy for such a new business?

7. Suppose a company follows the strategic management process with a degree of diligence. Yet, the company executives recognize that the business environment is rapidly changing. How might such a company adapt the strategic management process for such an uncertain environment?

8. To what extent are entrepreneurial marketing and the strategic management process consistent? Inconsistent? Explain.

9. Discuss the relationship between market ownership, value networks, and the trend toward integrated supply chains in today's market.

10. Discuss typical planning cycles other than the often-used annual cycle. How should rapid innovation and fast-paced change impact the frequency and duration of strategy planning?

11. The chapter related the BCG growth-share matrix to the PLC. Other than the pace of changes in the market, what are the similarities in the marketing mix between stars/the growth stage, cash cows/maturity, question marks/introduction, and dogs/decline?

12. How can moving from a question mark to a star (in the counterclockwise evolution around the growth-share matrix) be compared to crossing the chasm?

Endnotes

1. Based on: Jack Ewing, "Siemens Climbs Back," *Business Week* (June 5, 2000), pp. 79–82; Jack Ewing, "Siemens Proves Prudence Is a Virtue: It's Healthy, While Fast-Growth Rival ABB Is in a Shambles," *Business Week* (November 11, 2002), p. 33; *The Economist*, "Business: A European Giant Stirs; Conglomerates" (February 15, 2003), p. 65; Jack Ewing, "All Eyes on the Corner Office; The Race to Succeed Siemens' Longtime Chieftain Has Begun in Earnest," *Business Week* (March 1, 2004), p. 52; Jack Ewing, "Is Siemens Still German?; The Jobs are Going Where the Customers Seem to Be—Abroad," *Business Week* (May 17, 2004), p. 50; *PR Newswire*, "Siemens ultrasound number one in the U.S. for the fourth year in a row" (August 9, 2004).

2. Robert W. Bradford and J. Peter Duncan, *Simplified Strategic Planning* (Worcester, Mass.: Chandler House Press, 2000).

3. Gary T. Hamel and C.K. Prahalad, *Competing for the Future* (Boston, Mass.: Harvard Business School Press, 1994).

4. Adam M. Brandenburger and Barry J. Nalebuff, *Co-opetition* (New York: Currency Doubleday, 1996).

5. Peter Dickson, "Toward a General Theory of Competitive Rationality," *Journal of Marketing*, 56(1) (January 1992), pp. 69–83.

6. Hamel and Prahalad, *Competing for the Future.*

7. "Siemens acquires PLM leader UGS," *Manufacturing Business Technology*, 25(3) (March 2007), pp. 8–9.

8. Robert S. Kaplan and David P. Norton, "The Balanced Scorecard—Measures that Drive Performance," *Harvard Business Review* (January–February 1992), and "Putting the Balanced Scorecard to Work," *Harvard Business Review* (September–October 1993), pp. 134–142.

9. Paul Sherlock, *Rethinking Business to Business Marketing* (New York: The Free Press, 1991).

10. Lisa Bransten, "Start-Up Joins Hand-Held-Device Battle," *Wall Street Journal* (Eastern Edition) (May 9, 2002), p. B.5.

11. Hau L. Lee, "The Triple-A Supply Chain," *Harvard Business Review*, 82(10) (October 2004), pp. 102–113.

Chapter 6

Market Research and Competitive Analysis

OVERVIEW

As stressed in prior chapters, business-to-business marketing is different from consumer marketing, necessitating somewhat different approaches for understanding buyers than is commonly done in consumer markets. In this chapter we examine the market climate created by the influences of customers and competitors. In Chapter 3 we discussed the nature of the buying center and the business buying decision process to provide a framework for understanding buyers, their decisions, and the behaviors that impact them. The first section of this chapter demonstrates various methods to obtain that understanding. The second part of this chapter examines methods for understanding competitive activities in the market.

Well-developed marketing organizations nurture data acquisition from all sources. A major asset in the development of a competitive view is the ability to combine bits and pieces of information from multiple sources to form a larger picture of the competitive landscape. The ability to anticipate the type and range of competition in market segments is necessary to make informed judgments about a firm's ability to compete in those segments. Similarly, the design and development of a truly competitive offering depends, in part, on anticipating the value offered by competitors in those segments. Market research and competitive analysis develop information that increases the ability of marketers to make those informed judgments.

Example: IBM Relearns Its Customers' Perspective[1]

In 1993, Lou Gerstner took over the reigns at IBM, having previously been CEO at American Express. At the time, IBM was in a funk. Its stock price was slipping and it had lost its industry position in personal computers. Executive management at IBM was considering breaking the company into as many as a dozen separate businesses to reinstill competitive fervor in the operating units.

The old adage had been that "no one was ever fired for buying IBM." But IT managers couldn't count on that any more!

Gerstner examined the business and decided that IBM was stronger as an integrated company than as a bunch of separate businesses. He took IBM back to its roots to begin the turnaround and began visiting major customers personally, one on one. For second tier customers, he held meetings with CEOs of twenty or more customers at a time. He asked questions. He listened.

For the better part of a decade, IBM had moved away from this model of customer learning. Increasingly, it had called on lower and lower levels in the customer organizations, down to the IT manager level, and it lost touch with corporate customers' problems. Now Gerstner was setting the example of visiting and listening and prodding his marketers and salespeople to do the same. Gerstner nurtured— in fact required—his team to be sensitive to bits and pieces of market data. New products followed, as well as new software and service initiatives. One of the principal contributions Gerstner made was to create IBM Global Services, which quickly became one of the largest consulting organizations in the world. By 1996, IBM was back to being a major force in the information industry.

The important part of the strategy for the purposes of this chapter is the way that Gerstner pursued his initiation into the computer industry. His approach to learning the markets was to go to customers and find out what their problems were. Then he sought solutions to their problems and the customers responded. This typifies market research in business-to-business markets. It works because the markets are often oligopolies—the number of customer companies is relatively small. The more the marketer talks with and listens to customers, the greater her empathy for their situations and problems and the more likely that she will find something that can meet their needs.

Notice that the focus was on customers, not on competitors. By understanding customers, a strong competitive positioning evolved.

In 2002, Gerstner decided to retire, turning over the reigns to Sam Palmisano, a veteran IBM employee who joined the company in the mid-1970s. Palmisano, who came up through the IBM sales organization, pursues the customer-focused methods espoused by Gerstner. Since assuming the top position, Palmisano typically spends 60 percent of his time talking with customers. Out of these discussions, Palmisano has learned that IBM needs to further integrate the pieces of customer solutions that have typically been offered by its various business units[2].

Today IBM continues to perform well and to lead or mingle with the leaders in most major parts of the industry. One of the strongest parts of its business remains in services and consulting. Many industry reports[3] conclude that IBM Global Services is a leading "global market maker" for Customer Relationship Management (CRM), Service Oriented Architectures (SOA), and other consulting services. This demonstrates IBM's leadership in helping clients become on-demand businesses, with business processes that are integrated across their company as well as externally with key partners, suppliers, and customers. This gives them a natural way to continue to listen to their customers and learn where the new problems are cropping up.

LEARNING OBJECTIVES

By reading this chapter, you will

- Appreciate the rationale for market research in business-to-business markets.
- Understand the differences in market research between consumer and business-to-business marketing.
- Understand the kinds of market research methods employed in business-to-business marketing versus consumer marketing.
- Understand how current trends influence how market research is done in business-to-business marketing.

■ Understand the theoretical context guiding the collection of competitor data.

■ Know what kinds of data need to be collected on competitors and likely sources for these data.

■ Understand the effect of current trends on competitive information collection. Obtain practice in performing competitive analysis in a business-to-business setting.

INTRODUCTION

A marketing orientation necessitates that you know as much about customers, competitors, and the business environment as can be effectively and ethically collected. This implies that you will collect information about markets, your customers, your prospective customers, your customers' markets and customers, and your existing and potential competitors. All of this information collection and interpretation falls in the general domain of **market intelligence**. Market intelligence includes the results of both formal, planned investigations as well as the collection of data that, without centralized collection and informed interpretation, would appear as a number of random, unrelated events. The methods of collecting and interpreting these data are often quite different. The portion of market intelligence that involves the design of a research approach and the systematic collection, analysis, and interpretation of data on customers and channel members belongs to the subset of market intelligence known as **market research**. The other portion of marketing intelligence, less formal and seemingly random, most often includes activities directed at competitors and is known as **competitive intelligence** (Exhibit 6-1).

Market research is the systematic collection and interpretation of specific data related to the resolution of a specific problem or to satisfy a specific objective. Such efforts usually begin with a knowledge base, albeit sometimes rudimentary, that leads to the basic premise of the investigation.

Competitive Intelligence is the collection and informed interpretation of what might appear at first as a number of random, unrelated events.

Formal market research involves rigorous adherence to research design, careful data collection, careful analysis, and interpretation. This effort requires an informed starting point—knowing what the research problem and objectives are. Competitive intelligence gathering is less rigorous—often called "informal" research. Competitive intelligence efforts, seldom part of a formal plan, still require information assembly and interpretation discipline. However, the data collected may tend to be more qualitative; and the data collection is more of an ongoing process, rather than a series of projects with identifiable starting and ending points. The intent of all this effort, though, is to learn about the market, its players, and the directions the market is taking.

In this chapter we specifically address market research and competitive intelligence in business-to-business marketing. We begin with a review of the fundamentals of the market research process and the role it plays in the organization.

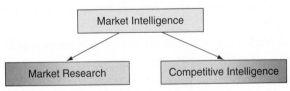

EXHIBIT 6-1   Portions of Market Intelligence

MARKET RESEARCH

In a customer-oriented organization, the marketing process begins with knowing the organization's customers and prospective customers, just as Lou Gerstner sought to do when he went to IBM and as Sam Palmisano did after taking over for Gerstner. To truly know customers, the business marketer needs to understand the following elements:

- *The customers' technologies and processes.* Learn your customers' technology—how it works and how they apply it. A willingness by the customer to apply technology will impact the application of the supplier's products.
- *The customers' products.* What is your customer going to use the product or service for? What will they expect of it? By understanding your customers' products and their fit in the market, you can better anticipate the needs of the customer.
- *The customers' markets and customers.* Your distinctive competency may well provide an opportunity for your customers in their market; but first you have to know what they are attempting to achieve. Know where the customer's next opportunity is and make it your next opportunity.
- *The customers' competitors.* This shouldn't be a surprise, but your customers' competitors are your customers also—or should be—unless they are excluded from considering your organization as a supplier by other considerations.
- *The customers' channels.* How do your customers reach their customers? What level of missionary sales effort, such as customer education and inventory assistance, do your customers provide? Can you assist with channel logistics, beyond the expected supply chain coordination, in any way? Are there buying habits in the end-user market that dictate a particular channel behavior that isn't ordinary (i.e., accompanying a companion product or offering, or a channel dictated by the way customers buy related products)? Often products that are accessories or supplies to an offering will flow in the primary channel as well as different service channels to effectively reach customers.
- *The customers' buying center and buying patterns.* How do your customers make decisions? Do they have several levels of decision making, or are decisions made quickly with little oversight? Are there patterns to their buying that you can correlate to other events, such as climate, holiday seasons, and natural calamities?
- *The customers' culture.* Just as you may treat a market or technology differently from your competitors in an attempt to differentiate yourself from them, your customers are doing the same thing. "Certain companies buy from certain companies." Tradition, long-term relationships, logistical considerations, common enemies, and many other factors contribute to the cultural makeup of your customers. There are some things some companies will be reluctant to do and some risks that they may not be willing to accept.

Knowing Your Customers

Knowing your customers includes knowing your customers'

- *Technologies and processes*
- *Products*
- *Markets and customers*
- *Competitors*
- *Channels*
- *Buying center and buying patterns*
- *Culture*

Many information sources must be combined to provide this level of customer understanding. Initial efforts include existing, though sometimes scattered, sources.

- The marketing manager may have had experience in the customer's company, perhaps as an engineer or salesperson. In such a case, the marketer understands customers because he or she *was* one!

An Example of Different Cultures and the Effect on Choices of New Markets

AT&T was once a leader in the development and use of computer technology. However, the U.S. government, who had granted the company a monopoly on the telephone service business in the United States—until the breakup of AT&T in 1984, heavily regulated AT&T.

AT&T knew a lot about computers—it had been making computers for its own use for 35 years. It considered the computer business one area in which it could effectively compete. Unfortunately, the culture within AT&T lacked the urgency needed to quickly develop and market cutting-edge products in a fast-paced market.

One approach to overcome its deficiencies was to acquire a company that could compete. AT&T acquired NCR in 1991 in an effort to address the banking computer market. However, the combination of the two companies was still unable to overcome their cultural differences and AT&T spun off NCR in 1996, leaving the enterprise computing market for good.

The current AT&T, which is based in San Antonio, Texas, was formed in 2005 by SBC Communications' purchase of its former parent company, AT&T Corp. As a part of the merger, SBC shed its name and took on the iconic AT&T moniker and the T stock-trading symbol (for "telephone").

Secondary data can be internal information compiled for other purposes, such as existing sales tracking information, as well as research conducted by someone else, such as a market research company, usually for a purpose somewhat different than the marketer has in mind. For instance, companies such as IDC, Gartner Group, and Jupiter perform generalized market research related to computer and software markets. They then sell the research reports to interested companies. The marketers who buy the reports do not have control over the kinds of questions that were asked or issues addressed. Secondary data can also be the results of a research effort developed for another reason.

Primary market research is the collection of data directly from respondents in the population in question. The marketer determines what data needs to be collected and sets out to obtain it.

- A marketer can talk with salespeople and customer service people who deal directly with the customers. She might talk with channel partners who also deal directly with customers.
- The marketer can obtain research from a research firm that has studied the customers and their markets.
- The news media (newspapers, local magazines, and so on) in the city or town of the customer may provide insight into the activities of the customer (as well as competitors).

The first two types of data, though useful, have unknown biases and are difficult to generalize. The last two types of data, often referred to as **secondary data**, do not always provide the necessary direct knowledge about specific customer needs, preferences, and behavior. Just as a local news story may be the result of public relations efforts in the community, much of this information originated for purposes other than competitive analysis. In such a case, the marketer needs **primary market research**.

Market Research Fundamentals

Market research is a powerful tool, but it is only a tool. Like any tool, it can be used properly, it can be abused, or it can be used to complete a task without providing the required result (ever been in the kitchen and, needing a screwdriver, ruin a butter knife?).

The steps of the market research process are shown in Exhibit 6-2. This is a general depiction of the market research process and is applicable in both consumer market research and business-to-business market research. The validity and usefulness of market research are strongly impacted by the quality and accuracy of each step in the process. Marketers should be reminded that market research results are a snapshot in time and that markets will change.

1. *Define the problem and research objectives*
   What decisions will be supported?
   What information is needed to make these decisions?
   Should the type of research be exploratory or conclusive?
2. *Design the research method*
   What respondents will be sought?
   What sampling method should be used?
   Design the research instrument.
3. *Collect the data*
   Control the quality of data collection.
   Enter data in database.
4. *Analyze the data and draw conclusions*
   Apply appropriate analysis techniques.
   Control for nonrandom error.
   Draw appropriate conclusions, given the results and quality of data.
5. *Present the findings*
   Apply information to decisions.

EXHIBIT 6-2   Steps in the Market Research Process

The following discussion summarizes some of the more elementary but salient points of the steps in the process. The discussion is presented as if the process involves two principal participants—the marketing manager and a market researcher. In reality, the marketing manager may take both roles, or several people may be involved on the side of the manager and several more on the side of the researcher.

DEFINE THE PROBLEM AND RESEARCH OBJECTIVES   In this first phase of the market research process, the marketer and researcher must define the problem and research objectives. One reason often cited for poor market research is a failure to separate symptoms of problems from the actual problem. Consider that poor sales are not really a problem, but a symptom of other offering shortcomings. The researcher must investigate the "problem" or purpose to know what "answers" are needed from the research. Without this guideline, the marketer and researcher can collect lots of information about markets without having much use for it.

DESIGN THE RESEARCH METHOD TO ACHIEVE THE RESEARCH OBJECTIVES   Who in the market—or what part of the market—has the information needed to support the decision process? The results of the research will be greatly impacted by the selection of respondents, or sample.

What is asked and how it is asked will also impact the results. Sample size will determine the accuracy of statistical analyses, but more importantly, the method of sampling and design of the research method (survey style; open-ended or closed-ended questions, delivery via mail, in person, or electronically; personal interview, etc.) must be tailored to the type of market segment under investigation. Oligopolistic business-to-business markets (only a few customers—see Chapter 2) will require an entirely different approach than market research in business-to-business markets with many buyers and sellers.

A *sample* is the members of the population to be respondents in a research study. If you want to obtain an accurate representation of the population, you will need to be careful about how a sample is selected. Ask your instructor to recommend a market research text to review sampling issues.

COLLECT THE DATA   In any primary market research effort, data collection has traditionally been the most expensive step because it is usually the most labor intensive step. The quality of data collection will be highly dependent on the knowledge, training, and attention to detail of the research personnel. In business-to-business market research where there is a need for in-depth personal interviewing, interviewers must have an adequate knowledge of the market, acquired through either personal experience or secondary research efforts prior to the interviewing process. The services of an outside market research firm may be appropriate, particularly when expertise in specific markets is desirable (see the box, "Working with Market Research Vendors").

ANALYZE THE DATA AND DRAW CONCLUSIONS   In doing good research it is necessary to remember what to do with the information collected and knowledge gained. While the type of research instrument determines the style and character of the information that is generated, the researcher must avoid drawing any conclusions not directly supported by the data or by the respondent group. Marketers need to be wary of **evidence seeking**—interpreting the data optimistically in a way that supports the conclusions the marketer wants to reach.

PRESENT THE FINDINGS   As simple as it may sound, applying the information to decisions can be difficult. One common failure, though occurring more often in consumer markets than in business-to-business markets, is failure to apply the findings or act on decisions in a timely manner.

Implications of Types of Decision Support

There are three basic decision types that research can be used to support: a *targeting decision*, a *design decision*, or a *go/no-go decision*, summarized in Exhibit 6-3. A thorough understanding of market segmentation supports **targeting decisions** while an understanding of customer needs and customer reactions to design variables supports **design decisions**. **Go/no-go decisions** are made before launch of a new strategy, product, or program and can occur at several different points before launch.

RESEARCH TO SUPPORT TARGETING DECISIONS   When selecting market segments to target, the researcher usually wants to have information that can be generalized to the market as a whole. Such information would characterize the whole market and provide estimates of the size of the segments that comprise it. Very often, a marketer will envision a new market for which little or no information is available or easily obtained. In such a case, the marketer wants to gather enough information about the segment or segments of interest to be confident that the identified market segments are large enough to deserve attention. To get generalizable information, the research must use sampling that is done well enough to determine the intricacies of the whole market sufficient to categorize respondents into groups representing market segments. The first attempt at

Targeting Decision	A thorough understanding of segmented markets supports the target decision process.
Design Decision	A thorough understanding of customer needs, reactions, and perceptions regarding features and attributes of the offer supports the design process.
Go/no-go Decision	Continuous information provides better decision making at critical stages or points in the development process.

EXHIBIT 6-3   Research Supports Three Types of Decision

Working with Market Research Vendors

Market researchers often need help from outside agencies. Market research vendors come in all shapes and sizes. Large ones often can provide resources to support integrated marketing programs. Smaller research firms often specialize in types of information collection, types of problems addressed, or markets studied. In working with market research vendors, common sense will go a long ways toward getting the most from the relationship. There are, however, some special circumstances that need to be kept in mind when dealing specifically with research vendors.

Research, by its nature, is a process of discovery. When negotiating a contract, enough flexibility needs to be built in so that the process can be changed as required. By the same token, the researchers need to understand that deadlines for decisions must be met. Early in the process, the client and the researchers should discuss what dimensions of the research are the highest priorities.

Then potential trade-offs between the dimensions of the research should be agreed upon. For instance, a potential trade-off may exist between level of uncertainty and the time required for data collection and analysis. The parties should discuss what levels of uncertainty are acceptable and preferred. They should also discuss the consequences if the research schedule should slip, as well as the advantages gained if the research is completed early. This will give the researcher a good sense of context so that the researcher can adapt the study design appropriately as events unfold. The parties may decide to build incentives into the research contract so that the research vendor will have good reason to strive for the preferable levels of uncertainty and timeliness, rather than settle for the merely acceptable levels. By talking about the trade-offs, the parties will tend to have more open communications as the project progresses, which also leads to better project outcomes.

Finally, marketers seeking the services of a research vendor usually need to specify the problems that need to be addressed rather than the specific tasks of the project. Professional researchers usually have a better understanding of the latest methodology than do marketing managers. Once vendors have submitted proposals, the managers can seek explanations from the vendors as to the advantages and disadvantages of the methods proposed.

segmentation will often be a product of the marketer's best educated guess about the market. The researcher must have a good idea of how the market will be segmented prior to starting the research. Unfortunately, it is not often possible to have a good idea about likely segments without doing some research. The implication of this is that good segmentation research is usually a two-stage research design. The first phase is **exploratory research** and produces the basis for effectively segmenting the market (usually based on differences in kinds of value sought—see Chapter 7). Secondary data can make a significant contribution to the exploratory phase.

Exploratory Market Research

How can you tell just by looking at a city's skyline how its business is faring? Just count the cranes!

"They are the immediate indicator for the state of the economy," says Leight Sparrow of www.vertical.net, the UK-based online magazine for crane cognoscenti. In 2007, 5–7 percent of all cranes were up in Dubai, Shanghai had about 1,200, and Spain was the true tower-crane hub. The big players in these markets are Liebherr, Manitowoc, and Potain. A recent article in *Construction Week* magazine said crane prices have jumped 30 percent this year, while the two major European manufacturers—Liebherr and Potain—were so backlogged that Italian and Chinese cranes were taking a growing share of the Gulf market. A new tower crane costs $100,000 to $1.9 million depending on the size. With demand so high the second-hand market is booming: The cranes being used to erect the BURJ Dubai were previously used on the PETRONAS Tower in Malaysia. See *Monocle*, January 2007. www.monocle.com

Before designing the project, the marketer and researcher need to decide whether the project is to be exploratory or conclusive. This decision depends on how much is already known about customers and prospects.

Exploratory research differs a great deal from conclusive research. Exploratory research is intended to get a sense of context and maybe some insight into possible relationships, trends, causes, and effects. Typical exploratory methods include analysis of secondary data, in-depth personal interviews, and focus groups. Conclusive (causal) research is theory-testing research. It answers questions such as, "Will our new product be attractive in the market?" or "Which message gets the most interest from our target audience?" or "Do customers prefer online technical support or waiting to have a technical support person visit them?" A conclusive study might use laboratory experiments; large-scale sampling for mailed or interview surveys, with multivariate analysis of this primary data; or direct observation of customer behavior.

In determining whether to do exploratory or conclusive research, the business marketer must first understand what is known about the intended target markets. Conclusive research alone may be sufficient if the marketer knows how a particular market works and wants to make some important choices about specific parts of the marketing plan. If the marketer knows only a little bit about how a market works and really is only guessing when making marketing decisions, then exploratory research is called for. Some other factors to consider are the cost, both in terms of money and time. Conclusive research is usually more costly in both money and time than exploratory research would be. However, exploratory research is not costless. Sometimes focus groups can be more costly and difficult to arrange than performing a series of phone interviews. Another strike against exploratory research is the difficulty in keeping bias out of the research. If a company decides to do a series of phone interviews instead of a carefully prepared mailed questionnaire, for instance, and uses one or two of its own marketers to do the interviews, the data can become very misleading. The interviewers may tend to hear only what they want to hear. Also, they may ask questions in such a way that they subtly lead the respondent to the answer most desired by the interviewer. If precision of the data and representativeness of the market are large issues, the marketer may want to "bite the bullet" and use more rigorous, conclusive research.

EXHIBIT 6-4   Defining the Purpose of the Research: Exploratory or Conclusive

The second phase is **conclusive research**. Conclusive research divides the sample into segments according to the segmentation basis developed in the first phase. It also tests to see whether the segments are indeed distinct. If the sample is representative, then the research can produce estimates of relative and absolute segment sizes. See Exhibit 6-4 for a discussion of exploratory research, compared to conclusive research. Other data about the segments are also collected in the same study to aid in choosing which segments to target. The additional data may include such things as strength of need, channels of distribution accessed, size of budget, and so on. All of these data help the decision maker envision the attractiveness of each segment.

RESEARCH TO SUPPORT DESIGN DECISIONS   Segmentation research is very different from the market research intended to provide insight for designing strategy, offering attributes, positioning, products, advertising, sales promotion, selling techniques, channel programs, or pricing. To design marketing strategy, or the offering, a company needs information for each targeted segment about

- benefits desired
- the nature of the buying decision process

- reactions to product, service
- communications methodology.

Notice that the segments have to be defined before this research can begin. Without the segments defined in advance, design-related research produces information for offerings without the benefit of specific segment wants; thus, they tend to be unfocused or generic.

It has been our experience that collecting data for both segmentation and design[4] at the same time is a bad idea. To design the offering, targeted to a group of customers, the marketer needs detailed, in-depth understanding of the customers' situation, needs and preferences, and buying behavior. This goes well beyond the level of detail required for most segmentation research. Trying to collect enough data to understand segmentation, plus enough data to design a good offering, requires more data than most respondents can provide in a reasonable amount of time.

RESEARCH TO SUPPORT GO/NO-GO DECISIONS   The third type of research is for go/no-go decisions. In the process of launching new initiatives (e.g., new products, new channel programs, new sales programs), market-related go/no-go decisions occur at two or three steps or stages, depending on how new the market is. There are also go/no-go decisions concerning the technological aspects of the product or the feasibility aspects of new programs.

The first go/no-go decision (see Exhibit 6-5) concerns whether the market opportunity is worth considering. If the opportunity has many new elements to the organization and the market is not well understood, this go/no-go decision point is necessary. To determine whether the opportunity is a "go," a quick assessment of the size of the potential market and the rate of market growth needs to be made. This requires data similar to the exploratory assessment of market segments, including *secondary data* sufficient to gauge the number of potential buyers of the product (or respondents to a new program).

The second go/no-go decision concerns whether the market is sufficiently interested in the offering concept. This decision occurs after the idea for the offering is well developed, but prior to the execution of the offering. Product engineering, development of promotion, and definition of channel support programs have not begun in earnest. Very often a product is being designed

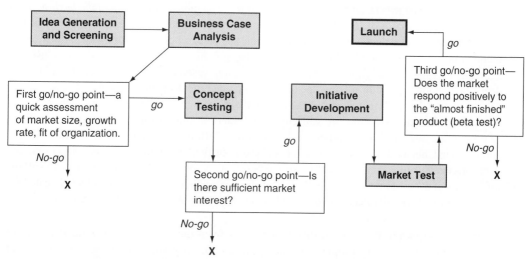

EXHIBIT 6-5 Go/No-Go Decision Points in the Marketing Initiative Development Process

*A **beta test** is a second test of a new product or technology, done at customer sites. An **alpha test** is a test done with a product or prototype internally within the company developing it. Alpha tests determine the viability of the product technology.*

for a particular customer with the participation of members of the customer's buying center; there is little need for a formal concept test. If the product or program is to be offered to a wider audience, the research will look more like a concept test for a consumer product.

The third go/no-go decision concerns whether the intended target market responds positively to the finished (or nearly finished) design of the offering or marketing program. When the company is developing a product or offering in collaboration with a key customer, this step occurs automatically. In other situations when there is no such collaboration, it is necessary to determine whether the intended target market will respond as desired and, if not, can simple changes be made to reach the desired effectiveness level. Many companies accomplish this as part of "**beta tests**" performed for technical reasons. In beta tests, the product or service is tested with a select group of real customers to see if the product works properly.

Designing the Research—Differences from Market Research in Consumer Markets

Market research in business markets has a different flavor than it has in consumer markets. In Chapter 1, we noted the differences between consumer markets and business-to-business markets. Given these peculiarities of business markets, marketers must address several problems that are specific to market research in business markets.

CONCENTRATED MARKETS   When a business marketer addresses customers who face oligopolistic markets, the traditional tools of quantitative market research lose their relevance: *Too few buyers exist* for estimation of population characteristics from statistical inference.[5] Data collection through large-sample surveys, such as are used in consumer research, cannot be performed. Data analysis techniques based on deriving unbiased estimation of population parameters and statistically testing their differences have little or no relevance. This means that business marketers need to use **personal interviews** for data collection when their customers face oligopolistic markets.

DIVERSITY OF INTERESTS IN THE BUYING CENTER   The *number of people in the buying center* produces another major difference from consumer market situations. In households, one or two people usually make decisions. A consumer market researcher can address questions to the member of the household most likely to make a decision in a product area and the response will generally be valid. In a buying center for an organization, several people may strongly influence a decision, making it difficult for any one of them to predict the decision's outcome. Further, if you could question them all, they may be able to give their preferences *at the time*, but such responses would not take into account any subsequent interaction among the buying center members (the buying center and its members' relationship to different elements of the value chain is addressed in Chapter 3). Consequently, it may be very difficult to predict an organization's buying decisions even from primary data. Perhaps the best that can be accomplished is to ask (1) will the offering meet the customer's needs and (2) does the customer currently have a budget allocated for addressing that particular need and then making do with results that are admittedly imperfect.

TECHNICAL EXPERTISE   A third difference arises from the *technical expertise that resides in the buying center.* For complex products, there is usually someone in the buying center who understands (or is believed to understand by other members of the buying center) the workings of the product or service technology. Accordingly, the language used in market research data collection instruments needs to reflect the technical nature of the product or service as understood by the target market. This becomes particularly important when the technical expert in the buying center comes from a different field than the technical people on the supplier side and may operate with a different specialized language. Market researchers then must translate the technical language of the supplier into the technical language of the buyer; similarly, they must translate the buyer's answer back into technical language the supplier can understand. At the same time, if the market research is also aimed at non-technical people within the buying center, the technical language of the supplier needs to be framed in the language usage that is understood by the buyers.

Jargon is any specialized language of a group that is used to improve the efficiency of communication among members of the group. Specific jargon does not necessarily have consistent meaning across different professional groups.

Designing the Research Approach—Other Special Circumstances in Market Research

Problems in performing market research in business markets worsen when two of the overarching trends we've been discussing since the first chapter—time compression and heightened uncertainty—have an effect. In addition, entrepreneurial marketing poses some special circumstances that the marketer must address. Under circumstances in which any or all three of these influences occur, the marketer is tempted to forego market research. This section suggests approaches that help the marketer to do appropriate research, rather than taking the risk of doing no research.

TIME COMPRESSION   Time compression can have several impacts. The first problem is the time pressure applied to the market research process. Market researchers must obtain data, analyze it, and make recommendations in periods that are often measured in weeks, or even days, rather than months. While technology is making the data collection and analysis less time consuming, analysis and interpretation of the data still require time for "human processing." Some things just take time.

Because most data collection methods obtain data for a "snapshot in time," time compression further reduces the duration for which research results are valid. Because the environment can change rapidly, much of this data has a short lifespan reflecting the state of the environment only so long as conditions are similar to the way they were at the time the data were collected.

UNCERTAINTY   While time compression itself is one source of *uncertainty*, other factors such as unforeseen competition and changing customer preferences also heighten uncertainty. Additionally, globalization of markets increases both the chance that new competition will arise and the chance that new customer segments will become evident. As competitors introduce new offerings at an increasing pace, reactions of buyers to these new choices become more and more unpredictable. Hence, new competition itself introduces new uncertainty in customers' preferences.

All this uncertainty drives marketers away from the use of market research, especially for innovative, complex products or services. For such products, prospective customers have a hard time reacting to concepts as they often cannot see the usefulness of a new product that is outside their experience. The complexity of many potential offerings makes it difficult for product developers to create representative prototypes to which respondents can react. Consequently, marketers and product developers often decide to spend their money where it will have the biggest bang for the buck—i.e., probably on product engineering—rather than on questionable research in which they will have little faith or trust. Still, it is important to get as much information as possible about customer preferences and needs as early as possible. To this end, the Marketing Operation Forecast (MOF) and the role of missionary sales/field marketing personnel are discussed in Chapters 11 and 12.

MARKET RESEARCH FOR ENTREPRENEURIAL MARKETING   By their nature, entrepreneurial situations involve both of the factors mentioned above—high uncertainty and time pressure. This combination requires the entrepreneurial marketer to take a "learn-as-you-go" approach to marketing, since there will be inadequate time for the marketer to perform a great deal of research. The research should be fast and conducted continuously to produce the constant learning that will allow marketing plans to be adapted rapidly.

MARKET RESEARCH WITH ONLINE DATA COLLECTION AND ANALYTICS SOFTWARE Online researchers such as Greenfield Online and Harris Interactive have made it much easier, cheaper, and faster to create surveys and collect data through the Internet and World Wide Web. Business-to-business marketers would avoid survey research (and still do in many cases, since the number of customers in many business markets is so small) because of cost and timeliness. Online surveying, though, removes many of these barriers and many marketers will find such techniques, when properly designed and managed, to be attractive and useful.

Companies like InsightExpress, Survey Monkey, and Zoomerang give marketers more control over their own survey creations. The drawback to these services is that marketers without much, if any, training as researchers can obtain useless or even misleading data. Accordingly, marketers need to add real research skills, particularly survey construction capabilities, to their bag of tools.

These advances in software still require a high level of expertise to use. Also, they require insightful managers to make sense of the results. Unfortunately, most business marketers face a situation where such support is an unreachable ideal. They must make decisions on research approaches and priorities that produce the "biggest bang for the buck," that is, that allow them to achieve effectiveness in an environment where resources are limited.

Practical Advice for Performing Market Research in Business-To-Business Markets

In the preceding sections, some of the problems of doing market research in business-to-business markets in today's turbulent environment have been highlighted. However, nothing has been said so far about how to address these problems. The following is a list of the key problems that must be overcome:

- Small number of prospective customers within many business markets
- Size, complexity, and informality of the buying center
- Unpredictability of buying center interactions
- Technical or complex nature of products in many business markets
- Short time horizons for making decisions
- Lack of time for respondents to participate
- Heightened uncertainty about market dynamics.

When a target market has a small number of buyers, the marketer must obtain data from enough of them to have data from an overwhelming majority of the market. In many cases, the largest three to five organizations will represent as much as 75 percent of the market or more. This means that the marketer or researcher must gain cooperation from potential respondents in these largest buying organizations and perhaps get a "representative" sample of the rest, making sure to cover any important market niches.

Addressing the next issue, technical or complex nature of the product, will actually help in getting cooperation from the respondents. One of the principal ways to foster cooperation is to show an understanding of the customer's business and respect for their technical capabilities. The researcher (or marketer, acting as the researcher) wants to make it easy and comfortable for the respondent to provide information. When the researcher has done her homework, learning as much as possible before talking with prospective respondents, respondents generally appreciate the fact that they do not have to translate too much for the researcher. In areas where the respondent has special knowledge and skills, the researcher should acknowledge the respondent's expertise, know enough to be able to ask intelligent questions, and let the respondent educate her.

In markets in which the marketer has experience and contacts, the marketer will generally take this approach naturally. We have noticed, though, that marketers' everyday contacts may occur at lower levels in the buying organization, since these people, such as design engineers or plant supervisors, have direct knowledge of product and service features that are desired. These are good contacts, necessary for understanding the important dimensions of the value sought by customers. Marketers should make special efforts, though, to make contacts at higher levels in the organization and throughout the buying center. Part of the marketer's job is to have brief meetings with upper-level managers, purchasing managers, R&D researchers, and corporate vice presidents to update them on new products and marketing initiatives and to learn about the buying center, its processes, and things it finds valuable.

All of this contact activity has two market research effects. First, it helps the marketer know the customer and its buying center intimately. Long-term contact with exchanges of bits and pieces of information builds a rich knowledge of what is valued and how the buying center processes work. Second, when the marketer needs a lot of information in a hurry, she is likely to have access to the people with the right information. Also, a context has been established which will make data gathering and interpretation easier—the "translation" barriers to market research will have been already breached.

CONDUCTING PERSONAL INTERVIEWS   One of the inescapable conclusions from the preceding discussion about performing market research in business markets is that personal interviews are appropriate in many circumstances. Sometimes, business marketers will need to hire a market research consultant or vendor to perform this research; often the marketer will decide to do the research with available resources in-house. If the marketer decides to do the interviews in-house, she should keep several guidelines in mind (see Exhibit 6-6).

First, if the research is more exploratory than conclusive, the questions should tend to be open ended. Such questions allow the respondents to give the questioner the benefit of their wisdom and insight. If the research is more toward the conclusive side, the questions should be designed more with multiple-choice answers. To get more insight, the researcher/marketer can then give respondents a chance to explain their answers.

Second, questions for all respondents should be the same. In exploratory research, the researcher should use follow-on questions to get rich data. In conclusive research, it is even more important to get each respondent's choice or score for each question. The questioner will need to

- Demonstrate an understanding of the respondent's organization
- If necessary, reassure confidentiality of source
- Ask open-ended question—have questions prepared to serve as an outline
- Have some follow-up probe questions scripted and ready, as well
- Lead in with an easy question or two to break the ice
- Ask the important questions early in the interview; then if you run out of time, you'll still have obtained the important material
- Don't overstay your welcome; if you run out of time, ask to finish up over the phone or by e-mail

To help get the most out of the interviews:

- Ask essentially the same questions of everybody interviewed
- Take care to ask for what you need to know, but be flexible—be a sponge
- Take good notes; write up a summary of the interview immediately after the interview, while it's fresh in your mind.

EXHIBIT 6-6   Improving Cooperation from Interview Respondents

be diligent in getting respondents to answer appropriately—too often the respondent will want to expound. The researcher should tolerate a certain amount of this, but in the end must induce the respondent to answer the question as it was asked.

Third, and perhaps most important, the researcher will usually have to strive for a low refusal rate by prospective interviewees, especially in oligopolistic markets. Since there are so few companies that comprise the vast majority of the market, even a single refusal could create an important "hole" in the marketer's knowledge. Exhibit 6-6 also shows several suggestions for improving cooperation from interview respondents.

ADDRESSING THE TOUGHER ISSUES   To summarize so far, having a network of customer contacts throughout the buying center—and periodically interviewing them, formally or informally—addresses several of the problems we have noted. The marketer will be able to

- obtain market research data from all of the relatively few customers that exist in an oligopolistic market;
- obtain information across the buying center;
- better translate the complex or technical nature of the respondents' information, as long as the marketer has done the homework;
- obtain data more quickly, because much of it has already been gathered through repeated, ongoing contacts; the marketer needs to only ask for quick responses to a limited list of questions; and
- avoid much of the problem with respondents' time compression because respondents know the marketer and trust that their time requirements will be honored; also, less information is sought at any one time, so quick responses are all that is usually necessary.

Three questions or problems remain.

- What methods are most effective in markets that are less concentrated, yet where more customers exist?
- What steps can you take to reduce uncertainty?
- What can you do about anticipating the interactions within the buying center?

When a customer market looks like monopolistic competition (usually before the emergence of a dominant group of players that eventually develop into an oligopoly), with many customers of varying sizes, but no customer that dominates its market, it becomes more difficult for the marketer to have a network of contacts that covers the market. While you still strive to establish a network of contacts among the largest firms in the market, contacts should be developed in other parts of the market as well. Customer size and distinctive competencies of niche players will likely be among segmentation variables, as behaviors are not likely to be consistent over the entire range of all market segments. The network should be built to represent the market as well as possible. This means that the marketer should try to develop contacts in firms that are *not* customers or even near-term prospects. They are cultivated for information purposes. The marketer can use the non-customer contacts to verify segmentation and targeting ideas. Also, it is often useful to have the perspective of someone who knows the market, but who sees the market from the perspective of an objective third party.

APPROPRIATE USE OF SURVEYS IN BUSINESS-TO-BUSINESS MARKETS   In markets in which many prospective customers exist, the distinctions between exploratory and conclusive research become pronounced. While exploratory research will take the form of qualitative interviews as with oligopolistic markets, conclusive research will generally involve surveys of one sort or another. A survey, administered by mailed or online questionnaire, can be an efficient way to gather the appropriate information from a sample that will generalize to the whole market. With appropriate survey construction, this can be done more quickly than collecting the same data through personal interviews, and analysis of the data will leave less room for interpretive mistakes. When done with such a survey, a conclusive research design for such markets will resemble conclusive research in consumer markets.

When the marketer must rely on surveys to obtain representative data, the problem of cooperation becomes prominent again, since the marketer will not use a network of personal contacts predisposed to cooperation. Providing **incentives for participation** is one approach to obtaining respondent participation. Very often, though, participants will view a small monetary incentive with disdain. Recently, researchers have turned to charitable donations, made in the respondent's name, as an incentive. Researchers have received high rates of cooperation when the donation is large enough, and the respondent is given a choice of recipients.

MANAGING UNCERTAINTY   Managing heightened uncertainty remains a concern. Often the answer lies not in better research, but in strategy designs that maintain flexibility and that have data collection and interpretation spelled out as strategy elements. On the research end, often care given to the research design can obtain information that is more useful for peering in the murky future. For instance, a researcher may face the task of thinking ahead beyond eighteen months in the future to what product configurations will be most attractive. Respondents will likely give spurious answers if asked about such features directly—they simply don't know what they will want that far into the future. However, by asking respondents about the problems they face and the trends in those problems, rather than whether a respondent has a need for particular new product features, the data gathered are likely to give the marketer more foresight into future needs.

MINIMIZE IMPACT OF TIME COMPRESSION   The issue of time compression, discussed previously, can be minimized through the use of market research companies that use respondent panels. Some national and international research companies recruit thousands of respondents to serve as respondent pools, or "panels." When a project comes along, a sample is selected from the pool to reflect the population that needs to be represented. These people receive the questionnaire and generally return it in a timely manner, all with a low refusal rate. When this process is managed over the Web, the speed and quality of the data are stunning. Results and data interpretation can be obtained within days or even hours. In a world where decisions must be made quickly, having real data from which to work, instead of questionable assumptions, can give the marketer better plans and better outcomes.

INTERACTIONS OF THE BUYING CENTER   Finally, we address the problem of the buying center interactions. Research on the outcome of past interactions may shed light on possible future outcomes. In other cases, the marketer will have to address the uncertainty caused by such possible interactions as simply another source of uncertainty: all the more reason to create strong relationships with all elements of the buying center.

SUMMARY OF MARKET RESEARCH

As we have seen, market research in business-to-business markets has the same general purposes and follows the same general process and guidelines as market research in consumer marketing. However, the execution of market research in business-to-business markets is often very different than market research in consumer markets. As the opening vignette pointed out, Lou Gerstner took a typical approach to learning about IBM's markets when he first took the reins at the large computer maker. He talked directly with a relatively small number of customers and used this information as the basis for revisions of IBM's strategies. Sam Palmisano, his successor, continues this approach to understanding customers and continues to drive strategy based on the understanding gained. Business-to-business market research often involves a great deal of person-to-person contact, open-ended questions, and a lot of listening. While competitive information is important, the effort to understand the markets starts with an understanding of customers.

Obtaining good customer information was the topic of this first section of the chapter. Once the marketer finds out how customers perceive and pursue value, she can move on to gaining an understanding of the competition, the standard against which customers judge what will be *superior* value.

COMPETITIVE ANALYSIS

Customer analysis is the place to start when doing an analysis of the business environment. There are two reasons for doing this. First, the point of competing is to create value for customers. Understanding how customers perceive value gets the marketer started in designing the offering. Second, customers can tell you who your competitors *really* are. All you have to do is ask. To discover competitors that are likely to exist in the near- to intermediate-term future ask customers who they think will likely have an offering that will interest them. If you are looking farther into the future, ask customers and prospects what kind of characteristics a strong competitor would be likely to have.

The Nature of Competition

Before getting into the basics of competitive analysis, we need to say a few words about the nature of competition. We have already described competition as providing superior value to targeted customers. But this does not convey a sense of the dynamic nature of competitive markets.

Markets seldom, if ever, reach an equilibrium state.[6] Rather, markets strive for equilibrium, particularly after periods of rapid growth, but are routinely upset by the innovation process. In Chapter 9, Innovation and Competitiveness, the innovation process is thoroughly discussed. For now though, note that you must expect innovation to occur whether it comes from known competitors, new (both expected and unexpected) competitors, or even from within your own company.

Innovation has the effect of changing market dynamics, sometimes radically. At other times, it merely continues the progression of the market with few changes in competitive positioning.

Markets evolve, sometimes in revolutionary ways. Current competitors are always a concern; even if they are weak, they can reinvent themselves in the future. New competitors are likely to spring up as existing companies diversify and entrepreneurs attempt to pursue the opportunities they perceive. The Internet makes many kinds of new venture competitors instantly viable. So the business marketer must anticipate abrupt changes in the competitive environment and try to prepare for them. Competitive analysis is a large part of this. However, in today's turbulent environment, competitive analysis must be done somewhat differently than it was done a decade ago. Many of the same ideas apply, but much more emphasis must be given to anticipating new competition from new ventures.

The Six Sources of Competition

Porter[7] characterized the several **sources of competition** that a company can face. Exhibit 6-7 shows the five sources that Porter suggested:

- existing direct competition,
- competition from channels,
- competition from upstream suppliers,
- competition from new entrants, and
- competition from substitutes.

We have added a sixth source: current partners that exist as a result of the development of value networks. In today's business environment, partnerships are formed to provide the pieces that complete the whole offering. In many cases, the partners are already competitors in other markets. Value networks are often temporary alliances of convenience in which either or both parties may

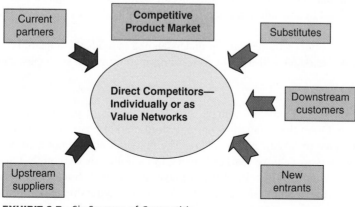

EXHIBIT 6-7   Six Sources of Competition

intend to sever relationships and go their own ways after more is learned about the market and internal strengths can be built. Technically, these partnerships are neither upstream nor downstream channel relationships, so we show them as a separate source of potential competition.

To start to understand competitors, then, the marketer must identify who the direct competitors are, either individually or as opposing value networks. Current partners must then be examined for their competitive potential. The marketer must also look upstream and downstream for any signs that existing suppliers or channel members have potential to become competitors. Next, the marketer must scan for indications that major companies from other industries are looking to enter the market (new entrants). Finally, the marketer should search for potential substitutes that could disrupt the existing industry. This disruption may come from some surprising sources. (See the boxed discussion, "Unexpected Competition—Antimatter Propulsion? Warp Drive?") Substitutes usually come from competing technologies, but not necessarily. The innovation could come in the form of a channel design substitute, making existing products more available or less expensive. Dell Computers offered such a channel design innovation in personal computers. By offering computers through direct sales rather than going through VARs or dealers, companies could buy computers more cheaply and easily than they could from vendors such as IBM and Hewlett Packard.

After these real entities are examined, the marketer can turn to building hypothetical configurations of start-ups or substitutes that might disrupt the marketer's place in the industry.

The marketer often knows direct competitors in familiar markets simply through experience. This may not be the case in emerging markets or when the marketer contemplates taking the company's offering to new markets. If the marketer knows who the direct competitors are, she can begin working on collecting data on them. In any case, though, the marketer must begin talking to customers and prospective customers as soon as possible. (Other sources for identifying potential competitors are discussed in the next main section, "Sources of Competitive Information.")

Information to Collect on Individual Competitors

Information about competitors' future actions and reactions reduces uncertainty. In particular, the marketer wants to identify threats and opportunities that emerge due to competitors' perceptions and activities. To find opportunities and threats, the marketer wants to first understand the direction that a competitor will take if the marketer's company does not change its strategy or tactics. Next, the marketer seeks to understand the competitor enough to anticipate how the competitor will react to strategies, programs, and tactics that the marketer may take in the foreseeable future.

Porter, again, offers a framework for understanding individual competitors. There are four areas in which the marketer will want to collect information: goals, strategies, capabilities, and assumptions.

COMPETITOR GOALS   **Goals**, of course, refer to the levels of performance the competitor wants to achieve. Often the competitor has a desired market position it wishes to obtain, for example, *dominance* or *largest market share*. The marketer should not assume that the competitor always wants to achieve market leadership or dominance, though. Large companies are often satisfied with merely being a major player in a market. Smaller companies are often satisfied with having a small share of a market or an ownership position in a small but

Unexpected Competition—Antimatter Propulsion? Warp Drive?

A few years ago, Technology Strategic Planning, Inc., a technology consulting firm, was performing competitive research for a client that makes chemical propulsion systems (engines) for space vehicles. NASA's mission to Mars was the subject of the research. Instead of investigating future advances in chemical technologies, the consultant examined large companies that were pursuing any kinds of propulsion systems. They found Mitsubishi working on antimatter technology. Antimatter subatomic particles are created in particle accelerators and can be trapped and stored. Recombining antimatter with matter releases a great deal of energy.

Competition from this unexpected technology achieved higher credibility when Technology Strategic Planning calculated the amount of antimatter produced in the world's particle accelerators. It would reach the amount needed for a round trip to Mars about the year 2016, the same time as NASA had scheduled for the Mars mission.

Source: Based on Christopher A. Sawyer, "The Case for Antimatter," *Automotive Industries* (February, 1996): 61.

profitable niche. The goals of the competitor give the marketer an idea of how hard the competitor will fight to pursue its strategy and how vehemently it will react if its market position is threatened.

COMPETITOR STRATEGIES   **Strategies** are the means that the competitor uses to achieve its goals. We can cast these in terms of target segments, desired responses in the marketplace, value offered, marketing mix employed, core competencies employed, and core competencies being acquired. This is the crux of the marketer's understanding of how the competitor will behave and react.

COMPETITOR CAPABILITIES   **Capabilities** are the resources, both financial and organizational, that can be brought to bear in pursuit of the competitor's strategies. A good reading of the competitor's financial statements may give clues to its future ability to fund major initiatives. It is also important to understand the competitor's culture and core competencies. Such issues as how flexible the competitor's organization is, how creative it is in designing new strategies, and how effective it is in implementation all give the marketer a sense of the competitor's tendencies and limitations.

Another indication of changing capabilities of competitors can be their activity at the patent office. New patents can be a major indication (though potentially late in the game) of the R&D focus of the organization. Naturally, this focus will be a result of how the company sees the future of the markets and how it expects to leverage its capabilities.

COMPETITOR ASSUMPTIONS   How a competitor views a market—the **assumptions** that have been made—is the most difficult dimension of competitive information to access. Executives of competitors have mental models of how their markets work. These models drive their choices of strategies and tactics. Seldom do competitors state their assumptions outside of internal business plans (although today more companies are publishing their views of the market mechanics on the Web—see the next section). Sometimes a CEO or other company executive explains her vision of the market in an article or interview for the trade or business press or she will give a presentation at a conference or trade show. More often, the marketer must infer a competitor's assumptions from the behavior of the competitor.

Within this framework, competitive analysis becomes an exercise much like solving a jigsaw puzzle. The marketer gathers bits and pieces of evidence. A competitor's actions and reactions to competitive dynamics are studied over time. The marketer needs to think about why the competitor did what it did. Over time, the competitor's motives and beliefs may become evident. Often the marketer never will get to the root of what drives the competitor. The marketer must remember that strategy is emergent as well as purposeful; often, something that looks purposeful was unintended. Also, competitors learn from their mistakes and successes, leading their belief systems to change. Consequently, the marketer faces a moving target when trying to fathom the competitor's assumptions. In the investigation of competitive assumptions, recognize also that your own assumptions act as a filter on a clear view of the market.

If the marketer learns that the competitor's assumptions are wrong, this knowledge can become a powerful lever. For example, a small printing company with three local weekly newspapers found that a regional chain of newspapers had acquired its principal competitor. The chain was purportedly offering advertising rates that the small printing company could not easily match. By quietly talking with its most important advertiser, the printer learned that the competitor was assuming that important accounts would want combination ads—ads that would run in several of its newspapers simultaneously. The competitor's advertising rates for ads that run only in a single newspaper were much higher. The printer, though, relied mostly on single-site retailers for whom the combination ads were of little or no use. The printer did not have to lower its rates and was actually able to take some business away from the chain, whose management was slow to learn about the true nature of the local market drivers.

Sources of Competitive Information

While competition has intensified over the last decade, the amount and quality of competitive information has kept pace. Some new sources of competitive information have even emerged.

THE CUSTOMER   The first source for competitive information, as was suggested earlier, is the end-use buyer. Customers and prospective customers can give anecdotal data on all four dimensions of competitive information: goals, strategies, capabilities, and assumptions. However, customers' perceptions of a competitor's capabilities may be somewhat myopic. The best way to acquire the data from customers is through normal cultivation of individual contacts. In the course of other discussions, the marketer can ask about comparisons between the marketer's offering and the competitors' offerings.

THE INTERNET   The obvious new source of competitive information is the Web. Most companies now have Web sites, even if these are only online "brochures," Web sites with basic information and little else. Competitors' own Web sites make it possible to quickly find information about all four dimensions of competitor analysis. Even capabilities can often be determined from a company's Web site. If the company is public, it often shows all its Securities and Exchange Commission (SEC) filings and recent quarterly and annual reports. In addition to capabilities, companies will often publish material describing their goals and strategies. This information helps prospective customers determine whether the company actively pursues the target segments and what the offerings for them are. Many companies also publish their mission statements for the same reason. Also, companies often publish their views of the industry and the market. This is done to give prospective customers and partners a sense of how they can work together into the future. It also gives insight into the company's beliefs about the market and, as previously discussed, can provide a competitive lever if the marketer believes the competitor is wrong about the workings of the market.

BUSINESS AND TRADE PRESS   A third good source of competitive information is the business and trade press. The business press includes articles written about a wide range of industries; the trade press sticks closely to one industry or set of related industries. Articles based on interviews and analysts' interpretation can give insight into all four dimensions of competitive analysis. In addition, the press can provide a history of past events or actions, which may also shed light on the competitor's tendencies.

TRADE SHOWS   Trade shows, a fourth source, can also provide a great deal of information to marketers. The trade show has booths and displays for any company of note within an industry. The importance of a competitor's product line relative to its other offerings may be obvious in the emphasis placed on it. The competitor's display is a view of how the competitor perceives the needs of the market—what assumptions it is making about the market. The marketer, or another person operating on the marketer's behalf, can make the rounds and get a close look at current products and programs. In the speaker sessions, which also are part of the show, competitors' executives or managers may give talks or make announcements that define or give clues to the competitors' goals, strategies, and assumptions. The hallways, coffee lounges, and bars in and around the conference hall and surrounding hotels may also have revealing conversations that are easily overheard without being nosy. (Chapter 15, Communicating with the Market, discusses the use of trade shows and the trade press to establish a corporate image.)

OTHER SOURCES   Other sources also provide insights into the four dimensions of competitive analysis. Many of them can be seen as outward indicators of trends and facts that lie beneath the visible surface. The business-to-business marketer may watch competitors' advertisements and publicity announcements. Classified advertising having to do with employment or real estate may also indicate changes in resource deployment that are a result of a change in strategic directions.

One common way of gathering and sifting through competitive information is to hire a consultant who does this on contract. Some consultants maintain extensive networks of contacts within their industries. Others have no immediate contacts but have good methodologies for obtaining information. As with any vendor, the marketer must check the credentials of such consultants to ensure that the consultant is not feeding more information back to some of the marketer's competitors. (The ethical implications involved in the collection of competitive information are discussed in Chapter 16, Business Ethics and Crisis Management.)

SUMMARY OF COMPETITIVE ANALYSIS

In a volatile, competitive environment, business-to-business marketers must learn as much as possible about competitors after they have come to understand something about their own customers. Competitive analysis sets the standard for customer value, which the marketer's firm must exceed. Competitive analysis is forward-looking. The marketer tries to anticipate competitors' future moves and reactions. The goal is to anticipate the threats to the marketer's strategy posed by competitors' strengths, as well as to identify opportunities presented by the constraints they face, their predisposition to certain behaviors, or other weaknesses in their offerings.

THOUGHTS TO TAKE WITH YOU INTO THE NEXT CHAPTER

Learning about the business environment is much like an education process. A great deal of studying is done early in the process, and then continuous learning is necessary. This chapter discussed the early studying that must be done, focusing on customers and competitors. Remember that all of this learning helps create and manage value for customers, so customers are the starting point in the analysis. Just as Lou Gerstner did when he started at IBM and just as Adobe did when it reorganized its company, everything starts with learning about value from the customer's perspective.

Chapter 11 presents one of the uses of this information—conducting forecasting. The chapter discusses on the practical aspects of forecasting, particularly the construction of a marketing operations forecast.

In the next chapter, we show you another major use of the information gathered in the analysis of the business environment. Information gathered about market segments and competitors that address them leads to decisions on choice of target segments and positioning. Then, in later chapters, the detailed information on customer needs and buying behavior obtained in the analysis helps in forming the marketing strategy, programs, and tactics.

Key Terms

alpha test *134*
assumptions *143*
beta test *134*
capabilities *143*
conclusive research *132*
design decision *130*
evidence seeking *130*

exploratory research *131*
goals *142*
go/no-go decision *130*
incentives for
   participation *139*
market intelligence *126*
personal interviews *134*

primary market
   research *128*
sample *129*
secondary data *128*
sources of competition *141*
strategies *143*
targeting decision *130*

Questions for Review and Discussion

1. Why is market research needed in business-to-business marketing? Why can't decisions always be made based on the manager's experience and intuition?

2. What factors make market research in business-to-business markets different from research in consumer markets? What are the resulting characteristics of business-to-business market research?

3. Compare the data requirements for go/no-go decisions, targeting decisions, and design decisions.

4. What are the differences between exploratory and conclusive research? When could exploratory research be used effectively without progressing to the use of conclusive research?

5. Why do the authors assert that research for segmenting markets and research for designing offerings aimed at target markets should be kept distinct, instead of run in the same research study?

6. In what kinds of markets would you want to use quantitative research similar to that often used in consumer research?

7. Why is it more difficult to do competitive analysis in today's market than it was a decade or so ago? Explain in terms of the six forces of competition.

8. From a general viewpoint, what are you trying to determine about competitors when doing competitive analysis?

9. How would you go about collecting information on each of the following competitor characteristics: goals, strategies, capabilities, and assumptions?

10. Describe how competitive analysis is like doing a jig-saw puzzle or creating a mosaic. Why is it like this?

11. Discuss the strategic implications of trade shows as sources of competitive information. What types of information will be available?

Endnotes

1. Based on Ira Sager, "How IBM Became a Growth Company Again," *Business Week* (December 9, 1996), pp. 154–162; and Brian Bergstein, "Aggressive Strategy for Market Growth Transforming IBM," *Seattle Times* (August 24, 2004), p. C.3.

2. "Leading Change When Business Is Good: An Interview" with Samuel J. Palmisano, *Harvard Business Review* (December 2004).

3. Jim Adams, Ed Mounib, Aditya Pai, Neil Stuart, Randy Thomas, and Paige Tomaszewicz, "Healthcare 2015: Win-Win or Lose-Lose? A Portrait and a Path to Successful Trans-formation"; OpenClinical 2007.

4. Yoram Wind, "Issues and Advances in Segmentation Research," *Journal of Marketing Research*, 15(3) (August 1978), pp. 317–337; A.C. Burns and R.F. Bush, *Marketing Research* (London: Prentice-Hall, 2001).

5. This does not mean that business marketers can get by without understanding statistical analy-ses. Recall that business marketers must under-stand their customers' customers. So a thorough understanding of the customers' markets usually requires a basic statistical knowledge to under-stand the secondary research available on con-sumer markets or large-population business markets.

6. This section is based on Peter Reid Dickson, "Toward a General Theory of Competitive Rationality," *Journal of Marketing*, 56(1) (January 1992), pp. 69–83.

7. Michael Porter, *Competitive Strategy* (New York: The Free Press, 1980).

Chapter 7

Segmenting, Targeting, and Positioning

OVERVIEW

In this chapter, we examine the process of segmentation, a process that partitions a market into subgroups based on similarities and differences in customer needs and perceptions of value. The notion of partitioning large, complex societal groups or markets into smaller subgroups for better management understanding is not unique to customer markets. The approach is conceptually no different than decentralized management of complex organizations. The goal is to improve understanding of and effectiveness in the subgroup, creating opportunities for more profitable relationships.

Segmentation affects the marketing strategy of the business-to-business firm through *targeting*, a process of selecting the best segments for the success of the organization, and through *positioning*, the establishment of competitive differentiation within targeted segments. In this chapter, we consider segmentation in terms of value and the value chain, and how different segmentation methods allow the formation of effective strategy. Two approaches for determining market segmentation are explored, an analytic approach and an innovation translation approach. Once market segments have been identified, the marketer reviews the likelihood of success in each segment, based on the values sought by the segment members and the values most likely to be successfully provided by the marketer's organization. Segments can be ranked by the highest level of return,[1] as viewed in light of the goals of the organization, and the willingness to commit resources. Those segments that demonstrate the highest potential for success become the targets of the organization's marketing efforts—they are the chosen target segments.

The creation of information by which these decisions are made—the information necessary for effective segmentation—is one of the major uses of market research and the competitive information (discussed in Chapter 6). Once target segments have been chosen, the process begins for designing strategy and offerings to engage each segment. The structure for this effort is the determination of positioning relative to competition.

The opening example shows how marketers at Panasonic positioned its offering for a segment of the larger market.

Example: Panasonic Targets the Rugged Laptop Segment[2]

In 1996, four Japanese personal computer (PC) makers, Fujitsu, Hitachi, NEC, and Sony, "invaded" the U.S. PC market. Unlike these four, Panasonic did not address the U.S. consumer market, even though Panasonic's parent company, Matsushita, had successful consumer computer offerings in Japan. In the United States, Panasonic targeted organizations that needed durable, portable computers. Priced at roughly twice that of a standard notebook, in 1999, Panasonic only sold 400,000 units worldwide. Panasonic margins were among the highest in the industry at a reported 30 percent gross margin per unit.

Would more customers be willing to pay the price? The U.S. Army equips a large number of personnel with standard business notebook computers. In Iraq and Afghanistan, however, the failure rate of these "business" notebooks was estimated at 80–90 percent. The cost of one notebook, plus the cost of its replacement or repair (including the field logistics to support the effort) could easily exceed the cost of a Toughbook. Learning from this experience, the Army purchased 7,500 Toughbook notebooks for use primarily in Iraq. The failure rate for those units was 8–10 percent. The Army has expressed a significant interest in Toughbook.

Panasonic's focus on the "rugged notebook" allowed it to have a clear, concise message and to structure distribution channels that provide value while not competing in the more aggressive consumer market nor conflicting with other offerings. Organizations that deployed significant numbers of notebooks to employees in the field who perform on-site customer service, field repairs, field sales, or other damage-susceptible active duty as might be encountered in police or military uses comprise a significant "niche" in the market. In these applications, customers want good performance that is not interrupted by frequent breakdowns.

When Panasonic launched the line in 1996, the communications messages all revolved around the durability of the machines. The notebook line is named Toughbook, which of course immediately communicates the key core benefit. Print advertising was simple, elegant, and pointed, with the notebook sitting on an anvil or shown in some other industrial-strength pose. It received a great deal of publicity from a well-designed promotional event in which one of the hosts of a television network morning show drove a Hummer over a Toughbook at the Comdex trade show. The advertising campaign "Own the Road" won an EFFIE award (from the New York American Marketing Association for effective advertising) in 1998.

The "toughbook" segment initially was too small for the larger competitors to see it as promising segment. By the mid-2000s, Panasonic's success drew attention and several new competitors. To keep ahead of the competition, Panasonic has continued to innovate to improve its offering, extend its product line, and address newly emergent subsegments. These subsegments, or "niches," include such Toughbooks in such situations as managing vegetation in utility right-of-way and managing inventory in shipping and warehousing. While it does not own the PC market as a whole, Panasonic continues to own this segment and it continues to be profitable in doing so.

LEARNING OBJECTIVES

By reading this chapter, you will:

- Reinforce your understanding of segmentation as a tool to manage markets and resources.
- Recognize segmentation as an effective management tool.
- Develop an understanding of segmentation based on the concepts of value and the value chain.
- Be introduced to the market information needs necessary for successful segmentation.
- Understand how segmentation supports business-to-business marketing decisions.

- Understand when and how an analytic approach to segmentation is useful.
- Understand customer involvement in business-to-business segment translation and evolution.
- Understand segment evaluation and the targeting process to maximize market opportunities.
- Strengthen your understanding of market-positioning philosophy by seeing positioning as a tool to enhance both customer and supplier value.

INTRODUCTION

Three of the most important concepts in marketing, whether in business-to-business marketing or consumer marketing, are **segmenting**, **targeting**, and **positioning**. The process of *segmenting* markets makes it possible to know a market well enough to tailor an offering to the specific needs of a few customers rather than creating an offering whose attributes are compromised (e.g., too little, too much, or not exactly as desired) in an attempt to appeal to a broad market. The process of *targeting* involves choosing segments to address based on matching the firm's strengths to the segments that will place the greatest value on these strengths and yield the greatest success. *Positioning* is the creation of greater value for targeted customers than is offered by competitors and the communication of that difference relative to other offerings aimed at the target market segment. This chapter shows how segmentation and the choice of target segments work when based on the concepts of value and the value chain, discussed in previous chapters. From these concepts, the criteria for a good **segmentation framework**—a method of segmentation used in understanding a given market—are derived, as well as criteria for the choice of a good set of target segments. Once target segments are chosen, the marketer determines how the offering for each of these segments ought to be positioned.

THE RELATIONSHIP BETWEEN SEGMENTING, TARGETING, AND POSITIONING

Recall that in business strategy, discussed in Chapter 5, the organization decides in what business to compete and how, generally, to compete. Well-defined market segments are distinct from each other in what they need or how they buy. Within each segment, the needs or buying behavior of individual buyers are very similar to those of the other members of the segment. In other words, it is desirable to create segments whose members tend to have homogeneous needs or buyer behavior within the market segment and distinctly different needs or buyer behavior when compared to members of other segments. With smaller size and reduced variability among its members, as compared to an unsegmented market, a good segmentation framework simplifies the approach to a market, allowing marketers to select segments for targeting where the firm can have the best advantage for success. Customers are also better served through the creation of offerings whose value is more closely aligned with their needs.

The Panasonic example illustrates these ideas well. The market segment that Panasonic discovered has only one primary value dimension—the need for durability. There is little variation within the segment on this dimension. The simplicity of the segmentation structure makes it easy to target and straightforward in providing the required value.

After alternative segments have been identified and understood, choosing target segments follows. It involves combining information about the opportunity within each segment and information about the organization's capability and desire to pursue each of the opportunities.

The analysis creates a measurement of the overall attractiveness of each segment. The marketer chooses the most attractive segments that the company can address.

In the Panasonic example, the durability laptop segment was chosen because of four main attractiveness factors. First, the need was obvious and it was important. Second, no competitor was doing a good job of meeting this need and none was expected to do so in the near future. Third, this need matched well with Panasonic's capability. Fourth, the segment was projected to grow quickly. The only drawback was the relatively small size of this segment, but even this worked in Panasonic's favor. Because Panasonic did not set out to dominate the entire U.S. market for laptops, the size of the durable segment was acceptable. Meanwhile, it *was* too small for the major competitors who were market-share driven or wanted to dominate the entire market. In this market, these distinctions gave Panasonic a competitive edge.

As part of the process of selecting segments to target, the marketer analyzes the value sought within each target segment, as well as the value provided by the principal competitors, and determines how to create a competitive position to address each targeted segment. The positioning of an offering for a segment is the definition of which dimensions of value will be emphasized. The purpose is to offer more value than competitors on some key dimension or dimensions. Positioning establishes the framework for the marketing strategy. It defines the product or service features to be emphasized, the general message to be communicated to selected audiences, the channels that will be used to create value for the buyer at the point of sale, and the price level that the customer should see.

Panasonic positions itself well for the durable laptop market. First, the product is well suited to this market. Second, Panasonic has done well in communicating its message through advertising and publicity. Third, Panasonic has done a solid job in supporting its channels with specialized software and sales promotion. And fourth, the price tag meets expectations without charging too much of a premium. The following discussion examines additional details of the relationship between segmenting, targeting, and positioning.

MARKET SEGMENTATION

The concept of market segmentation has been around for a long time.[3] In practice there is much confusion surrounding the idea.[4] This is unfortunate, as the segmentation process is intended to reduce confusion and assist marketers to better understand how to serve particular markets. In this section we examine the basic ideas of segmentation and then we examine segmentation in the context of business-to-business marketing. We then note important implications and current ideas on the practical aspects of measuring and analyzing segmentation.

Basic Framework of Segmentation

FINDING GROUPS WITH SIMILARITIES IN WHAT THEY BUY OR HOW THEY ACT As described earlier, segmentation involves dividing a market into subgroups or categories of customers in such a way that the marketer is more able to serve particular needs and thus gains a competitive advantage. Broad segments, such as those in consumer mass markets, require products that appeal to the large population of the segment. Selecting smaller segments reduces the number of potential customers that one offering must satisfy. The offering may then be defined with more specific attributes that have value to that smaller customer group rather than with a compromised offering that can only almost satisfy the members of a larger market. This is not intended to imply that a greater number of smaller segments is always better than a few large segments. Markets can become oversegmented. Oversegmentation can result in fragmentation and diversity that make it difficult to profitably serve the smaller markets.

Generally, marketers will strive to create segments that have characteristics of **measurability**, **accessibility**, **substantiality**, and **actionability**. In business-to-business markets, *measurability* is important because marketers need to understand the size, value needs, and purchasing characteristics of a particular segment. If the potential success of marketing to segments cannot be measured, it becomes difficult to not only choose among alternative segments but to design offerings that provide superior value for members of a segment. *Accessibility* is a measure of the marketer's ability to communicate with the market segment and reach them with distribution channels in a manner that makes serving the segment possible. *Substantiality* implies a market segment that desires the particular value offering an organization presents, such that the segment is profitable enough to serve differentially from other segments. *Actionability* is a measure of the capabilities of the organization to create a total offering with a competitive advantage with respect to the specific needs of the segment.

A reminder here is appropriate. The discussion above specifically refers to the total offering, not just "a product." Similar, if not identical, products are marketed to different segments with different total offerings for each segment. Economic utility, form, time, place, and possession contribute to the differentiation of the offering. In consumer markets, this *economic utility differentiation* leads to the same product being offered at specialty retailers and at warehouse clubs. In business-to-business markets, economic utility differentiation can lead to customer-specific supply chain requirements. In this view, it may be appropriate to recognize that supply chain productivity and efficiency based on customer standards is often a defining parameter in business-to-business markets.

NEED FOR MEASURABILITY CREATES INFORMATION NEEDS   This discussion of segmentation implies that information about the prospective markets is readily available. This available information is not only the outcome of market research efforts, but also the product of information collection that attempts to forecast markets. Forecasts are predictions—there are no guarantees. Many processes, both quantitative and qualitative, are used in the effort to predict market behavior over time, though few, if any, are specific. When in doubt as to the needs of a market, it is always best to go to the source of the need—the customer.

The oligopolistic nature of many business-to-business markets offers the opportunity to discuss needs with every potential customer in a way that is not feasible with mass markets. A benefit of positive relationships with customers is the availability of information. Business customers, while tempered by proprietary concerns, will have forecasts of their own markets used in the customer's business planning decisions. Suppliers must be able to effectively provide offerings that match the full needs of the plan. These needs may be technical (assistance in the most effective user of technology in design and development) or logistical (the planning necessary to serve diverse supply chain requirements).

TYPICAL BASES FOR BUSINESS-TO-BUSINESS SEGMENTATION   There are many **bases for segmentation**, some straightforward, some obtuse. A business must choose the segmentation strategy that makes the best use of its strengths and positions it effectively against competitors. Exhibit 7-1 shows the typical bases for segmenting business-to-business markets. In the opening example in this chapter, Panasonic identified a segment based on preferences of the customers, borne out of a special need for portability and durability of the computers. While other potential customers in the market had a need for portability, their need for durability was not so acute as it was for those targeted by Panasonic. Because many potential users' buying patterns were substantially different from mass-market computers (government, law enforcement, and so on), Panasonic

- *By product offered*: A company may treat all customers who offer the same kind of product as a market segment.
- *By geographic region*: Customers located in the same geographic area may be treated as a market segment.
- *By industry in which the customer participates*: All companies in the same industry group may be treated as belonging to a market segment.
- *By size of customer's company*: Companies of the same general size may be treated as belonging to a market segment.
- *By size of account*: A company may treat all its customers who order roughly the same amounts from the company as a market segment.
- *By buying behavior or preferences*: Segments may consist of companies whose buying centers act in similar fashions or whose needs are very similar.
- *By technology used by customer*: All companies that use the same general product or process technology may be treated as a segment.
- *By process and supply chain requirements*: Companies may have differing standards of inventory control and on-time performance as well as a need to control elements of the value network that is providing the offering.

EXHIBIT 7-1 Common Bases for Segmentation of Business-to-Business Markets

developed specialized marketing channels—providers of economic utility—to reach those buyers. It turns out that, no matter how segments are initially defined, the marketer should almost always be looking for special, common needs that can be addressed by the marketer's company.

Value-Based Segmentation

No matter which of the segmentation bases in Exhibit 7-1 is chosen by a business, business-to-business marketers, like consumer marketers, should target segments that have similar needs or buying behavior among their members. If most companies in a target market want the same thing, a great deal can be saved on costs by providing one product that is well designed and offering it with efficient and appropriate communications and sales methods. On the other hand, if after segments are defined, every company in a target market segment were to think and act uniquely, it would be very costly to meet the needs of multiple customers within this segment, suggesting that a new segmentation strategy should be investigated.

A more complete and often more effective way to think of segments is to say that segments should be based on differences in value sought. While simply defined—value is the sum of the benefits minus the sum of the costs—the perception of value will not remain constant across many customers. Exhibits 7-2a and b show the value concept again and the difference between two combinations of value chains and offerings. The first combination addresses a second segment whose members vary considerably in the kinds of value they seek. The second combination is built to provide value to a segment whose members all seek similar sorts of value. The offering and value chain for the first combination display considerably more complexity and, hence, will be more difficult to construct and probably will be more costly to execute. The implication is simple. Companies should try to choose and address segments that are homogeneous in the kinds of value sought, rather than heterogeneous. The marketing organization will then find it easier to discern the needs of the customers and translate these into an offering that provides superior value, enabling the marketing organization to be better able to manage its costs and businesses.

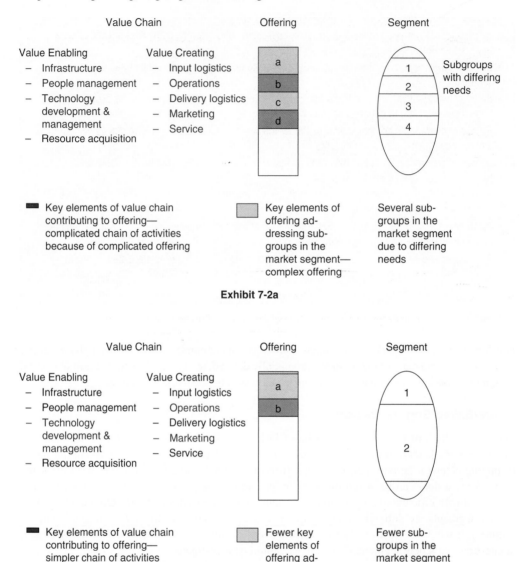

Exhibit 7-2a

Exhibit 7-2b

EXHIBIT 7-2 Segments and the Value Chain

The Process of Determining Segmentation

Two useful ways of determining a segmentation framework to employ are in general use in business-to-business marketing. They are, first, an analytic approach and, second, an *innovation translation* approach. The approach to use depends on the situation that the company faces. Marketers tend to use an analytic approach when they face a market with many customers or an unfamiliar market they are trying to enter. When a marketer has only a few large customers and is looking to extend its existing offering into new customer groups, the marketer often takes an innovation translation approach. Both approaches work well under the right circumstances. In some instances, a combination of the two approaches often would improve the segmentation and, hence, the positioning and strategy that result.

ANALYTIC APPROACH TO DETERMINE A SEGMENTATION FRAMEWORK An **analytic approach** employs research and data interpretation to derive a segmentation framework.[5] The approach attempts to develop two sets of information. The first set has to do with the relative size and growth of considered segments. These data help support decisions of which segments to target as well as whether or not it is a good idea to proceed with the project at all. The second set of data has to do with an individual segment's needs and buying behavior. These data are much richer in terms of the value sought by segment members. Combined, these two sets of data support design decisions on products, services, communications messages, media choices, selling approaches, channel design, and pricing.

The first type of information—having to do with segment size and growth—must often be gathered quickly, particularly for decisions made early in the planning process regarding likely target segments and go/no-go decisions. To aid in analyzing segments and making these decisions within a compressed time frame, the marketer must often rely heavily on secondary data. Government or trade organizations collect much of these secondary data. These agencies collect data so that many people and organizations can use them for various purposes. The data are usually arranged by industry, as embodied in the **North American Industry Classification System (NAICS)** code (see the accompanying box and Exhibit 7-3), by geographical location, and perhaps by

*The **North American Industry Classification System (NAICS)** code is a scheme of industry classifications designed and used by the U.S. government, as well as Canada and Mexico. To see a full description, go to http://www.census.gov/naics/.*

11	Agriculture, Forestry, Fishing, and Hunting	53	Real Estate and Rental and Leasing
21	Mining, Quarrying, and Oil and Gas Extraction	54	Professional, Scientific, and Technical Services
22	Utilities	55	Management of Companies and Enterprises
23	Construction	56	Administrative and Support and Waste Management and Remediation Services
31–33	Manufacturing	61	Educational Services
42	Wholesale Trade	62	Health Care and Social Assistance
44–45	Retail Trade	71	Arts, Entertainment, and Recreation
48–49	Transportation and Warehousing	72	Accommodation and Food Services
51	Information	81	Other Services (except Public Administration)
52	Finance and Insurance	92	Public Administration

EXHIBIT 7-3 Top-Level Industry Groups in the North American Industrial Classification System (NAICS)
Source: www.census.gov/eos/www/naics/index.html

size of company (i.e., the data are usually arranged demographically). The marketer, however, would usually like to have the data arranged in more fine-grained fashion so that they are closely linked to differences in value sought. Consequently, to use the data quickly, the marketer will need to make some reasonable assumptions to convert the demographic data to usable estimates.

Before discussing the second type of data, consider the following hypothetical example to show what the marketer might have to do.

Suppose the marketer was investigating entering the market for online surveys for small business to assess customer satisfaction. The marketer's company provides online surveys for larger companies for various kinds of market research. He has gotten wind of this potentially unmet need among smaller companies. In initial talks with CEOs of small companies, the marketer believes that several possible segments exist among companies that recognize they have a need:

- Companies that are receiving frequent customer complaints and that are losing occasional customers. This segment can be designated as *Segment 1: Major Turnaround.*
- Companies that believe that their relationships with customers are generally weakening and are seeking to stop deterioration before it is too late; designated as *Segment 2: Stopping Deterioration.*
- Companies that have high levels of customer satisfaction but that believe they are facing increasingly competitive markets in which they must achieve ever-higher levels of customer satisfaction if they are to remain competitive. This segment can be designated as *Segment 3: Competitive Improvement.*
- Companies that believe they have problems in specific areas, such as meeting delivery schedules or performing effective customer training, and that seek to improve performance in these specific areas; designated *Segment 4: Specific Area Improvement.*

It should be obvious from the foregoing listing of categories above that it is unlikely that the marketer will find secondary data that will break out the numbers of small companies into these groupings. The marketer will need to find a way to make reasonable assumptions about how large each of the groups is and how fast they are growing. One way might be to talk with several small business consultants to get their opinions of how large these segments are. Another might be to examine third-party financial data such as that provided by Dunn and Bradstreet to get a breakdown of financial performance categories and use these as rough approximations of sizes for the segments.

Suppose that the marketer finds data on the number of small businesses from the U.S. Bureau of the Census and develops a forecast of segment growth. The marketer believes that the relevant size range for small businesses is 50–500 employees: below 50 and they are not large enough to see the $5,000 per year price as worthwhile; while above 500 and they are already likely to have a customer satisfaction tracking solution in place if they desire one. The hypothetical data are shown in Exhibit 7-4.

On the basis of Exhibit 7-4, the marketer estimates that by 2012, the *stopping deterioration* segment will become the largest of the first three segments, at 156,000 companies ($0.2 \times 390,000 = 78,000$ companies in 2010; $+100$ percent $= 156,000$ companies in 2012). In addition, the *specific area improvement* segment of the market will increase to 292,500 companies ($0.3 \times 390,000 = 117,000$ companies in 2010; $+150$ percent $= 292,500$ companies in 2012). This information and the resulting calculations give the marketer an estimate of relative segment size, both now and in the future. The segment sizes for 2010 and 2012 are shown in Exhibit 7-4.

From secondary data:	
Number of U.S. businesses with more than 50 and fewer than 500 employees	390,000
From quick survey of consultants:	
Segment 1: *Major Turnaround.* Assumed percentage of small businesses with customer satisfaction problems	10%
Segment 2: *Stopping Deterioration.* Assumed percentage of small businesses seeking to stop deterioration in customer satisfaction	20%
Segment 3: *Competitive Improvement.* Assumed percentage of small businesses seeking to improve competitive performance	30%
Segment 4: *Specific Area Improvement.* Assumed percentage of small businesses seeking to improve specific functional areas contributing to customer satisfaction (can overlap with above categories)	30%
From a Delphi estimate of a small business consultants:	
Segment 1: Assumed percentage increase in *major turnaround* segment by year 2012	100%
Segment 2: Assumed percentage increase in *stopping deterioration* segment by 2012	100%
Segment 3: Assumed percentage increase (decrease) in *competitive improvement* segment by 2012	(50%)
Segment 4: Assumed percentage increase in *specific area improvement* segment by 2012	150%

EXHIBIT 7-4   Hypothetical Data for Segmentation for Online Customer Satisfaction Survey Service
Source: Number of businesses is projected from United States Bureau of the Census, U.S. County Business Patterns (2006). Other data are hypothetical.

With these estimates in mind, the marketer can evaluate the segmentation framework with respect to *measurability*, *accessibility*, *substantiality*, and *actionability.* First, concerning measurability, the estimates shown in Exhibit 7-5 illustrate that the segments in this framework can be measured. The estimates could be refined with more primary research, if need be. In terms of accessibility, assume in this hypothetical example that the segments as defined can be reached through normal distribution and communications channels. Small businesses, whether financially well off or financially strapped, can be contacted through mail, print, and Internet media; data can be provided to them through physical or digital distribution channels (further research may show preferences for certain types of media and channels within the segments). With respect to substantiality, assume that the sizes of these segments are large enough to warrant consideration, given the goals of the research supplier. The marketer will later need to examine more closely the sustainability of profits within segments that are chosen. Finally, concerning actionability, assume that the needs of each segment can be met by an offering that the marketer feels his company can provide. Accordingly, the segmentation framework is one that is viable for the software supplier.

Segment	Number of Small Businesses in 2010	Number of Small Businesses in 2012	Percentage Increase (Decrease) from 2010 to 2012
Segment 1: *Major Turnaround*	39,000	78,000	100
Segment 2: *Stopping Deterioration*	78,000	156,000	100
Segment 3: *Competitive Improvement*	117,000	58,500	(50)
Segment 4: *Specific Area Improvements*	117,000	292,500	150

EXHIBIT 7-5   Hypothetical Sizes of Market Segments for Online Customer Satisfaction Survey Service

This simple example shows how an analytic approach might be used in making quick estimates of segment size and growth. This is not enough information for choosing segments, but it is a start. The marketer will need to develop and use information on needs within the segments, competitors' offerings and strategies for addressing the segments, and his own company's strengths and weaknesses in providing value to the segments.

The second type of data—data on the needs and buying behavior exhibited within individual market segments—needs to be mostly primary data. These data are used early in the planning process to suggest the bases for segmentation. They are also used for suggesting assumptions the marketer might apply to secondary data to determine market size and growth, as was done in the preceding example. For these two purposes, data gathering can be fairly quick, particularly if the marketer has a good network of contacts in the relevant market. However, data on needs and buying behavior are also used for design decisions, starting with decisions on positioning. These decisions require the development of in-depth information and, hence, require more time. The decisions themselves, though, also take some time to reach a conclusion, so there generally is more time for acquiring and digesting primary data (though this is still subject to pressure from the time compression trend, discussed in previous chapters).

Using effective market research techniques, the marketer can obtain data on the prospective customers' needs, buying center behavior, reactions to messages, reactions to pricing options, and channel preferences. During this data gathering and analysis, the marketer may discover information that calls into question the original choice of target segments. Such discoveries ought to be anticipated; the decision process should allow for performing some iterations that change the emphasis among target segments or even discard a segment from consideration. Before the investigation starts, the manager needs to predetermine what kinds of negative information will trigger reconsideration of the targeting decisions. If such controls are not in place, too much effort may be spent in unnecessary reconsideration of prior decisions, rather than in proactive problem solving.

Before we follow the example to the stage of choosing target segments, let's take a look at the other approach to segmenting markets, the innovation translation approach.

SEGMENTATION BY INNOVATION TRANSLATION   In markets in which only a few customers exist, a company may provide an offering to only one or two large customers. In time, the company may decide to look for additional customers who are attracted to the offering or to an offering that is similar to the original. The process of looking for these new customers is really a process of verifying the existence of a segment by translating the technology of the offering to additional customers.

When a supplier's technology or offering is familiar to a market, customers may find new uses for the product or service without additional assistance from the supplier; or the supplier and customer together may find a new use through collaboration with each other. This new use may or may not be pursued as a new market segment for the supplier. The supplier can undertake a market development effort to determine the validity of the new segment. Stated another way, the supplier will need to validate the new use of the product by translating the new use to other customers with similar needs. Hence, a successful *innovation translation* of new business can create a new target market. Many new market segments are established through this exact process. Segmentation by **innovation translation** emphasizes the nature of many business-to-business market segments—they exist because a customer pulled technology through a relationship with a supplier rather than a supplier having pushed a new offering to the customer.

The marketer, with the help of field marketers (i.e., missionary salespeople) and their headquarters counterparts, must be well coached to recognize the importance of information about how their products are being used, as well as to recognize new translatable business opportunities. Once the opportunity is recognized, the headquarters marketing team should develop a marketing plan focused on serving the new segment. This plan should, of course, develop translation tools that expand on the distinctive features or competencies that make the offering the ideal choice in this new market, as well as further defining potential players in the market. These translation tools (data sheets for new product variations, examples of the "new business" application, press releases, collateral materials, etc.) should aid the field marketing team in implementing the translation of the innovation to new customers. Ultimately, should the new segment progress in a manner that the supplier's offering "owns" the market, customers automatically know the offering as the standard.

One barrier to discovering new segments that may have to be overcome is the resistance encountered from new customers who are wary of the marketer's prior relationship with one of their principal competitors. In markets with a few large players, success at one customer may not lead to success at another, even if the rational needs are similar. In oligopolies, players in the market often resist ideas and developments that have their beginnings at a direct competitor. This resistance can result from an extreme concern about proprietary information. If the offering is well tailored to the competitive need, the customer who is the target of the translation may be suspicious of the level and type of communications that take place between the suppliers and the first customer. Cultural and competitive factors can also play a large role. Some oligopolistic competitors avoid any sign of imitating major competitors, particularly if customers can discern who was "first" in the market.

Obviously, such resistance creates an additional burden on the field market development team or missionary sales force. Before they can assess whether a market segment can be developed, they must overcome the second customer's reservations. This is another reason for establishing a strong field market development organization so that the preparatory work for such translation efforts has already been done when the marketer decides it is time to attempt a translation.

Essential to the translation segmentation process and the missionary sales approach to market development is an understanding of the role of **field market development (FMD) personnel** and their relationship to direct sales, end users, and headquarters marketing personnel. This marketing effort requires a value-added or value-based price approach to be margin supportable. Suppliers whose offerings require significant customer education to take full advantage of the value offering will employ a field marketing team whose compensation and position structure enable the team to spend the time with customers in the education process. This is significantly different from the role of a direct sales team. As these issues relate to field sales and other aspects of business-to-business promotion, they are dealt with in greater detail in later chapters.

Summary of Segmentation

Two approaches to segmentation, the analytic approach and the translation approach, have been discussed. To review, the analytic approach seems to emerge when the marketer faces a market with many customers or when the marketer is looking to enter a new market in which his company has little or no experience. The analytic approach can be helped by introducing some elements of translation, particularly in developing in-depth information on value sought and buying behavior within segments. Translation can be helped by some analysis, as well. The marketer and the field missionary sales force may want to collaborate on gathering data from the field and on interpreting the data to suggest possible new market segments. This analysis may lead the missionary sales force to target high-potential segments even though these might not be the easiest for gaining initial access. Whether the marketer uses a process that is largely analytical or largely translation, the next step is to choose target segments.

CHOOSING TARGET SEGMENTS

Once segments are defined, the process of identifying the best opportunities for the organization begins. Of the segments chosen to address, the marketer may decide that one or a few should be targeted as primary, that is, they receive emphasis. To make these choices requires application of criteria in two stages. First, the marketer makes a judgment of how attractive each segment is; then a group of segments is chosen that allows organizational objectives to be met.

Attractiveness of Segments

Exhibit 7-6 shows the factors to be taken into consideration in determining the **attractiveness** of each segment. Notice that attractiveness is determined from information that comes from all the elements of an environmental analysis.

Attractiveness is obviously not a concept that can be easily quantified. Some organizations may want to allocate weights to the various factors and then assign attractiveness scores based on a qualitative assessment for each segment.

- Size of Segment
- Growth Rate of Segment
- Intensity of Unmet Need(s)
- Reachability of Segment through Communications Channels
- Readiness of Segment to Seek and Adopt a Solution
- Likelihood of Competitive Intensity
- Sufficiency of Channel Reach
- Likely Value Contribution by Channel(s)
- Match Between Segment Needs and Supplier's Strengths
- Differentiability of Supplier's Offering
- Opportunity to Achieve Strategic Goal by Addressing Segment
- Opportunity to Achieve Learning Goal by Addressing Segment

EXHIBIT 7-6 Factors in Assessing Segment Attractiveness

MARKET ATTRACTIVENESS   Segments that are large and growing fast are usually more attractive than smaller or slower-growing segments, all other things being equal. As part of the effort made in "knowing the market," the marketer can estimate the size and growth rates of various segments. At this point, qualitative judgments about the priority of needs as seen by the market segment are appropriate. In other words, how important is the marketer's offering when compared to the other opportunities or solutions under consideration by the customer? The answer to this may show up in the level of urgency displayed by the customer, whether or not the customer is willing to take the lead in a new development or application, and/or whether the customer is likely to outsource solutions to difficulties or develop its own solutions.

Boeing and Airbus are facing this kind of a question in considering the segment of the commercial airplane market for "superjumbos."[6] The question is not so much whether a market exists for super jumbos—jumbo jets with 500+ seats—but whether the market is attractive enough to warrant design of a completely new plane. Boeing believes that airlines will move away from the hub-and-spoke model that currently dominates air traffic routing patterns. It believes airlines will migrate to longer, direct routes, requiring mid-sized fuel-efficient planes. Hence, Boeing does not believe the segment is attractive enough to warrant a new super jumbo design. Airbus is counting on the hub-and-spoke to have staying power as a dominant model at least in the Middle East and Asia, so Airbus has proceeded with a super jumbo design.[7]

Early indications seem to bear out both interpretations of the market to some degree. Airbus has built a 555-seat new jet, the A380, which it first tested in 2005 and began to ship in limited numbers in the late 2000s (first few units in 2007).[8] By mid-2005, it had acquired commitments for over 100 aircraft, indicating that demand may be sufficiently high to warrant the $13 billion development effort. Boeing has seen orders for its venerable 747 passenger plane slow considerably (freighter versions do better) since 2000. To compete in the super jumbo market, Boeing modified the existing 747 to create a 450-seat "stretch" 747.[9] Meanwhile, preorders have been brisk for the Boeing 787 "Dreamliner," a 250-seat jetliner capable of flying nineteen hours nonstop, launched in 2009. Airbus has countered with its own mid-sized, long range jet, the A350. Early orders for the A350 have confirmed that this market segment is also probably viable.

However, there is still uncertainty left to resolve. For instance, in the market segment for super jumbo jets, the economic turmoil of 2008–2009 caused many airlines to cancel or renegotiate their orders. This economic upheaval, coupled with the technical and production problems that delayed introduction of all new products, illustrates the problems that many business-to-business marketers have in trying to anticipate the future. Time horizons are often so long—development work on the A380 began in the mid-1990s—that research data only provide a glimmer of what will occur.

Adaptability may be very important when considering market segments for a new product or service. If potential customers are able to easily adopt a new product or service because they already have in place the required infrastructure for adoption, they are more likely to act on an intention to buy. Related to this may be the existence of relationships with existing buying center members. Again, potential customers are able to act more quickly if the participants already understand their buying center roles and are used to fulfilling those roles.

Available budget also adds to attractiveness of a market segment. A prospective customer may indeed want the product, but, if the buying center cannot access available funds, the intention to buy may go unfulfilled.

COMPETITIVE ATTRACTIVENESS—CHOOSING YOUR BATTLES   A good competitive analysis will provide the marketer with information on the existence or likely existence of strong competition vying for business from segment members. The marketer must think ahead to how strong the competition is likely to be. Just because a competitor's offering to the market segment is currently weak does not mean that this will remain the case. Also, a market segment that is currently unaddressed by a competitor may be pursued vigorously once the competitor realizes there is potential in the market.

A segment is competitively attractive if there are significant barriers to entry for other competitors. For instance, suppose it is apparent that the first company to enter a market segment is likely to acquire critical mass of customers quickly, leaving little room for new competitors to enter. This market would then be competitively attractive to the first entry only, as the marketer should recognize the "first" in a market could create a substantial defense from competitive intrusion.

CHANNEL ATTRACTIVENESS   The ideal situation is to find segments that are not already served by well-established marketing channels, but could be addressed by channels that are looking for new business and can readily adapt. The channel power situation in such a case is favorable. The next best situation would be segments that are already addressed by existing channels, but in which no channel members are dominant. The marketer positions the new offering as a competitive advantage to the channel members. Two kinds of segments vie for the honor of *least* attractive: those segments for which no suitable channels address them currently and for which development of new channels would be difficult and those segments for which well-established channels exist with one or a few dominant channel members. The marketer will face a difficult power position in trying to access these segments through the dominant channel members.

When there are not any obvious suitable channels, a market view of competition is mandatory. Even when the offering is new to the market, customers will have already been satisfying the existing need with less than ideal solutions and may be in the habit of seeking these solutions through particular channels. The appropriate channel may be the one in which customers expect to find solutions rather than the channel that is readily accessible or available.

COMPETITIVE ATTRACTIVENESS—SUPPLY CHAINS AS A DISTINCTION   Integrated supply chains provide important value to final buyers. Supply chains create value in lower costs by mitigating the bullwhip effect. Also, if information is shared conscientiously within the supply chain, the right products can be developed and produced to fulfill final buyers' particular needs. Consequently, a company can provide distinctive value for customers by having a well-run, integrated supply chain.

As a product category matures, the cost, time, and place benefits provided by an integrated supply chain are likely to increase. Dell's supply chain allows it to customize computers for customers' specific desires and deliver them rapidly. This is typical of the kind of value that is sought by many market segments when the market is mature.

At first glance, a firm that produces and markets components or raw materials may seem to have limited need to understand segments among final buyers—the component supplier merely has to meet the product specifications, along with quality targets and delivery schedules. However, if the component supplier makes the effort to understand the final buyer segments, it may be able to find creative ways to meet the needs of the final buyer that had not been anticipated by the supply chain driver. The component supplier could then avoid the trap of supplying a standardized, undifferentiated product. The component supplier may also find other segments that could want similar component parts in the after market, thus creating a new opportunity that would have been otherwise ignored.

INTERNAL ATTRACTIVENESS—PLAYING TO YOUR STRENGTHS The marketer's environmental analysis identifies the company's current core competencies and those that it is building for the future. When a segment's most important needs can be met by using the company's core competencies, then the segment is more attractive. The Panasonic example at the beginning of the chapter illustrates this point. Panasonic was very good at creating sturdy portable computers. It also had proprietary technology for a touch screen interface. This interface proved to be very useful in field-use situations where ruggedness was also needed. Accordingly, Panasonic was well matched to the market segment it identified.

ATTRACTIVENESS—OTHER CONSIDERATIONS Other parts of the environmental analysis may lead the marketer to rate a segment higher or lower in attractiveness. The analysis of public policy, for instance, may lead the marketer to downgrade the attractiveness of a segment because meeting the segment's needs may encounter more government regulation. In the forestry industry, for instance, addressing a market segment focused on using high-quality wood for luxury interior designs may have become less attractive with more regulation that protects the high-quality wood found in old-growth forests.

The organization's goals may have a significant impact on how attractiveness is assessed. Suppose a company's goal is to be the leader in its industry. Then the segments addressed will probably either have to reach a minimal size or be the market leaders or market owners in the segments they serve. The industry also probably has one or more closely watched segments that reflect the health and direction of the industry. If a company wants to be recognized as the industry leader, it must participate in those segments, even if doing so is not particularly attractive strictly on profitability grounds. For instance, to be recognized as a leader in the automotive tire manufacturing industry, a company such as Goodyear or Michelin must be a major supplier of original equipment tires to vehicle manufacturers. Since this is a rather closed, oligopolistic market with significant entry barriers, some tire manufacturers, such as Cooper Tire, will not be recognized as leaders as they do not participate in the OEM market but focus on the second tier or aftermarket for replacement tires.

Choosing Targets

Once segments have been assessed for attractiveness, segments need to be chosen to target. If the marketer takes the analytic approach, a rational approach for choosing must be followed. If the marketer takes a translation approach, based on translating existing business, some analysis can aid in the selection of the next trial customer or customer type. In either case, the marketer needs to take a careful look at the objectives that he is attempting to meet. The choice of segments must at least allow those objectives to be met.

PROCESS FOR CHOOSING TARGET SEGMENTS ANALYTICALLY The main idea for choosing segments analytically is to start with the most attractive segments and to target as many as are required to assure that the organization will meet both financial and nonfinancial objectives. Most sets of objectives include a desired sales level and a desired growth rate in sales. The objectives include a profitability level and a growth rate for profits, as well.

Nonfinancial goals such as recognition as the market leader, learning about a line of business that is new to the company, reduction of risk by spreading the sources of revenue, or achieving synergy across other marketing programs may be relevant to the attractiveness of segments. The marketer should rank attractiveness by choosing the most attractive segment and any others that are relevant for special reasons such as those already noted. The marketer should then ask whether the company could meet its goals by targeting only these segments. If the marketer does not believe that the company stands a reasonable chance of meeting its objectives, the marketer should look to the next most attractive segment on the list. After adding this segment (or perhaps a group of related segments), the marketer should again determine the likelihood of meeting the stated objectives. This process should continue until the marketer is satisfied that the objectives will be met or until there are no more attractive segments.

Return to the example of the online customer satisfaction survey service. Exhibit 7-7 shows the factors contributing to the attractiveness of the four segments discussed earlier. The first three variables concern customer and market considerations. The next, competitive attractiveness, then channel reach and communications reach. All considerations having to do with the match between customer needs and company capabilities have been combined into one variable. An additional variable, sensitivity to price, has been added. For each variable, a score has been assessed on a 5-point scale, with 5 being most attractive and 1 being least attractive.

The scores are summed and listed at the bottom of the table. Notice that each variable was weighted equally. A marketer might weigh the variables differently depending on how important each is judged to be to the selection of target segments. Other variables could be applied as well, depending on the situation.

Attributes	Segments			
Scores on 5-Point Scale	Segment 1: Major Turnaround	Segment 2: Stopping Deterioration	Segment 3: Competitive Improvement	Segment 4: Specific Area Improvement
Potential size year 2010 (in $ million)	2 $195.0	3 $390.0	4 $585.0	4 $975.0
Growth, percent increase by 2012	4 100%	4 100%	1 (50%)	5 150%
Need strength	5	4	3.5	3.5 (High variance)
Competitive strength	3	3	4	3 (High variance)
Channel reach	5	5	5	5
Communications reach	4	4	4	4
Capability fit	2	5	5	2
Price sensitivity	2	3	4	3
Overall attractiveness (sum of attribute scores)	27	31	30.5	29.5

EXHIBIT 7-7 Segment Attractiveness for Hypothetical Example   *Source*: Based on Peter Doyle and John Saunders, "Market Segmentation and Positioning in Specialized Industrial Markets," *Journal of Marketing*, 49(2) (Spring 1985), p. 30, table format.

In this hypothetical example, the second segment receives the highest score, followed by the third segment, the fourth segment, and the first segment. To pick target segments, the marketer would first select the second segment, comprised of small businesses with deteriorating performance, whose managers are seeking a turnaround. The marketer would then compare the size of this segment to the company's objectives. Assume that the company is seeking $2 million in operating profits per year. If the company's operating profit margin on its products is typically 20 percent of the price paid by ultimate customers (assumed to be $5,000 in this case), then sales must be $10 million per year ($2 million divided by 0.2). The marketer compares the $10 million needed to the $390 million current market potential, which is expected to grow to $780 million within two years. What happens if the marketer is uncomfortable with the prospects of obtaining 2–3 percent of market potential during the first year of addressing this market segment? The marketer does not know how fast customers in this segment will adopt the new service and how quickly competition will enter the market. On the basis of prior product introductions, she may feel that 10 percent of the market potential is the maximum sales that will be realized in the first year of an early market. If competitors enter the market, the chances of reaching the target profit level may dissipate quickly as competitors take part of the business and price competition erodes margins. The marketer would then be left addressing only one segment and not reaching desired profit levels (even if sales levels are reached). Accordingly, the marketer would probably decide to address the next most attractive segment as well, the segment of small companies seeking to improve competitive performance. Together these two segments represent about $975 million in market potential for 2010 and $1.073 billion in 2012. The marketer would probably be much more comfortable that the objective of $10 million annual sales could be reached.

At this point, the marketer would probably stop adding segments to be targeted. Objectives are reachable with the targets already chosen. The other two segments, while attractive, still have some major drawbacks. Both the specific area improvement segment and the segment needing a major turnaround in customer satisfaction present problems in the fit with the company's capabilities. For whatever reasons, the marketer has scored this category as a 2. Given the offering that can be provided, the value that can be delivered will probably not satisfy these customers. Accordingly, in this hypothetical example, the company will probably target only the two most attractive segments.

Looking at the process again in general, if a marketer reaches the point at which there are no more attractive segments and objectives still appear unreachable, then the process reverts to an earlier decision point. The marketer may try defining segments differently in search of greater opportunities. Alternatively, the marketer may seek to change the objectives of the organization related to that particular market segment.

Changing objectives may be difficult if upper-level management is unwilling to alter the objectives. The part of this process that is most problematic may be assessing whether objectives can be met or not. At this point in the analysis and planning process, there is probably not enough information to do a good forecast of revenues, let alone of profits. There is probably a great deal of uncertainty in anticipating sales and profits that are likely from any given segment. Also, without a strategy and offering fully defined, it will be difficult to get an accurate idea of what market response the company can expect in each segment. Accordingly, this assessment will probably need to be done qualitatively by examining the market potential for each segment and by making reasonable assumptions about the level of market response and the costs involved. This analysis can be refined later, after more data are gathered about the segments chosen and after the offering is fully developed for each segment. The marketing operations forecast (Chapter 11) can provide significant insight to market conditions and the likelihood of succeeding with translations of the new offering.

It should be noted that the actual design, development, and commercialization of the total offering are taking shape at the same time as, and with significant input from, this market segmenting and targeting effort. This luxury—developing the offering as more is learned about specific target markets—is afforded only to those organizations that operate from a marketing concept. Organizations that develop a new offering from the point of view of their own needs and then look for customers to fit to the offering have no such luxury.

UNCERTAINTY AND TIME COMPRESSION—THE NEED TO USE ANALYSIS AND TRANSLATION TOGETHER   The problem in choosing target segments based on reaching these objectives is that we do not really know whether our best offering will meet the objectives. We do not know at this point in the analysis whether we can grow fast enough to reach target sales growth, sales levels, and profitability. To compound this problem, the marketer generally will not have enough time to perform the analysis necessary to remove the uncertainty.

A decision-making approach in which the marketer is somewhat confident must be used to make choices quickly and at least somewhat accurately. Whether an analytic approach or a translation approach, some conscious effort needs to be spent on choosing segments to meet goals if the outcome is to be good. We believe that either approach—analytic or translation—can be improved under conditions of heightened uncertainty and time compression by adding elements from the other approach. So, if a marketer gravitates toward the analytic approach, he will benefit from adding elements of translation into the choice of target markets. Similarly, if the marketer tends to use a translation approach, the choice of target markets will improve with the addition of some analysis into the process.

In the first instance, the marketer takes an analytic approach, but time compression does not allow much collection and analysis of data. It is also highly likely in fast-moving, emergent markets that the nature of likely competition will be largely unknown. So, it is not certain the extent to which competitive action in the segment will allow large market share or high profitability. Instead of trying to obtain more data when there is not much good data to be found, the marketer can make the targeting decision by choosing tentative target segments. This would probably involve more segments being targeted than might have been chosen otherwise. In addition, the strategy and offerings chosen may involve some investment in flexibility until results of the strategy implementation indicate which segments are likely to be better performers. The strategy would involve reassessment of segment attractiveness after six months or so. At that time, the company might invest more heavily in pursuit of some segments and pull out of others.

Suppose a marketer uses a translation approach. The company has developed a product that works for one large customer and is now looking to translate this business into other segments, usually within the same industry initially. A close look at which elements of value are best addressed in the relationship with the first customer—that is, by analyzing the value obtained by the first customer—may give some clues as to which types of customers or customer situations to look for as the next best translation. Then the translation process of the missionary sales force can be more closely directed in market segments that are more likely to bear fruit.

POSITIONING

For each target segment, the members of that segment will have one or more value dimensions that are most important to them and are likely part of the defining parameters of the segment. Recall that in the Panasonic case the targeted customers had "durability" as their most important value dimension. The marketer designs an offering for each segment that creates value for segment members, thus differentiating the offering from competitors. Panasonic created the

ToughBook, which is more durable than other laptops. Through **differentiation** and communication, the marketer attempts to obtain the segment members' perception that his offering is better than the competitors' on one or more key value dimensions. Panasonic used a combination of ads and other promotion to get across its message of superior durability. The perception that prospective customers (and existing customers, too) have of the competitive offerings, in relation to each other, is the positioning of the offerings. In the Panasonic case, customers see the Panasonic Toughbook as more durable than the competing brands.

Positioning, then, is foremost something that occurs in the mind of the prospect or the customer. Marketers attempt to influence this positioning, but, ultimately, it is the customer that creates "position." Marketers have very real limits on "positioning" their products and offerings. The potential customer's perception of position is influenced by many factors: articles in trade journals, discussions with other buyers, discussions with salespeople, advertising from all relevant competitors, presentations at trade shows, and product trials, just to name a few. Suppliers that are part of companies with multiple divisions may find that the positioning held by prospective customers has been set by another division whose products may be totally unrelated to the market in question. Initially, prospects will perceive the marketer's communications with a skeptical eye. Seldom would they consider the marketer an objective source of evaluative information about his own product. If credibility is required for the prospect to accept a communicated message, then the marketer must find ways to build that credibility.

The situation is somewhat different for the existing customer. Positioning ultimately depends on the customer's own experience with the product, the service, and all other dealings with the supplier and the supplier's agents (such as resellers). Communication can help the customer pay attention to important aspects of his experience. Communication can also help customers set expectations and interpret results of their usage of the product or service. In the end, though, customers' beliefs depend on the value they perceive that they have received; so, good positioning comes down to some very simple principles:

- Provide better value than competitors on one or more key dimensions of value, as perceived by your prospects and customers.
- Communicate the differentiation that you provide in such a way that the prospect and customer have high but reachable expectations.
- Deliver on your promises and occasionally find ways to surpass your customers' expectations.

These sound simple but, in reality, are difficult to execute. To be successful, marketers need to find what their companies do best and focus on building superior value from those strengths. The execution of this positioning begins with a **positioning statement** which is the succinct statement of the positioning the company hopes to achieve in the minds of its target customers.

FURTHER ISSUES IN SEGMENTATION, TARGETING, AND POSITIONING

The basics of segmentation are mostly straightforward; yet applying them is difficult because market structures are seldom simple. This complexity arises because business-to-business customers are trying to differentiate and adapt themselves to their own complex, changing markets. The business environment that both marketers and their customers face presents complexities and turbulent changes. When marketers develop segmentation frameworks, choose target segments, and develop their positioning strategies, they often have to adapt to this complexity and accommodate this turbulence. What follows is a discussion of two situations that influence marketers to think and act beyond the realm of simple, static segmentation.

Segmentation and Positioning Based on the Technology Adoption Life Cycle

As discussed in Chapter 2, propensity to adopt innovations underlies the new technology adoption curve.[10] Moore's ideas about propensity to adopt have implications for identifying segmentation, choosing target segments, and positioning. Moore suggests that business-to-business companies can divide their markets into adoption groupings, as presented in the box—"Adoption Categories in the Technology Adoption Life Cycle."

Moore observed that markets for innovations evolve in a regular pattern. The segments of adopters of an innovation—technophiles through laggards—enter a market in regular succession, one after another, and this succession drives the growth and evolution of that market. Early in the life cycle for a product category based on an innovative technology, buyers always come from technophiles and visionaries (innovators and early adopters in Rogers' terms). After visionaries have bought the product and the infrastructure has developed to support it, pragmatists begin to enter the market. Once the market has been established and specialized uses have emerged, the conservatives enter. Laggards may enter the market after prices have come down for specialized uses or costs of not adopting have risen so high that laggards can no longer afford not to adopt.

All of this suggests that a marketer who markets a product based on a technological innovation needs to have a sense of where the offering is located on the TALC. This will give clues to the kinds of segments to address in the marketer's near future.

When a marketer uses the TALC as a guideline for segmenting, targeting, and positioning, a strategy of innovation translation creates a focused process that identifies potential customer **niches**. This process must begin prior to reaching the "tornado"—the period of rapid growth in sales. Efforts to develop business from new customers—often called simply "business development"—based on a strategy of innovation translation, become important after the first adopters (the technophiles in the market) are satisfied. A major function of missionary sellers is business development, educating customers and assisting in the most productive application of the supplier's new technologies. Using the TALC as a guiding concept forces the marketers and business developers to think about how the market will evolve and how their efforts will influence the type of organization that the supplier designs to market the offering. As such, the organization and its responsibilities change

*A **niche** is a segment that is relatively small with fairly well-defined boundaries. The term is often used in a way that suggests that the niche can be served mostly or entirely by a single supplier.*

Adoption Categories in the Technology Adoption Life Cycle

Technophiles adopt the very newest technologies, just to try them out and experiment. These adopters do not require a fully developed product or offering.

Visionaries see the competitive advantages they can build in their organization with the new technology. They buy before the product or offering is standardized and require a custom offering built around the new technology.

Pragmatists want to gain competitive advantage through new technology, but will not buy until they believe the product is easily adopted with minimum upheaval. They will distrust the references from visionaries. They need a fully developed offering.

Conservatives tend to adopt only when it costs them not to adopt. They need to be convinced that the offering is exactly what they need.

Laggards will find reasons not to adopt, even when all evidence says they should.

as the offering evolves. The TALC and the adoption environment of the customer thus have significant impact on the design of business development efforts.

Positioning a Product Line

Product lines are groups of products that are sold together or that address similar market segments. For instance, a machine tool manufacturer[11] may have a line of products that perform related functions, such as tools for cutting sheet metal, stamping patterns or holes into the sheet metal, and shaping the sheet metal by bending or twisting. The same manufacturer may have different models of each tool, as well. At one end of the line may be machine tools with less throughput and fewer computer-controlled features. At the other end of the line may be high throughput, multifunction computer-controlled machine tools. These various models allow the tool manufacturer to address many different segments. In each segment, the buyers are looking to obtain machine tools that fabricate parts out of metal or plastic. However, the uses of the tools are different, requiring different combinations of features and differing purchasing criteria.

In most cases, the supplier will want to maintain consistency in the brand's image and positioning across most or all of the segments. There are several reasons for this. First, many of the competitors will be the same from segment to segment. Each of these will have fairly consistent strengths and weaknesses, allowing the supplier to occupy similar positions relative to these competitors in all the segments. Second, efficiencies can be obtained in product design, manufacturing, communications, training, service, and other elements if positioning is similar across all segments. Third, customers in closely related segments communicate with each other and pay attention to the same information sources. In many cases, the same buying center may be buying different products for differing situations: the people doing the buying are the same; the difference in the segments comes from the usage situation. Maintaining consistency in positioning across segments then makes it easier for customers to understand the supplier's position and to reinforce the positioning relative to each other. Indeed, many buying center members go to other companies in other segments as their careers progress. As they move from segment to segment, they take their beliefs along and expect suppliers to provide similar types of value from segment to segment. As long as all this "cross fertilization" is occurring, the supplier is wise to use it to advantage rather than create confusion.

When the supplying organization is multiproduct or multidivisioned, the overall corporate positioning strategy and how that relates to the positioning of a line of products must be considered. Product line positioning must be supportive of the corporate or brand positioning effort. In most cases, a supplier company will have a few value dimensions that are common differentiators for all its products. These usually derive from the company's distinctive competencies. For instance, the manufacturer of the machine tools may differentiate its products on lowest cost of ownership and flexibility in application. Obviously, this gives the manufacturer the opportunity to make this a common theme in its communications for the entire line of products (similar to Panasonic's use of durability as the common theme for its line of notebook computers).

In some cases, the supplier will want to establish a **flagship product**—a product in the line that is well known and conveys the positioning for the whole line. An example would be Hewlett-Packard's Laserjet printer for small business. The product produces high-quality output and is easy to use. The product name has become a brand name that extends over several models. This positioning has become a central theme for all of HP's laser printers, for its inkjet printers, and for its accessory products such as scanners, as well.

This approach is possible when an initial product has achieved notoriety. A company might establish a flagship product after the product line has been established, but this is more difficult to do. It requires the existence of a large segment that can be addressed by the flagship and a clear and enduring advantage that can be embodied by the product and its offering. If the advantage is transitory, the flagship will not obtain the credibility to assume the positioning mantle."

This discussion of product line positioning demonstrates the concept of market ownership noted by McKenna.[12] Setting a high standard, continuous innovation, thoroughly satisfying a particular niche market segment, and creating credible dominance are factors that help define ownership.

THOUGHTS TO TAKE WITH YOU INTO THE NEXT CHAPTER

The first part of this chapter discussed two approaches to determining segments—an analytic approach and an innovation translation approach. The analytic approach involves the use of secondary and primary research, plus the judicious application of informed assumptions. A marketer is most prone to use it when the market has many customers or when the marketer is entering a market in which he has little experience. The innovation translation approach involves efforts to find new segments based on translating an offering that has already been adopted by one or a few customers. It involves the use of missionary salespeople or business development specialists to look for and validate new market segments.

Once segments have been identified, the marketer chooses some of them to target. This is done by determining how attractive each segment is and then choosing the most attractive segments. Ideally, the marketer continues to add segments to the list of targets until he feels certain that the organization's objectives can be met. If the marketer does not reach such a point, then objectives or the segmentation framework needs to be rethought.

Once the target segments are determined, the marketer needs to determine the positioning for each. Ideally, the positioning for one segment should not conflict or undermine the positioning for any other segment. While the positioning effort is the responsibility of the marketer, the positioning result is in the mind of the customer. The marketer attempts to aid the customer in establishing this position in the customer's mind. The marketer does this by first making sure the offering delivers superior value to the targeted customers. Second, the marketer communicates a message to targeted customers that emphasizes the key dimensions of value that create the desired position relative to competitors.

As noted above in the final section of this chapter, markets are complex and ever-changing. The process of finding a segmentation framework, choosing target segments, and developing positioning is difficult to do well but rewarding when accomplished, as illustrated by Panasonic in the opening example.

Key Terms

accessibility *152*

actionability *152*

analytic approach (to segmentation) *155*

attractiveness (of segments) *160*

bases for segmentation *152*

differentiation *167*

field market development (FMD) personnel *159*

flagship product *169*

innovation translation approach (to segmentation) *159*

measurability *152*

niche *168*

North American Industry Classification System (NAICS) *155*

positioning *150*

positioning statement *167*

product line *169*

segmentation framework *150*

segmenting *150*

substantiality *152*

targeting *150*

Questions for Review and Discussion

1. Consider the following segmentation basis variables and note potential strengths and weaknesses of employing each in a segmentation framework:
   a. Demographics
   b. Technology
   c. Culture of technology adoption
   d. Perceived value subject to industry standards
   e. Point of technology adoption of the customers' customers.

2. How do the concepts of value and the value chain define how marketers should try to segment markets?

3. What is the difference between the analytic approach to segmentation and the innovation translation approach to segmentation?

4. What factors do you think will influence how strong the airlines' perceived need will be for super jumbo jets seating 600+ passengers in the year 2013?

5. Why would you say the market for super jumbo jets is a *market segment*, even though the customers—the airlines—are the same customers who also buy jumbo jets and other kinds of airliners?

6. In Exhibit 7-7, the last column of the table shows that there is a lot of variation in the strength of the need perceived by segment members and in the strength of competition in meeting functional improvement needs within this segment. Why

would these observations argue against choosing this segment as a target segment?

7. What should a marketer do if, in choosing target segments, he or she runs out of attractive segments to add to the list of targeted segments and it does not appear that objectives can be met?

8. Why can marketers only hope to influence positioning and not create it?

9. Compare the importance of positioning in business-to-business markets with positioning in consumer markets.

10. How is positioning an offering for new customers different from positioning for existing customers?

11. Explain why mass markets require offerings with fewer distinctions than niche markets.

12. What is the difference between a niche and a market segment?

13. How is McKenna's philosophy of market ownership, discussed in Chapter 2, reinforced by the TALC positioning strategies suggested in this chapter?

14. Define the business segments addressed and positioning of your business school or marketing program. What could your school do to change or improve your target segments chosen? Your positioning?

Endnotes

1. Whatever is the highest degree of "return" will be based on what the organizational goals are. These will not be the same for all competitors in a market, nor will they remain constant over time for each competitor.

2. Based on Geoffrey James, "Standing Tough," *Marketing Computers*, 20(3) (March 2000), pp. 34–42; Frank Tiboni, "Building Tough Notebooks" (sic), *Federal Computer Week*, www.fcw.com (May 17, 2004); Edward F. Moltzen and Mario Morejon, "Toughest Notebook Challenge—Trips, Drops and Spills, Oh My! Panasonic, Dell, Toshiba, and Acer Put Their Notebooks to the Test. Which One Survived?" *CRN* (1251) (October 15, 2007), p. 32.

3. Wendell R. Smith, "Product Differentiation and Market Segmentation as Alternative Marketing

Strategies," *Journal of Marketing*, 21(1) (July 1956), p. 4.

4. See Peter R. Dickson and James L. Ginter, "Market Segmentation, Product Differentiation, and Marketing Strategy," *Journal of Marketing*, 51(2) (April 1987), pp. 1–10; and John Berrigan and Carl Finkbeiner, *Segmentation Marketing* (New York: HarperBusiness, 1992).

5. See Peter Doyle and John Saunders, "Market Segmentation and Positioning in Specialized Industrial Markets," *Journal of Marketing*, 49(2) (Spring 1985), pp. 24–32, for an illustration.

6. Andy Reinhardt, John Rossant, and Frederik Balfour, "Boeing Gets Blown Sideways," *Business Week*, 16 (October 2000), p. 62.

7. Carol Matlack, "Mega Plane Airbus' A380 Is the Biggest Superjumbo Ever, and Airlines Have

Ordered More Than 120 Already. A Brilliant Leap, or a Great Folly?" *Business Week* (3857) (November 10, 2003), p. 88.

8. Kevin Done, "New Delay to Airbus A380 Jet Deliveries," *Financial Times* (May 14, 2008), p. 21.

9. James Gunsalus and Rishaad Salamat, "Boeing to Launch Stretched 747 to Fight Jumbo Airbus," *Chicago Sun-Times* (June 14, 2005), p. 58.

10. Geoffrey A. Moore, *Inside the Tornado* (New York: HarperCollins Publishers, Inc., 1995).

11. For the uninitiated, machine tools are those devices and equipment, usually capital items, employed by manufacturers that perform the mentioned functions on raw materials and components in the process of adding value. The products of machine tool manufacturers then are "the products that make the products."

12. Regis McKenna, "Marketing Is Everything," *Harvard Business Review* (January–February 1991).

Chapter 8

Developing the Product, Service, and Value of the Offering

OVERVIEW

In previous chapters, we discussed the context, market environment, and behavioral aspects of business-to-business markets. The elements of corporate and marketing strategy, and market research have been examined. Regard these facets of marketing as the tools of the trade. In this chapter you will begin to see how many of these elements pull together into a plan to develop and position the product and offering. The development process for new products and offerings is examined and positioning in the market is discussed as an integral part of the development process.

In the following examples, the focus is on product failures. Very large organizations still make mistakes in product development and commercialization. You may recognize some of the consumer products as "icons" of business failures, while the business-to-business failures may be more obscure. Regardless of the market, many of these examples, though complex offerings, are in hindsight a failure of one of the basic tenets of new product development. The examples start with, appropriately, the Edsel, an historic and probably the best-known product failure, albeit a consumer product. An old example by today's standards, the Edsel set a standard by which many other "failures" are measured. Every company, business-to-business or consumer oriented has had its Edsel. The Edsel is an icon.

The Best and the Brightest Still Have Product Failures

In August 1957, Ford Motor Company introduced a car to the American market from an entirely new division of the company—the Edsel. The vehicle was conceived as a mid-priced vehicle positioned above the Mercury but below the Lincoln, aimed at General Motors Buick and Oldsmobile line. The vehicle had been conceived in the early 1950s and developed through the middle of the decade. The mid-priced market was growing when it was conceived, but by the time the car was introduced, the economy had taken a dive. The mood in America was hardly upbeat. On the day that the Edsel was introduced, the Soviet Union announced that they had a missile that could reach America.[1] By the end of 1960, the Edsel was gone, never to effectively compete in a mid-priced market that evaporated with

173

the declining economy. The Edsel, a $350 million loss, in 1957 dollars, for Ford Motor Company, was to become an icon for failure. As early as the 1960s, a cartoon of the SST, the American response to the supersonic passenger aircraft, the Concorde, was shown, with an Edsel-like "horse-collar" grill, attempting to take off.[2]

Not to be outdone in the product failure game, in the 1960s RCA decided to take on IBM in the mainframe computer business. Codenamed "Project Intercept," the effort was the largest ever undertaken by RCA. In September 1971, after a loss of $500 million, RCA eliminated 8,000 jobs, backed away from an installed base of about 500 customers, and ended the computer effort. RCA stock rose on the news. The Edsel had been replaced, if not in the minds of consumers, at least in the dollars-lost competition.[3]

In the early 1980s, Apple Computer introduced the Lisa, a new desktop system aimed at business-to-business markets. Probably put off by its $10 thousand price tag and ineffective business-to-business channel, business users were not impressed and stuck with IBM, the established business supplier with the relationships and service they expected.

In an attempt to translate success in business-to-business markets into the consumer market, IBM introduced the PCjr. The classic IBM keyboard, once the standard by which others were measured, was not included. Instead, the "Chiclet" keyboard, with oval, rocking keys was the standard. Also, the computer was not expandable—a benchmark feature of previous IBM desktop computers. Dead wrong for the market, this product cost IBM $100 million. A pittance.

In 1981, Xerox, the recognized owner of the office copier market, introduced the Star System—a desktop computer system that used little graphic images as symbols of functions and a small palm-sized device to move the curser around the monochrome screen. The system received little support—after all, Xerox was a copier company. Who could be bothered with a "little" computer with a graphical user interface and that silly mouse to navigate around those little images?

New Coke, DuPont's leather substitute Corfam, RCA videodisc players, the Susan B. Anthony dollar coin (even the U.S. federal government competes in the product failure competition), the Apple Newton, WebVan,—the list goes on. How do so many companies with access to the best resources create such money losers?

LEARNING OBJECTIVES

By reading this chapter, you will:

- Understand the importance of customer and supplier involvement in the development of new offerings.
- Know the role of marketing in the development process, particularly in a market-driven firm, as the source of direction and definition.
- Recognize the concept of the value network as a powerful tool in creating market ownership.

INTRODUCTION

Each of the product failures noted in the opening example has an element of marketing failure associated with it. Whether an obscure business-to-business product that few consumers have heard of or a well-known icon of failure, research has shown that the largest single reason for the failure of new products and services in the marketplace is a lack of a thoroughly developed and executed marketing plan.[4] In this chapter we look at the relationship between technology, products, and marketing. Note that, in the marketplace, customers seek solutions, not technologies or products. Offerings are perceived by the value they deliver, not by the specific technology that makes them work. We will see, however, that products, technology, and marketing are significantly woven together in business-to-business markets.

Business-to-business marketing organizations are influenced by the technology of the products they offer and the longevity, or survival, of that technology in the market. Succeeding technologies as well as multiple product life cycles (PLCs) must be measured and planned to ensure the ongoing nature of the organization. While at first glance, a particular technology may be viewed as the mainstay of an organization, long-run successful organizations recognize that the customer acquires the technology for its solution value, not for the technology itself. This view can be difficult to accept among members of a technology-based organization who are proud of their technical accomplishments and believe that the technology is the key to their success. The supplying organization then must recognize the value that the technology provides *from the customer view.*[5] A supplier's new product development should focus on the market of the customer, not the current product or product line of the supplier.

THE PRODUCT LIFE CYCLE

The generalized product life cycle, shown in Exhibit 8-1 (modified slightly from Exhibit 2-4) is useful as a device to relate many concepts of marketing. Life cycle management makes some basic assumptions about offerings.[6] These assumptions vary from the generalized case depending on changes in the market environment and the pace of innovation:

- All products and offerings have a limited life.
- All products pass through different stages of evolution. For each of these stages, there is an idealized marketing mix that best fits the environment in that stage when the life cycle is viewed from the viewpoint of a product category.
- The different stages offer the organization different opportunities and threats, and market segmentation and targeting should reflect the changes.
- Profits vary over the life cycle, contributing to the need to modify the marketing mix. Profits classically peak in the late growth–early maturity time frame.

With our understanding of business-to-business markets and market environmental factors, let us consider the implications of these assumptions.

In markets that are slow to change, accepted products have longer periods of viable application, passing through the stages more slowly. Basic commodities fit the generalized life cycle with a greatly elongated maturity phase, potentially many years long; while products in fast-paced markets, such as computer processors, experience a full life cycle in a much shorter time span.

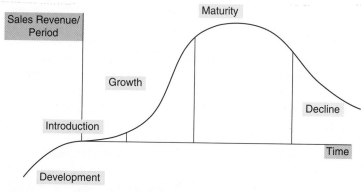

EXHIBIT 8-1 The Product Life Cycle

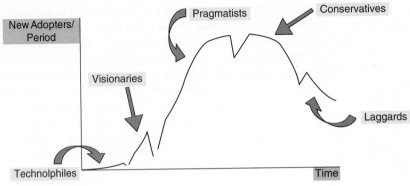

EXHIBIT 8-2 The Technology Adoption Life Cycle

Within market segments, products and services evolve through the use of new technologies, materials, and manufacturing methods. This may not change the functionality of the product offering but may change the costs to provide it. New technologies are accepted at a different pace by different market segments. This can cause discontinuities such as those demonstrated by the technology adoption life cycle, Exhibit 8-2, repeated here for convenience from Exhibit 2-5.

THE PRODUCT LIFE CYCLE AND LIFE STAGES OF OFFERINGS[7]

The generalized marketing mix implications of the PLC, familiar to many students, are discussed here. Within this framework, this discussion is treated from the view of business-to-business offerings. Note that, as shown in Exhibit 8-1, *five* stages of the PLC are considered: development, introduction, growth, maturity, and decline. Also note that, while in Exhibit 8-1 a line distinguishes all borders between stages except the development–introduction boundary, these transitions are more likely to be "fuzzy" in application, which will be discussed in detail later.

Offering Development Stage

*The marketing mix in the **development stage** requires some attention. The product is not completely defined, and profits do not exist; though a target price or value point is being considered. Promotion, beyond the selling effort at the customer, may be oriented toward publicity about technological development. If the product development is a result of a significant collaboration with the customer and involves elements that the customer considers proprietary, the customer will have a voice in any promotional efforts.*

While not always shown in exhibits of the PLC, the **development stage** as shown provides a visual reminder of the complexity and potential need for collaboration in the development of new offerings. During this period, the organization spends R&D, prototyping, field testing, and trial use resources (dollars, personnel, opportunity costs, emotional investment, and etc.) to prepare the offering to correctly address the customer need. This investment does not necessarily end with the introduction of the offering. Realize, too, that revenues may actually begin before the development stage is completed. Very often, a supplier developing a product will obtain a development partner to help defray the development costs. In other cases, a supplier may take "pre-orders" before the completion of the final product. In most cases, these revenues do not fully offset the development costs, so the net income is still negative.

Depending on the degree of customer involvement in the development, a specific introduction time for the offering may not exist. If the development is a mutual effort of both the customer and the supplier, as is often the case in business-to-business markets, inclusion into the customer's product may occur before introduction to the general market. This can be the result of an agreement in which the customer has exclusive rights to the offering early in its life or, perhaps, the result of other potential users developing a wait-and-see attitude toward a new technology.

With high-learning products, those that require the customer to rethink current practices and/or take on new manufacturing techniques (such as disruptive innovations—see Chapter 9), the supplier may spend significant resources developing the training and education of customers at many levels. The customer's manufacturing operations need to learn the techniques and nuances of the new offering and the customer's product service organization may require training to adequately satisfy field service requirements. Potentially, all elements of the buying center may require a break-in period to make using the new offering a routine event. The corresponding elements of the supplier value chain become a major part of the training process as different portions of both organizations adapt to the new situation.

Unlike education and training of various parts of the customer organization as described for high-learning products, low-involvement or low-learning products are more likely to follow a more traditional path. Resource commitments to training will likely end at the start of the product introduction stage of the PLC, the assumption being that, for low-learning products, the customer and the general market will adapt more quickly.

Offering Introduction Stage

Many decisions about the offering (its flexibility for translation to other market segments, the ability to incorporate additional product attributes in future versions, the commitment of manufacturing resources, and etc.) are made through the development stage and into the introduction stage of the PLC. The **introduction stage** of the PLC is one of low sales volume for reasons on both sides of the supplier–customer relationship, and many of these factors become key elements in how the new offering is positioned in and priced to the market. During this stage, the supplier experiences the growing pains of commercial manufacturing and/or mainstream involvement as a member of the customer supply chain—often a major part of the new offering. If many of the elements of the new offering have been outsourced or are the result of a **unique or first time value network**, the logistical process experiences a significant learning curve. The customer faces the same learning curve as it incorporates the offering into its operations.

Contextually, the management of the supplying organization must make a conscious decision about market ownership. If the new offering is consistent with previous offerings in that it is the next generation that satisfies an evolving need in the market, then the concept of market ownership[8] is likely recognized and pursued.

If the offering is independently developed in full or partial isolation from the potential customer base, and presents a high-learning situation to the market, early users are limited to innovators or technophiles who are willing to accept change and are attracted to innovation. Under these circumstances, price strategy is more about positioning in the market than about profitability. Certainly, price should not be dictated by early manufacturing or delivery costs. During the

*During the **introduction stage**, profits are negative or, at best, break through to the positive side near the end of the stage. The product is somewhat basic, as competition has yet to force a need for differentiation. Price and positioning are strongly related. Promotion is used to build awareness, and distribution is necessary for other than large OEM customers.*

*Just as members of the customer organization must learn about the new product, supplier personnel also must understand any new portions of the value network. If, in the development process, designers in the supplying firm elect to outsource elements of the product in a different manner than previous offerings, a **unique or first time value network** is created, associated with the new offering. Members of the new value network experience a learning curve as they may not have delivered an offering to this particular customer as a part of this team before.*

introductory stage, profits are unlikely or may break through to the positive side. This is dependent on many factors, not the least of which is how the pricing scenario is expected to play out through the life cycle as well as the potential threat of competition in the market.

During the introduction stage, promotion is used to "announce" the offering. If the development was the result of collaboration with a customer, then promotional tools that feature the customer's use of the offering, with the customer's consent, are appropriate. If the product is an innovative effort and the customer owns its market, promotion certainly wants to build awareness among other members of that market. Field marketing (missionary sales) efforts should be focused in this area. With low-learning offerings, it may be appropriate to use sampling to encourage trial.

During the introductory stage, the place element of the marketing mix is influenced by whether the offering is collaboratively developed and introduced or it is an individual development. If it is a collaborative effort between supplier and customer in an OEM relationship, product distribution and channel design have likely been part of the development process. As the innovated offering is translated to other users and market segments and the market "knows" the product, additional marketing channels or supply chains evolve to meet the needs of new adopters. Late majority or conservative adopters who are not likely to have the learning needs or volume to justify a missionary or direct sales effort will seek channels more likely to provide inventory and ordering convenience.

In circumstances in which the product does not have a pre-established customer or is not the result of a collaborative effort (likely a low-learning product), the development of distribution channels by the supplier, targeted at potential market segments, may be the only means of product delivery.

*In the **growth stage**, profits increase rapidly as new customers accept the product. More adopter categories accept the offering. The need for product differentiation becomes apparent, as competitors seek to distinguish offerings. Market penetration pricing may be appropriate as competition puts pressure on high margins. Distribution channels, particularly for low-learning products, become important in the training and education of customers. Promotion is used to remind and reinforce purchase decisions.*

Offering Growth Stage

The good news in this stage is that the target market has accepted your new offering. The bad news is that success usually attracts competition, and your organization must get through the transition from introduction to growth or, as described by Moore, cross the chasm.[9] Recall that in Chapter 5 we developed an analogy between the stages of the PLC and the stages of the growth-share matrix. The transition to the growth stage is not unlike the successful development of a *question mark* into a *star.* As with a star, significant investment is required to grow with the market, including the investment required to keep ahead of new competitive entries, meet new supply and manufacturing demands, and meet price challenges to the value position of the product.

An offering that grows from the introduction stage to the **growth stage** crosses several boundaries. The early majority (Rogers) or pragmatists (Moore) have accepted the product, economies of scale in manufacturing may be necessary, product differentiation will now require distinctive attributes, and profits are rising.

PRODUCT ACCEPTANCE   When a product enters the growth stage, it is an indication that the market recognizes and accepts it as a legitimate proposition. Customers who had taken a wait-and-see approach (i.e., pragmatists) now recognize that benefits outweigh the risks associated with use of something new. Often, in business-to-business markets, the new product has been incorporated into the offering of a competitor of the pragmatist and the market has recognized the increased value. The pragmatist must now play catch-up with the visionaries. The pragmatist may seek a way to leapfrog (i.e., jump ahead of) competition through application of the next generation of evolutionary product. A supplier firm should anticipate the business opportunities present in these situations with next-generation offerings that capitalize on the learning curve of the original innovative offering.

PRODUCT DIFFERENTIATION   The next version of the offering may very well be offered by your direct (new or otherwise) competitor. Market entry, including the development of additional attributes is easier for the competitor. While it may not be known as the market owner, the competitor has a competitive offering that costs less to develop (they piggy-backed on your development curve); the offering likely is differentiated from your offering with features and attributes, though still compatible with your established standard; and the competitor has a proven market.

At this point, total offering attributes become increasingly important. The relationship that the innovative firm has with the technophile or visionary customer base contributes to market ownership—the reputation for innovation has value in the marketplace. Warranties, services, design assistance to incorporate the offering into customers' products, and experience in the market segment all add to the value of the offering.

ECONOMIES OF SCALE   Success in the growth stage is as dependent on the ability to supply in large quantity as it is on the acceptance of the offering in the marketplace. Recall that business-to-business demand is leveraged and volatile. The rapid growth of sales in the growth stage is not the result of many small users accepting the offering, as it would be in consumer markets. Growth is likely the result of the business-to-business customer specifying the new product for inclusion in its own offering. This specification creates a sudden jump in volume coincident with the start of production by the customer of its new product. The existing manufacturing capacity, style, or culture of the innovator may not be able to handle the resultant increase in volume.

To further examine the complexities of this situation, consider the PLC for silicon pressure sensors as described in the following example.[10]

As a major innovator and developer of the micromachining process, Sensacon Corporation has successfully developed a growing market for the micromachined pressure sensor. Sensacon, a high-technology, start-up operation, has begun to deliver on the profitability promises that management made to investors. By avoiding large-scale manufacturing, fixed costs were kept relatively low throughout the introductory period. Sensors were etched and assembled without much automation. Labor was added or reduced through the use of an agency that provided skilled temporary assembly workers. Users of the sensors were technology oriented themselves, and volumes were such that the inconsistencies that resulted from hand assembly could be adjusted in the users' operations. Sensacon's annual production was in the range of 5,000 units. Most applications of the sensor had been in self-contained under water breathing apparatus (SCUBA) diving equipment used to measure pressure underwater and in medical devices used to measure blood pressure.

The Sensacon breakthrough came when the sensor was selected for use in an automatic tire pressure monitor. Automobile and truck manufacturers had been looking for a cost-effective system to monitor tire pressures for some time, and the controversy over tire failures on SUVs had prompted two manufacturers to specify systems for all of the SUVs they produce. The combined volume of the two companies was forecast to reach over one million vehicles. With four sensors on each vehicle, the sensor volume would be over four million units. Sensacon had been selected to supply approximately 50 percent of this volume. The remaining volume was divided up among three competitors. Sensacon *monthly* sales volume at the start of tire monitor production would exceed the most recent *annual* volumes experienced by the company and was expected to reach an annual rate of approximately two million units. Initial shipments were to begin in six months. Sensacon employees and investors were ecstatic.

To be sure, the SUV manufacturers did not select Sensacon automatically. Competitors were entering the sensor market as the potential profitability was a very attractive lure. Sensacon executives were aggressive in the price to the SUV manufacturers as they wanted to establish a leadership position in this new market segment. Recognizing the newly arrived competition, Sensacon had started development of the next-generation offering, SensorSUV. The aggressive price to the manufacturers did not concern Sensacon as it was believed that the experience curve combined with economies of scale in manufacturing would create the necessary low-cost position to enable profits at the aggressive price.

About three days after the new contract was announced, manufacturing management attempted to scale up production of the existing sensor. In anticipation of a production tryout, additional space had been leased and temporary workers were added to the regular workforce. Unfortunately, even with added automated etching and manufacturing for the brass enclosure and increased facilities and labor, the tryout could not meet anywhere near the volumes hoped for. In addition, the part-to-part variability of the sensors was outside of the SUV manufacturers' specification. While Sensacon technology was up to the challenge, its manufacturing was not.

A task force of key Sensacon personnel was assembled. It soon became obvious that the sensor would have to undergo a complete redesign to enable high-volume manufacturing. The necessary changes in the sensor included redesign of the sensor itself for automated handling and machine insertion into the enclosure; redesign of the enclosure and investigation of new materials, like plastics, to replace the brass enclosure; new manufacturing expertise in high-volume plastic molding and assembly; and new high-volume, production-capable sealing techniques to protect the sensor core from the environment. Sensacon management began the search for a qualified independent contract manufacturer. Hoping to eventually develop its own capabilities later in the contract period, immediate time pressures from customers did not allow Sensacon the luxury of developing its own high-volume manufacturing facility.

Concurrent with the revelation that a significant product redesign is necessary, Sensacon is overwhelmed with inquiries from its new customers. Contract and procurement provisions, supply chain requirements, as well as a significantly more complex and larger buying center have exceeded Sensacon organizational capabilities. The staff that served a small number of healthcare and SCUBA equipment manufacturers is unable to serve the new customer base.

In this example, the impact of the new business extends not only to manufacturing and product design but to the culture of Sensacon as well. Once a small specialty product company, Sensacon now must redesign itself organizationally. Crossing into the growth stage can be traumatic.

Offering Maturity Stage

Offerings that move from the growth stage to the **maturity stage** often have become "standards" in business-to-business markets. While manufacturers work to maintain distinctions from their horizontal competitors, the market owner is already beginning the replacement of the offering with the next-generation product. This is not, however, to say that maturity is an undesirable stage of the life cycle. In terms of the growth-share matrix analogy, a business in maturity is a cash cow for the successful market participant and is often capable of generating significant cash for development of other opportunities.

During early maturity, profits may continue to rise slightly and the competitors who are now in the market have **economies of scale**. Proliferation of new product versions previously experienced in the growth stage usually declines and, depending on the market circumstances, domestic manufacturers may be faced with foreign competition. Because competitors have economies of scale and the market is no longer growing as it had been, price becomes a more important part of the marketing mix as manufacturers attempt to keep their facilities operating at the most profitable volumes. Promotion stresses the reliability and reputation of the supplier as well as unique product attributes. When overall sales stop growing, if any one participant in the market desires increased sales it will have to come at the expense of another participant.

Recall that business-to-business demand is more volatile than consumer demand. This places added pressure on markets in the maturity stage. Early adopters of the initial product begin to replace it in their next-generation product with newer generations of the offering or, quite possibly, new offerings with significantly different capabilities. Suppliers must continue after the customer's initial specification and purchase to make the entire relationship routine so that they are already in a collaborative role when the product they supply is upgraded or replaced by the customer design process.

During maturity, marketing may focus on protecting market share. While this is a desirable strategy in the short term, it is not a substitute for innovation and self-initiated offering development and replacement programs. Sales volume lost as old customers (pragmatists and early majority) discontinue use and move to newer offerings is not replaced by conservative or late majority adopters. Sales volume declines rapidly during this period unless business lost (core churn) is replaced by new business or translations of other successes.

*During the **maturity stage**, profits will have peaked and competition may begin to fight over market share. Promotion is used to reinforce buying decisions and often focuses on supplier reputation and value. Distribution efforts intensify to reach all possible subsegments of the market. New customers will not replace the volumes lost as old customers move to newer offerings. Price is a major part of the marketing mix.*

Offering Decline Stage

As an offering transitions to the **decline stage**, less-productive or weaker competitors drop out of the market, either through consolidation or by leaving the industry. A few competitors with highly efficient manufacturing capabilities or large commitments to customers may actively seek acquisition of the other players. For those competitors that remain in a declining market, efforts become focused on keeping manufacturing facilities running at productive utilization rates. Price, particularly associated with long-term contracts, becomes a major part of the marketing mix. The product line is reduced to minimize production variation and improve economies of scale. Promotion is generally reduced to minimal levels necessary to maintain existing customer communications.

*When an offering or business enters the **decline stage**, promotion is reduced to the minimal levels that will accommodate existing customers. Consolidation usually occurs among suppliers, and price becomes a major part of the marketing mix.*

Depending on the circumstances of the company, a business in decline is often viewed as a dog and is either harvested or divested.

PRODUCT ELIMINATION CONCERNS   In theory, an ongoing business works to develop the next-generation offering in its market. A decision to eliminate an existing product in decline has implications beyond the immediate profitability of the product. (Chapter 11 discusses management of multiple products at different points in the PLC, particularly as related to market ownership.) New products replace the declining revenue from a product at the end of its life. Not a simple financial decision, eliminating a product can have an impact not just on the organization, but on the organization's customers as well. The product elimination decision should be examined through the view of all stakeholders; customers, ancillary products and services of the organization, and the likely replacement of the offering with a new product.

Some customers may be dependent on the product. If the selling organization is determined to eliminate the product from its portfolio, discussion with existing customers must include assurances of supply for their needs. If the relationship has been one of mutual development, a replacement product has been anticipated and the assurance of supply will be for a specific period of time while the new offering ramps up. If no replacement product is anticipated and the customer relationship is jeopardized, there are some choices:

- The seller can divest of the product, introducing the existing customer base to the acquiring organization. This provides an assurance of supply to the customer and can increase the value of the acquisition to the acquiring firm.
- The seller can sell the business to the customer.
- The seller can introduce the customer to the remaining suppliers (likely to have been the sellers' competitors) in the market for the eliminated product. As unlikely as this seems, it can assist the selling organization with the overall ongoing relationship with the customer.

A primary concern is to eliminate the product without eliminating the customer relationship.

BASIC NEW PRODUCT DEVELOPMENT PROCESS

Most readers are probably familiar with the basic concepts of the steps of the new product development (NPD) process. To review, the stages and a brief explanation of the traditional NPD model follow:

STAGE 1: IDEA GENERATION   New ideas come from many sources. The organization must collect these and bring them to consideration, at least periodically. Ideally, an organization operating under the marketing concept looks to customer needs for new product ideas. Unfortunately, this is not always the case, though in business-to-business markets, the highest percentage of new product ideas originates with customers.[11] This should not be a surprise when the relationship-based nature of the organizational buying process is compared to the consumer process. The business-to-business marketer is much closer to the needs and wants of the customer and more able to anticipate the customer need for new offerings and solutions.

STAGE 2: PRODUCT SCREENING   A select, multidisciplinary team reviews descriptions of potential projects to determine those that warrant continuation. While business literature provides several models for the makeup of the team, the primary concern is to select members who are at ease with change. Each new product idea usually needs a product champion, intrapreneur, or evangelist to successfully get beyond this second stage.

Criteria for screening new ideas generally include the nature of the opportunity weighed against the organization's capabilities and the expected costs. A "ballpark" estimate of market needs and the capability of the new idea to meet those needs is performed.

most important step !

STAGE 3: BUSINESS CASE ANALYSIS   Ideas that survive the second stage must have the business plan developed more fully. The business plan must have both a market and a technical assessment. Later in this chapter, we discuss the high failure rate of new projects that do not have a complete market assessment associated with the business plan. The probable revenues and costs are analyzed to determine the likely financial contribution of each project. If it appears likely that minimum financial targets will be met, the project continues. The organization begins to consider additional attributes that will comprise the total offering.

When products are the result of collaboration between supplier and customer, the initial market application is usually assured. The design process integrates the product into the offerings of the customer. If the collaborative nature of the product has led to a design considered proprietary by the customer, the supplier may be limited from taking the product or its technology to other potential customers, at least for a period of time. Should this occur, translation to other customers and segments is delayed and the business case analysis must consider that the product is a custom design for one customer, at least for the specified time period.

Information for estimates: Note that all of the information required to make a good go/no-go decision is not immediately available to marketers. Inputs from other parts of the organization, accounting and finance, manufacturing, and so on, are an integral part of the decision. This is easier in a market-driven organization where all parts of the company recognize the need for change. Marketers often must "market" new product development efforts in their own organization—often a major responsibility of the marketing team.

STAGE 4: PRODUCT/STRATEGY/PLAN DEVELOPMENT   In this stage, after the business analysis has shown a justifiable case for further expenditures, the product technology is further developed and refined. Meanwhile, the product's strategy and implementation plans are developed. The market assessment developed as part of the previous stage becomes the starting point for the detailed marketing plan. The ability to have several levels of offering, depending on customer need, may be considered at this point.

In many business-to-business product development efforts, the collaboration between supplier and customer results in a custom product unique to the needs and circumstances of the customer. The scenario under which this collaboration operates is one in which the supplier performs most of the R&D while the customer provides input to the operational needs of the product, testing various iterations of it in the process. The outcome of this effort is a well-defined product specification written by the customer that is well matched by the custom offering of the supplier. The early collaboration is advantageous to both customer and supplier. The customer is assured of the full understanding and cooperation of the supplier. The specification, influenced by the collaborating supplier, is written to the supplier's competencies and technologies. Competitors must be willing to match the specification as an "or equivalent" offering.

STAGE 5: TEST MARKET   If the new product is intended for a broad market rather than the result of a collaboration with a specific customer, a limited release of the early product is trial launched in a "beta" test or the final product is released into limited markets or with selected prime customers. The purposes for doing these full-scale tests is to fine-tune the product, fine-tune the strategy, build the market's early awareness, and get final feedback on the product's viability in the marketplace.

Basic New Product Development Process

Stage 1: Idea Generation

New ideas come from many sources. Ideally, an organization operating under the marketing concept looks to customer needs for new product ideas.

Stage 2: Product Screening

A select, multidisciplinary team reviews descriptions of potential projects to determine those that warrant continuation.

Stage 3: Business Case Analysis

Ideas that survive the second stage must have the business plan, including both a market and technical assessment, developed more fully.

Stage 4: Product/Strategy/Plan Development

The product's strategy and implementation plans are developed.

Stage 5: Test Market

If the new product is intended for a broad market, a limited release of the early product is trial launched.

Stage 6: Product Launch

Promotion efforts aimed at target markets may be used to create awareness, interest, and early trials.

Stage 7: Hand Off to the Innovation Translation/Customer Education Team

With a high-learning or custom product, significant missionary effort is required to assist the customer base in achieving maximum value from the offering.

Proprietary disclosure agreements aid both the supplier and the customer. Customers working with suppliers in development of new products want assurance that the supplier is not taking any product or market information to competitors. With this assurance of nondisclosure from suppliers, customers are able to exchange proprietary data during the development process. In reciprocation, suppliers are often assured of receiving 100 percent of the business for a period of time. Suppliers are aided by disclosure agreements as they allow the supplier to be on the cutting edge of offerings in its customers' markets. After the agreed-upon period of time, the supplier may translate the product application to other potential customers.

In most business-to-business collaborative relationships, the summary in the previous paragraph is not a likely scenario. If the offering is the result of an ongoing relationship with a major customer, the first-use testing is limited to that customer. As noted earlier, there may be proprietary customer features that have been incorporated into the offering. The customer organization may have objections if features of its new product, contributed by the supplier product, become known to the market prior to market introduction. While some collaborative efforts include **proprietary disclosure agreements**, many collaborations are less formal. Suppliers should proceed with any market testing or awareness efforts with extreme caution. Inadvertently disclosing the product plans or technology of a customer can lead to an end of a business relationship.

STAGE 6: PRODUCT LAUNCH   If the new product is intended for a broad market, it is fully released once all the fine-tuning is complete. Promotion efforts aimed at target markets may be used to create awareness, interest, and early trials. Depending on the degree of newness to the market (from a market perspective), the education portion of the marketing plan should begin just prior to the launch. A public relations effort coordinated with the preparation of articles and features in technical journals should be considered as a start of the customer education process.

If the new product is a customized, collaborative effort with a particular customer an introduction to the market is still possible. The timing of such an introduction, however, should be determined by the launch of the customer's product and be done with the customer's concurrence. A well-timed and targeted promotional effort that features the customer's offering should be well received by the customer. A premature promotional effort has all of the same risks as those discussed for beta test fine-tuning.

STAGE 7: HAND OFF TO THE INNOVATION TRANSLATION/CUSTOMER EDUCATION TEAM Once market introduction is complete, full-scale customer education can begin. With a high-learning or custom product, significant missionary effort is required to assist the customer base in achieving maximum value from the offering. Utilizing the **innovation translation approach** to segmentation (discussed in Chapter 7), marketers attempt to translate the success to other potential customers.

With low-learning products or those introduced to a broad market, customer education efforts are not as extensive. Because of the more rapid adoption of the low-learning product by the market, product management specialists become involved more quickly.

*The **Innovation translation approach** is used to validate a new market segment. When new business is realized as a result of collaboration with a customer, the product is a customized offering. Translation to other potential customers validates the existence of the market segment. Without this process, the new business is an isolated application of the design and development efforts of the supplier. Translation activities are usually the responsibility of missionary sellers or market development specialists. Chapters 7 and 11 discuss the translation approach in greater detail.*

Customer/Market Orientation

There are generally two approaches to effectively developing new products or services. One way is to focus on the technology or the product first. In this approach, the product is developed with little or no customer input and introduced to the market. The second way is to extensively involve existing and prospective customers throughout the process. It would appear that these are two ends of a continuum. However, the amount of customer input usually represents a philosophy. An engineering-driven philosophy tends to minimize customer input; a customer orientation tends to maximize it.

This is not to say that the first approach is entirely without merit; this approach has many supporters (if only by accident), particularly in high-technology organizations. In many circumstances, a customer orientation resides just below the technology-oriented surface or can be adapted to it. Consider this example: Suppose members of an engineering team require a particular type of design software but cannot find a suitable vendor. The alternatives are to settle for what is available or develop the software themselves. The internal development leads to recognition that they are not the only engineering team that has a need for such software. Members of the team split away from the original engineering group and start their own company to provide such software. These engineers have been customer oriented, even if they are not likely to recognize it! Though they have not performed any extensive market analysis, they have discovered other potential users for the software. As long as there are other potential customers like themselves, they understand customers already. Unfortunately, this is not likely to lead to translation of the innovation to other market segments. The narrow focus of a technology or engineering approach can often ignore other potential markets, leading to what some critics have called an incestuous or closed market.

It is critical for the engineer or entrepreneur to maintain a customer-oriented approach when new markets are addressed. One of the comments we hear most often from business-to-business marketers is about the frustration they experience in dealing with engineering staffs that have little, if any, customer focus. We have also experienced this with many technically oriented students. Ironically, many first-time marketers that are initially product driven become customer oriented over time. This transformation can occur suddenly and with some difficulty when a product is unsuccessful and the responsible marketers decide to talk to potential customers to see what went wrong. Under severe time pressures, marketers that believe they are customer oriented may purposely launch a new product with little customer input, just so they can get something quickly into the marketplace. After launch, which is typically small in scale, they obtain a great deal of feedback from users and nonadopters. They quickly come out with succeeding versions of the product. Each version more closely conforms to the desires of prospective customer market segments. This approach may be used in emerging markets where little is known about how customers will react to the new product. Competitors have not yet emerged, so there is some time for quick adaptation. Perhaps market segmentation has not yet become evident. Unfortunately, the customer may resent being presented with a product that has no value in his view. The outcome is new versions of the technology that are more suitable to the customer. The principal implication here is that paying attention to customer needs makes for better products. The supplier could have saved time, money, and competitive exposure had the customer been consulted at the start of the process.

Team Approach

About ten years ago, strategic management visionaries began decrying the "silo" approach to the management of the firm. The functional approach to management, in which marketing, engineering, product research, manufacturing, customer service, sales, and so on operated separately in "silos," was seen as particularly dysfunctional when it came to generating and launching new products. To break down the silos, small, cross-functional teams were espoused as appropriate for managing both the creative effort and cross-functional coordination required in new product development, launch, and management. Indeed, many companies have found this team approach beneficial. Recent examples can be found in such companies as Cisco Systems, IBM, Chrysler, and others.

There are some facets of the team approach that need discussion. A new idea seldom survives the hurdles of repeated business metrics without a champion to father it. The commitment of an entrepreneurial approach by the "champion" (often referred to as the intrapreneur) assists the development through organizational hurdles. Products that are more likely to disrupt conventional processes and thinking in the firm require support at higher levels with each succeeding stage of the development process. This is understandable, as greater disruptions may strike at many levels in the organization. Individuals may feel that their current jobs are threatened or that they will have to learn a new technology or way of doing things. There is less short-term risk in slowing or ending a new product development as each development stage is exposed to measurements of business potential. The composition of the NPD team should reflect these different demands and recognize the need for an internal marketing program.

Invest in the Early Stages

One of the ways to help with this process is to use rigorous market-driven standards early in the development process. Cooper[12] lays out the rationale and research findings relevant here. He explains that the idea of the staged approach to NPD is to identify and weed out likely new product losers early in the process. The early stages are relatively less expensive than the later stages. In many instances, the potential market segments may be described as potentially high growth, but the firm may have little existing presence. The Boston Consulting Group Growth-Share Matrix[13] characterizes these opportunities as "question marks," usually requiring significant commitment (of management—the intrapreneur again), competency (of the organization, distinctively from the competition), and heavy investment for success. If a bad fit is identified early on, the heavy expenditures for development and launch of a product failure can be avoided. By the same token, if a company is willing to take on additional levels of risk, it may decide to pursue one or more projects with potentially high payoffs.

Stage Gates and Phase Reviews

Cooper's conclusion is that progression from stage to stage ought to be governed by use of carefully constructed **stage gates**. These gates are prespecified milestones that must be reached—and approved by a high-level manager or executive—before the project can continue. The gates have two qualitative aspects: technical milestones and market or business milestones. Again, Cooper has found that adherence to such stage gates produces superior performance.

Experience suggests that such rigorous adherence to stage gates is practiced much less often than is ideal, particularly on the market or business side. The principal reasons for this are uncertainty and scarce resources. Given limited budgets, it is very tempting for the NPD manager to put as much effort into R&D as possible. The firm has much more control over internal technical developments. Also, the market is usually more difficult to interpret than is the technical performance of a product. Consequently, higher priority is placed on what can be influenced directly and budgets for market analysis go wanting.

Whenever we encourage the use of lists or stages in business, we are concerned that they will be applied as a recipe or prescription, without consideration for the context or intent of the process. It should be emphasized that the stage gate system is a process to facilitate NPD. It is not a checklist of functional items that must be done by each department before the project is handed off to the next group. The process is multidisciplinary, requiring the use of cross-functional teams in the development effort. Each stage is market driven but includes technical, financial, and production activities. With a strong focus on quality in each element of each stage, the development team stays in touch with the changing market and customer needs.

A modification of the stage gates approach is to reduce the number of stages to three or four phases. Instead of having to pass a stage gate at the end of the idea generation stage, then the business case stage, then again at the end of the product development stage, and so on, a project might face phase review gates only at the end of idea generation, concept development and testing, and commercialization planning and preparation. This cuts down on the time wasted in scheduling and running stage gate reviews. Yet it still maintains a degree of control and risk management at key points.[14]

Stage gates are simply checkpoints after each stage of the product development process. The ongoing NPD process is interrupted at certain milestones to ensure that the original goals and objectives are still viable and that the development is still forecast to meet the expectations that were created as a part of its initial approval. The stage gate process is fairly rigorous but is a flexible process to keep NPD on track. While a development may not continue to meet initial expectations, continuous marketing input may point the NPD team to additional or substitute opportunities.

Concurrent Development

One of the concerns about "lists" in business is the implication that things happen sequentially. Large strides have been taken to improve "time to market" for new products through the recognition that it is possible to conduct many elements of the development concurrently. First to market, often key in market ownership, has exploitable advantages. The first entry into a new market often is able to define the parameters of the market, setting the standard for others who follow.

Concurrent development is simple in concept but hard to do. The idea is to identify activities that can be done simultaneously, in parallel rather than serially. The development effort is divided into modules that can be developed separately, but with continuous communications between the module developers. The unifying nature of teams is also critical to effective concurrent development. Communication and coordination between the teams working on the modules must be maintained during development.

Opportunity costs are the measurement of those business opportunities that are not pursued because resources have been committed to the new product development. NPD teams may use several different criteria to make these judgments, such as internal rate of return, net present value, and market scenarios.

When a new product idea presents relatively high development risk but relatively low **opportunity costs** (high risks, not that much to gain by working on something else), it may not be particularly advantageous to speed up the development process.[15] Stage gate management can become particularly important as a way to ensure that development criteria are met, providing milestones that re-examine the risk-reward ratio of the project.

No Shortcuts

One of Cooper's primary conclusions is that effective NPD relies on doing the right things right. There are no shortcuts to be taken, no activities to be ignored. The chance of catastrophic failure can be minimized by enlightened application of the above principles. Failure likelihood goes up as "rules" are broken.

THE ROLE OF MARKETING IN THE PRODUCT DEVELOPMENT PROCESS

Ideally, in a market-driven organization, marketing is responsible for the definition of new offerings based on a continuous review of customer needs. As customer needs evolve over the period of the product development, the goals of the development evolve. Thus, marketing is responsible for the direction and outcomes of the product development process.

The responsibilities of marketing go far beyond the customer interface. Unfortunately, many NPD efforts minimize the resources committed to marketing while maximizing product and technology development. Research has shown that the marketing effort is often the most deficient part of the new product plan.[16] In 22 percent of development projects studied (including firms that considered themselves "market driven"), there was no detailed marketing study at all. In another 46 percent of the projects, the marketing plan was considered to be poorly done. In all projects analyzed in the study, a full 74 percent had no market study or plan or had a plan that was judged as seriously deficient. This deficiency in marketing effort continued through the development process to the product launch, where, even in a sales- or product-driven organization, you would expect significant input from marketing. Test-marketing or trial-selling efforts were deficient or omitted in 58 percent of the studied projects. Also, 52 percent of the projects failed to have adequate business or financial plans. In these same projects, however, technical assessments, in-house testing, and pilot production efforts were judged to be sufficient for the task—*reinforcing the dangers of a product or technology focus.*

Where should the marketing effort, particularly in "market-driven" firms, show up? In the first chapter, we characterized marketing as the driving force, the "heart and soul" of the organization. In this context, marketing has a responsibility to drive the NPD process.

Marketing Defines the Outcomes

The responsibility of marketing is well defined by Sherlock.[17] The following are the ways in which marketing must serve the organization:

- *Understand the technology in depth.* This is not meant to imply that marketers must have technical degrees but that they must know the value of the technology, its strengths and weaknesses, *from the viewpoint of the user.* Marketers need to know the science in such a way that they can recognize opportunities in customer needs and the limitations of technology capabilities.

- *Define and redefine current and future customer needs.* The continuous evolution of customer needs creates a dynamic, sometimes volatile environment. An offering cannot be accurately defined at the beginning of the process and, without modification to the definition, be correct for the market at the end of the process. In a long period of development as partners, the supplier and customer will discover and evaluate many different aspects of the total offering. The needs of stakeholders in the buying center will evolve, requiring the attention of members of the supplier's value chain. Marketing must provide definition of customer's needs, continuously updated, to research and development and manufacturing in the supplier organization. The timeliness and quality of the information about customer needs is a reflection of the quality of the relationship with the customer.

- *Motivate other company departments and organizations.* The marketers, whether headquarters or field personnel, must be closely associated with the customer and should champion the supplier's development effort toward the best interests of the customer. To the rest of the organization, the marketer should "be" the customer! Business-to-business customers expect this, and the degree to which the development effort meets specific customer needs is evidence of the success of the effort. Marketing can make progress toward this synergy by involving as many corporate technology and development participants with the customer as possible. This not only establishes direct communications between members of the value chain and the buying center but also instills in the participants a sense of ownership of the effort to satisfy customer needs.

- *Screen and select ideas from all sources.* Marketers should know their own companies well enough to know their strengths and weaknesses. The strengths are tools that can be used to bring value to customers. Marketers should also know the intricacies and nuances of their customers. What businesses are they in? What synergies are possible? What competencies of the customer's can be matched to strengths of the marketers' companies to create distinctive offerings?

- *Guide the new product development with the continuous redefinition of current and future customer needs already noted.* Accomplishing this step is far easier when the organization is contextually prepared for the redefined parameters. This will be assisted significantly by the participant ownership already described.

- *Reward the efforts of the technical and support staff.* When the new offering is introduced and perhaps at milestones along the way, the marketer should reward the participants. Have a party. Get a wall plaque. Create an event. Positive exposure and association with the current success bode well for cooperation in the future. Also, make the reward known to the customer, not only elevating the work of the participant but also demonstrating to the customer his importance in the supplier's organization. If there was significant collaboration with participants from the customer, reward them too!

- *Catalyze company resources to get the right talent on the job—be willing to cross traditional company boundaries.* Marketing is responsible for a collaborative and synergistic relationship with other parts of the supplier organization. Marketers should cultivate relationships throughout their organization. Each of these relationships can become a positive igniter in the search for the best result for customers. Having working relationships throughout the organization is another resource the marketer can bring to bear on customer needs.

The level of responsibility prescribed here for the marketing organization is difficult to grasp for an organization that is not truly market driven. Firms that operate under the product or sales concept[18] often have an internal culture that views the marketing effort as an expense rather than a defining paradigm.

REDUCING THE RISK OF NEW PRODUCT FAILURES

New products have an element of risk associated with them. To reduce this risk, firms can utilize many of the development tools described here or any number of other processes described by a large body of research about NPD. Unfortunately, even with careful planning by organizations that engage in NPD, there are still product failures.

Why Do New Products Fail?

If the marketing effort in the organization is responsible for the process outcome, as we have described, then responsibility for the failure of the process also rests with marketing. Indeed, poor marketing (or no marketing effort at all) is a major cause of product failures. Consider the study by Cooper, noted earlier, that found that 22 percent of NPD projects surveyed had no detailed market study performed. While this may be a frightening prospect for true marketers, many managers do not even realize that they have missed a part of the development process. To improve the chances of new product success, let us look at some causes of new product failures.

THE MISSING MARKETING PLAN   At the outset of many NPD projects, assumptions are made about technology, manufacturability, and markets. These assumptions are often necessary to get the project off the ground, to get resources committed to begin the first stages of investigation and development.[19] These assumptions—market size, value as perceived by the customer, growth rates, and desirability of features—that are often used to justify the initial effort can become ingrained in the project. Studies have shown that once approved, project funds are most often used to validate technological assumptions, but not market assumptions. In fact, 78 percent of total resources expended go to technological and manufacturing activities.[20]

NO REAL NEED EXISTS   Some products are the answer to a question that nobody has asked. These types of failures are often associated with executive attachment to a technology or idea. The development proceeds in isolation, with little attention to the real needs of the market. With strong executive attachment, market research results can be overlooked or interpreted to support the opinions of management. Cooper reports that this accounts for 28 percent of product failures.

THE MARKET SIZE IS OVERESTIMATED OR A "ME TOO" PRODUCT FAILS TO PENETRATE THE MARKET   Few marketing efforts can maintain an exclusive hold on a market. In oligopolistic late growth or maturity situations, expecting much more than 30 percent market share can be overly optimistic. In new markets, once the offering is successful and competition seeks a piece of the action, the innovator that had "all" of the (small) market during introduction is certainly faced with losing share—while gaining volume as the market grows.

Overestimating market size has implications beyond lower-than-expected sales revenues. Initial market estimates are used throughout the organization. Whether to attract investors, plan facility development and expansion, or staff the organization, inflated estimates lead to unfulfilled expectations. Very large organizations may impose higher benchmarks of success than

smaller, more nimble or productive firms. Even if the offering is successful beyond the introduction stage, less than anticipated sales results tarnish the entire project and, in the case of a
start-up, the entire organization. "Me too" products face a double whammy: market leadership is
usually not an attribute associated with followers. The inability of "me too" products to significantly penetrate existing markets contributes to 24 percent of new product failures, second only
to there being no real need for the product.[21]

THE OFFERING FAILS TO MEET NEEDS ADEQUATELY   Accounting for 15 percent of new
product failures,[22] products that do not work right can be the result of poorly defined needs—a
marketing deficiency; poor product performance—a technology flop; or a combination—the
product technology would have worked but the offering was rushed to market before all the bugs
were worked out. Timing linked to competitive product launches can suffer in this manner.

In high-technology industries, technophiles and innovators are usually quite forgiving with
regard to new product ship dates. These market segments recognize that the offering is new and
subject to a slow and possibly cumbersome introductory period and are able to adjust the timing
of their own offering to meet supplier schedules. They are usually not dependent on economies
of scale, while their product is likely dependent on the new technology.

High-volume industries, particularly those that serve consumer markets and have major
economies of scale and high fixed costs, usually can tolerate neither inadequate product performance nor inexact delivery schedules. These industries (e.g., consumer electronics, automotive)
adopt technologies later in the life cycle. Only proven technologies are incorporated into their value
network.

In some cases, the product may meet end use needs, but the needs of the channel are not
met by the supplier's offering or business model. In the 1980s, for example, Monsanto believed
it could translate its Saflex product from the automobile windshield market to the new home
construction market. Saflex is a plastic sheet that allows glass laminators to make a safer, sturdier
form of glass by sandwiching the Saflex between two plates of glass. In the new home market,
Saflex glass for windows would be safer and provide more insulation than plain glass. However,
it would cost more and required thicker window frames. Wholesalers and homebuilders were not
convinced that consumers would want to pay higher prices for the glass and did not want to carry
inventory of wider frames for products with unproven demand.[23] Monsanto discontinued the
translation effort when its test market showed the channel problems.

MARKET WILL NOT PAY   13 percent of product failures are the result of a price squeeze[24]—
either the costs of development and marketing were higher than expected or the market price
adjusted to the new supply. What is important to recognize is that a price that the market is
unwilling to accept is a symptom of other problems. Had there been an effective marketing plan,
the market price of the offering would have been studied such that the change as a result of the
increased supply—the market elasticity—would be anticipated. Competitive reactions should
also be anticipated. It is not unusual for existing suppliers to a market to adjust price downward
when faced with a new competitor.

CONTRARY PERCEPTIONS OF INNOVATION   The degree to which a new offering is an innovation
impacts the positioning of that offering in the market. When the supplier perceives the offering as a
breakthrough innovation but the customer perceives the offering as an incremental product, there
will be a mismatch of perceived value, unlikely to result in an adoption of the product by the
customer. When the opposite is true, the supplier regards the innovation as an incremental product

> - No Marketing plan
> - No real needs exists for the product
> - The market size is overestimated
> - A "me too" product fails to penetrate the market
> - The product does not fully meet customer needs
> - Market will not pay
>
> A good marketing plan is a solution to all of these!

EXHIBIT 8-3 Why New Products Fail

but the customer perceives a breakthrough innovation, there is still a mismatch but one of significant value to the customer. Unfortunately, unimpressed supplier management may not provide the necessary resources to the product to enable it to fulfill its potential in the market. The contrary perception of the level of innovation and thus value in the market creates shadowed and delusionary products,[25] further discussed in Chapter 9. Exhibit 8-3 summarizes this list of reasons for product failures.

COLLABORATORS

Fans of old war movies probably have a negative impression associated with the word *collaborator*. **Collaborators** were those who worked with the enemy for their own (perhaps) short-term benefit. The second meaning of *collaborate* in the dictionary is "aid or cooperate traitorously." However, developing a collaborative relationship in business can be very positive—if you are the successful collaborator.

We have repeatedly discussed and referred to the total effective value of the firm, as viewed by the customer or client. Sherlock's term for this complete and total impression, appropriately, is "value image."[26] Value image, similar in concept to market positioning but with a much broader vision, can have a great impact on the likelihood of success in business-to-business relationships. Let us take this concept one step further.

Delivering customer value encompasses more than providing the latest technology, though continuously providing adequate customer value assumes that innovators expand the technology envelope. Successful technology companies, such as Cisco Systems, 3Com, and others, were founded on technology but, as we have noted, cannot rely on technology to maintain a market advantage. As these companies establish successful markets, competition increases, tightening margins and forcing a closer look at research and development funding. What are the alternatives? Why not have someone else fund and manage your early-term, high-risk research and development?

Enter the high-technology start-up company. As companies like Cisco Systems develop market ownership, they attract a cadre of smaller companies (satellites? corporate groupies?) that follow their market. Some of these smaller companies are satisfied to pick up a few crumbs along the way, while others invest (emotionally and financially) in the next-generation technology that will replace or threaten or enhance the Cisco portfolio. Cisco is faced with a dilemma. These satellites provide real value to Cisco's customers. They can fill in the gaps in Cisco's product line, and they often rely on Cisco to help establish customer contact. At the same time Cisco is partnering with the smaller company, the smaller company is hoping to gain a foothold in Cisco's market and, with its new technology, capture market share. While all this is going on, Cisco must continue to invest in R&D—if not to push the technology envelope, then as a defensive measure.

Collect enough satellites in your market, and the situation can be downright threatening. The answer: Cisco reduces R&D expenditures and encourages R&D by the smaller companies through their partnering, or collaboration. Part of the attraction for the small company to become involved is encouragement from Cisco that, when the R&D effort is proven in the market, Cisco would be interested in an acquisition. Cisco gets to select from an array of new technologies that impact its market without the associated development costs or introduction risks.

The result? Cisco acquires one (or a few) of the satellite start-up companies. The start-up goes the way of many high-technology start-ups—become acquired by larger, established firms. The other satellites go the way of many other start-ups—out of the market. For the winner(s), this collaboration has been successful. They partnered with "the enemy" and, over the long term (for a start-up), won. For the other companies, the collaboration held a context closer to that traditional old war movie.

In this narration, the customer for the satellite was, tactically, the Cisco customer and, strategically, Cisco. The value of the satellite to Cisco had to be marketed in such a way that Cisco had confidence in the long-term relationship. From an investor view, the customer was always Cisco. In a new venture, a relationship with a large company with coattails to success may be a greater asset than a marketing partner or a customer partner. They can be a *collaborator*. Not all collaborators win.

Collaborations or partnerships are not new to business. Different patterns of mutual development between organizations have always existed. The patterns, or business models, have changed with changing market conditions. In the next section, we compare the concept of value networks, introduced in Chapter 2 with the more traditional vertical integration model of creating value as we discuss the "make or buy" decision.

MAKE-OR-BUY DECISIONS

Closely related to the product development process and marketing's role in it is the "make-or-buy" decision. The degree to which an organization incorporates new or unique components into its products, combined with the potential proprietary nature of those components, creates the need for a sourcing decision. When market conditions allowed it, many organizations preferred to vertically integrate back into the manufacture of parts and materials. Early in the twentieth century, Henry Ford manufactured his own steel, glass, and tires for his company's vehicles—there just wasn't anyone else capable of supplying the company needs. The advent of electronics and home electrical products in the 1920s demonstrated the need for plastic materials, not just for insulators but also in radio cabinets and the bases for vacuum tubes. The volumes associated with these consumer applications justified the backward integration into the manufacture of circuit board and plastic materials by General Electric. During the period of rapid growth of the automobile market, General Motors integrated into the manufacture (often through acquisition) of many vehicle components. Market conditions during this period of heavy vertical integration—the early twentieth century—may not have given these early pioneers much choice. Many of the products that were the subject of the integration were not available from another source, or, if they were, **proprietary information** considerations

Proprietary information is data that, while not protected by patents, is not available to the general public and has significant value to the owner. Trade secrets, process techniques, and formulas (think Mrs. Field's Cookies and Coke syrup) are a significant part of the value of organizations. Maintaining the secrecy of proprietary information can be a significant motivation in make-or-buy decisions. Organizations that outsource part of their offering to another firm risk the loss of this secrecy.

It can happen. Polaroid, faced with significant capital investment resulting from the success of its "instant" camera, contracted production of film to a reputable source for photographic supplies—Eastman Kodak. Later, Kodak entered the market with its own instant camera. Polaroid claimed that Kodak used proprietary information learned from the manufacture of Polaroid film in the development and manufacture of the Kodak camera. The courts agreed, and Kodak was forced to leave the instant camera market.

prevented the company from outsourcing the components. Both of these factors remain a consideration in vertical integration versus outsource decisions in today's market.

Vertical integration has attributes that speak in its favor. An integrated supply chain provides assured sources for components and materials. The development back into the manufacture of components and materials can also lead to profitable business opportunities. Until recently divested by General Electric, GE Plastics has been one of the pre-eminent suppliers of engineering plastics (though they have left the circuit board material business). However, vertical integration can also lead to the development of large, sprawling organizations. (Business portfolio management is discussed in Chapter 5.) To many people, large size implies bureaucracy, and bureaucracy implies slow movement, often devoid of innovation. While this is not meant to imply that very large organizations cannot respond to rapidly changing markets, it does indicate the involvement of a different decision-making process.

Large, vertically integrated organizations have an investment in the current form and method of conducting business and manufacturing products. New technologies, while not overlooked from an R&D perspective, may not survive the internal standards of the business model if they do not utilize existing facilities or "fit" the current idea of what business the organization is in (often mistakenly defined by what the organization produces). This myopia has been demonstrated countless times[27]—from ice houses to refrigerators, from vacuum tubes to solid state devices, from photographic film to digital imaging. Investment in infrastructure can slow the response to change.

Factors in the Decision

Let us return to the Sensacon example (earlier in this chapter) to demonstrate some of the factors in a make-or-buy decision. Keep in mind that a make-or-buy decision has greater implications than just attempting the lowest production cost. The development of a successful value network may include many make-or-buy decisions.

> Sensacon has invested in new technology to create the next-generation sensor, to be called SensorSUV. The new technology gives SensorSUV a faster response time and greater resistance to shock and vibration, both features in which the market has expressed interest. This new distinction is primarily the result of the incorporation of a new component into SensorSUV. While the technology of the component is not, by itself, new, it is the first time it has been used in the sensor market and Sensacon has modified the component somewhat. Should Sensacon manufacture this "new" component itself or purchase it from an outside source?

First, Sensacon must assess the component's contribution to SensorSUV's value as *perceived by the customer* (see Exhibit 8-4, Make-or-Buy Decisions). If the component has only a minor role in the value of SensorSUV, Sensacon then must decide if it is unique to the sensor market. If the component is unique, it is in the best interest of Sensacon to either develop a partner relationship with qualified suppliers to produce the component or encourage potential collaborators to develop the market for the component. In either case, the partner or collaborator will have to be assured of purchases from Sensacon and an opportunity to further develop, with other sensor manufacturers, market applications for the component after a specified period of exclusive use by Sensacon. Because the component's role in the value of Sensacon's product is minor and technology based, it would not usually be a good decision for Sensacon to make the

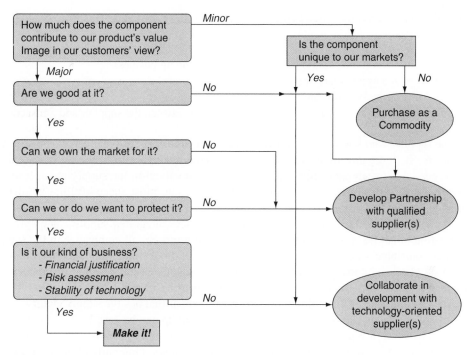

EXHIBIT 8-4   Make-or-Buy Decisions

component itself. If the component plays a minor role in the value of SensorSUV and is not unique to the sensor market, Sensacon should treat the component as a commodity purchase.

If Sensacon determines that the component plays a major role in the value of the SensorSUV, an entirely different decision path is necessary. Since the component contributes significant value to Sensacon's end product, it may be in Sensacon's best interest to manufacture the component itself. Sensacon is, however, in the sensor business, not the component business, and may not have a distinctive competence in the manufacture of the new component. If Sensacon is not good at the manufacture of the component, then the sourcing alternatives become the same as the *Minor/Yes* decision flow in Exhibit 8-4,—either source from a partner or encourage a collaboration.

What if Sensacon decides that it has the unique competency required to manufacture the component successfully? This may be a diversification decision. Using the parameters of market ownership,[28] Sensacon must now decide if it can "own" the market for the component and if it wants to protect the proprietary nature of the component (patents, trade secrets, etc.). If either answer is "no," Sensacon should look to outsource the component through a supplying partner. It is only at this point, after the market-driven considerations, that Sensacon should fully examine the business case for manufacturing the component itself.

Supplier Role in the Decision

Throughout this make-or-buy decision process, the potential supplier (either partner or collaborator) should be involved with Sensacon to determine what value it can provide as a supplier that will exceed the value that Sensacon can produce for itself. This level of supplier-delivered value will

- Allow Sensacon to invest in other areas closer to its main business
- Be recognized as a resource by the customer (Sensacon)
- Develop a business opportunity for the supplier
- Create or reinforce a potentially strong relationship between the supplier and Sensacon.

The supplier who knows the culture and competencies of its customer can create win-win situations for both organizations. The role of the potential supplier to Sensacon is a scenario that is repeated between each supplier–customer pair involved in the supply chain leading, ultimately, to the consumer, and is, in fact, what makes up most successful market-driven business-to-business relationships.

McGrath goes so far as to say that in markets where integrated supply chains prevail, the cross-functional team developing a product should represent all companies in the supply chain that contribute value to the product. In the Sensacon example, any subcomponent or material suppliers to be involved in the manufacture of the new sensor should be represented in the team. This collaboration is enabled and enhanced by currently available Web-based software. The outcome of this collaboration is a new sensor that has the supply chain already designed and in place. The time to introduction and ramp up can be greatly shortened, while the value built into the product can be maximized.[29] The box *Microsoft Integrates XBox Supply* demonstrates another example of the dangers of outsourcing parts of an offering that are critical to success.

Microsoft Integrates XBox Supply

When Microsoft (MS) introduced the original Xbox, business analysts declared a battle royal between the PlayStation 2 from Sony and the new Microsoft product.

It didn't happen that way.

Late to market outside the United States by almost two years, notably because of component supply problems, by the time MS had sold 1.5 million Xboxes, Sony had already sold 20 million PS2s worldwide. (One strategic view is that the first company to sell 10 million units will lead the market.) Nvidia, the graphics chip supplier for the Xbox ran late finishing the custom design for the Xbox, and contract manufacturer Flextronics initially had difficulty assembling the console.

Peter Moore, Corporate VP for the Xbox division says this won't happen again. Microsoft has taken steps to get to market significantly ahead of the new Sony PlayStation 3—particularly in foreign markets. To introduce in Europe, Japan, and the United States simultaneously, MS has added two contract manufacturers, Wistron and Celestica in addition to Flextronics, to manufacture the Xbox 360 at three different factories in China. Additional contract manufacturing alone doesn't completely solve the problem.

MS recognized that certain components of the Xbox 360 were unique and, should supply problems develop, there would be no alternative sources. Notably, Microsoft was completely dependent on chip designs from Intel and Nvidia. To lower costs as well as insure supply of volumes of components, MS wanted greater control of the chip designs. Neither Intel nor Nvidia was willing to give MS ownership of the designs and greater control over the chip sourcing and thus withdrew as suppliers to the new program. This opened the door for new partners.

IBM and ATI Technologies agreed to give MS ownership of the new unique designs. MS, working with these new partners, now had extensive expertise as well as control of the final product. Essentially, MS eliminated a bottleneck in the supply chain by now being able to source manufacturing of the chips directly. They had greater control, or, to put it another way, they had greater control of price, margins, and design of the components.

Microsoft "integration" into the chips for the new Xbox solves another problem that plagued the original Xbox, the availability of an adequate assortment of compatible games. The earlier completion of the new chip designs allows simultaneous development of games.

Microsoft recognized that to insure the "destiny" of the Xbox it would need greater integration into key parts of the product. The entire supply chain for all parts of the total offering must place the same priorities on the supply of components. The alternative, as Microsoft learned, is to "make" rather than "buy."

Source: Dean Takahashi, *The San Joe Mercury News* (August 16, 2005), p. B1.

THOUGHTS TO TAKE WITH YOU INTO THE NEXT CHAPTER

In this chapter we have looked at the PLC as a tool to better understand the pressures placed on offerings by different aspects of the market environment and the methods by which the marketing mix can be used to respond. While the PLC is a generalized case, it provides a framework around which to build product management theory. The PLC may be used as a representation of sales revenue over time for individual products or product lines but is most often applicable to product or market categories. Through this view, an analogy to product categories as strategic business units in portfolio management is possible. Buying behavior, profitability, and competitive threats as well as perceived value vary over the life cycle.

The NPD process has been discussed in what we hope is not a bureaucratic context. Marketing is the defining force in NPD and thus bears significant attention in the review of why new products fail. New ideas must be considered from the view of the market and not be just a good idea for the offering firm. The failure to apply adequate marketing practice in new product planning is the single largest factor in new offering failures. The value of the offering *as perceived by the customer* cannot be overemphasized.

In the next chapter, we examine entrepreneurial orientation and the innovation process and their impact on the competitiveness of the firm. The pace of innovation contributes to the trend away from vertical integration and toward the application of the value network concept in offering development. The "make-or-buy" decision is crucial to the long range planning of innovative organizations and requires marketing's insight and knowledge of customer perceptions of value. In Chapter 9, the management of innovation and the importance of business-to-business brands in the creation of industry standards are discussed.

Key Terms

collaborators *192*
decline stage *181*
development stage *176*
economies of scale *181*
growth stage *178*

introduction stage *177*
maturity stage *181*
opportunity costs *188*
proprietary disclosure
    agreements *184*

proprietary information *193*
stage gates *187*
unique or first time value
    network *177*

Questions for Review and Discussion

1. Review the generalized product life cycle as shown in Exhibit 8-1. How well does the PLC model work for rapidly changing technologies? Markets? Why?

2. At what point in the PLC are the following product categories?

   Railroads   Gasoline   Commercial aircraft
   Desktop computers   Genetic engineering

3. How can executive attachment to a technology lead to product failure?

4. How does the fast pace of markets impact make or buy decisions?

5. What are the implications of outsourcing significant parts of an offering that will have a very long maturity stage in its PLC?

6. What are the implications of vertically integrating to provide most all of the elements of value for a product category that competes in a highly competitive technology market?

7. What role does marketing play in the NPD process? What are marketing's responsibilities?

8. How are the attitude and culture of the NPD team related to the number of successful developments?

9. Is it better to invest heavily in the early stages of NPD or toward the end of the process? Why?

10. If misunderstood or misapplied, what are potential pitfalls of the stage gate method of managing NPD?

11. Using Exhibit 8-3, explain how effective marketing can overcome each listed reason for product failures.

Endnotes

1. Robert Lacey, *Ford, The Men and the Machine* (Ballantine Books, 1986), p. 513.

2. Ibid., p. 516.

3. Isadore Barmash, *Great American Business Disasters* (Playboy Press, 1972), p. 241.

4. Robert G. Cooper, *Winning at New Products* (Reading, Mass.: Addison-Wesley, 1993).

5. Recognizing the customer's view cannot be overemphasized. Chapter 1 discusses viewpoint as a major contributor to misunderstanding and misapplication of the value chain concept.

6. Phillip Kotler, *Marketing Management, The Millennium Edition*, 10th ed. (Upper Saddle River, N.J.: Prentice Hall, 2000), pp. 301–304.

7. Recall that "the offering" consists of many elements of product, service, installation, finance, and so on.

8. The strategic implications of market ownership are discussed in Chapter 5.

9. Geoffrey Moore, *Crossing the Chasm* (New York: Harper Collins, 1991).

10. We believe some explanation is necessary here. Silicon pressure sensors are produced through a process called micromachining, similar to the process that makes integrated circuits. This process is used to manufacture many types of microstructures, referred to in the industry as micromachined electromechanical systems—MEMS. Without belaboring the technology or the jargon, these products are arguably at the chasm. This example is a compilation of the experiences of more than one company in this market. Simplifications have been made for academic clarity, and care has been taken to prevent any direct relationship with any single market participant.

11. Kotler, *Marketing Management*, p. 335.

12. Cooper, *Winning at New Products*.

13. The BCG Matrix is discussed in Chapter 5.

14. Catherine Kitcho, *From Idea to Launch at Internet Speed: How to Identify and Develop Profitable Opportunities* (Mountain View, Calif.: Pele Publications, 2001).

15. V. Kasdturi Rangan and Kevin Bartus, "New Product Commercialization: Common Mistakes," *Harvard Business School* (Note 594–127, 1994, 63–75).

16. Cooper, *Winning at New Products*, p. 24.

17. Paul Sherlock, *Rethinking Business-to-Business Marketing* (New York: The Free Press, 1991), p. 84.

18. Kotler, *Marketing Management*, p. 25.

19. Cooper, *Winning at New Products*, p. 25.

20. Ibid., p. 26.

21. Ibid., p. 27.

22. Ibid., p. 28.

23. Eric Berggren and Thomas Nacher, "Introducing New Products Can Be Hazardous to Your Company: Use the Right New-Solutions Delivery Tools," *Academy of Management Executive*, 15(3) (August, 2001), pp. 94–95.

24. Cooper, *Winning at New Products*, p. 28.

25. Rangan and Bartus, "New Product Commercialization."

26. Sherlock, *Rethinking Business-to-Business Marketing*.

27. Theodore Levitt, "Marketing Myopia," *Harvard Business Review* (July–August 1960).

28. Regis McKenna, "Marketing Is Everything," *Harvard Business Review* (January–February 1991).

29. Michael E. McGrath, *Next Generation Product Development: How to Increase Productivity, Cut Costs, and Reduce Cycle Times* (New York: McGraw-Hill, 2004).

Chapter 9

Innovation and Competitiveness

OVERVIEW

In this chapter we address two methods by which marketing creates competitive advantage for the business-to-business firm: entrepreneurial orientation and innovation. We separate these out from other chapters because too often they are thought to be part of a single element of the marketing mix—product, particularly through new product development and product management. We wish to emphasize that innovation and brand building need to extend across all elements of marketing.

Indeed, new product development is extremely important in getting a key portion of value right for customers. In new product development, marketing can and should add its own innovative contribution to the structuring of the product and service portions of the offering. However, recent studies that have examined the successes and failures in business—many of which are companies engaged in business-to-business marketing—show that broad-based innovativeness is a key to high performance. Maintaining or increasing a degree of differentiation from competitors can be accomplished through innovating in the channel structure, the pricing structure, or even the communication strategy, as well as in the product. As we saw in the last chapter, the opportunity for product innovation becomes reduced during the mature portion of the product life cycle. If the company is not careful, it resorts to shaving margins to maintain competitiveness. Finding a way to innovate elsewhere in the offering, away from "product," may be the only way to maintain margins. Indeed, adopting world-class supply management practices can be viewed as a form of non-product innovativeness.

Innovativeness can be viewed as the key element of an entrepreneurial orientation; so, in this chapter we discuss innovation in the context of marketing entrepreneurially. Entrepreneurial orientation includes proactiveness, controlled risk taking, and opportunity seeking, as well as innovation. In this chapter, we discuss how the marketing function of the firm can approach all elements of marketing with an entrepreneurial orientation.

The methods discussed in this chapter build sustainable competitive advantage deep within the company's inner workings. Competitive advantage in the company's offerings comes as the result of attention paid to building these links in the company's value chain.

In the opening example, we show how Sun Microsystems created a platform for generating new initiatives that address emerging needs in new markets. The innovative effort actually has two stages: the building of the partner community framework and the formation of new marketing programs. Innovation at both levels involves much more than product innovation; the whole effort is very entrepreneurial in character.

Example: Sun Creates an Innovative Partner Network[1]

In March 2000, Sun Microsystems launched iForce, a networked community of Sun partners, including software developers, VARs, systems integrators, and peripheral equipment suppliers. The idea was to provide business customers with a single entity to go to for e-business or other network systems. iForce is a good illustration of a non-product innovation.

While Sun had its share of problems in the early 2000s, the iForce initiative survived and evolved. The principal benefit provided by iForce was a one-stop shop for enterprise or service provider customers. Because all the elements of the offering are "under one roof," and are marketed together as a bundled offering, the customer saves time and some expense in acquiring and using a customized solution. Sun provides services and facilities that make it attractive for partners and customers to participate. For Sun's business partners, Sun provides financing, operations services, and global marketing. It provides discounts and consulting services for start-up Internet companies. Sun has also built test and proving facilities, called iForce Ready Centers, where partners, customers, and Sun technicians can experiment with and build customized systems for customers that can then be scaled and translated to the customer's own facilities. Customer problems are addressed by all parties concerned using Sun methods or development approaches created by other Sun integrator partners, if more applicable.

Much of the revenue and margin produced in sales generated by iForce goes to the partners. Sun makes money on sales of equipment, operating systems software, some consulting, and eventually on returns from venture capital activity associated with the initiative.

By not overspecifying the nature of the partnership program at the outset, Sun facilitated other sorts of innovations. In the first six months after launch, the partnership framework produced a specific initiative focused on wireless systems called, appropriately enough, iForce Wireless. This initiative targeted telecommunications companies and wireless service providers, offering combined packages of hardware, software, applications, and integration services.

Over the first five years of the 2000s, Sun suffered severe sales declines. Competition for the remaining business was fierce; customers sought low-cost network servers based on Intel microprocessors and Linux operating system (Sun offered servers with its own SPARC chips and Solaris operating system). As sales slid, Sun survived in part by moving a number of remaining channel accounts in-house and reducing its support for the channel. Sun's channel partners remember this treatment. Even with the attempts to integrate and rationalize the network under the iForce umbrella in 2004 and 2005, some partners want more in the way of integration of development efforts, sales efforts, and information. As the economy improves, though, Sun is working to improve partner margins, support their transition to include a higher level of service, and open the channels of communication. In the spring of 2005, Sun introduced an iForce program to match channel partners with Sun salespeople to address many larger accounts. This gave the partners access to Sun business worth several billion dollars in yearly revenue.

LEARNING OBJECTIVES

By reading this chapter, you will:

- Understand the application of entrepreneurial marketing and innovation in order to compete in business-to-business markets.
- Obtain an understanding of how innovation relates to entrepreneurial marketing.

- Gain a sense of how innovation can be accomplished in all elements of the offering.
- Understand how to implement innovation and entrepreneurial marketing in business-to-business marketing.
- Gain a sense of how current trends in business-to-business markets are affecting the concepts and implementation of innovation and entrepreneurial marketing.

INTRODUCTION

The nature of the business environment in business-to-business markets is constant change. Customers constantly want new and better products and services from their suppliers. Competitors are constantly trying new strategies and tactics for winning over customers. As Dickson notes,[2] there is no equilibrium; some competitor will always come along with something better that changes the relationships in the market.

To cope with this dynamic frenzy, business-to-business marketers must either find market niches that they can lock up so tightly that they face no significant threat of competition or they must compete just as hard as the other businesses in the market. The first alternative is at least limited in scope, if it exists at all. This means that marketers must compete by continually trying to create more value for both existing and new customers. In this chapter, we discuss a way to do this by acting entrepreneurially.

An entrepreneurial approach to competing involves four key elements: seeking opportunities, innovating, acting proactively, and taking controlled risks. In the discussion in the second part of this chapter, we go into some depth on the why and the how of innovating.

In the opening example, Sun Microsystems noticed that its customers were becoming overwhelmed with the intricacies, choices, and uncertainties involved in building e-commerce systems. To bring all the pieces together in one place, Sun formed the iForce partner network and developed programs to support it technically and with marketing assistance. Over time, Sun continued to build this network and found innovative ways to support it. This example illustrates some of the key ideas in this chapter. Sun acted entrepreneurially through nonproduct marketing innovation. It controlled the risks involved by innovating in steps, obtaining feedback, and revising the innovation. It continued to incrementally innovate to improve the value for its partners and for customers. The innovations built on each other and enabled further innovations, by Sun and its partners. Finally, they gave it a brand name and continued to support the brand. As the initiative builds new aspects (e.g., the iForce Wireless program and the partnership with direct sales), the iForce brand will acquire a stronger reputation among partners and customers. This will help Sun compete against the likes of IBM and Hewlett-Packard. Even assuming Oracle's efforts to acquire Sun are successful, iForce will help Oracle or Sun in its competitive efforts.

MARKETING ENTREPRENEURIALLY

Entrepreneurial marketing is the undertaking of a marketing strategy that actively pursues a new opportunity and has relatively high levels of innovation, proactivity, and controlled risk taking.

The methods of the entrepreneur add more to organizational performance than just energizing it through an entrepreneurial vision. Company executives can enhance performance by fostering an environment in which the organization does **entrepreneurial marketing**.[3] Even if the company's upper-level management does not create such an environment, the individual business marketer can still improve performance by incorporating entrepreneurial methods into his approach (within the constraints imposed by the organization).

What does it mean to market entrepreneurially? People generally think of entrepreneurship as the act of starting a new company. However, this is perhaps too simplistic a view. Managers and employees within a company can act as if their organization is a high-growth start-up with the result that their organization shows at least some of the flexibility and boldness of a start-up. Accordingly, we can identify characteristics that indicate that an act is more or less entrepreneurial. Research done by marketing and management scholars has come to the point of defining entrepreneurial activity as having three or four dimensions.[4] For our purposes, the key dimensions of entrepreneurship can be thought of as **innovation**, **proactivity**, **controlled risk taking**, and **opportunity seeking**.[5]

Innovation is creating something new and making it useful. The fact that somebody uses the new thing for some particular purpose distinguishes an innovation from an invention. Innovation can also be taking something that already exists and making it better, so that it provides more value to customers than it did before. *Proactivity* is doing something before others do it. Innovations, by their nature, are proactive, but entrepreneurs can do things that are not necessarily new. They might do something before their competitors do it, and this by definition is also being proactive. *Controlled risk taking* is a combination of knowing what the risks really are, taking moderate risks in which the worst case is survivable, and finding ways to manage the risks to increase the chances of success and reduce the consequences of failure. Finally, *opportunity seeking* is largely self-explanatory. Note that people and companies that are more entrepreneurial tend to actively look for opportunities and are constantly evaluating how attractive prospective opportunities are.

With this in mind, we can begin to see what entrepreneurial marketing is like. For any one entrepreneurial event, there is a cycle of activity. The cycle begins with opportunity recognition (Exhibit 9-1). Then an initial design is produced to address the opportunity. The design is developed and tested on prospective users and customers, and their reactions are evaluated and incorporated into the design. Meanwhile, the resources for pursuing this opportunity are being gathered. The project grows; choices are made; the capability to produce and deliver is ramped up; and the product, service, or program is launched. After launch, feedback is received, analyzed, and acted upon. In the feedback, new opportunities are sought and can trigger the cycle anew.

For this event to be successful, certain things must be done. First, the opportunity must be kept firmly in mind. The vision of the opportunity may change as feedback is received, but realization of the opportunity is the goal. Too often, new ventures lose focus as the team members see new opportunities galore and they try to find ways to pursue them. Second, producing a successful design involves combining established technology with recent technology (we use a broad definition here: *technology* is any way of doing something; it is not limited to hardware or software—see the discussion later in this chapter). The new technology may take a fair amount of creative work. The mind-set here must be a willingness to change or do things differently in order to pursue the opportunity. "Whatever it takes" must be done to make the opportunity "happen."

Obviously, these first two strictures or guidelines connote the "opportunity seeking" and "innovation" portion of entrepreneurial orientation. Innovation without proactivity, though, can drag on forever inside the organization without ever seeing the market. The

Innovation is the creation of something new and commercially useful or the improvement of something to make it more useful. It might involve the application of science or technology, but does not have to.

Proactivity is doing something before others do it. Taking the lead in a market or in a new development, even when the offering that will become obsolete by your action is your own, is a key element in market ownership.

Controlled risk taking is not "bet-the-farm" risk taking. Rather, entrepreneurial risk taking is knowing what the risks are and doing something to control the risk.

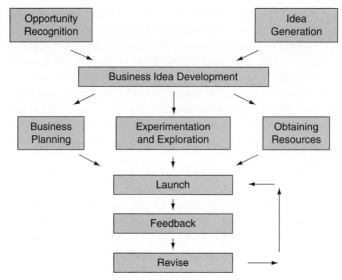

EXHIBIT 9-1 Entrepreneurial Cycle

entrepreneur or marketer has to get the innovation into the market, first to test it, and then to pursue the opportunity full bore. Taking too long can kill momentum; the development team gets comfortable (or bored) with tweaking the product or program to "get it right." Taking the new design to the market becomes a psychological hurdle that is too high to get over easily. Taking too long can also lead to being pre-empted by competition or by the customers themselves. The window of opportunity may close for a number of reasons.

Proactivity, then, involves doing things to reduce the time to market. Once in the market, proactivity involves doing things to rapidly improve the offering before the competition can improve theirs.

Though risk taking is often seen as the ultimate role or characteristic of the entrepreneur, most entrepreneurs do not see themselves as taking huge risks. Either they do not know enough about the chances for failure or they believe that they have enough control over the situation to manage the probability that their project will fall short of expectations. Successful entrepreneurs find ways to make things work, and they trust in their abilities to do so. Thus, entrepreneurial marketing is done in a way that minimizes the resources that are put at risk.

One way that marketers reduce the chance of failure is by obtaining as much information as possible before launching full scale. However, waiting too long can create a risk that an opportunity will be missed.[6] Another way that information can be gathered while being proactive is to run one or more "experiments."[7] These are trial runs in which the new business, new product, or new program is launched on a minimal scale in the market, usually in a small, controllable portion of the market. The results can be assessed and a revised offering launched into the larger market, eventually. In many cases, this can produce a full-scale launch more effectively than a launch based on extensive research.

Changing the Rules

The ultimate way of reducing risk, or at least changing everybody's risk, is to change the rules of the market, as discussed in Chapter 5. Recall that Hamel and Prahalad argued for competitive strategy that changes the relationships among the participants in a market, so that the "rules" determining competitive advantage are changed.[8] However risky, changing the rules is almost always entrepreneurial on the other three dimensions (proactivity, innovation, and opportunity seeking), as well, and can have a substantial payoff. It is usually very proactive in that action is taken before other competitors act. If the new rules come to be adopted by the market, the action may have the effect of upsetting the current competitive balance, starting the process of being recognized as the market owner. As for the innovation dimension, changing the rules almost always involves an innovation of some sort, whether it is innovation in the product or elsewhere in the offering.

Entrepreneurial marketing, then, is the undertaking of a marketing strategy that actively pursues a new opportunity and has relatively high levels of innovation, proactivity, and controlled risk taking. It stands to reason that it improves the marketer's chance of success because it creates new value that tends to be higher than the value offered by competitors.

Practical Aspects of Creating an Entrepreneurial Orientation

Over the past decade or so, many companies have said they wanted to "be more entrepreneurial" but have not gotten beyond paying lip service to the concept. The question arises how an entrepreneurial orientation should be fostered, particularly in business-to-business marketing. We discuss four key elements to inducing an entrepreneurial way of doing things within the marketing function: hiring the right kinds of people, directing the right kinds of activities, removing impediments, and providing the right incentives.

HIRING THE RIGHT KINDS OF PEOPLE   Hiring people who are comfortable acting entrepreneurially means looking for many characteristics that are common for most management or professional positions in today's business world. Good communication skills and an ability to work well with small, diverse teams are valued skills in most career positions. They are equally important for implementing an entrepreneurial orientation. Three key traits stand out, though, as likely indicators of someone who will be comfortable in an entrepreneurial environment. First is the ability to persistently pursue a passion. The marketer will want to be surrounded with team members who can get excited about business, treat it as a venture, and work hard to make it succeed. The second trait is a comfort with trying new things, making mistakes, and learning from them. This does not mean that the person is careless or sloppy. Complete learning comes in part from a comparison of expectations to actual results and trying to understand why there is a variance. This means that the person will be comfortable with the detail of setting objectives and then measuring results against those objectives. The important aspect, though, is that the person will not see mistakes as personally threatening. The third trait is a bias for action. Proactivity requires taking action in a quick but prepared way. Unprepared action tends to be reckless; overpreparation, of course, creates delay. The characteristic required strikes a balance between the two.

DIRECTING APPROPRIATE ACTIVITIES   We discuss innovation at length in the next major section of this chapter, so here we discuss activities that identify opportunities, create proactivity, and take controlled risks.

Opportunity recognition comes in part from formal activities to analyze potential markets and match unmet needs to a company's existing or expected core competencies. These are similar to the kinds of activities discussed in Chapters 5 through 7. Specific analytic methods for opportunity recognition can also be found in trade and research journals.[9] An adjunct to analytic techniques is an opportunity-oriented way of looking at the world. This involves cultivating a constant sensitivity to unmet customer needs and possible partnership combinations that can create new kinds of value. Managers can help their less-experienced marketing staff learn how to build a network of contacts for information collection (see Chapter 6).

Marketers should also develop contact networks aimed at facilitating execution of marketing activities (see the box, "Contact Network for Execution"). This will help in instituting proactivity as a way of doing things. Controlling the results of planning activities also enhances proactivity. Plans should seldom be more than a few pages in length and should have a series of action items specified.

The key activity for controlling risks is to establish learning mechanisms. This means trying new initiatives on a limited scale and assessing the results. Such assessment should be directed both at internal operations and at customers' perceptions of value. The Sun iForce program illustrates this kind of learning. Sun was able to observe the efforts of its actions in setting up the community of partners and learned what worked and what did not. Sun also learned what was valuable both to its partners and to customers, and this led to new initiatives in solutions developed for customer problems and changed methods of combining VAR sales activities with Sun's direct sales force.

REMOVING IMPEDIMENTS   Two principal impediments are often imposed by existing organizations. The first is a requirement for extensive justification. The second is a tendency to punish failure.

Opportunity seeking and proactivity are obviously hindered by a requirement for over-analysis. Controlled risk taking—and hence learning—is stifled if the organization demotes, ostracizes, or fires individuals who take risks that fail. These impediments need to be addressed by company executives. A marketing manager can do his best to shield employees from short-sighted company policies, but these policies would eventually limit the manager's ability to operate entrepreneurially.

PROVIDING INCENTIVES   Over the past decade, companies have gotten used to providing incentives to employees through profit-sharing bonuses and stock options. The economic slow-down of the early 2000s demonstrated the downside (literally) of these types of incentives. Accordingly, a range of incentives needs to be considered, including cash, equity, and non-monetary rewards. The keys, as always when providing incentives, are to provide appropriate incentives, to award the incentives for doing the right things, and to provide the rewards soon enough after the actions to be real reinforcement for the desired activity.

Contact Network for Execution

Just as marketers develop a network of contacts for information collection, they will need to form a network of contacts for getting things done. It pays to determine ahead of time who within the organization is responsible for such things as graphics design, support of missionary sales, sales training, and document production. These contacts will be internal to the firm but may also include outsiders such as consultants, ad agencies, and contacts among distributors. By cultivating these contacts during planning, the marketer can make execution go smoothly when the time comes.

COMPETING THROUGH INNOVATION

The entrepreneurial element of innovation is central to the continuing ability of the company to win customers and reap financial performance benefits. In the last chapter, we discussed product innovation through the new product development (NPD) process. In this chapter, though, we want to emphasize that innovation in the non-product elements of the offering can be just as important—sometimes even more important—than product innovation. Indeed, Christensen and Raynor assert that most disruptive innovations (explained below) are not product or technology innovations so much as they are business model innovations, the product innovations that are part of the new model being rather modest in scope.[10] An example is Dell Computers' choice of a direct channel—selling personal computers over an 800-number phone line.

Value comes from all elements of the offering. Maintaining or increasing a degree of differentiation from competitors can be accomplished through innovating in the channel structure, the pricing structure, or even the communication strategy surrounding the product. As was shown in the last chapter, the opportunity for product innovation becomes reduced during the mature portion of the product life cycle. If the company is not careful, it will resort to shaving margins to maintain competitiveness. Finding a way to innovate elsewhere in the offering, away from "product," may be the only way to maintain margins.

Innovation can be viewed not just as the creation of new things but also as new and better ways of doing what has been done before. Depending on viewpoint, all the following can be legitimate innovations:

Designing for more efficient production

Less use of raw materials

Reduced environmental impact

More effective marketing communication or selling

More effective distribution systems.

From this view, innovation is a significant contributor to productivity and, thus, is a significant contributor to our economic well-being and growth. In fact, at the macro level, innovation drives a free market economy. New products, services, retailers, other channel intermediaries, communications methods, and forms—all come from innovation. New ideas are the outcome of innovative effort. Our society "makes progress" through innovation.

Innovation across the Offering

Managing innovation is an important function of the firm. In the prior chapter, we discussed new product development and product management at length. New product development is extremely important in getting a key portion of value right for customers. The last chapter discussed an NPD process that moved from idea generation through several stages to arrive at a commercially offered product, managed on an ongoing basis. We can think of this process being extended to the other aspects of the offering. Our experience tells us though, that companies rarely spend the same kind of effort—nor do they have the same kind of process—for innovating in the other elements of the offering and value chain.

Before getting started, some definitions are in order. First, we want to be clear on what we mean by **technology**. As defined earlier, technology is a way of accomplishing something, based on scientific principles

*For our discussion, **technology** is not limited to items that comprise a manufactured product or those tools used in the performance of a service. Technology is a way of accomplishing something.*

or knowledge. Scientific principles can be found in all disciplines of inquiry, so this is a very broad characterization of technology.[11] Technology is not limited to the mechanisms that comprise a manufactured product or the code that comprises a software program. We can think of the marketing activities chosen by the firm as a technology to perform marketing. Similarly, innovation is not limited to changes of products or services. *Innovation* is a change in any technology and must be useful and potentially commercialized—innovation is invention in commercial use.

With these definitions as background, consider what is required for building a process that will facilitate and drive innovation across the offering(s) of the company. Recall from Chapter 5 that the firm must have a clear mission and goals, and executive management must recognize the necessity of change to meet those goals. In other words, executive management and strategy makers must recognize a need to be innovative and must make a conscious choice to do so. Innovation is so important for the long-term health of the company that top-level management must drive it. This strategy decision must cover what technologies to pursue, what kind of innovation will be pursued to address these technologies, and how to pursue this innovation.

If the company is going to pursue innovation—and it is a rare company that would not—the company must adopt a predisposition for trying new things. The culture and reward structure must accommodate and assist people who seek to innovate, whether they succeed or fail. Failure in innovating is positive, as long as (1) something valuable is learned and (2) it does not kill the company. Most innovations can be tried initially on a small scale without pursuing "bet-the-company" risks. Without adoption of policies that reward innovation and support "useful" failure, creating a culture of innovation is an uphill battle. This inclination to innovate must extend beyond the R&D part of the organization, because R&D only addresses part of the offering.

Once the organization is on its way to instilling an innovation inclination, executive management and strategy makers must choose where and how to innovate, as already mentioned. In Chapter 5, we stated that company executives make the strategic decision to pursue major business opportunities. Given the choice of business, innovation initiatives to pursue these will probably be obvious; and indeed the expected contributions of innovation were considered in the choice of opportunities. Given the innovative directions and businesses to pursue, strategy makers then determine "how innovative" the company needs to be.

Over the past twenty years, researchers and practitioners have observed that "big" innovations differ greatly from "small" innovations.[12] The field has come to distinguish two ends of the spectrum in terms of *radical innovation* and *incremental innovation.* **Incremental innovations** take the existing product and offering and make small-step improvements to the original design. Incremental improvements add up to produce a great deal of change in an offering over time. **Radical innovations**, on the other hand, can produce large changes in the functions and performance of a product or offering. Radical innovations can be so radical that they create an essentially different kind of product or offering with a new combination of types of value produced. These have come to be called **breakthrough innovations**,[13] although common usage of the term is inconsistent. Sometimes *breakthrough* is used to mean any extreme change in performance or costs, including a large improvement in existing benefits or costs, without changing the product's basic architecture or the offering's principal benefits. At other times, the term is used to strictly mean that the technology architecture has changed drastically or that benefit structure is essentially different and vastly better. No matter how the terms are defined or used, the implication is clear: different kinds of innovation behave differently and require different kinds of organizational treatment.

A way of thinking about innovation with useful implications has emerged over the past decade or so. Christensen distinguishes between *disruptive innovation* and *sustaining innovation.*[14] **Sustaining innovation** is innovation that improves the existing dominant technology, products, or offerings. It serves the needs of higher-end customers who already purchase similar products, but who want more value from these products. Sustaining innovation can be incremental changes or radical changes—but it is still innovation that stays on the same technology vector. In comparison, Christensen describes **disruptive innovation** as introducing a product or business idea that creates a new kind of value. Customers addressed by the disruptive innovation can be segments that are overserved by the products previously available. Or they might be customers whose needs are substantially different from the needs of existing customers. Initially, the new offering usually offers performance below that of the existing technology. The newly addressed segments do not represent an attractive business for the established companies competing with existing products. Hence, the disruptively innovative company gains a foothold by serving the new customers. Eventually, though, the new type of offering supplants the old as rapid technology advancement on the newcomer technology outstrips the capabilities of the established, mature technology.

Christensen argues that existing market leaders find it very difficult to pursue disruptive technologies. The leaders' infrastructure and operations are all geared toward pursuit and support of the existing direction in technology. Even the leaders' customers are all invested in receiving benefits from the existing technology; if a supplier produces an offering based on new technology, the customers will tend to redirect the supplier back to the established technology. Suppliers of the new technology must target different customer groups than the current leaders in order to succeed.

Christensen, in his analysis of the disk drive industry, has shown—and later he and Raynor reiterate[15]—that disruptive technology is *not necessarily radical innovation.* Incremental innovation may be the initiator of the disruptive innovation. Similarly, radical innovation does not have to be disruptive. It may simply improve the performance and benefit package of the existing architecture and offering but do so in one large leap. Take word processing in the early 1980s, for example. One might argue that the introduction of electronic, stand-alone word processors was a radical innovation over the electric typewriter. The word processors offered by Wang, Olivetti, Xerox, and IBM were far better and more useful than the standard IBM Selectric, but they were still, after all, typewriters. Meanwhile, word-processing software was offered as a product to be used on the desktop personal computer, linked by printer cable to a dot matrix or daisy-wheel printer. It was not as versatile as the trained typist with the stand-alone word processor, but it worked and gave the amateur typist the ability to create a usable, changeable document without burdening the administrative assistant or going through the typing pool.

Word-processing software was not a particularly radical innovation. It had been around for years, making it possible for someone to write documents using his company's mainframe or minicomputer. The initial market was not in the office products market; it was the individual professional (or even the student) who wanted to write her own documents. Over time, the software got better through incremental innovation. As professional staff learned that they could write, edit, and print their own documents faster and better than sending repeated drafts through a typing pool, the typing pool went away. As the remaining office staff started using the other mainstay programs of the PC—databases, graphics, and spreadsheets—and as offices invested in relatively expensive laser printers, administrative staff made the switch to multifunction PCs from their old, single-function word processors. The heyday of the stand-alone word processor was over within a few years.

The disruptive technology was the word-processing software; the innovation was incremental. The effect on the office products market was far-reaching. The radical innovation was probably going from the electric typewriter to the electronic typewriter. This was a sustaining innovation in Christensen's terms.

Accordingly, the firm needs to decide to address disruptive innovation if it is to survive in the long run. Without doing this, a new entrant will eventually replace the old technology for most of the market. The decision is not whether to pursue disruptive technology. The decision is *how* to pursue it and *to what extent*.

The company must also determine whether the innovation it will pursue is radical or incremental. Whether disruptive or sustaining, radical innovation requires different kinds of development and commercialization efforts than incremental innovation does.[16]

A corporate or business strategy that intends to "change the rules of the industry or marketplace," as discussed in Chapter 5, almost always needs to pursue breakthrough or disruptive innovation and to be proactive rather than reactive. The goals of the strategy makers and the circumstances of the business environment dictate how aggressive the company needs to be in this pursuit. In any case, the business strategy sets the innovation context within which the marketer has to operate.

Pursuit of Disruptive Technologies

Christensen and Raynor[17] say that disruptive strategies should be pursued when a product technology has developed to the point where mainstream customers' needs are overfulfilled. At this point, there is likely to be an emerging segment looking for lower performance, but new benefits. Assuming that the executive management of the firm decides to pursue disruptive technology to some extent, the question becomes "what does this mean for marketing?" within the firm. Christensen makes a compelling case that implementation of such a directive involves five things:[18]

1. Separate the project or business unit responsible for pursuing disruptive innovation from the existing company with its established customers and business model. Find new customers who really want the offering.
2. Address the new business with a small business unit appropriate in size for the small market size of the initial opportunity.
3. Use an iterative, exploratory approach for finding the right market and the right way of addressing the market.
4. Use processes and decision-making rules appropriate to the new business model; do not use the processes and rules of the existing organization, as these were not likely designed for an emerging business, nor will they facilitate changes.
5. Develop the markets that want the offering; do not try to find the breakthrough technology advance that makes the disruptive technology competitive in the old mainstream market. Eventually the new markets will evolve together into a new mainstream of their own.

These prescriptions suggest that the business-to-business marketer who finds himself in the pursuit of disruptive innovation (whether in the product, service, or in other elements of the offering) should be in a small business unit pursuing an uncertain opportunity (if it is not an uncertain opportunity, the innovation is probably not disruptive). If the marketer observes that his organization lacks autonomy from a large organization, then he should start looking for ways to change this situation. The large organization will usually impose its systems, values, and metrics on the new venture and unwittingly kill it. Even a supposedly enlightened organization that gives the new venture its own criteria for support will be tempted to change its mind later and impose revenue and profit objectives that are impossible to meet.

From Pistons to Fuel Cells

Kolbenschmidt Pierburg AG is the world's second largest supplier of pistons to manufacturers of internal combustion engines—auto and truck, gasoline and diesel. Annual sales are $1.8 billion, with revenues forecast to hit $3 billion in 2005. Because of demand for products in North America, the company will build a new U.S. production line, part of a $50 million capital investment.

How does this company spend R&D dollars? Certainly to maintain the position that its internal combustion engine components command in the market, but also by anticipating the future needs of the market. Kolbenschmidt has established a new business segment within its organization devoted to the development of clean, efficient fuel cells. Dr. Dieter Siepler, chairman of the Kolbenschmidt executive board, thinks it makes good business sense. Siepler says that Kolbenschmidt is confident that, by 2010, fuel cell power trains will be a viable alternative to traditional systems, with annual revenues forecast to start at $140 million.

Kolbenschmidt is a stakeholder in the future of the internal combustion engine. More importantly, the company's management recognizes that that stake is not in the product form but in the satisfaction of customer needs.

Source: Lindsay Brooke, "Piston Supplier Invests in Fuel Cells," *Automotive Industries* (April 2001).

The box "From Pistons to Fuel Cells" describes the innovative effort of Kolbenschmidt Pierburg AG. Notice that the kind of innovation pursued will probably involve a changeover in the infrastructure, that is, the innovation pursued is probably disruptive. Kolbenschmidt Pierburg AG will have to be careful how it manages its efforts, or it may be tempted to stay with the old line of business and lose out to the new, even though it has addressed the new technology directly.

If the marketer is indeed located in an autonomous venture with a cost structure and reasonable revenue targets of its own, then the question becomes how to accomplish the innovation required. One key is to take a learning approach. This is very different than an approach to execute a marketing plan. The premise of the learning plan is that uncertain markets are unknowable at first. Resources have to be allocated to trial, error, learning, and reconfiguration.

There are two important parts of this learning approach—called **discovery-based planning** by Christensen.[19] The first is gathering as much market and customer data as possible. The discussion in Chapter 6 described the establishment of a network of customers and industry contacts that become the sources for a large part of the customer data that need to be collected. This needs to be done in this case as well, but it is a network of different kinds of contacts that must be built. In particular, current customers in an established business are generally poor information sources about future direction. They are often focused on the day-to-day effort of maintaining the existing offering. They tend to not see the innovative uses of new products or the value of new services or other changes in the offering. For disruptive technologies, most of the customers emerge in new markets and segments; and the marketer will not have a good idea of what these segments are. Consequently, the marketer needs to cast widely for new, useful contacts. These contacts should be similar to the kinds of people von Hippel calls "**lead users**."[20] These are not necessarily the market leaders. Rather, they are users who have vision, who can anticipate what kinds of needs will arise among potential customers in the future. In this case, though, the lead user has to be someone who can anticipate what kinds of users will even exist in the future. Customer organizations that rely on innovation as a driving force in the competitiveness of the firm will have separately managed and rewarded groups in their organizations. These groups will have a different focus, interested in changing rather than maintaining the status quo. When presenting innovative offerings, marketers will find these parts of the customer organizations their strongest allies. This mirrors quite well the adoption process defined by the TALC.

The second important part of discovery-based planning is the judicious use of trial and error. Many users will not be able to give usable information on the nature of their needs and buying behavior until they become familiar with the offering and have had a chance to see how their organization would benefit from it. Consequently, the innovating company must run a sequence of trial offerings. In each one, user feedback is sought on the value provided by all aspects of the offering. It is important to systematically collect this feedback and learn as much as possible about what will best provide value to the customers. Firms that recognize the need for continuous innovation, both as suppliers and customers, will have these relationships as part of an ongoing effort.

Pursuit of Sustaining Innovation

Most innovation is what Christensen calls **sustaining innovation**. Such innovations are changes, radical or incremental, that make somewhat predictable improvements to existing technologies. *Radical sustaining innovation* increases performance or costs dramatically but within the same technology direction. *Incremental sustaining innovation* makes small changes along predictable vectors. While most innovation is sustaining innovation, most sustaining innovation is incremental in nature. To compete for any length of time within an industry, a company must pursue sustaining innovation.

When the marketer is in the situation of competing through sustaining innovations, a rigorous and disciplined process of managing innovation is possible and necessary. The principal characteristic of this situation is that customers can provide a good idea of what they want, how it will be used, and how they will acquire it. Through the process of market ownership, value is provided to customers through a well-established extended value chain.[21]

With this in mind, the process for preparing the periodic marketing plan can be used as the framework for instituting innovation throughout the offering. Just as the company has a process for development of new products, the annual marketing plan (or plan done on some other periodic basis) can be treated as the process for marketing's R&D. The purpose of the planning process should be to evaluate the market, evaluate past marketing efforts, recognize evolutionary developments, and find new ways to create value for customers.

The periodic nature of the planning process is important. **Time pacing** of planned organization change—setting strict time tables for new versions of products, operations, strategies, and so on—has been found to work well in fast-paced business environments in focusing the company's efforts and setting expectations for customers.[22] It has been found to be extremely useful in dictating the rules of engagement in a competitive market, particularly from the point of view of the market owner. Business-to-business marketers can use time pacing in their attempts to achieve incremental innovation across all elements of the offering. The rules for doing periodic marketing plans should state that each plan will include improved value in all elements of the offering. Not only will customers come to expect periodic improvements in the value they receive from such things as service or pricing plans, but the sales force, channels, and partners will learn to expect new programs and support as well. Too often, business-to-business marketing planning focuses innovative attention on products and markets to the exclusion of innovation in the other elements of the offering. Time pacing of non-product innovation will take the marketers out of product-centric marketing planning and help them refocus on pursuing multiple avenues to improved value for customers.

Practical Aspects of Accomplishing Innovation

In this discussion of innovation so far, we have described the need for the company's strategy makers to decide what businesses and technologies to pursue and to decide whether they are working on disruptive innovation or sustaining innovation. Disruptive innovation requires an autonomous organizational unit with its own mission, processes, and metrics. Sustaining innovation requires attention to constant customer inputs and time pacing applied through the marketing plan. Just as was done in the first section of this chapter, we now turn to some practical aspects of implementing innovation across the offering. Again, we will discuss this in terms of obtaining the right people, directing the right activities, removing impediments, and providing incentives.

OBTAINING THE RIGHT KINDS OF PEOPLE   Innovation occurs in either a project format or through ongoing management of the marketing function of the company. Projects often result in special purpose teams assembled for the duration of the project. If upper-level management assembles the team, then the marketer may have no choice of with whom he must work. If given the choice of people for the team or when hiring for the ongoing marketing function, it is important to match the type of person to the type of innovation being pursued.[23] Someone who takes a visionary, extensive redesign approach to every problem would not be appropriate for incremental innovation. Someone who takes an impatient, results-oriented approach may become frustrated in a setting with so much uncertainty and uneven progress as displayed by disruptive or radical innovation.

Other than this distinction, the marketing manager will want to include (hire, if appropriate) people who are creative and innovative. Note that innovativeness is focused on usefulness or value for the customer. This is not "variety seeking" for its own sake. Another trait to try to avoid in team members is a strong tendency toward being territorial. Because of the fluid nature of innovation and the tendency to change directions if needed, a strong sense of territory can be detrimental. A new offering will need a champion to gain adoption within the organization. However, when the feelings of ownership become too strong, the person will stand in the way of adapting the innovation or even scrapping it when the need arises.

DIRECTING THE RIGHT ACTIVITIES   We have already discussed ways to obtain customer information when working on disruptive innovation or sustaining innovation. Both involve establishing networks of relationships with people who can supply information. The biggest difference is who is included. In a disruptive innovation effort, the network must be broad and focused on insightful customers and industry watchers. In a sustaining innovation effort, the network is focused more on customers, partners, and channel members within the markets of interest.

A current trend in innovation efforts is the use of collaborators and partners in innovation efforts. The opening example describing Sun Microsystems' efforts to develop the iForce initiative is an example of collaborative development, all under the directive efforts of one company. It should be noted again that this innovative effort extends across the entire offering; it is not limited to innovation in product, service, channels, or any other part of the offering.

A key aspect of getting the activities right is matching the activities to the type of innovation. Recall that the distinction between sustaining and disruptive innovation makes a difference in how the innovation is addressed. Radical innovation needs autonomy and constant updating of the vision of the future market.[24] This is particularly true when the radical innovation is disruptive. Even when the radical innovation is a sustaining innovation, there is still considerable uncertainty in how the configuration of the offering will eventually stabilize. Indeed,

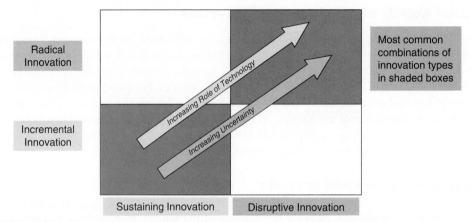

EXHIBIT 9-2   Relationship between Radical/Incremental and Disruptive/Sustaining Innovation

market uncertainty exists as well, although not to the extent of market uncertainty under disruptive innovation. Accordingly, there is probably good reason to address radical sustaining innovation with an autonomous business unit. While the relationship is not perfect, there tends to be more incremental change associated with sustaining innovations and disruptive change has more radical innovation (see Exhibit 9-2). Hence, the autonomous units tend to be associated more with disruptive change than with sustaining change. The applicability of time pacing for radical innovation, even when the innovation is sustaining, is questionable. There are just too many uncertainties about how long it will take to configure the new offering.

Rangan and Bartus point out that a large problem in product commercialization is the match between the company's beliefs about the innovation and customers' beliefs.[25] They say that mismatches occur when marketers believe the innovation to be radical while the customers believe it to be incremental, and vice versa. When the market sees the innovation as radical while the company sees it as incremental, the company is likely to miss a major opportunity. Rangan and Bartus call these products "shadow" products because they hide in the shadows of the products the company feels are more important. When the market sees the innovation as incremental while the company sees it as radical, the company will spend too much on promoting it and will lose credibility in the eyes of the customers. These products Rangan and Bartus call "delusional."

While these are useful characterizations, we need to break down these mismatches and misperceptions further, because the way to address the problem depends on the source(s) of the misperception. First, the innovating supplier and the marketer working for the supplier can misread the importance that customers will place on the innovation. The marketer can also misread the customers' ease or difficulty in adopting the innovation. The innovating supplier is not the only party that can misperceive importance or ease of adoption: the customer can have misperceptions as well. Pragmatist or conservative customers may not believe that an innovation can change their competitive advantage as much as it really can. Also, they may have misgivings about adoption that are really quite easily handled. Exhibit 9-3 shows these different sources of misperceptions and some differences in how a company might try to overcome them.

IMPEDIMENTS AND INCENTIVES   The impediments to instilling innovation in an organization are similar to the impediments we discussed for the rest of entrepreneurial marketing. One

Type of Innovation	Supplier Perception/Misperception	Customer Perception/Misperception	Approach to Solving
Radical	Accurate	Inaccurate—Not radical	Education, demonstration
	Accurate	Inaccurate—Difficult to adopt	Education, demonstration, target by TALC
	Inaccurate—Not radical	Accurate	Listen to customers & prospects; reposition
	Inaccurate—Easy to adopt	Accurate—Hard to adopt	Listen to customers and prospects; create rest of offering that eases adoption
Incremental	Accurate	Inaccurate—Hard to adopt	Education, demonstration, target those with greatest need
	Inaccurate—Not incremental	Accurate	Listen to customers and prospects; reposition; scale back effort

EXHIBIT 9-3 Perceptions and Misperceptions of Innovations

impediment is holding managers accountable for justifying their projects when there are no results data available or secondary data that are usable. A second is overzealous punishment of failure. Upper-level management must set the guidelines and the tone for removing these impediments.

Similarly, incentives need to be provided for being innovative. In the entrepreneurial marketing section it was mentioned that the incentives need to be set at the right level, using the right forms, and delivered in time to reinforce the right behavior. These statements are equally applicable for instilling innovation in the offering.

Note if your company is strictly known as a technology company, technology innovation is necessary, though not sufficient, for success. The argument that "we are focused on our high-technology product—that's why customers buy from us" is a dangerous position. In fact, the technology-oriented organization will have branding as a more important task, as their product is expected to make a value statement rather than be a "me-too" product. The "me-too" organization can focus on manufacturing efficiencies, distribution economies, and alternative cost (read "lower") positions with purchasing departments. Ironically, the technology-oriented company must establish a brand position or become a low-cost producer of maturing products.

THOUGHTS TO TAKE WITH YOU INTO THE NEXT CHAPTER

Planning and executing the marketing activities that create an offering can be competitively impotent if the marketer treats it as only a cookbook exercise. To make the offering competitive on an ongoing basis, the business-to-business marketer needs to attack the competition with several tools. We have discussed some of the most important concepts and tools in this chapter.

Innovation gives the marketer the opportunity to produce more value for customers and to continue to do so over time. As markets mature, it becomes more and more important for marketers to look for non-product ways to innovate. As discussed in this chapter, it is necessary to have a sense of what kind of innovation is being pursued. This dictates the approach to the development of innovations in the offering.

Innovation is a key part of marketing entrepreneurially. By marketing with innovation, proactive efforts, controlled risk taking, and attention to opportunities, marketers should be able to compete on both value and time. Adopting an entrepreneurial orientation involves setting the expectations for the marketers that they will need to act entrepreneurially and then setting the structure and incentives so that marketers will be motivated to be entrepreneurial.

As you go to Chapter 10, and beyond, be thinking about how to innovate and act entrepreneurially in the particular element of business-to-business marketing addressed in each chapter.

Key Terms

breakthrough innovation *208*
controlled risk taking *203*
discovery-based planning *211*
disruptive innovation *209*
entrepreneurial marketing *202*

incremental innovation *208*
innovation *203*
lead users *211*
opportunity seeking *203*
proactivity *203*

radical innovation *208*
sustaining innovation *209*
technology *207*
time pacing *212*

Questions for Review and Discussion

1. Why would taking an entrepreneurial orientation in business-to-business marketing yield better competitiveness for a company than would a more reactive, risk-averse approach?

2. How does innovation differ from proactivity?

3. Why is controlled risk taking more competitively attractive than strictly risk-averse behavior?

4. What is the difference between radical innovation and disruptive innovation?

5. Why is an autonomous organizational unit the appropriate way to pursue disruptive innovation?

6. Why should a marketing manager try to enhance and direct incremental, non-product innovation? Since it is incremental, why not just let it happen on its own?

7. Compare the marketing mix and customs of an innovation-oriented firm and a market share-driven firm. What prevents a share-driven firm from also being a leader in innovation?

8. Referring to Question 7, what suggestions could you make to a share-driven firm that also wants to be known as the innovator in the market?

Endnotes

1. Based on H.M. Fattah, "Second Rising?" *Marketing Computers* 21(3) (March 2001), pp. 34–36; iForce Web site: http://www.iforce.com; Jim Kerstetter and Peter Burrows, "Sun: A CEO's Last Stand," *Business Week* (3893) (July 26, 2004), pp. 64–70; and on Elizabeth Montalbano, "Sun Engages Channel," *CRN* (1147) (May 16, 2005), p. 6.

2. Peter R. Dickson, "Toward a General Theory of Competitive Rationality," *Journal of Marketing* (January 1992), pp. 69–83.

3. Michael H. Morris, Minet Schindehutte, and Raymond LaForge, "Entrepreneurial Marketing: A Construct for Integrating Emerging Entrepreneurship and Marketing Perspectives," *Journal of Marketing Theory and Practice*, 10(4) (2002), pp. 1–19.

4. Danny Miller and Peter H. Friesen, "Innovation in Conservative and Entrepreneurial Firms: Two Models of Strategic Momentum," *Strategic Management Journal*, 3 (1982), pp. 1–25;

Michael H. Morris and Gordon W. Paul, "The Relationship Between Entrepreneurship and Marketing in Established Firms," *Journal of Business Venturing*, 2 (1987), pp. 247–259; Jeffrey G. Covin and Dennis P. Slevin, "Strategic Management of Small Firms in Hostile and Benign Environments," *Strategic Management Journal*, 10 (1989), pp. 75–87.

5. Morris, Schindehutte, and LaForge, "Entrepreneurial Marketing," add three other dimensions—resource leveraging, value creation, and customer intensity. In this text, these dimensions are included in the other four or are an integral part of the general approach to marketing espoused in this text.

6. Peter R. Dickson and Joseph J. Giglierano, "Missing the Boat and Sinking the Boat," *Journal of Marketing* (Summer 1986).

7. Thomas J. Peters and Robert H. Waterman, *In Search of Excellence* (New York: Harper and Row, 1982).

8. Gary Hamel and C.K. Prahalad, *Competing for the Future* (Boston, Mass.: Harvard Business School Press, 1994).

9. Thomas C. O'Brien and Terry J. Fadem, "Identifying New Business Opportunities," *Research Technology Management* (September–October 1999), pp. 15–19.

10. Clayton M. Christensen and Michael E. Raynor, *The Innovator's Solution: Creating and Sustaining Successful Growth* (Boston, Mass.: Harvard Business School Press, 2003), Chapter 2.

11. This is consistent with Porter's view of technology in the value chain, found in Michael E. Porter, *Competitive Advantage: Creating and Sustaining Superior Performance* (New York: The Free Press, 1985), Chapter 5.

12. C.f. James M. Utterback, "Radical Innovation and Corporate Regeneration," *Research Technology Management* 37(4) (1994), p. 10.

13. C.f. Gina Colarelli O'Connor, "Market Learning and Radical Innovation: A Cross Case Comparison of Eight Radical Innovation Projects," *Journal of Product Innovation Management* 15(2) (1998), pp. 151–166.

14. Clayton M. Christensen, *The Innovator's Dilemma* (New York: HarperCollins, 1997); and Christensen and Raynor, *The Innovator's Solution.*

15. Christensen and Raynor, *The Innovator's Solution*, p. 66.

16. V. Kasturi Rangan and Kevin Bartus, "New Product Commercialization: Common Mistakes," *Harvard Business School* (Note 594-127, 1994, 63–75).

17. Christensen and Raynor, *The Innovator's Solution.*

18. Ibid.

19. Ibid.

20. Eric von Hippel, "Lead Users: A Source of Novel Product Concepts," *Management Science* (July 1986), pp. 791–805.

21. Christensen calls this a value network. His idea is similar to our notion of a value network but is more limited. We also see the partners who are contributing something to the offering, rather than just the suppliers who make materials and components that are aggregated into final products.

22. Kathleen M. Eisenhardt and Shona Brown, "Time Pacing: Competing in Markets that Won't Stand Still," *Harvard Business Review* (March–April 1998), pp. 59–69; and Connie J.G. Gersick, "Pacing Strategic Change: The Case of a New Venture," *Academy of Management Journal*, 37(1) (1994), pp. 9–45.

23. Rangan and Bartus, "New Product Commercialization," p. 70.

24. O'Connor, "Market Learning and Radical Innovation."

25. Rangan and Bartus, "New Product Commercialization," p. 71.

Chapter *10*

Pricing in Business-to-Business Marketing

OVERVIEW

Price is a key component of value. Customer-oriented pricing involves setting prices that reflect the customer's perception of the worth of the offering. This is set by the customer's own value chain and cost structure. Prices charged by competitors influence the perceived maximum that customers will pay.

This chapter first reviews some basic ideas about setting prices in light of maximum prices that can be obtained for a given offering and costs that must be covered to make a profit. Basic concepts of demand, supply, and price elasticity of demand are reviewed in light of their contribution to pricing.

The next sections discuss the management of pricing as part of the marketing mix. Strategic aspects of pricing include objectives of pricing, price development for new products or services, and price throughout the product life cycle. Tactical pricing includes pricing of bundled products (bundles of several products for a single price), competitive bidding, and changing prices.

The next section concerns negotiated price. In the final section the general trends in business-to-business markets and how marketers must adapt their pricing efforts are discussed. We revisit the trends of time compression, hypercompetition, and the growth in the use of the Internet.

Intel Changes Its Competitive Pricing for Microprocessors[1]

In the past, Intel Corporation had used a price-skimming approach for microprocessors. New processors would be introduced and offered at a high price level. The OEM buyer—Hewlett-Packard, Dell, IBM, for instance—would buy relatively few processors for a relatively few computers that would be offered to high-end users—corporate specialty users in finance, engineering, network serving, and Web hosting. After these first needs had been fulfilled, and as software development was catching up to the capabilities of the new processor technology, Intel would drop prices and the OEMs would offer computers to users whose need for speed was not so immediate as the first users, but who were willing to wait for lower prices and more functionality. As prices came down, Intel would drop prices on its prior processor to the point at which late majority and laggard buyers of low-priced computer equipment would purchase.

Meanwhile, competitors, principally Advanced Micro Devices (AMD) and Cyrix, introduced compatible processors priced under the Intel price points. Since competitors were playing catch-up, Intel was able to minimize the competitive influence of these low-cost alternatives by continuing to enhance the speed and functionality of Intel processors. This market ownership by Intel controlled the pace of innovation to maximize Intel profitability while squeezing the competition.

At the end of the decade (1990s), AMD processors reached (and in some views, surpassed) the performance levels of the most capable Intel chips. AMD began an identity program and the Athlon-brand processor became a viable alternative at the premium end of the market. AMD had solved some earlier production problems to reach the point where competitive processors could be shipped in quantity and on time, giving the OEMs a solid second source of microprocessors. The significance of this should not be minimized; AMD was able to price Athlon processors for the premium market, greatly improving the company's overall financial performance.

As Intel introduced the Pentium 4 in late 2000, the U.S. economy and much of the world economy were entering a slowdown. Sales of workstations and personal computers slowed considerably, causing inventories to escalate and PC makers', as well as chipmakers', earnings to fall.

Intel used the downturn as an opportunity to rejuvenate its competitive advantage. It dropped prices quickly on its high-end processors. Prices on its 1.5 GHz Pentium 4 processor dropped from $795 in December 2000 to $519 in April 2001. Similarly, the 1.4 GHz Pentium 4 was priced at $574 in December and reduced to $300 in April. AMD, of course, followed suit with similar reductions in its line of processors.

Aggressively lower prices were not Intel's only strategic move made to improve competitive position. Intel, like most other technology companies during the period, actively cut costs. A program to trim the workforce by 5,000 employees through attrition had to be enhanced with a "voluntary separation program" in which workers were offered incentives to depart (it seems that during a downturn workers want to keep their jobs and not feed the normal attrition rate). Even while earnings were declining, though, Intel announced that it would not reduce R&D spending, nor would it slow its capital spending plans. Because it had the resources, Intel wanted to be ready with new products when the economy rebounded. Also, during a downturn, capital projects, such as new plants and equipment, can be obtained for lower cost than during boom times. So, when the economy improved, Intel could produce products with a cost advantage, which would allow it more price flexibility while maintaining higher profitability.

This is close to what actually happened as recession of the early 2000s played out. Intel was able to continue its price pressure on AMD. AMD was hurt badly, having to lay off about 2,000 employees in 2001 through 2003. Intel was also able to introduce the Centrino version of the Pentium 4, which was specially designed to easily enable wireless connection of laptop computers to the Internet, via Wi-Fi technology. This new product revived PC sales and, since AMD did not have a quick competitive answer to the Centrino, it revived Intel's profitability.

AMD, however, did not fade quietly into the night. AMD countered with its own product innovation by beating Intel in offering high-end 64-bit microprocessors—the Opteron and next-generation Athlon—which were quickly adopted by computer manufacturers in the next generation of servers. Thus AMD's share of this market rose to 17.8 percent from 16.6 percent over two years. Intel's answer for server processors did not reach the market until 2007. In this way, AMD countered price competition in some of its aging product lines through successful product innovation. The company was able to compete in the low-margin product lines because it produces high-margin products needed in another market segment, thus sustain this business for an extended period of time.

New Intel CEO Paul Otellini has announced a market-driven strategy aimed at the convergence of computing and entertainment and enabling mobile computing applications. Instead of the Pentium brand, Intel will transition to three brands, the existing Centrino brand, a brand named Viiv that focuses on home computing and electronics, and Core, a brand aimed at applications of Intel's new dual core processors.

Intel and AMD are both trying to avoid the debilitating effects of direct price competition by pursuing extensive product innovation. Now Intel has restructured the better part of its business strategy to compete in the future. How should AMD now respond?

LEARNING OBJECTIVES

By reading this chapter, you will:

- Remember the basics of pricing from your marketing principles course.

- Understand the relationship between perceived value and price.

- Understand the relationship between cost and price.

- Gain a sense of what aspects of business-to-business pricing are strategic and which are tactical, and how to address these aspects.

- Understand how negotiated pricing works; gain a sense of strategies for maintaining margin and customer relationships in negotiated pricing.

- Learn how to avoid dropping price as a short-term tactic.

- Gain an appreciation for the effects of current trends on pricing.

INTRODUCTION

Price is an important part of a broader set of strategic initiatives that includes product strategy and communications. Customers respond to the price changes made by suppliers. Competitors react as well, provided the changes are recognized as benefiting the entire industry. Price changes, when followed by competitors, establish a price leader in a market. All competitors may not have the interests or market position to profit as much from the changes made by a market leader, but not following the changes would be more costly than "going along" with the market. As pricing ideas are discussed throughout this chapter, some of the nuances of price as strategy, not tactic, will come more clearly into focus.

Price makes it possible for transactions to take place. The customer receives benefits from the product or service offered in exchange for the exchange price. The supplier receives the price paid by the customer in exchange for the product or service offered. Both parties expect that the outcome of the transaction will enhance their total value. *Neither the customer nor the supplier will act unless the price makes it worthwhile for both parties.*

For the marketer, pricing is situational and depends on strategic purposes and the business environment. In many cases, the price element of the offering includes such things as providing financing, setting financing terms, allowing for several methods of payment, establishing payment terms and schedules, allowing price adjustments for activities performed by the customer or services provided by the supplier, or calculating exchange rates to allow for payments in any of several currencies. *All of these elements of price are part of the total offering and a consideration in the customer's buying process.*

Business-to-business pricing differs considerably from pricing in consumer marketing. When consumers make purchases, price is a deliberate contributing factor to the final decision and is usually a predetermined suggested list price. The elements that contribute benefits beyond the core product, such as a convenient retail location, adequate product assortment, and an easy payment method may be part of the shopping experience but are not usually foremost in the decision process. Few consumers associate waiting times (either at checkout counters or for delivery), or quantity (consumers seldom can take advantage of volume discounts, and if they could, would likely patronize a different seller), as elements of price. Consumer decisions related to the economic utility (form, time, place, possession) of an offering are viewed as either convenient or not. Consumer markets, characterized as operating under monopolistic competition, generally have little variation in the offerings in any particular product category. As a result, in consumer products, price is often used as an attractive feature of the offering and thus is a major part of the marketing mix.

In business-to-business markets, all costs (indirect and direct) as well as the direct benefits from the offering are considered in the decision process. Price levels for business-to-business offerings are evaluated objectively in light of the customer's value chain, while consumers evaluate prices and costs in light of their perceptions of acceptable price levels—often determined by the relative position of competitive offerings. Price strategies in business-to-business markets must consider that professional purchasing people who are skilled at extracting value from transactions are part of the customer buying center. Business-to-business pricing involves competitive bidding and negotiating much more than does pricing in consumer markets. The psychological aspects of pricing in business-to-business marketing are subdued, though still present, when compared to consumer marketing.

Pricing is one of the easiest marketing variables to change and one of the most difficult to do well. Too often, cutting price becomes the "magic word" that allows the marketer or seller[2] to sell a mismatched product or service to an otherwise unwilling customer. While the short-term consequences of price-cutting may be positive—the company gets the business of a new customer or keeps the business of a dissatisfied customer, the long-term results can be bitter. The lowered price becomes a surrogate for other problems associated with the product or relationship. Recall the discussion of the misuse of the value chain concept from Chapter 1. Recognizing value from the supplier point of view can lead to a failure to see what customers perceive as value. Constantly giving price concessions to win over customers undermines margins, which in turn means few resources for investing in the growth of the business.

Continuously relying on cutting price is habit forming. Sellers start to see it as an easy to implement first resort. Marketers start basing their marketing programs on elaborate, costly, and ever-more-frequent promotion plans, built around price reductions, used to support channels or "incentivize" customers (who, predictably, stockpile enough of the product to see them through the period during which no promotion is run—a practice that intensifies the bullwhip effect). Customers become addicted, too. They get to the point where reduced price always becomes a major concession sought in negotiation; and once the precedent has been established it has become the benchmark to which future negotiations refer. Recognize also that business won primarily through price concessions can be lost the same way.

In this chapter we discuss concepts and methods in pricing that, hopefully, can avoid the kind of pricing that results in prematurely collapsing profits. Note, though, that understanding customers, their needs, and buying decision processes and preparing good offerings for them go a long way toward supporting prices that lead to profitability. Profitable pricing is the outcome and reward of doing a good job in the rest of the areas of marketing.

Setting prices is often caught up with the supplier's efforts to build a relationship with customers. Setting prices, then, has to address the competing interests of establishing goodwill with customers (a pressure to give the customer price breaks—a win for the customer) and extracting the maximum profit from transactions (a pressure to charge as much as "the market will bear"—a win for the supplier). Balancing these two competing forces is where creativity comes into play. This becomes particularly necessary when sellers are negotiating with customers and a concession on price seems to be the thing that will close the deal. Stability of the relationship between the two parties is likely only when the outcome of the negotiation is a win–win situation.

Finally, this chapter discusses some of the effects of our three current trends: time compression, hypercompetition, and the Internet. Time compression does not allow companies to fully understand customers and markets and how they respond to price levels and changes. Time compression also places a great deal of pressure on marketers, sellers, and business development people to negotiate and reach closure quickly. Hypercompetition makes it difficult for companies to maintain differentiated positioning. Without differentiation and with low-price oriented competitors working hard to win customers, business-to-business marketers face increased pressure to improve the value of their offerings.

PRICING BASICS

Cost-based pricing is the determination of price by figuring costs of offering a product or service and then adding on a standard percentage profit. An alternative method is to determine a price that will yield a targeted rate of return on capital invested in the offering. Several problems arise with either procedure. First, costs per unit usually depend on volume and the volume is set arbitrarily. Second, many cost categories are added based on a "standard rate" that may have no relationship to actual costs required or incurred. Third, and most important, the price has no relationship to customers' perceptions of the worth of the offering. Customers might be willing to pay much more for the offering, or much less. Either way, the marketer loses.

Many of the factors mentioned that contribute to cost-based pricing are addressed by market-savvy firms as determinants of whether the firm should be in the business in the first place. (See "ParkerHannifin Discovers Value Pricing," below.)

At its most basic, a price is an indicator of the worth of the offering. A customer looks at the price of the offering and asks three general questions: "Are the benefits received worth the price being charged?" "Can we obtain the same benefits for a better price?" and "Can we obtain the same benefits at a lower cost by producing the item ourselves (vertical integration—see 'Make-or-Buy Decisions' in Chapter 8)?" If the customer has a budget constraint, which is usually the case, an additional question is this: "Can we pay the price?" In simple terms, the marketer's job in pricing is to set a price that obtains positive responses to the questions about whether the benefits are worth the price and whether the customer can afford the price. The marketer must also set the price so that the customer cannot obtain more value from some other supplier's offering. As market conditions change, the marketer may have to change prices for existing offerings to maintain or improve the attractiveness of the offering.

Setting and changing prices, when done well, involves a combination of analysis and creativity. The analysis part must address both customers' perceptions of value relative to competition and the supplier's cost structure. We have observed that, too often, the analysis is incomplete, focusing solely on internal costs and profits. To really understand a customer's perceptions of value, including the perception of price, marketers often need to understand the customer's cost structure.

The creativity part is often incomplete itself. The marketer must use all the elements of pricing as part of the jigsaw puzzle of the offering (Exhibit 10-1) to create superior value for customers. Xerox's pricing in its early days is a classic example of how creative pricing can add to value instead of subtracting from it. To overcome customers' negative reaction to the purchase price of the first photocopy machines, Xerox provided a leasing option for the equipment. The reduced cash flow burden at the time of acquisition made the cost more palatable and reduced the customer's risk: If they did not like the new technology, they could return it without having tied up a significant amount of cash. Of course, customers found that they soon relied heavily on photocopying and adopted the technology wholeheartedly.

Pricing based on customers' perceived value—**value-based pricing**— is not the easiest way to establish prices but creates prices that are consistent with the marketer's strategy. This stands in contrast to **cost-based pricing**, which is often (and mistakenly) used in business-to-business marketing. Cost-based pricing runs the risk of losing profits or pricing too high for the market.[3] Costs are important in determining profit levels from different pricing alternatives, and they matter when downward pressure on prices puts price level in jeopardy of falling below costs. Beyond these considerations,

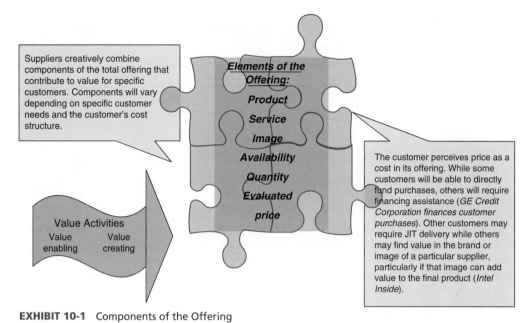

Suppliers creatively combine components of the total offering that contribute to value for specific customers. Components will vary depending on specific customer needs and the customer's cost structure.

Elements of the Offering:

Product

Service

Image

Availability

Quantity

Evaluated price

The customer perceives price as a cost in its offering. While some customers will be able to directly fund purchases, others will require financing assistance (*GE Credit Corporation finances customer purchases*). Other customers may require JIT delivery while others may find value in the brand or image of a particular supplier, particularly if that image can add value to the final product (*Intel Inside*).

Value Activities

Value enabling   Value creating

EXHIBIT 10-1   Components of the Offering

cost has little to do with price.[4] When profitability is threatened, marketers need to understand what costs are relevant and what consequences will result from setting prices at levels near cost levels; but different stakeholders within the supplier organization may have different perceptions of what those costs levels actually are. Usually, though, costs should have nothing to do with setting price levels. When price and cost are not supportive, the imbalance is usually a symptom of a larger, strategic problem, not a tactical difficulty.

Pricing to Reflect Customer Value

To set prices, the marketer must understand the way customers perceive value. This is more complex than simply charging what the market will bear. It involves balancing the concerns of customer value, supplier profitability, customer goodwill, and long-term relationships. At the core of these considerations are the customers' perceptions that there is a price that is appropriate for the benefits customers will receive from the offering and that there is a maximum price that they will be willing to pay for that offering.

   Recall that customers evaluate the value of an offering by considering both the benefits they receive and the costs they incur from acquiring something offered. Part of the cost consideration is the price paid for the **total offering**. The other part is the cost of acquisition and use of the product or service that is acquired in the offering. We have combined these two elements of cost into what we call **evaluated price**. Evaluated price can be very different from the price that is charged or the value exchanged. Exhibit 10-2

*The **total offering** is the offering that provides a complete solution to the buyer's needs. This may include financing, delivery, service, or, based on the buyer's preference, only the core product. Different customers may have different views as to what the value of the total offering is, depending on the value each customer places on items of value beyond the core product (see Chapter 1).*

*The **evaluated price** is the price of the offering, from the view of the customer, after all costs associated with the total offering are evaluated.*

- Actual price paid/value exchanged at time of purchase (viewed as cost by customer)
- Cost of locational convenience, that is, shipping and associated costs
- Handling and storage costs incurred by customer, that is, refrigeration and other environmental requirements, training for special handling, obsolescence, damage, inventory shrinkage, other logistical costs, etc.
- Inventory financing/holding costs
- Environmental impact/disposal costs or value
- If capital equipment
  - Financing
  - Customer installation costs
  - Installation, maintenance, and facilities costs
  - Cost of obsolescence/removal/disposal of old equipment
  - Employee/operator retraining

All of these costs are arguably quantifiable. Additional factors, value image, goodwill, reputation, and so on, are less quantifiable but also significantly contribute to the customer's view of evaluated price.

EXHIBIT 10-2   Potential Costs Considered in Evaluated Price, as Considered from the Customer's View

describes some potential costs included in the evaluated price. Note that many of these costs occur over the life of the product, not at the time of initial purchase. Exhibit 10-3 describes a situation in which a comparison of the charged prices of two raw materials shows a big advantage for the first material. However, when the evaluated price of the two materials is compared, the second material comes out the clear winner.

The customer considers value to be the difference between benefits and evaluated price. For the customer to continue to consider the offering as a viable alternative, the difference

How do you convince a customer to substitute a higher-priced product for a low-priced product? Value.

Consider the experience of manufacturers that use small motors in their products—in particular, small appliances and power tools. Historically, these small motors were manufactured with die-cast metal frames. Simply stated, die-cast metal parts are essentially the result of molten metal poured into a mold, cooled, and then removed from the mold. The metal raw materials used often cost very little, say $.50 per pound.

Suppose you are the field marketer for a company that makes engineering plastics. (Engineering plastics are not like the disposable "picnic" plastics. Engineering plastics have physical properties that make them a viable substitute for metals in many applications.) Your next development effort is to work with a major manufacturer of small appliances to convince the manufacturer to switch from metal, at $.50/pound, to engineering plastic, at $2.50/pound. How are you going to pull this off? The place to start is by knowing your customer's business and having a credible relationship with stakeholders in the buying center. You see, when the total offering is examined, the plastic is cheaper than the metal. How?

When die-cast metal parts come out of the mold, they have a very rough surface. Motor frames require smooth bearing-like surfaces at many points. This means the metal part must be put through a machining step to make each critical surface smooth. Motor frames also must have ways to attach other parts to them—casting cannot produce the necessary holes with screw threads; another machining step is required for each hole or screw thread. The metal part still is not ready to be a motor frame. Many metals rust. (Even if a zinc alloy, corrosion may be a problem in some applications.) A surface treatment may be necessary to prevent rust or corrosion. If the design is such that the motor frame is part of the

EXHIBIT 10-3   Evaluated Price—Where Does Value Come from?

appliance housing, it will require an aesthetic coating or paint to match the design of the appliance. Several steps are necessary to create a usable motor frame.

Plastic parts are made by melting the plastic and injecting it, under pressure, into a mold. The nature of the engineering plastic is that it will flow into tiny details in the mold. Intricate designs are possible, reducing the number of other parts that must be attached; they get molded as part of the motor frame. What screw holes are still required are molded in at the same time. Engineering plastics will not rust and can be colored before molding; no painting of finished parts is required. The motor frame is finished when it comes out of the mold.

The $2.50/pound material creates a less expensive part than the $.50/pound material, though a view based strictly on material price would have never recognized the possibility. The total offering approach builds real value for the customer and new business for the supplier.

Today, the majority of all small power tool and appliance motors are made with engineering plastic frames. That new business was translated to many manufacturers and is now the accepted way to build small motors.

Note: Apologies to engineers familiar with these manufacturing processes for our simplification to create academic clarity!

EXHIBIT 10-3   (continued)

between benefits and evaluated price must be positive; the evaluated price cannot be considered to be more than the benefits.

Exhibit 10-3 shows the evaluated price compared to the benefits and how customers make choices from competing alternatives based on value. After the customer determines the value of each offering, she makes a selection based on which alternative she perceives to offer the most value. Suppose a company was considering contracting with a computer systems supplier for an automated ordering system; the company's employees could order their own systems interactively through an online catalog. The customer has the option of installing a system in which users can order from a constrained list of options. Alternatively, the supplier can establish an ordering process in which users have far more choice in the hardware and software they can order. The benefits of the second option—the one with more choices for users—make it appear to offer more benefits than the first. However, the evaluated price of the second option might be high enough to make the first option more attractive; in the second option, users might order desktop systems with such a wide array of hardware and software that the customer's IT department would incur a huge cost in integrating all the systems into its network. The end result would look very much like the situation depicted in Exhibit 10-4, in which the option with the lower benefits might have the higher value. If the marketer understands the customer's situation, then she can structure the offering so that a calculation of benefits minus evaluated price works out best for the customer.

So what is the maximum price that a marketer can charge for her product or service? If there is no competition, it is the price at which benefits are just noticeably more than the evaluated price, that is, the point at which there is a noticeable value for the offering. If the marketer wishes to establish or maintain a relationship with customers, then she will probably charge a price at a level where customers believe they are getting a "fair" price and are willing to work with this supplier in the future. This "fair price" level may be somewhat nebulous, but, if the marketer knows well the beneficial value of the offering as well as the customers, she will have a sense of where this price stands. If there is some sort of competition—and there usually is—the customer will likely use the price charged by competitors as a reference point. If the marketer's offering creates more benefits than the competitors' offerings, then customers will be

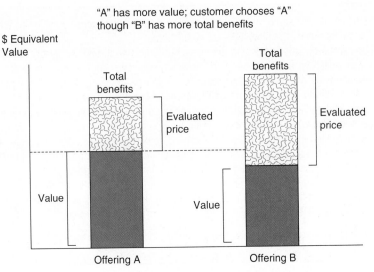

EXHIBIT 10-4   Customer's Perception of Value and Evaluated Price

willing to pay a premium; if not as much as competitors' offerings, then customers will be only willing to pay a discounted price. Again, the marketer must have a good understanding of customers' perceptions to know how much premium or discount is appropriate.

Most pricing situations involve setting prices below the maximum that can be charged, but not all situations. Whenever a supplier is engaged in a single transaction in which future relationship is not an issue, or when the supplier is expected to extract maximum revenue from

Parker Hannifin Discovers Value Pricing

Parker Hannifin was founded in 1918 as a manufacturer of hydraulic brakes for trucks. Today, Parker is a leading producer of over 800,000 industrial components used in everything from space shuttles to ocean-going vessels. In 2001, Donald Washkewicz became CEO, having risen through the ranks from his first employment with Parker as a college graduate. Like many U.S. manufacturers, Parker faced increased global price competition as well as price pressure from customers.

Parker Hannifin pricing policy was straightforward—determine cost and add a standard markup—usually about 35 percent. Managers with price authority loved it—it was easy and it gave them a degree of price autonomy. Unfortunately, the strategy was completely unrelated to customer value. If Parker developed a way to lower the production cost of a part, the lower cost translated directly to a lower price. If a product development led to an improved version, the same standard markup applied. This scenario was true throughout Parker Hannifin, which had revenues near $10 billion.

Mr. Washkewicz ordered a complete corporate review of every price. He established a new senior position for pricing and employed many outside consultants. There was, of course, pushback from managers accustomed to the traditional process, so much so that Mr. Washkewicz created a list of the fifty most common reasons why his strategy wouldn't work. He told company managers that if they could come up with an original reason, he would listen; otherwise get on board. The result: since 2002, operating income increased by $200 million, helping net income to soar from $130 million in 2002 to $673 million in 2007. In the same period, Parker shares rose 88 percent.

(continued)

How?

Price to value. All items were placed in one of five categories. "A" items were high-volume commodity-like products where there was at least one large direct competitor influencing market prices; "B" items were partially differentiable products where differentiation added value for customers, and so on, through "E" items that were special custom-designed or "legacy" products only available from Parker Hannifin. Services such as customization of products, customer education, special delivery factors such as location and timing were considered as value-added elements for the customer. Parker discovered that about a third of its products fell into niches where there was limited or no competition.

Customers whose purchase price went up were not happy, though many understood the new approach. (Customers of generic items appreciated the new lower prices, such as a 15 percent decrease in hydraulic replacement filters.) In one example, a manufacturer of auto engine components balked at increases of 10–20 percent on fifty different items and rebid the parts from Hannifin competitors. Of the fifty parts, the customer ended up switching only three items to competitors. Parker had been under-market on forty-seven of the items. In another instance, Ingersoll-Rand Co., maker of the compact "Bobcat" line of loaders and excavators, objected when the Parker price for its new hydraulic fan motors was higher than expected—enough that there was a "CEO to CEO" conversation. However, in the end, Parker showed that the new item, designed for the application, replaced eleven separate parts, fit in a smaller area, was easier to install, and eliminated several hydraulic connections, reducing the risk of leaks. The customer's evaluated price significantly favored Parker. (See Exhibit 10-3, Where Does Value Come From?)

Source: Timothy Aeppel, "Seeking Perfect Prices, CEO Tears Up the Rules," *The Wall Street Journal* (March 27, 2007).

a transaction, the supplier can maximize profit by charging at the point where value to the customer, minus the price, is zero. The electric power market of the early 2000s illustrated both the situation and the limits of this practice. The United States' power-generating capacity had reached a point where spot shortages occurred. Distribution systems had to buy power on the wholesale spot market and prices for this power can be extremely high. Accordingly, high costs of power were passed on to ratepayers. Suppliers, however, faced regulatory and judicial review of these pricing practices. The end users' representatives pursued investigations into price "gouging"—unfairly taking advantage of the shortage—that might have been done by some suppliers. In several of these cases, end users won judgments against these suppliers.

A VALUE-COST MODEL OF THE CUSTOMER   Business customers purchase products and services to aid in the creation of value for their own customers. A marketer working for a supplier can better understand the price the customer will be willing to pay by understanding her customer's own value chain in a **value-cost model**. The value-cost model is a diagram of the customer's value chain showing the key elements that contribute to value for the customer's customer and the key elements that contribute to the customer's costs. The supplier's marketer might want to diagram the way that the customer creates value, that is, to map the value chain used by this customer. When several customers in the same market have a similar value chain, a value map can be used as typical for that segment. If the customers in the market vary considerably in their value chain configurations, the marketer may want to map out typical configurations for the market segments that are identifiable and, to whatever extent is possible, understand why participants in the same market have dissimilar value maps. The main idea is to understand what activities are done by her customers that are linked together to create value.

Once the marketer has a sense of her customers' typical value chain, the marketer needs to overlay the costs that her customers incur in performing these activities. Working backward from

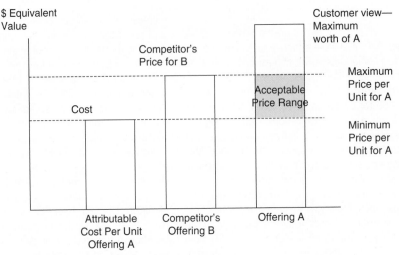

EXHIBIT 10-5   Maximum and Minimum Price

Revenues are simply the actual price received for the product multiplied by the number of items sold.

the **revenues** obtained by customers, the marketer can see what activities subtract the most from her customers' profitability. By paying particular attention to the point in the value chain at which the marketer's product or service enters into the customer's value chain, the marketer can approximate how important the product or service is to the customer's creation of value. The level of importance in the overall customer value map will be an indication of what the customer can afford and how sensitive the customer is likely to be to changes in the supplier's price. (See box "Parker Hannifin Discovers Value Pricing.")

Customers' perceived value, relative to competitors' offerings, establishes the appropriate price to be charged. Customer-oriented pricing, then, is based on an understanding of these perceptions held by the customer. The lower the price charged, the greater the value as perceived by the customer. However, there is a *minimum price* that can be charged. In the long run, the minimum price is a price that covers the supplier's relevant costs (see Exhibit 10-5). Contribution to profitability comes from setting a price higher than the level at which relevant costs are just covered. The question becomes, then, what costs are relevant?

RELEVANT COSTS

Think of ongoing costs and ongoing revenue as the cash flow associated with the incremental activities required specifically to offer the product or service in question. Revenues from the product are reduced by only those costs directly attributable to the product.

To understand which costs are relevant in the calculation of profitability, the marketer must think in terms of paying for **ongoing costs** out of **ongoing revenue**. It also helps to think of the act of setting price as a strategic decision. In thinking about costs, we are only concerned with the costs that are consequences of that decision. Thus the timing of when pricing decisions are made has much to do with what costs are relevant. Relevant costs are those that meet the following criteria:[5]

Resultant

Realized

Forward-looking incremental

Avoidable

Resultant costs are those costs that result from the in-process decision. Pricing is often part of a decision that affects two or more of the four Ps. For instance, pricing may be part of the launch of a new product, so a pricing decision is part of a decision to pursue development and launch of a new product. In this case, the relevant costs are those associated with the development, manufacture, marketing, operations, and partnerships done or formed because of the new product. If the marketer is only going to change price, the relevant costs of this decision are the costs of continuing to offer the product. The de facto decision is whether to continue or not and thus the resultant costs are those involved with going forward.

Realized costs are actual costs incurred. Not included are costs that are allocated for accounting reasons but are not directly traceable to the decision being made. Thus overhead costs allocated based on accounting averages are not "real" costs and are not relevant. However, actual increased costs that are attributable, such as the number of staff, production equipment, office space, and utilities, are relevant as long as they are attributable to the decision being made at that time.

Forward-looking incremental costs are the costs that will be incurred (forward looking) for the next unit or units of product or service that will be sold when the decision is implemented (the costs of the incremental units); that is, they are the next costs to be incurred. For instance, suppose a new product has been on the market for six months when the competition drops its prices significantly. If we dropped our price to match the competitor's, the price would drop below the level where it is recovering each new unit's share of the R&D *previously* expended on the product. This R&D cost would not be relevant for decision making because it is not forward looking. Consideration of incremental costs defined in this way ensures, again, that the actual costs resulting from the decision will be considered.

Avoidable costs are those costs that would not be incurred—that is, costs that would be avoided—if the decision were not made, for example, if the product or program were not launched. Avoidability becomes a concern when the marketing manager is considering a price reduction. The manager must determine at what point the price does not cover costs. Suppose that a product manager is considering matching a competitor's price reduction on certain product models. In calculating the price at which the revenue is too low to cover cost, the manager's salary is unavoidable (assuming he remains employed). Accordingly, the product manager could drop the price below the point where the product manager's salary would be fully recovered.

This may seem counterintuitive, because any manager wants to cover all costs. Think about the example shown in Exhibit 10-6. Suppose the product manager, Bill, gets paid a salary of $100,000. Suppose also that Bill will not be fired, even if his product, Product A, is discontinued—the cost of paying Bill is unavoidable (he is employed notwithstanding the success or failure of Product A). Now suppose Bill expects that he will sell 100 units of Product A, that is, if you spread the cost of Bill's salary across the 100 units, each unit will cover $1,000 of Bill's salary. Suppose also that the other costs (incremental, attributable, and avoidable) are $6,000 per unit. And suppose that the original price of Product A and its competitor is $10,000 per unit.

Now the competitor comes along and drops the price on his product to $6,500, which is $500 below the price at which Bill's salary is fully covered. Assume that if Bill matches the price cut, he will still sell 100 units (but if he does not fully match the price cut, he will sell no units). The profit calculation would go as follows:

Revenue = 100 units × $6,500/unit = $650,000.

Total cost = [100 units × ($6,000 per unit)] + $100,000 [Bill's salary] = $700,000

Total profit (loss) = $650,000 − $700,000 = ($50,000)

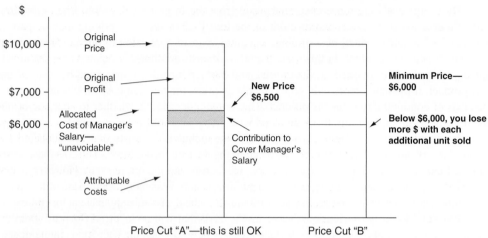

EXHIBIT 10-6   Price Cut Example—How Low Can You Go?

This is still a smaller loss by $50,000 than the company would have lost if it discontinued the product or did not change the price (in either case, the company's revenue would have been $0, since no units would have been sold) and thus lost the whole $100,000 it will pay to Bill. Following this logic, Bill could cut his price on Product A down to $6,001 and still contribute something to cover part of his salary, reducing the loss. If he prices below $6,000, the loss goes higher than $100,000 and the company would have been better off just discontinuing the product. In other words, as long as Bill's salary is unavoidable (covered as a result of other profitable products managed by Bill), it is irrelevant to the incremental pricing decision. Any cost that will be paid anyway, regardless of the decision made, is similarly unavoidable and irrelevant to the decision.

Contribution Analysis

Contribution margin can be viewed as the difference between ongoing attributable costs and ongoing attributable revenue.

From the supplier's point of view, price needs to be set in such a way that contribution margin is positive. **Contribution margin** for a product (this could also be for an offering, for a new marketing program, or for a customer) is the revenue less the avoidable costs that are directly attributable to the product in question. It is called contribution margin because it represents the portion of revenue that "contributes" to coverage of fixed costs, indirect costs, and profit, that is, value in excess of variable and directly attributable costs. Contribution margin is calculated as shown in the following equation:

$$TC = [(P - VC) \times Q] - AC$$

where

TC = Total contribution to fixed costs, overhead, and profit

P = Price

VC = Variable cost per unit

Q = Quantity sold

AC = Other attributable costs (costs incurred by undertaking the action)

Marketers need to be careful in deciding which costs are relevant and which are not. If, for instance, the accounting department has given you a standard percentage that is "your share" of overhead costs or indirect costs, it is *not* a relevant cost for contribution margin calculations.

Demand Functions and Pricing

All of the preceding discussion has dealt with pricing on a "per unit" basis. The marketer is interested, though, in the effect of the offering and marketing program on total sales and profits in the market. The concepts of demand, equilibrium prices, and elasticity—often presented as the foundations of pricing management—are conceptually useful but largely impossible to quantify and use in real-life situations. In practice, marketers generally do not have enough time or data to fully analyze demand-price effects and so must use assumptions and quick approximations to make informed decisions. The theory does generally help understand market behavior, even if exact forecasts cannot be made.

Recall from your economic principles course that a **demand curve** shows what quantity of products or services will be sold in a market at different price levels. An industry **supply curve** shows how much product will be produced in an industry at different levels of price (see Exhibit 10-7).

In theory, the intersection of a demand curve and a supply curve (the sum of individual supply curves for firms in a given market) gives the equilibrium price and quantity of products in that market.[6] This equilibrium point is a theoretical state or condition that markets will tend to move toward. When a marketer is looking to set prices for the first time for a new product or for a product entering a new market, an estimated demand curve could, in theory, help assess what sales to expect.

The problem with this approach is that demand curves and supply curves are abstractions that often defy estimation. Because demand is derived in business-to-business markets, forecasting demand at different market prices is a herculean task. Supply curves are difficult to forecast as well, due to the complex interplay of input costs and the uncertainty about what competitors will actually participate in a market. Instead of estimating a demand curve, it is probably best to get a sense of what a majority of the customers project they will buy in the foreseeable future as well as attempt to get a sense of how sensitive to price they are. This provides a "limited version" of a demand schedule over a narrow range; this is about the best that a more rigorously estimated demand schedule could do in contributing to decisions on pricing in any case.

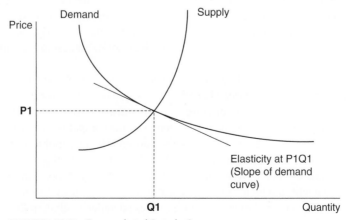

EXHIBIT 10-7 Demand and Supply Curves

The concept of *elasticity* is useful when thinking about the effects of a price change; however, the context of business-to-business markets must be kept in mind. **Elasticity** refers to the tendency of demand to react to changes in price; generally higher prices yield lower demand, and vice versa. In business markets, there is likely to be a significant difference between short-term and long-term demand. In the short run, a customer may have little choice but to stay with its initial order because products and services purchased, often incorporated by design into the customer's offering to its customers, are so dependent on one another. Thus, when a marketer raises prices, the customers are not likely to change their demand level much in the short term. Choosing instead to maintain the relationships they have built in their markets, they suffer lower profits for the time being. However, in time, a customer's product and production plans can be changed to revise its input combinations. This, then, results in lower demand (or no demand) for the marketer's offering. In the short term, business-to-business demand is inelastic; in the long term, it can be very elastic.

Another difference between short-term and long-term elasticity occurs because of switching costs and derived demand. Think back to the example in Exhibit 10-3. Suppose the manufacturer of small motors was faced with a sharp price increase in metals. In the short run, to continue to meet its commitments to its customers, it might be very difficult for the manufacturer to switch from zinc to plastic as the material for the motor frames. The manufacturer would pay the increased cost of the zinc. The manufacturer would probably not reduce its quantity purchased either, since that amount depends on the demand for small motors. In the short run, the manufacturer absorbs most of the increased cost of the materials but begins seriously looking for alternatives. The price of the metal has approached the maximum price that the manufacturer is willing to pay. After an investigation of the price and costs of alternatives—in this case, the evaluated price of the plastic alternative, the manufacturer undertakes the switch. So, while the short-term reaction to price is inelastic, in this case, the long-term elasticity reflects "on-off" demand. Once the evaluated price has exceeded the relevant maximum, the buyer simply, through replacement of the product, "turns the buying switch to off," ceasing her demand for the product. (Note that in this instance, the zinc metal is replaced by plastic—not another metal.)

A short-term reaction to a price decrease followed by a long-term reaction may be just the opposite effect. Suppose an office supply dealer reduces prices on printer paper (passing through a reduced cost from paper suppliers). The dealer's customers may react quite noticeably, buying large quantities of paper, particularly if they believe the price will increase again in the near future. They are simply stockpiling extra paper when it can be purchased at a low price, pulling future demand into the present. The primary impact has been to temporarily move product through the channel at a faster pace The customers still use the paper at the same rate, or nearly so, even if the price remains low. Just because the price of paper is lower does not mean customers will write more or longer documents.

In addition to concepts of demand and elasticity, it is important for the marketer to consider competitive reactions to price changes. Just as it may be easy for a company to change its prices, it is probably equally easy for competitors to do so. A price cut to take away business from competitors may simply be matched or exceeded by the competitor, resulting in lost margin for all with little shift in market share. Firms are particularly susceptible to this trap when a product has passed through the maturity stage of the PLC and market sales volumes decline. Cuts in price may have little effect on overall number of units sold. Any increase in sales will come at the expense of a competitor, which can be expected to vigorously defend its market share.

To anticipate competitors' price reactions requires an understanding of their cost structures and their tendencies to participate in industry price changes. In the Intel example, Intel was anticipating that competitors might not be willing to fully match price cuts.[7] If the competitors do match the price cuts, Intel is counting on them to suffer more than Intel from the lost profitability.

In summary, there are several lessons that the marketer can take away from the economic fundamentals of price:

1. Demand levels will be different at different levels of price; different market segments will have different price sensitivity based on segment members' perceptions of the benefits from the product or service in question: in most markets, one price does not fit all segments.
2. Changes in price yield reactions from customers, which are different in the short term from their long-term reactions: short-term reactions are usually constrained by customers' situations; longer-range reactions allow greater flexibility. In other circumstances, customers may shift the timing of their expenditures in response to short-term price changes; their longer-term reactions may show less elasticity.
3. Changes in price will yield reactions from competitors: It is important to pay attention to their communications as well, since these may give clues to how they are viewing the market, prices, and other pressures that may influence future actions.

MANAGING PRICE AS PART OF MARKETING STRATEGY

These ideas form a framework for thinking about pricing, but at some point the marketer must take what is known and what is assumed about customers and competitors and she must make price decisions. Again, the principal price decisions are what prices to set, how to change prices when necessary, and what the other elements of pricing should be—payment terms, financing, and so on. Pricing is situational, depending on strategic purposes and market circumstances.

Internally, price is a part of positioning, so the marketer must set prices to be consistent with the other elements of the offering for positioning purposes. Beyond its role in positioning, there are several strategic purposes for which pricing is a crucial element. The marketer will want to use price to obtain specific reactions from customers, competitors, distribution channels, or from the direct sales force. The instances we discuss are pricing to introduce a new product, pricing to use the experience curve or learning curve to achieve advantage, and pricing when engaged in translation segmentation. Before getting into the discussions of these circumstances, though, it is necessary to discuss the strategic context for pricing decisions.

When the marketer makes price decisions to address a change in competition, to win over certain customers, or to achieve some other short-term objectives, pricing is being used as a tactical tool. Price is a marvelous (and dangerous) incentive for motivating customers to take action. As a tactical decision, marketers will need to decide what discounts will be given, to whom, and how. Other price conventions also need to be observed. In many markets, customers choose suppliers based on competitive bidding. Another tactical issue is how to approach changing prices to reflect market conditions. All these tactical issues in pricing are discussed in the section of this chapter that follows managing price as part of marketing strategy.

Strategic Context of Pricing

Setting prices to achieve strategic purposes takes place within the context of the business environment and the strategy chosen to address that environment. As shown in prior chapters, pricing is examined through the PLC and the TALC. The environment, however, does not fully define the strategy to be taken. Companies have choices of what sorts of strategies they will follow. Accordingly, how pricing contributes to different kinds of purposes or objectives is examined.

PRICING OBJECTIVES   As previously discussed, the strategic management process sets out objectives and strategic purposes for the firm to address. In setting objectives for marketing strategies and programs, the marketer will realize that some objectives are addressed directly with pricing strategies. These objectives have come to be called *pricing objectives*, but are really broader objectives in which price plays a key role; other marketing elements are usually key components as well. Exhibit 10-8 shows several objectives whose achievement depends on pricing.

The marketer must address the first two strategic purposes—achieving a target level of profitability and building goodwill in a market—no matter what. Price levels must obtain enough revenue volume and margin to satisfy the company's strategic concerns. The marketer also needs to determine pricing that is consistent with a desired level of goodwill or relationship building. As noted earlier, there is a maximum price that customers will accept for an offering. Generally, even though customers agree to pay this price, they will not subsequently enter into a close relationship with the supplier that charges such prices because they believe the supplier is exploiting their need. If the marketer wishes to develop relationships with customers, price levels must fall within ranges that are acceptable or attractive to the customers.

For each of the purposes listed in Exhibit 10-8, it is obvious that there are other elements of the marketing mix involved. For instance, in encouraging the sale of complementary products, the supplier must communicate so that the customer will know that the complementary products are available and why, together, the products provide more value. Also, the complementary products must work well together, implying that product design and execution are also necessary. Availability implies some sort of channel support. In fact, for most of these objectives, addressing them with price alone is usually inadequate, leading to lost sales and lost profitability. Accordingly, the role of pricing in accomplishing those objectives, then, needs to be understood. The following sections examine situations where price plays a key role in achieving a strategic purpose.

Strategic Purposes

- Achieving a target level of profitability
- Building goodwill, or relationships, in a market or among certain customers
- Penetration of a new market or segment
- Maximizing profit for a new product
- Keeping competitors out of an existing customer base

Tactical Purposes

- Winning the business of a new, important customer
- Penetrating a new account
- Reducing inventory levels
- Keeping the business of disgruntled customers
- Encouraging customers to try a product or service
- Encouraging sales of complementary products

EXHIBIT 10-8   Several Marketing Objectives Addressed by Pricing

Pricing throughout the Product Life Cycle and the Technology Adoption Life Cycle

Pricing is situational, depending on strategic purposes and market circumstances. Both of these parts of the situation are heavily influenced by market evolution as the PLC and TALC progress. Customers' perceptions of needs and value change during this market evolution. Concurrently, the competitive environment changes as well. Strategies—and the role of pricing in those strategies—should evolve as the markets evolve.

As previously noted, life cycles for a product category, not for individual models or incremental innovations within that category, are the context of PLC discussion. When a new product category is introduced into a market, only the innovators—customers who accept offerings early in the PLC—will be interested in adopting so early. When offering a new product, the marketer is trying to obtain adoption from innovators (technophiles, if it is a technology product), who usually do not have big budgets and who do not really *need* the product anyway; they just want to try it to see what it will do. At this early stage, few if any competitors exist, so pricing can be set commensurate with perceived value. However, value may not yet be readily apparent. (Recall the discussion of shadow and delusional products in Chapter 9; value must be understood from the customer's viewpoint.) At this early stage, pricing is constrained more by customer perceptions than by competitive pressures and the objectives pursued by marketers may focus more on learning about needs and building early references than on creating cash flow.

In the next stage of adoption, the offering is usually custom-built and is still undergoing rapid improvement in design and performance. Pricing has to accommodate several competing purposes. To some extent, the supplier may try to obtain trial and will want to price for penetration. In these circumstances, customer organizations usually provide a forecast of usage that the supplier can use in financial and capacity planning efforts. The supplier is also trying to pay for ongoing R&D costs, plus customization costs and training costs. If the design and development process has not been part of a collaboration or partnership between the supplier and the customer, then R&D, customization, and customer training will tend to push the price up. Unfortunately, if this occurs, the development may have occurred in isolation, away from the continuous feedback process described in Chapter 8 as necessary for successful new product development. Visionaries will also see the new product as something that can provide a competitive advantage in their business and so will tend to place a high value on it, justifying relatively high prices. Still, there is often a desire to learn something about the technology and the market, so the marketer may be asked to reduce price in exchange for learning (see Pricing in Translation Mode, below). In general, whether the product is a system, a component part, a material, or a service, volumes will be low and development costs will still be high. Pricing at this early stage will tend to be relatively high.

In getting across the chasm, or the market development gap, the first pragmatist buyers may need additional incentive to spur adoption of the product. Beyond these initial pragmatist buyers, though, the dynamic interaction of market segmentation, price sensitivity, innovation, competition, and marketing strategies can send pricing in many different directions. In some markets, rapid growth may be spurred by reductions in pricing. In segments where the marketer encounters competition, price will have to be set to reflect the competitive pressures, pushing price levels down. In technology markets during the growth phase, as standards emerge, the dominant players will be able to price their products at a premium, since their products will have more value. In other market segments, growth may be so rapid that even with several competitors, there is no great pressure downward on prices, at least until growth slows. At the end of the growth period, but before maturity, competition will generally become more intense and will tend to drive prices down. During this period, product differentiation opportunities begin to disappear. Bloomberg is a company offering a service that may be reaching this stage of the life cycle. See the description of their situation in the box, "Bloomberg's One Size Fits All," and consider whether they will have to change their strategy, including their pricing.

Two key drivers are at work: the drive to integrate features to improve performance and the drive to reduce costs. Intel is a good example of a company that has pursued both improvement directions simultaneously. They have built communications, graphics, and memory cache capabilities into their chip sets. Meanwhile, they have pursued production efficiency improvements and labor cost savings to drive costs down. This approach worked very well for the market segment of customers who were not likely to upgrade their computers but were more likely to purchase a complete replacement. This segment consisted of those who wanted computers of high volume, low cost, but with limited upgrade capability and flexibility.

As the market evolves into maturity, there is often a consolidation among participants. The structure of the supply base begins to appear oligopolistic. A few dominant players begin to exercise the ability to control (or, at least, strongly influence) the market. The dominant suppliers control pricing and often they do so by investing in productivity enhancements that enable cost reductions so that they can drive prices lower. A current trend in business markets to accomplish this is the outsourcing of technology development. Companies will find low cost sources of undifferentiated product or service modules. While cost leadership is important, there is a danger of losing control here, perhaps outsourcing a process or technology that should be incorporated as a distinctive competency of the firm. Performance improvement through technology integration is

Bloomberg's One Size Fits All

Bloomberg LP is a private company that provides financial information to the investment community. Money managers, corporate financial managers, investment advisors, and Wall Street brokerages all obtain detailed analysis from Michael Bloomberg's empire. Bloomberg started the business in 1981 and has built it into the leader in the industry.

Bloomberg's clients have a private connection to the financial network. The data and analyses are displayed in real time on a personal computer at the end of the network wire coming into the business. The price was a flat $1,285 per month fee per terminal during the late 1990s. Competition from net start-ups and from Reuters arose in the late 1990s. Prices for these competitors were generally lower than Bloomberg's, but the quality of the information still made Bloomberg the preferred alternative.

As the economy entered recession in 2001–2002, the financial services industry took a serious downturn and the real value of Bloomberg's service

became evident. Reuters and some of the weaker start-ups took the brunt of the lost sales. It turns out that Reuters' customer service was lacking to the extent that when a customer could no longer subscribe to both Reuters and Bloomberg, they generally chose to eliminate their subscription to Reuters. During this period, Bloomberg's sales actually increased while Reuters lost sales. Bloomberg was actually able to increase its price by $100 per month.

Sources: Based on Tom Lowry, "The Bloomberg Machine," *Business Week* (23 April 2001), pp. 76–84; Charles Goldsmith, "Reuters Banks on Messaging—Company Hopes Service Will Help It Regain Edge Lost to Rival Bloomberg," *Asian Wall Street Journal* (October 15, 2002), p. A10; Charles Goldsmith and Kay Larsen, "Reuters Group Faces Up to Its Own Bad News and Financial Data—Squeezed by Rivals, U.K. Company Tries to Revamp Culture and Content—Yankee Boss on London's Fleet Street," *Wall Street Journal* (Europe) (February 18, 2003), p. A1; David Litterick, "Cost-Cutting Puts Reuters into Black," *The Daily Telegraph* (London) (February 18, 2004), p. 32.

an important source of competitive advantage at this point in the PLC. When a company outsources a portion of the technology, even if it is not core technology, it runs the risk of losing its ability to fully integrate the technology with other parts of its products and, hence, it loses a portion of its unique value.

Pricing during maturity depends upon how much the supplier can differentiate its offering. Since product features offer little chance for differentiation, much of the possible differentiation arises in the relationship between the supplier and the customer. If the supplier can create this non-product differentiation, it can charge a price that earns something of a premium. If its relationships are not strong or cannot be strengthened, the supplier needs to be able to drive costs down to stay competitive and profitable.

As the market moves into decline, pricing depends upon the market segments still served and the number of suppliers still competing for a piece of the pie. Because of unique switching costs, some users may continue to use old equipment or supplies from an earlier era. A premium price may be possible for such customers, but there is an upper limit set by the switching costs. Other customers will stay with older products as long as they can get a low price. Depending on the supplier's cost structure, it may still be profitable to serve these customers.

Price Models

Different price models are often traditional in some businesses—consider the "standard" markups used by many wholesaling and retailing organizations, called "cost plus" pricing. Penetration pricing, discussed below, is often the price model used by a firm that has a business strategy of maintaining a "low-cost producer" position in its markets. Which came first—the penetration scenario or the low-cost producer strategy? With the range of pricing options so wide, it is important for the marketer to understand what circumstances favor the differing approaches.

Setting price is sometimes considered science and at other times, an art form. Software programs aid in price determination through business and market modeling—all that is necessary is that the correct data be input to the selected business model. Prices, arrived at through a number of factors, generally are either *cost based* or *market based*. Cost-based pricing, discussed earlier, assumes that the costs associated with the creation of the offering, plus whatever margin goals apply, will yield a final price that will be acceptable to the market and profitable for the firm. Cost-based pricing, analogous to product or production-oriented views of markets, sees the important elements of the value chain as those that benefit the firm. Cost-based pricing ignores what level of value the customer perceives. (See the box, "Parker Hannifin Discovers Value Pricing.") Potential competitive activity in the market is easily overlooked, contributing to a myopic view of the business. Market-based pricing is "standard" to the marketing concept and market-driven, market–ownership oriented firms. As part of the product development, the value of the offering as perceived by the customer is understood. The price is a major part of the positioning strategy.

Penetration Pricing and Price Skimming

The PLC and the TALC will define the business environment the marketer faces and will influence the purposes the marketer pursues. When a supplier is introducing a new product ahead of the competition, the introduction may be aimed at maximizing profit in the short run until competitors overcome the supplier (which would be a purpose pursued by a nondominant competitor in the earlier stages of the PLC); or it may be aimed at maximizing profit segment by segment as the product achieves wider adoption (a purpose pursued by a dominant competitor in the late growth or maturity stages of the PLC). Alternatively, the marketer may want to achieve a rapid adoption by customers in which the supplier obtains a large, defensible market share (a purpose pursued by a company in the growth stage hoping to become a dominant competitor).

Price skimming is charging relatively high prices that take advantage of early customers' strong need for the new product. Since the benefits of the product are so attractive and/or important to them, customers are willing to pay higher prices. Without competitors offering similar products, the supplier can charge a skimming price and these first customers will pay the premium. **Penetration pricing**, on the other hand, is charging relatively low prices to entice as many buyers into the early market as possible.

Suppose a marketer is about to launch a new offering that provides superior value to competitors' current offering and believes that competitors will not be able to match the new offering for several months at least. Penetration pricing would make sense if the marketer further believes the following:

1. The market can be dominated by gaining early customer commitments.
2. Key large customers will commit early rather than waiting for a competitor if they believe that they are getting the best price now.
3. A learning curve effect will result from early adoptions all coming to the marketer's company, allowing cost or quality improvements that give the marketer's offering a competitive advantage over forthcoming entrants.

Penetration pricing requires that a large group of customers are sensitive to low prices. This is most prevalent in markets that have evolved enough for customers to understand the value of an offering. In early markets, this may not be the case (see the earlier section on pricing throughout the PLC).

If the marketer already dominates the market and serious competition is not likely to materialize—either because of a dominant lead in technology or airtight patent protection—then the marketer can set skimming prices that obtain purchases from the early price-insensitive customers. After this segment has been largely sold, the next highest price-insensitive segment may be addressed with a lower price; then the next, and so on, as if peeling the layers of an onion. This is a profit maximization approach followed by many market leaders in the past. It has an element of risk, though, if the market leader does not realize that some unforeseen competitor is going to undermine this strategy. AMD was able to take advantage of Intel in the market for low-end microprocessors in this way. Intel did not realize that the market would be so strong and allowed AMD to undercut its pricing on the Pentium II and Pentium III with powerful but inexpensive Athlon processors. Intel countered with newer Celeron processors, but only after AMD was able to establish entry into the market.

Another circumstance calling for skimming prices is when the company wants to maximize short-term profits. It has a temporary lead in the market but does not expect to be able to compete over the long term. This would be the case with a small company entering a market ahead of the market leader, who is likely to be in the market within, say, six months. The small company could make as much profit as possible by charging a skimming price for the most price-insensitive customers. In the meantime, it is looking for the next market opportunity because it knows the current situation will not last once the leader enters the market. In many circumstances, this company may end up selling the product technology or even the company to the market leader. The generalized market conditions for the success of either skimming or penetration pricing are summarized in Exhibit 10-9.

Price-skimming strategy

- With skimming, the value of the offering as perceived by the market must reflect the high price.
- The market is somewhat inelastic.
- The marketer has a sustainable market advantage over any possible competition via patents, availability.
- Competitive entry is difficult if not altogether blocked.
- Production methods must be profitable at the lower volumes—economies of scale may not be feasible or desirable.

Penetration strategy

- The market is somewhat elastic.
- A low existing price level acts as a barrier against competition.
- Economies of scale in manufacturing as well as distribution are necessary.

EXHIBIT 10-9   Market Conditions Necessary for the Success of Skimming or Penetration Pricing

LEARNING CURVE EFFECT   A special case of penetration pricing occurs when management in a company believes that competitive advantage can be achieved through running down a **learning curve**. The learning curve concept says that as more product units (or service units) are produced and sold, unit costs can be reduced through the learning that has occurred. As they obtain experience, companies learn how to produce products with more quality; they learn how to handle inputs more efficiently; they learn how to distribute products more efficiently; and they learn how to provide service more efficiently and effectively.

Repetition leads to learning more efficient ways to complete the same task. This is the principle behind the **learning curve**. *Just as with individual tasks, the more you do something, the better you get at it (if not, why practice?); organizations (teams) will improve performance through learning.*

The conditions for effective use of this strategy are fairly restrictive and relatively rare.

- There must be enough prospective customers, with high enough quantity demand, who are price sensitive and who will adopt if the price is right. This suggests that pragmatists must be ready to buy; any earlier in the PLC or the TALC, there may not be enough buyers.
- There must be ample opportunity for learning to occur, and enough future demand for the product that the learning can be of benefit.
- There must be sufficient time to learn. Learning is a function of both volume and time for assimilation of new knowledge.
- There must be a sufficient lead over the competition to avoid direct price competition. If a competitor can match price, then learning will not occur as fast and the competitor will learn just as quickly.
- There must not be a competitor who will come along in the near future with a process innovation that will start a new learning curve. If this occurs, the cost savings may not be enough to match the unit costs for the competitor, no matter how much learning has occurred. Meanwhile, the supplier on the original learning curve may have built up switching costs to the point that it cannot easily adopt the technological innovation of the competitor to pursue the new learning curve.

- If conditions are ripe for a learning curve strategy, the marketer must ensure that the learning takes place. It is not enough just to set the low price and then sit back and wait for nature to take its course. The marketer must meet with the relevant managers in the areas of the firm where learning is to occur and obtain their cooperation in pursuing the necessary process improvements.

CHOICES ARE NOT ALWAYS AVAILABLE   Not every firm will have the plethora of pricing options discussed. A small firm operating before the chasm will have neither the ability to manufacture in large quantities—economies of scale—nor a market large enough to absorb the volume. Technophiles and visionaries comprise most of the market for firms before the chasm. In these circumstances, the company will likely view skimming as the only pricing scenario that can work.

As the firm approaches the chasm, new facilities and organizational development must be concurrent with the development of expanded markets. As pragmatists become interested in the offering, volume demands will increase, requiring new product designs capable of high-volume production, larger sales and marketing team to educate and train potential customers, and an expanded organization to support these needs—all typical of a firm about to cross the chasm. These circumstances, combined with the entrance of competition in the new market, force a reconsideration of penetration pricing.

Conversely, consider the large established (but still innovative) firm. If the new product fits with existing manufacturing capabilities, the large firm likely will introduce the product with penetration pricing. This assumes a product and corporate infrastructure that is immediately across the chasm and an available pragmatist market. If the new product is significantly different from current products—a disruptive innovation as perceived by the firm, the product may be introduced using price skimming to technophiles or visionaries.

The second alternative above, a disruptive innovation using price skimming, is not a natural capability of established firms with existing infrastructure and markets, particularly if they are product driven. While the firm may, with ongoing R&D, have the new product mostly developed and "on the shelf" it is unlikely that it will be introduced if it obsoletes the existing offerings and manufacturing facilities. This situation often leads to what is called the "second in, low cost producer" (or just "low-cost producer"). The large, established, market-oriented firm will be aware of new developments in its market. The new, small "before the chasm" competitor may enter the market with an innovative product using skim pricing. There is no motivation for the larger organization to enter the market until the demand is proven—as the product crosses the chasm. When this occurs, the large firm jumps in with penetration pricing and the facilities and organization to support it. Thus, the large firm is not the first in the market, but upon entry is the volume leader, without having risked the initial market introduction. A spin-off of this concept occurs when the large company acquires the smaller company as the smaller company nears the chasm. R&D costs are translated to acquisition costs.

Pricing in Translation Mode

One of the key ideas discussed in earlier chapters is that business-to-business marketers learn about new segments through the process of translation—developing new markets for new business successes. The supplier and customer will embark on a mutual development effort to see whether the needs of the customer can be met reasonably and profitably. The marketer will need to negotiate a price for the product and for the service of developing it. The customer will want to be credited for the assistance it provides to the supplier in specifying the product, trying it and testing it under varying conditions, and generally in providing the platform for launching a successful new business. Successful translation efforts lead to established "list" prices for core offerings.

An alternative to pricing in this type of activity, particularly if there are many unknowns and the parties are interested in quantifying risks, is to separate the components. First, the development activity should be treated as a consulting service. However, the service cannot be charged at a full consulting rate since the customer is, in effect, consulting back to the supplier developing the product. The product itself can still be priced on a value basis. The price could be set initially at a preliminary rate when the contract is first signed and then adjusted based on value at some specified future date. Some part of the deal might be structured in a way that pays the customer a royalty on future sales of the product to new customers.

Pricing for International Marketing Efforts

A key trend over the past twenty years has been the move to marketing of products across national boundaries. International or global reach raises some interesting pricing challenges including how to set prices in different currencies and whether to charge global prices or prices that differ by region or country.

The problem faced by companies operating internationally is that customers, competition, and channel structures differ greatly from country to country. Market conditions may call for lower prices outside the company's home country, or the competitive situation may be such that the company can charge higher prices and make more profit. Often the costs incurred in opening foreign markets reduce contribution margins to the point where prices must be raised to make any contribution at all; and, of course, these higher prices may or may not reflect the value perceived by customers in the new market.

As a company does more and more business in foreign markets, it will face increasing pressure to regularize its prices from country to country. The global customer will look to minimize its costs by buying products wherever the price and shipping costs are the least in combination. They may negotiate to conduct a transaction for products or services in one country and receive delivery at the location of usage. Smaller companies may also take advantage of this cross-border arbitrage by buying through global distributors who accomplish much the same purpose.

The problem faced by the marketer is similar to the problem of addressing multiple market segments. Maximizing profit by addressing the segments separately only works when segments can be separated from each other. If they cannot, at least relative to price, then the marketer must decide how to address the combined segments as one market. To do so, the marketer needs to address the portion of the market that is most important, given the company's competitive position and its goals. If this makes the price too high for other segments (geographic segments, in this case), then the company must live with the meager earnings from these other segments. When conditions change and the company can address the segments differentially, then the pricing strategy can change accordingly.

MANAGING PRICING TACTICS

Companies face changing business environments that require fast reactions. Often, pricing is the first thing that can be changed to fend off a competitive threat or take advantage of an opportunity. Business-to-business marketers need to keep in mind that the tactics employed must be consistent with overall positioning and must still reach a balance between value for customers and profitability for the company. The issues discussed here usually arise in business-to-business marketing as a way to implement some strategic direction or to obtain a short-term reaction from customers, competitors, channels, or the company's own sales personnel and, thus, are tactical in nature.

BUNDLING   In business-to-business marketing, bundling is principally a tactical pricing move, rather than a strategic one. Price **bundling** is when several products or services are sold together as a package for one price. The reasoning behind bundling in consumer marketing is to create the impression that the bundle has value and is a good bargain. It induces consumers to buy products, services, or features that they would not buy when sold separately. In business-to-business buying, the customer usually has information and professional purchasing personnel who know what the bundled products are worth individually and who will attempt to bundle or unbundle purchases as fits their need. Bundling is a way to sweeten a deal to close a sale or to move some old inventory while minimizing transaction costs. In other circumstances, bundling of materials, parts, or components can lead to serious price discrimination issues. Suppliers who consider bundling to close a deal may find that, in the long term, they have compromised the price structure integrity of one or more product lines.

Discounts and Allowances

Discounts and allowances are reductions in price for some special reason. Discounts are usually given as a reward incentive for some action taken by the buyer during the transaction. Thus, a discount may be given for paying promptly in cash or buying in quantity. An allowance is a credit against price given to channel members in exchange for some logistical or marketing activity that they perform. For instance, an allowance may be given for prospecting new accounts, for providing after-sale service, or for advertising. The key is determining what needs to be done to influence the final customer's buying decision and then providing sufficient incentive for the channel intermediary to perform the necessary activities.

The problem with discounts and allowances is that customers and resellers get used to them and expect them. Communication that accompanies such reductions in price must be clear that the reductions are offered only for specific purposes. Even so, powerful customers and resellers may insist that the reduced pricing should be the norm.

Competitive Bidding

In many markets, the method of choosing suppliers is through competitive bidding. Participation in markets that buy through bidding is a strategic decision for the supplier.

Suppliers are likely to face competitive bidding situations when the core product is indistinguishable from the offering of direct competition. Many agricultural products (commodities) and products that are in the mature stage of the PLC, when purchased in quantity, are sought through competitive bidding. Competitive bidding may also be the format when a customer is selecting a supplier for general use items such as office supplies. The contract that is awarded may not be for specific items but rather for a defined set of terms for a specified period of time. As different parts of the organization require those items, they are authorized to make direct purchases as needed, often through a predetermined Web page.

Government agencies have perhaps the most convoluted bidding processes. Government purchasing has an agenda beyond obtaining the lowest price. The bidding process is designed to avoid favoritism to any potential supplier, creating a level playing field for all potential candidates. Other requirements related to social agenda, such as location where the work will be performed, the number and type of subcontractors, whether workers are unionized, and so on, are often parts of the process.

Bidding can be arranged in a number of different ways, but two main types of competitive bidding are common: **sealed bid** and **open bid**.[8] Sealed bid, or closed bid, pricing involves placement of private bids by prospective suppliers. Usually, the lowest bid wins the contract, but not always. In many cases, the customer evaluates the total offering and chooses the supplier it considers to offer the best package. In some cases, the customer provides feedback to bidders and accepts revised bids. This begins to look a lot like open bidding; however, the customer may allow significant time for revisions between bidding rounds. In open bidding, competing suppliers see each others' bids. The idea, of course, is to let competition drive the offered price to its lowest possible level (or to drive the package of product and service benefits to its highest possible level for a relatively low cost). If the bidding is limited to price offers and little time is allowed for revised bids, the process begins to look like an auction. In a real-time auction, the customer also benefits from the competitive emotions that build as the bidding progresses. The customer may actually get a sizable discount that results from a supplier's desire to beat a major competitor in a public forum.

In sealed bid pricing, the marketing manager needs to do significant analysis in preparing a bid. Since the customer usually specifies the amount of business it wishes to acquire, the sales volume is usually a given. The supplier's costs are usually a straightforward calculation based on this volume. However, the marketer needs to be careful to consider ancillary costs, such as the impact on production schedules or special training costs for service people. The creative part of preparing the bid comes in determining the price level. This requires understanding the customer's perceptions of value to ensure that a reasonable price is bid. More important is having a sense of how the competitors will bid. Past experience in bidding against competitors will provide some sense of their proclivities in bidding relative to costs and perceived value. From this information the marketer can construct a table of probabilities of the likelihood of winning the bid at certain prices. Exhibit 10-10 shows a table of possible bids, probabilities for winning, and expected profits in a hypothetical proposal and bid situation in which a bid is being prepared for, say, a market research project.

Cost	Bid	Profit	Probability of Winning Bid	Expected Profit
$20,000	$20,000	$0	.2	$0
$20,000	$22,000	$2,000	.5	$1,000
$20,000	$24,000	$4,000	.7	$2,800
$20,000	$26,000	$6,000	.5	$3,000
$20,000	**$28,000**	**$8,000**	**.4**	**$3,200**
$20,000	$30,000	$10,000	.3	$3,000
$20,000	$32,000	$12,000	.2	$2,400

EXHIBIT 10-10   Hypothetical Example of Profit Expectations in a Competitive Bidding Situation   *Source*: Based on table construction shown in Michel H. Morris and Gene Morris, *Market-Oriented Pricing: Strategies for Management* (New York: Quorum Books, 1990), p. 120.

The basic idea in determining a bid price is to find the price at which the expected profitability is maximized. Expected profit at a given price is calculated as:

$$E(PF) = PW(Pr) \times PF(Pr)$$

where

$PF(Pr)$ = Profit at price Pr

$PW(Pr)$ = Probability of winning the bid at price Pr

$E(PF)$ = Expected profit

In the example in Exhibit 10-10, the probabilities of winning the bidding are shown as low at very low bids, since the credibility of the project being successfully completed is likely to be questioned by the customer at these low levels. In this hypothetical situation, the highest expected profit is at a price of $28,000. This would be the bid price to use. Managerial judgment, of course, may adjust this up or down for any of several reasons. The marketer may believe that this particular instance is unique and that the competitor will bid higher (or lower) than usual. Perhaps the marketer believes that this particular request for bid will draw entrants into the market that do not usually participate, requiring a higher (or lower) bid to win. In any case, the determination of a best bid based on the calculation of a highest expected profit at least provides a place to start.

Competitive bidding purchase processes vary considerably from situation to situation. It should be noted, though, that the work of the sales team, and including missionary sellers, might be able to favorably influence the request for bids. If a relationship between supplier and seller is effective, the supplier's team may help the buying center to specify a solution that closely resembles the offering of the supplier. The request for bid, then, would ask for bids on a project that the supplier is well prepared to provide; other competitors will probably be less able to meet the requirements sought. Thus, even though the project goes out for bid, the customer has largely already made the decision of which supplier will be chosen.

INITIATING PRICE CHANGES   Once the marketing plan has been finalized, the company will implement the plan and price levels will be set. As events unfold, the business-to-business marketer will need to react and change the marketing activities to match changes in the market and to take advantage of opportunities that arise. Price levels will need to be reviewed, and, at

Defending Supplier Advantage

In many industries, it is common practice that when a new supplier has bid below a current supplier for a piece of existing business, the current supplier—the defending source—gets a "second look." This is an acknowledgment of the costs involved for the customer in switching suppliers for an existing piece of business. Many of the initial start-up concerns related to logistics, invoicing, JIT services, and even the packaging methods of shipments will have to be re-established with the new supplier. Recall the "make the transaction routine" portion of the buying decision process; the more comfortable a customer is dealing with the friendly routine of a competent supplier, the less likely that supplier will be faced with a price threat. If the current supplier has not put a "friendly routine" in place, things could be much different.

times, prices will need to be changed. The key thing to keep in mind is that changes in prices induce reactions from customers and competitors.

Events that would change the structure of demand or the nature of competition, and that might cause a marketer to re-evaluate prices, include competitors' changes in prices; changes in customers' perceptions of the value of an offering, either positive or negative; entrance of a new competitor into the market; introduction of the next generation of products, making the current generation less valuable to customers; and exit of a competitor from the market, which in turn changes customers' perceptions of the relative value of the remaining offerings in the market. Events that would change cost structures in such a way that prices might be affected include the introduction of new process technology that reduces the supplier's costs, allowing reduction of prices; and increases in costs for all competitors such that the industry's supply curve shifts (see Exhibit 10-11 in which an across-the-board increase in costs shifts the industry supply curve to the left). Notice that an increase in costs that affects only the marketer's company will generally not have an effect on prices because the industry supply curve is not affected. No other competitors see the increase, and so they will continue to compete at what was a competitively set price. In time, there may even be a price shift downward as market shares redistribute and some competitors realize cost reductions from higher volumes. In a competitive market, these cost savings may be passed on to customers. However, the effect is not likely to last long. As other factors in the dynamic market shift, the effect of the unique cost increase will likely be superseded by other changes.

Summary of Managing Price

Pricing needs to be consistent with both business unit strategy and marketing strategy. In certain circumstances, pricing is a key component of strategy in that it builds and uses competitive advantage. General price levels are set when business unit strategy is designed; specific price levels and price schedules are set in the design of marketing strategy and tactics. As the marketing strategy is managed, the marketer must monitor competitive prices and the reactions from customers. Price changes will usually need to be considered as the business environment changes.

One of the key purposes of pricing is the creation of profitability. Prices are set to achieve profits, but the implementation of those prices needs to be done so that desired profit levels will

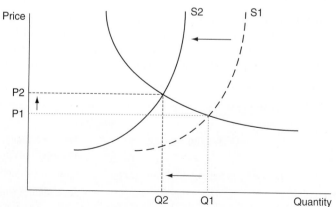

EXHIBIT 10-11   Effect of an Industry Increase in Costs

indeed result. In many business-to-business markets, prices are negotiated at least to some degree. The next section discusses the negotiation process and how it can be managed to maintain profitable prices.

PRICING IMPLEMENTATION: THE CASE OF NEGOTIATED PRICING

In many instances, the development of a price list, along with a set of consistently applied price discounts and allowances, represents the whole of the implementation phase in the management of pricing. This is especially the case when prices are implemented through an established network of distributors. Very often, though, for large purchases, customized offerings, and for new products or services, the final price of an offering will be negotiated between the two (or more) parties. This, of course, happens much more frequently in business-to-business marketing than it does in consumer marketing. Another large difference between consumer and business-to-business situations is that most business-to-business negotiations occur within the context of a relationship between buyer and supplier, or at least they have the potential of becoming a relationship. As already stated, the difficulty in dynamic pricing, that is, pricing through negotiation, is that it must address both the goals of building relationships and building profits *simultaneously*.

This takes a great deal of skill and usually falls to the seller to implement, at least in part. Some companies give their sellers complete authority to negotiate and agree on prices. Other companies give their sellers limited authority, requiring price approval from a sales manager for larger deals. Still other companies require sellers to obtain approval on all prices. In a market sensitive company, pricing authority often rest exclusively with marketing management. In certain other situations, higher-level executives for both the supplier and the customer complete the negotiations.

A problem that can arise is that sellers think of negotiation as part of "closing the sale." The temptation for the seller is to cut price to close the deal.[9] This may significantly improve the value provided to the customer but can play havoc with meeting profitability targets and has future implications that may not be seen by those very close to the situation. With attention to some basic ideas in negotiation, the marketer can implement pricing such that both a price associated with the customer's perceived value and the supplier's margin can be maintained.

Two Types of Situations

Sellers and marketers face two general types of negotiating situations, based on the extent to which a relationship with the customer is involved. As seen in Exhibit 10-12, when there is no relationship, nor even a slim chance of one developing, the situation can be treated as a stand-alone transaction. When the supplier has a relationship with the customer or has a reasonable

	Situation	
	Stand-alone Transaction	**Balanced between Transaction and Relationship**
Effective bargaining styles	Competitive; problem solving	Problem solving; compromising
Effective approach	Use of leverage	Seek common interests

EXHIBIT 10-12   Two Types of Negotiating Situations in Business-to-Business Sales

hope of building a relationship, then negotiation must be done while balancing the concerns of profitability and enhancing the relationship.[10]

The first situation, the stand-alone transaction, occurs when a company is making a one-time unique offering, such as selling off excess inventory of discontinued product. Another common stand-alone transaction occurs when a supplier attempts to get the business of a company whose primary objective is always price.[11] To be chosen by the customer, the supplier must meet minimum quality and delivery requirements and then is expected to offer as low a price as possible. The buyer generally is in a position of leverage, usually as a high-volume purchaser with multiple sources of supply. This would typically occur when the offering is in the mature phase of the PLC. The customer uses professional buying expertise and often "hard-ball" negotiating tactics to push the price as low as possible.

In the stand-alone transaction, a negotiator with a competitive style or one with a problem-solving style would best represent the prospective supplier. The negotiator with a competitive style will tend to extract as much profit out of the deal as possible and will be able to match any hardball tactics used by the customer. There is always the risk that a clash of competitive styles will kill a potential deal; upper-level management of the supplier company will have to decide whether it can tolerate this risk and any potential adverse outcomes. Even if the deal is signed, there may be little goodwill left between the parties. Since this is a single transaction, though, this should not matter.

A problem-solving approach may also work well in this situation, particularly if the customer's negotiator also takes a problem-solving approach. Problem solvers tend to think beyond the surface issues of the negotiation and look for unique solutions that improve the benefits received by both parties. Even though the situation is a single transaction, the result can be unexpectedly positive for both the buyer and the seller.[12]

The other kind of situation involves a transaction with long-term consequences. In the best of circumstances, it involves a customer with a different attitude than the price-oriented customer just described. In general, this is a customer that wants to receive the best value package possible but that also sees the potential benefit from establishing a lasting relationship with suppliers, so that the suppliers know the customer's business and can be proactive in providing value. This situation can occur in any stage of the PLC, including maturity.

A problem-solving approach works best in the second situation, where transaction concerns are balanced with relationship concerns. Good creative problem solvers will find ways to enhance the relationship with each successive negotiation session. A compromising style and approach will also tend to produce positive outcomes but may not produce the unique outcomes of the problem solver.

The marketer must be cautious to correctly identify the situation. Customers may appear to seek value and seem to want to pursue long-term relationships. However, as negotiations develop, it becomes clear that lowest price is an overriding concern. Such customers really want the benefits of both high value from a relationship and low price. This is a dangerous sort of relationship in which to become involved. The switching costs for the supplier become too great to easily leave the relationship, while the profit from a long-term relationship never materializes.

Preparation for Negotiation

Obviously, to do a good job of negotiating, the company should prepare as much as possible. It helps to think in terms of the stages involved in a negotiation and to do what is necessary in each stage to make a favorable transition into each subsequent stage. Negotiation involves teamwork in most instances. At a minimum, the negotiating team includes a marketing role and a seller role. Exhibit 10-13 shows the stages and substages of the negotiation process.

Preparation
    Data collection and analysis
    Determination of negotiation strategy
Information Exchange
    Elicit information not yet obtained
    Test hypotheses about nature of situation
Engage in Negotiation
    Opening
    Discussing positions
    Concessions
    Closing
Obtain Commitment

EXHIBIT 10-13   Stages in the Negotiation Process
in Business-to-Business Sales

Most companies do a reasonably good job of preparing their sales teams to present the offering and show its benefits. This requires understanding of the customers' needs, buying center interactions, and the buying decision process. Some of this preparation serves the price negotiation process as well. Knowing customers' needs and their relative importance gives the sales team an idea of what issues the customer will bargain hardest on and the ones on which they will be most likely to make concessions. Other kinds of preparation questions to address include the following:[13]

- Who has the authority to make a final decision?
- What are the bargaining styles of the individuals most likely to participate in the bargaining decision process?
- Will the situation be perceived as a transaction, part of a relationship, or a balanced combination of the two?
- What evaluated price range is the customer expecting?

Data about the customer can be obtained using typical market research and market operation forecasting methods. Whatever is not known can be obtained through contact with customers during the prenegotiation period. In addition, the marketing analyst's cost and value model of the customer's business will have been used already to set price levels for the product and offering. This same model can give the sales team an idea of what the customer's acceptable price range will be. The newer the market or the newer the customer, the more general will be the cost or value model. In any case, though, it can give the sales team a starting point from which to negotiate.

The second part of the preparation phase involves determining the negotiation strategy. The first part of the strategy-making stage is framing of the negotiating situation, estimating the objectives of the other side, and determining the likely negotiation style to be employed by the other side. Once the nature of the transaction has been recognized, the negotiating team's goal should be to bring the most appropriate bargaining style to bear.

Determining goals is the next step. If the marketing analyst has done the homework, an acceptable price range should be laid out—from the supplier's viewpoint as well as from the customer's. Also, the homework should indicate what issues are likely to be key for the customer and on which issues the customer is likely to be willing to compromise or make concessions. With this in mind, the supplier's negotiating team needs to determine what issues—including price—are most important and how these issues are prioritized.

The team then needs to determine where it has leverage and where the customer has leverage. A party in the negotiation has **leverage** when it has the power to get the other side to accede to its position. Leverage comes from an unequal distribution of importance or need—one side needs the deal more than the other side. For instance, if the customer has alternative suppliers available, the customer tends to have leverage. If the customer needs immediate delivery so that it can meet a tight production deadline, the supplier tends to have leverage. Even if the negotiating team decides that it has some leverage, it may choose not to use it for reasons of enhancing a relationship.

The bargaining strategy may even extend to anticipation of the kinds of concessions that will be attempted. Concessions work best in an "if . . . then" format, such as "if you are willing to wait an extra month for delivery, then we can come down in price per unit by 5 percent." This is called **integrative bargaining**, an approach in which multiple dimensions are considered simultaneously.[14] The negotiation team may want to identify important issues for the customer that can be easily accommodated. They can then offer concessions on these issues to obtain reciprocal concessions from the customer in areas that are important to the supplier.

In preparing for the closing stage, the supplier's negotiator avoids the temptation to give in on price to complete the contract. The negotiation team may prepare one or more final "pot sweeteners" that can be reserved for deployment to close a deal. These are based on the customer's important non-price needs that the negotiating team has discovered. Ideally, these are high value for the customer and low cost for the supplier. If the deal closes before these concessions are reached, the negotiator can add in one or more of them as a special bonus (especially if they are low cost). This could help cement a relationship with the customer.

The outcome of all this preparation is a game plan for undertaking the bargaining. All of the participants on the negotiation team now have an idea of what they are trying to accomplish and what their roles are. The plan helps the team to concentrate on reaching their goals rather than on simply achieving the minimum deal they will accept. Lastly, it sets out information areas that need to be filled in with information from the customer. After the negotiation team goes through an information-exchange stage, the negotiation plan is updated to reflect new information.

Last Thoughts on Negotiation

Note one last piece of preparation: when involved in a stand-alone transaction—particularly with a large, leverage-holding, price-oriented customer, the negotiator needs to know when to walk away from a deal. With the price-oriented customer, the negotiator should not fool herself into thinking that a contract taken now at minimal profit or even a loss could build into a relationship in the future. The purchasing department will always push for price concessions, even if the supplier has a relationship with other members of the buying center. When dealing with a price-oriented customer who has leverage, the supplier should have a cost structure that creates profit; this is the only way to consistently win in this situation.

PRICING AND THE CHANGING BUSINESS ENVIRONMENT

Throughout this text, we have explored how the trends occurring in the business environment require business-to-business marketers to change and adapt. In particular, we have examined the effects of time compression, hypercompetition, and the growth in use of the Internet. In this concluding section of this chapter, this examination continues.

Pricing, Time Compression, Hypercompetition, and the Internet

Time compression affects the time that marketers have for analyzing industry conditions and customer reactions. It also puts pressure on marketers, salespeople, and customers to negotiate quickly so products and services become available before market conditions change. Obviously, pricing is not done as well as it could be when time compression prevails. When time compression interacts with the ease that prices can be changed, the effect is insidious.

Under time pressures, marketers are forced to try to react to quickly changing customer needs or rapidly developing competitor actions. Product features and channel programs take time to develop, so a quick reaction is difficult. Changes in sales force methods take time to disseminate within the organization, but these can probably be done more quickly than product changes. Promotional messages delivered over the Web can be changed fairly quickly, but messages going out through other media take time to develop. Price changes can be implemented very rapidly, though. If a marketer believes that a response to a competitive move must be immediate, the quickest way to respond is to drop prices.

Related to time compression are the trends of hypercompetition and increased use of the Internet. Hypercompetition increases the number of competitors vying for the same customer. It also means having to compare the marketer's value against some very different value packages involving substitute products or services offered. A marketer can address time compression and hypercompetition through more attention to constant preparation. This means, in part, constantly collecting information about customers' value-cost models and paying constant attention to the customers' customers and their perceptions of value. As much as possible, the analyses we have discussed need to be done on an ongoing basis rather than as ad hoc analyses. This allows setting of prices more quickly and gives negotiators more information when they begin the negotiation process. This may seem to the marketer like overattention to tactical information. However, time compression is so prevalent and pricing is so crucial to profitability that constant preparation is truly a strategic activity. Also, both quicker price quotes and better presentation of value for customers relative to competitors help address the problems of hypercompetition.

Increased use of the Internet has both beneficial effects on pricing and some drawbacks. Internet communication through e-mail and shared Web sites can increase communication and preparation. In collaborative circumstances, in which both the transaction and the relationship are important to both parties, increased sharing of information facilitates more creative solutions. In the situation in which three or more parties are involved and relationships are important, such communication facilitates better coordination.

A trend facilitated by the Internet is the use of auctions, particularly in supply chain transactions. Auctions are a two-edged sword, having both benefits and drawbacks. The key to maximizing benefits for all parties and minimizing the drawbacks is to use auctions in appropriate circumstances. Auctions are good for transactions involving undifferentiated commodities. Used outside this context, the benefits of relationships become minimized or circumvented.

Marketers in offering their products or services can use auctions. Marketers may also encounter auctions used by buyers to obtain products or services. When a buyer–seller relationship already exists and one party or the other begins using an auction, the trust in the relationship is called into question. The buyer or seller using an auction is saying, "We think we can get a better price; you've been holding out on us." An auction is better used for one-time transactions or for obtaining a first supplier (buyer) in a new line of business that may develop into a relationship. An example of a one-time transaction might be the case of a supplier with excess or obsolete inventory. Rather than contacting individual resellers or customers, the marketer may announce an auction and direct the inventory to the customer or reseller who values it most.

THOUGHTS TO TAKE WITH YOU INTO THE NEXT CHAPTER

In this chapter we have focused on price as part of a total offering—the value statement to the customer. The key idea is to set price level in such a way that superior value is created for customers. Recall that value is composed of benefits received by customers less the customers' costs. These costs include the price of the product or service. The marketer tries to set the price and structure the customers' costs so that customers receive more value than they would receive from the marketer's competitors. On the other side of the transaction, though, price must be set so that the supplier establishes profitability. Price must be set to cover the relevant costs and contribute to profit. To accomplish value-based pricing, then, the marketer needs to understand both the customers' perceptions of value and the marketer's own costs.

We have discussed the ways for managing prices in a competitive environment that changes as the supplier's market evolves and how the marketer's pricing must be consistent with business and marketing strategies pursued by the marketer's company. In some instances, as with penetration pricing and price skimming, price plays a key role in accomplishing strategic purposes. Pricing tactics also play an important role in implementing marketing strategies.

In business-to-business markets, marketers must often face the prospect of implementing their pricing through price negotiations with customers. We have discussed the importance of preparation for such negotiations as the core means of ensuring that negotiation is successful in creating customer value and supplier profitability.

As you move into future chapters concerning selling and relationships, keep in mind the seller's role in the negotiation process. In many cases, the seller is the primary person for maintaining profitable pricing in the presence of the customer. Think about how the marketer, the missionary seller, and the sales representative can work together to build relationships with customers and still manage to create a strong negotiating position.

Key Terms

avoidable costs *229*
bundling *242*
contribution margin *230*
cost-based pricing *222*
demand curve *231*
elasticity *232*
evaluated price *223*
forward-looking incremental
    costs *229*

integrative bargaining *249*
learning curve *239*
leverage *249*
ongoing costs *228*
ongoing revenues *228*
open bid *243*
penetration pricing *238*
price skimming *238*
realized costs *229*

resultant costs *229*
revenues *228*
sealed bid *243*
supply curve *231*
total offering *223*
value-based pricing *222*
value-cost model *227*

Questions for Review and Discussion

1. In general, what is the maximum price that can be charged for a product or service?
2. What is the maximum price that can be charged for your product when you have direct competitors but your product is differentiated, that is, it provides more benefits than competitors provide?
3. Under what kinds of circumstances would a marketer want to charge a price less than the maximum price possible for the offering?
4. In general, what is the minimum price that can be charged for a product or service?
5. When would R&D costs be a relevant cost to consider in pricing decisions?

6. Suppose you were considering a price increase. What kind of difference would you expect between short-term elasticity and long-term elasticity in response to your price increase?

7. Under what general conditions would you want to use a price-skimming strategy? A penetration price strategy?

8. Under what conditions would you switch from a skimming strategy to a penetration strategy? What elements of the marketing mix other than price would be involved?

9. The chapter relates the "second in, low-cost producer" to the acquisition of small technology companies by large firms as two strategies that have potentially similar strategic outcomes. In a fast-paced market, which strategy would be most effective for (a) an established, large manufacturer of consumer products, and (b) a large high-technology network equipment manufacturer?

10. Discuss the organizational and marketing-mix changes required when a small company hits the chasm. From question 9, above, of the two strategies discussed, which would be the most appropriate in today's marketplace?

11. Suppose your company is the market leader in a fast-growing market. Your product is differentiated in that it provides more and better benefits than your competitors'. How would you price your product?

12. In competitive bidding, what factors would enter into your determination of a bid to offer?

13. Why is preparation for negotiation so important to effective pricing?

14. Explain the major differences between negotiation in a single-transaction situation and negotiation in a balanced-concern situation.

15. Explain why time compression causes problems for price negotiations even when both parties have an interest in enhancing a relationship.

16. Explain "evaluated price."

Endnotes

1. Based in part on Cliff Edwards, "Intel Inside the War Room," *Business Week* (April 30, 2001), p. 40; Maija Pesola, "Chip Growth 'Best Since 2000,' " *National Post* (September 30, 2003), p. FP10; Edward F. Moltzen, "AMD, Intel Rev Their Engines as Race Heats Up," *CRN* (1103) (July 5–12, 2004), p. 41; Cliff Edwards, "Inside Intel," *Business Week* (January 9, 2006), pp. 47–54.

2. We use the term *seller* for efficiency's sake instead of using the generic, and more awkward, "*salesperson.*"

3. Michel H. Morris and Gene Morris, *Market-Oriented Pricing: Strategies for Management* (New York: Quorum Books, 1990), pp. 87–93.

4. Paul Sherlock, *Rethinking Business to Business Marketing* (New York: The Free Press, 1991).

5. Based on Thomas T. Nagle and Reed K. Holden, *The Strategy and Tactics of Pricing: A Guide to Profitable Decision Making*, 2nd ed. (Upper Saddle River; N.J.: Prentice Hall, 1995), Chapter 2.

6. See, for instance, Jack Hirshleifer and Amihai Glazer, *Price Theory and Applications* (Englewood Cliffs, N.J.: Prentice Hall, 1992).

7. Indeed, AMD tried to *unilaterally increase its prices* on memory chips, only to see a net loss of revenue and profits.

8. Morris and Morris, *Market-Oriented Pricing*, p. 119.

9. Nagle and Holden, *The Strategy and Tactics of Pricing*, pp. 190–191.

10. G. Richard Shell, *Bargaining for Advantage: Negotiation Strategies for Reasonable People* (New York: Penguin Putnam, 1999).

11. Nagle and Holden, *The Strategy and Tactics of Pricing*, p. 193.

12. Roger Fisher and William Ury, *Getting to Yes: Negotiating Agreement Without Giving In* (New York: Viking Penguin, 1981); and Shell, *Bargaining for Advantage*.

13. Shell, *Bargaining for Advantage*.

14. Ibid., p. 169.

Chapter *11*

Business Development and Planning

OVERVIEW

The practices of innovation, product development, and pricing often combine to make it possible for companies to seek increased business beyond their current market segments and customers. This effort can be the result of an innovation the organization has not previously offered, the recognition that a current company offering is in maturity and its market is still innovating, or any combination of these factors. In these circumstances, depending on the degree of difference or innovation of the new offering, the firm seeks to replace older products in target markets (sustaining innovation), enter market segments where the firm may have a presence but not with this type of offering (incremental innovation), or enter new markets where the firm is not known and the offered technology has not yet been accepted (disruptive innovation, from the viewpoint of one or all of the stakeholders).

This chapter focuses on the organizational changes necessary to achieve these goals, the market knowledge and planning that are required for success, and the strategy that reinforces the delivery of goals.

Sensacon—Continuation of a Hypothetical Example

Consider the situation faced by Sensacon, the company developed and referenced in previous chapters. Recall that Sensacon, a major innovator and developer of micromachined devices, successfully developed a small growing market for its innovative pressure sensor design. Initially, the market was comprised primarily of visionaries; typical applications were in SCUBA (self-contained under water breathing apparatus) equipment and health-care devices. Both market segments were ideal targets for Sensacon as market demand and Sensacon manufacturing capabilities (high variable costs, no economies of scale) were well matched.

In the product development stage and the introductory stage of the product life cycle, the Sensacon staff of technology-savvy "customer engineers" had worked closely with customers. The creation of the pressure sensor was dominated by the specific customer needs of the visionary market. Product changes were mostly incremental, as the customers in this market segment were interested in the performance of the sensor and were willing to design their products to accommodate the Sensacon product. The customers' low-volume products provided an excellent proving ground for the Sensacon technology. Customers acquiesced to time delays and initial delivery problems; investors anxious to see positive cash flow at Sensacon expressed the only sense of urgency.

The size of Sensacon markets skyrocketed when they were selected, as one of four companies, to supply tire pressure sensors for SUVs.[1] The volume demands on Sensacon manufacturing and customer support would now reach two million units annually, up from five thousand units. As previously discussed, Sensacon was faced with the typical factors faced by a small company moving into "the big time." Sensacon—and the technology it was developing—was crossing the chasm.

Manufacturing development, significant product redesign for volume manufacturing, and support for significantly larger and more complex customer buying centers became necessities of the transition. The small staff that had been successful in creating value for technophiles and visionaries—moving R&D invention to market innovation—was overwhelmed by the volume of new customer inquiries and application requirements. Additional marketing resources were added to interface with customer demands in all phases—supply chain organization and development, customer education in the proper application of the sensor, and so on—all required development and coordination. Sensacon learned a new way of doing business.

While Sensacon made the transition to the growth stage of the PLC, senior marketing management recognized that steps must be taken to avoid the trap of Sensacon being a one-product one-market company. Sensacon developed a field market development team and approached the SUV manufacturers with application designs for all vehicles, not just SUVs, and also approached other vehicle manufacturers. The process began of translating this new business success to additional opportunities. Customers were soon found that were interested in the development of handheld tire pressure sensors for car owners and heavy-duty models for tire shops. Soon, Sensacon found it necessary to develop a new marketing channel for the product as dealers and tire repair shops needed service and replacement parts—and the training to use them. An additional channel to reach vehicle owners that wanted to upgrade older vehicles was also developed.

As the sensor moved through the PLC, the nature of support changed. In introduction, close collaboration and mutual design efforts were required to bring the innovation to market. As Sensacon crossed the chasm, field market development (FMD) teams were deployed to translate the success to additional customers. Supporting the original equipment manufacturer (OEM) effort was not enough. The Sensacon total offering included the training and deployment of service personnel at the consumer level. And as, eventually, competition entered the market, a consumer positioning effort was deployed to attract aftermarket customers. Though the core product did not change (other than those changes that made it possible to mass-produce it), the marketing organization, at each transition through the adopter categories, evolved to meet different customer needs and opportunities.

LEARNING OBJECTIVES

By reading this chapter, you will:

- Understand the distinctions between "line" functions and "development" functions in an organization.
- Recognize how the level of innovation of an offering can determine the part of an organization that is responsible for its success.
- Understand the distinctions between *New Business*, *Translation*, and *Core Churn* categories of business and the business-to-business marketing resources necessary to support each effort.
- Understand the different efforts involved with launching new products and managing mature business both at the organizational and customer level.

■ Understand the different types of forecasts and the integration of market information into the organization.

■ Understand the value, use, and development of a market operations forecast, and the launch of new business efforts, segmentation by translation, and core churn management.

■ Recognize the changing roles played by marketing professionals as an offering evolves in the market.

INTRODUCTION

As discussed in both the strategy chapter and the innovation chapter, businesses with different goals, that is, managing a cash cow versus developing a question mark into a star, require different approaches to marketing and different performance measurements. Also, within organizations, different departments and sections will have different business responsibilities related to the role the department or section plays in the creation of the total offering.

Offerings that are early in the PLC will interest different market segments than offerings in later stages. Customer education and service needs change as the product evolves. Notwithstanding the changing market, marketing has three primary **goals** at every stage of the life cycle.

• Obtain new customers.
• Continue to meet the needs of existing customers.
• Coordinate offerings that are in different stages of the PLC and manage them such that the business' prospects are not tied to the PLC for a single product or for a cluster of related products.

At each PLC stage, marketing must be concerned with acquiring new customers and obtaining sales from existing customers. New customers can be further segmented into new adopters and customers that have previously adopted another company's offering. As described by the TALC concept, the market segments most interested in adopting the offering change over time. These different new adopter segments are not always served best by the same design of marketing operation that addressed the previously targeted segment. Existing customers' needs are also evolving as they adapt to their own changing customer markets. The levels of codevelopment, service, and education required to satisfy the customer need for a total offering evolves, as the product becomes known in the market. The marketing and market support organization that is appropriate in the rapid growth stage may be overly elaborate, or possibly not margin supportable, in later stages. As the business targets more and more segments with offerings in different stages of the PLC, the management of multiple forms of marketing operations becomes increasingly complex.

This chapter focuses on the management of individual products and services in a dynamic environment, the role that business development plays through the PLC, and the organizational structures most appropriate to these changing market efforts. Because business environments are dynamic, few products live forever. Most successful products have observable life cycles—they are developed, introduced to the market, their sales grow, the product-market matures, and eventually their sales decline as customers' preferences change and new offerings supplant the existing ones. Most business-to-business marketers must change their marketing strategies, programs, and tactics to accommodate this life cycle.

Important in creating marketing strategy for evolving products is the concept of **business development**. Marketing professionals often apply the concept of business development, but it has

Business Development is the search for opportunities and the structuring of business entities to exploit those opportunities with current or near term organizational capabilities.

not obtained universal agreement among professionals as to what "business development" really is. Consequently, "business development" means different things to different people. This chapter establishes the following definition: *Business development entails the search for opportunities and the structuring of business entities to exploit those opportunities with current or near-term organizational capabilities.* Business development involves analysis of markets and market segments, including discussions with potential partners to understand their direction and the needs of their markets. Business development then extends to creation and maintenance of relationships with partners that could include customers, channel members, or suppliers of complementary products and services.

As previously discussed, R&D, product development, and innovative efforts are most effective when the team responsible for these functions is specialized—focused on particular demands rather than attempting to provide invention, innovation, business development, and customer service for an offering in a "cradle to grave" approach. The definition of success for products at different points in the PLC changes: market introduction and customer awareness early in the PLC, then followed by market penetration and market ownership, and, eventually, the profitable management of a product in decline. A "specialist" approach is not only more likely to be successful because of the type of resources committed to it, but by the ability to measure its results.

FORECASTING MARKETS

The first step in the development effort is gaining as much knowledge as possible about the marketplace. Knowledge of "what's out there" is a primary tool in effective business development efforts.

The question "what's out there?" and the processes of market research and competitive analysis have been previously discussed. All of the information gathered is of little use if it is merely a snapshot of today. Markets change. Predictions of the future or, as business organizations prefer to describe the practice, forecasts are created more often than they are believed. (How often do you listen to a weather forecast with the idea in mind that it will influence what you will do the next day, then completely forget it and do what you want without consideration for the forecast?) The same could be said for market forecasts. The credibility and reliability of forecasts are directly dependent on the quality of the information used to create the forecast (naturally) and whether or not the creator is invested in the forecast being "good" (as opposed to useful).

What Makes a "Good Forecast" Different from a "Useful" Forecast?

Under the best of circumstances, a forecast can be in the ballpark—close enough to be an aid in making business decisions. A good forecast is one that was created through generally accepted methods. Procedures were followed. Good forecasts can be wrong, but are defended as good because they were done the right way. Good forecasts can be good and still be inaccurate. A cynic might say that this is a somewhat bureaucratic approach, focused on process rather than results.

A useful forecast is a forecast that contributes data to decision making. There is a temptation here to use the term *accurate* in place of *useful*. Experienced forecasters know that forecasts are, at best, useful and, by their very nature, not exact.

Notwithstanding the lighthearted (but usually accurate) view of forecasts and forecasters presented in the box "What Can Be Said about Forecasts and Forecasters?" the usefulness of forecasts depends on recognizing many factors that contribute to the qualitative rather than the quantitative nature of the forecast. The marketer must recognize the value of applying managerial judgment that comes out of experience and familiarity with the market. When the person charged with doing the forecast has little experience in the market being forecast, she would do well to seek the opinion of those who do have such experience. Experienced forecasters try to account for the following factors that will cause markets to change direction.

- *Technological change*: Can technological change be accurately forecast? In high technology, Moore's Law is often used as a tool to demonstrate the positive growth potential of the silicon electronics business. Most forecasts of technology incorporate growth, often based on the philosophy of Moore's Law. But, Moore's Law is a forecast of growth, not change. Did prognostications about the vacuum tube industry forecast the demise of that technology as the mainstay of electronic signal processing or was the growth of solid-state electronics as a replacement technology myopically ignored?
- *Time horizons*: The longer the time frame of the forecast, the less accurate and less useful the forecast is likely to be. How far into the future should a forecast look? What is the nature of change in customers' markets? Does the market embrace new methods and technologies, or is it resistant to change? How quickly can customers react to changes in the market? If an offering is part of an enabling technology, what delivery time frame is required to meet the customer's development and production schedules?
- *Barriers to entry or exit*: Never assume that the barriers to entry in an existing business will prevent another competitor from showing up in the market. Breakthroughs happen (how did the current organizations get in the market?) Also, never minimize the staying power of a competitor, particularly one who has a significant investment (financially, culturally, image, etc.) in serving the market need.
- *Elasticity of demand*: Directly associated with technology replacement, demand in business-to-business markets is somewhat volatile. As previously discussed, this volatility can defy conventional wisdom. Changing technology forces offerings through the adopter stages more rapidly as
  - early adopters embrace newer technologies
  - suppliers elect to abandon "late cash cows and dogs" faster, preferring to commit resources to new products or markets, in search of higher growth rates.

  Demand for offerings is influenced by changes in target markets, as technology products move from early adopters to markets whose participants are more closely associated with "proven" rather than "new" technology. This can be viewed as the dramatic increase in demand, as demonstrated by increased growth rate in the PLC and the shift from visionaries to pragmatists in the TALC.
- *Forecast expenditures*: What level of resources (how much time/money/energy) do you want to spend to improve forecast accuracy? Conditions in developing markets demand rapid decision making. Committing greater financial resources to obtain more accurate information also often creates an additional expenditure of time. The market opportunity may slip away before enough data is accumulated to enable a comfortable decision. It pays to recognize when wanting more data is just another way to avoid making a decision.

What Can Be Said about Forecasts and Forecasters?

Many marketers do not enjoy developing forecasts. The very act of forecasting asks the forecaster to make claims about things that cannot possibly, without the capability of time travel, be known. Forecasting, then, sets the forecaster up to be wrong. In the context of forecasting, however, wrong can be acceptable. Consider the following "rules" of forecasts:

1. Forecasting is difficult, especially if it's about the future.
2. When completed, all forecasts are wrong, you just cannot know by how much and in which direction.

3. State all forecasts to the third decimal place to prove you have a sense of humor.
4. When presenting data, provide either volume or timing, never both.
5. Compensating errors can make your day.
6. The best defense is a good offense, so, if you have to forecast, do it often.
7. If you get it right, never let your manager forget it.

Source: Adapted from Paul Dickson, *The Official Rules* (New York: Dell, 1978), pp. 53–55. Dickson credits Edgar R. Fiedler with Fiedler's 25 Forecasting Rules, appearing in the June, 1977, issue of *Across the Board*, the magazine of The Conference Board.

Forecast Types and Techniques

Ways of performing forecasts differ according to the type of forecast. Some different types of forecasts as well as some forecast techniques often encountered in organizations follow:

- *Strategic forecast*: Generally, a long-range business forecast associated with macroplanning efforts. Strategic forecasts usually have a stronger element of "top-down" input, with a major effort to reconcile reality with the strategic direction. These forecasts usually involve three- to five- (maybe ten-) year periods, reviewed and revised annually.
- *Marketing planning forecasts*: Usually associated with a particular product or market, these forecasts are the ones with which many marketers are most familiar. Marketing planning (a plan to determine needs and satisfy wants generated from those needs) often has significant data inputs from market research and competitive analysis, while attempting to project what customers will do. These plans usually involve one- to three-year periods, with annual review and revision, though quarterly and semiannual reviews are not uncommon.
- *Marketing operation forecasts (MOFs)*: The least formalized but often the most widely used, the **marketing operation forecast** is usually the responsibility of the field operation, sometimes in conjunction with brand/product/market specialists from headquarters. Under many themes and designations, operational forecasts, tactical in nature, are an ingredient in sales forecasts for territories, the tool used to judge performance for **missionary sellers** or field marketing operatives, and a major source of market information in business development efforts. These forecasts usually involve one- to three-year periods, reviewed and revised at least monthly, and include major elements of market research and intuition (based on knowing the market) in their development. The actual length of the one- to-three-year period is influenced by the product or technology life cycle and the rate of new product adoption. The marketing operation forecast is presented as a tool to gather timely data related to the logistics of current and future business and technology as well as the competitive environment. This kind of forecasting is essential to effective marketing management throughout the PLC.
- *Sales forecasts*: Shorter range than MOFs, sales forecasts are valuable for logistics, manufacturing, and material resource planning. While marketing operation forecasts and

sales forecasts may at first glance seem very similar, major distinctions include the way data are collected and the techniques used in analysis. Sales forecasts include a stronger element of history; they more often are used to track existing sales patterns and apply those patterns to the future. As a result, statistical data manipulation plays a major role in development of useful information, and there is an assumption that future market activities will follow the pattern of the current market. Predictive models (e.g., rolling average, econometric models)[2] are used to develop data of value not just for sales management but for logistics, manufacturing, and materials requirement planning (MRP) managers as well. Herein lays a major difference between MOFs and sales forecasts. Very little history or statistical manipulation is used in MOF development. While "no statistician should ever undertake analysis of a market without drawing fully and continuously on the knowledge of the marketing management,"[3] marketers must realize that sales forecasts are not good substitutes for MOFs. A brief summary of a few predictive models,[4] used for sales forecasting, appears in Exhibit 11-1. Note the quantitative rather than qualitative nature of several models.

Marketing Operation Forecasts in Depth

What are the data that make up a good *marketing-based* operational forecast? First, create the ideal list of the types of information a marketer wants to see when she picks up a forecast developed by the field marketing operation and obtained at the customer level.[5]

Rolling Averages

Forecast for the next period is a weighted average of a preset number of prior periods.
- Data: existing sales figures
- Averaging decreases impact and awareness of turning points
- Not predictive of turning points
- Appropriate for large-volume, low-value markets, ineffective with low volume, "lumpy" markets (large single purchases—facilities, infrastructure, etc.)

Econometric Models

Forecasts are based on relationships derived through statistical analysis.
- Useful for coverage of several years
- Requires prediction of many independent variables
- A study of history applied forward
- Lumpy markets can be modeled
- Provides information about broad categories: not effective for single brands or share data

Delphi Approach

Forecasts are from a panel of experts who are systematically polled.
- Executive opinion polling, with feedback provided to respondents to enable "correction" to the mean
- Selection of respondents critical to validity of results; stability over time improves usefulness of predictions
- A qualitative, intuitive model, useful for trends, not specific brands or offerings
- May have value in business-to-business marketing because of the oligopolistic nature of markets, ability to acquire informed respondents

EXHIBIT 11-1   Predictive Models

Marketers would like to know answers to the question "how much" about *current business*—much the same as a sales report:

- How much will customers buy of what they are now already buying? What customers currently buy is part of the suppliers' internal sales data. How the volume of customers' purchases will vary, based on factors in their market, is information usually available from customers. This business volume is usually referred to as the **core business** at a particular customer.
- How much will customers pay for it? If selling price for the current business is not fixed by contract, list price, or other agreement, marketing will be interested in any changes in the customers' value perception of the offering.

Timing of purchases will be important to marketing, not because a particular sales quota must be reached, but because marketing and support resources have to be allocated to obtain the purchase and enable delivery. The ideal MOF answers the "when will . . .?" questions:

- When will customers buy the noted (forecasted) volume?
- When will customers' purchases peak? Declining purchases could be a sign of a change in the customers' market, leading to new product introductions by customers. The customers' new products may or may not utilize the same materials or components. Business volume that was previously considered core may begin to erode.
- When will customers consider new technology? If the marketing organization has a new product or offering, when are customers likely to entertain a change in the current offering? What is the life cycle of the customers' existing offering, when will they be in the next design cycle to replace the offering, and will they consider a new technology for inclusion in the new offering? Customer culture in regards to the risks of new technology adoption will influence the likelihood that new technology will be considered.
- When will customers start buying from a competitor (or from the marketer's organization)? Have the customers, in a search for lower-cost supply, rebid the business? If an organization is the existing source, will the customer purchase from an additional supplier to avoid dependence on one source or has the current supplier been able to capitalize on another defending supplier's difficulties and will now be a second source for the purchases? An effective and well-informed sales force, by the way, usually answers these questions, but the answers should be independently confirmed by marketing.
- When will customers buy new technology? Incorporating new technology into the next-generation design is only part of the process; when will customers actually require delivery of production volumes of the new technology? New products may have a period of slow growth when market segments move to the next-generation product. Rapid growth follows the short-term decline in sales. Can the supplier organization sustain both the slow sales period and then the rapid growth? In terms of the MOF, purchases of new technology offerings are often referred to as "new business." The net business to customers is not entirely new, as the customer reduces purchases of what the supplier (assuming the selected supplier continues as the selected supplier for the replacement technology) previously considered "core."
- When will customers stop buying the existing stuff? If customers are introducing a new offering to their market, how long will the existing offering be continued? As noted, there is likely to be an overlap as volume of the new product ramps up and the old product winds down. Replacing the old core business with new business is often referred to as **core churn**.

Many customer organizations are spread around the globe. It is not unusual for design and development operations to be in one location while manufacturing is at remote sites where costs are lower. If the customer organization uses contractors for manufacturing, new products may be outsourced from different contract manufacturers. Changes made to accommodate decreasing volumes of older products and increasing volumes of the new offering will not always take place at the same physical location. Separate or unique supply chains and logistical systems may be required during the transition period. Marketers will want to know:

- Where will the existing stuff be shipped (stored, consigned, etc.) if a change occurs as a result of the new manufacturing plan.

This leaves a set of "who" questions that marketing must address. The customer contacts that provide most other pieces of the MOF can also provide these answers:

- Who will actually manufacture or incorporate your products? (Do they use contract providers? Will the contract providers have favorite sources other than yours?)
- Who are the primary specifying and buying influences, and where are they?
- Who are the customers' competitors?

Additional "what" questions that need to be answered for the MOF include:

- What are the customers going to use the product for or in?
- What is the customers' market like—does your organization understand it?
- What R&D is necessary on your part to satisfy needs?
- What kind of new business is this to the supplier? Is this business a translation of an existing success, a new market, a new product, or both a new market and product? Can other opportunities be located that this application success can be translated to? (Exhibit 11-2 and the box "New Business, Translation, and Core Churn" further define these terms.) These translation efforts are a particular function of the field marketing specialist or missionary seller.
- What else might be unusual about this business?

Products

		New	Existing
Markets	**New**	New business	Translation
	Existing	Core churn	Core

EXHIBIT 11-2 Business Development Tracking Grid

New Business, Translation, and Core Churn

Real New business is the result of a major R&D, product development, and/or marketing effort, if done from a marketing viewpoint, in conjunction with the customer. This partnership with the customer results in first-time applications or adoptions of technologies.

Translation business occurs when the customer specification is not a first of a kind application. Though it may be new in the view of that customer, it is not "new" to your organization; it's merely a translation of a previous success.

Core Churn occurs when the translation business at a customer replaces an application of your older technology. This "new" business certainly required an effort by the team to get the business; however, it shouldn't require as large an effort—assuming the translation tools were adequate. Unfortunately, the organization does not experience an increase in business equal to the sales of the replacement. The organization realizes the net of the old and new volumes. (See also Exhibit 11-2.)

Consider the power of this level of information. Remember, this is a tactical forecast. This forecast should be accessible throughout the organization.

With this level of tactical information, bottoms-up forecasting for strategic purposes becomes not only less cumbersome but more accurate. The real power of this information, though, lies in the planning that it facilitates. Once the marketing manager knows what, when, and how customers will be considering, buying, ordering, and using the manager's products and services, the manager can direct the marketing effort. If more resources are needed, the manager can begin the process of obtaining the authority and funding to hire new employees, hire consultants or agencies, and schedule customer visits or whatever is required. If the nature of the support changes, the manager can adopt the organization style or model that will best serve the needs of both customers and the supplier.

Several groups within the organization will find this information useful: manufacturing, R&D, scheduling, logistical support, customer service, and so on. If the supplying organization is engaged in a business that markets products to companies that use contract manufacturers or have several geographically dispersed manufacturing locations, they are likely to have such a logistical tracking system already. To clarify and perhaps simplify the nature of the MOF, consider the scenario in the box "Back to Pacific Drives . . ."

Operational forecasts of this detail can be difficult, not because the necessary information is not available but because obtaining it can be time consuming and will be viewed by a field seller as getting in the way of selling. This will be aggravated if there is no formal missionary sales structure. If there is an existing missionary sales structure, they will need to be motivated to contribute to the MOF, probably through compensation based on their participation. (A review of the philosophy of compensation—you get what you reward—is included in Chapter 12.) For offerings in the high growth part of the cycle, a field marketing team is in the best position to gather and organize this information. A field marketing team may be a burden to late-maturity or decline offerings where the customer base is knowledgeable and innovation of the offering is not likely. (The next generation of offering that will replace this mature product is in the translation or high growth stage of the cycle.)

Exhibit 11-3 is an example of a concise way to handle all of this market information so that it is useful to many company entities. Enterprise software now exists to do "automatically" what was a once-a-month computerized report. With the advent of corporate Intranets, this data can be readily updated and available. Market factors that impact forecasts, such as regional economies, world economic conditions, interest rates, and other factors that can impact business levels, can be added to the report, but these factors are beyond the scope of this analysis.

Customer Name	Application	Our Product	Annual Volume	First Year Volume	Close Date	Run	New/ Translation	Competition	Competitive Product	Ship to/ Manufacturer Location	Threat Assessment (%)
Ajax Computer	Printer	MX272	35,000	4,000	July 2007	24 months	Trans	Zigma	Z-44	Ajax/Mexico	70
Sensacon	Pressure sensor	PX400	200,000	50,000	August 2007	36 months	New	Amron	AM27	Sensacon/ Vermont	80
Sensacon	Sensor retainer	PX410	200,000	50,000	August 2007	36 months	New	Amron	AM30	Sensacon/ Vermont	80
CarryAll	Luggage closure	CL2	10,000	8,000	February 2008	24 Months	Trans	Klincon	Zip2	To be determined	50
Widget Inc.	Stepping motor	PX401	100,000	45,000	April 2008	48 months	New	UniMem	UM503	To be determined	60
Palo Alto Computer	Desktop computer	PD1000	60,000	30,000	April 2008	18 months	Trans	UniMem	UM300	Palo Alto/ Texas	60
NBM Computer	Notebook computer	PDN1005	75,000	20,000	April 2008	24 months	New	Coastal drives	CDX	NBM/ Singapore	20
FunLine	Game console	PD1000	200,000	70,000	July 2008	24 months	Trans	UniMem	UM300	Precision Mfg/Taiwan	60
Spartan Computer	Internet appliance	PD1000	6000	5000	January 2009	24 months	Trans	UniMem	To be determined	To be determined	50

EXHIBIT 11-3 Data Chart for Marketing Operations Forecast

First-of-a-Kind Application, Translation of a Previous Success, or Replacement for Existing Business?

All new business is good—right? But what kind of new business is it? Different types of "new business" will require different resources of the organization. Note the eighth column of Exhibit 11-3: "New/Translation." This indicates the category of new business the application falls into from the marketer's perspective. Is the application new business, a translation from a previous success, or incremental business as the application is a replacement for an existing piece of core business? In other words, beyond the actual sales volume, what qualitative value does the application have to the selling organization and how should the marketing effort be managed?

Real New Business is the result of a major R&D, product development, and/or marketing effort, particularly if the offering is the result of partnering with the customer. This partnership with the customer results in first-time applications or adoptions of technologies. Many parts of the organization are involved. Can it be manufactured? Can we support the volume? The missionary seller gets a lot of help. The supplier is going to want to brag about this piece of business after the customer introduces its product to the market, hoping to attract additional customers interested in the same value and function. These are the applications and efforts that everyone in the organization finds the most exciting. Most "new business," however, is not *real* new business.

What if the new customer specification is not a first-of-a-kind application? This is true for the majority of new business. While a partnership with the customer may have developed a specification for your company's product, and it may be new in the view of that customer, it is not "new" to your organization; that is, it is not a new technology, product, or use of a product. It is merely a **translation** of a previous success. As an example, let us say that working with Hewlett-Packard, you develop a *new* high-capacity storage device for HP's personal computers. Business with HP (in this instance) is real new business. Your headquarters storage device product specialist (or whatever title is used) develops a set of marketing tools for the field team to take this initial success and translate it to other customers. Missionary sellers eagerly take these

Back to Pacific Drives . . .

The missionary seller, working over a period of eighteen months, develops a major piece of business with a Silicon Valley computer company. Pacific Drives brand is specified on the drawings for new models of the computer company's network servers, though the "or equivalent" phrase follows the specification.

Over this eighteen-month period, many company disciplines will want to be notified of what is going on. Manufacturing will want to plan resources and schedule manufacturing. Logistical support will want to plan when and where to ship. Your missionary seller (a marketing position) has done an exemplary job. Except . . .

Like many companies, your customer has remote manufacturing sites. If the customer's new server line is successful, production will start in Ireland six months after initial manufacturing. Perhaps your sales team in these sales territories would like to know what is going on. They may have some interesting information to contribute to a better plan to serve this piece of business.

For instance, one of the potential contract manufacturers contemplating a bid for the business has a cozy relationship with your major competitor, DynaDrives, who has extended special credit terms.

Oh, by the way, two years ago, during a shortage, you cut off the contract manufacturer because of slow payment.

How does this change the business and, hence, the forecast? Can you influence who/what/where/when? You can only if you know about it.

translation tools to their other customers in the PC business—Sony, Gateway, Dell, and so on. With this assistance (training, education, design application, and so forth) these other PC manufacturers begin to use the new storage device. While new business to the missionary seller and the customer, these applications are translations of the storage device offering that was originally successful at HP.

What if the translation business at Gateway replaces an application of your older technology storage devices? Is this business still considered new? It certainly requires an effort by the team to get the business; however, it should not require as large an effort as the HP application because the relationship with the customer is stable and the technology has been previously developed. The supplier's technical application specialists, rather than R&D personnel, assist in the technical support effort for the customer. Unfortunately, the organization does not experience an increase in business equal to the sales of the new device at Gateway. The organization realizes the net of the old and new business volumes. This replacement business, core churn, is necessary, important, and critical to market ownership but not as glamorous to the team as "real new business." The organization needs all three types of new business—real, translation, and churn. Each type has different implications for margins, customer support, and product development—the entire marketing mix.

MANAGING PRODUCTS THROUGH THE PRODUCT LIFE CYCLE

In prior chapters, it was noted that the product life cycle is a useful tool for thinking about marketing strategy, but does not provide specific prescriptions for action, nor does it provide specific predictions of changes in market parameters, such as product sales. Presented here is a quick summary of the PLC stages and how they relate to the TALC for technology innovations, followed by more depth on the implications for managing three aspects of business-to-business marketing—marketing strategy, business development, and marketing organization.

Interrelating the TALC and the PLC

Exhibit 11-4 (similar to Exhibit 2-7) shows the PLC and TALC superimposed. As previously noted, the PLC is most usable when viewed from the perspective of a product category, rather than at the level of an individual product model or version. Customers are best understood for strategy purposes based on their perceptions, thoughts, and feelings concerning the category of the product. For instance, in the hypothetical Sensacon example from the opening vignette of this chapter, the initial customers for the pressure sensor devices were visionaries in the SCUBA and health-care devices markets. Later customers were pragmatists in the automotive market. These later customers were pragmatists with respect to pressure sensors—they were nonadopters with respect to the early versions of the pressure sensors that were too costly and ill-adapted to the automotive market. Sensacon must first segment the prospective customers in the market based on their predispositions to adopt the product category.

SUMMARY OF PLC CONCEPT   Exhibit 11-5 shows the life cycle of a product being divided into five stages: development, introduction, growth, maturity, and decline.

In the *development stage* of the PLC, efforts focus on moving invention to innovation, often with the encouragement of a specific partner or customer. These development partnerships (or contracts or maybe development grants from government agencies) can supply

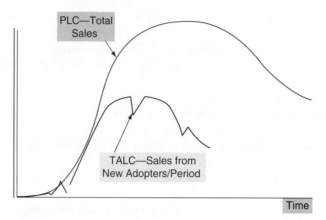

EXHIBIT 11-4   The TALC and PLC Superimposed

dev.

funds for development or may take the form of a guaranteed first sale of the outcome. Usually, development costs exceed development revenue, but not always. The customers at this stage are the technophiles in the TALC and some early visionaries.

Once the product in its early incarnations has been tested with early customers, the product will enter the *introduction stage*. In this stage of the PLC, with feedback from technophiles and visionaries, development work continues to improve the product. The improvements to the product can be either radical or incremental innovations; in either case, the product moves closer to broad commercialization (over time, though, these changes shift toward incremental changes and the design of the product begins to stabilize in form and function). In terms of the TALC, the customers in this stage will generally remain visionaries. Sales of these early products start to grow. The products and market growth become more visible to other potential players in this market—potential customers, potential competitors, potential suppliers, and potential channels.

At the end of the introduction stage, visionary new adopters become scarcer. The companies competing to supply the new products in this market will face the "chasm" of having to find pragmatist adopters to fuel continued sales growth. Pragmatists have different requirements from visionaries—a stable, valuable product with full supplier support infrastructure; and solid assurance that the product and infrastructure will perform and support future evolution of the product. If the supplier companies can provide this "whole product," the assurance of

intro

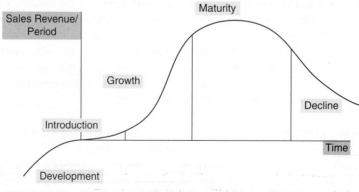

EXHIBIT 11-5   The Product Life Cycle

minimal adoption trauma, and the assurance of future support, the product can move beyond the introduction stage.

In the Sensacon example, the company has introduced the pressure sensor to visionaries in the SCUBA and blood pressure device markets. As Sensacon becomes comfortable with the capabilities of its offering, so will potential users. Sensacon searches for opportunities that will carry the technology—and the company—across the chasm. Shortly afterward, the company pitched new business in the SUV market and had to go through a series of demonstrations and trials to prove the effectiveness of the product design. Recall that SUV manufacturers perceived a high level of need and urgency. The vehicle rollover problems, mostly attributed to Firestone tires on Ford SUVs, could be lessened with a low tire pressure warning to the vehicle driver. Sensacon had found its "beachhead" pragmatist segment. Once the manufacturing and quality problems associated with manufacturing in quantity were addressed, Sensacon could realize rapid increases in sales, as did the other competing manufacturers. The growth period of the PLC had started.

In the *growth stage,* product innovation continues, but the product moves toward a consistent architecture and the type of innovation tends more toward incremental than radical. Initially in the growth stage, product innovation is focused on developing a standard that will be accepted by many customers, leading to an ownership position. As the growth stage progresses, new competitors enter the fray, some with innovative products and others with me-too products trying to profit from getting a "piece of the action." *{ growth 1*

There are actually two phases to the growth stage. In the first phase, growth is driven by new segments of pragmatists adopting the product category for the first time. Later in the growth stage, a second phase occurs as many of those early adopters buy more of the product. Often their second purchases greatly increase in volume and dollars over their first purchases as they increase the use of the initial product or translate the success to additional products in their line. Eventually, sales in these pragmatist markets begin to stabilize.

The reduction in the growth of sales puts pressure on the competitors in the market. The competitors that will survive and prosper are those who have adapted to the predominant technology standards and who have developed their operations to deliver value and manage costs. The competitors who do not have a competitive advantage will begin to fail. Some will be acquired by better-positioned companies; some will struggle to find other businesses to enter; others will go out of business. Even as Sensacon focuses on improving its products and its operations to compete in the growth stage of the micromachined pressure sensor device market, it must be thinking ahead to the second phase of growth, in which competitive pressures will increase.

The growth stage transitions to the *mature stage* when markets begin to become saturated and when the preponderance of buyers have incorporated the product into their "standard way of doing things." These repeat buyers make up the *core* business for Sensacon. The growth stage may be extended if the transition from pragmatists to conservatives is smooth and price levels do not erode. In other cases, price erosion may turn into sales decline, which can be only partly offset by volume growth as conservatives begin to adopt. In either case, the competitors must adapt their product innovation and marketing tactics once again as the market changes. *{ maturity*

Eventually, the PLC enters decline. In the *decline stage,* customers have begun shifting demand to other products or solving their needs in some other way. For example, the market for handheld calculators is well past maturity. As more handheld devices have calculators built into them, such as personal digital assistants and cell phones, there are fewer instances where someone wants stand-alone calculating capability at their fingertips. Competitors decide whether they *{ decline* will continue to address the market or leave the business. Those that do remain may continue to pursue some incremental product innovations, perhaps aimed at niche markets (big button and display calculators for vision and dexterity impaired individuals, and so on). These niche markets may sustain a few survivors in the business.

Marketing throughout the Product Life Cycle

The PLC and the TALC provide general guidance on how to market in an evolving environment. Different customer groups (segmentation via adoption inclination) become prominent as the PLC or TALC progresses and marketing strategy must change to address these different groups as they emerge. At the same time, competition and infrastructure in these markets are also changing and marketing strategy must adapt to these changes as well. At any point in the PLC or TALC, there are still major uncertainties about customers, competitors, and technology. Continued analysis and exploration are required to gain insight into evolving opportunities.

The conclusion in this situation is that marketing strategy and marketing operations can be only partly derived from good marketing analysis. Exploration and partnership building are also necessary to proactively discover opportunities and develop the businesses necessary to pursue them. Recall from the discussion earlier in the chapter that business development is the part of marketing that involves finding opportunities and working out methods of exploiting those opportunities. Business development involves research, experimentation, and analysis. Business development differs from strategic planning in that it becomes an active exploratory dialog with potential partners. Those partners can be customers, channel members, external alliance partners, or subdivisions or departments internal to the company. The next section delves into the implications of melding the general guidelines of the PLC and TALC with the proactiveness of business development.

MARKETING STRATEGY AND BUSINESS DEVELOPMENT THROUGH THE PLC

Development Stage   In the development stage, the marketing strategy is to "find a marketing strategy." In other words, the company that is working on early-stage products in a new product category must learn about customers, find initial target markets, and begin exploring how to shape the business to pursue the opportunity. Technology development, marketing strategy development, and business development are thus all the same in this first stage. These efforts help find development customers who will be the test cases for first products as they move beyond the prototype phase. This early effort involves much experimentation and perhaps false starts. Entrepreneurial organizations find that they are in search of a market for a new technology. At this stage, markets may not know of the possibilities of the technology and technology owners may not know of those markets in need. In business-to-business markets, conventional market research efforts will not suffice. The entrepreneur must simultaneously approach many potential markets in a learning process, as visionaries are not concentrated in any one market, but exist throughout all markets.[6]

Some revenue may be generated by marketing or business development activities that get partnerships, contracts, development grants from government, or prelaunch sales from prospective customers. These activities may indeed generate revenue. However, the goals of early marketing or business development are to generate information about customers, generate product and business designs, and begin to build trust with important partners. Too much of an emphasis on early revenue and profit can distract the organization from these goals.

In the development stage, the value proposition and positioning evolve. A key element of the value offered to visionaries is the access to early-stage products and upgrades that can change the customer's strategy toward its own customers. Visionaries will see this value; pragmatists will take a wait and see approach. Pricing will not be a major factor in the marketing mix until the new product is considered for a large market. Through the development period, the nature of discussions is to anticipate price after the chasm is crossed.

Introduction Stage   When the product has been developed enough that it demonstrates initial value to customers, the product enters the *introduction stage*. In most business-to-business markets, the early stage launch of a product is somewhat informal. The purposes of marketing strategy or business development efforts will be to get exposure and begin to educate potential customers about the technology, its near-term products, and potential benefits. In the process, marketing or business development will make it easy for prospective visionary customers to self-select and come forward voluntarily. Good activities for accomplishing education and early discussions are participation in trade shows, information-rich Web sites, and "Webinars"—online multimedia seminars. Business development efforts should also include direct contact with companies that the marketer feels have a high likelihood of being good visionary customers.

This business development effort in the introduction stage illustrates the difference between personal selling and business development. If the early-stage company were to focus on personal selling in the introduction period, the classical sales management approach would be to screen prospective customers, focusing on those that showed immediate sales potential. Once the salesperson determines that a potential customer is a pragmatist who wants to wait for more evidence of performance before adopting, the salesperson would note the prospect's future interest, mark the account for later follow-up, and move on to another prospect. This approach is short-sighted in the early stages of the PLC. The uncertainty of customer adoption and revenue requires a missionary or "evangelist" approach to the market. These individuals ideally will be part of a business development organization that will hand off the offering to FMDs for translation after the initial beachhead is established.

If there are potentially many customers for the company's early product, the company may go through a formal launch process later in the introduction stage. The activities for this formal launch will involve marketing that goes beyond business development. The target market will still be visionaries and may be confined to a limited number of industries. Sensacon did this in the introduction stage of the pressure sensor PLC: They addressed markets in SCUBA and medical devices, launching early versions of their products at trade shows in these industries, accompanied by appropriate marketing communications and selling efforts.

As noted above, a key element of marketing strategy and business development is the search for the first pragmatist market segments that can serve as a beachhead for crossing the chasm. This effort during the introduction period involves analysis of potential market segments and talking with prospective customers to find pragmatists with a crying need. In this early stage, the offering will usually involve a fair amount of customization.

Business development has identified the first customers to be targeted and probably the potential follow-on segments. In products for which few customers exist, business potential beyond the first launch customer is not automatic. A handful of targeted customers, in some cases only one, may be the extent of the market. The transition between the launch customer and the next customer can be traumatic. The level of collaboration that exists with the launch customer is not always present with follow-on customers.

Several factors impact the success of the organization as the chasm is approached.

- Is manufacturing ready to take on additional demand? In a large company with economies of scale, this may not be an issue, but a smaller company will need a plan to scale up with the increased demand.
- What level of design support will be necessary to both scale up the manufacturing effort and satisfy customization demands from new customers?
- Is the support staff capable of meeting the needs of an increased volume of customers?
- What pricing strategy will support the manufacturing volume or service needs of the new customers? (Review Chapter 10, the basic parameters of pricing an innovative product.)

In the Sensacon case, their discussions with SUV manufacturers identified the pragmatist's requirements and the urgent need. It should be noted that this represented new business for Sensacon, not a translation from its existing products. In some cases, crossing the chasm may involve a translation of a product application from a visionary customer to a larger pragmatist customer group. Such a translation would involve validating the application and making the adjustments in the offering to address the pragmatist market segment. This was not the case in Sensacon. The new pragmatist segment required a re-engineering of the product and creation of new manufacturing and logistics operations.

Growth Stage   When the suppliers have a successful beachhead with pragmatist adopters, marketing strategy and the business development portion of marketing strategy must recognize the advantages of market ownership and work to create a "defacto" standard in the market. Success brings competitive imitation and the emergence of complementary products to serve peripheral customer needs, solidifying the offerings' ownership position. As products become standardized, business development efforts will start shifting more toward translation efforts. Missionary sellers or FMDs will tend to perform a lot of the business development effort. However, there will also be a fair amount of effort aimed at developing new business. For instance, Sensacon may look to translate the SUV pressure sensor success to another market, such as the aircraft market. The first effort to enter this market might focus on large commercial aircraft, requiring a major engineering effort of the product and new specifications for manufacturing and delivery logistics. This would represent *new business* for Sensacon. If then, Sensacon translated this new aircraft pressure sensor product to executive jets and small private aircraft, this business might represent translation business. Large account business development specialists might pioneer the original entry into the commercial aircraft market. Field marketing teams might accomplish the translation to the other aircraft markets.

Marketing strategy during the translation period would tend to focus on making it easier to find and approach new pragmatist market segments. Marketing communications would be aimed at generating awareness and understanding of the advantages of Sensacon sensors—building brand identity in order to compete against the new entrants that are in the market or who will soon enter. Pricing will take into account competitive dynamics as well as customer perceptions of value. A fair amount of effort may go into developing channel relationships, particularly if the large-volume adopters have ancillary needs in the aftermarket. In the Sensacon example, aftermarket channels become an important source of new business (translation business) requiring careful selection, development, and support of these channel partnerships.

Market Ownership and Field Market Development

Market ownership doesn't just happen. The marketer must develop an organization that will serve the diverse needs of different adopters, including design assistance, application education, and offering customization to specific requirements of differing customers. In a pragmatic customer organization that values proven technology and incremental change, the supplier mentors the new application of the offering through the customer organization. Each stakeholder in the buying center has a specific need and concern related to the adoption. This complexity can be unwieldy without a marketing organization design to accommodate it. At this stage, marketing and customer service become more prominent as the means to compete. A strong missionary sales effort, for example, FMD personnel, is essential for successful market ownership. (See "Operations and Organizational Structures to Manage Simultaneous Product Life Cycles," below.)

The second phase of the growth stage arrives when core business maintenance is a major field marketing responsibility. This does not mean that business development goes away as an important activity, though. As new versions of the product are developed and new applications emerge, sizable market development efforts are required to create growth though core churn. For instance, tire pressure sensors may move from OEM applications to aftermarket installations. This will require customer research, education, and development of new value propositions to gain new business within the custom auto and auto service markets.

At this point, some of the business development staff will shift their focus to work on other technologies or innovations in other PLC or TALCs. Meanwhile, field market development has full responsibility for continued translation efforts. Since products have tended toward standardization by this time, this new business will tend to be translation and/or core maintenance business, although some opportunities may require new channel, product, or service supplier partnerships that are so different as to constitute real new business. Marketing strategy during the second phase of the growth stage focuses on caring for existing customers and winning customers away from other suppliers.

Market Ownership   Market ownership comes from a three-pronged attack. First, the company must stay close to the front in product development. Second, the company needs to be recognized as the owner of the market. This comes from taking good care of customers, advancing the value provided, and good branding communications (see the box "Market Ownership and Field Market Development"). Third, the product must be the defacto standard in the market. Third-party companies adopting the owner's operating standards, connectivity, and methodology demonstrate market ownership. The owner's standard becomes dominant as all market participants adopt it.

Maturity Stage   When the slow-down occurs in growth as pragmatist customers become saturated, the company must be positioned to survive the inevitable shakeout of competitors. After the shakeout of competitors and considerable decline in the rate of sales growth, the PLC has reached the *maturity stage*. New customers are conservatives. Conservatives represent a relatively sizable portion of sales only if the pragmatists do not engage heavily in repeat sales. Some product categories have little in repeat sales, such as the enterprise resource planning market. Other markets are sustained through periodic repeat purchasing by almost all buyers in the market, such as the business markets for laptop computers, cell phones, and PDAs.

Marketing during maturity focuses on reselling products to existing customers. Competitive efforts focus on taking or defending market share from other competitors. If a supplier is relatively small, a reasonable strategy is to find a niche that it can dominate and defend. This may be a market niche that is comprised of conservatives entering the market. An example of a conservative-driven niche might be the market for software to run medical offices. This is essentially a specialized application that runs on existing software and equipment—the market would not likely tolerate the risks and reliability difficulties associated with new or emerging technologies. While the opportunity is not huge, it is large enough to support several decent-sized software companies.

In maturity, the successful large suppliers will be those that focus innovation for low-cost production. The supplier with the most staying power wins the market share battle in maturity, and that usually is the low-cost producer. Efficient ordering systems and streamlined logistics aligned with supplier needs become competitive advantages. Remaining business development efforts, at this stage of the PLC, have two aspects. First, business development must contribute to the company's strategy for competing in the maturity stage of the PLC. A typical strategy is to seek development of ancillary business opportunities, in service and support, associated with the primary business. The effort noted in the box "Caterpillar Grows through Services" is typical of this type of effort. Second, business development must look ahead, as noted above, to the next generation new business.

In the maturity stage, core business and core churn take on increased importance. Whether a company is large and addresses several mainstream market segments or whether the company is small and addresses a defensible market niche, the company must expend selling effort to protect core business from its competitors as well as get existing customers to seek additional or replacement products and services (core churn) for aging products. Much of it is accomplished through the established sales force. This "caretaker" function is an important part of the marketing effort, focusing on building and maintaining relationships with customers and partners.

Business development activity has now come full circle. It is focused on finding opportunities for new technology development. Eventually, the old PLC will die out. A market owner will have proactively designed this demise to be coincident with newer products entering the growth stage. An important role for business development is to develop the transition from current offering to next-generation offering with large-volume pragmatists. In some cases, new markets emerge that are related to the company's mainstream PLCs. In the past ten to fifteen years, many companies facing maturing or mature lines of business have found new growth in services. Lou Gerstner's key contribution as CEO of IBM in the mid-1990s was the shift of

Caterpillar Grows through Services

In 1973, Ford Motor Company requested that Caterpillar provide rebuilt engines for Ford's truck division. Caterpillar accommodated its customer and by early 1980s found that this service had potential as a continual income producer. Over the years, Caterpillar treated remanufacturing as an ancillary business, but continued to slowly invest.

By 2000, remanufacturing opportunities were beginning to emerge in cost-squeezed industrial markets. In overseas markets, such as China, new equipment was still too pricey, but lower cost refurbished equipment was affordable. Caterpillar had invested in operations to the point where it was positioned to take advantage of these new opportunities.

Today, Caterpillar is actively pursuing remanufacturing and other services as key elements of its growth strategy.

emphasis from computer systems to IT services. Similarly, as discussed in the box, Caterpillar has seen a new growth opportunity in its remanufacturing services. When such opportunities are not available, the company must look for other lines of business and it must start this effort in the maturity stage of the current PLC, if not sooner.

Decline Stage   Eventually, the PLC enters *decline*. By this time, the offering should no longer be the focus of a field market team since the customers know the product. Some users will stay with the older technology just because it works well and meets their needs. If there are any new customers, they are skeptics (laggards). Their numbers are relatively few, but not insignificant. For a marketer who wants to address a niche market, finding skeptics who will adopt an old technology (usually one hidden in some other product, e.g., microprocessors imbedded in the power train control systems of automobiles) may be a viable market with few competitors. Ultimately, from the consumer viewpoint, these innovations are invisible—merely an improvement in the final product in which they serve.

Marketing at this stage depends on keeping existing customers satisfied and managing costs. Often, a company decides that it is not cost effective to pursue a line of business that is in decline and thus sell it to another company. The companies that stay in the business, or that enter it as the result of an acquisition, will use very tightly targeted communications so that money is not wasted communicating with noncustomers. The price is set at a level low enough to discourage the customers from looking to switch to new technologies.

For late maturity and declining products, FMD will be nonexistent, with sales efforts rewarded through short-term reward systems (i.e., commission selling). Since the support needs for offerings at this stage are primarily logistical in nature, the most effective marketing effort will not be provided by an organization focused on translation efforts. The company that stays in the late-cycle business uses a sales-oriented suborganization or separate department entirely. Many of these products have achieved commodity status, thus marketers tend to sell and distribute through industrial distribution. However, many products in the decline stage are now sold through Web-based marketing.

Business development at this stage has two possible directions. First, in looking for new customers, business development is concerned about finding the most efficient channels that reach the skeptics. Such channels are needed because very often the skeptics are small businesses that are addressing small niches that they can easily defend. Hence, they do not have the need or the budget to buy more up-to-date equipment or services. A second direction of business development is to find the other companies that might be interested in buying the line of business in the declining stage of the life cycle.

ORGANIZING TO MANAGE SIMULTANEOUS PRODUCT LIFE CYCLES

Up until now the discussion has followed a single product life cycle. However, most companies attempt to manage a series of products that are in various stages of their own PLCs. To maintain the viability of the company, it needs to take a "pipeline" approach to the collection of businesses and products pursued. Ideally a company would simultaneously have a balance of products in early stages of the PLC, in middle stages of the PLC, and in maturity and decline. This ensures that as some products reach decline there are products that come through the pipeline to take their place and provide stability and growth in revenues and profits.

The company can take one of two general alternatives to the organization of its marketing based on this pipeline analogy. On the one hand, the company can assign a marketing team to a product or product line and carry out the product's marketing from cradle to grave. The second alternative is to organize by customer adopter type within the PLC. Thus, when a product is in the introduction stage, the marketing team that does product introductions takes control. When the product moves into the growth stage, the team that grows product lines takes over, and so forth.

As shown in the above section, a product-centric organization must begin marketing in the early part of the life cycle by using an approach that focuses on finding early development customers and partnerships. This moves to marketing based on finding visionaries and a first pragmatist niche. Once the chasm is crossed, the same marketing organization must focus on finding and developing new segments. When growth takes off, the marketing focus is on stuffing the channel and selling upgrades to first customers. At the change to maturity, the marketing effort requires routinization and fine-grained product differentiation. Changing to decline requires product line trimming, cost savings, and selling off of products or whole product lines.

Using Specialists

A product-centric organization requires the marketers to wear many hats and learn new techniques as the product passes through the different stages of the PLC. Suppose the range of marketing activities is divided into research or analysis, product development, new business development, translation business development, core churn business development, selling and sales support, channel development or management, market communication, and customer care. Exhibit 11-6 shows how the emphasis of activities might change as a

Activity	Development Stage	Intro Stage	Chasm and Early Growth	Tornado—Later Growth	Maturity Stage	Decline Stage
Research and Analysis	▲	▲	▲	▲	▲	▲
Product Development	▲	▲	▲	▲	▲	
New Business Development	▲	▲	▲			
Translation Business Development		▲	▲	▲		
Core Churn Business Development				▲	▲	▲
Selling and Sales Support			▲	▲	▲	
Channel Development and Management			▲	▲	▲	▲
Market Communication			▲	▲	▲	
Customer Service					▲	

EXHIBIT 11-6 Activities Emphasized at Stages of the PLC for a Hypothetical Product

company's product progresses through the PLC. It becomes obvious that a marketing team assigned to this hypothetical product will have to learn to be proficient in new sets of activities every time the PLC hits a transition, rather than specialists in the activities and customers suited for each stage.

This still does not capture the level of complexity involved in marketing through the PLC. The nature of activities that continue to be emphasized from stage to stage also changes. For instance, marketing's role in product development early in the PLC is focused on finding and specifying the elements of the core product. Later, this effort shifts to finding features that are desired by various market segments, which will result in product versions in the product line aimed at those particular segments. If the marketing team continues to focus on finding the breakthrough features later in the life cycle, effort and time will be wasted and opportunities will be missed.

The tendency for the product-centric marketing organization will be to (1) keep doing what it knows best, which will be ill-suited to the next batch of customers, and (2) not learn the new activities that are better suited to next adopters. Either tendency—especially the combination of the two—is a recipe for acrimony, sleepless nights, pink slips, and reason to review Levitt's "Marketing Myopia" again.

caution

The alternative is to have a set of marketing organizations—specialists—for each adoption stage. As a product (remember, this is a class of products, not individual versions or models) moves from stage to stage, the product is handed off to a new team, who is good at handling this stage of the PLC and dealing with these kinds of customers. This approach has the advantage of bringing marketers with appropriate expertise into the fray. Generally, it will not take these marketers long to get acclimated to the new product. They must be careful, though, to look for the right prospective customers. For instance, pragmatists for one product may not be the same pragmatists who adopted the last product. However, the principles of addressing pragmatist markets will tend to be very similar from one situation to the next.

Business Development Bands through the PLC

To summarize so far, the marketing organization should be configured around the different kinds of adopters. This will bring specialized knowledge to bear for each type of adopter. Different pieces of the marketing organization will have different goals and objectives to achieve and will address these goals with different sets of activities. It follows, then, that the motivation and compensation should be structured to reward the performance of specified activities and the achievement of particular objectives.

Exhibit 11-7 shows the PLC with three horizontal bands, each indicating an area of different marketing focus.

The first band, the *Range of Initial Business Development for Each Offering*, employs business development teams focused on the innovators or visionaries in potential customer organizations. This focus is not limited to existing customers and relationships—the team will be prospecting for the first successful partner for the new product. The new offering is generating little revenue and little, if any, profit. The team is interested in initiating that *first piece of new business* that may be the beachhead of a new product line, market segment, or even a new star SBU for the company. The individuals most likely to be successful in this band are team players with a sense of market ownership. These teams will

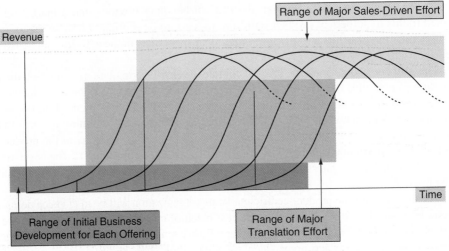

EXHIBIT 11-7 Business Development Bands over the Product Life Cycle

be motivated through compensation that rewards business development activities rather than selling activities. Rather than commission, compensation will tend toward salary with bonus potential.

The second band in Exhibit 11-7, the *"range of major translation effort,"* is the period when FMD specialists or missionary sales, coordinated by headquarters marketing effort, seek customers for offerings "proven once" in the first band. A major tool of this effort is the marketing operation forecast discussed extensively in the first half of this chapter. The FMD focus is market development within a specialized area (territory, product line, etc.). Successful translation of the proven-once new business leads to the establishment of new market segments— segmentation through translation. (Individual compensation, roles, and the continuum from sales to marketing functions are further detailed in Chapter 12, "The Business-to-Business Sales Force.")

Exhibit 11-7 shows the *"range of major sales-driven effort"* as the third and final band. At first glance, this type of representation, the results-compensated sales-driven role, is unfortunately applied in the earlier bands by many organizations. However, in the context of this strategy, there are two functions of this role: (1) maintain ongoing successful relationships with buying customers, a traditional sales-driven approach and (2) interface with the organization marketing effort to prepare purchasing organizations for new business, translation, or core churn changes that may be on the horizon. FMDs are working with customers or partners in that many have remote manufacturing locations or use contract manufacturers, as well as manufacturing at the location where the developments take place. These logistical endpoints—nodes in the supply chain—when they occur in the territory are the responsibility of the seller.

At this point it may seem like there is a redundant field team in this scenario—the FMDs and the field sales team. However, when the functions and responsibilities of the two teams are understood, there is little overlap, but a strong need for an integrated effort. The pivotal tool in this integrated effort is the MOF. Additionally, the overall strategy of the organization must be one of value pricing to enable the margins necessary to support the education and development efforts of the teams.

THOUGHTS TO TAKE WITH YOU INTO THE NEXT CHAPTER

This chapter has focused on market forecasts and business development. The focus has been on the practical aspects of forecasting, particularly the construction of a marketing operations forecast. The MOF starts with customers and what they are likely to do in the near future: how much they will buy of what kinds of products, when they will buy, when they will need delivery, and when they will need support. This provides information sufficient for planning the execution of marketing programs and tactics. Information provided by forecasts and the MOF about market segments and competitors leads to decisions on choice of target segments, positioning, and customer needs and buying behavior. The marketing information obtained in the analysis helps in forming the marketing strategy, programs, and tactics.

"Business development" is a function that is not always clearly defined and, when defined, changes at the same pace as the market. Different organizations, processes, and techniques prove most successful at different stages in the life of an offering. Changing markets and customer needs drive the concept of continuous organizational change. The most successful organizations recognize that one structure and reward system cannot perform at "ownership" level throughout the PLC. Utilizing the principles of division of labor, the marketing organization is subdivided into specialized groups most competent at working with customers at specific points in a PLC. Customer relationships are more stable, as adopter categories for specific innovations tend to be stable and the productivity of customer as well as supplier resources are maximized.

Key Terms

business development *255*

core business *260*

core churn *260*

goals *255*

marketing operation forecast (MOF) *258*

missionary seller *258*

translation *264*

translation tools *265*

FMD = Field Market Development

Questions for Review and Discussion

1. List the uses for forecasts in business-to-business marketing.
2. What are the different kinds of forecasts used in business-to-business marketing?
3. Who has primary responsibility for developing the marketing operations forecast? Why?
4. How is a marketing operations forecast used differently than a sales forecast?
5. What is business development? How does it differ from personal selling?
6. Describe the role of the field market development person in an organization whose focus is technophiles and visionaries.
7. Describe the role of the field market development person in an organization whose focus is pragmatists.
8. Why is the role of the FMD diminished for products in maturity and decline?

9. As an offering moves across the chasm, what strategies will be necessary to insure market ownership?
10. How do the goals of market "ownership" and market "share leadership" differ?
11. Describe how "real new business" is analogous to diversification.
12. When is core churn also new business?
13. How does business development change as the PLC progresses through its stages?
14. Why should a marketing organization be oriented toward different types of adopters rather than specializing in different products?
15. How should compensation be used to motivate and reward business development activities, such as field market development? Why?
16. List the roles and responsibilities of the three different bands in the management of simultaneous life cycles.

Endnotes

1. Additional details of the Sensacon market and the company's development are included in Chapters 8 and 10. The entire "Sensacon Story" is repeated as a discussion case in the case study portion of this book.

2. E.J. Davis, *Practical Sales Forecasting* (London: McGraw Hill, UK Ltd., 1988), p. 203.

3. Ibid., p. 128.

4. Ibid., pp. 203–222.

5. "Field Marketing Operation" personnel titles vary by industry. We have seen missionary sellers, market development specialists, customer and product evangelists, customer engineers, and so on. What is important to recognize is that this individual is delivering value to the customer, is compensated by a relatively stable salary (with some bonus potential), *and is part of the marketing organization.*

6. Shu-Yuan Wu, *The Learning-by-Experimentation Process for Market Creation*, 19th Annual UIC Research Symposium on Marketing and Entrepreneurship, August 2005, San Francisco.

Chapter *12*

Business-to-Business Selling

Developing and Managing the Customer Relationship

OVERVIEW

Previous chapters stressed the importance of relationships and the value they add to business-to-business offerings. This chapter's focus is on the seller, who performs the sales function of the firm and makes that relationship a reality. The discussion concentrates on the different roles that sellers can play, depending on the culture of both supplier and customer and the level of involvement of the buying center. The term *seller* is used often in this text to simplify "salesperson" nomenclature. While not used in this text as an exclusive replacement, seller is interchangeable with saleswoman, salesman, and salesperson.

The business-to-business selling process is more time consuming and, ultimately, more personal than the consumer process. In business-to-business selling, the complexities of successful selling require the buyer and seller to develop mutual respect and trust, a luxury that sellers in consumer markets seldom have the opportunity to achieve.

The role of the business-to-business seller changes with the expectations of different customers and the nature of the offering. This chapter reinforces the notion that there is not necessarily a "way to sell," but there is certainly a way that customers want to buy. Ultimately, the most successful way to develop a sales organization is to match the way the customers want to buy.

The opening example tells the story of how Hewlett-Packard lost one of its strengths—selling to corporations—and began rebuilding that competency to regain a competitive edge in the computer industry.

HP Returns to Its Original Selling Competency[1]

In 2005, Mark Hurd became the new CEO of computer giant Hewlett-Packard (HP), replacing Carly Fiorina, who was removed by HP's board of directors after five lackluster years. One of the things that Mr. Hurd observed was the ineffectiveness of the sales force targeted at corporate customers. Customers complained that they had too many points of contact with HP and were not sure who to go to when they were interested in particular products or services. Furthermore, they felt that HP's response time to requests for service or information was too long.

Mr. Hurd learned that several factors appeared to contribute to the sales force's problems. First, the sales force was organized as a stand-alone entity. Salespeople represented several product lines at once. The combination of these two organizational design features made the sales force accountable mostly to the sales management infrastructure, with little responsiveness to the product divisions. In addition, sales teams selling to corporations were larger than their counterparts selling for competitors. The bureaucracy within the sales organization was another factor stifling sales team effectiveness. Ten layers of management slowed decision making. The red tape faced by the individual salespeople constrained the amount of time they could spend with customers. HP estimated that its salespeople spent about 30 percent of their work time in front of customers.

After reviewing the situation, Mr. Hurd and HP's senior sales executives began restructuring the sales force in five key ways:

- A large portion of corporate sales was relocated to within the product line divisions (accountability to product marketing).
- A single sales rep became responsible for most of the largest accounts and sales teams were reduced in size from an average of four people to three (one-stop focus for customers).
- Sales meetings were confined to Mondays, so sales reps could be on the road for more time during the week (organize to sell rather than manage).
- Information technology used by the sales organization was upgraded and software for tracking sales leads and the sales process was standardized on a single system (marketing operation forecasting—Chapter 11).
- The compensation structure was reorganized from commissions based on revenue to better reflect sales profitability (rewards more aligned with desired outcomes).

The result was more time spent in front of customers, better response time to customer requests, and more sales wins. The improvements showed promise and represented the start of a restructuring process to regain HP's competitive edge in selling.

LEARNING OBJECTIVES

By reading this chapter, you will:

- Understand the roles of sales and the seller in business-to-business organizations.
- Understand the differences between selling in business-to-business markets and selling in consumer markets.
- Understand the basics of effective business-to-business sales force organization.
- Recognize the different types of sales representation that are most appropriate for offerings under different customer buying patterns.
- Understand the internal and external relationships necessary for successful sales and market development personnel.
- Recognize the different levels of selling associated with product types, rewards, and seller performance.
- Reinforce the necessity of understanding customers' needs and preferences in the building of a sustained organizational relationship.

INTRODUCTION

The opening vignette describing HP's efforts to reorganize and re-energize its enterprise sales force illustrates the importance of managing sales in business-to-business marketing. The seller in business-to-business markets plays a much larger role in the sales process than the seller of consumer products. In consumer markets, relationships between sellers and customers are usually brief, one-time events, with little personal information exchanged between the participants in the transaction. While some consumer product sellers may develop a clientele who return for repeat purchases, the relationship is sporadic. In business-to-business selling, however, the nature of the purchase and the characteristics of the process require an ongoing relationship between the seller and all of the stakeholders in the buying center. At HP, the company had shifted from emphasis in selling to other businesses to excellence in selling to consumers. The company relied on its small systems computer sales and printer business to generate most of its profits. However, the company discovered that this was not enough to sustain the company in the long run. HP would have to regain its excellence in business-to-business sales to thrive in the future. Excellence in business-to-business selling begins with an understanding of customers, their needs, and their decision processes. Mark Hurd began his tenure at HP by talking with 400 of their largest customers to understand their thinking, their problems, and their concerns about working with HP.

As discussed in Chapter 3, the buying process in business-to-business markets evolves through more intricate phases than the consumer purchase process. Before getting involved in the specifics of business-to-business selling, a look at the role of selling in general is in order.

THE NATURE OF SALES AND SELLERS

Everyone has an idea of what sales "is." When the word *salesperson* is heard, most people have an immediate image of a sales stereotype based on individual experiences with salespeople they have dealt with or have heard about. The car salesperson, the insurance broker, and the real estate agent—almost every entity the consumer deals with will have a selling role associated with it. The diversity of these roles and the skills required to be successful make it almost impossible for any particular stereotype to accurately reflect the reality of the profession. However, most people will form their impressions from a limited sample and then generalize these into stereotypes. Unfortunately, this leaves most people with a far too narrow view of selling.[2] To fully understand the nature of the sales function, a broader perspective is necessary.

Selling is a natural function. Everyone sells. In social situations, people find themselves trying to "sell" to the rest of the group where to go to party that night; children try to "sell" parents on why they need that new bicycle; and, at work, employees sell their skills and accomplishments to the boss. At its most elementary level, selling is persuading.[3]

The form the persuasion takes and the style with which it is applied determine the success of the effort. Customers resent "pushy" sellers who they believe are attempting to force something on them that they do not need. Whether the resentment is the result of a seller who does not regard the needs of the customer as most important (fit the market to the product—a sales era strategy; see the later discussion on the evolution of sales philosophies) or whether there is a mismatch in acceptable persuasion techniques, the customer still feels resentment toward the seller. Better sellers, then, attempt to understand customers' personality and behavior variables and work to satisfy the intangible as well as the tangible needs of the buyer.

Selling creates value for both the buyer and the seller. The sales process instigates the principle of exchange, in which both the buyer and the seller possess greater value after the transaction. While at first appearing elementary, the review of this concept can be a grounding force for sellers and their managers who get caught up in the "meet the quota at any costs" short-term sales approach. In fact, in relationship-based sales organizations that operate with a strong sense of partnering with customers, the seller's role is often viewed as that of a value creator.[4]

Sellers are the frontline personnel, the first line of one-on-one communication with the prospective customer. The seller is an important part of the organization's value image.[5] Beyond "first impressions," the customer makes many judgments about the selling organization based on the image and presentation of the seller. In the customer's eyes, the seller *is* the selling organization. Conversely, if the seller competes well within his organization for organizational resources for his customers, the seller is the customer in the eyes of the selling organization. Sellers, particularly in partnering roles, are often called upon as the liaison to manage both intrafirm and interfirm conflicts.[6] Sellers, thus, are often in the role of **boundary personnel**, the diplomats of the organization.

Boundary personnel is the term given to individuals in the organization who operate, as a significant part of their responsibilities, spanning the boundaries of their own organizations and those of customers. Both buyers and sellers have boundary roles. Actual job titles and levels in the company can vary, but the function of liaison and/or diplomat can be a major asset to the relationship between buyer and seller and, in some instances, across internal boundaries within the customer buying center.

Characteristics of Business-to-Business Selling

As summarized in Exhibit 12-1, business-to-business selling situations are different from consumer selling in many ways. In business-to-business markets, the seller spends time building and nurturing the personal and business relationship with several individuals throughout the buying center.

REPEATED, ONGOING RELATIONSHIP   The relationship between the seller and buying center members is often a series of **dyadic interactions**. The seller builds the enhancing elements of the relationship and minimizes the threats to the relationship over the course of these interactions. As the duration and complexity of the relationship grows, the seller must convince the buyer of the seller's interest in the success of the buying organization and of the buyer as an individual. The repeated, ongoing nature of the relationship can eventually permit the seller to be a motivator (though not necessarily the prime mover) in new solutions for the buying organization.

Dyadic interactions are one-on-one meetings or sessions between stakeholders in the buying center and the seller or other individuals in the selling organization's value chain. A typical "sales call" by a seller on a buyer would qualify as a dyadic interaction, as would a meeting between a field marketing representative and the project manager of a new development effort in the buying organization.

SOLUTION ORIENTED, TOTAL SYSTEM EFFORT   A natural outcome of the seller's focus on the success of the buyer and the buying organization (though cause and effect could probably be argued) is a solution-oriented, "total system" effort or total offering approach. As repeated throughout and a major theme of this book, customers buy solutions, not technologies or core products. This approach, of

- Repeated, ongoing relationships
- Solution-oriented, total system effort
- Long time period before selling effort pays off
- Continuous adjustment of needs
- Creativity of seller in problem solving often demanded by buyer

EXHIBIT 12-1   Business-to-Business Selling Characteristics

course, requires the seller and the selling organization to fully understand the customer, including the customer's market environment and culture as well as every facet of the differing needs of the buying center. The successful seller also understands the different motivating elements between members of the customer buying center. These factors contribute to a level of "knowing" that reinforces the relationship with the customer and assists the seller to develop and nurture an appropriate solution.

LONG TIME PERIOD BEFORE SELLING EFFORT PAYS OFF   In most consumer selling situations, the seller will know in a matter of minutes whether the sales effort has been successful. In business-to-business sales situations, the outcome of the effort may not be known for months or even years. For example, the complexity of decisions in the design of a new electric power-generating facility may extend the period for selecting turbine suppliers for several months or longer. As described in Chapter 3 from a behavioral context and again in the discussion of the marketing operation forecast in Chapter 11, the solution provider selection process is time consuming. Throughout the development period, astute sellers use the development period to reinforce the value of their offering versus potential competition

CONTINUOUS ADJUSTMENT OF NEEDS   Sellers and selling organizations must be flexible and responsive to the changing needs of customers, particularly if the selling organization has joined with the customer in a mutual development effort. The next-generation solution that results from the application development process may not be what was initially envisioned. The specific needs of customers evolve as they learn more about the product and how it can be applied to their needs. The development process is usually an education for both the buying and the selling organization.

CREATIVITY DEMANDED OF SELLER BY BUYER   Business-to-business customers, particularly large ones who may specify the use of significant quantities of the selling organization's products, expect an innovative and creative approach to their needs. They do not appreciate being offered exactly the same solution as another customer, even if the success of the offering at the other customer is what attracted them to the supplier in the first place.

Approaching each customer's problems in a way that can be recognized as unique has subtle advantages to the seller. Unique offerings to customers who are in competition with each other can relieve the seller of many concerns regarding pricing and price discrimination. Unique offerings may very well have different costs associated with them. Depending on the customer's view of single versus multiple sources for purchases, the buying organization may prefer a unique offering from the seller, perhaps enhancing the exclusivity of its own offering.

THE ROLE OF SALES IN A MODERN ORGANIZATION

"Nothing happens until somebody buys (sells) something." This statement, and variations on the theme, is as true today as it has ever been. While new communications technologies such as the Internet and new management tools such as customer database management software have the capability to make the task more productive, buying and selling are still at the heart of business.

Relationship Sales and Marketing

The term *relationship selling* has been used frequently in recent years to describe the context of business-to-business selling. Unfortunately, there seems to be no clear definition for the term.

Often the "relationship" between seller and buyer is sometimes considered to be far less important in low-involvement, low-technology sales than it is in more involved situations. This is not necessarily the case. In fact, given homogeneous products late in the PLC, the case could be made that the buyer–seller relationship is one of the important differentiators between competing suppliers. "The relationship" between buyer and seller is always important though the nature of the relationship and the expectations of the parties involved change under different circumstances.

DEFINING WHAT A RELATIONSHIP IS Successful relationships between suppliers and business customers involve mutual respect, trust, and authenticity. At this level of relationship, the business-to-business seller must demonstrate an authentic interest in the success of the customer as an individual and the customer's organization. Customers who place a high value on business relationships reciprocate in kind.

As is true with all marketing, relationship marketing is based on the concept of exchange. The intricacy and complexity of the exchange directly impact the nature of the relationship. Different levels of relationship associated with different levels of intricacy or complexity can be seen as follows:[7]

Switching costs are the costs to the buying organization of changing suppliers after an initial selection has been made and supply has begun. Switching costs result from, among other things, changes in logistical requirements, engineering and design, and services. Switching costs can create barriers to exit for firms, contributing to a customer feeling locked in to a particular supplier. Appropriately, incurring high switching costs should be mutually beneficial to both parties.

Relational exchange is the term given to customer–supplier relationships where the interaction recognizes the long-term benefit of the combination. Interdependence is an accepted, even fostered element of the relationship.

• *Discrete exchange.* Interaction is of a short duration, with a minimum of involvement. Applicable in one-time-only exchanges, these transactions have very low **switching costs**. There is little reason or motivation for any loyalty. Economy or necessity is often the primary motivation, with little interest by either party in an extension of the relationship. Sellers need not be much more than order takers.

• *Differentiating an undifferentiated product.* In competitive situations with homogeneous products, suppliers seek to differentiate the total offering with the strength of the relationship between individuals and organizations. In these circumstances, the relationship often involves a greater degree of social interaction rather than collaboration or partnering in a new development. Ownership of the relationship is at the individual level, often fostered by the seller. The seller is in the role of a persuader or, in the case of continuing existing business, a sustainer.

• *Multiple transactions.* Interaction is repeated, and individual transactions tend to merge into an ongoing **relational exchange**. In these situations, there is usually mutually high investment by supplier and customer. Both social and economic interaction occurs, and both parties see strategic implications in continuing the relationship. Mutual benefits exist. The goals of the buying and selling organizations have evolved to be interdependent. Beyond persuasion, sellers become problem solvers and effective resources for the customer. The seller in this role has opportunities to encourage and motivate customers toward processes, technologies, and techniques that reinforce the use of its offerings.

• *Collaboration or partnering.* A level of intimacy is proactively sought by both parties. In business-to-business markets, organizations interested in obtaining the best value from their suppliers view the suppliers' representatives, whether sellers or marketers, as resources. The parties involved work toward bringing the capabilities of the supplying firm and the customer firm together to provide value for each party. Both buyer and seller view the relationship as a potential element in their competitive advantage.[8] These relationships are strategic in nature, fostered by senior management in both organizations. The relationship is dynamic, with each organization actively seeking opportunities for the other. In many cases, these relationships lead to joint operations or ventures that are mutually beneficial. At the extreme, this level of collaboration can lead to acquisition of one party by the other.[9] The selling role in this context is one of relationship/value creation.

RELATIONSHIPS AND ATTITUDE In practice, a major element of many relationships is attitude rather than behavior.[10] For instance, in the HP situation discussed in the opening vignette, Mark Hurd felt that a key component of revamping the HP sales force was to change the attitudes of salespeople from passive sellers to proactive relationship builders.

The attitude and culture of an organization and how these are reflected in the attitude of individual sellers and marketers will imply certain behaviors toward customers. All relationships are not on the partnering level, nor should they be. Relationships imply investment by both parties and not all suppliers or customers will perceive the other party as a viable investment. Many sales and marketing relationships, while having elements of both social interaction and partnering, are haphazard rather than planned. The costs and benefits of complex relationships vary and are often very difficult to quantify. Like any relationship, both parties must want the relationship to work. In some instances, buyers will not want any type of relationship other than that which is purely transaction-based. Though this is not the norm, selling organizations must be willing to accept this view.

RELATIONSHIPS AND LOYALTY The basis for long-term relationships is satisfaction with prior experiences between the parties. (Note that this relationship can be either individually based or organizationally based. Obviously, organizations will seek to ensure that the relationship grows beyond the individuals involved to protect the firms from employee job changes.) The longer the relationship has had to mature, the greater its stability. Loyal customers remain loyal after an unsatisfactory experience.[11] Recall the relationship of Ford Motor Company and Firestone, used in Chapter 1, Exhibit 1-2. The relationship between Ford and Firestone dates back to a close friendship between the two companies' founders. The severing of the relationship as a result of the Firestone tire debacle is surprising, and Firestone tires are not likely to be found on many new Ford products in the near future.

RELATIONSHIPS AND CORPORATE CULTURE Increases in competition and the ever-shorter life span of new technology are contributing to the evolution from product selling to offering selling (i.e., transaction-based to relationship-based sales). The diversity of choices available to customers makes it more difficult to be the seller of the customer's choice. Depending on the philosophy of marketing or culture under which the firm operates (see Chapter 1 and Exhibit 12-2, "The Philosophies of Marketing"), sellers will be focused on different objectives and be expected to perform different tasks.[12] Corporate culture and the level of importance in the firm's marketing mix given to customer relationships will determine the approach of the seller. In product- or sales-driven organizations, sellers are measured and rewarded by the short-term results obtained.

Seller objectives are focused on meeting the needs of the selling organization—selling more now. If the organization is truly customer or market driven, the seller is measured and rewarded with longer-range goals in mind. Seller objectives are focused on satisfying customer needs. Exhibit 12-3 discusses the success that Kinko's business-to-business sales force had when management transformed order takers into relationship-creating sellers. One of the key things that Kinko's management did was change the nature of the objectives for which sellers were accountable.

Different eras in business history have spawned different marketing eras or philosophies: These eras or philosophies assist in the understanding of marketing and its role in business and society. All organizations, however, have not moved on to the marketing or societal marketing theme. Depending on corporate culture and marketing environment, some firms continue today to embrace earlier philosophies.

- *Production era and product era:* Management focus was on maximizing consumption, making sales the objective of sellers. Production efficiency has high value, while, with little or no effort to understand customer needs, customization is almost nonexistent. In the production era, supply was not always able to keep up with demand. Early beginnings of product differentiation occurred in the product era. Sellers are order takers.
- *Sales era:* Sellers still focus on making sales, and maximizing consumption is still important, though some attention is paid to customer needs. "Fit the market to the product." Sellers use persuasive techniques, often interpreted as a hard-sell approach.
- *Marketing era:* The primary objective of the sales force is satisfying customer needs. Conceptually, this marketing philosophy works to maximize choice in the market. Differentiation efforts extend to the total offering.
- *Societal/partnering/value network era:* (Many terms have been used to describe this era.) The sales force objective is to build stable, long-term relationships. Conceptually, this marketing philosophy works to maximize relationship or life quality.

EXHIBIT 12-2   The Philosophies of Marketing

Four Forms of Seller Roles

Given the preceding discussion on the components of and types of relationships, seller role patterns can be defined for different organizational cultures and types of offerings.[13] These roles vary by complexity of skills required of the seller, proactivity, and the degree to which the relationship is transactional or value creating, as discussed in the following sections.

THE ORDER TAKER   The **order taker's** primary role is taking orders and ensuring timely delivery of the correct products. The buyer's need for product and the seller's need for short-term sales results are the driving factors in the relationship. Most selling efforts are concentrated on making potential customers aware of stable product offerings. A major part of the marketing mix is place, providing locational convenience and timely delivery. Product types associated with this type of selling are usually in the late maturity or decline stage of the PLC and/or of common usage knowledge, such as those products often sold through industrial distributors to customers whose volume doesn't justify a direct relationship. Users may be conservatives or laggards as described by the TALC, generally avoiding risk associated with innovative offerings. Little, if any, customer education is required to obtain maximum value from the product, as the market is familiar with the technology. Sellers are rewarded based on short-term results. Product- and sales-driven selling organizations that rely on this type of transactional selling are unlikely to have the skills or approach to handle more sophisticated, innovative offerings.

At first glance, it may seem like the order taker can be replaced to a large extent by a Web site. In many instances, this may be possible. Certainly, a well-developed Web site can prove a valuable productivity-enhancing asset to both buyers and sellers. However, this works as long as the Internet-based relationships are primarily transactional. When there is an element of personal

In 1998, Kinko's was still an independent company: it was the twenty-four-hour copy shop for business travelers who lost their luggage and students whose dog ate their homework and it obtained approximately 20 percent of revenues from business clients. Efforts to attract business customers were largely left to the discretion of each local copy shop. Kinko's headquarters provided little assistance for business-to-business selling efforts. As a result, sellers were little more than order takers, an extension of the retail shop, waiting for customers to come to them. Business-to-business sales were small, one-time corporate deals. There was little repeat business, and new business was difficult to forecast.

Kinko's management recognized that it had to turn its sales force from a collection of hardly managed order takers into a team of relationship-creating, problem-solving sellers. Business-to-business sales were reorganized. Management created a focus and goals. Sellers were encouraged to find long-term, profitable relationships with large customers. Marketing tools were created that helped sellers approach higher levels of management in potential customer organizations, enabling discussions of continuous duplicating services, rather than overflow copy making. A new Intranet site was developed with information on the new sales process, frequently asked questions, customer case studies, and aids for new employees approaching unfamiliar customers and customer types. To effectively use these new tools, the newly created 500-person sales organization was trained in a seven-step sales process that focused on building value for customers. Key to the success of the process was continuous communication with customers. They were no longer to be treated as "some people who need a rush set of copies" but as business partners who had selected Kinko's as the provider of choice for their copying and duplicating needs.

The results? Not only did sales increase more than 50 percent but sellers reported that the new process, with common measurements, procedures, and more clearly defined offerings, assisted in creating lasting relationships. Having gone from order takers to relationship builders/problem solvers proved very satisfying. Turnover was lower, and sellers were excited about future prospects. Sales? Results were 110 percent of plan. Not bad for an organization that had not met its sales targets for the three previous years.

EXHIBIT 12-3 Kinko's Prints a Business-to-Business Plan   *Source:* Based on Andy Cohen, "Copy Cats," *Sales & Marketing Management* (August 2000), pp. 50–58.

service required, Web-based systems have not yet proven to be good substitutes. The quality and depth of the selling relationship become major differentiating elements of the marketing mix.

In the example about Kinko's, the company's business-to-business sales organization, before the change described, was made up primarily of order takers. As described in the opening, this reactive sales model can make repeat business subject to significant reselling effort. If the buyer feels that it has been the proactive party in the transaction, it is more likely to seek assistance from any providers who could meet the customer's requirements. Since no close relationship exists between buyer and seller, the buyer would not be inclined to define its future purchases with a single provider who knows the customer's business intimately.

One type of the order taker role is the inside sales or customer service specialist. The individual in this position seldom meets customers in person. The relationship is usually over the telephone or via e-mail. The primary functions of the position are to administer the sales order system of the supplier and to facilitate the logistics needs of the customer. Many of the commitments related to availability and delivery made by the field selling organization are satisfied by the efforts of the inside sales team. Known by many titles (sales service specialist, order facilitator, customer service representative, etc.), these individuals are often the backbone of internal customer order handling. In the case of routine purchases, the inside sales team is often the direct contact for the customer. Once a customer buying pattern is established, a proficient sales service specialist anticipates orders and proactively solicits routine business buyers in the customer organization. The inside sales team serves the field seller by freeing time for relationship building and value creation and serves the customer by always being available to take, track, and expedite orders.

THE PERSUADER/SUSTAINER The development of the order taker relationship into a major differentiating element of the marketing mix leads to the **persuader/sustainer** role for the seller. In this role, short-term results are still the primary sales orientation. However, the seller takes a more proactive role in the relationship.

As a persuader, the seller continuously informs and updates customers about products and offerings. The persuader attempts to convince the customer of the value of the product versus competitors' products, though the focus is still on the needs of the selling organization. Though a hard-sell approach is of diminishing value in business-to-business sales, the persuader often resorts to such techniques to obtain orders now rather than later. In this selling situation, product types, though similar to the order taker scenario, are still evolving and thus have an added degree of heterogeneity. Some customer education may be necessary. The product is likely in the maturity stage, and differentiation from horizontal competition does not rest solely on price.

As a sustainer, the seller has a responsibility beyond that of obtaining short-term sales to include maintaining and nurturing an existing relationship with established customers. In the circumstances described here, customers look to the supplier for help in making the best selection among heterogeneous offerings. As described in Chapter 11 and in Exhibit 12-4, "New Business,

---

Different types of "new business" require different seller resources. Real new business is the result of a major R&D, product development, and/or marketing effort, usually in conjunction with a customer. This results in first-time applications or adoptions of technologies. Many parts of the organization are involved. These are the applications and efforts that everyone in the organization finds the most exciting. Seller resources required for *real* new business include training with the product, training on matching customer needs to product capabilities, prospecting assistance, and other market intelligence. *Real* new business produces new revenue but usually incurs greater selling costs than either translation or core churn.

Most "new business," of course, is not *real* new business, not a "first of its kind" application of new products or technologies. While a partnership with the customer may have developed a specification for your company's product, and it may be new in the view of that customer, it is not "new" to your organization. It is merely a translation of a previous success with another customer. In translation business, sellers must be accustomed to the new products and uses among prior customers. Some prospecting assistance may be required. The revenue is new to the company, and the costs will not be as great as with real new business.

What if the translation business replaces an application of your older technology product? Is this business still considered new? It certainly requires an effort by the team to get the business, however, it should not require as large an effort—assuming the translation tools were adequate and the customer relationship has been at least sustained. Unfortunately, the organization does not experience an increase in business volume equal to the sales of the new product. The seller realizes the net of the old and new volumes. This replacement business, core churn, is necessary, important, and critical to market ownership but not as glamorous to the team as *real* new business. Such selling effort requires some new resources in terms of product and usage knowledge but generates the lowest level of the three in the way of additional selling costs.

The organization needs all three types of new business—real, translation, and churn. Each type has different implications for margins, customer support, and product development—the entire marketing mix.

EXHIBIT 12-4 New Business, Translation, and Churn

Translation, and Churn," this sales role is most likely to deal with business that would be described as core churn. Because of the differentiable nature of the product and the variety of alternatives, the sustainer must actively recognize the role of sales in maintaining the positioning and image of the selling organization. The activities of sellers for enlightened industrial distributors and supply chain service providers fit this category.

THE MOTIVATOR/PROBLEM SOLVER Customers rely on sellers for advice, particularly as product offerings become more innovative and complex or require a significant degree of customer education to obtain full value. Under these circumstances, the persuader/sustainer evolves into the **motivator/problem solver**. This is not, however, automatic. The selling organization must be market driven—sensitive to customer needs. The type of offering described (complex, innovative) and the need to assist customers in maximizing the value received would seem to naturally apply to products in the introduction or growth stage of the PLC. Depending on the level of customer education necessary and the level of customer interest in new and innovative offerings, typical customers are visionaries or pragmatists. In this scenario, the selling organization has a much different task than in prior role descriptions.

The motivator/problem solver is part of a sales force whose primary objective is satisfying customer needs. This is accomplished less through short-term sales goals and more through the ability to create unique customer solutions through matching of supplier capabilities with customer needs. The seller is expected to fully understand the customer organization, its culture, buying habits, processes, and its customers. This level of knowledge assists in anticipating customer needs or recognizing problems where seller solutions can be applied. This type of business often fits the description of translation business—often proving the segment through discovery.

The motivator/problem solver is most certainly considered a resource by the customer. Customers, as described earlier in this chapter, demand creativity and commitment on the part of the seller. The motivational aspect of this selling role consists of the seller's ability to encourage customer product development personnel to incorporate the offerings of the supplier. Involvement begins early in the new-task buying process. The closer the relationship between supplier and customer, the earlier in the buying decision process this influence can be applied.

For the motivator/problem solver approach to be successful, the seller must expand the sphere of influence to a greater number of stakeholders in the buying center. This is a major distinction between this role and the role of the persuader/sustainer. This proactive approach begins to take on the appearance of field market development. Sales management, recognizing that compensation must be tied to results, is challenged as a larger quantity of seller resources become committed to development of solutions rather than maintaining existing sales. (Compensation is discussed later in this chapter.) When the supplier has a line of products that require significant customer education, the likelihood increases that the customer development process will require considerable attention.

The complexity of motivator/problem solver objectives has led management in many organizations to recognize the value of splitting the functions into a sales role and a missionary sales or field marketing role. When this occurs, it is important that the field marketer's reporting arrangement is to the marketing organization, freeing the individual from short-term sales objectives (the title of the field marketer position varies and sometimes holds little descriptive evidence of the job function—i.e., customer engineer, product evangelist, etc. See "Missionary Sellers/Field Marketers" section).

The example of Kinko's, described above in Exhibit 12-3, readily demonstrates the value of the motivator/problem solver role even with products and offerings that, at first glance, may seem generic. After the rebuilding of Kinko's business-to-business sales force (and continuing after the acquisition by Fedex), new business-to-business customers were not likely to see the service provided as generic, particularly since the offering was tailored to the individual needs of the customer.

THE RELATIONSHIP/VALUE CREATOR In the **relationship/value creator** role, sellers are expected to build and maintain relationships with all elements of the customer buying center. The relationship between supplier and customer develops into a partnership that is mutually inspiring and stimulating. Both supplier and customer recognize that for each of them their own success is tied to the other party's success. Rather than an individual seller effort, these relationships are often built by sales and marketing *teams*.[14] Value is created by both customer and supplier teams, and each appreciates the value of the other. In this role, the selling objective is to creatively join supplier capabilities with customer needs. The outcome of this effort would be "new business" development (as opposed to translation or core churn).

The partnering role of value creation adds many different tasks to the responsibilities of the seller. The seller becomes a liaison between elements of the supplier value chain and the customer buying center. In this role, the seller is a diplomat, a manager of conflicts, a resource allocation expert, and a director of a team whose mission it is to provide value to both organizations. There is no mention of maximizing short-term sales or use of persuasion tactics.[15] In fact, short-term results are often sacrificed to build the relationship and the associated long-term benefits.

At this level of relationship, there is not anything that is not the seller's job. A crucial element of success in this type of customer–supplier relationship is the commitment of senior management of *both* firms. Customers must be equally interested in relationships at this level. It is important that all members of the team, both customer and supplier, understand the nature of the relationship.[16]

The relationship/value creator is a more sophisticated sales approach than other role models described here. The seller must be solution oriented for the needs of both the customer and the supplier. This more sophisticated approach requires a more complex set of seller and selling organization skills. This context is not served by the typical sales training advice on selling tactics. Suppliers and their sellers must have a strategic vision of the customer's industry and the clientele fit in it.

Knowledge of the customer's market environment, an understanding of the nature of the customer's business and the customer's approach, is also important. (See Chapter 6, regarding *knowing your markets*, which is also summarized in Exhibit 12-5.) Individual seller capabilities

---

Knowing your markets includes knowing:
- *The customers' technologies*
- *The customers' products*
- *The customers' markets and customers*
- *The customers' competitors*
- *The customers' channels*
- *The customers' buying center and buying patterns*
- *The customers' culture*

EXHIBIT 12-5 Knowing Your Markets *Note:* Chapter 6 discusses *knowing your markets* in greater detail.

Order Taker	Takes orders; ensures correct and timely delivery of offering. Major effort in the "place" marketing mix variable.
Persuader/ Sustainer	Proactive role in relationship. Informs customers about offerings and ongoing updates. Attempts to convince customer of value of offering, though the focus is still on needs of selling organization.
Motivator/ Problem Solver	Focus on the needs of the customer organization, potentially creating unique customer solutions through match of supplier capabilities with customer needs. Considered a resource by the customer.
Relationship/ Value Creator	Build and maintain partnership with all elements of the customer buying center. Supplier–customer relationship is mutually inspiring and stimulating; both parties recognize an equity in the other's success.

EXHIBIT 12-6   Summary of Different Seller Roles

should also include strong interpersonal skills, business analysis skills, and problem-solving skills. The nature of different seller roles is summarized in Exhibit 12-6.

Other Types of Selling Roles

As discussed throughout this text, the customer decision process and usage situation for many business-to-business products and services are so complex that several other selling-related roles are needed to successfully deliver value to the customer. The two most important of these are the missionary salesperson and the post-sale customer service provider.

MISSIONARY SELLERS/FIELD MARKETERS   The four models of seller roles described evolve from simple order taking into complete immersion in the internal organization of the customer. When the supplier–customer relationship is complex—such that significant sales and business development are ongoing or when the development period is significantly long, regardless of the existing sales relationship—it is inappropriate to expect sellers, compensated on commission with a short-term focus, to be responsible for the development effort. In these cases, creation of a FMD team can separate the long- and short-term efforts into more appropriate field functions. Missionary sellers/field marketers are known by several position titles (customer engineers, product evangelists, market development specialists, to name a few) but are best categorized as field marketers.

Field marketers are critical in finding new prospective customers, finding and testing new market segments to address, and in developing new business within existing customer accounts. As discussed in Chapter 3, the initial phase of the customer's decision process may extend over a relatively long period of time, particularly when the product or service includes significant learning or represents a significant departure from the way that the customer is used to operating. The

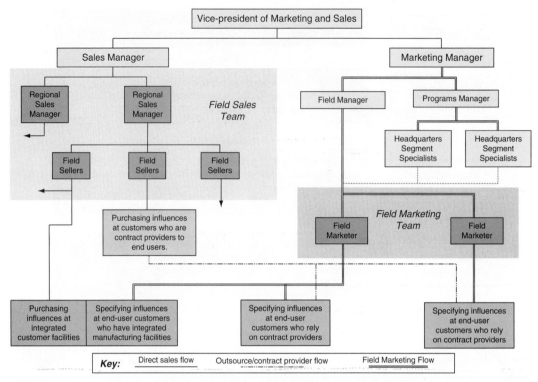

EXHIBIT 12-7 Organizational Relationship Between Field Sales and Field Marketing

missionary salesperson then must be adept at building relationships and participating with those relationships to create value for both parties.

Recall that, as mentioned in the endnotes of Chapter 3, missionary sellers are part of the marketing organization. Exhibit 12-7 shows a typical organization that uses the dual field approach of sales and marketing. The field marketing team, consisting of missionary salespeople or FMDs, reports to the marketing manager through a field manager. The missionary salespeople or FMDs can be located in headquarters but are more effective as field positions, sharing regional facilities with the field sales team. The primary functions of missionary salespeople or FMDs are as relationship/value creators, working with members of the buying center at the specifying customer.

The field sales organization shown in Exhibit 12-7 has a primary role of either motivators/ problem solvers or persuader/sustainers. Purchasing influences in integrated customer organizations that buy directly from the seller, as well as influences at contract providers who supply to the specifying customer, make up the primary field sales relationships.

As described in Chapter 11, these field marketers are often the individuals who are responsible for the marketing operations forecast. As part of the marketing operation, these marketers can rely on the entire marketing management chain to reinforce value creation efforts at various levels of the customer organization, leaving the sales organization to concentrate on short-term revenue generation. Additionally, the entire organization relies on these individuals to deliver the necessary information contained in the MOF. Regardless of level, the purposes pursued are the same: to obtain information, to establish rapport, to educate, and to explore ways that the supplier can create value for the customer.

POST-SALE CUSTOMER SERVICE   For many relationships, the customer organization needs considerable attention and assistance from the supplier organization to effectively use the products or services it purchases. Effective customer service can make the difference between delivering superior value to the customer and having a customer that is not fully satisfied. Customer service done right is expected; done wrong is a disaster. Service requirements can cover a range of needs, including product or process design assistance, marketing planning and execution assistance, installation, training, troubleshooting, repair, and upgrades. In some cases, suppliers provide customers with assistance in product design and management.

Two principal problems must be addressed to provide good customer service in business-to-business markets. First, the service has to be useful and appropriate for the customer. In many business markets, the customers are few in number and their needs unique. Accordingly, the customer service staff must be skilled in tailoring its service to the customer's special needs—major customers may be provided with dedicated, specialized service personnel within the supplier organization. In other markets, the customers are numerous and varied. Customer service personnel must be able to handle service requests quickly and appropriately.

The second principal problem to be addressed is that service must be provided in a cost-effective manner. Service costs are usually imbedded in the price of the offering, unless the customer specifically declines that level of packaged value. When service is sold as a separate offering, the offering can be subject to close scrutiny by the customer. Still, the service organization must be able to manage costs in such a way that profitability is maintained.

Customer service situations are opportunities to build and reinforce the customer relationship, not cost-based situations to be avoided. A product problem that could become a major issue can be transformed into a service success, creating "a fan" of the customer. Poor customer service only reinforces the initial difficulties that caused the customer to seek aid in the first place. Because customer service can be so important to providing value to customers, the marketer should be involved in the design of the service offering or in directing the personal interaction required between service provider and customer.

This task of building customer relationships through service is made more difficult when the service delivery model does not provide for continuity of contact between the customer and individual service personnel. It is important that the service organization have some sort of institutional memory. Suppose, for example, a technical problem arises at a customer site. If the service organization has a database of interaction histories, the service person that gets the call can see the service history and have more information on which to base a solution.

Customer relationship management software and services have been developed and deployed in recent years that have greatly improved suppliers' ability to deliver good service. The software keeps track of all orders and service provided. It gives any service personnel updated information on the complete history of every customer. It tracks current order progress and current service progress. It further gives callback schedules and reminders.

Good service people can also initiate the customer decision process for future purchases. A good CRM system (automated or not) prepares the service people to recognize opportunities through observation of other customer problems and to begin the collaboration between customer and supplier toward finding a solution.

Note that CRM software is not a replacement for an effective MOF, as the MOF, created by the marketing organization, is an essential tool of the entire organization, not just the sales organization. The MOF provides information to effectively plan and develop marketing efforts over a longer time frame. Boundary personnel must recognize the necessity of providing correct and timely information to the forecast effort and management at every level must reinforce this posture.

Management Perspective

In all of the roles discussed, management must consider what the selling organization is trying to accomplish and match that with what the best information available says that the customer organization is trying to accomplish. The most sophisticated seller role does not automatically work with all customers. Developing a sales force and establishing the context for the sales relationship require an understanding of what is seen as having value by both the supplier and the customer.

Exhibit 12-8 generalizes the correlation of value and relationship complexity. While this summary is a generalized case, it does illustrate that the appropriate sales force design is dependent on many factors, often situational. In Exhibit 12-8, the shading of transactional sales and relationship sales bars is not intended to imply that relationships have no significance in transactional sales. In fact, a strong case can be made that the buyer–seller relationship may be one of the strongest factors by which the product is differentiated from the horizontal competition.

The increasing complexity of the buyer–seller relationship can be based on many factors, such as the size of the buying center, the need for customer training, design assistance, and the overall attitude and approach to relationships by the customer organization. Responsibilities and coincident training needs of the seller will vary with the expected role type the seller will play. As the sales relationships depicted in Exhibit 12-8 become more reliant on a value orientation and an increasing complexity of the buyer–seller relationship, the demands on the skills of the

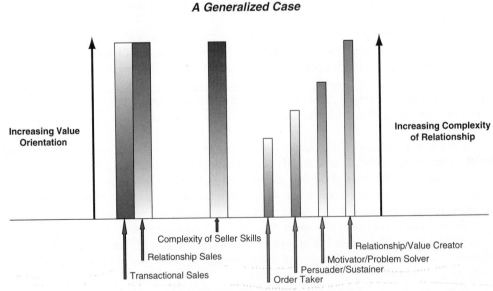

A Generalized Case

Degree of shading indicates relative degree of importance.

EXHIBIT 12-8   Correlation of Value and Complexity of Relationships

seller increase. The seller roles will be a reflection of management commitment and support. Based on the commitment of senior management in both the supplier and customer organizations, the relationship/value creator role is far more likely to create value with technophile and innovator customers and sellers.

THE MUTUAL NEEDS OF BUYER AND SELLER

In effective dyadic relationships, the creation of value is not limited to the immediate task at hand. Both buyer and seller will have expectations of the role each will play and how individual and organizational needs will be met. The most effective relationship is one in which the individuals involved recognize the factors that make each other a success. What defines success, however, is broader than satisfactorily completing the immediate task and varies with the individuals involved. With this in mind, consider that organizational buyers and sellers have three needs to satisfy:

1. The needs of the job function
2. The needs of the organization
3. The individual needs of the buyer and seller.

The Needs of the Job Function

At the most elementary level, each member of the buying center in the customer organization as well as each member of the value creation team in the supplier organization has a specific, short-term job to perform. Tactical sales trainings and purchasing seminars cover the necessary content of "good selling and buying." This section is not intended to elaborate in this area. The emphasis is with the context or attitude of the effort. In most selling efforts, it is no longer adequate to "just sell" and not be concerned with satisfying customer needs beyond the immediate transaction, just as in buying, it is not wise to leverage a supplier in a manner that threatens long-term survival. Exhibit 12-9 takes a look at some of these issues.

Both sides of the relationship have job-related tasks that must be performed to achieve a minimum degree of success. Other members of each organization rely on them to meet day-to-day expectations associated with the job function. Within the selling organization, these expectations depend on the type of seller roles employed. Within the buying organization, role types are determined by the complexity of the purchase, from new task to routine repurchase. The number of participants in the buying center and the value creation team will change, depending on the purchase complexity and frequency of the purchase. In a customer-sensitive organization, the selling team becomes a mirror of the buying team. In other words, sellers will sell the way buyers want to buy.

The Needs of the Organization

The needs of the supplier and customer organizations extend beyond the short-term needs of the job functions of buyers and sellers. Members of the buying organization will place demands on the selling organization that will be focused by the buying center through the seller. Sellers then need to be not only competent in representation of their product or offering, but must represent the image, culture, and value potential of all elements of the company they represent. Sellers have an obligation to their organization on a day-to-day basis, to be goodwill

Though the relationship has received attention lately, the automotive industry has always talked of the Tier 1 supplier base as a group of critically important suppliers. To reduce their own design and development costs, the auto makers have encouraged suppliers to take on development of vehicle modules—suspension systems, interior seating systems, climate control, and other subsystems. Though suppliers would incur higher costs as a result, they were assured that their efforts would be considered at price-setting time. In other words, the ideal partnership is building relationships that create value for both parties.

There have been a few problems. It seems that as soon as the overall automotive market turns down or one auto maker gets into a profit squeeze, suppliers are asked to make up the difference. The first episode was in 1992 when Jose Ignacio Lopez, then purchasing chief for General Motors, forced, with the threat of losing the business, suppliers to cut costs. This began an all-out war between GM and suppliers that lasted through much of the 1990s. Supplier relationships crumbled. GM never realized the savings that Lopez projected, and supplier quality and performance declined. Even after Lopez left GM for VW, his name became an icon for relationship busting and price cutting.

During the period that GM was damaging relationships, Chrysler had come from near bankruptcy into a period of prosperity. Chrysler insisted that it knew the value of supplier relationships, as suppliers could make or break the company. Suppliers were encouraged to work with Chrysler to find cost savings, and both supplier and Chrysler shared in the outcome. Suppliers rated Chrysler as their favorite customer. In 2000, however, Chrysler, then part of DaimlerChrysler since 1998, was in trouble. Group CEO Dieter Zetsche announced that, effective immediately, Chrysler would reduce all purchasing contract prices by 5 percent. Under the new rules, if a supplier shipped goods, they were agreeing to the new terms. In effect, Chrysler "did a Lopez." In fact, trade press editorials soon had headlines like "Lopez All Over Again." Some industry commentators called it extortion. Suppliers, however, sent their own shock back to Chrysler. Seventy percent of Chrysler suppliers said no. Supplier commentary was similar to this: "They can't say partnership in good times when we spend development funds and then say cut margins when they have a problem. We can't afford it. It does not benefit us in the long run. Quality and warranty costs will suffer." They did.

The debate over long-term relationships versus transaction-based relationships goes on. GM is still haunted by supplier memories of Lopez. No customer will establish good working relationships with suppliers as long as they treat them as commodities. Customers too, must be responsible for the long-term benefit of supplier relationships. GM and Chrysler found out. Kinko's figured it out. Next?

EXHIBIT 12-9   Relationships Have to Work Both Ways Update   *Sources*: Based on several reports: Mark Yost, "Suppliers Say Ghost of GM's Lopez Haunts Online Auctions," *The Wall Street Journal/Dow Jones Newswires* (March 8, 2000); Lindsay Brooke, "It's Not Business, It's Extortion," *Automotive Industries* (March 2001), p. 7; Ron Harbour, "Nothing to Give Back," *Automotive Industries* (March 2001), p. 16; Maryann Keller, "Lopez All Over Again?" *Automotive Industries* (March 2001), p. 19; Gerry Kobe, "Supplier Squeeze," *Automotive Industries* (March 2001), pp. 26–30.

ambassadors and crisis management specialists. In the eyes of the customer, the seller *is* the selling organization.

Just as customers will place demands on sellers that are beyond traditional transactional roles, the supplier will expect its sellers to have an extensive familiarity with the backgrounds of their customers. The seller is the first source of information about the customer. Sellers will have an obligation to their own organization to know not only what customers buy and how/when they will use it, but will be expected to understand the customers' businesses well enough to anticipate, with an adequate degree of confidence, how decisions will be made (refer again to Exhibit 12-5, Knowing Your Markets).

Buying activities of customers also extend beyond just a transactional nature. It's up to the seller to recognize the organizational demands placed on each stakeholder in the buying center and to be a part of the resolution of those demands. As discussed earlier in this chapter, attitude is a major factor in the successful relationship. Both sellers and buyers need to recognize that they are the first level of interaction in the business-to-business relationship.

The Individual Needs of the Buyer and Seller

Beyond job function and organizational needs, individuals in buying and selling roles will have career, personal, and professional needs that are part of their goals. Sellers that recognize the mutual nature of these needs can be far more effective in building relationships and creating value for both organizations.

For professionals, rewards and goals go beyond monetary compensation. Individual needs related to career advancement, recognition, professional organization membership, and office holding and authoring of journal articles and features are all possible goals or needs felt by different members of the organization. Particularly in situations where the offering will be a result of a joint development effort by supplier and customer, there will be opportunities to recognize individuals in both organizations. As the new business is prepared for translation to additional users, contributors can be acknowledged by sponsorship of technical papers featuring the participants as authors.

Buyers may also have aspirations that are related to how they are perceived in their roles ("make me a hero in my organization") or how they are perceived by family and personal relationships. Sellers have opportunities to play a role in the attainment of these goals. There may even be opportunities, within the bounds of ethics and good taste, to impact perception in the home environment (see Exhibit 12-10, Fruits, Flowers, Potted Plants, and Chocolate).

A substantial part of relationship building is getting to know the customer beyond the work environment. Still, an accepted part of the sales relationship is business entertainment. Entertainment can take the form of meals, attendance at conferences, tickets to sporting events, and similar gratuities. Many companies will have policies that limit the extent of these events to prevent abuses from either buyer or seller.

Sellers often will find that they have pulled customers away from their families with business-related meetings, trips, or occasional sporting events. This doesn't help the customers with their family relationships. In an effort to turn the home conversation from "are you going to the baseball game with those business buddies again tonight?" into something positive, many astute sellers will reward the home environment with delivery of flowers, candy, fruit baskets, or other tokens of appreciation. The intended message: "We recognize your sacrifice for our business—we just wanted to let you know we appreciate it." Hopefully, this turns the conversation into something like this: "You're going to the conference with them—hey the flowers they sent were beautiful."

Some care should be taken in this venture. Don't send house plants to people who have serious allergies, and avoid candy if someone is on a diet. Most of all, be sure to let the business associate know that the gesture will happen. As the story goes, a few years ago, a major airline forgot this part. As part of an effort to lure more business travelers, the airline offered a "spouse flies free" to business travelers. They thought they had a very successful promotion until they mailed "thank you for flying with us" cards to the homes of business travelers. Rumor has it that not so many spouses had actually made those trips!

EXHIBIT 12-10 Fruits, Flowers, Potted Plants, and Chocolate

Selling Structures

A *direct sales force* consists of personal field sellers directly employed by the supplier of the offering and support staff and resources. Sellers' responsibility may be defined by product or customer type, geographic region, or another segmentation scheme that meets customer needs and creates a manageable workload for the seller. The most costly type of selling structure is direct sales.

A *manufacturers' representative* is an independent businessperson who acts as a supplier's agent or representative in a particular market segment. Manufacturers' representatives usually represent several noncompeting manufacturers

who rely on the "rep" for account coverage. Reps do not take ownership of the goods they represent. Reps are compensated by commissions on the products they sell.

A *distributor* represents manufacturers' goods by taking ownership and providing local inventory to businesses in the region. Distributors provide many other business services involved with form, time, place, and possession—the four types of economic utility. Distributors make money by buying products from suppliers at wholesale prices and reselling them to final customers with distributor's markup (added margin).

SELLING—THE STRUCTURE

Should the business-to-business supplier employ its own **direct sales force**, establish an agreement with a **manufacturers' representative**, or rely on **distributors** for sales coverage? The answer to this question depends on the nature of the offering, the concentration of customers, and the manner in which customers want to buy the product or service. Chapter 14 focuses on the rationale for using distributors and the development of various types of marketing channels. This chapter examines the underlying principles behind the use of either direct sellers or manufacturers' representatives or, in some circumstances, a combination of both.

*A sales **call pattern** is a sequence or cycle of sales calls typical for a given type of product or customer. It is dependent on the type of selling involved with a product and the type of customer base. Products with similar buying styles, habits, customer types, and selling intensity may be grouped together and represented by the same seller. An equipment product line that is a new task purchase, possibly requiring a capital investment decision by the customer would not fit the same call pattern as items that are routine purchases such as supplies and materials. Matching call patterns is an important consideration in sales force design.*

Sales Force Organization

The direct sales force can be organized in several different ways. This brief summary describes only the most common types of organization. The most common sales force organization is by geographic territory. Firms with multiple products may organize by product, particularly when different products do not have the same customer base or **call pattern**. When a firm has a large concentration of customers in a particular area—such as the automobile industry in Detroit, the computer industry in Silicon Valley, or the oil and gas industry in Houston, the sales team may be organized to focus on that particular customer type. An extension of this type of organization may be the "national accounts" or "account manager" position. This is useful when one customer has many locations that are served on a daily basis by many different sellers. Such a situation would occur with a customer like IBM, with major facilities and buying centers throughout the world. An account manager is the coordinator of all the individual efforts. Of course, depending on the collection of products and offerings, different suppliers may elect to use any combination of these types of organization. Whatever sales organization structure is used, firms must recognize that the organization should match the buying habits and patterns of customers, not the convenience of the firm.

All of the factors already mentioned that differentiate sales organizations can be used to determine the correct manufacturers' representative for a supplier.

When the firm cannot afford a direct sales force, when call patterns for a new product will be significantly different from existing patterns, or when customer facilities are not concentrated in a manageable geography, contract representation may be the best alternative. Often, firms that have sales teams serving geographic concentrations of customers utilize manufacturers' representatives in other market areas with few customers, ensuring complete coverage for the firm's products.

DIRECT SALES FORCE

This section starts with an in-depth discussion of the direct sales force. Manufacturers' representatives are discussed later in this chapter. An in-depth discussion of distributors occurs in Chapter 14.

The average value-added sales call costs the seller's company over $200.[17] The approximate number of in-person **sales calls** that a professional seller makes in a day is four. This is down from almost five calls per day twenty years ago. What contributes to these numbers?

A sales call is an in-person meeting between the seller and stakeholder(s) in the customer buying center. The meeting may be dyadic or involve several members of each organization.

The cost of sales calls varies greatly, depending on the type of product or service, the travel involved, and many other factors. Costs per sales call include all the costs of putting a direct sales force in the field, such as the purchase or lease and operation of a company-provided vehicle, travel expenses and expense accounts, cellular phones/faxes/laptop computers, and, of course, the seller's compensation. The average cost of each in-person meeting with the customer is further influenced by the fact that sellers, on average, spend slightly more than a third of their time with customers. The same study notes that sellers spend approximately one quarter of their time performing administrative duties (paperwork, meetings, and so on) and almost one third of their time traveling or waiting to see customers.[18]

Sales managers are always in search of methods to improve the sales productivity statistics quoted above. One of the numbers noted, four sales calls per day, may at first look to be moving in the wrong direction. Quite the contrary; through the more effective application of widely available communications capabilities (phone, fax, e-mail, teleconferencing, and so on) and the availability of large quantities of standard information from electronic sources such as the Internet, sales force productivity has improved.

Sales Force Deployment

Effective deployment of a company's sales force requires knowing the market sales potential, compiling these estimates into sales estimates for specific customers in specific territories, and evaluating trends that may impact this forecast. Knowing the market potential is often the result of a **top–down forecast**, while market estimates for individual customers, if the territories are already staffed, are usually the result of a **bottom–up forecast**. (A more in-depth discussion of forecasts, including the bottom-up marketing operations forecast, can be found in Chapter 11.)

A top–down forecast is often the result of research efforts to forecast market potential, starting with a "whole market" forecast and reducing it to the specific segment(s) in question. A bottom–up forecast starts with an analysis of how much product can be sold to each customer in a particular region or territory. The forecasts are rationalized with the business objectives of the organization. In a market-driven organization, this is often part of the MOF.

Some trends can be anticipated; others cannot. Natural disasters, wars, political crises, financial market upheaval—all of these can impact the design of the sales force structure. The newness of the offering—its distinction or degree of innovation in the market—and the existence of ongoing relationships with potential customers can impact the outcome. Smaller organizations placing new technology in the market may not have an extensive relationship base. Managers will have to estimate the acceptance of the offering as it moves through the adopter categories.

The next step is to determine how many sellers will be needed to bring about the sales forecast, consistent with the resources of the firm. The nature of the offering, the learning curve, and the required level of customer education to get maximum value from the offering will have significant influence on the **intensity of territory design** and skill levels of the sellers. Managers are expected to estimate the average length of sales calls, travel time between calls, and the number of calls per customer per sales period (customers must be prioritized). The offering position in the PLC will influence the length of each sales call and the number of missionary or development sales calls that will be necessary to turn potential customers into buying accounts.

Intensity of territory design refers to the number of sellers in a given region. If customer education is a major consideration, sellers will be required to spend greater amounts of time with each customer. As the customer base learns how to use the full value of the offering and the purchase becomes routine, less attention to each account will be required. While this can appear as an opportunity to increase seller productivity, it may be a false indication; in most instances it would be preferred to have new, additional offerings rather than change the nature of the seller relationship.

This last factor, the amount of missionary or development effort required to create a success, has significant influence on seller selection and compensation. Organizations that require a significantly large missionary effort from their sales force but still need day-to-day short-term sales results may find it appropriate to split the responsibilities between a short-term-focused seller and a long-term-focused field marketer. This "double field team" can be costly. Small and/or start-up organizations without a strong base of core business may find it more appropriate to focus on the missionary role, regardless of position title, and provide appropriate compensation.

Sales Force Compensation

Rewards for sellers take various forms as part of an overall motivation package. Rewards can include sales contests, better territories, higher salary, better company car, and similar monetary and personal or ego gratification. Different activities of the seller will be pursued with different levels of enthusiasm depending on the expected reward. Studies have shown[19] that sellers' motivation is derived from their beliefs about whether an expended effort will lead to a given amount of improved outcome (expectancy); their belief that an improvement in a particular area of performance will lead to a corresponding increase in a given reward (instrumentality); and the desirability of the offered reward, relative to other levels of achievement and reward already obtained by the individual seller (valence perceptions). At the risk of oversimplification, a summary of the preceding statement could be that, generally, *you get what you reward.* Thus, in the process of designing a compensation plan for sellers, managers must assess the job performance and behavior that will most benefit the overall marketing and sales objectives of the firm.

STRAIGHT-COMMISSION COMPENSATION PROGRAMS   Many managers believe that sellers are primarily motivated by money and, thus, will favor compensation plans that are directly tied to sales obtained *and paid for.* While money is a major motivator, this style of compensation must be consistent with the objectives of the organization and fit with the type of product offered.

Commission-only plans are most appropriate for products and services where repeat efforts are necessary to sustain customer purchases. Frequently ordered items (routine rebuy), such as consumables and other supplies and materials and parts easily replaced by horizontal competition, are such items. These are low-involvement, low-learning offerings, often in the maturity or the decline stage of the PLC. The selling role is order taker or persuader/sustainer. Referring again to Exhibit 12-8, the value of these sales roles is correlated to products with few if any adoption issues, late in the PLC, with the least complex product-related value statement. "Product related" is an important distinction. As described in "Four Models of Seller Roles" earlier in the chapter, the buyer–seller relationship can be a major differentiating factor in these sales.

With commission-only compensation plans, rewards are linked to short-term, repeated performance. Sellers most likely will concentrate their efforts with customer accounts that have a pattern of frequent and substantial purchases. If the seller is meeting organizational and personal objectives, there will be little incentive to develop new accounts or introduce new innovations to existing accounts. Sales managers find that they have little leverage or control with which to persuade sellers to engage in sales development efforts or even perform routine administrative tasks. The seller considers any diversion from the time spent with preferred customers an opportunity cost. In an attempt to exert some level of control, at least with regard to the attention paid to different products in the product line, variable commission rates are used. More profitable products have higher commission rates, hopefully encouraging sellers to focus on those products. Offerings that require a significant time period for adoption or customer learning may be inappropriate products for a full-commission sales force.

Straight-commission plans can also be a problem for sellers. Consistent with the personal needs of the seller, the variability of compensation may not fit well with personal income requirements. Negative changes in the economic climate will also cause instability in the income stream. In an effort to reduce this variability, firms will allow sellers to borrow, or draw, from future commissions, providing a stable income stream.

Straight-commission compensation is inappropriate during the initial period of sales training and new seller familiarization with customers and territories. Unless coming from an identical position with similar customers and products, new sellers should be given time to acclimate to the position.

STRAIGHT-SALARY COMPENSATION PLANS   Straight-salary plans overcome many of the disadvantages of straight-commission plans. Management has significantly greater influence and control over the activities of the sales force, because how the seller spends time will not directly impact compensation. Managers can direct sellers to develop new territories or broaden their customer bases without impeding the ability of the sellers to earn a living. The time-intensive efforts associated with relationship building, market research, sales promotions and publicity, and solving customer problems do not get in the way.

Selling roles that are required to provide design and engineering assistance are more appropriately compensated with salary plans. The motivator/problem solver and the relationship/value creator are roles typical of straight-salary compensation. Appropriate offerings for straight-salary plans are products and services that have long gestation periods, high learning, and are in the introduction and growth stage of the PLC. An increasing value orientation and complexity of the customer relationship also increase the need for additional management control and stability. Salary plans are also appropriate where management cannot reasonably determine the direct impact of individual sellers on sales results.

The most significant objection that sales managers have to salary plans is the lack of financial rewards tied directly to sales results. Straight-salary plans may attract sellers who are security oriented rather than achievement oriented. Sellers who are compensated by straight-salary plans will not always see a direct link between specific sales performance and reward. As with commission plans, the style of compensation must be consistent with the objectives of the organization and fit with the type of product offered.

COMBINATION COMPENSATION PLANS   Combinations of salary and bonus or commission are the most frequently used and popular of seller compensation plans.[20] Properly designed, they can deliver most of the advantages of both straight-salary and straight-commission plans while avoiding many of the disadvantages of both. Whether the plan uses a salary plus commission or a salary plus bonus depends on the degree of flexibility and control desired by management.

Salary-plus-commission plans operate much the same as straight-commission plans with compensation tied directly to sales outcomes. The salary portion of the plan validates management direction with regard to administrative duties and customer problem solving and service, while the commission portion provides the seller with an opportunity to increase compensation through increased levels of effort. The commission portion of the package is usually paid as earned and is part of the seller's regular income stream. The ratio of salary to commission in the total compensation package should reflect what management believes to be the objectives of the organization and the territory.

Bonus plans provide management with an increased degree of flexibility. Bonuses are paid for exemplary performance, meeting specific goals (sales, marketing, or administrative), and reaching specific levels of performance. A bonus is paid when the benchmark is surpassed rather than on a continuing basis. The bonus, then, is an additional incentive rather than a regular part of the compensation plan. The ratio of salary to bonus in such plans is usually greater than the ratio of salary to commission in those plans. Bonuses are paid only when a specific goal is reached and then usually at the end of the measurement period—quarterly or annually.

A final note about seller compensation is appropriate. There are many myths associated with seller compensation and its relationship to performance. Compensation plans are not the only motivational tool available to managers; not all sellers prefer high-risk or leveraged compensation plans; and sellers are not motivated only by money. Professional sellers are results oriented but not just short-term sales results. Successful sellers are oriented toward commitment and accountability. As with other employees in different roles, sellers will be motivated by effective leadership, acknowledgment, and reward.

MANUFACTURERS' REPRESENTATIVES

The "rep" in business-to-business marketing jargon is an independent business person who has specialized in a market segment or collection of segments that have common users or call patterns. Reps act as agents for firms in particular markets or regions. They carry no inventory and take no ownership of the goods they represent. The firms they represent are known as their *principals.* When the rep's customer makes a purchase, the terms of sale are often between the principal and the buyer. From a transactional viewpoint, the rep is not in the middle of the sale. The rep is compensated for the sale by the principal, after the sale is culminated or "**booked.**"

*When is a sale **booked**? Many organizations will have different policies regarding when a sale is "booked" for commission purposes. In most instances, a sale is not considered complete until the customer has paid the invoice. Reps then, just like direct commission sellers, must wait for all terms of a sale to be concluded to receive their compensation.*

The value of a good manufacturers' representative is in existing relationships with customers. Established reps have ongoing, successful relationships with buying organizations in the market segments in which they specialize. In selecting a rep, suppliers will seek out those who already have good relationships with potential customers—often determined by asking the customers who they might recommend as the local rep for the product or product line.

Because of their ongoing relationship with customers, they already understand the nature of the markets in which they compete. Little time is needed to get "up to speed," except possibly with the principal's product line. Since it is in the best interest of the rep to keep the lines of products represented current, the rep may solicit a new principal for a potential relationship as a way to complete or extend an existing product line. In these circumstances, little time is required to explain the supplier's product line. The rep usually has a target buyer already in mind.

In the short term, there are few costs associated with the use of manufacturers' representatives. Since all compensation is commission related, all selling costs are variable. The **fixed costs of sales** are covered by the rep, spread out over the commissions earned from all products and organizations represented. Thus, adding another product is efficient from the perspective of the rep when call patterns required by the new offering match those of existing products. From the perspective of the principal, no investment is necessary to establish a competent sales force. The lack of any significant fixed costs makes the use of manufacturers' reps very attractive for small firms that cannot afford full-time sellers, firms who may have full-time sellers in areas of customer concentration but require coverage in territories where sales volume does not warrant a direct seller, and firms introducing new products or entering new territories.

*The **fixed cost of sales** includes administrative overhead and field selling expenses. Administrative overhead includes all management and administrative salaries, the salaries of planners and sales support people, the cost of sales literature, and other special costs that cannot be linked directly to an individual transaction, such as prospect seminars, sales meetings, attending industry conferences, and so on.*

Over the long term, particularly when a rep is very successful with the products of the principal, the mutual advantages of the relationship change. When sales volumes increase, the principal does not recognize any economies of scale in the selling process. At some point, selling costs associated with using the rep will exceed the costs of placing a direct sales force in the same territory. When this becomes significant, sales managers often believe that a direct sales force will better represent their products because they will be focused solely on their products and will more aggressively represent the firm. Many reps half jokingly say that they want to be successful for the principals they represent but not so successful that they lose the product line to a direct sales force! Suppliers that rely on reps as the primary sales force often must be reminded about the reason they selected to use reps in the first place. The principal is compensating the rep for their knowledge of the industry and their relationships with customers. While responsibility for sales in a territory may be transferred with the termination of the rep's contract, relationships are not so easily transferred.[21]

Market Conditions that Favor Manufacturers' Representatives or a Direct Sales Force

Exhibit 12-11 compares the market conditions that tend to favor either a manufacturers' representative or a direct sales force. While much of this information is a summary of the information already discussed, there are a few situations, along with the trade-offs involved that bear special note.

TECHNICALLY COMPLEX PRODUCTS   Products, services, or total offerings that are complex will favor the use of a direct sales force. Whether because of the need for integration into other products or a steep learning curve associated with a new technology, reps will be more successful with standardized or generic products. This can lead to undesirable trade-offs.

Suppliers of high-technology, high-learning products are often small companies that may not have the financial ability to invest in a direct sales force. Using manufacturers' representatives may not be ideal but may be the only choice because of the low fixed costs. When reps are to be used to represent these types of products, a technical background or education is very important. The culture and environment of the rep and the target market must be supportive of new technology.

LONG LEAD TIMES   Whether because of the technically complex nature of the offering or the time to actually build and book the offering, long gestation periods tend to favor a direct sales force. The selling organization must have the financial wherewithal to support fixed selling expenses incurred

Appropriate for Direct Sales Force When	Appropriate for Manufacturers' Representative When
• The product is technically complex • The selling situation requires a specialized background that reps do not usually have, e.g., scientific or special technical • Control of the seller is important—the organization selects, trains, and controls personnel • Long lead times for results are common—direct sellers have more patience (and more budget) through the long sales cycles • Significant missionary work is required to build relationships • Significant prospecting for new customers is required • The customer base is highly concentrated • Explicit customer feedback is desired for innovations, new products, competitive information • High fixed costs exist, but with economies of scale	• The product is standardized or generic • For technical products, a general technical education or background is important • Control of personnel is less important—reps are independent business people • Short sales cycles are common, or long sales cycles without much pre-sale service required • The reps have other complementary lines • Reps have established relationships with target customer segments • The selling effort required for the product matches reps' existing call patterns • The market is dispersed and/or when the market consists of many small customers • Customer feedback is less critical (can stand the filter or time delay) • Low fixed costs are required

EXHIBIT 12-11 Comparison of Appropriate Market Conditions for a Direct Sales Force and Manufacturers' Representatives

during the period between customer specification and sale of the product. Manufacturers' representatives are not likely to be interested in waiting through long design, development, and build cycles to realize any compensation for their efforts.

If the selling organization finds that reps are to be used under these conditions, compensation becomes less straightforward than straight commission. Variations based on when a sale is booked or payments based on progress or goals reached are among the alternatives. The selling organization is at risk as funds will be expended before an actual sale is made.

SELECTION, TRAINING, AND CONTROL A manufacturer selects, trains, and has direct control over its own sales force. Sellers can be selected who become aligned with the goals of the organization and "fit" with the culture and environment. Sellers will be trained at the discretion of the manufacturer not only in particulars of the offering but in the internal relationships, behaviors, and expectations of the organization. The sales manager, to the extent allowed by the compensation plan used, will have significant influence and control over the activities of the seller. Such will not be the case with reps.

Reps are independent business people, either in business for themselves or part of a manufacturers' representation firm. They are directly responsible for their success or failure. Their efforts are spread over many products or product lines. The time spent with the products of any particular manufacturer will be directly dependent on what they believe will be a short-term success.

MISSIONARY WORK REQUIRED If a missionary selling effort is required to educate customers or build relationships in a new market segment or territory, a direct sales force or field marketing organization is almost always required. Few reps are likely to take on new markets or building new relationships unless long-term benefits will accrue to the rep. Keep in mind that reps are selected in large part because of their existing relationships. If a principal finds that the manufacturers' rep is often asked to approach new markets, it may be appropriate to question the process that selected the rep in the first place.

EXPLICIT CUSTOMER FEEDBACK DESIRED   Collaboration with customers, whether as part of a value network or an individual effort, will require explicit communication between supplier and customer. Situations that would normally require motivator/problem solver or relationship/value creator sales roles usually require the use of a direct sales force.

There can be alternatives. If the supplier can accept less timely or filtered customer feedback, using a rep may still be possible. This is not likely in the development of first-of-a-kind new business. A more likely scenario would be the use of the manufacturers' representative for direct selling and a direct field marketing or missionary sales effort for joint development efforts.

Combinations of Representation

The "explicit customer feedback" scenario described above leads into a representation pattern that occurs often. Many firms will use manufacturers' representatives or, as described in the next chapter, industrial distributors for their products. These relationships are focused on the short-term selling needs of the firm, usually fitting the role descriptions of order takers or persuader/sustainers.

How do these firms partner with customers to develop new products or "push the envelope" in their markets? Does the use of reps preclude a firm from taking an ownership role in a market? Firms that rely on reps and distribution for selling support will usually have a direct field marketing or missionary sales organization. This releases the missionary seller from day-to-day sales and account maintenance responsibilities to focus on longer-term R&D issues with customers. The selling effort also benefits because sellers have been freed from development responsibilities. A typical example of this type of arrangement can be seen in the sales arrangements of manufacturers of communication equipment (e.g., telephone switching devices and so on); computer workstations; and other products that have quick product delivery, installation, service and training as part of the offering. Sales and local inventory are accomplished by the distributor while installation, training, and service are provided by the missionary seller.

THOUGHTS TO TAKE WITH YOU INTO THE NEXT CHAPTER

Basic selling is persuasion. This chapter has presented the basic role of selling and several levels of complexity that become the selling model named here as the relationship/value creator. Throughout this text, the discussion has focused on the value network and the total offering that can be provided to the customer buying center. Elements of the value network, when brought forward to the customer by the seller, represent the supplier's approach to satisfying the needs of stakeholders in the customer buying center. The seller represents the different solutions to the different stakeholders and returns the feedback about each value element to the appropriate part of the supplier network.

Based on the complexity necessary to create a successful selling situation, a direct sales force or a manufacturers' representative is used. The greater the complexity of the offering and the greater the collaboration between supplier and customer organizations, the more likely a direct sales force will be used. The discussion has also revealed the role that missionary sales or business development personnel can play in complex relationships, relieving the seller, either direct or rep, of the need to be concerned with longer-term developments. Also discussed were the types of compensation appropriate in these different circumstances.

A direct sales force to handle short-term situations combined with a missionary seller for a long-term focus is just one marketing channel design that can be successful when it matches the way the customer organization works. The next chapter examines marketing channels and, more generally, value networks, their appropriate design and development, and looks at a variety of business-to-business channel and network designs that may be appropriate in certain circumstances. Different types of channels, channel intermediaries, and partners will be discussed, and their role in long- and short-term relationships examined. In going forward, consider the three needs that buyers and sellers work to satisfy—the needs of the job function, the needs of the organization, and personal needs. All must be considered not only in successful relationship selling, but in value network development as well.

Key Terms

booked [sale] *302*
bottom–up forecast *299*
boundary personnel *282*
call pattern *298*
direct sales force *298*
distributor *298*

dyadic interactions *282*
fixed costs of sales *303*
intensity of territory design *300*
manufacturers' representative *298*
motivator/problem solver *289*
order taker *286*

persuader/sustainer *288*
relational exchange *284*
relationship/value creator *290*
sales call *299*
switching costs *284*
top–down forecast *299*

Questions for Review and Discussion

1. Compare the role of a seller in consumer markets with a seller in business-to-business markets.

2. How is the repeated, ongoing relationship in business-to-business selling an advantage for both the seller and the buyer?

3. Explain why a dyadic relationship between buyer and seller may be of value to order takers.

4. As a product moves through the PLC, how does the nature and complexity of customer support change?

5. Discuss how the changes examined in Question 4 are related to technology adoption.

6. Refer to footnote 13, related to the levels of selling. Of the four forms of seller roles described in this chapter, which would you assign Level A? Level B? Level C?

7. Characterize the differences between the seller role of a motivator/problem solver and the seller role of a relationship/value creator.

8. Many sales managers claim, "Our sellers are the first line of defense and the first line of offense in the supplier–customer relationship." What does this statement mean? What role types are the sellers likely operating in?

9. Suppose you are the marketing manager for a small company marketing a new product that requires extensive collaboration with the customer before the customer will adopt it. What are the advantages and disadvantages of selling your product through manufacturer's representatives?

10. What are the three areas of mutual needs of buyers and sellers?

11. One-to-one marketing has been a goal for marketers over the past two decades. One-to-one marketing is, in essence, treating each customer as a segment of one and marketing directly to that customer. In business-to-business marketing, how close do you think most companies can come to implementing one-to-one marketing?

12. What risks must be considered when changing representation from manufacturers' representatives to a direct sales force?

13. At what level of sales success would you consider making the switch described in Question 11? What are the factors you must consider to make such a decision?

14. Consider the relationship between DaimlerChrysler and its suppliers described in Exhibit 12-9. Chrysler was in trouble and needed cost reductions. Think of some ways that Chrysler could have obtained the reduced costs and maintained a strong working relationship with its suppliers.

Endnotes

1. Pui-Wing Tam, "System Reboot—Hurd's Big Challenge at H-P: Overhauling Corporate Sales," *Wall Street Journal* (Eastern Edition) (April 3, 2006), p. A.1.

2. Gilbert A. Churchill Jr., Neil M Ford, and Orville C. Walker, *Sales Force Management*, 2nd ed. (Homewood, Ill.: Richard D. Irwin, 1985), pp. 4–7.

3. V. R. Buzzotta, R. E. Lefton, and Manuel Sherberg, *Effective Selling through Psychology* (Cambridge, Mass.: Ballinger Publishing/Harper & Row, 1982), p. 3.

4. Barton A. Weitz and Kevin D. Bradford, "Personal Selling and Sales Management: A Relationship Marketing Perspective," *Journal of the Academy of Marketing Science*, 27(2) (1999), pp. 241–254.

5. Paul Sherlock, *Rethinking Business to Business Marketing* (New York: The Free Press, 1991).

6. Weitz and Bradford, "Personal Selling and Sales Management," p. 244.

7. Michael H. Morris, Janine Brunyee, and Michael Page, "Relationship Marketing in Practice," *Industrial Marketing Management* 27 (1998), pp. 359–371, 361.

8. Arun Sharma, Nikolaos Tzokas, Michael Saren, and Panagiotis Kyziridis, "Antecedents and Consequences of Relationship Marketing," *Industrial Marketing Management* 28 (1999), pp. 601–611.

9. Morris et al. proposes a common working definition for all relationships, defining relationships as "a strategic orientation adopted by both buyer and seller organizations, which represents a commitment to long-term mutually beneficial collaboration." This is similar to the collaboration or partnering definition discussed here, but we do not concur with its universal application.

10. Morris et al., "Relationship Marketing in Practice," p. 369.

11. Sharma et al., "Antecedents and Consequences of Relationship."

12. Weitz and Bradford, "Personal Selling and Sales Management," p. 242.

13. Sherlock suggested three "levels" of selling, A, B, and C, in Rethinking Business to Business Marketing. C level was doing everything right but just maintaining the landscape, B level was all of C level plus the ability to establish and maintain the customer relationship, and A level was all of B level plus the ability to live up to the customer's archetypical model of seller. This description has proven useful to demonstrate some of the psychological aspects of selling but does not consider all of the factors noted here.

14. Weitz and Bradford, "Personal Selling and Sales Management."

15. Ibid., p. 244.

16. Sharma et al., "Antecedents and Consequences of Relationship," p. 605.

17. Michele Marchetti, "What a Sales Call Costs," *Sales and Marketing Management* (Bill Communications Inc.; www.salesandmarketing.com, 2001).

18. Philip Kotler, *Marketing Management: The Millennium Edition*, 10th ed. (Upper Saddle River, N.J.: Prentice Hall, 2000), pp. 620–632.

19. Churchill, et al., *Sales Force Management*, pp. 434–450.

20. Ibid., p. 467.

21. The termination of the manufacturers' representative contract does not terminate commissions to the rep. The rep is usually compensated for ongoing core business and also receives a portion of the commissions on new business that will close shortly, the presumption being that the business would not have happened if it were not for the efforts of the rep. We know of one situation in which a rep developed a very lucrative business for a principal, the business becoming the largest single contributor to the rep's sales volume. The principal noted that the commissions paid to the rep were multiples of the costs that were forecast if a direct sales office, fully staffed, were placed in the territory. The rep lost the product line. To achieve the same level of coverage, the principal hired two full-time sellers and administrative help and transferred two design engineers from headquarters to the sales office. The principal may have failed to recognize that the rep had a very productive and efficient relationship with the customer base.

Chapter 13

Business-to-Business Branding

Creating and Fostering the Brand

OVERVIEW

Brand management is one way that marketing creates competitive advantage for the business-to-business firm. Looking at branding in this light is a novelty for industrial companies because branding innovation in the past has always been hidden behind product innovations. In recent years, it has become clear that branding could also make a difference for industrial companies that sell large bulldozers or small screws.

Brands only exist in the minds of the customer. Many companies have demonstrated that being known and having positive brand associations could be extremely important in competitive situations. *Branding adds value* for the customer because it makes the buying decision process easier and helps him to reduce the risk of buying the wrong product. On the other side, branding helps the companies because it adds value to their intangible assets and can create price premiums. Business-to-business companies with high brand value such as Microsoft, IBM, GE, and Intel (see Exhibit 13-1, Brand Value) stand out, but many lesser-known companies have also discovered that effective branding increases the total value to customers and also is of value in mergers and acquisitions.

Branding is a distinct way of *differentiation*: Do you sell ordinary pumps or do you sell branded pumps? Do you sell commodities or solutions? Brand management has become an integral part of managing business-to-business companies. When an OEM identifies a supplier brand in its product, some of the market power shifts away from the OEM to the supplier, allowing supplier companies to become visible in markets where they wouldn't ordinarily have a presence.

Branding can be viewed as a key element of an entrepreneurial orientation where value creation and value usage come together at any point of the PLC and help the company to differentiate themselves from the others.

Brand building requires attention across all the elements of marketing. Branding is just as important in business-to-business marketing as it is in consumer marketing. As manufacturers' consumer brands lose market power to private brands, strong brands in business-to-business markets receive favorable treatment in the customers' buying decision process. However, to create a strong brand goes

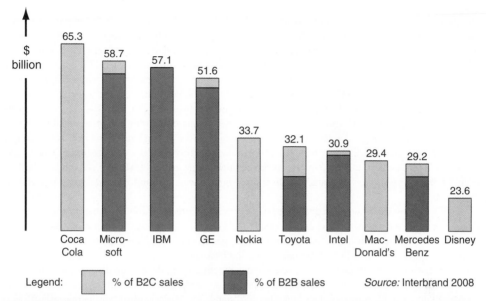

EXHIBIT 13-1   Brand Value of Top Ten Companies (Based on Interbrand Best Global Brands 2007)
Source: David Kiley, "Best Global Brands," *Business Week* (August 6, 2007); includes also two
ingredient brands: Microsoft and Intel

far beyond building awareness for the brand name; rather, it takes mastery of all the
elements in the offering that contribute to value for customers, which of course takes
time to establish. A strong brand is something for new companies and new market
entrants to strive to build; it is something for established companies to nurture,
protect, and use with care. This discussion addresses methods of making a brand
into a standard and generally building brand strength. The methods discussed in this
chapter build sustainable competitive advantage deep within the company's inner
workings.

In the opening example, ITT Corporation, a global engineering and
manufacturing company, demonstrates the need for a single corporate brand initiative
for the emerging market in China. Building a unified approach with a clear stated
value proposition raises the possibilities for engaging successfully at home and
abroad. Branding plays an important role in markets, internally, and by attracting
qualified employees worldwide as well.

Example: ITT Industries—Brand Engineering in China[1]

Strong global brands have never been as important as they are now in China. No matter how powerful
and highly recognized some local brands may be, it is difficult for diverse names to compete against
those operating under a single corporate brand umbrella. That is why ITT Industries (ITT), a New York-
based diversified global engineering and manufacturing company, is now rolling out its extensive
rebranding strategy in China—linking the parent brand to the individual attributes of diverse ITT
products, including Goulds, Flowtronex, Wedeco, Flygt, Bell and Gossett, and Lowara.

ITT Corporation is a global engineering and manufacturing company with leading positions in
the markets it serves, generating 2008 sales of about $10 billion. ITT is the world's premier supplier of

pumps, systems and services to move, control, and treat water and other fluids. The company is a major supplier of sophisticated military defense systems and provides advanced technical and operational services to a broad range of government agencies. ITT also produces electrical connectors used in telecommunications, computing, aerospace, and industrial applications. Further, ITT makes industrial components for a number of other markets, including transportation, construction, and aerospace. Based in White Plains, New York, ITT employs approximately 39,000 people around the world.

"Brand without performance is empty, but performance without brand is like a cry in the wilderness," says Thomas Martin, ITT senior vice-president and director of corporate relations. "ITT is in urgent need of creating a single strong brand worldwide, especially in China, and now is a good time to do it," Martin emphasizes. The idea of the rebranding initiative results from research ITT conducted among its 200 customers, and employees, worldwide toward the end of 2004. "We got valuable findings from the interviews, which indicated the diversified brands were not uniformly designed in the past," says Martin.

ITT employees know much about the business they are directly involved in, but do not know what ITT does around the world. Among employees, ITT is viewed as a "generic" corporation, and employee allegiance is aligned with individual business units, which constrains the sharing of ideas. A strong corporate brand could help ITT attract and retain the best talent during its global business expansion. This is increasingly important in China, where the competition for talent is rapidly intensifying.

These are, however, only the internal benefits. According to the research, ITT customers are unclear about what the company does and what ITT stands for. Historically, after the big reshuffling of ITT in the 1980s, many of the ITT businesses went to market as individual brands, which watered down the brand identity. The segmentation is seen clearly in the China market.

The multiple brand strategy seems to be particularly dangerous as ITT's better-branded competitors in various markets in China, including Siemens, GE, and Northrop Grumman, strive to seize business opportunities there. "There will be tremendous investments made in infrastructure, health care, water; GE can approach China as one company and form a company-to-country relationship," said Jeff Immelt, GE's chief executive officer (CEO), in Business Week in March 2005. The former CEO with Siemens AG, Klaus Kleinfeld, also noted that China is the most important market for Siemens.

From December 2005, the branding campaign, called "Engineered for Life," officially kicked off worldwide with a new uniform branding guideline. It covers all aspects, including name cards, product brochures, building signs, corporate stationery, and Web sites, and aims to give all employees, customers, and shareholders a clear picture of what ITT stands for.

Dong Ruiping, external affairs director with ITT Industrial China Investment Co Ltd., says, "2007 was a critical year for the execution of the branding campaign in China." There is no better test of ITT's rebranding strategy than the China market. "China offers us a greater chance than Europe and the United States, ITT's major markets," says Martin.

In recent years, industries related to ITT's businesses, including water treatment, construction, manufacturing, and mining, have grown rapidly in China. Take water treatment for example. The world is running out of clean water, and China is no exception. In the country's recently endorsed 11th Five-Year Plan (2006–2010) for the Peoples Republic of China, water cleaning and water recycling in cities and rural areas have been given great attention. "ITT has a series of biological, filtration and disinfection technologies and equipment to preserve increasingly precious water," says Martin. "We are also good at moving water from plentiful areas to thirsty communities, which could meet the nation's demand as well."

ITT has provided pumps, mixers, and expertise to more than 250 wastewater treatment installations throughout China, including one in Zhaojiabang that began operation in 2007. In the station, thirteen submersible Flygt pumps manage the flow of sewage and rainwater, meaning downtown Shanghai is better able to manage wastewater after a heavy storm, enhancing the city's image as a metropolitan and commercial centre. The 2008 Beijing Olympics also spawns immense opportunities for ITT. The company secured a major project to develop the kayaking and canoeing course in the water park for the games in Shunyi, a district on the outskirts of the capital. The project will also utilize six Flygt submersible pumps. "ITT has extensive experience in supporting the kayaking and canoeing courses at the Olympic Games, with its pumping systems installed in the kayak projects in Atlanta, Barcelona, Sydney and Athens for previous Olympics," says Martin.

In 2007, ITT was very successful globally and sales in China grew by 40 percent year-on-year, but Ms. Dong refuses to disclose relevant figures in China. "They are sensitive. What we can say is sales and profits have kept increasing here, driven by organic growth instead of acquisitions," she says. ITT has invested more than US$125 million in China. "We will continuously increase our investment here and try to provide localized solutions," Dong says.

ITT is not alone in transforming a multiple brand into a single one. U.S.-based Ingersoll Rand, a diversified company, rolled out its branding initiatives last year, including the deletion of the hyphen previously used between the two parts of its name and refreshing the company's logo. "It's vital to create the image that Ingersoll Rand is a well-integrated company, as the whole is greater than the sum of its parts," says Herbert L. Henkel, CEO of the company.

LEARNING OBJECTIVES

By reading this chapter, you will:

- Understand the creation and application of brand management in order to compete successfully in business-to-business markets.
- Have obtained an understanding of how branding relates to entrepreneurial marketing and gained a sense of how branding can be accomplished in all elements of the offering.
- Understand how to implement brand management in business-to-business marketing.
- Have developed insights in the concepts of competing and winning over a long time frame through building and managing brand strength in a business-to-business environment.

INTRODUCTION

When Friedrich Krupp, who extended the running time on train wheels by tenfold, put his famous steel rings on his products and registered them as trademark in 1875, his business customers could easily distinguish the "right" products from imitations and fakes. Brands help people to organize their thinking and reduce their risk of purchasing "wrong" products, both in the consumer and business world.

In the opening example, ITT Corporation recognized that its customers were seeking a sure way to get trusted product from one qualified supplier. The ITT unified branding approach was the response. To align the product brand approach under one umbrella brand, ITT formed a recognizable corporation with diversified product offerings. ITT also benefited from this brand alignment for its internal understanding and its recruiting efforts worldwide. This example illustrates some of the key ideas in this chapter. ITT acted entrepreneurially through branding innovation. They reduced risks for the customers and opened the doors for new markets and new employees. This kind of branding innovation has to be seen as a continuous process to adapt to the customer requirements and the changing environment. The theme of competing over time in a changing environment through branding as a key competitive tool in business-to-business marketing is discussed in the last section of this chapter.

HOLISITC BRANDING

The concept of branding can add more to organizational performance than just putting a logo, an advertisement, or a tag line under a company name. Company executives can enhance performance and create value all along the value chain for themselves and the customers by creating and implementing marketing programs, processes, and activities that are intersecting and interdependent. It is therefore necessary to have a broad, integrated perspective to assure consistency of the comprehensive approaches. Relationship marketing, integrated marketing, and internal marketing are components of the **holistic** approach. Knowing that the brand influences any buying decision internally and externally needs an approach that can open doors even before the seller knocks on the door.[2] A brand is not the campaign and the classy brochures; it is the way the customer perceives your action. Brand perception is influenced by everything the company does that comes in contact with the customer: the way the receptionists answer the phone or the service technician solves your problem.

*A **holistic** approach is one that emphasizes the total offering— the functional relationships between all of the pieces. This is consistent with the earlier definition of a total offering—the offering that provides a complete solution to the buyer's needs; this may include financing, delivery, service, and so on.*

Characteristics of Business-to Business Branding

The proliferation of similar products and services, increasing competition, and incredible price pressures are among the numerous powerful forces that make business-to-business brand building a crucial factor. Brands can help to differentiate, reduce the risk and complexity, and compensate price pressures by offering additional value. The most important **brand functions** are as follows:

*A **Brand** is a collection of experiences and associations attached to a company, organization, product, or service; more specifically, brand refers to the concrete symbols such as a name, logo, slogan, and design scheme. A brand is a symbolic embodiment of all the information connected to a company, organization, product, or service.*

• *Increased information efficiency*: Branded products make it easier for the customer to gather and process information. Bundling information about the manufacturers and origin of a product in the form of a brand helps customers to more quickly find their way in a new or confusing product environment. Moreover, branded products have recognition value. Customers can repeatedly find trusted brands quickly and easily.

• *Risk reduction*: Choosing a branded product reduces the customer's risk of making the wrong purchasing decision. Brands create trust in the expected performance of the product, and provide continuity in the predictability of the product benefits. Especially in business-to-business marketing, brands can help to ensure and legitimize buying decisions, since buyers often have a penchant for avoiding risk.

• *Value-added or image benefit creation*: For consumers, the value added or image benefit usually lies in the subjective, self-expressive value that brands can provide them. In a business-to-business environment the additional value provided by brands is usually not anchored in purely self-expressive values. Nonetheless, it can be very important. Through a brand you do not only present your employees to the world but also the whole corporation. The brand is the shorthand for the value image of the company.

In light of these three main functions, it becomes apparent that brands and branding have high importance as methods that a business can use to compete. Certain contextual factors enhance the importance of the brand functions. The supplier industry structure and the number of competitors increase brand relevance in monolithic markets with low numbers of competitors. Also the complexity of the buying process and the size of the buying center make brands more relevant. The more recognized a brand is among members of the buying center, the more likely that the "hurdles" for approval will be lessened. When offering a clearly visible "public" product offering, brand is very relevant. Branding is particularly important in new task buying situations where "a way it is now done" doesn't exist. Yet, there are still only a few successful business-to-business brands that already prove the potential in that area.

The Role of Business-to-Business Brands

In many industries branding is undervalued, leaving a gap with huge unrealized brand potential. Not only could companies profit from a tremendous first-mover advantage by deciding to jump onto the brand wagon, future-oriented companies may even be able to set the business standard with their brands. The establishment of a brand as the defacto standard in a market segment is one of the critical ingredients in market ownership. Discussed in Chapter 5; the three elements of market ownership are repeated in the box below.

The role of brands in business-to-business marketing can be summarized[3] as follows:

- *Differentiate*—Brands are an effective and compelling means to "decommoditize" product categories that are highly undifferentiated.
- *Secure future business*—Quite often it is important to establish brands for your products or services in order to prepare for the future. There are many business areas where only those companies survived that chose to brand their products from the beginning.
- *Create brand loyalty*—Brands assist companies in transitioning from a transaction-based selling model to one that is relationship based. The customer always comes first. **Brand loyalty** is created when the business manages to consistently deliver on what its brand promises.
- *Differentiate marketing efforts*—Businesses with strong brands can benefit from increased communications effectiveness. Marketing efforts will be more readily accepted than those of complete no-name products and services.

Market Ownership

In "Marketing Is Everything," McKenna discusses owning a market. From his discussion, we can form three indicators of market ownership:

1. Market owners define a market niche as theirs and work toward dominating it. Their brand is immediately identified as the standard in that market. Examples are Hewlett-Packard Laser-Jet printers and GE Lexan Polycarbonate Resin. These branded products are defacto standards in their industries. Competitors to both products note their equivalence to those offerings.
2. Market owners continue to evolve their offerings with the next generation as defined by the value presented to the customer.

3. Market owners benefit from other organizations developing ancillary products and markets that serve the owners' customer base. Third parties define their products as compatible with market owner. In this ancillary product development process, the market owner may be consulted by the developer to ensure compatibility with future products. The owner thus gains insight to other points of view about its market.

Market share is not a defining parameter that leads to market ownership, as is often mistakenly implied. Market share is more likely a result of, not a cause of, ownership.

Source: Regis McKenna, "Marketing Is Everything," *Harvard Business Review* (January–February 1991).

- *Create preferences*—Brand preference at its best leads to the rejection of competitive brands. Marketers who are naïve of the relationship aspects of business-to-business markets may believe that this is true only for consumer markets. A strong brand, however, will act as a barrier to people switching to competitors products.
- *Command price premium*—A business with well-known brands can command premium prices for their products and services. It makes it automatically less susceptible to competitive forces. That business-to-business brands are valuable resources is also reflected in the acquisition prices. Brands can balloon these prices tremendously.
- *Create brand image*—Brands enable companies' value propositions to be more emotive and compelling. Above all, a positive brand image also appeals to all other stakeholders—it makes it even easier to recruit and retain talent.
- *Increase sales*—The main goal of most business is to prosper. Companies with strong brands can benefit not only from higher margins but also from high sales volume.

Not only are there considerable benefits for industrial companies in building strong brands, there are serious penalties for those who do not. The alternative is to be continuously challenged through customer price cutting, discounts, and cost reduction programs (Exhibit 13-2).

THE BRANDING TRIANGLE   As trust builds, the relationship between the buyer and supplier moves into partnerships that recognize that the goals of both organizations can best be met by working together. To illustrate this we developed the **branding triangle** (Exhibit 13-3).

The branding triangle[4] illustrates visually the marketing-related connections between a company, its collaborators, and its customers. Collaborators refer not only to employees but also to wholesalers, dealers, ad agencies, and so on. The triangle aims to act as a common field to the intersecting market participants. It is essential to provide a consistent picture of the company and its brands across all different media and to all stakeholders. Only then is it possible to guide their perception throughout the huge flow of different pieces of information. Nowadays brand management—especially in business to business—is not only related to one product, service, or

EXHIBIT 13-2   The Role of Business-to-Business Brands

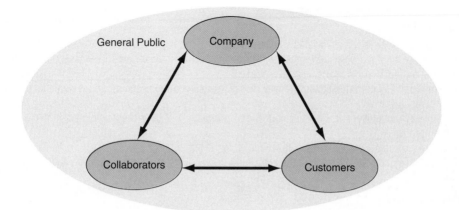

EXHIBIT 13-3   The Branding Triangle

market offering but rather to the whole company—the value image[5]—itself. Therefore, it is important to recognize the value that a comprehensive brand portfolio together with a corporate brand can provide. It is important to find the right combination of presenting your company geared to the respective target groups and stakeholders while keeping the necessary consistent value statement outside as well as inside the company.

The company stands for everything, the tangible and intangible; whether it is service or product, it incorporates the history as well as the prospective future. The image of the company, from its foundation to the present, is usually mainly formed by external marketing communications. Few customers or other stakeholders deliberately make efforts to find out everything there is to know about a company. They usually only know what the company "tells them." Not less important of course is the performance of the employees and other related cooperators. What picture are they drawing in the customer's minds? If they internalized the message of the brand they are representing, guided by effective internal marketing communication, that necessary consistency is assured. So you see the brand is the one thing that connects everything across all touch points. Brands are, at the same time, multifaceted but fragile figures. It is much easier to dilute or even to ruin a brand than to build one.

Yet, many business decisions on a daily basis are based on opinions that do not precisely reflect the real situation of the brand. In times where marketplaces change so rapidly it is absolutely crucial to base every important decision on accurate, current, relevant, and objective information in order to protect the brand. To ensure consistent performance, some kind of brand checklist, Exhibit 13-4, can be very helpful. If you are about to make extensive decisions in which the life of a brand is at stake you should rigorously stick to that checklist.[6]

BRANDING DIMENSIONS

A successful brand is a statement of who and what the company is. To take full advantage of its brands as strategic devices, branding must be the thread running through the subject of marketing. To regard brand management as merely managing design or advertising seems to be too superficial and tends to shorten the brand's life expectancy. A company must be prepared to carry out a considerable amount of marketing and brand planning.

Brand Identity

- Do you have clear values associated with your brand?
- Are you presenting a clear and consistent brand identity to your target audiences? (logo, colors, designs, etc)
- Do your branding communications convey messages that communicate important elements of value your company delivers?
- Do company employees know what your brand promises and their responsibilities in living up to those promises?
- Does your company keep its promises embodied in the brand?
- Do you have control over trademarks and brand marks? Do you control over how these elements are used?

Brand Awareness

- Does your audience recognize your name? Your logo?
- Do your target audiences remember you when they are considering purchasing?
- Do your target audiences recall your brand whenever they think about your type of product?

Competitive Positioning

- Do you understand your positioning in the marketplace?
- Does your brand have differentiating benefits associated with it in customers' minds?
- Do you intended customers believe your intended positioning in the marketplace?

Process

- Does your company review the consistency between your operations and culture and your brand values?
- Do you review your communications, branding, and perceived brand image periodically?
- Is this done systematically? Do you measure your brand equity?

EXHIBIT 13-4   Branding Checklist   *Source*: Nick Pauley Design Brand Check (2008) download under http://www.pauleydesign.co.uk/PD_gd_brandcheck.pdf

Brand management is the organizational framework that systematically manages the planning, development, implementation, and evaluation of the brand strategy

Brand management, therefore, is the organizational framework that systematically manages the planning, development, implementation, and evaluation of the brand strategy.[7] The development of a holistic brand strategy has to involve all levels of marketing management. Such a holistic perspective can also provide valuable insights into the process of capturing customer value. In a world where product offerings are getting more similar, brands are one of the few opportunities for making a difference. Brands can help by:

- Greater willingness to try products and services
- Less time needed to close the sale after offering
- Greater likelihood that a product is purchased
- Willingness to pay a price premium
- Less sensitivity to price increases.

These benefits clearly show the power of brand equity. There are many definitions about brand equity available; all their drivers refer to perceived quality, name awareness, brand association, and brand loyalty. There are various ways to measure brand equity. In Exhibit 13-1 we have highlighted the most important business-to-business companies. To increase the brand equity, a consistent impression of the company relationship is needed (Exhibit 13-5).

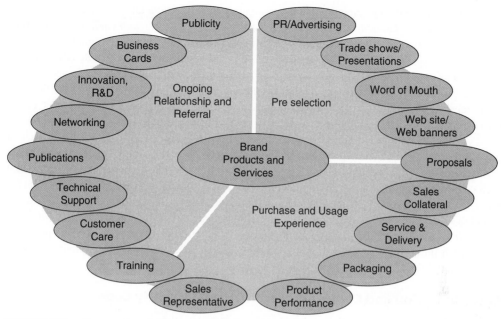

EXHIBIT 13-5 The Brand Customer Relationship

Brand Strategy

A brand strategy can be defined as the choice of common and distinctive brand elements a company applies across the company itself and the various products and services it sells. It reflects the number and nature of new and existing brand elements while at the same time guiding decisions on how to brand new products. To put it in other words, the brand strategy lays out a future image for the company to aim for, providing a plan of action and criteria against which to judge it. It is based on certain future goals. Among others, the most common goals related to the customers are to increase brand awareness, create a positive **brand image,** and to establish brand preferences and brand loyalty. The brand strategy also aims at increasing the appeal and attraction of the company in the eyes of the stakeholders, who underpin the management of the company, and to give the employees criteria with which to judge the value of their own actions.

To structure and manage their portfolio of brands is one of the biggest challenges businesses face nowadays.

BRAND ARCHITECTURE   To develop a company-owned brand architecture is essential since it defines the relationship between brands, the corporate entity, and product and services. For business-to-business companies, defining the brand hierarchy to pursue is the most important aspect of the branding strategy. Brand architecture normally evolves starting with a brand that is strongly associated with a distinctive asset such as the technological innovation or the founding of the company. With diversification and mergers and acquisition activities, the company offering ends up with a mix of brands without consistency with the

Brand strategy: Your brand is one of the most valuable assets of your company. You can make it the driving force behind your business. In order to plan and implement a brand strategy, the current state of your business must first be understood so that you can uncover the needs and issues that are unique to your company and your industry. It's only by gaining this understanding, and aligning it with the company's vision, that the brand strategy can be revealed.

broader company message. Keeping the brand architecture consistent and understandable for the customer is the key element. Companies can stretch their brand by *width* (individual to corporate), *length* (low to high end), and *depth* (national to international). Companies can have individual brands or brand families and everything could be put under a corporate brand. Brand strategy and brand architecture have to be adjacent. If a company approaches various separate and diverse market segments, individual brands may be the most favorable. If a company approaches a whole industry, a family brand makes sense. If there is no consistent brand management, companies end up with a mixed or hybrid structure of brands.

A good example of thorough brand consistency is General Electric. Since the launch of their corporate logo, all new products or divisions must be part of the GE culture and brand architecture—a "branded house" as referred in Exhibit 13-6. Other companies are successful with other architectures. In hybrid architectures, such as is shown with AKZO NOBEL, consistency as well as diversity is implemented. As a result of many mergers and acquisitions, the business-to-business Daimler AG has had to manage many truck brands around the world, to benefit from the brand equity and goodwill acquired and with the physical assets. The positioning of each individual brand is important to the value of the offerings in local markets. As a result, maintaining a "house of brands" is a necessity.

Communication and Corporate Identity/Visual Identity Code

Now that we have covered the potential strategic options that companies can apply in an industrial context, it is time to move on to the more concrete brand elements. Brand elements are the visual and sometimes even physical devices that serve to identify and differentiate a company product or service. The adequate choice and coordination of them is crucial when it comes to brand equity. When building a strong brand the following brand elements are key:

- Name
- Logo
- Tagline (or slogan)
- Brand story.

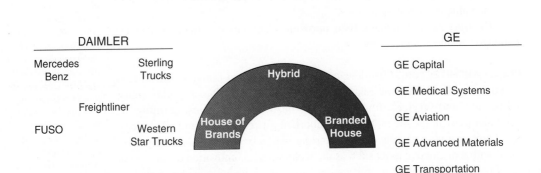

EXHIBIT 13-6 Brand Architecture Spectrum

The formal brand elements like name, logotype, and slogan taken together form the visual identity of a brand or company. They should reflect the brand essence, brand personality, and corporate culture of the business.

The visual identity has to be designed with a long-term perspective. In order to assure the consistency of the brand performance, it is also very helpful to define branding guidelines that exactly specify the use of each brand element. Such a guideline is called **visual identity code.** This visual identity code for the brand elements should follow a set of choice criteria in order to reduce the risk of diluting or weakening the brand:

- *Available*—They should be available and usable across all intended markets. Today it is also very important to check the availability of the Internet domain for possible brand names.
- *Meaningful*—Ideally the brand elements should capture the essence of the brand and communicate something about the nature of the business.
- *Memorable*—Good brand elements are distinctive and should be easy to remember. Brand names should be moreover easy to read and spell.
- *Protectable*—It is essential that the brand elements, especially the brand name, can be legally protected in all countries in which the brand will be marketed.
- *Future oriented*—Well-chosen brand elements can position companies for growth, change, and success. To be future oriented also means to check the adaptability and updatability of the brand elements.
- *Positive*—Effective brand elements can evoke positive associations in the markets served.
- *Transferable*—Is it possible to use the brand element to introduce new products in the same or different market.

The first four criteria can be characterized as "**brand building**" since they are concerned with major implications when choosing and creating the brand elements in the first place. The latter three are more defensive. They are important for the general value and brand equity creation. In making a business brand, marketers have many choices of brand elements to identify with their products and services.

Because of its targeted nature, it is usually much less costly to implement a branding strategy for business-to-business companies than for businesses in the consumer market. The content of business-to-business brand communications is also different compared to consumer markets. The primary purpose of consumer branding content is to create awareness and an emotional experience that leads to brand preference, while business-to-business content serves important practical and pragmatic functions. Communicating too many complex details about the company, though, should be avoided, as this would leave the audience with information indigestion. The communication tools should ideally focus on the advantages of a product or

Visual Identity Code—Corporate Identity

Contrary to popular belief, the term *corporate identity* refers to more than just the design of a company's logotype and stationery—it is a blanket-term that refers to the particular way that an organization presents itself and interacts with its staff and public. An organization's identity is the sum total of its history, beliefs, environment, and visual appearance (stationery, architecture, uniforms, signage, website, brochures, etc.) and is shaped by the nature of its technology, its ownership, its people, its ethical and cultural values, and its strategies.

service as well as the explicit needs that are being met by the offer. These needs can include reducing costs, time, overhead and improving productivity and/or quality; they also can increase flexibility and expandability.

Assuming that your customers and prospects as well as the press are as interested in and as knowledgeable as you are about your product or even your product category can lead to misguided communication efforts. Customers are not interested in the product itself; they usually are interested in a solution of their problems—the total offering. Before a company can come up with a customized solution that highlights and promotes any kind of specific capabilities the company may have, you have to uncover the explicit needs of the customers. Yet, many companies in the business-to-business realm still inundate prospective customers with volumes of paper expounding their competencies and capabilities.

In business-to-business marketing, especially when applying a corporate brand strategy, effective segmentation and targeting is key. Information that is important to your investors is usually not likely to motivate your prospects. A company with a diversified spectrum of products and services has to acknowledge that different target groups often value different benefits. One communication strategy rarely fits all.

Also, participants in a business-to-business buying center will vary in their involvement and motivation in the decision-making process. Consequently, it is unlikely that all members of the buying center will be equally interested in the same brand values. The selling strategies employed by companies in business markets should be underpinned by a clear understanding of the information processing that occurs as business-to-business purchasers make their decisions. While the nature of many industrial products and markets may call for an emphasis on functional brand values there is a need to recognize that organizational purchasers are still influenced by emotional considerations such as trust, security, and peace of mind (see Chapter 3 for further discussion of organizational behavior and individual decision making).

Brand value communication that demonstrates an understanding of the psychological concerns of industrial buyers can be a powerful source of differentiation in markets dominated by a focus on functionality. Brand communication that does not recognize the value attached to intangible brand elements by different buying center members may undermine the sales process. Successful business-to-business brand communication requires strategies that incorporate brand values to appeal to the social and psychological as well as the rational concerns of the different organizational buyers involved.

To establish an appropriate communication strategy it is essential to concisely know who your message is meant for. The solution is to adopt a holistic perspective that takes into consideration that business-to-business market encounters are complex interactions affected by multiple players. Such holistic marketing perspective requires external, internal, and interactive marketing, as shown by the branding triangle in Exhibit 13-3.

The branding triangle clearly illustrates the intersecting relationships of the three most important market participants: company, customer, and collaborators (employees, partners). **External marketing** relates to the regular work of pricing, distributing, and promoting of products and services to customers. **Internal marketing** describes all actions that train and motivate collaborators to become true brand ambassadors. The company directly affects external and internal communication efforts while **interactive marketing** is primarily affected by internal marketing activities. The branding triangle is showing the equivalent importance of all three communication approaches. It is no longer enough to merely rely on external marketing efforts if you want to establish a successful brand. Yet, there are still many industrial companies that do not effectively communicate their brand essence and values internally to their employees. If no one takes the time to explain the effect of the brand, especially the brand promise, to employees, branding efforts are in most cases doomed to failure. It is essential to realize the internal implications and develop internal brand programs and training to educate collaborators on what the brand represents, where the company is going with its brand, and what steps need to be taken to get there.

Brand building tools are the means of marketing communication by which companies aim to inform, persuade, and remind customers—directly or indirectly—about their products and brands. In a way, they act as the "voice" of the brand and create a platform to establish a dialog and build relationships with customers. The brand building tools are not fundamentally different in consumer and business-to-business areas. The marketing communications program is made up of the same major modes of communication, but the market conditions are very different:

- Personal selling
- Direct marketing
- Public relations
- Advertising
- Sales promotion.

However, priorities typically vary significantly. In business-to-business markets, the focus is typically set on the first one—personal selling. But understanding the concept of "brand" as holistic experience also conveys, "everything matters." Therefore, all elements in the marketing communications mix are potential tools for building brand equity. They contribute to brand equity in many ways: by creating awareness of the brand, linking the desired associations to the brand image, eliciting positive brand judgments or emotions, and/or facilitating a stronger customer–brand relationship. The box "From Earth-Moving Equipment to Boots" describes the innovative branding effort of Caterpillar, Inc. Notice that the kind of brand consistency involves employees on all levels and positions.

Companies should periodically check the performance of their branding efforts. Caterpillar is successful because the company has been vigilant in maintaining consistency of its image in the consumer market with its image in the business market. A failure to maintain standards of excellence in one market will reflect across all markets.

MEASURING EQUITY AND VALUE

Although the value of a brand cannot be measured precisely, it is important to establish estimates that provide a frame of reference when developing brand building programs and budgets. Some marketers regard brand equity measurement and brand valuation as equal although they need to be distinguished from each other. Over the last two decades a vast number of brand evaluation models have been developed.[8] Most of them fall into the following categories (Exhibit 13-7):

- *Research-based evaluations*—Brand equity measurement is a behavioral approach that puts a financial value on brands. Researchers measure customer behaviors and attitudes that have an impact on the brands. The perceptual brand metrics include awareness (unaided and top of mind), knowledge, familiarity, relevance, satisfaction, and recommendation.
- *Financially driven approaches*—Brand valuation is used to estimate the total financial value of a brand. The estimation of the financial value of a brand is partially based on subjective judgments of knowledgeable people in an organization. It usually involves straightforward logic. First, you have to identify the earnings stream of each major market

EXHIBIT 13-7 CAT Footwear

From Earth-Moving Equipment to Boots

Let us take a look at Caterpillar. For more than eighty years, the earth-moving equipment of Caterpillar Inc. has boldly shaped the world's landscape and infrastructure. It is one of the few high-profile brands that are prominent and successful in two very different fields. In the business-to-business area, the stylish yellow-tabbed CAT logo is best-known as the symbol of the leading global manufacturer of construction and mining equipment, diesel and natural gas engines, and industrial gas turbines.

The history of Caterpillar dates back to the late nineteenth century, when Daniel Best and Benjamin Holt were experimenting with ways to fulfill the promise that steam tractors made for farming. The Best and Holt families collectively had pioneered track-type tractors and the gasoline-powered tractor engine. In 1925 the Holt Manufacturing Company and the C.L. Best Tractor Company merged to form the Caterpillar Tractor Corporation. In 2007, the company gained sales revenues of US$44.9 billion and a profit of about US$4 billion. Today, CAT is truly a global brand. Approximately half of all sales and target customers are outside the United States. The products and

components of this global supplier and leading U.S. exporter are manufactured in 49 U.S. facilities and 59 other locations in 22 countries around the globe.

As a technology leader, the construction-equipment giant is represented worldwide by a global dealer network that serves customers in more than 200 countries. The mostly independent and locally owned dealerships provide CAT with a key competitive edge since customers deal with people they know and trust while benefiting from the international knowledge and resources of the company.

The company sets a strong focus on testing and quality processes that aim to secure its reputation for reliability, durability, and high quality. Caterpillar products are premium priced and are regarded as more effective and money saving in the long term because their systems are proven to work harder and longer than competitive products. Faced with the threat of potential brand erosion and customer confusion due to decentralized divisions the company decided to develop a program to secure and foster the integrity of its corporate image. The result was the "One Voice" campaign that put a strong focus on the corporate brand strategy.

The strength of this iconic American brand, moreover, has been extended very successfully to consumer markets. Prior to 1994, to most consumers, the brand was more familiar on a range of expensive heavy-duty boots and associated apparel. The strength and extraordinary appeal of the Caterpillar brand in business to customer lies in its brand heritage for rugged durability. CAT footwear, for instance, combines the rugged durability of work shoes with the easy comfort of casual footwear.

carrying the brand. Those are then divided according to the following criteria: those attributable to the brand, to the fixed assets, and to other intangibles. After capitalizing the earnings attributable to the brand, you get the estimate value for that brand in the product market. This is especially important for companies that base their growth on acquiring and building diversified brand portfolios. The usual way is to subtract the book value from the market value and attribute the difference to brand equity.

- *Combined approaches*—These approaches are using behavior and financial brand valuation methods combined. One of the best-known combined approaches is from Interbrand Corporation, a global branding consultancy. The method—although not publicly open, which is now recognized by auditors and tax authorities in many countries, defines the brand value[9] as the net present value of future profits attributable to the brand. The valuation model, according to our understanding, integrates three core processes: financial analysis (with focus on additional cash flow created through the brand), market analysis (determining particularly the generated and achievable price premium), and brand analysis (analyzing brand recognition, brand loyalty, and so on).

COMPETING THROUGH BRANDING

The unifying theme in this chapter is that branding can create competitive strength in a business-to-business environment. Market ownership has a perceptual dimension. Being recognized as the owner of a market conveys a competitive advantage whenever a customer is trying to decide whose offering to choose or whether to purchase the next offering from the same supplier as the last purchase. As was noted in Chapter 3, business buyers are people, too. They develop beliefs (associations) and preferences. They remember some things and do not remember others. When they lack information and do not have time to search, they fill in the blanks from what they already know.

In general, building strong brands requires time to establish trust and confidence. There are certain circumstances in which a supplier's product can quickly become a standard, but the general case requires time for extended interaction between customer and supplier. In this way, **brand building** in business-to-business marketing differs somewhat from branding in consumer markets—strong brands are built through careful establishment of a relationship with each customer and prospective customer. Marketing communications has a role in business-to-business brand building, but it is not nearly as short term and product centered as it is in consumer marketing.

In this section of the chapter the discussion describes how, under certain circumstances, a supplier obtains the status of being a standard for its market. Then the discussion moves to consideration of how strong brands can be built in circumstances where it is not conducive to build an industry standard. Then we will introduce the ingredient branding concept.

Importance of Brand in Business-to-Business Buyer Behavior

Re-examine the buying decision process discussed in Chapter 3. As the following sequence of steps in a typical buying decision process illustrates, a recognized brand name with positive associations attached has an advantage at each stage of the decision process, even under high-learning (high-involvement) purchase situations.

- *Determine that a need exists.* Missionary salespeople from a well-known and well-respected company may have entry into the buying center to discuss new products, which triggers the buyers' recognition that they indeed have such a need. Missionary salespeople from an unknown or start-up company may not be given such an opportunity or may have to work harder to obtain entry.
- *Determine product specifications.* The designers for the customer may design around component products from a well-known supplier; thus the recognized brand may be the standard by which the specifications are set. Assistance and design input from missionary sellers of the known brand will be strongly considered. The well-known supplier often has permission to participate at a more intense level than the unknown supplier. An unrecognized brand will probably have to go through extensive testing and competition against other products before the designers feel secure in specifying it as a standard.
- *Acquire solution providers.* The list of suppliers from whom to invite bids will most likely include the well-known companies. If the list of proposals does not include a branded player, the buyer may specifically request a bid from a brand name player so that a benchmark is established or so that upper-level management will sign off on the proposals allowing the selection process to proceed.
- *Cull the bids/proposals to a short list.* The well-known supplier gets the benefit of the doubt for inclusion on the short list or may be included for comparison purposes. If a choice exists between a recognized brand and an unknown supplier, all other things being equal, the name brand will usually get the nod.
- *Evaluate the short list, or get revised proposals/bids.* Evaluations of name brands are given more weight or are trusted more than proposals from lesser-known companies.
- *Cut the short list to finalists.* Again, the name brand may be included for comparison, may get the benefit of the doubt, may be evaluated higher because its figures are better known or trusted, and may win any ties. The brand name may be included to give the lesser-known brands more legitimacy. (It is easier to explain the list to upper-level management if it includes at least one name that is known.)
- *Presentations.* The name brand may be treated with more deference or respect; holes in the presentation may be assumed away. The claims from lesser-known companies may be subjected to closer scrutiny.
- *Final evaluation and choice.* The well-known company wins ties. Higher price for name brand may be tolerated if the brand means higher value to customers (e.g., Intel); the name brand may have more negotiating power to obtain various concessions from the buyer; and trust of the name brand will be a factor to consider.
- *Postpurchase relationship.* If satisfaction is good with the well-known company, there is no reason to switch. If there is minor dissatisfaction with the name brand company, the customer may doubt whether the situation could be improved with another supplier. For a lesser-known supplier company, the customer may be inclined to seek outside help or switch suppliers entirely more quickly if results do not live up to the customer's expectations.

In each stage, in each instance of a customer decision, the advantage for a well-known supplier may be small. The accumulated effect in any one customer decision, though, can add up to a sizable advantage. Over time, too, having a slight advantage in a large number of customer decisions will result in a sizable number of wins for the well-known company.

Branding as a Standard

The ideal state for a marketer to reach is to have her product or service specified as the **standard**. Every other potential competitor then has to show it meets or exceeds the specifications and that its overall offering has better value. Even if the brand has not been attributed standard status, having a known and respected brand brings competitive strength into the buying process.

Industrial products are often established by initial users as a defacto standard for that product type. Just as one might say "make a Xerox" when we actually mean make a *copy* (using equipment from Canon, Kodak, or another manufacturer), brands such as Loctite (anaerobic adhesives), Velcro (plastic hook fasteners), Plexiglas (brand of acrylic sheet), and others have set industrial standards. While generic forms of these products exist, the brand itself has become jargon for the type of product and the expectation for product performance.

Under these circumstances, brands become a specification standard, often noted in "engineering call-outs" as "Velcro #XXX or equivalent" or "Lexan 500 or equivalent" (*engineering call-outs* is a "shorthand" term simply referring to design engineers' specification of materials and parts on the engineering drawings of devices). The use of the brand as the standard creates shortcuts for purchasing and engineering, but also could lead to brand proliferation and the loss of differentiation; therefore, the understanding of its development and conscious brand management is required for continuous success. (All trademarks, such as Xerox, Velcro, Plexiglas, Makrolon, and Lexan, are owned by their respective companies.)

How does a manufacturer's brand become a standard? The following discussion offers some possibilities.

FIRST WITH NEW TECHNOLOGY A new technology often requires extensive manufacturer assistance for application (the role of missionary sales is critical to the product's success). Branding of the product at this point reinforces its use as jargon (what else will the customer call it—manufacturer X new product number XXX?) The customer needs to be told what to call the thing. Future similar or copycat products will be called by the first manufacturer's brand. (At this point, it becomes critical for the first manufacturer to take steps to formally and legally protect the brand, while not discouraging its *informal* use in discussions. Note that many of the product names mentioned here are trademarks of their respective manufacturers.)

Return again to Sensacon and the supply of the SensorSUV to sport utility vehicle manufacturers (Chapter 8). Customer laboratories, or an independent investigatory body as selected by design engineering, will be asked to verify the performance of SensorSUV, based on samples and performance data supplied by Sensacon. The lab will work with the manufacturer to develop the standard, based on the accepted performance of the sensors as previously approved. Once this standard specification is completed and accepted, copycat products will be required to meet it. This standard is "owned" by the first manufacturer—Sensacon. The copycat manufacturer will always be faced with the question "Does your sensor do everything that SensorSUV does?" (Important even if the customer does not necessarily need all the things that SensorSUV can do, tailoring of the product—also known as cost reducing—occurs later in the life cycle and is motivated by a customer need to reduce the manufacturing cost of the product that has had the sensor incorporated into it.)

BEING BEST WITH SERVICE   When it absolutely, positively has to be there overnight, we "FedEx it"—whether it goes via UPS, DHL, or some other carrier. FedEx established a service niche that is not questioned under any circumstance and thus helped create this standard. This level of commitment must also be applied to tangible products, parts, components, and so on. Sensacon must realize that the technology edge does not suffice to create the brand. Market ownership is necessary. (Market share *does not* equal market ownership.) Why did the customer specify Sensacon? Without excellent service, product education, application assistance, and general application development hand-holding, the customer would find other devices (not copies or direct replacements for Sensacon but devices that can fill the need when included as part of the design process) that meet the requirements.

The danger of a customer using alternative devices in the design of its product is particularly acute when the alternative is a proven product in the eyes of the designer. Whenever there is any doubt, the customer is likely to use what it is already familiar with. A new adhesive may be entirely appropriate (e.g., less costly, lighter weight, etc.) to hold an assembly together, but it is only as good as the confidence that the customer has in it.

INNOVATING THE NEED—NOT THE TECHNOLOGY   As SensorSUV matures and becomes known throughout the customer base, less application development is necessary on the part of Sensacon. However, users of SensorSUV will begin to look to the next generation of *their* product and how it can be enhanced. This enhancement can lead to a need for a next generation sensor. This next generation product, if it is to be truly new, may require new technology, style, and materials and/or have different performance requirements. By serving the need and not the product, the SensorSUV brand becomes known as a solution rather than a component part.[10]

Internal marketing is more than the part of the marketing effort that creates newsletters inside of the organization. Just as positioning products in target markets, is an important part of brand building, positioning the product and organization with employees and internal stakeholders is critical. These stakeholders are the "face" of the organization and its brands. Their attitude, appearance, and belief in brand are contextually important the brand message.

LIVING THE BRAND   Contextually, many of the above-mentioned elements are integrated into a strong market-driven organization. As these elements contribute to brand differentiation, the effort must be greater than an external campaign. **Internal marketing** plays an important role in brand consistency. This must spread across not just product and OEM channels, but must be in installation, service, logistics, after-sale communications, and so on.[11]

Defending the Brand

Obviously, if SensorSUV is a profitable item, there will be imitators, either copycats trying to be the low-cost producer or modifiers trying to slightly move the technology envelope—at least enough to meet all the properties of SensorSUV while enhancing their own product's attractiveness. A key idea for defending the brand is to "reach out and touch" *everyone* at all levels of the customer organization. Some thoughts on how to make defending the brand easier follow.

• *Market up.* As the specifying influence moves through the process of establishing SensorSUV as the product of choice, the missionary seller should build relationships with management above the influencers to reinforce the decision process (as well as to learn more about what is going on at the customer—but that is another topic).

• *Market down.* SensorSUV will have to pass several hurdles in the customer's organization. Laboratories will test the product; manufacturing will manipulate the product; and purchasing will, eventually, buy the product. Technicians in the lab will appreciate attention from the missionary sellers. The lab personnel are often ignored, not only by specifying influences but by suppliers. Yet, lab people can make or break a product. (Do you test that fabric horizontally or vertically for the flammability test? Does color make a difference? What is the value image of this supplier? Who are they? How long did the samples take to get here? etc.)

- *Market sideways.* The first specifier of SensorSUV should not be the only specifier. If SensorSUV is used in a breakthrough (or otherwise significant) customer product, that customer product should (with the customer's concurrence) be used as a demonstration of SensorSUV's capabilities. This translation of an initial success should be featured in print promotion, at trade shows, and at any other promotion opportunity in which influencers at other potential customers can be exposed. Make SensorSUV a wagon that people want to ride. ("Nobody ever got fired for specifying SensorSUV.")

The SensorSUV example operates in a market where the customers are manufacturers of SUVs. The customers face a market that is an oligopoly; this means that SensorSUV faces a market in which it has only a few potential customers. Specification of a component part in the design for a new vehicle almost automatically makes that brand a standard. Becoming a standard when the customers' market is characterized by monopolistic competition is more difficult and time consuming. Because each customer is looking for unique ways to differentiate itself and because there are a lot of customers, it is difficult to get agreement among the industry participants to declare something as a standard. In many industries, there are standards bodies comprised of customers and suppliers. To avoid accusations of antitrust collusion, these standards groups work hard to create standards that do not convey monopoly status or unfair advantage to any of the participants. Very often, standards bodies will continue to confer until the market has largely declared a winner. At other times, standards are written so that only product interfaces are standard; the product itself can be unique. In other cases, a standard must be declared before the industry can move ahead. In such cases, a neutral solution is usually found in which all participants can choose to participate.

SUBORDINATE BRANDS   Earlier in the discussion of brand architecture (Exhibit 13-6) we noted that "corporate" or family brands seek to provide overall consistency. As consumers, we have overall impressions of the Intel and AMD brands, but both companies have established additional brands to aid the positioning of various products. When we hear *Intel Core* or *Phenom II* we understand the reference to a high-end computer processor. On the other hand, when hearing Intel *Celeron* and the AMD *Sempron* we recognize a lower performance, albeit lower cost processor. These *subordinate brands* serve to protect the premium Intel Core and Phenom brand positioning. In a price war, the first combatants are Celeron and Sempron.

Many business-to-business companies have established the same branding strategy. Companies such as 3M and General Electric continually reinforce their corporate image. However, within GE product lines will be strategic brands that define price points and overall value. Imitators in the markets served by GE and 3M will often use price as a major part of their total offering, particularly when the established brand is known as the "standard" in that industry (see "branding as a standard" above). Competitors try to be "as good as" the standard but at a lower price. Particularly in the growth stage, customers will not be as aware of the overall value of the industry standard, or may not need "all" of its properties. In many instances, rather than ignore this less than premium market, suppliers will create subordinate brands to offer. These brands are used to not only provide broader market coverage, but to protect high-end brands that have premium price and positioning. Typical examples are the 3M *Spartan* brand (to broaden the line and protect *Scotch*) and GE Noryl Resin (to broaden the GE Plastics line and protect Lexan polycarbonate resin). Not just a product strategy or just a price strategy, these subordinate brands are part of an integrated long-term market strategy.

BUILDING A STRONG BRAND

Strong brands take time to build unless special circumstances prevail. A start-up or young company without a brand reputation has the opportunity to become a standard in markets like the one faced by Sensacon. In other markets, principally early markets in which there is no established competition, a young company can also build market ownership and brand reputation quickly. Without special circumstances, the company must expend considerable effort to build a strong reputation. In established markets in which young companies compete against companies with strong brands, young companies are at a disadvantage because they have no brand recognition or reputation. Consequently, from an early point in time, the young company needs to think about whether and how it should build its brand. In general, unless a company is going to be a low-cost, low-price supplier, a strong brand reputation will translate into competitive advantage.

For established companies, strong brands are an asset to be enhanced and supported. A company with a poor reputation will find it difficult to overcome that reputation for two reasons. First, proposals offered will be discounted in the minds of the buying center. Consequently, even if the company has solved the problems that have led to a poor reputation, it will receive relatively few chances to prove its mettle. Second, when it does obtain the chance to prove it has solved its problems and it performs well, the customer may be inclined to diminish the positive results based on past history. It will take a series of positive outcomes before the blemished reputation of the past dissipates.

Brand strength is generally made up of brand recognition or **awareness**, quality of the products or services, and the customers' positive beliefs—**associations**—linked to the brand.[12] In business-to-business markets, awareness adds little until the company's value chain is established so that superior value is created for customers.[13] So, building brand strength is a relatively long-term process that revolves around building value for customers first, from which come positive associations about the product and company, and then building broader awareness.

Note that positioning is a particular aspect of brand building. It involves matching the product and directed message with the most important needs of the target market segment (see segmentation, Chapter 7). It is a position that is maintained for a period of time and evolves into a set of associations linked to the brand. The essentials of brand building include creating strong products and communicating this to the appropriate target markets.

Building Associations

Brands are basically symbols. People use symbols to represent clusters or bundles of information that are related to the things the symbols stand for. They can then efficiently compare and evaluate alternatives by considering the symbols that represent those alternatives. People in a buying center tend to make holistic judgments concerning the entity represented by the symbol, based on all the associations attached in their minds to those symbols. The most powerful associations come from customers' direct experiences. If these are numerous and positive, the holistic evaluation will be positive. The ideal situation is for everyone in the buying center to have at least a few positive experiences with the company and its products or services. If the experiences of the people in the buying center have not been uniformly positive then the political dealings within the buying center can be detrimental. This suggests that the sales team and service personnel have an important impact not only on the immediate outcome of a customer's buying decision but on the outcome of future situations as well. The effect of advertising and other less-personal communications has an impact on brand perceptions but without the robust and durable character of personal contacts.

Brand associations are not so hard to create as they are to control. Every time customers interact with a supplier, use its product, or interact with a customer service person, impressions are formed. Every time they see an advertisement, hear a news story, or talk to someone who has an opinion, impressions are formed. However, memory is selective. They may not remember what the marketer wants them to remember, so the marketer has to try to be as consistent as possible in all the messages delivered. These messages also have to be consistent with the customers' own experiences. Ultimately, customers' experiences with the product or service will be the things that they will remember most. Accordingly, making those usage experiences as positive as possible is critical for the marketer.

The communications part of association building, then, has to do with managing expectations. Too much hype can create expectations that are hard to meet. This is one of the problems that Apple faced with its Newton. Everyone was expecting this wondrous device, when wondrous was not about to be delivered until version 3 or so. Underplaying the value created by the company's new product is also problematic. If customers do not believe they will get much value, then few will be inclined to try it. This is not as bad as overblown hype where the aftereffects of unmet promises can live on for years. In planning the effort to build a strong brand, then, the marketer must first understand what associations customers currently have about the company and its offerings. Then, the marketer must decide what associations the company would want customers and prospective customers to have in the future. The marketer must then determine what combination of experiences and messages is most likely to achieve the desired change in the customers' and prospects' minds.

Quality

Quality is the only type of association that is directly related to profitability, as determined by researchers in the area of strategic management.[14]

Quality has special meaning: it is *perceived* quality from the point of view of the customer. Further, quality can be thought of as the ability to provide appropriate value from the customer's point of view. Hence, "durability" when durability is not needed is not quality; "aesthetically pleasing" when aesthetics are not valued is not quality; and so on. So, high quality means having the ability to perform very well on the most important dimensions *as determined by targeted customers*.

To create quality, companies must know their targeted customers very well to understand what it is that means quality to them. Second, the company must have a fair amount of creativity to be able to turn the customer's vision of quality into a product or service while being able to keep costs under control.

If the marketer wants to create associations that denote quality, it is important that the company communicate this; and the product has to perform when the customer uses it, or the service must provide superior satisfaction.

Ingredient Branding

Ingredient branding—or "InBranding"[15]—is one of the most promising branding strategies for business-to-business companies. Generally, it is exactly what the name implies: an essential ingredient or component of a product that has its own brand identity.

Ingredient branding is a special form of cobranding—the joint presence of at least two or more brands on a single product or service. The scope of possible cobranding approaches can range from a mere temporary joint promotional effort up to the organizational linked development of completely new and innovative products. The regular cobranding approach is mainly used for consumer products and services; application in business-to-business marketing tends to be quite restricted. An example of industrial cobranding is the joint venture of Pitney Bowes and Royal Mail (UK postal system), to offer customized document management and mailroom-related services in the UK; another is the alliance of Amazon.de with DHL in order for each to benefit from the positive image of the partner.

Examples of popular ingredient branding range from clothing (Gore-Tex, Lycra), carpets (Stainmaster), diet soft drinks (NutraSweet), and packaging (TetraPak) to bicycle gears (Shimano), sound systems (Dolby), as well as gasoline and chemicals (Techron, Microban) promoting the inclusion of a value-enhancing, branded ingredient. Of course, we cannot leave out the ultimate, widely quoted best practice example of ingredient branding which we will consider in detail at the end of this chapter: Intel. In the following section we will provide you with the basic information on how InBranding works and how to position it in the overall marketing concept.

While ingredient branding is a form of multistage branding, most business-to-business companies only use single-stage marketing approaches. They direct their marketing efforts only to the next stage in the value chain, to their direct customers. Multistage or ingredient branding is directed at two or more downstream stages of the value channel.

The basic underlying promotional principle that makes ingredient branding work is the pull principle. According to the pull principle, the manufacturers of the ingredient brand direct their communication efforts directly to the final consumers, thereby bypassing the manufacturers of the finished product. The main idea is to create consumer demand for the ingredient at the retail level, so that consumers pull the product through the distribution channel, forcing middle stages to use the ingredient. In some very successful cases, the ingredient brand may even become the standard in the product category.

Exhibit 13-8 displays the push–pull principle. A push strategy means that an ingredient manufacturer concentrates his marketing efforts on promoting his products to the manufacturers of the finished goods. In order to support the branded ingredient effectively, a manufacturer should always use a coordinated push and pull program. The pull strategy helps consumers to understand the importance and advantages of the InBrand while the push strategy aims to strive for full support by all channel members. Without the support of the subsequent stages of the value chain, an ingredient branding strategy can rarely be successful.

General targets of ingredient branding approaches are materials or parts that enter into final branded products, but lose their individual identity on the way. In order to step out of such an anonymous position, manufacturers attempt to establish ingredient brands that increase awareness and preference for their products.

Not every ingredient can be successfully pushed or pulled. Does anybody really care about what kind of lubricants his favorite car brand uses in its manufacturing process? Not really, so it is obvious that there are certain requirements and restrictions that have to be taken into consideration when thinking about implementing an ingredient branding strategy. The most important aspect is that the "ingredient" should capture an essential part of the end product. Intel processors, for instance, are regarded as the "heart" of the personal computer. The ingredient should be perceived as important and relevant by consumers and, thus, contribute to the performance and success of the end product. The InBrand has to be clearly marked with a

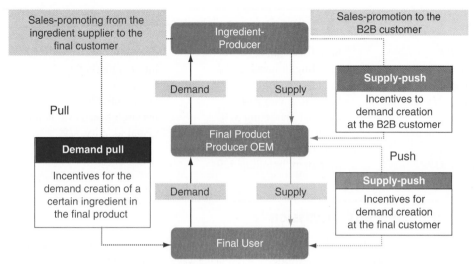

EXHIBIT 13-8 Push and Pull by InBranding *Source*: Philip Kotler and Waldemar Pfoertsch, *B2B Brand Management* (Heidelberg, NY: Springer Publishing September 2006)

distinctive symbol or logo on the end product. Consumers need to be aware that the respective product contains this ingredient.

In addition, brand alliances provide companies with a large number of potential advantages. By capturing two sources of brand equity, brand alliances can tremendously enhance the value proposition and points of differentiation of all products and services involved. With equally strong and complementary brand associations, the impact of cobranding can be even greater than expected. Such beneficial synergy effects of combined brand power might also allow greater freedom to stretch.

THOUGHTS TO TAKE WITH YOU INTO THE NEXT CHAPTER

Introducing the brand management paradigm to business-to-business companies is a great step forward, but requires the reallocation of resources and the hiring of professional marketing managers. Currently there are not too many marketing experts who understand branding, except if they have business-to-business experience.

Branding gives the marketers the opportunity to produce more value for the customer and the company. As discussed in this chapter, it is necessary to understand the principles of branding, apply them in the business situation, and continuously modify them.

Branding is a key part of marketing entrepreneurially. By marketing with branding, proactive efforts, controlled risk taking, and attention to opportunities, marketers should be able to compete on both value and time. Applying branding and measuring results is a crucial step of enhancing the company's future perspectives.

In reading Chapter 14, and beyond, you should keep in mind what branding can provide to business-to-business marketing. Chapter 15, on communicating with the market will deepen your understanding of business-to-business value creation and give you key ideas to keep in mind when you land in a challenging job in one of these arenas.

Key Terms

associations *328*

awareness *328*

brand architecture *317*

brand building *319*

brand functions *312*

brand management *316*

brand image *317*

brand strategy *317*

brand strength *328*

branding dimensions *315*

branding triangle *314*

buyer behavior *324*

external marketing *320*

financially driven approaches *321*

holistic branding *312*

ingredient branding *329*

interactive marketing *320*

internal marketing *326*

loyalty *313*

push–pull *330*

research-based evaluation *321*

visual identity *319*

Questions for Review and Discussion

1. What are the benefits created by branding?
2. How does business-to-business branding differ from consumer products branding?
3. Why should you approach branding in a holistic way?
4. What are the important business-to-business brand functions?
5. What roles do brands play for a company's offering?
6. Why should marketing apply the branding triangle?
7. Why should a business-to-business marketer care about building a strong brand?
8. Why is it advantageous to have your brand designated as a standard by a customer's purchasing process?
9. How are positive associations for a brand established in the memory of persons in the customer's buying center?

10. Can a business-to-business marketer be innovative in the way a brand is built?
11. What are requirements for ingredient brandings, and what are current examples?
12. What industries are more inclined to use ingredient branding?
13. Many positive aspects of ingredient branding have been discussed. What are some of the potential problems?
14. Why is it important to choose an ingredient branding partner carefully? What factors must be considered beyond short-term market effectiveness?

Endnotes

1. Based on China Daily Report (April 17, 2006), p. 3; Hoovers Report ITT (2007); ITT Corporation Press release White Plains, N.Y. (March 19, 2008).
2. Philip Kotler and Waldemar Pfoertsch, *B2B Brand Management* (Heidelberg, NY: Springer Publishing, September 2006).
3. Adapted from D.A. Aaker and E. Joachimsthaler, *Brand Leadership* (New York: The Free Press, 2000).
4. Kotler and Pfoertsch, *B2B Brand Management*, p. 55.
5. See Chapter 3.
6. Nick Pauley Design Brand Check (2008) download under http://www.pauleydesign.co.uk/PD_gd_brandcheck.pdf

7. Kotler and Pfoertsch, *B2B Brand Management*, p. 66.
8. David A. Aaker, "Measuring Brand Equity Across Products and Markets," *California Management Review*, 38 (Spring 1996), pp. 102–120.
9. Singfat Chu and Hean Tat Keh, "Brand Value Creation: Analysis of the Interbrand-Business Week Brand Value Rankings," *Marketing Letters*, 17 (2006), pp. 323–331.
10. If your company is strictly known as a technology company, technology innovation is necessary, though not sufficient, for success. The argument that "we are focused on our high-technology product—that's why customers buy from us" is a dangerous position. In fact, the technology-oriented organization will have branding as a

more important task, as their product is expected to make a value statement rather than be a "me-too" product. The "me-too" organization can focus on manufacturing efficiencies, distribution economies, and alternative cost (read "lower") positions with purchasing departments. Ironically, the technology-oriented company must establish a brand position or become a low-cost producer of maturing products.

11. Kotler and Pfoertsch, *B2B Brand Management*, p. 125. As an example, Canon insists that its repair personnel wear a white shirt and tie, not only as a sign of their professionalism, but to reinforce the ease of use and service of their products. It just wouldn't be right for the repairperson to show up greasy and dirty, covered in toner, from the last repair.

12. David A. Aaker, *Building Strong Brands* (New York: The Free Press, 1996).

13. Kathryn Dennis, "A Q&A with Regis McKenna," *Marketing Computers*, 20(12) (December 2000), p. 38.

14. C.f. Robert D. Buzzell and Bradley T. Gale, *The PIMS Principles* (New York: The Free Press, 1987).

15. Waldemar Pfoertsch, Cheryl Ann Luczak, Frederik Beuk, and Jennifer D. Chandler, "InBranding: Development of a Conceptual Model," *Academy of Marketing Studies Journal*, 11(2) (2007), pp. 123–135.

Chapter *14*

Channel Relationships and Supply Chains

OVERVIEW

We discussed buyer and seller behavior in business-to-business relationships, market research and competitive analysis, and new product development and pricing in previous chapters—all in the context of delivering value to the customer. In this chapter, we focus on that delivery function. Marketing channel intermediaries are necessary to make the connection between customer and supplier. Whether done through intermediaries or directly between supplier and customer, the functions and activities that form this channel comprise the "place" component of the marketing mix. This chapter's examination of the complexities of marketing channels and how the different elements come together includes an emphasis on the development of networks of partners to create value for customers.

Effective marketing channel designs and efficient business logistics systems are often the elements of an offering that provide the winning edge in competitive situations. A well-designed and well-developed marketing channel effectively provides, in a manner and form acceptable to the customer, attributes in the offering that reach beyond the core product. The logistics system, part of the channel design, delivers the core product at the right time and place, again as determined by the customer. Customers in different target markets require different combinations of channel services. As a result, unique channel designs are often required to effectively satisfy different markets. The opening story, a classic example, demonstrates how a successful company targeted a new market but did not develop a new marketing channel to reach that market.

The Apple Lisa

In 1983, Apple Computer introduced the Lisa computer. This new desktop computer was the first major new product to follow the successful Apple II line of personal computers. The Lisa initially had a $10,000 price tag. Priced at this level, the system was obviously meant for large commercial or

334

business users. Apple introduced the Lisa through the same channel that had been successful with the Apple II computer line.

The Lisa was a major sales disappointment. Apple, the company that earlier had successfully introduced the personal computer to an embryonic market, had now failed with its first premium, business-oriented computer. While Apple enthusiasts were stunned, potential business customers seemed uninterested.

What happened? Among other problems, Apple failed to recognize that the business target market would have a different set of needs and expectations associated with the purchase of a computer.[1] Different target markets usually demand a different set of services and, thus, a channel design focused at providing those services. The marketing channel for the Apple II line of computers, comprised of independent computer dealers, had contributed to the success of the product. The target markets for these early computers were schools and, to a large extent, home users. The home Apple user was likely to be more interested in the computer as a technology device in itself than in the functionality of the device. This hobby or enthusiast attitude—the technophiles of the home computer market—was well served by the independent dealer network as many had entered the business as would-be "hackers" themselves. Business users, however, want the computer itself to be "invisible" while accomplishing the required business support tasks. Differences from the home market in user training, product information, product support, financing, delivery, and many other facets of the total offering, combined with a lack of awareness or ability of independent channel members to satisfy these needs, contributed to this major product failure for Apple. Had Apple recognized this difference, it should have been obvious that its current channel design was ill-equipped to approach the business market. Was Lisa a "good product"? Because of the poor channel design, we will never really know.

LEARNING OBJECTIVES

By reading this chapter, you will:

- Understand the principles of market channel design and the delivery of economic utility—form, time, place, and possession—to customers.

- Understand value networks and the relationship to marketing channels.

- Understand classical vertical integration patterns and the value network alternative.

- Understand the fundamentals of business logistics and how these principles are being applied in today's global supply chains.

- Recognize the importance of building channel relationships from the view of providing economic utility and developing sustainable value networks.

- Have gained an understanding of how the Internet can enhance the value that marketing channels can provide to customers.

- Have obtained an appreciation for the limits of applying information technology to enhance marketing channels.

- Know when and how the Internet can provide competitive advantage by enhancing marketing channels and when application of Internet technologies will not provide a competitive advantage.

INTRODUCTION

Primary channel participants are those intermediaries such as wholesalers, distributors, retailers, agents, and brokers who are part of the proactive marketing design of the channel. These intermediaries can have responsibilities associated with presale customer contact, sales, customer service, and transactions in the channel. Primary channel participants form a vital link between the supplier and the final user of goods and services.

Ancillary channel members are those businesses and service providers whose efforts have been traditionally viewed as somewhat generic but without which the channel could not work. Marketers often do not consider which trucking company products will be shipped on, just that the channel design will include trucking as part of its logistical requirements. A similar approach is used regarding financing, storage, promotion, and other facilitating services. Marketers specify the function in the channel design, not necessarily the specific provider.

A direct channel is formed when the supplier markets and sells directly to the buying organization or end user. No additional primary intermediaries are involved.

Marketing channels comprise the *place* element of the marketing mix. A **marketing channel** is the means to manage the presale contact, transaction, and fulfillment activities between the supplier and the final buyer. The original supplier of a product or service can provide the channel value, or the value may be provided through one or more channel intermediaries—organizations that perform channel functions between the original supplier and the final buyer. Without the place element of the four Ps—whether supplied directly or through intermediaries—the customer cannot realize the value contained in the supplier's product or service.

Place involves many organizations—**primary channel participants** and **ancillary channel members**—that are independently owned and operated. These organizations, while participating in the channel, may very well have internal goals that are not always consistent with the goals of the channel leader. Combine this with a natural resistance to change among well-established operating organizations, and *place* becomes a very difficult part of the marketing mix to alter.

The channel is usually direct in supplier–customer relationships in which the volume of business is large, particularly in relationships between a supplier and an original equipment manufacturer. The sales force, market development, customer service operation, and delivery system of the manufacturer form a **direct channel** with appropriate corresponding parts of the customer organization. For instance, Dana Corporation, a major manufacturer of transmissions and chassis components to the automotive industry, does not go through intermediaries to supply automobile parts to General Motors. Rather, they form a direct channel in which Dana sales and marketing personnel work directly with GM engineers, buyers, and other stakeholders in the buying center. General Motors places orders directly with Dana; Dana manufactures and ships the parts directly to GM; and Dana personnel handle the GM account.

When the target market segment is not oligopolistic—not dominated by a few, large participants, suppliers may not be able to provide the total offering desired by the market and still provide superior value. The high handling costs and smaller order quantities associated with serving the many geographically dispersed and smaller customers in such target markets make it unlikely that the costs of a direct relationship will be recovered. In such circumstances, channel designs other than direct channels are necessary.

THE RATIONALE FOR MARKETING CHANNELS

Why have channel intermediaries? Couldn't the supplier do directly everything that channel members could? The answer lies partially in the economic theory of division of labor. A specialist is usually more adept at providing a service when that service is the main offering of the business. When serving dispersed customers who buy a large assortment of goods associated with the market segment, but buy in small quantities, intermediaries often have efficiencies, special skills, or special circumstances that upstream suppliers do not have.

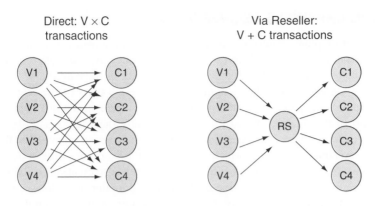

Direct: V × C transactions   Via Reseller: V + C transactions

V = Vendors; C = Customers; RS = Reseller

EXHIBIT 14-1   Channels Can Create Efficiency

Another example of the value of intermediaries is the reduction in transaction costs and complexity. As shown in Exhibit 14-1, the number of transactions is cut considerably by selling through a distributor, reducing overall selling costs and the opportunities for error. The ability of the intermediary to purchase in quantity to serve a bundle of small users, rather than each user making a direct purchase, lowers costs to users because the intermediary can take advantage of quantity-scaled pricing.

Customers in different market segments may have different expectations about the level of services that are provided with purchases. As a result, different target segments may require differing channel structures. The classic example of the Apple Lisa illustrates what can happen when the target segment wants and expects services that the channel is not able to provide. The existing Apple channel served home users who usually purchased individual units, but the target market for the Lisa was large- and medium-sized businesses more likely to purchase in large quantities. The home user was likely an innovator or early adopter of home computers, somewhat enamored with the technology. The institutional buyer, however, was likely far more pragmatic, requiring functionality and ease of use instead of hot technology.

Apple's existing consumer product channel was not particularly well suited to the value sought by the target market. We can see how this might be done better, though, using the Dana example. The relationship with large customers—the OEM market—requires a particular set of services and is identified as a separate target market in the Dana segmentation scheme. The product is custom tailored to the specific customer application. While Dana may supply, for instance, the four-wheel drive transfer case for SUVs to both GM and Ford, the designs are the result of collaboration with each customer and are unique. However, these transfer cases are not only delivered in large quantities as components to the vehicle manufacturers' assembly facilities, but enter the service market—repair shops—as well. The service and repair segment has very different demands related to economic utility. Repair shops want one component, individually packaged and locally available for quick delivery. Thus, the marketing channels for these two segments—the OEM segment and the service segment—must deliver different levels of form, time, place, and possession value (see "dual distribution" later in this chapter).

MARKETING CHANNELS DELIVER VALUE

Successful marketing plans require significant channel development and planning, if they are to provide superior value as perceived by the final customer. As we have seen in the Apple example, the importance of "how the customer gets the product" is often overlooked by both novice and experienced marketers, and the recognition that different parts of the offering (services, financing, and so on) may require separate and unique channel activities is often ignored.

In the rest of this section, we examine more closely the value generally provided by channels. This reinforces why channel design and management are so important to the marketing strategy and its execution. Channels principally provide the four kinds of economic utility that we have discussed many times throughout this text. Channels also create costs, both for the supplier and for the customer, in the creation of this utility. Supplier- and channel-incurred costs must be recouped from revenue in a way that they have a minimum effect on the price that can be charged. Customer costs associated with the channel subtract from the total value realized by the customer. Accordingly, channels must be designed and managed in a way that controls channel costs and allocates the savings among customers, channel members, and suppliers.

Economic Utility

The ideal product not only satisfies core customer needs but also is part of a total offering that is provided in the correct quantity, at the right time and place, and in a manner that fits the routine of the customer. This sort of value provided by the offering has been called *economic utility* and has four parts—*form*, *time*, *place*, and *possession*. Often, the supplier can create differentiation by uniquely providing these four kinds of value through the marketing channel. At a minimum, all four elements of value must be created for the marketing strategy to succeed.

Form, time, place, and possession in business-to-business markets are described subsequently. Economic utility is part of place in the four Ps of marketing. The relationship between the four Ps, the total offering, and economic utility is discussed in Chapter 1.

FORM Form utility is the usable quantity or mode of the product most preferred by the customer. This may be an individual item on a retailer's shelf in the consumer market. In an industrial setting, it might be a specified lot size of industrial components with convenient packaging, containerization, or **palletizing** to accommodate the operations of a customer's manufacturing facility.

Palletizing is the arranging and securing of products on pallets—platforms that can be easily stacked and moved by forklifts—so that the products can be handled, shipped, and deployed for use quickly and easily. Many customers have a particular style or design of pallet that works with the material handling equipment in their facilities. Suppliers are required to provide shipment of goods on compatible pallets.

TIME Time utility describes the availability of the product when the customer needs it. In the consumer market, this may be reflected in a retailer's store hours. In business-to-business markets, just-in-time (JIT) delivery service aimed at minimizing raw materials inventory at the customer is an example.

PLACE Place utility, also known as *locational convenience*, is provided in the consumer market by retailers as several stores in a region or stores clustered with similar outlets of competitors, as demonstrated by the clusters of competing automobile dealers at various "auto rows." In business-to-business markets, place utility might be demonstrated by delivery of component parts directly to the customer's manufacturing site.

POSSESSION Possession is the methodology by which the customer obtains ownership or the right to use of the product or service. In consumer markets, possession may be the variety of methods a customer may pay for an item—cash, check, credit card, or retailer-provided financing. In business-to-business markets, the financing of customer purchases can be a major part of the total offering.

While each of these four types of utility can vary in complexity and degree of intricacy, provision for them must be in every marketing channel. The responsibility for satisfying customer needs associated with form, time, place, and possession may be shifted to other channel members (distributors, wholesalers, manufacturers, etc.), but the functions cannot be eliminated from the channel; if these functions are not provided, chaos in the delivery of value would result.

Channel Flows and Activities That Create Value

How are these economic utilities—the aspects of channel value—created? Suppliers or channel intermediaries may provide one or more of the following services in their effort to provide economic utility:

Marketing and sales flows

- Creating product assortments aligned with customer demand rather than with the manufacturer's product line
- Communicating with customers in both a sales role and as a communication channel between customer and supplier (in the Apple Lisa example, the Apple retailer was unprepared for the buying culture of large institutions)
- Setting and negotiating prices

Product and ownership flows

- Taking temporary ownership, transferring title, handling government documentation and registration, and so on

Installation, training, and service flows

- Providing before and after sales services to customers (the Apple dealer's role in the education process for home users was quite different from the training needs of institutional buyers who would need basic training for actual users of the computer)
- Installing and maintaining complex systems (the institutional buyer would expect installation and testing on-site for all locations)
- Providing systems and services support to channel members (the independent dealer is unlikely to have the staff to support ongoing inquiries from the numerous users of the institution's systems)

Ancillary flows

- Providing financing for customers or for suppliers (the institutional buyer would have different finance needs than the usual Apple user)

Contracted transportation, handling, and storage services

- Contracted promotion services
- Arranging for insurance, financial protection
- Managing information gathering, analysis, and dissemination

*The **channel pattern** is the particular design or arrangement of various intermediaries that perform channel functions. Different circumstances in the target market environment may call for different channel patterns, that is, different types of intermediaries to meet specific requirements. Different types of channel patterns are discussed in the "Channel Design" section.*

These services, shown in Exhibit 14-2a, exist to a varying degree in most channels, but the **channel pattern** that performs the service changes. In the

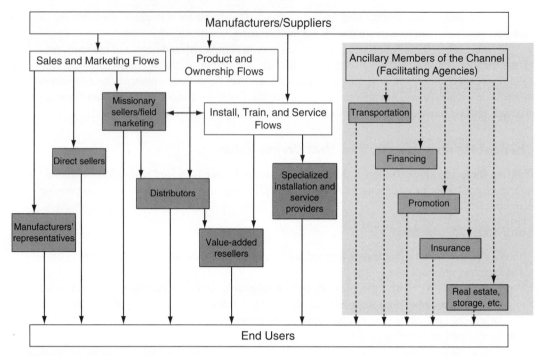

Note: This Exhibit is not intended to imply that all channels contain all flows shown or that all possible flows are shown here.

EXHIBIT 14-2A Marketing Channel Flows—Supplier to Customer

Trade credit is the payment term provided to end users by distributors and other channel intermediaries to finance purchases. Particularly in the purchase of components and materials, small business-to-business customers will rely on trade credit as a way to finance operations.

Different target markets have different expectations regarding the availability and duration of trade credit. Channel members should be aware of market expectations with regard to credit services and manu-facturers should be prepared to grant terms to distributors that aid in this part of the total offering.

Dana example earlier in this chapter, sales and marketing would flow through direct sellers for very large accounts (e.g., GM, Ford), while the service channel would use distributors able to provide the specific needs of repair personnel. Missionary sellers assist the distributors in assortment and quantity decisions and provide product training to distribution personnel.

In the Dana direct channel, customer-specific product flows from the man-ufacturer (Dana) to the customer (GM, Ford) directly. Shipments are likely in large quantities, palletized per customer requirements, and are aided by a contract transportation services provider—an ancillary channel member. Ownership transfers directly between Dana and the end users (note that, in the interests of legibility, a direct line from "ownership" and "end user" is not shown in Exhibit 14-2a). Exhibit 14-2b shows various flows from the customer to the supplier. Naturally, payment flows are of great importance. Payment does not necessarily follow the same path (albeit, in reverse) as product, whether the manufacturer has an in-house financing operation or uses ancillary channel members who provide financing services. The level of importance of the finan-cial institution in the channel is directly related to the level of importance of financing as part of the total offering. Many small businesses rely on the availability of **trade credit** to finance operations.

Previous chapters have discussed the importance of marketers knowing all aspects of the markets served. A major source of customer and market information is the participants in the marketing channel. As shown in Exhibit 14-2b, *all*

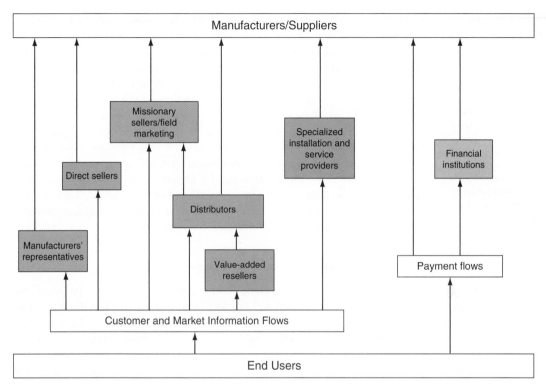

Note: This Exhibit is not intended to imply that all channels contain all flows shown or that all possible flows are shown here.

EXHIBIT 14-2B Marketing Channel Flows—Customer to Supplier

participants, not just those directly related to the supplier, can be a source of information. Channel members' proximity to customers provides a direct source of potentially detailed information that contributes to "bottom-up" market analysis such as the marketing operation forecast discussed in Chapter 11.

Marketing Channels Meet Customer Needs and Expectations

Marketing channel flows of possession, ownership, promotion, negotiation, financing, risk-taking, and market information are organized by intermediaries comprising marketing channels so that goods and services are provided to customers in the form and at the time desired. Just as consumers have favorite methods that meet their particular needs to purchase products and services, businesses have a preferred way they "buy." While the core product may be similar in many cases, different target markets have different expectations of the total offering.

Depending on the resources of the firm and the needs of the target markets, channel designs may include a direct sales force, the use of independent intermediaries (wholesalers, brokers, distributors, manufacturers' representatives, etc.), or any combination of these options, as previously shown in Exhibit 14-2a. These options, often referred to as *channel patterns*, include dealer networks, franchise systems, Internet broker systems, and other various forms of contractual relationships beyond the scope of this discussion. Additionally, there are ancillary functions that every channel design must provide, including but not limited to transportation

Vertical Integration, as used here, refers to the degree of ownership a firm has of its marketing channel. The firm may own distributors of its products and may actually own the organizations that provide ancillary services, such as transportation, inventory control, and financing. Ownership of these facilitating agencies can be efficient through economies of scale but "expensive" when a change in channel design or services are required.

services, insurance, and other financial services. A very large firm with an established channel infrastructure will often elect to perform all of these ancillary services itself. While this may have significant economies of scale, this **vertical integration** limits flexibility. Today, companies desiring greater flexibility often seek specialists to perform ancillary tasks, allowing the firm to concentrate on development of its markets. In the last ten years, we have seen the emergence of "business logistics" providers—grown-up transportation companies who realize that they have more to offer than just moving goods (see Exhibit 14-3 for a discussion of services provided by UPS and FedEx). This channel design technique, called **functional spin-off**, assumes that ancillary services are provided most efficiently by experts in each service[2]—a basic application of the principle of division of labor. For many small firms, using a service provided through functional spin-off allows a lower capital investment, greater flexibility, and a broader range of long-term options.

Industrial Distributors Serve Industrial End Users

Why would an industrial end user want to purchase from a distributor? Wouldn't products cost less by purchasing directly from the manufacturer? For very large customers, when the supplier or manufacturer has the advantage of logistical economies of scale, this is likely true. Suppliers, however, are often unwilling or unable, at a reasonable cost, to provide many services for medium or small customers or those who have irregular usage patterns. Distributors fill the gap, giving attention to and building relationships with medium and small users. These industrial distributors

Two key logistics-driven initiatives employed by United Parcel Service (UPS) put increased pressure on FedEx, formerly Federal Express, in two areas in which they compete. First, UPS has built its capability for providing overnight delivery. The improvements to UPS's system involved integrating overnight airfreight with short- to medium-haul ground transportation via UPS's ubiquitous brown trucks. While FedEx still leads in the overnight express market, UPS, through the integration with its existing ground transport infrastructure, has grown significantly.

The second initiative, begun in 1994, is a logistics services line of business offered for medium- and large-sized companies. Logistics services include supply chain and distribution systems design and management. The group applies new technology where needed, but focuses on achieving desired results with whatever methods are appropriate. This line of business has landed several major global companies as customers and produced dramatic cost and time savings. Meanwhile, FedEx has had to revamp its logistics service operation.

FedEx, through a major expansion of its system, now competes with UPS directly in its ground delivery system. Both companies have forward integrated, acquiring small business and consumer service companies Kinko's (FedEx) and Mailboxes, Etc. (UPS). Each company has used its unique capabilities to compete in the other's primary market. Each is sensitive to and responds directly to the competitive actions of the other. What will be the next battleground?

The lessons from this rivalry include the following:

- Core competencies in logistics can produce competitive advantage.
- New competitive strengths can be built through patient development of new core competencies.
- Traditional markets must be actively and creatively defended.

EXHIBIT 14-3 UPS and FedEx Compete through Focus on Logistics Capabilities *Source:* Charles Haddad, "Ground Wars," *Business Week* (May 21, 2001), pp. 64–68.

develop an understanding of the smaller customers' business that the supplying manufacturer could not achieve through the relationship possible within the profit margins provided by the small purchase volume. The distributor spreads the costs associated with the relationship over several products and product lines, often from many different suppliers. Small- to medium-sized purchasers (these may be large organizations that purchase small volumes of certain items) can receive better customer service from a modern industrial distributor. Within this context, distributors can serve customers in many ways:

- *Provide fast delivery.* Distributors maintain a local inventory of the products from suppliers they represent. Arrangements can be made with customers to provide regular JIT deliveries, allowing the customer to avoid a large resource commitment to incoming inventory.
- *Provide segment-based product assortment.* Distributors can provide "one-stop shopping" to small- and medium-sized industrial customers. A small electronics assembly company may need a variety of components, from circuit board materials to computer chips and all the ancillary components in between. The distributor maintains a product line focused on the needs of its served markets, creating product assortments from many sources.
- *Provide local credit.* Small businesses often find it difficult to obtain financing, particularly during periods of tight money. Most distributors provide trade credit for established customers. It is not unusual for unique payment terms to be a significant part of a distributor's total offering. In many instances, the credit-granting capability of the distributor becomes a major competitive feature.
- *Provide product information.* The electronics assembler in the earlier example may require advice on the application of components or may need instruction about the proper use of supplies. The assembler might be switching to a new soldering method that requires the handling of new solvents. The distributor not only will be a source for the solder, solvents, and ancillary equipment but also will be able to advise regarding their proper use.
- *Assist in buying decisions.* Our electronics assembler may need assistance in the selection of technically equal components from two different manufacturers. The distributor can assist in this selection process. The assembler will seek well-known industrial brands at the inception of a project but may seek an alternative supply as production increases. This not only helps to develop lower cost alternatives but also provides the assembler with a second source of goods should a calamity befall the manufacturer of the industry standard. Distributors of well-known industrial brands seek to include a generic equivalent in their product line. The distributor can then provide both products to the assembler, preventing the assembler from obtaining the generic product from another source. Manufacturers of industry standard products attempt to dissuade their distributors from offering an alternative but often have little choice in the matter. (In consumer markets, distributors often advise retailers regarding "hot sellers" and avoiding "turkeys" from a manufacturer's line. It is in the best interest of the distributor to have profitable, successful customers—that is how the distributor can be sure of getting paid!)
- *Anticipate needs.* By maintaining a close relationship with customers, the distributor can anticipate future needs and have inventory available in a timely manner. Through the relationship, the distributor can know new business opportunities that the customer is pursuing and, in a coordinating effort with the customer, have the necessary materials and supplies available at the right time. The distributor essentially becomes the materials-handling specialist for the customer—another example of functional spin-off, this time by the customer.

Industrial Distributors Serve Industrial Suppliers

Manufacturers benefit from distributor channels, particularly when the manufacturer recognizes the proactive role distribution can play in a well-designed marketing channel. Distributors perform many functions for manufacturers that enable the manufacturers to reach market segments that would be prohibitively expensive to reach otherwise:

- *Buy and hold inventory.* Distributors purchase goods from manufacturers. In this context, distributors are customers of the manufacturers, selecting, buying, and *paying* for goods. With the purchased goods, the distributor provides local inventory for the manufacturer's smaller customers whose order volume and frequency make them too costly to serve directly. The manufacturer is relieved of the financial and logistical responsibility of holding local inventory in the form required by these customers.
- *Combine manufacturers' outputs.* The customers served by distributors usually purchase products of more than one manufacturer from the distributor. The distributor serves many manufacturers by providing assortment and selection to customers based on the needs of the customer segment, not the product line offering of any one manufacturer. In our earlier electronics assembler example, the distributor provides products related to the assembler's business. This may include supplies, such as solder and solvents, worker protective clothing, and electrical components, such as computer processors and memory chips. Manufacturers with narrow product lines may find that distribution with complementary products is the only way to gain exposure with potential customers.
- *Share credit risk.* Manufacturers often provide credit terms to their distributors to enable them to carry and hold inventory. This actually becomes a service to the manufacturer. The risks associated with credit terms extended to the distributor (assuming an ongoing relationship between the manufacturer and the distributor) are significantly less than the risks associated with extension of credit to the many small customers who rely on the distributor for trade credit. The credit granted to the distributor is a significant factor in the distributor's ability to grant credit to its customers.
- *Share selling risk.* Though distributors are often independent businesses who are customers of the manufacturers via the purchase of goods, there is also an underlying assumption that the goods purchased are marketable by the distributor and that marketability has been developed in large part by the manufacturer. The manufacturer is served by this shared risk and partnership—both parties have a stake in the success of the product.
- *Forecast market needs.* Since distributors are much closer to the markets they serve, they are able to provide manufacturers with realistic forecasts of business activity. This enables the manufacturer to better schedule its own production activities.
- *Provide market information.* Beyond market operations forecasts, discussed in Chapter 11, distributors can have a better understanding of unmet customer needs. Working with the manufacturer, new products and services can be devised that enhance the value of both parties to the ultimate customer.

The factors just described and summarized in Exhibit14-4 point to the partnership between distributors and manufacturers. When both sides recognize the possibilities that a strong partnership can create, the customer wins.

Seller Benefits	Buyer Benefits
Buy and hold inventory.	Provide fast delivery.
Combine supplier outputs (reduce discrepancy of assortment).	Provide market segment-based product assortment.
Share credit risk.	Provide local credit.
Share selling risk.	Provide product information.
Forecast market needs.	Assist in buying decisions.
Provide market information.	Anticipate needs.

EXHIBIT 14-4   Enhanced Customer Service—Distributors Serve both Buyers and Sellers

Value Networks Are Marketing Channels

We can think of a value network as encompassing a distribution channel, as shown in Exhibit 14-5. The key thing to recognize is that the distribution channel is only a portion of the value network in most cases. The value network includes the supply chain feeding into the supplier, the partners providing product and service components of the offering, and the distribution channel reaching the final buyer. All of these elements combine to form a final offering for the final customer as well as having a role in contributing value for the final customer.

Recall that value for customers is the sum of the benefits minus the sum of the customer's costs. The incorporation of channel elements into the offering creates certain benefits and imposes certain costs upon customers, which, of course, they evaluate when choosing among competitors' offerings. Before designing channels and determining how channels will be managed, the marketer must understand how channels contribute to value in the offering.

Return to the opening example of the Apple Lisa and the ways that the existing Apple channel could not provide value for the intended target market—corporate buyers of computer systems. Apple Computer's independent dealer network was adept at providing support and services to the Apple II target market but was unable to satisfy the *same needs* of a larger, more intricate target market.

Apple and the iPhone

The Apple entry into the telecommunications market with the iPhone is far more successful than the Lisa was in the business computing market. Just selling the hardware wasn't enough. Apple recognized that customers would need the specialized service capabilities of a major telecommunications carrier and a unique delivery channel. The telecommunications business is a large but specialty market with significant government oversight and regulation. Apple could enter the business directly, though this would require either acquisition or business development, but the market was already undergoing consolidation. Apple created a marketing channel with AT&T, an experienced player with established credentials. Consider all of the factors shown in Exhibit 14-4. Combined, the two organizations can provide a level of service that each independently would be hard-pressed to match. The outcome: a value network that has enhanced the offerings of both companies. Visit www.apple.com/iphone/enterprise and review what you now understand as the value of building and managing relationships. How many of these factors has Apple built in to the "value" of the iphone business-to-business positioning effort?

Does anybody even remember the Lisa?

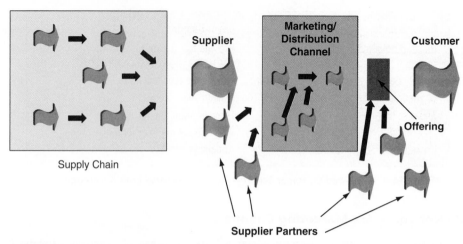

EXHIBIT 14-5 A Value Network

The same needs? Generally speaking, yes, but not the same expectations and demands. Just as consumers have favorite methods that meet their particular needs to purchase products and services, businesses have a preferred way they "buy." While the core product may be similar in many cases, different target markets will have different expectations of the total offering. Look at each of the following channel activities.

USER TRAINING   The home computer buyer most likely purchases a computer for individual use or use within the immediate family. This user seeks out the computer dealer to discuss the features and capabilities of the product. The user does not need "computer for dummies" training. The corporate customer, however, is unlikely to go to the independent computer shop to discuss the purchase. More likely, the institution's buying center has a diverse set of needs and the actual users of the computer want to know how to use "this thing" (remember, this was in 1983). The computer systems supplier is expected to go to the institutional customer. Training in computer fundamentals is necessary on a large scale.

PRODUCT INFORMATION   The home user's enthusiasm for the computer is accompanied by a knowledge of the computer obtained from magazines, user groups, and other sources. At the time of the Lisa introduction, the home user was likely an early adopter of home computing technology. The dealer's role in the education process was probably limited to product technology alternatives and options. An institutional buyer, however, likely expresses needs in terms of what the computer can accomplish, rather than how it accomplishes it. This is an important distinction. While technophiles purchase technology just because it is new, business users are far more pragmatic, requiring functionality and ease of use over technology.

PRODUCT SUPPORT AND DELIVERY   For the home market, the dealer is likely to discuss the product technology with the customer and provide one-on-one technical support. Outside of making sure the buyer leaves the shop with all the necessary cables and computer accessories, the dealer usually does not play a large role in the computer installation. The institutional buyer, however, expects installation and on-site testing for all locations. This is a different expertise and service context than the technical product support at the shop. Often, channel designs for products that require on-site installation and service have separate channel intermediaries to accomplish these needs. Exhibit 14-2a, previously discussed, shows some of the possible channel flows and participants.

FINANCING   A large purchase by the home computer user might include a printer and an external storage device. The extent of financing provided by the independent dealer might be the acceptance of third-party credit cards (Visa, MasterCard, American Express, and so on).

The institutional buying center may have particular finance needs. The acquisition of many computers may be more acceptable as a lease rather than as a purchase, or the buyer might want a payment plan spread over several years. The independent dealer is unlikely to have the financial capability to support the financing portion of the offering.

Apple's existing consumer product channel was not particularly well suited to the value sought by the target market. The product itself may have been very well suited to the target market (debatable, but possible in this case). The different types of value discussed, though—the other kinds of value sought by the market segment—could not be delivered by the channel and so the marketing of the Lisa was problematic. Compare Apple's partnerships to offer iPhones to its partnerships for the Lisa (see box "Apple and the iPhone"). For the iPhone, telecom partners are positioned much better for both consumer and business markets than were Lisa's consumer retailers positioned for business customers.

THE ELEVATION OF BUSINESS LOGISTICS MANAGEMENT TO SUPPLY CHAIN MANAGEMENT

Up to this point in this chapter, the discussion has been focused on the rationale, economic utility, and design of marketing channels. The actual movement and storage of goods, major ingredients in the marketing channel, have been relegated to the mention of ancillary members of the channel. The management of the movement, sorting, and storage of goods in the marketing channel is called **logistics**.

Historically, logistics has been conceived and implemented as an important tactical function focused mostly on meeting customer service goals as efficiently as possible. In today's business environment, logistics design and management is often included in what has come to be called **supply chain management**. The goal of supply chain management is to create value for customers through effective and efficient flow of materials, components, finished goods, and services. The supply chain extends from raw materials through to end-use customers. In theory, the difference between logistics management and supply chain management is that supply chain management can create competitive advantage through the creation of superior value to customers. This value can come from any of the kinds of utility discussed above and in any combination. Logistics on the other hand focuses on value principally through time and place utility, provided at minimum cost. Conceivably, supply chain management could provide higher value to customers, allowing the company to charge premium prices.

Another substantial difference between logistics and supply chain management concerns scope. Logistics deals with materials and goods storage and movement. Supply chain includes these, but also includes dynamics in materials sourcing, production, and service delivery. Supply chain management combines the disciplines of channel management and logistics management. As will be discussed shortly, the theoretical promise of supply chain management has not yet been reached in most instances. Supply chain management still tends to focus on attaining cost efficiencies, even if they tend to detract from customer value. Marketers must recognize that supply chain systems are competitive tools that assist in differentiating the total offering. Like other parts of the total offering, the definitions and requirements for performance will be determined by the customer. Though professional logisticians or supply chain managers will have responsibility for the design and development of the specifics of logistics or supply chain systems, marketers will provide critical input in such efforts.

The Physical Distribution Concept—A Cost–Service Relationship

In designing logistics systems, the economic utilities comprise the kinds of objectives that must be met in performing logistical operations: meeting customer form needs, meeting customer time needs, meeting customer place needs, and meeting customer possession needs. The logistics system must get the right products to customers, in the right quantities, in the right place, at the right time. Logistics must do this in ways that transfer ownership to customers (and to channel intermediaries) at the appropriate time and place.

Logistics systems design includes decisions on inventory management, transportation modes and scheduling, warehouse size and location, physical handling systems, and information handling systems. System design is aimed at minimizing costs while maintaining a given level of customer service. In this effort, managers are concerned with the simultaneous management of three elements:[3]

- Inventory
- Transportation
- Warehousing.

The lowest system cost of these three elements combined will not necessarily be a result of the lowest possible cost of each element. The balance of these three elements to minimize costs at a given level of customer service is called the **physical distribution concept**.

INVENTORY MANAGEMENT   Inventory management is often the largest cost associated with any logistics system. Channel members have significant investment in inventory, and that investment usually implies carrying and finance charges as well as the costs associated with storing and assorting the inventory. Recognizing the high costs associated with large quantities of inventory, tools to minimize these costs are used. Tools such as JIT inventory management, JIT manufacturing and facility location, and electronic data interchange (whether in private networks or facilitated by the Web) are employed. The lower quantity of inventory that can be maintained at any time leads to lower inventory costs. However, lower inventory levels often lead to more frequent and thus more costly transportation.

TRANSPORTATION   Transportation decisions traditionally have involved the choice of water, air, rail, truck, or pipeline utilization, depending on the nature of the product. Slower transportation methods usually have lower costs, with airfreight the highest cost method. Slow transportation methods imply that safety stocks—the amount of inventory available between the time of reordering and the arrival of new inventory—must be of larger quantities than with rapid transportation methods. While other factors can impact lead times, such as particular product and manufacturing circumstances and optimal quantity order sizes, if transportation costs are minimized without regard for the impact on the total system, inventory carrying costs increase.

WAREHOUSING   As the level of inventory increases so does the cost to store it. If low-cost transportation leads to an increased inventory level, then warehouse costs are also increased. If warehouse costs are minimized, transportation costs increase, particularly as suppliers attempt to avoid "stockouts"—running out of goods just as a buyer may require delivery.

Depending on the nature of the products and the goals of the channel design, channel management focuses on two functions of warehousing. The first of these is product flow or movement, and the second is product storage. Channel designs that focus on rapid movement of goods rather than on storage of large quantities of goods use facilities optimized as **distribution centers**. Channel designs that accept slow movement and focus on storage of goods use facilities optimized as **warehouses**.

Distribution centers are optimized to move product through the facility, creating assortment in the process. Materials flowing into the center are immediately redirected to customers. The discrepancy of assortment is reduced, and goods are held for a minimal period of time. Depending on the nature of the goods and the lead times associated with their creation, rapid transportation may be used to replace the need for significant safety stocks.

Warehouses are optimized as storage and assortment creation facilities. If the nature of the goods is such that long-term storage creates an optimal logistical pattern, warehouses are employed. Because inventory quantities are usually larger when the longer-term storage is used, transportation costs can be reduced.

MATERIAL REQUIREMENTS PLANNING   The storage, movement, and assortment of goods in business logistics systems are part of the **materials requirements planning (MRP)** effort, which is now often included within enterprise resource planning systems. While an extensive discussion of MRP practice is beyond the scope of this text, business-to-business marketers should understand the goals of MRP and how suppliers can create value for customers in this area.

Materials resource planning efforts involve many stakeholders in the organization, often some of the same stakeholders that contributed to the buying decision in the buying center. MRP requires forecasting demand on an ongoing basis, aimed at minimizing business logistics costs and the impact of the bullwhip effect while maximizing customer service. Purchasing, manufacturing, transportation, and marketing contribute information to synchronize the various needs of each part of the organization. MRP responsibilities usually reside in the purchasing department of the organization. Successful MRP efforts involve purchasing professionals in the management of the entire supply chain. This presents another opportunity for the supplier to influence the specification and selection process of the buyer.

LOGISTICS AS A COMPETITIVE EDGE   Logistics have become an important part of competitive advantage in most product-oriented industries. Getting the product to the customer faster means that needs of end users can be met more quickly. In the case of component parts, getting the products into the production process faster means that supplier production schedules can more closely match end customer demand, thus reducing inventories, carrying costs, and waste. The discussion of the rivalry between FedEx and UPS, shown in Exhibit 14-3, illustrates the importance of logistics in building or maintaining competitive position.

Economic Utility of Business-to-Business Markets

The examples noted demonstrate the broad array of methods that can be used to provide economic utility in a channel. Note also how different the methods are for business-to-business markets versus consumer markets. In mass consumer markets, economic utility is provided, with much

*Customers should not be required to match the channel and logistics design of the supplier. Suppliers should develop channel designs that seamlessly match the operation of customers. For small customers, this usually involves the use of industrial distributors. For large customers, this involves matching delivery time and methods, palletizing, and other requirements. We use the term **differentially invisible** to imply that the customer should not be required to adapt to the supplier—the process should be invisible. This level of service, part of the total offering, can be a competitive differentiating factor.*

speculation, by a channel design that attempts to anticipate consumer needs. In business-to-business markets, economic utility is often the result of a specific demand by a particular customer—part of "the way a customer buys."

Chapter 3 discussed the process flow model of the buying decision process. The *Deliver Solution Stage* and the *End-game Stage* (as shown in Exhibit 3-3 in Chapter 3), contain elements related to the transactional aspects of the process, shown as analogous to *Make the Transaction Routine* and *Resell the Job* of the classical industrial buyers' decision process. The marketing channel design is a direct result of recognizing and accommodating the materials planning, handling, inventory, scheduling, and invoicing needs of the customer. Part of building a long-lasting relationship with customers is developing a marketing channel that is **differentially invisible** to the customer. A differentially invisible channel meets all of the logistical parameters of the customer. The merging of the two systems is so smooth that the customer does not recognize any differences in operation or style. This can be a significant advantage should the customer ever consider changing suppliers, as customers can incur significant costs associated with changing or adding suppliers. In oligopolistic markets, a supplying firm may have a different customized "routine" for each major customer, as well as a standardized routine for smaller customers. Each of these parts of the total offering is an opportunity to create value for the customer while demonstrating a differential advantage versus the competition.

The box "Supply Chain Design Eliminates Local Inventory" illustrates how a logistics design can create value for a customer and extend business opportunities for channel members.

CHANNEL DESIGN

With value for customers firmly in mind, the business-to-business marketer must design a working channel structure as part of the marketing strategy and plan. Sherlock suggests that the marketer must start with an understanding of the final customer and determine what channel-provided value the customer wants.[4] Then the marketer can begin to design the channel that delivers this value. This sounds like an obvious, even trivial, approach. Too often, though, the marketer begins at the doors of her own company and designs forward to "reach" the customer. Taking this approach, as we saw with the Apple Lisa, can have damaging results.

Intensity of distribution refers to the level of locational convenience required by the target market. Specialty products are usually in exclusive distribution while mature, generic products (whose marketing mix puts more emphasis on convenience factors) are usually in intensive distribution, creating horizontal competitors in the channel.

As we just said, the marketer must know what the customer wants. The marketer must extend this analysis upstream as well. The environmental analysis must also include an analysis of existing and potential marketing channels. The information desired is similar to that collected for customers—their needs, their buying behavior, how they view value, the nature of their buying centers, and so on—but includes an analysis of the value they provide and their internal value chains that produce that value.

In designing the channel, the marketer must decide whether to go through intermediaries or go through a direct channel. Other decisions include the level of **intensity of distribution** (how many distributors within a territory), the kinds of channel partners to obtain, how the channel flows will be structured, and, most importantly, how competitive advantage will be built. Recall from

Supply Chain Design Eliminates Local Inventory

Prior to 1995, J.C. Penney, the large retailer, would routinely hold up to six months of dress shirts in inventory at its regional warehouses and another three months at its stores. This inventory level made it necessary to forecast sales of colors, styles, and the number of shirts well in advance of actual customer purchases. A mistake in these areas was often in place for an entire selling season. This was costly not just from a logistics point of view but also from a customer service standpoint. Today, thanks to a supply chain designed with J.C. Penney's major shirt supplier, stores hold almost no inventory of dress shirts while maintaining the desired level of customer service.

TAL Apparel Ltd., a Hong Kong shirt maker, major J.C. Penney supplier and maker of one out of every eight dress shirts sold in the United States, works directly with retail stores to maintain the most efficient level of inventory. When a shirt is purchased in a Penney retail store, the transaction is downloaded at a TAL factory. A replacement for the purchased shirt is added to the package to be shipped to that retail store. In this process, J.C. Penney corporate decision makers are absent.

Through the 1990s, TAL recognized that new competition from mainland China garment producers could impact its business and sought methods other than price to maintain its relationship with customers. At the time, J.C. Penney kept almost nine months of inventory—roughly twice the level of competitors. TAL proposed a direct link from the customer (the J.C. Penney store) to the manufacturer. Penney, using its own warehouses and employees, spent 29 cents per shirt to sort TAL incoming shipments for distribution to individual stores. TAL could do it at the factory for 14 cents.

By understanding its customer's inventory situation, TAL proposed that Penney turn it all over to them, suggesting that TAL could respond more quickly than Penney to consumer demands. This was a bold step—it was asking Penney to outsource the inventory management of dress shirts. Management resisted, worried about shipping errors, technology incompatibilities, and so on. The proposal sat for years, until senior management began pushing for greater efficiencies throughout the system.

To be done properly such a step includes sales forecasting not just volumes, but styles, colors and variances by region across the country. TAL studied the market for J.C. Penney and, working with IBM as a software and hardware supplier, developed the inventory system from point-of-sale to manufacture. Data is continuously collected from Penney sales and sent directly to TAL. The data is run through the computer model developed specifically for this purpose. TAL then determines how many shirts—by style, color, and size—to make. TAL then sends the shirts directly to the retail store. There is no need for regional inventory, and each assorted shipment is tailored to the forecast demand of the individual retail stores.

While initially reluctant, J.C. Penney has now turned the entire operation, including the design of new shirt styles and subsequent market testing, to TAL.

What happens if a store sells out of a particular style, size, or color? After all, TAL computers determine the ideal inventory for each shirt. If two shirts, in a particular style, size, and color, is the forecast ideal inventory level in a store, what happens if both sell on the same day? TAL manufactures two replacement shirts, ships one by the regular process, and ships the other by air to quickly replenish the store. TAL pays the shipping, Penney gets billed for the shirts, and the customer (Penney and its customer, the consumer) relationship is maintained.

Rodney Birkins, vice president for sourcing of J.C. Penney Private Brands, say the results have been "phenomenal." While on a routine basis, under the old system, Penney would have thousands of shirts warehoused all over the country, the new system cuts inventory to "zero."

Sources: Gabriel Kahn, "Made to Measure: Invisible Supplier Has Penney's Shirts All Buttoned Up," *The Wall Street Journal* (September 11, 2003) Case Studies: IBM boosts quality and productivity at TAL, IBM case studies online, http://www-0-7.ibmcom/hk/e-business/case_studies/manufacturing (April 29, 2007).

Dual distribution is a channel pattern that uses more than one channel design, each intended to reach a different target market. Incorporation of dual distribution is a decision to reach multiple market segments with different economic utility needs. The Dana example earlier in this chapter is an example of dual distribution. Two different channel designs, one direct to the OEM market, the other through intermediaries that reach the service parts market, provide coverage to market segments based on the buying requirements of each segment.

Multidistribution is the deployment of multiple channels of the same design in a given territory. Multidistribution is a decision about the intensity of product placement or distribution.

Chapter 10 that we suggest that marketers innovate across the offering to create competitive advantage. Designing channels is one area where large advantages can be created.

When a manufacturer selects more than one channel intermediary at the same level—such as two industrial distributors in the same market, horizontal competition is created. This channel pattern is called **multidistribution**. The multiple distributors serve the same market segment and compete for the same customers. Manufacturers selecting multidistribution are increasing the *intensity of distribution* for their products. Recall from your principles of marketing course that intensity of distribution refers to the degree to which a product is available from one (exclusive), a few (selective), or several sources (intensive distribution). Multidistribution occurs later in the life cycle of a product when generic forms may be available in the market and locational convenience is of prime importance in the marketing mix.

Reduce Discrepancy of Assortment

Another service provided by channel intermediaries is the creation of assortments based on customer needs rather than on manufacturer product lines. Industrial end users who purchase through channel intermediaries select the intermediary that has a product line representative of the needs of the end-user business. A nursery supplying landscaping services businesses purchases supplies—fertilizer, soil additives, agricultural chemicals, and flower pots—from a distributor who has specialized in supply to the nursery market. It is unlikely that the nursery buyer could find a manufacturer with a product line that included all of these items. Most manufacturers produce a large quantity of a few items, and most end users purchase a small quantity of a diverse set of items that serve many aspects of the business. The distributor has sought to create an assortment of items needed by the nursery market segment. By carrying the products of several producers, the distributor creates a "one-stop shop" for nurseries. This effort transforms *the manufacturers' assortment* into a *market assortment*. By reducing the discrepancy of assortment, the distributor has saved the end user the cost and time of dealing with multiple suppliers.[5]

The creation of market-based assortments serves producers and users. Suppliers seek channel members that carry complementary product lines. The value of a single product is enhanced by the availability of associated items from a single source. Producers also seek intermediaries that have product lines that include items from recognized market owners or well-known industrial brands. The association with the market standard bearer becomes a positive attribute for the producer of the lesser-known product.

When Use of Distributor Channels Is a Good Channel Design

When is it appropriate to use a distributor, and what products are good candidates for distributor channels? Distribution, as part of the "place" of the marketing four Ps, does not stand alone but must be fully integrated with the other parts of the marketing mix. The previous discussion centered on the four economic utilities and how manufacturers and distributors can serve each others' needs. The following discussion examines other factors that are necessary and appropriate for successful distributor channels.

MARKETING MIX ISSUES Obviously, some products are appropriate for distributor channels while others would be unsuccessful in the market if distributor channels were selected. Traditionally, products that favor the use of distributor channels require local stock, are somewhat generic, and have very low unit value. This traditional view of distribution can be limiting, and there is often a predisposition against distributors by manufacturers as low tech or unqualified. Customers in each market segment will have an expected channel of delivery for product, service, and all other marketing channel flows. Competitor efforts will also influence channel design. With this in mind, let us examine when use of distributor channels is appropriate. In the following discussion, while each factor is discussed individually, they are seldom solitary influences in the marketplace.

FACTORS FAVORING USE OF DISTRIBUTOR CHANNELS

- *Product requires local stock.* Certain products require local and immediate accessibility. Certainly this is the case with food stuffs, but it also applies to certain industrial chemicals, components used in construction trades, and any product (or service) for which shelf life or perishability is a consideration.
- *Small product line, unable to support a direct sales force.* Regardless of other factors involved, companies with limited product offerings just may not be able to afford their own sales force. Distributors who have compatible product lines and established relationships with appropriate customers will be sought out to carry the limited line.
- *Product is somewhat generic.* While few marketers relish admitting that their product is substitutable, those who are in such markets should realize that they can be the substitute for the competitors' products. Goods in the maturity stage of the PLC are often sold based on accessibility and/or availability. Local stock and established distributor–customer relationships are the deciding factors in these sales. Margins on generic or easily substitutable products may be insufficient to support a direct sales force.
- *Product has low unit value.* Similar to generic products, items that are relatively inexpensive on a unit basis and are sold to many customers but seldom in high volume are likely candidates for distributor channels. Office supplies are an example of this category.
- *Product is near the end of its product life cycle.* Beyond availability issues, products that are in the mature or decline stage seldom need significant customer education for proper application. As a product matures, channel redesign is often an important tool to maintain profitability. It is easier to place a product into distributor channels as the need for customer education or missionary sales lessens.
- *Customers are widely dispersed.* The logistics expense of serving customers who are geographically spread out can be a real problem. Depending on the volume of purchase by each customer, distributor channels are usually a more effective channel design. Often, a manufacturer will have dual channel designs—distributor channels for small-volume, dispersed customers and direct sales for the few very high volume accounts in the same geographic region.
- *Local repackaging, sizing, or fabrication is required.* The steel industry relies on steel service centers to cut, blank, and perform some first-stage processing on products shipped to the centers in very large rolls. Customers of the service centers are able to purchase custom-formed components that are more readily incorporated into their operations. Many chemical and plastics manufacturers ship their products to distributors in bulk railcars where the distributor repackages into 25 kg to 500 kg packages (solids) or large drums or gallon

containers. These smaller sizes allow customers to purchase in smaller lots and lower their investment in inventory and risk from spoilage and obsolescence. A significant portion of distributor margins are derived from the different prices for the bulk versus packaged products.

- *Many small buyers.* Similar to the situation with geographically dispersed buyers, many small-volume buyers will create a transaction nightmare for a volume-oriented manufacturer. Distributors can take over the small but frequent transactions on a routine basis.

FACTORS NOT FAVORING USE OF DISTRIBUTOR CHANNELS

- *Product is highly customized.* When individual customer applications of products require customization, shorter channels are more appropriate. Close contact by design, manufacturing, and engineering personnel in both the supplier and customer organizations is essential to application success. Distributor channel services like local inventory and rapid delivery are more suited to products that have a more generic nature.
- *Product is new or innovative.* The application of new products often requires that customers be educated in the most efficient use or service. The role of missionary sales is very important. While distributors can be used for logistical needs, the application development efforts necessary to deliver full value to the customer are best handled directly by the supplying firm.
- *Product is technically sophisticated.* Complex or technically sophisticated products, similar to the situation for new or innovative products, require advice and counsel in their correct application (see the subsequent glazing example).
- *Significant missionary selling is required.* If part of the total offering involves high-service and design assistance, distributor channels may be suitable only for the logistical needs of the product. Many of the product types already noted fall into this category, but the list is not exhaustive. Regardless of other factors, a manufacturer may elect to promote products through missionary sales while spinning off logistics to independent distributors.
- *Manufacturer requires control over product application.* Regardless of the degree of innovation, some manufacturers may not be comfortable with leaving application counseling about their products to third parties. Pharmaceutical companies' use of "detail persons" calling on physicians is an obvious example. Prescription drugs are specified for patients by physicians, requiring the "detail" person to provide up to date and accurate application information. The product flows to pharmacies through distributors who maintain local inventory and provide timely delivery. Other products that have significant liability issues that manufacturers wish to control also fall into this category. Consider manufacturers of bullet-resistant glazing (better known as bulletproof glass—only their legal counsel won't let them say "proof"). Application of these products in banks, gas station kiosks, and similar locations requires careful product specification and installation to be fully effective. Manufacturers wish to reduce their vulnerability through control of all aspects of the product application.
- *Geographic concentration of large buyers.* Regardless of other product characteristics, when the customer base is made up of a few geographically concentrated large users (typical oligopolistic markets), shorter channels better meet customer needs. Large-volume deliveries, price structure, and other service factors favor direct relationships. The same product may be represented by independent distributors in areas of lesser customer concentration.

OTHER CIRCUMSTANCES There are many less obvious but equally important possibilities favoring the use of distributors. When an offering requires extensive sales effort directed at buying professionals (purchasing agents, buyers) because there are many direct competitors, existing buyer–seller relationships may be critical in gaining acceptance by the customer. If sourcing decisions of a product type or within a particular market segment rely primarily on the relationship aspects of the total offering, it may be necessary to use distributor channels to penetrate the market. In these circumstances, the distributor's existing relationship with the industrial end user becomes the primary competitive feature.

Another possibility that seems to defy the logic of when to use distributor channels is the case of a new business. Whether offering an innovative new product or a product with several substitutes in the market, new companies without the resources to place their own sales team in the field may find that a distributor channel is the only affordable way to reach certain segments. Similarly, an existing business-to-business manufacturer about to enter a new market may find distributor channels particularly attractive. Customers in the new markets may have significantly different buying patterns than existing customers. The direct sales force of the business-to-business manufacturer may be well trained and organized but only in relation to the existing products and markets. Placing the new product in distributor channels avoids distracting the direct sellers from their normal call pattern and customer base.

When customer buying patterns indicate that customers expect to find the offering in distributor channels, it is necessary to also use distributors. If known competitors use distributor channels and your company expects to reach the same market, it may be necessary to use distributors. The channel relationships for the product or service type may be already established, and customers are unwilling to establish different habits. Even if the product is the next-generation innovation targeted to replace existing offerings in the segment, users of the established product expect their needs to be satisfied by the same distribution pattern.

Often, particularly with smaller customers, purchases through distributors are preferred. The smaller industrial end user may be taking full advantage of the inventory services and trade credit available from the distributor, taking advantage of the complete solution offered. To penetrate this customer it may be efficient to join the buying pattern rather than compete with it. Exhibit 14-6 summarizes factors favoring or not favoring the use of distributor channels.

Favoring	Not Favoring
Product requires local stock.	Product is highly customized.
Product line is small, unable to support direct sales.	Product is new or innovative.
Product is somewhat generic.	Product is technically sophisticated.
Product has low unit value.	Significant missionary selling is required.
Product is near end of PLC.	Manufacturer requires control over product application.
Customers are widely dispersed.	Large buyers are geographically concentrated.
Local repackaging, sizing, or fabrication is required.	
Market has many small-volume buyers.	
Product requires extensive sales effort directed at buying professionals.	
Start-up venture or established company is entering a new market.	
Competition uses distributors.	
Customers prefer distributors.	

EXHIBIT 14-6 Factors Favoring Use or Not Favoring Use of Distributor Channels

Vertical Integration versus Finding the Right Channel Partner

Throughout this chapter we have referred to industrial distributors with the idea that when you need one, one will be readily available. This is not always the case. Traditional patterns of distribution will vary depending on many factors, not the least of which is whether or not there is a distributor capable or willing to take on the product line. This availability can be problematic when designing international channels. In some instances, manufacturers may be forced to forward integrate because of the unavailability of fully developed distribution channels. In developing economies an integrated system of industrial distributors may not exist. It may be necessary to establish a distribution subsidiary, wholly owned by the manufacturer. This creates special concerns of channel control, time to market, and flexibility. These concerns may be magnified when the manufacturer faces distribution infrastructures at different levels of development in the different regions or countries where distribution is required. The market ultimately determines most effective channel design, based not only on those factors shown in Exhibit 14-6 but also on the economic and industrial development of the target market and on customer expectations

DISTRIBUTION AND THE PRODUCT LIFE CYCLE

The preceding factors address a combination of marketing mix variables and how they can impact the use of distribution. These factors may exist alone or in combination with others. Consider these factors as they relate to the PLC.

Introductory Stage

Early in the PLC (introduction) a start-up with a new product may not have the resources to fund a direct channel. A start-up organization may often be the least able, from a marketing view, to use a distributor for many of the other marketing mix variables previously noted. While contrary to conventional wisdom, it may be appropriate that start-ups in this position seek additional financing from their investors to build the appropriate sales force.[6] This sales force will most likely take on the organizational style of missionary sales or an application development team while business logistics functions can be handled by independent distribution. As already noted, an established manufacturer may also use distribution for a new product if the target market is not consistent with the existing markets served by the manufacturer's sales force.

Promotion as it relates to marketing channels during the introductory stage consists primarily of establishing brand awareness. New brands must prove viable not only in the market but also to channel intermediaries. Listing allowances and discounts may be required to gain acceptance among intermediaries.

Growth Stage

Once an offering has proven its worth in the marketplace, obtaining distribution is much easier. Distributors want successful products and will readily accept an offering that their customers are likely to want. During this period, missionary sellers can help establish the product in distribution and build loyalty with the distributor sellers by providing customer and seller training and sales leads, particularly with high-learning products. When the supplier goal is to position as the industry standard, loyalty built by a strong missionary effort at this time will help fend off imitators in the future.

In technology markets, the marketer may enlist the services of value-added resellers during the growth phase. VARs have established relationships with technology buyers and provide technology and integration services that are needed to complete the offering. One problem that can arise with VARs is that, as the market begins to expand rapidly, the VARs may want to continue to participate as high-volume resellers. This is fine as long as they have the capability to do so, but VARs may not have the ability to handle large volumes, the desire to open new markets, nor the willingness to reduce prices. Consequently, they may be a bad fit for fast-growing markets.

The channel manager or marketing manager must continually communicate with the VARs to let them know how the market is evolving so that changes in channel patterns do not come as a surprise. The wise manager will continue to work with the best VARs, setting them up for the next set of new products coming through the pipeline as they become ready to market to the VARs' traditional target segments.

Maturity or Decline Stages

A product that has reached the maturity or decline stage of the PLC may require an entirely redesigned marketing channel. A product that has moved into the low-learning stage as customers become more familiar with its use and no longer need applications development support may be placed in distribution for the first time. If the product has become an industrial commodity (with several "or equivalents"), margins will be less than during its added-value stage, possibly not able to support the development effort employed during higher-learning periods. Distribution will be able to handle the new buying criteria more efficiently than direct sales. (New buying criteria may relate to locational convenience, JIT, low cost in small volumes, and so on.)

During maturity and decline, particularly when there are a number of alternative products, suppliers use a number of trade promotions to keep products in the forefront of seller efforts. Rebates to channel members, special volume discounts, and sales incentive contests are all used to attract and keep sellers' attention.

MANAGING CHANNELS OF DISTRIBUTION

Once the channel strategy has been designed, the marketer must execute the plan. The kinds of activities included are selection of channel partners and building relationships with them, running channel programs to keep them motivated and performing to the plan, and reshaping the channel strategy as the market changes.

Selecting and Caring for Distributors

Selecting a distributor has some of the same elements as selecting a manufacturers' representative (see Chapter 12). Like manufacturers' reps, distributors—even those that are part of nationwide distribution companies—are designed to have regional impact. Nationwide distributor organizations need to be examined region by region. It is rare to find a national distributor who is equally strong in all regions where they compete. Regionally based distributors or a combination of national and regional players may be better able to serve your particular needs. In any event, here are some basic points to remember:

- Ask potential customers who they would recommend. Who better to recommend a distributor with successful relationships?
- Determine which distributor fits marketing plan goals. While logistical concerns may be a perfect match, the goals and aspirations of the distributor should be aligned with yours. Contextual differences may not surface early in the relationship but will be difficult to resolve later. A simple example, particularly for aggressive, growth-oriented companies, is a distributor who is willing to sacrifice growth to maintain higher margins.

- Make calls with them. This can be part of the selection process as well as part of the relationship-building process after selection. If acceptable to the distributor, make customer calls with some of its sales force before the contract is signed. Remember that your distributors are both customers and sales assets. Making customer calls with them, often in a missionary role, is an essential part of building the relationship and protects your company from being isolated from your ultimate customers. (Many distributors will be cautious about letting the customer–manufacturer relationship get too cozy.)
- Make calls on them. As we have said, your distributors are also your customers, particularly if they distribute products for your competitors. Build the relationship at all levels.
- Train and support them well and often, at both your facilities and theirs. Your training and education of your distributor can increase the comfort level with your products and your organization. Show them your facilities, not only to provide product and service training but so that individuals from each organization can develop connections beyond e-mail and telephones. Make them feel like a part of your team.

Superordinate goals are those goals that go beyond a single intermediary, are desirable to many of the channel members, and are unobtainable through the effort of a single channel member. Cooperation and mutual understanding between intermediaries are necessary to achieve these goals. Since the goals are considered laudable by many of the channel members, the process of obtaining them fosters teamwork and cooperation.

TEAM PLAYERS Different channel designs exist for different markets. Some are the result of years of unintentional channel design that has become customary in a particular market while others are tightly designed with significant (and sometimes resented) control at many levels. Regardless of the details of the channel design, channel members must recognize that they are part of a team whose individual goals can be enhanced through agreement with the system goals. Any channel member at any particular level can maximize profits or performance as an individual entity. Successful channels are the result of teamwork—the creation of a win–win situation. Channel performance that is consistent with the needs and wants of the target market and internally consistent with the goals and objectives of members requires a contextual approach that recognizes and develops both individual member and **superordinate goals**.

To understand this dual-purpose goal setting, students must recognize and understand the channel from the perspective of each member. Factors that can improve the performance of a retailer are often costly to manufacturers and wholesalers (increased promotion, local inventory, rapid shipping, and so on). While acceptable to the retailer, these factors decrease the profitability of the channel for other members. Thus, channel management must include a balance that is acceptable to all members.

Power and Conflict in Marketing Channels

Power in marketing channels usually results when one channel member (Member A) is dependent on another member (Member B). The dependent member, A, is not completely free to select its own direction on all issues. Member B then has influence and control over Member A with regard to the issues in which A is dependent on B. The dependence may not be just monetary but may include specialized knowledge, skills, and market access. Thus, the portfolio of resources and skills that a channel member commits to the channel effort can have a significant impact on how the channel relationship is managed and controlled.

BASES OF POWER Power can be classified as deriving from bases of resources and skills. The *bases of power*[7] include reward, coercion, legitimate, expertise, identification, and information power. For discussion purposes, these bases are broken into categories. *Soft* bases are comprised of expertise, identification, and information power; and *hard* bases are comprised of the remaining reward, coercion, and legitimate bases.[8]

Hard power bases are usually quantifiable and specific. Rewards can be margin rates, incentive programs, and special monetary promotions through the channel. Rewards may be specifically related to performance in product sales results or territory coverage. Coercive power, effective only when there is a significant imbalance in the channel, often takes the form of punishment for a lack of performance or results. Legitimate power stems from a contractual agreement that is enforceable by a third party or, in highly intraorganizational channels (i.e., a corporate or contractual vertical marketing channel), a strong feeling of obligation or commitment. Continuous use of hard power bases often leads to greater conflict as members feel *required* to perform rather than *invited* to perform.

Soft power bases are more qualitative in nature than hard bases. Product and market expertise and information are shared between channel members in the recognition that improved channel performance can be of benefit to all members. Identification power exists when one channel member possesses an image, reputation, or position in the market that makes belonging to that channel system a positive asset. This association may be related to brands, channel support, or prestige market positioning. In business-to-business markets, identification power can be associated with exemplary assistance provided to channel members by a manufacturer's missionary sellers as well as a manufacturer's brands being the industry standard in target markets. Agreement on goals and the understanding of win–win outcomes are important in the effective application of soft power bases.

As is often the case, mutual dependence exists between members such that an imbalance that leads to conflict can be avoided. Many marketing channels are often combinations of independent businesses attempting to meet channel goals while also meeting the goals of the individual business. Unfortunately, these goals are not always in complete alignment. Goal incompatibility and its variants are among the primary causes of channel conflict. Older, established channel members who have "proven their mettle" may have as a primary goal stabilizing profit margins at the highest level, while newer, less-known intermediaries have a more aggressive posture in the market. Other conflict igniters are territory issues, where suppliers may reserve **house accounts** for a direct selling function, and **product line maintenance** issues. The scenario of adding a second source for a product type, discussed in this chapter, can lead to conflict between channel members if there is an expectation of loyalty that has been lost or not earned. While many conflict resolution techniques are available, their details are generally beyond the scope of this text. The following discussion looks at channel design, leadership, and control as elements in channel power and conflict.

Channel Patterns and Control

Traditionally, channel power was the realm of the large manufacturer at the top of the channel. Manufacturers who desired greater power and control over channels would either forward integrate into corporate vertical marketing systems or enter into contractual relationships in which goal setting included superordinate goals. As manufacturers moved to establish control of channels, economies of scale in buying were created that began to influence intermediaries who were not aligned with a vertical marketing system. The outcome was the joining of **horizontal competitors** (intermediaries at the same level in a channel, usually existing in multidistribution) into buying groups to create the scale necessary to compete with corporate systems.

Exhibit 14-7 shows the organization of several traditional vertical marketing systems (VMSs) and the addition of value networks, arranged in order of dependence on or degree of supplier control (increasing left to right) and dependence on mutually beneficial relationships

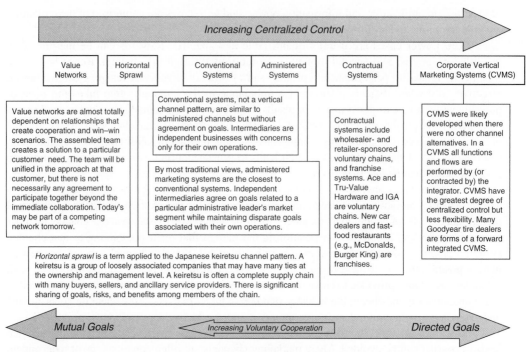

EXHIBIT 14-7 Control and Cooperation in Vertical Marketing Systems

(increasing right to left). The following discussion characterizes these channel patterns from the viewpoint of channel control and the importance of mutually beneficial relationships.

Historically, a large manufacturer's size and financial power gave it the privilege to strongly influence, if not control, the marketing channel. Manufacturers that desired greater control or were unable to achieve distribution goals through independent intermediaries would integrate operations, forming a **corporate vertical marketing system (CVMS)**. This provides centralized control but limits flexibility and requires a significant capital investment.

Contractual channels aim at control through binding agreements with otherwise independent intermediaries. Of these systems, probably the greatest control exists with franchisors in franchise systems. However, even with the significantly controlling contractual agreements that exist in franchises, franchisees are independent business owners, not employees of the franchisor. (Among the most interesting contractual channels are the farm producer co-ops—see "Finding More Uses for Cranberries"). Contractual systems are voluntary; there is no unified ownership. Most contractual arrangements were created to develop competitive buying positions. Faced with competition from large, vertically integrated organizations, independent channel members formed voluntary chains. (Voluntary chains were started at the wholesale level as well as at the retail level. The main difference is where the motivation for the cooperative effort came from and is not significant to this discussion.) In the grocery industry, the Independent Grocers Alliance (IGA) is among the best-known system, while Ace, Tru-Value, Pro, and Sentry Hardware are all types of voluntary chains. Toro, the outdoor equipment manufacturer, uses contractual channels (franchises) for commercial outdoor equipment; and McKesson, the pharmaceutical wholesaler, has over 3,300 independent retailers that are part of its voluntary chain.[9]

Finding More Uses for Cranberries

Imagine that you are the owner of a cranberry bog. Your big market consists of one day a year—Thanksgiving—and everyone does not like cranberries on turkey. You dream of cranberries on cereal in the morning, cranberry-apple juice as a breakfast drink and a cocktail mixer. As the owner of just one bog you might find it difficult to develop new uses for cranberries, but as a member of a consortium of bog owners, resources could be pooled and risks minimized in a way that you could afford product and market development efforts.

Your dream is the vision that many farm producer cooperatives have been built on. Ocean Spray, Sunkist, LandO'Lakes, and others are co-ops established to expand the markets for basic commodities and establish quality standards that could be reflected as premium brands in the marketplace.

To be part of the co-op, growers must meet certain quality standards associated with their particular produce and agree to certain resale terms. At the inception of many co-ops, growers were very interested in joining as there was significant upside potential—more markets would be available and price and quality would be stabilized. With time, the co-ops developed channel power positions that benefited their members both in the markets for their products and the markets for farm equipment and supplies. Farm co-ops are big business. Consider this the next time you have whipped cream and cranberries on your ice cream. A farm-producer co-op may have marketed all three products!

Because of their voluntary nature, contractual channels require a greater degree of cooperation and mutual goal setting to be effective. This is more true with administered channels, whose composition and level of commitment by intermediaries are not legally binding. **Administered channel intermediaries** are independent businesses who have agreed to marketing goals and programs developed by other companies. General Electric used administered channels for major appliances in consumer markets and industrial components and motors in industrial markets. Owens & Minor, Baxter, and several other hospital supply distributors provide JIT "stockless" inventory services to their customers. A sophisticated refinement of JIT systems, stockless systems provide supplies in quantities as small as single units to care stations within client hospitals.

Known for the implied business camaraderie that exists between suppliers and customers, **keiretsu** systems often have little contractual control. Sometimes called **horizontal sprawl**, the keiretsu consists of a very flat channel pattern, with few, if any, vertical layers. Each supplier has a direct relationship with the customer. Ancillary providers in the pattern are also members of the keiretsu, such that shipping, financing, and other services are available to members at favorable terms. The favorable consideration is part of the relationship; members recognize that what is good for other members will be good for the entire group, strengthening the keiretsu for all. (In the United States, this may be contrary to antitrust law.) Operating without centralized control, the composition of the keiretsu is dependent on members recognizing the value of long-term cooperative relationships and win–win attitudes.

Value networks are similar to the keiretsu at any given customer or solution development. However, members of value networks are often part of a specific network for only that development program or customer application. The success of the network rests on members understanding that they must respect and value other members' positions; they could very likely be competing with others as members of different networks. While sometimes appearing ad hoc, value networks provide ultimate member flexibility; particularly important are fast-changing, high-technology markets.

CHANNELS AND THE INTERNET

Throughout this text, we have explored the effects of the Internet on business-to-business marketing. One area that appeared to have potential for great change stemming from rapid adoption of Internet technology is the area of business-to-business channels and supply chains. At the height of the dot-com bubble, Web technology had the potential to bring significant portions of business transactions online in a very short period of time. A sizable portion of this online activity would be channel transactions.

Many companies that formed to change the nature of business-to-business channels never got to profitability and hence disappeared—either by being acquired or by simply closing their doors. (See Chapter 3, "Covisint: The Importance of Adapting to Customers' Buying Behavior.") However, this does not mean that Web-based technology has not had an impact on business-to-business channels. Many companies have adopted new technology that enables today's agile and efficient supply chains. This area continues to hold promise, though planners and pundits now take a more realistic view of it.

The Internet's Emerging Role in Business-to-Business Marketing Channels

If we look at the Internet and the Web as enhancements to information flow, we can then think about how the technology can affect channels. As we noted earlier, channels provide value for business-to-business customers by creating form, time, place, and possession utilities. All of these utilities can be enhanced through better and faster channel flows. Rapid flow of order data between resellers and suppliers can closely track demand patterns for different product models. The supplier can create better forecasts of demand for different models and thus provide better product assortments in real time. Better information flow also allows the execution of JIT manufacturing and supply. This improves time utility for end-use customers, since they can receive a product in days or even hours from the time they ordered it, instead of waiting weeks or months. Real-time information can give suppliers more information about geographic demand patterns, allowing more inventory to be placed downstream near locations where customers actually need the product. Thus, place utility is improved (and time utility as well); and, of course, this gets products into the possession of customers earlier. Analysts have also argued that sharing real-time demand data has reduced the bullwhip effect over the past decade.[10]

In addition to these ways of creating value, the Web also reduces channel costs. Management of channel relationships using Web applications squeezes costs out of the channel in several ways. First, when considering ordering, inventory tracking, billing, and payment, the accuracy of using the Web to manage data reduces a great deal of the costs associated with error checking and corrections. Second, better information makes forecasting more accurate, reducing inventory costs. Better information also makes timing of orders more manageable so that quantity and payment discounts can be obtained on a higher proportion of orders.

Companies are also learning that value can be produced for customers by reducing customer costs through the use of Web-enhanced order processing and fulfillment tracking. For instance, four oil pipeline companies in the United States formed a joint venture project, called "Transport4." This effort, headed by Colonial Oil of Atlanta, created a Web-based ordering and scheduling facility for shipments of oil products. Oil producers, industrial oil buyers, oil distributors, or any other institutional customer could go to the password-protected site to schedule and route oil shipments from point of origin to any destination served by the four member pipelines. Prior to the existence of the joint venture, a customer would have to arrange such a shipment by EDI, phone, fax, or mail. The worst part of the old system was that each pipeline company was a separate entity with its own product codes, data interchange protocols, and ordering and scheduling procedures. The joint venture allows the customer to order and schedule across all four pipelines in one step. Confirmation is immediate. In the past, a complicated order might take a week or more to finalize. Now it can be done in a matter of minutes.[11]

Since its inception, Transport4 has grown to seven pipelines. After hurricanes Katrina and Rita in 2005, Transport4 became an important component in bringing the oil distribution industry quickly back into service in the Gulf Coast.[12] Transport4 has added new services, including an online auction capability.[13]

Companies are discovering that Web-automated channels provide better value to the end customer. Lower channel and inventory costs, plus an ability to forecast demand more accurately, mean that fewer stockouts and back orders occur for products moved through the channel. Customers may benefit directly through reduced transaction costs. Value to customers may also be enhanced from channel cost savings that are reinvested in such things as filling out product lines and increasing inventory of complementary products; this results in customers receiving more value from product availability. Suppliers or channel members might also invest cost savings into enhanced customer service.

What Has Happened to New Types of Channels

New channel structures emerge as more companies obtain experience with the Web and as more entrepreneurs are exposed to Web-enabled commerce. All of these channel arrangements have the same general purposes as traditional channel structures: providing the appropriate selection of the right products and making them available to end-use buyers, efficiently handling ordering and order processing, and facilitating fast delivery at the lowest cost possible.

In our prior work,[14] we reported two general types of business-to-business channels that were beginning to emerge shortly before the dot-com bubble burst: affiliate networks and hubs. An **affiliate network** is a sales channel more than it is a distribution channel. Affiliates show a link on their Web sites that refer a prospective customer to the Web site of a marketer. If the customer buys something from the marketer, the affiliate receives some sort of compensation for the referral. A network of affiliates can potentially generate an enormous number of referrals—sales leads—to the marketer who resides at the center of the network, and theoretically has great potential for generating sizable sales numbers.

Hubs,[15] or portals as they are often called, are a generic class of Web sites that "make markets"—bring buyers and sellers together to facilitate transactions—in a business-to-business context. They can be one of several types: catalog, auction, exchange, or barter. *Catalog hubs* serve as agglomerators, in which the products from several vendors' catalogs are combined in a searchable database. *Auction hubs* match buyers and sellers in an online analogy of real-world auctions. *Exchange hubs* act as clearing centers for bringing buyers and sellers together. Commodity-like products are offered in a setting where buyers and sellers indicate the products (or services) they want to trade and the prices they seek. *Barter hubs* act like exchanges, except that "prices" are nonmonetary. Buyers and sellers each exchange something of value (the exchange may involve a bartered service or product, plus some amount of money). Generally, hubs make money by charging processing, handling, and marketing fees.

Since 2000, however, Internet businesses have run through a series of problems. Business-to-business marketers have faced problems related to—but not identical to—problems faced by consumer businesses. Both sectors faced dramatic shrinkage in funding as the investment community re-evaluated the future profitability of Internet and Web-based businesses.

The concept of affiliate networks has caught on much more in consumer markets than in business-to-business markets. Affiliate networks for business marketers tend to be too costly to manage well. Participation in a network is usually not attractive for potential affiliates because it does not generate enough revenue to be worthwhile.

For business-to-business hubs or portals, two interrelated problems emerged.[16] First, relationships require more off-line attention than online business models assumed. It is not enough to cut transaction costs if barriers that arise in supplier–customer relationships detract more from the value produced. Second, because relatively few potential users actually used the online market exchange sites, volume did not rise to levels that produced profits for the market exchange companies. New companies found low-entry barriers in the technology: almost anyone could set up a market exchange site. As a result, too many exchanges were chasing too few transactions. Chemdex, as an example, hoped to "make a market" in the life sciences industry. While it was one of the first, it soon found thirty-seven other companies competing for the same business. Ventro, the owner of Chemdex, discontinued the site in December 2000.[17] To add to these problems, many businesses have relied on advertising to supplement their online revenue streams. Many advertisers have come to realize that the returns from online advertising often do not warrant the expense.[18] A combination of declining returns from advertising and reduced advertising as the economy slowed has produced a precipitous drop in advertising revenue.

The end result was that new online businesses, the different kinds of hubs mentioned earlier, often did not fare well. They did not acquire enough participants to reach critical mass, that is, enough transaction volume to be profitable. Most are out of business or running at greatly reduced activity levels. The business models in which a single company runs an automated supply chain or distribution system have fared better. However, even these have proven to take longer and involve more investment than was originally anticipated.

Future Adoption of Information Technology for Channel Management

The exuberance of the dotcom era has now been replaced with post-collapse caution. Even so, the best business ideas from this period, enabled by innovative technology, are slowly taking hold. For instance, while portals did not generally fare well in the early 2000s, some exchange hubs have evolved and thrived in specialized markets. Global Healthcare Exchange has come to be well established in medical products sold to hospitals and clinics.[19] The potential gains from exchange hubs are so great that the costs of implementation are offset for many users. Quadrem Global eMarketplace—another exchange hub that operates in the oil and gas, mining, minerals, and other industries—has built a business that appears to be sustainable.[20] Taking small steps to prove the concept to potential adopters seems to be working in this case.

Notwithstanding these difficulties, Internet and Web-enabled businesses and supply chains still hold promise. As a cluster of technologies that fully integrates supply chain management, we are probably still in the visionary part of the TALC. However, beachhead niches are starting to emerge and we may see a chasm crossing in the near future.

THOUGHTS TO TAKE WITH YOU INTO THE NEXT CHAPTER

Channels create and enhance value for business customers. They provide value in terms of making the right products and services available, by giving buyers an appropriate level of choice, by providing products and services in the appropriate quantities, and by doing so at appropriate levels of cost. To do this, channel members perform a variety of tasks. The combination provided by any individual channel member is dependent on the nature of the product and the way that customers expect to obtain it. The combination may include such activities as forecasting market needs, performing market research, buying products that create a selection, holding inventory, creating product bundles or performing final assembly, providing service, setting or negotiating prices, communicating with and selling to buyers, facilitating transactions, moving products, providing financing, and establishing relationships with customers.

To create value for final buyers, suppliers need to understand those buyers, understand the perspective of potential channel members, and then design a channel structure that is as appropriate as possible, that is, it provides superior value to final buyers and that makes appropriate profit levels for channel members and for the supplier. Once the design is in place, the marketer must recruit and choose individual channel members to implement this design. In most cases, the marketer must then work to establish a relationship with channel partners. One of the most pressing environmental changes that must be addressed today is changing technology. As the Web changes the way that business channels are structured and managed, the business marketer must adapt. A proactive rather than reactive approach is called for. The risk of "missing the boat" is too great otherwise.

Key Terms

administered channel
   intermediaries *361*
affiliates *363*
ancillary channel members *336*
channel pattern *339*
contractual channel *360*
corporate vertical marketing
   system *360*
differentially invisible *350*
direct channel *336*
distribution centers *349*
dual distribution *352*
form *338*

functional spin-off *342*
horizontal competition *359*
horizontal sprawl *361*
house accounts *359*
hubs *363*
intensity of distribution *350*
keiretsu *361*
logistics *347*
marketing channel *336*
materials requirements planning
   (MRP) *349*
multidistribution *352*
palletizing *338*

physical distribution concept *348*
place *338*
possession *338*
primary channel participants *336*
product line maintenance *359*
superordinate goals *358*
supply chain *347*
supply chain management *347*
time *338*
trade credit *340*
vertical integration *342*
vertical marketing system *359*
warehouses *349*

Questions for Review and Discussion

1. Does a company that markets directly to other companies have a channel? Why or why not?
2. Why can channel structure differ between segments even though the products are the same?
3. Explain the four kinds of economic utility.
4. When a channel provides financing to customers, what kind of economic utility is it providing? Explain.
5. When a channel provides training for the customer's personnel, what kind of economic utility is being provided? Explain.

6. What does it mean for a channel to "reduce the discrepancy of assortment"?
7. Why is carrying extra inventory so costly for suppliers or channel members?
8. What are three reasons that a business-to-business marketer may want to market through channel intermediaries rather than market directly?
9. Review the opening example of Apple and the Lisa computer. Using Exhibit 14-2a, determine what path Apple used to get the Lisa to its market. Compare that to the path you think may have been more appropriate.

10. What sorts of risks does an industrial distributor share with the supplier?

11. Suppose that a start-up company is offering an innovative product that management hopes will establish a new product category. What forces will tend to lead the company to market the product through channel intermediaries rather than directly? What characteristics of an early market will tend to lead the company to market the product directly to final customers?

12. What are key causes of channel conflict?

13. What are the chief differences between an administered channel and a value network?

14. What kinds of value can be provided by Web applications that manage channel transactions?

15. What kinds of value would channels provide that cannot be substantially enhanced through Web applications?

16. Using Exhibit 14-4, review the Apple Lisa and compare how well the factors were addressed. Note how much better developed was the channel for the iphone in meeting customer needs as they pertained to "the way the customer buys."

Endnotes

1. Louis W. Stern, Adel I. El-Ansary, and James R. Brown, *Management in Marketing Channels* (Upper Saddle River, N.J.: Prentice-Hall, 1988), chapter 8, Instructor's Manual Discussion.

2. Louis W. Stern, Adel I. El-Ansary, and James R. Brown, *Management in Marketing Channels* (Upper Saddle River, N.J.: Prentice-Hall, 1988), chapter 8.

3. Lou E. Pelton, David Strutton, and James R. Lumpkin, *Marketing Channels, A Relationship Management Approach* (Chicago: Irwin, 1997), pp. 301–311.

4. Paul Sherlock, *Rethinking Business to Business Marketing* (New York: The Free Press/Macmillan, 1991), chapter 10.

5. Stern and El-Ansary, *Marketing Channels*, p. 5.

6. Sherlock, *Rethinking Business to Business Marketing*.

7. Stern and El-Ansary, *Marketing Channels*, pp. 268–283.

8. The first three bases—reward, coercion and legitimate—are often referred to as *mediated* power bases while the remaining are called *nonmediated* bases.

9. Stern and El-Ansary, *Marketing Channels*, pp. 331–334.

10. Thomas F. Siems, "Who Supplied My Cheese? Supply Chain Management in the Global Economy," *Business Economics*, 40(4) (October 2005), pp. 6–21.

11. Sean Donahue, "Pipe Dreams," *Business 2.0* (January 2000), pp. 90–95.

12. Anonymous, "Transport4 Launches T4 Online Auctions," *Pipeline & Gas Journal*, 234(1) (January 2007), p. 12.

13. Barton Brown, "A Web of Pipeline Communications," *Pipeline & Gas Journal* 230(4) (April 2003), p. 14.

14. Robert Vitale and Joseph Giglierano, *Business to Business Marketing: Analysis and Practice in a Dynamic Environment* (Mason, Ohio.: South-Western Publishing, 2002).

15. A good early description of emerging models appeared in an article by Don Tapscott, David Ticoll, and Alex Lowy, "The Rise of the Business Web," *Business 2.0* (November, 1999), pp. 198–208.

16. Elise Ackerman, "Businesses Hit Rough Spots on Internet Journey," *San Jose Mercury News* (February 26, 2001), pp. 1E, 10E.

17. Cecelia Kang, "Online Supply Exchanges Refocus their Strategies," *San Jose Mercury News* (February 26, 2001), pp. 1E, 10E.

18. Jennifer Rewick, "Beyond Banners," *The Wall Street Journal* (October 23, 2000), p. R38.

19. Gary H. Anthes, "On the Mend," *Computerworld*, 39(4) (January 2005), p. 35.

20. Susan Avery, "Rio Tinto Purchasing Uses E-Marketplace for Supply Chain Efficiency," *Purchasing*, 136(6) (April 2007), p. 35.

Chapter *15*

Communicating with the Market

OVERVIEW

All relationships depend on reliable and timely communications. Throughout this book we have stressed the importance of building customer relationships at many levels. In Chapter 12 we emphasized the importance of the personal selling portion of the promotion mix. While personal selling plays a critical role in communication with customers, the other three elements of the **promotion mix—advertising, sales promotion**, and **public relations**—are required for the specialized role that they play in the communication process. In this chapter, the discussion will focus on these three elements and their value in business-to-business markets. Not only does each element of the promotion mix have a specialized role, but the synergies between the elements combine to provide a unified message to the marketplace. As discussed in Chapter 13, marketing communication is a key component for building a strong brand.

This chapter starts with an overview of promotion and the differences between consumer products promotion and business-to-business promotion. After the overview, the discussion turns to achieving different outcomes with combinations of the elements of the promotion mix. There are some forms of business-to-business communication that defy categorization into only one of the elements of the promotion mix. In discussion of the management of promotion, we will examine how definition of outcomes desired rather than process employed is more likely to provide insight into the promotion needs of the situation.

The implementation of positioning and differentiation strategies, as determined by the strategic plan of the organization, is in large part the purview of the promotion effort. The chapter will conclude with a discussion of the value creation elements of promotion.

Andersen Consulting Does a Quick Transformation to Accenture[1]

After nearly three years in a courtroom squabble, on August 7, 2000, the arbitrator finally ruled that Andersen Consulting could split from Arthur Andersen, the accounting firm. The $1 billion price was deemed reasonable, but one condition seemed a monumental challenge: Andersen Consulting could no longer use the Andersen name (not too bad, so far: they were already moving to change the name), and the name had to change by January 1, 2001. The split meant Andersen Consulting had to change its name in 129 days and not "disappear" in the process.

Arthur Andersen had an excellent reputation as a business consulting organization, when in 1989, the partners decided to institutionalize the consulting arm of the firm with a separate public identity. The consultancy was still a part of the firm, contributing to the firm's overall financial performance. Disagreements arose concerning the strategic directions of the firm, allocation of resources, and clashing cultures; and Andersen Consulting filed for arbitration in 1997.

Over the years, Andersen Consulting had redirected its consulting efforts from general management consulting to focus more on enterprise-level IT consulting. As client companies changed over to business operations that relied on information technology and enterprise resource planning systems, Andersen Consulting became the integration engine that accomplished the restructuring. Now Andersen Consulting was faced with the task of continuing in this business, building on its past success and reputation, without losing its identity when the name changed. And it did not yet have a new name.

The task was Herculean on three fronts. First, a new name had to be found that conveyed the strengths and vision of the new company. Meanwhile, the name had to be available, the URL—the Web address—had to be available, and the name had to have no negative connotations in any of the sixty or so countries in which Andersen Consulting did business. Second, the logistics of changing the name on all the company's materials was enormous: business cards, letterhead, brochures, paychecks, and signage, as well as all the company's advertising and corporate communications materials. Third, the changeover had to be communicated to customers, prospective customers, and the world at large in such a way that all these audiences would take notice and maintained positive memory associations with the new name. The changeover had to be done well, too. If the changeover was managed poorly, people would notice and Andersen Consulting would have to begin life as a new company digging its way out of a credibility hole.

Andersen Consulting started by seeking suggestions for names from its executives and employees, as well as from hired consultants. By October, after culling 2,677 entries, the partners and their hired consultants, Landor Associates, chose the name Accenture. The name was originally the suggestion of a senior manager in Oslo, Norway.

Andersen Consulting launched an advertising campaign that "teased" the audience, suggesting a name change was coming. The name officially changed on January 1, and Accenture launched an extensive campaign to make the change very visible. It involved advertising in several media, a public relations campaign, and the culmination of the physical changes to identity materials throughout the company. The logistics campaign had been implemented by fifty employee teams. To accomplish all this, Accenture employed the project management skills that were the core of its consulting business.

The results, of course, will not be fully known for a while, maybe for years. The early results, though, indicated that Accenture was on the right track, particularly in light of the demise of Arthur Anderson through the Enron debacle. A majority of target audience members realize that the name is changing and the Accenture name is gradually acquiring memory associations. In all, Accenture's efforts stand as a good example of what it takes to accomplish such a name change.

LEARNING OBJECTIVES

By reading this chapter, you will

- Understand the distinctions between personal selling and the nonpersonal types of promotion.
- Understand the differences between promotion in consumer markets and promotion in business-to-business markets.

- Understand the role of promotion in providing value, information, and education to customers and influencing the buying decision process.

- Have become familiar with the kinds of promotion used in business-to-business marketing and their uses.

- Gain a sense of how to manage promotion in conjunction with the other elements of marketing strategy and the offering.

- Understand how promotion can assist the development of a firm's strategic positioning.

- Gain a sense of how publicity and Internet communications can play special roles in business-to-business marketing.

INTRODUCTION

In Chapter 12, we discussed personal selling, which is, of course, face-to-face communication. Business-to-business marketers also use other, less personal media to communicate with the market. All forms of communication, called the *promotion mix* in most marketing principles texts, are generally grouped into four categories: personal selling, advertising, sales promotion, and public relations. In business-to-business marketing, there are some forms of communication that defy such categorization. The communication effort does not fit nicely into any one element of the promotion mix. For instance, participation in industry trade shows and conferences employs all four categories of communication: salespeople are on duty at the booth and interact with customers (personal selling); brochures on products and marketing programs are given away (advertising); other sales premiums—promotional items such as T-shirts, coffee mugs, and so on—are given away to provide incentives for customers to visit the booth (sales promotion); and the company president, wearing the company's polo shirt and sun visor, sits on a discussion panel in a seminar session to expound on the company's vision of the industry's future (public relations). At the same time, company technical professionals are presenting a paper on the company's newest technology breakthrough at the conference that is a part of the trade show. The object of all this communication is to help the members of the buying center move through their buying decision process and, strategically, position the firm in the minds of customers.

  This chapter concerns all the methods of communication that are not personal selling. In many organizations, these promotional efforts are known as *marketing communications* ("marcom") or, in large organizations when public relations are handled at the corporate level, advertising and sales promotion (A&SP). For brevity, we use the term **nonpersonal communications** to describe these promotional efforts.

  In the opening example, Andersen Consulting was faced with a monumental communication task as it moved to quickly change its name to Accenture. In doing so, Accenture and its consultants followed the main guidelines for good communications. They started by choosing a name that would communicate a desired message. Then they used multiple methods to deliver the message that the name was changing. The campaign was sequenced in such a way that it got the attention of the target audiences and primed them for the name change. Repeated messages in differing forms reinforced the message so that audience members' memory would be enhanced. All the while, the company kept in mind the role of the company's name and the impact of these messages on the buying decision process.

*The term **nonpersonal communications** refers to the elements of the promotion mix other than personal sales, such as advertising, sales promotion, and public relations. Depending on organizational structure, nonpersonal communications may be known as marketing communications (marcom) or advertising & sales promotion (A&SP).*

Communications contribute to the marketer's delivery of value to customers. Without communications the customer might not realize that the supplier has a solution for his problem or is willing to work with him to develop a solution. The customer might not fully understand how much value the supplier's solution truly provides.

A COMMUNICATIONS MODEL

There are three key ideas in providing value through communications. First, the members of the buying center respond to messages; media are only *a means of delivering messages*. Second, messages must be crafted to assist members of the buying center to *progress through* the buying decision process. Third, messages must be crafted *to implement the positioning* chosen in the design of marketing strategy. Keep these three ideas in mind through the following discussion of the communications model, shown in Exhibit 15-1.

Losing Meaning in the Translation

The simplest communications model, *sender-encode-medium-decode-receiver*, is familiar to many students. As shown in Exhibit 15-1, there are several areas of this model that require particular attention. Note that the sender and the encoding process are not separate. As the sender creates a message, that message is placed into "code" that has meaning to the sender as an accurate representation of the message. The message can be received accurately only by a receiver who "decodes" the message the same way it was encoded. In personal communications (everyday conversation), this is not *usually* a problem, though you can probably recall having asked someone to rephrase something he or she said because you did not understand it. While this

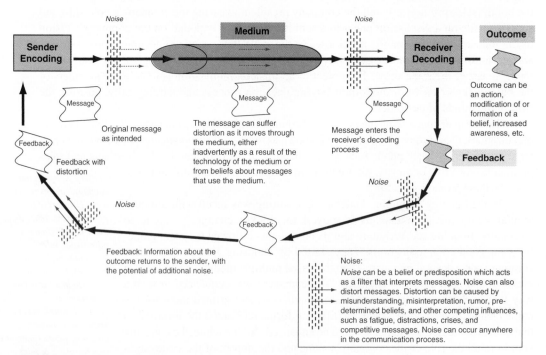

EXHIBIT 15-1 A Model of the Communication Process

sounds simple, many market segments have their own languages, usually referred to as the **jargon** of the market or discipline. Jargon improves communication efficiency within a group, but tends to isolate the group from outsiders and may have the effect of intimidating non-group members. Jargon across industries may have the same alphanumeric form but mean something completely different, adding confusion to the isolation and intimidation (see box, "Now What Did That Really Mean?"). In business-to-business marketing, messages must be encoded in the language of the receiver or customer if the goal is to assist the customer through the decision process.

Jargon is any specialized language of a group that is used to improve the efficiency of communication among members of the group. A price paid for this efficiency within the group is to separate the group from nonmembers who may not have experience with or knowledge of the language.

Media Can Impact the Message

The means of transmission selected for the message will have an impact on how the message is received. Receivers may prejudge messages because of previous experiences, or beliefs about certain media, or the medium's technology may have a distorting impact on the message. For example, the telemarketer whose call is abruptly cut short may have had the deal of a lifetime, but the receiver absolutely would not tolerate interrupting phone calls. Or perhaps the upper-level management of a company perceives that time spent at conventions and technical conferences is not productive, so the engineering staff is not provided with any budget to attend. Whether reasonable or not, different customers and markets have established methods by which they obtain information. The medium used in a market segment must be an accepted conduit for information and must be consistent with the positioning of the firm and its offering.

Feedback

In any marketing communication effort, it is critical for the marketing manager to know whether the message was received by the targeted audience as intended. In consumer markets, because of the heavy dependence on advertising (a monologue),[2] sales results are often the first indication of a message not performing as designed. In rapidly changing markets, the time lapse associated with waiting for sales results is too great to effectively add correction to the message. When advertising

---

Now What Did That Really Mean?

Different things mean different things in different industries. In the chemical industry, ABS is *acrylonitrile-butadiene-styrene*, a widely used plastic for consumer products. In the automotive industry, ABS is *antilock brake systems*. Again, in the auto industry, rear windows are *backlites* (tail lamps *are* called tail lamps). PC is a desktop computer, but is also *politically correct* in social situations. How many different meanings can you think of for "10K"?

Colloquial expressions in some languages can cause communication difficulties. In the United States, we say that someone who has accepted responsibility for a situation has *stepped up to the bar*. And of course, when a concept or idea is not anticipated to be successful, *that dog won't hunt.*

In common language, many words imply meanings not intended. When polled as to the meaning of the word *compromise*, students most often reply *to give up*. Yet, compromise is often the outcome of negotiations aimed at creating win–win situations that work for all involved, enabling all parties to commit to an agreed-on direction, goal, or *common promise*. Compromise can thus be defined as doing what works!

Direct response requests—reader surveys, questionnaires, and warranty registrations—are forms of customer feedback. The difficulty with these types of feedback is that they require an active interest by the customer in providing feedback. This implies that only a portion of the total market for the product is providing information. The behavioral aspects of those customers who will make an effort to provide feedback may be significantly different than the entire market segment.

Selective exposure, selective attention, and selective retention are different behaviors associated with message perception. As with any behavioral element, there is a degree of subjectivity, based often on the receptiveness or attentiveness of the receiver.

Selective exposure refers to the actual media to which the receiver may be exposed. Different stakeholders in the buying center will experience different types of media exposure. Just as McDonald's places commercials during Saturday morning cartoons focused on fun meals and Ronald McDonald and commercials focused on family relationships on the evening news, business-to-business marketers must recognize the media that the target audience is regularly exposed to (magazines, business press, etc.).

is a significant form of promotion, firms must use other means to solicit feedback. Still, even with the use of **direct response requests** inserted in promotions, feedback through the Internet, toll-free access to customer service, and other means, feedback is often only available through a proactive choice of the customer.

One of the advantages of the personal selling and strong relationship aspects of marketing in business-to-business markets is the opportunity for immediate, personal feedback through the field sales and marketing team. When the relationship is also the medium that carries the message, feedback is immediate. The ongoing dialog with customers reduces the opportunities for distortion and misunderstanding.

Noise

Jargon and the other factors noted that create distortion or inaccuracies in messages are commonly combined into the category of **noise**. Noise can be a belief or predisposition that acts as a filter that interprets messages. Noise can also distort messages. Distortion is caused by misunderstanding, misinterpretation, rumor, beliefs, and other competing influences—such as fatigue, distractions, crises, and competitive messages—and can exist at several different places in the communication process. Whenever the message is interpreted, either for transmission through media or creation of an outcome, the possibility exists that the message will be changed. As the target audience for many types of promotion, customers screen incoming messages based on timing, their individual interests, the needs of their job function, or the immediate needs of the task at hand. Other messages get screened out. Receivers, to protect themselves from message overload, only pay attention to useful information. Thus, noise in the communication process can be a situational factor. The successful message must be created to survive the influences of media, break through the screening process, *and* be accurately perceived by the receiver.

Customer perception, then, is both selective and subjective.[3] Message interpretation is subject to **selective exposure**, **selective attention**, and **selective retention**. Successful promotion, as in other parts of the marketing mix, requires business-to-business marketers to make judgments about the behavior of customers.

Capabilities of Promotion

In the next section, we examine the strengths and weaknesses of different elements of the promotion mix. Marketers must understand the limitations of promotion as well as its capabilities. Exhibit 15-2 lists purposes that can and cannot be pursued with most promotional efforts. As you study this material, recall that promotion must be contextually consistent with the overall marketing effort and support the positioning of the offering and the organization. Recognize that the promotion mix is the implementation of the communication strategy. Every part of the promotional effort should be designed to communicate effectively with the customer under specific circumstances. There are not good or bad elements of the promotion mix, just inappropriate elements or combinations of elements for the task at hand.

What Promotion Can Do	What Promotion Cannot Do?
• Inform about availability • Persuade trial • Encourage repurchase • Communicate advantages • Establish awareness • Aid in securing channels • Assist in creating brand preference • Build image • Move product to balance production • Support selling efforts.	• Sell products that do not meet needs • Convince customers that an inferior product is superior • Convince customers to go out of their way to purchase when comparable goods are more readily available • Convince customers to pay more than perceived value • Overcome a weak marketing strategy • Substitute for a bad product.

EXHIBIT 15-2 Capabilities of Promotional Efforts

THE ELEMENTS OF THE PROMOTION MIX

How are messages delivered to audiences? A variety of methods exists. We start with general categories of the promotion mix from a marketing principles course—personal selling, advertising, sales promotion, and public relations—and then discuss common, useful methods, often a mix of elements, in business-to-business settings.

Personal Selling

Chapter 12 discussed personal selling in depth. Recall that personal selling is individualized communications, often a series of dyadic interactions—one-on-one conversations between the seller and customer. The seller's message can be tailored and adapted to the particular needs of the customer. Often the marketer can reach several individuals at once in a setting that resembles one-on-one interaction. Executive seminars or "Webinars"—seminars conducted online—have both scripted and interactive components. Even when economies of scale can be leveraged in the seminar or Webinar setting, personal selling reaches a relatively small audience at any one time. Because of the closeness of the personal interactions in sales, personal selling is the primary driver in building effective relationships.

Personal selling is the most costly communication method on a cost-per-contact basis. Many companies use nonpersonal communications in the early part of the decision process for prospective customers, because, to build awareness, it is more cost effective than contacting customers with sellers. Advertising, sales promotion, and publicity help make buying center members aware and interested in the supplier's offering and help draw them to contact the supplier to begin including the supplier in the buying decision process.

Advertising

As consumers, we believe we are experts in advertising, or at least in how to surf around or through it! While advertising is most important in consumer markets, it still has a role in business-to-business markets.

Selective attention is a protective method receivers use to prevent overload. Based on an individual's ability to process and store messages, only useful information is seen. The successful message may be a reinforcement of a previous decision or may address an immediate need. Either consciously or not, receivers only take interest in information that has immediate value.

Selective retention is the measurement of the "storage function"—the quantity or portion of a message retained and the time span over which it is recalled. Because of timing or other circumstances, receivers will not recall messages that have no immediate use, though they may be of value at a later time. Several reminder techniques, such as leave-behind brochures and other sales paraphernalia (coffee mugs, pens, paperweights, etc.), are used to address this issue.

Advertising is usually a monologue—impersonal mass communication without any direct feedback mechanism. When mass communication is used, the message must be short, to the point, yet general enough to be understood by a broad range of recipients. Advertising is effective at establishing awareness in and providing general information to the target market. In both the consumer buying decision process and the business-to-business buying decision process, advertising's impersonal, nonspecific nature is not usually effective when the final purchase choice is made at the point of sale.

Initially, advertising costs can be high from both a production and a placement viewpoint. However, once created, advertisements are most often used several times, spreading the production costs over more than one use of the ad. Also, while the **media buy**—the cost of airing or placing the advertisement—can be expensive, the size of the audience reached results in a relatively low cost per exposure.

*The **media buy** is the selection of where and when the advertisement will be distributed. Considerations should include not only how people are exposed to the message but whether they are the right people. Business magazines and trade journals track the decision-level authority and influence of the professionals who are regular readers and use that data to influence advertisers regarding the frequency and placement of ads in their publications.*

Sales Promotion

Sales promotion is often considered the "all other" category in the promotion mix. Sales promotions are incentives that are used to enhance the value of an offering over a specified period of time. As consumers, we know sales promotions as coupons, rebates, point-of-purchase displays, samples, and contests. While these are the sales promotion focus of consumer markets and are also used in business-to-business markets, additional categories such as promotional allowances, sales meetings, conventions and trade shows, exhibits, and cooperative advertising are more often the focus in business-to-business markets.

Sales promotion can be divided into three general categories based on the results desired.[4]

- Sales promotion focused on sales team support
- Sales promotion focused on middlemen support—these "push" promotions are used to influence channel members with regard to their operating variables, such as inventory levels, payment timing, cooperative promotion participation, and so on.
- Sales promotion focused on customers to shift the time of purchases, stimulate trial, or encourage continued use of a product—normally known as "pull" sales promotions.

The discussion that follows focuses on the first two of these three categories. The third category—sales promotion focused on customers to shift the time of purchase, stimulate trial, or encourage continued use of a product—is contextually more consistent with consumer marketing. Consumer rebates encourage purchase during the period of the promotion, often borrowing sales from later periods. Samples or bundled products (e.g., a sample jar of a new jelly attached to a jar of peanut butter) seek to get customers to try new products. These direct to consumer sales promotion tactics have only limited use in business-to-business markets.

SALES PROMOTION FOCUSED ON THE SALES TEAM Company or organization internal marketing programs often have a large element focused on internal motivation and annual or seasonal themes. Annual sales and marketing meetings are often the kickoff events for these programs, aimed at bringing everyone together in support of the common theme. While a major internal promotion effort, the sales meeting affords the opportunity for all members of the field team to interact with headquarters counterparts and be a part of the planning of the strategy that they implement. It is at this time that many sales incentives and contests are introduced and training in new products, merchandising programs, and support materials takes place.

SALES PROMOTION FOCUSED ON CHANNEL INTERMEDIARIES   The correct promotional allowance to middlemen can make or break efforts to get product through a distributor channel. Rewards to channel members for cooperation with seasonal promotion plans are essential to get middlemen focused on products. The necessity of these promotions is most often obvious very early in the product life cycle and again in the maturity and decline stages when a product is likely to face horizontal competition.

Early in the PLC, incentives to middlemen may be necessary to get new products accepted by the marketing channel. Listing allowances, incentives that provide for the costs associated with adding a new product to the industrial distributor's line, are common. Merchandising assistance and training for the distribution sales force, particularly with new offerings, are important sales promotion efforts. Coincident with the push promotional effort through the channel must be the pull effort with end users of the product. Recall from Chapters 12 and 14 that distribution sellers, often more involved in transactional sales, most likely are rewarded on a short-term commission basis so they pay close attention to how they spend their valuable time. The distributors must be convinced of a ready market for the new product before encumbering their sellers with the additional time commitments of training and customer development.

As the popularity and profitability of the new product grows, competitors will be attracted to the market. Distribution will recognize the benefits of belonging to the channel for the product. It is shortly after this recognition that the distributor seeks a second source for the product in an effort to protect customers from relying on a single source or using other distributors for a second source of the product type. In these circumstances, when products face horizontal competition, sales incentives in the form of sales contests, volume bonuses, and rebates to the distributor or directly to sellers can maintain focus on the product.

Firms that use distributors for products must recognize that, regardless of the product position in the PLC, the distributor and the distributor sellers are an extension of the sales team of the firm. Sales and marketing meetings at the distributor level provide an opportunity to develop and improve relationships with distributors while giving them the opportunity to feel a part of the organization. These meetings and seminars operate for the distributors the same as the national sales and marketing meetings operate for the firm's sales team. New products are introduced; and training in new products, merchandising programs, and support materials takes place.

Public Relations

The intent of public relations (PR) and publicity is to develop a positive image of the company or product line through nonsponsored (nonpaid) messages. Public relations covers all efforts to obtain the attention and favorable coverage of the firm's business by third-party media and publics. Companies engage in publicity to transmit a message that is viewed, interpreted, and retransmitted by news organizations, reporters, and media "luminaries"—news commentators that have developed reputations and are recognized personalities or expert authorities. In the world of new media, these luminaries increasingly include "bloggers"—media commentators

*Public stakeholders are those public entities that have a vested interest in the financial performance and/or social responsibility demonstrated by the firm. These **publics** or public stakeholders may be large retirement systems with significant financial holdings in the stock of the firm, mutual fund managers whose funds are invested, government agencies charged with regulating portions of the firm's business practices, and public interest groups whose agenda can be advanced or damaged by actions of the firm.*

that post Web logs, or "blogs," that offer a running commentary on topics of interest. Since the message of PR has been digested by the media and **public stakeholders** and supposedly evaluated on its merits, the retransmitted message reported in the media gains credibility. Very often, the reach and attention-getting ability of the media extend far beyond the reach and impact that a company can buy with advertising. Well-executed PR efforts, then, have the potential to obtain much higher levels of response than can equivalent expenditures in advertising. Within this definition, PR is somewhat analogous to organized word of mouth!

At times, management will need to be persuaded that publicity or an ongoing PR effort has value. The results of these efforts develop over long time periods, making them difficult to quantify. In addition to the difficulties associated with measuring results, PR efforts are difficult to control because so much of the message will be interpreted and reinterpreted by other parties who will have their own level of knowledge and perception and may have their own agenda regarding the message. These difficulties contribute to a lower regard for PR among some business-to-business marketers. This is unfortunate, as publicity and public relations can serve the organization well, particularly during difficult times.

PUBLIC RELATIONS ACTIVITIES   PR activities include press releases, special events, press tours, public appearances by company executives and participation in media dialog as industry observers and experts, participation in trade shows and conferences, and any number of other

Guerrilla marketing is the use of attention-getting small events intended to get the company noticed, to build small pockets of sales, and to obtain word-of-mouth diffusion of a message. It might involve passing out free samples or promotional merchandise in public places or engaging in small bits of "street theater" to attract attention. The idea is to generate grass-roots level excitement while spending a minimum amount of money. Small companies or start-ups often rely on guerrilla marketing.

activities intended to obtain public recognition or notice (see **guerrilla marketing**). Note that we have included trade shows and conferences as, at least in part, a PR activity. While this is not the traditional definition, the outcomes of trade shows and conferences contribute significantly to the corporate image or PR effort. These events thus serve as an example of the overlap of different elements of the promotion mix. The purposes of these activities are to generate awareness, credibility, and reassurance of legitimacy and quality, as well as to convey differentiation on a few important dimensions. Note that all of these intended outcomes contribute to the value image and/or branding effort of the firm.

Messages to be conveyed through PR cannot be complex: media coverage and interpretation will tend to simplify the message transmitted from the company. The exception to this is evaluative expositions coming from media luminaries, who can go into great detail in examining a company and its offerings. However, so much evaluation and interpretation go into media luminaries' reporting that a company cannot count on a complex message to be retransmitted in whole.

EFFECTIVENESS IN PUBLIC RELATIONS   Two major dimensions of effort underlie effective PR. The first is effective management of relationships with the media. The second is creativity. In both areas, prudent management often looks outside of the organization to professional PR agencies. A good PR agency is "worth its weight in gold" for managing media relationships (i.e., it is worth the hefty retainer it will charge for its efforts). This technique may be the only way you have of exercising any control of how the

PR gets repeated in the marketplace. The right agency has established relationships with reporters, editors, and Internet luminaries who influence the media that the target market is exposed to. The media editors who make decisions about the content of their reporting trust the agency to give them newsworthy information and rely on the agency to filter out unsupported "hype". Good PR representatives have nurtured the relationship with editors, reporters, and luminaries and know the customs and nuances of the market. They know how often they can contact editors without wearing out their welcome and know how to diplomatically introduce new ideas to the media. Good agencies have the contacts and the credibility to schedule press tours that draw the best reporters, industry analysts, financial analysts, and industry luminaries.

As previously noted, management can be reluctant to hire the services of a full-time PR agency. Too often, companies that are new to publicity underestimate the value of a good agency, believing that they do not need such relationships with the media or that a summer intern can come close to replicating an agency's efforts for a tenth of the cost. Many companies, large and small, have learned that the need for an existing positive public image can occur without warning. Then it is too late. Very few companies can ignore the need for a good public image. Those that do must have an unassailable market position.

WHEN THE IMAGE UNRAVELS   What happens when the firm is faced with a serious PR problem? While the management of crisis situations is a major focus of Chapter 16, an understanding now of the fundamental concepts of PR is appropriate. In the preceding discussion, public relations was defined as having a long-term focus with little management or control over the actual reporting of the news or event and a reliance on (or fear of) the trust and credibility of the secondary sources—the reporting media personalities. Recognizing these conditions should also foster the recognition that just handling a bad situation does not suffice; closing the barn door after the animals are already out does nothing to address the main problem! An ongoing PR effort that has built relationships with the media and established a positive corporate value image can create a significant predisposition to forgiveness from the market.

Knowing these fundamental concepts, why do some firms do so poorly when faced with a serious image problem? It has been our experience that, because of the long wait for a payoff (that may never be quantifiable), management spends promotion dollars on elements of the promotion mix that have immediate, measurable impact. This predicament is aggravated by the short-term business measurements used to reward many managers. Though a positive public image can contribute to, among other things, the recruitment of employees and location and development of facilities, these outcomes are seldom quantifiable. The PR effort may never be missed—until it is needed.

PROMOTIONAL METHODS IN BUSINESS-TO-BUSINESS MARKETING

The methods used most often in business-to-business marketing are effective because they are designed for use when there are relatively few people in the audience and the audience is looking for specialized information on several dimensions. Nonpersonal communications—advertising, sales promotion, and public relations—can have a positive influence on the way the buying center progresses through the buying decision process. Care must be exercised to ensure that messages are appropriate. This means that messages must be appropriate for the type of individual, appropriate for the role in the buying center, and appropriate for the stage in the buying decision process. There are two principal challenges in accomplishing this—aside from the *creative* challenge of creating compelling, effective messages. First, the marketer needs a thorough understanding of the customer, that is, what the behaviors of people are in the buying center, what their roles are in the decision process, and what motivates them. We have, of course, stressed this understanding throughout the text. The second challenge is to keep all these messages consistent. The marketer may be able to target certain roles in the buying center by placing communications in certain media, but this does not assure that people in one role are not reading messages aimed at someone else in the buying center. This is particularly true for print advertising, sponsored articles, or contributed material in trade magazines and for Web site content. People in many different roles read trade magazines: executives, managers, technical people, and purchasing managers. Web sites, by their nature, attract all sorts of viewers.

In business-to-business marketing, different types of nonpersonal communication can be designed to have a significant effect at several points in the buying decision process, as can be seen in Exhibit 15-3. The types of promotion used must have an order—a map or sequence—associated with their placement. A trade journal editor may be willing to mention a new offering in an editorial about changes in a particular market or include the offering in the "new products" section of the magazine but would not consider either action if the offering had already been featured in a print advertisement. The news would not be new.

As Exhibit 15-3 shows, communications early in the buying process among the members of the buying center can influence and motivate to recognize a problem and to seek a solution. In earlier chapters, we have discussed how sellers and missionary salespeople can influence this aspect of the buying decision process. A coordinated effort of nonpersonal methods can also influence buying center members' perceptions. For instance, a print ad in a trade journal may catch the attention of a product designer, creating a level of awareness that assists the missionary sales effort and starting the process of thinking about embedding new capabilities in his product.

In the next stage of the buying decision process, nonpersonal communication can provide a great deal of information as members of the buying center collect information and compare offerings and suppliers. During this information search phase, nonpersonal communication may

In the Process Flow Stages . . .	Non-Personal Communication Can . . .	Using . . .

Definition Stage
  Problem definition
  Solution definition
  Product specification
	Help identify problems;
	provide info for defining solutions;
	help customers remember vendors
		Advertising; web site; trade show participation; publicity

Selection Stage
  Solution provider search
  Acquire solution provider(s)
	Provide info on vendor; provide info on products and partners	Web site; direct mail

Deliver Solution Stage
  Customize as needed
  Install/test/train
	Deliver service and training info	Web site

Endgame Stage
  Operate solution
  Reach end result
  Evaluate outcomes
  Determine next set of needs
	Provide reinforcement; deliver service info; share performance data for evaluation	Web site; advertising; public relations

EXHIBIT 15-3   The Buying Decision Process and Potentially Effective Methods of Nonpersonal Communications

influence the direction that the decision process takes. For instance, information on a Web site may be enough for a process engineer to make early comparisons among alternative system components and to decide to keep the vendor's product in his consideration set. The process engineer may have decided to look at the Web site because he received a well-designed direct mail piece or read a product review in a trade magazine.

During the next stage, in which selection of a vendor occurs, the participants may remember communications they have seen before; or an executive may remember an ad for one of the companies on the short list of suppliers that he is to approve for final proposals for a project. In these instances, nonpersonal communication may not have access to decision makers *during the stage*. However, a well-designed ad that the decision maker has seen before may have created a high enough level of recognition in the decision maker's memory that it has a positive influence on the decision, small though the effect may be. Also during selection, a sales promotion offering may induce the customer to try a product or service to see whether it holds value or not. For instance, an office supply dealer may send an e-mail coupon to an administrative assistant that provides a 15 percent discount for trying the dealer for next month's order, plus a "special gift" for the administrative assistant. This may be enough to induce the administrative assistant to make the decision to try the dealer (without feeling guilty about receiving the special gift, because the company has received a discount in the deal, too).

As Exhibit 15-3 shows, after a sale has been made, the supplier's communications could reinforce the idea that the customer made a good choice. Promotion that features a customer's new use of the firm's offering not only reinforces the customer's selection but also encourages other similar users in the market (often competitors of the first customer) to examine the value provided by the offering. This can lead to translation opportunities for the firm and good exposure for the customer's products—assuming the customer is amenable to having its products featured in the promotion. And, of course, nonpersonal information may be provided that helps the customer to use the product.

Convergence of the Promotion Mix

In the following discussion, the methods and devices of business-to-business promotion are discussed. Each of these methods or devices follows the basic tenets of the four elements of the promotion mix—personal sales, advertising, sales promotion, and publicity. However, it can be difficult to specify these efforts as fitting into only one of the promotion mix variables as they are a mix, or combination, of many different parts of the promotion mix. Therefore, the discussion of these methods focuses not necessarily only on the process by which promotion mix variables are used, but on the desired outcomes of the promotional effort. After we discuss several of these important promotional tools, we return to the Sensacon[5] example, used in Chapters 8, 11, and 13, to aid in understanding them.

Print Promotion

One of the key methods of communicating with customers in business-to-business markets is through printed promotion. In most industries, there are several trade publications that reach members of a buying center. When stakeholders in various positions find an ad for a product or service they like, they often save the magazine issue, download a file from the magazine Web site, or clip the ad. This provides extended memory beyond what can be kept in their heads.

There are other kinds of publications that run print advertising, principally business magazines and industry directories. Advertising run in these vehicles has slightly different purposes than ads run in trade journals, such as a longer time focus, and, hence, the execution will be different.

ADVERTISING IN TRADE JOURNALS   Most industry segments have several journals, magazines, or newsletters reporting developments, events, conditions, and trends in the industry. Audiences for the major publications cover large proportions of the membership of the major buying centers for companies within the industry. One of the difficulties with trade publications is that the audiences are diverse; executives, as well as design engineers and administrative staff, are likely to read many of the same publications. It is therefore difficult to create ads that appeal to all or many roles in the buying center.

In creating print ads, the marketer and his advertising agency should target specific members of buying centers and the stage of the buying process that most will be in at the time. The message should convey *key benefits* important to the buying center member at this stage in the process and should be delivered in language most compelling to those benefits. This means that product advertising does *not always convey product attributes*. This can be very difficult for technology-oriented product managers to accept. For instance, a small manufacturer of emission control equipment in the semiconductor industry was targeting process engineers with print ads that conveyed a great deal of information on product features, technology, and specifications—read: *boring*. They changed the ad design to focus on cost savings (a key benefit sought by process engineers when looking for system upgrades) and ran it with the headline "Be a Cost-Saving Hero"—read: *attention getting*. The company quadrupled its information inquiries from the engineers! Again, customers do not buy technology; they buy solutions, so doesn't it make sense to promote solution-creating capabilities?

In business-to-business marketing, careful consideration should be given to the amount of technical data that is included in the promotion. In making this decision, the marketing manager should be aware of the attitude and behavior of the individuals in the target audience. Complex data can be left to separate documents available on request; often made available as downloads from the marketer's Web site.

In general, advertising in trade journals requires some effort to break through the noise, but this noise level is usually only moderate. At times, though, the noise level can rise precipitously. During the Internet boom of 1999–2000, for instance, trade magazines such as *Business 2.0* and *The Industry Standard* greatly expanded the number of pages printed, mostly with more ads. This made it difficult for individual companies to get noticed in amongst all this noise.[6]

DIRECTORY ADVERTISING   When members of the buying center are looking to build a list of suppliers to approach for an **RFP**, **RFQ**, or **RFB**, they often turn to an industry directory. A well-placed ad in the appropriate directory for the marketer's industry can generate significant new leads. A clear statement of the principal products offered and the key points of differentiation attract more attention than a simple listing in the directory. A problem with directories is that they are usually compiled less frequently than product introductions, so the directory ad needs to be fairly generic, yet convey points of differentiation. Often this amounts to stating the company's general positioning, as well as pointing out the company's key product lines. Additional information is made available through a referral to the company's Web site.

CONSUMER MEDIA   Sometimes, important members of the buying center are not reachable through trade media or other traditional business-to-business media. In other instances, the marketer wants to reach a broad audience and convey a message in a way that evokes an

Billboards in Business-to-Business Promotion

It may not sound like a good idea at first, but billboards—outdoor advertising—can play a role in business-to-business promotion. When a principal stakeholder in the buying center is not reachable through other means and a thought-provoking message can be developed without complexity, billboards may be a good choice.

Located on major commuter routes, the billboards will be seen by all passers, but as long as that executive who is the target of the ad sees it, it has done its job.

This is one time when a slow, congested commute is a good thing!

emotional response. In such circumstances, advertising in consumer media may be appropriate. Broadcast advertising—radio and television—may be the most effective way to reach a general business audience. Consumer media may also be appropriate when targeting small businesses that do not have a strong tie to an industry or to a profession, or, as described in the box, "Billboards in Business-to-Business Promotion," when a message that will be widely viewed will, in fact, have a narrow target audience.

A problem with consumer media that business-to-business marketers may not be used to encountering is the high noise level. Consumers have erected high barriers to attention and it is easy for advertisements to get lost in the clutter. The ad agency must work at producing ads that get attention. At that point it is crucial to not get carried away in the creative effort and undermine the message or to convey unintended messages that undermine the company's positioning.

SENSACON APPLICATIONS OF PRINT ADVERTISING   To briefly review, recall that Sensacon is a company at the chasm of the technology adoption life cycle. It just completed a major development of its pressure sensor technology for application as tire pressure sensors on SUVs. The size of this new business forced the remaking of the company. Sensacon has the opportunity to become the industry standard for tire pressure sensors but must first position its product and company as the market owner. The task is to communicate Sensacon technology and leadership beyond the SUVs and the two manufacturers that have specified its product.

Now, consider the communication needs of Sensacon. What advertising should Sensacon engage in? Recall that Sensacon is a new supplier to the vehicle industry—many participants may not be aware of Sensacon capabilities or presence. The first task then would be an awareness campaign in major trade journals. However, a review of exactly what Sensacon wants to accomplish and where it is now is critical.

Having a print ad is, in itself, of little use if it does not convey a well thought out, consistent message. Recall that management at Sensacon has named its new product SensorSUV. While this *brand name* differentiates the product from other Sensacon products, it does little to identify the product with potential customers. What does the product do, sense the presence of SUVs? No, the device monitors tire pressure. This is not a feature that the industry is likely to limit to SUVs. By knowing the nature of the vehicle industry, Sensacon realizes that this feature is likely to spread to other types of vehicles: sports cars, family sedans, and anywhere remote tire pressure sensing may be a desirable attribute or feature. The name needs to be changed to something more indicative of what customers will identify with.

Sensacon retains an advertising agency and, among other tasks, the agency works to rename the offering. SensorSUV becomes *InflationGuard*. Print ads to broaden awareness among vehicle designers and engineers (a sizable group, who tend to pay attention to trade magazine advertising) are developed that focus on the ease of use, low cost, and safety advantages of InflationGuard. The ads feature scenes of vehicles that use Sensacon tire pressure sensors (with the concurrence of the vehicle manufacturer), perhaps SUVs in rugged terrain or loaded for a family camping trip, with a caption that reads "Vacations are to get away from worries about pressure." Perhaps an inset picture of the sensor in a tire is part of the ad.

Which journals should the ad be placed in? What exposure does Sensacon want? Since Sensacon and its customers must prepare the tire service industry for these devices, print ads in service industry journals, in addition to vehicle and tire manufacturer journals, are appropriate. The tire service industry may also be an appropriate audience for direct mail (discussed subsequently), though with a different message. Service, repair, and replacement procedures and advice are distributed by Sensacon to all tire dealers on industry mailing lists, advising them of procedures and reassuring them that Sensacon will be available to assist in their service efforts.

Corporate Advertising

There is value for the firm to achieve an image distinct from competition. Corporate advertising is a promotional effort undertaken to enhance the value image or positioning of the firm itself. Corporate advertising is not specifically related to any product of the firm. In this view, corporate advertising is not unlike the institutional advertising done by many supermarkets in consumer markets. By advertising the store, the firm adds brand recognition to all of its house and private brands without the expense of specific promotions that would challenge nationally known brands.

The use of corporate advertising can provide outcomes that would be difficult for specific product-related promotion.[7]

- A company's reputation impacts the chance of getting a first hearing at a new account, and can help overcome problems at an existing account; a degree of forgiveness can exist.
- Community concessions and subsidies, particularly when a firm seeks to expand or create new facilities, can be enhanced.
- All things being equal (such as "average" sellers from all competitors), the larger, well-known company will get the business over the lesser-known smaller competitor. Thus, a smaller company should spend what might be limited promotion dollars to select and train good sales representatives, to overcome the larger competitor's average seller, rather than spend money on advertising.

Company reputations help selling and marketing efforts most when the offering is complex or the risk to the customer is high. When either of these circumstances exists, customers seek suppliers who are willing to address needs in a collaborative manner. The customer seeks a partner to share risk and to be able to help with recovery if something should go wrong. Similarly, a customer favors the well-positioned supplier when it is less familiar with the technology or market or the task at hand is not well defined. All of these reasons were important for Accenture. When the name of the firm was changed, Accenture's management wanted to leverage the strong reputation they had as Andersen Consulting. To do this, they relied in part on corporate advertising to get the attention of buying center members and attach their beliefs to the new name.

After being recognized and accepted in the market, Accenture moved to develop its own image separate from Anderson Consulting—a move that was to be fortuitous.

Direct Mail

Direct mail advertising has several attractive features for the marketer. First, in many circumstances, it can be closely targeted to some important audience characteristics. Second, its effectiveness can be fairly easily measured by determining the proportion of targeted individuals who respond. Third, it is relatively inexpensive.

Direct mail also has its disadvantages. The most important of these is that a large portion of the target audience can easily ignore it. At its worst, direct mail is annoyance that undermines customer perceptions of the positioning of the offering. In general, though, direct mail is expected, and, while not exactly cherished by customers, it can be a good source of information when it is well done.

Sales and Support Literature

As has been mentioned before, much of the communication effort in business-to-business marketing centers on face-to-face personal selling and customer service. These efforts can be greatly aided with well-executed printed materials. Often called collateral materials, these materials are useful early in the customer's buying decision process, when buying center members are collecting and comparing information about several suppliers; they are useful during the customer's review of supplier's proposals, since they help clarify and remind the buying center members of vendor's key differentiators; and they are useful at the end of the process when the buyers are considering their next purchases.

Good sales support literature serves two general purposes: it tells the customer about benefits they will receive, and it gives them enough information that they can determine how the product or service will work. This helps the buying center members think about how the offering can be integrated into their own operation. There are several types of printed materials that are lumped into this category. Each type has a particular function and capability suited to specific circumstances.

CATALOGS, PRODUCT BROCHURES, AND DATA SHEETS The use of catalogs, brochures, and data sheets implies that the product or product line is relatively stable. Offerings that are evolving, either through R&D by the supplier or in conjunction with customers, are not likely to be featured in catalogs. As sales support material, catalogs, brochures, and data sheets provide excellent **leave-behind materials** for sellers but are most effective in transactional sales in which the seller role is that of an order taker or persuader/sustainer.

CAPABILITIES BROCHURES When the seller's role is that of a problem solver or relationship/value creator, standard products are less likely to be the focus of the sales effort. Catalogs and product brochures are less likely to be as valuable. This is similar to the situation faced by service companies. Collateral materials for service organizations focus on the capabilities of the firm and may include testimonials from satisfied customers. The relationship between customer and supplier in a collaborative development effort is not very different. The customer is not necessarily interested in a specific product form as he is in the capabilities of the supplier as a collaborator.

Leave-behind materials are items that sellers can give to customers following an in-person sales call. Leave-behind materials do not necessarily have to stand alone—the seller explains the literature and the value points to the customer.

Another very similar type of promotional material is called the seller stand-in. Seller stand-in materials are often used in direct mail campaigns. This type of material must be self-supporting—the seller will not be able to emphasize or explain its relevance to the customer's needs.

TECHNICAL BULLETINS, TEST REPORTS, AND APPLICATION HISTORIES   Technical bulletins, test reports, and application histories are excellent design guides and problem solvers for customers. Customers in collaborative relationships with suppliers are interested in information that will make their effort easier, timelier, and more productive. Technical information that assists the customer with integration of the product or design features into his product, best practices data, and application histories—case studies of other successful applications of the product or technology—can be very useful. For example, a paint manufacturer may have a specific treatment process to get certain paint grades to stick to otherwise unpaintable surfaces. The *best practices information*, the technical data relating to the chemistry and surface preparation, could be in a technical bulletin. Application histories show unique and notable applications of the technology. Printed advertisements used in trade journals, as previously described, that have been replaced by newer examples often become part of application histories. Web page designers should incorporate easy access to these materials, either to the general public or with opt-in methods. Opt-in features of online newsletters and customer information systems are discussed later in this chapter.

The technical bulletin and the application history, though used in the same manner, usually are positioned differently. Traditionally, the technical bulletin is hardly ever a four-color glossy advertisement reprint, while the application history starts out as exactly that. With the advent of the Internet, technical bulletins and application histories are not only easily updated but are more readily available to customers.

SENSACON APPLICATIONS OF SALES AND SUPPORT LITERATURE   InflationGuard is a new product with great potential but with only two customers—the SUV manufacturers who have awarded Sensacon the business. Marketing managers at Sensacon want to capitalize on this development effort in what they believe to be an expanding market. The Sensacon field team has the task of *translating* this *new business* success to other customers. (New business, translation, and core churn are discussed in Chapter 11 and again in Chapter 12.) The headquarters market segment specialists (see Exhibit 12-2 for a perspective of where the headquarters market segment specialist fits into the organization) are responsible for developing the translation tools that will assist the field team.

Appropriate translation tools targeted at vehicle manufacturers include a capabilities brochure introducing Sensacon; a technical bulletin focused on the ease of adaptability of InflationGuard to other tires and vehicles beyond SUVs; and an application history featuring the current SUV success story, partially culled from the print advertisement discussed earlier. As Sensacon adapts InflationGuard to more vehicles and tires, the updated data can be made available through the Internet.

Translation tools for the aftermarket—tire service and repair facilities and SUV dealers—require a different approach because these channels get information from different sources. Sensacon plans to develop an aftermarket version of InflationGuard. Individual customers will be able to have the product installed on their vehicles by a certified dealer. This is, however, several months away. In the meantime, Sensacon will seek one or more tire manufacturers as partners, training the field personnel to handle Sensacon inquiries.

Channel Promotions

When Sensacon does decide to enter the aftermarket, there may be several options. Collaboration with a company that already has established aftermarket channels—a tire manufacturer or automotive accessory company—may be the correct choice. Whichever channel design Sensacon pursues, an appropriate promotion plan will be necessary. Sensacon will need to consider various sales promotion techniques focused on middlemen, as discussed earlier in this chapter.

Promotional Merchandise

Premiums, as they are called, are merchandise items given away to customers, prospects, channel members, media representatives, and other stakeholders or interested parties. Premiums are a form of sales promotion, usually intended to augment other promotions. Sales promotions serve, in consumer marketing, as short-term inducements to purchase, while, in business-to-business marketing, they are intended to get action other than a sale. Most business-to-business transactions are too complex and valuable for a sales promotion incentive to provide much inducement. Rather, sales promotions are used to provide incentive for small, intermediate actions in the buying decision process, such as an incentive to visit a trade show booth, an incentive to fill out a questionnaire, an incentive to visit a Web site, or an incentive to remember a brand name when it is time to put together a list of suppliers to invite to make a proposal.

Premium merchandise, something of limited but noticeable value, is provided, and some reciprocal action is expected or hoped for. Premium merchandise is given away at trade shows with the most interesting and unique items encouraging a lot of visits to booths. Sellers give out premium merchandise on customer calls as they make excellent leave-behind items. The incentive is for remembering the company and the seller and for establishing positive feelings about either or both. Often, a small premium is sent with a direct mail piece, providing incentive for the recipient to call for more information or to set up an appointment with a seller.

Premium merchandise that is unique should be chosen in order to get attention and memory. However, the nature of the premium should, if possible, be related to the product or service offered and should provide value to the customers in their role in the buying center. This is often difficult to do and might require very different kinds of merchandise for, say, engineers and managers. More often, the marketer finds it necessary to simply find merchandise that is unique and valuable and has a clever use of the brand logo emblazoned on the merchandise.

PUBLIC RELATIONS, TRADE SHOWS, CONFERENCES, AND CORPORATE POSITIONING

Trade shows and conferences, usually considered short-term sales promotions, are great opportunities to initiate and reinforce the positioning of a firm relative to other industry participants. In this section, we examine how these promotional methods are used in an overall integrated marketing communications plan (IMC). First, let us review the basics of trade shows and participation in them.

Trade Shows and Conferences

Trade shows are considered by some to be a great excuse to travel to a major city at the company's expense. They are much more than that. Anyone who thinks that is all that trade shows are has never worked in a show booth or tried to absorb all that is going on at the show. Attendance at industry trade shows is expected of any serious player in the market segment. Also, all but the smallest companies are expected to exhibit. This is important. Without visibility at the industry show, it is far more difficult to build awareness among potential customers.

At times, it may be difficult to decide which trade shows to attend. In some industries, particularly if the industry is doing well financially, several shows spring up, each claiming to be "the" show to attend. Many large shows divide into regional shows, lowering travel expenses, making it possible for more people to attend. This, of course, means more shows for exhibitors who then experience increased costs. The process of selecting shows to attend and/or participate in includes but is not limited to an analysis of the following:

- What shows are considered important by customers in their markets.
- What shows are considered notable by industry and financial analysts who track the industry or firm of the marketer.
- What shows are likely to have the best audience for announcements, conference presentations, and technical sessions.
- What shows are likely to be attended by customer or industry luminaries who are part of the target audience of the firm.

If a marketer's customers have trade shows, the marketer should also attend. The opportunity to see what the marketer's customers consider to be important, not only to their customers but also among their competitors, should not be passed up. If the marketer's customers in different segments have shows, he should attend and, maybe, exhibit. This sounds like a lot of trade shows. However, with all of the marketer's potential customers in one place, why wouldn't he attend and, possibly, exhibit?

WHO SHOULD ATTEND   The trade show is not a party for marketing and sales staff but is an opportunity to educate members of the firm about the business, particularly the new employees. Everyone that the organization can afford to send should attend the show. This includes support staff, technical staff, production staff, marketing and sales, and senior executives. Firms that operate under the marketing or societal marketing concept recognize the importance of all team members contextually understanding the markets in which the firm competes. Of course, attendance at the show helps cement relationships among the staff and with customers and distributors as well.

Individuals should have a plan of attendance that includes learning as much as possible about what impacts their role in the organization. Technical conferences or seminars usually occur simultaneously with trade shows. Advanced programs are available such that attendance at appropriate events can be scheduled. Traditional with many trade shows, particularly in the high-technology or consumer products arena, are press conferences about new product introductions or new business alliances. While the information presented at these events is not likely to be startling or reveal any proprietary information, the *spin* placed on the presentation can be telling.

HAVING AN EXHIBIT   Why would anyone actually want to spend hours at a show booth at a trade show? As stated in the last paragraph, there will not be any new information that a well-informed marketer does not already know. However, in the industry trade show, current and potential customers visit the show to learn about suppliers and their offerings. If the trade show in question is the marketer's customers' industry trade show, the marketer's presence is noted as support and commitment to the segment. Besides, not all of the marketer's horizontal competitors recognize the importance of attending shows other than those in their own industry. The marketer's effort may be rewarded by having his customer base all to himself, avoiding comparisons with his competition!

Having exhibits at the customers' trade shows provides an opportunity to identify and start relationships with customers that may be new to the market, as well as to reinforce relationships with existing customers. If the marketer's company is entering a new market, an exhibit at that market's show is a good way to begin the market development efforts.

If the marketer's firm is about to announce a new product for a particular market segment or collaboration with a major customer that will result in a new offering, it makes more sense to do this at the customer's show. Consider that all of the potential customers will be there with an interest in what the marketer's company has to offer and what value it can contribute. This may make more sense than using the marketer's industry's trade show when all of his horizontal competitors will be present looking for potential weaknesses to exploit.

STAGING THE EXHIBIT   Technically competent people who can explain offerings *without relying on jargon* should be at the booth. The booth staff should be well coached so that they are aware of the goals of the exhibit and aware of what not to do—or reveal! Sales and marketing staff are naturally gregarious and enjoy engaging people in conversation, while technical staff may not be fully aware of the strategic importance of certain information. It is sometimes startling how much proprietary information can be obtained in a conversation with a poorly trained or poorly briefed person at a trade show.

In a well-attended, lively trade show, marketers find it difficult to obtain customers' attention and memory. This is a good place to consider well-done publicity events as part of the booth activities. Trade shows are a place where a good deal of silliness and drama can be staged to obtain attention. Marketers need to be mindful of the company's image and the positioning of its products. Too much silliness or the wrong kind can convey the wrong message if a marketer is not careful.

Whenever possible, products or applications of the company's technology or capabilities should be available to *touch and feel* in the booth. Just as with print advertisements in trade journals, featuring customer applications (with their concurrence) can be very effective. If the marketer's firm is the market owner in a segment, the product trade name should be prominently displayed and reinforced in conversation. However, if the marketer's company is not the market owner, use of the generic name for the offering may be more appropriate even if the firm has its own brand name. If there is little chance of establishing the marketer's brand, there is no reason to help with the reinforcement of the competitor's brand name.

WHEN THE SHOW IS OVER, CAPITALIZE ON THE EFFORT   When the show is over, everyone goes home, proud of a job well done; but, the effort is really only starting. The show will have generated many inquiries about the company's products and capabilities. These leads should be made available as soon as possible to field teams for appropriate follow-up. Unless contacts specify otherwise, "as soon as possible" should be measured in days, not weeks or months. As with any promotional effort that creates customer expectations, failure to respond to inquiries in a timely manner is more damaging than not accepting the inquiry itself. If the marketer's firm is unable to respond quickly due to anticipated inquiry volume of other planned events (i.e., the company's national sales meeting, etc.), individuals who have made inquiries should be advised of the delay. Those who cannot wait should get immediate attention.

To improve response time, many firms hire **fulfillment firms**. These organizations specialize in responding to inquiries. A direct mail or Internet response immediately after the show, handled by the fulfillment organization "buys some time," as well as serving as a reminder to keep the firm and its offering uppermost in the customer's mind until the field team can respond.

Fulfillment firms specialize in timely response to customer inquiries. Requests for product literature and any other follow-up that can be handled through the use of printed materials or premiums are requests that can be appropriately contracted to fulfillment firms. Should a recall or product advisory become necessary, fulfillment firms can be called on to handle the increased number of inquiries placed to company phones, e-mail, and Web sites.

Shortly after the show is over, an evaluation of the costs per lead generated should be made. This evaluation should be performed again six months later, or at least before the next show. With the day-to-day pressures in many business environments, the six-month review of cost per legitimate lead may never happen. This is unfortunate, as this evaluation can provide guidance as to what to do, or what not to do, with the next show. If there were many leads, but very few proved legitimate, then an in-booth screening method may be appropriate. If the company is giving away a popular premium, the marketer may want to qualify recipients—but without denying the premium to someone who may not appear qualified.

Public Relations and Positioning

Press conferences and technical conferences coincident with trade shows are an excellent tool to build the positioning of the firm and the offering. Many of the promotional methods described here may seem focused at large, financially capable firms well positioned to take advantage of the trade show environment. While that is not strictly the case, what alternatives are there for the small firm that is not yet established in the market or does not have the financial ability or the existing positioning to attract interest at a trade show? The careful use of publicity can help to overcome these limitations. First, management in the small firm must recognize that the firm cannot directly take on large competitors and develop appropriate strategy. A market niche must be developed in which the capabilities of the firm can be demonstrated. This can be particularly challenging for a small, high-technology company.

High-technology companies do not become high-technology companies by accident. Most start-up organizations believe they have a unique product. The challenge is to remake the positioning of the firm from one of offering a unique technology product to one that is known for applying technology to customer needs. Publicity and a good PR consultant are the tools to accomplish this. Consider the assets of the high-tech company. What are they? The founders of the organization have—or at least believe they have and are able to convince investors that they have—a distinctive competence in their field. Usually, this competence is put to work developing the technology of the product. While this is necessary, it is not usually sufficient to position the firm as a leader in the market. Let us again consider the Sensacon example.

SENSACON APPLICATIONS OF PUBLIC RELATIONS, TRADE SHOWS, AND POSITIONING
Prior to winning the InflationGuard business, Sensacon engineers and developers spent years developing the application in collaboration with customers. In the selection stage of the buying decision process (see Exhibit 15-3), manufacturers of SUVs had to find sources with the capabilities to solve the tire pressure monitor problem. These capabilities had to be not only in technology, but also in the ability to support the SUV unit volume requirements and to work with the culture of a mass production-oriented customer—not something for which high-technology companies are known. SUV manufacturers had to believe that Sensacon was capable of meeting the standard. Among other factors, Sensacon management used publicity and corporate positioning to establish its positioning in the market.

Shortly after becoming established, it became apparent to Sensacon management that the company competency was in the application of very precise micromachining technology to large-volume applications. However, large customers were not likely to trust this capability without some tangible evidence. To support the business needs of the firm, management focused on two low-volume but technically complex target markets—SCUBA equipment and medical devices. In both markets, Sensacon could prove the technology without investing in high-volume manufacturing. With the assistance of a PR consultant, Sensacon developed a strategy to position the company as the technology leader in the market.

First, the founders of the company and a select set of technical employees were supported in active membership in all related professional societies. This support included both financial incentives and time commitments; the active membership became part of the job description for these individuals. Soon, Sensacon representatives were chairing technical committees and conferences. This was only the start. Technical papers were written for presentation at conferences focusing on Sensacon technology and its potential in the marketplace. Hypothetical examples of high-volume applications of the technology were demonstrated at associated trade shows. (A delicate balance was necessary between revealing proprietary information and presenting technically enlightening information.) Through the relationships of the PR consultant, Sensacon was able to get mentioned as an up-and-coming organization by editors of trade journals and magazines. Technical papers authored by Sensacon employees were accepted for publication in peer-reviewed professional journals. As momentum developed, Sensacon experts were asked to contribute signed articles about pressure sensor developments to trade journals in that market segment. In reprint form, the signed articles were used as leave-behind sales support items. After approximately two years, Sensacon was the technology icon in the pressure sensor industry.

TECHNICAL PAPERS   A comment about the use of technical papers for publicity and corporate positioning is appropriate. Creating technical papers implies writing ability, speaking ability (if the paper is to be presented at a conference), and technical capability. Without all three capabilities, the effort is not likely to create the intended results. Strategically, selection of authors to represent the firm in these endeavors must consider the capabilities of the individuals. The firm must provide adequate support or coaching of individuals, and the individuals must be willing to be coached. As we maintain from Chapter 1, in a market-driven firm, everyone is part of the marketing effort. Here are some simple guidelines for successful use of technical writing and presentations under the circumstances described here:

- As author or coauthor, the exposure within the company *and* the industry is a good career-enhancing opportunity. Give it the best effort possible.
- Recognize that conference presentations are not only about the technology. Keeping the audience awake and interested is also important. Also, be aware that the paper may be used as a leave-behind brochure or a signed article in a trade journal—more good career exposure, if it is done right.
- Avoid product claims that cannot be verified or accomplished within the parameters of the claim. Again, never create an expectation that cannot be delivered.
- Make the technical papers accessible on your Web site. For less technical audiences, create summary papers that get across the key features and differentiating benefits.
- Do not present the paper if any of the following circumstances exist:

    1. The product is still not ready for market.
    2. You do not want to stimulate the competition.
    3. The product is in joint development with a customer who considers the effort proprietary.
    4. The strategy is to target a small number of selected accounts.
    5. You cannot handle the volume of inquiries that may be generated.
    6. You are not a good speaker.

INTERNET AND WEB COMMUNICATIONS IN BUSINESS-TO-BUSINESS MARKETING

In Chapter 14, we discussed the transactional use of the Web in business-to-business marketing—how the Internet is being used to facilitate product sales and channel functions. Business marketers also make use of the Web for communicating with customers and channel members: this is the other major use of the Web. Even though many Web-only businesses failed or were acquired during 2000 and 2001, the Internet and Web still have appeal for these two uses. Many companies—both new Internet-oriented companies and established "brick-and-mortar" companies—make extensive use of the Internet and Web for these two purposes. Usage and importance of these methods are increasing, as evidenced in a survey by MarketingProfs and Forrester Research in 2007.[8] Respondents to the survey indicated that e-mail marketing would be the most commonly used communications method in 2008 (84 percent of respondents would use[9]) and over half would use such methods as search marketing and Webinars.[10]

At this point, we need to make a distinction between Web communications and Internet communications. Web communications are communications messages and methods used through Web sites. Internet communications include not only Web communications, but also include e-mail and some other less-used Internet tools. Consequently, unless we are being more specific, we use the term *Internet communications* to include Web and e-mail communications.

For communicating with business customers, the biggest advantage the Internet offers is low-cost interactivity. Unlike other nonpersonal communications methods, Web sites and e-mail messages can quickly convey messages back and forth between sender and receiver. While not always as rich a communication medium as personal selling, Web sites and e-mail messages can address large portions of the customer's buying decision process for a lot less cost. In many instances, the buying decision process requires interaction with a seller, but Internet communications can effectively address other portions of the process at far lower cost than would have been incurred without the site. After the dotcom bust of 2000 and 2001, the businesses and technologies that survived have grown much more sophisticated. Web sites and complex online business processes can be constructed and launched for about one-tenth of the cost of less capable processes that were proffered pre-2001. Today's business-to-business communications over the Web are more interactive, more esthetically pleasing, and much more closely attuned to customers' buying decision processes than before.

Internet communications must be approached the same way as any kind of marketing communications (contrary to some common wisdom, the Internet has not changed the basic rules). The marketer needs to understand buyers, the buying center, and how decisions are made. The role of Internet communications can then be determined in assisting buyers in moving through the decision process. Internet methods must then be coordinated with other communications methods. Messages, most of all, must be coordinated so that target audiences receive the messages that inform and prompt the appropriate action. Marketers should also track the relative effectiveness of the multiple Internet communications methods used so that the marketer can tell what methods are working and what ones are not. The Web, through the use of software for analysis of **server logs**, affords the ability to run experiments with alternative messages and presentations. After only a short period of time, the alternative that is most effective can be determined and fully deployed.

A *server log is a computer file that records every action taken by every visitor to a Web site. Analysis of a log file can tell the marketer what parts of the site get the most traffic, how long visitors stay on a page, and what patterns are evident in visitors' interaction with the site.*

Web Site

Almost all business-to-business marketers use a Web site in their marketing efforts and indeed most now have fairly complex sites. For many, it has become their core communication method. It has become standard practice in information search for customers to view material on suppliers' Web sites. Companies learned very early that the Web was an efficient way to display and distribute brochures and product data sheets without incurring printing and mailing costs. Web sites today have far greater communicative abilities than this, though. A good Web site can address most all the purposes and objectives we have discussed for nonpersonal communications in a business-to-business setting. By providing concise information about customer problems and solutions that are provided by the supplier, a Web site can help members of the customer buying center do the following:

- recognize and understand their problems;
- collect and compare information about alternative solutions and costs;
- collect and compare information about alternative suppliers, their partners, and their successful delivery of value to prior customers; and
- easily and quickly obtain such things as training materials, user manuals, and troubleshooting guides for use during the installation, testing, and use of the supplier's product or service.

Many marketers have added **product configurators** to their sites over the past few years. A configurator is an interactive program that lets the prospective customer choose from among product attribute alternatives to configure a product that the customer believes will best meet his needs. The configurator then provides supporting information, such as system requirements and quotes a price. For products that are relatively inexpensive, such as a laptop computer or a data router, the Web site often has a feature that lets the customer place an order for the product the customer just configured.

Marketers find it most difficult to provide value for different market segments. The promise of Web site design is to provide a uniquely defined user experience. Even though a great deal of progress has been made in this regard, this is still difficult to do. Two ways to distinguish market segments are by the viewer's industry or by the type of product that interests the viewer. Many Web sites do these quite well already. Most companies do less well in trying to segment by type of buying center member or by the stage of the buying decision process in which they find themselves. Companies have often done well to distinguish types of customers by existing versus prospective customers, allowing access to a secured extranet that has more detailed information pertaining to their particular account. Prospective customers may be divided into segments by level of interest: site visitors with a higher level of interest sign up for a free "membership" which gives them access to a portion of the site that is for "members only." Another way of segmenting by level of interest is to have visitors that are more interested sign up for free e-mail newsletters or even free "Webinars"—Web seminars. These methods of addressing segments still do not distinguish by type of role in the buying center or situation in the decision process. A Web site that is truly customer centric in its design would allow a visitor to enter a portion of the site based on his role or situation. For a hypothetical description of how this might work, see the sidebar entitled "A Website Tailored for Buying Center Roles."

In addition to targeting, other considerations must be kept in mind when designing Web communications. The Web site should be attractive without requiring annoyingly long download times. Many business-to-business Web sites are built with eye-popping graphics and animation, but the value of this is questionable for most companies. With broadband connections, these generally load quickly enough, but are still distracting for someone who wants usable information quickly. Interactivity should be designed at appropriate levels. Too often, Web sites are designed around the supplier's organization and offerings rather than around the customers' needs and buying behavior.

Attracting Visitors to a Web Site

A Web site will have little impact if existing and prospective customers do not visit it. Consequently, a sizable effort must be made to bring the right kind of visitors to the Web site. These efforts usually require the marketer to combine and coordinate marketing communications efforts that include both online and off-line methods.

This is one area that has undergone considerable change over the last several years.

The marketer has several communications techniques that can be used to contact and attract visitors to the Web site. With Google and Yahoo! dominating the search processes of prospective customers, "search engine optimization" has become a necessity for any marketer who relies on the Web to draw new prospects. Search engine optimization (**SEO**) involves designing the site so that search engines find the Web site and associate it with key words and phrases. So when someone searches for these key words or phases, the marketer's website is listed very high on the search results list.

SEO requires the home page and other high traffic pages in the site to present concise content that reflects benefits, products, or services sought by the prospective customer. It is

A Website Tailored for Buying Center Roles

For instance, suppose a vice president of customer service is exploring options for CRM systems. The vice president or his delegated manager looking for options has a different agenda in looking for information on CRM system providers than does the IT project manager who is involved in choosing and implementing a system. The VP wants to know about improvement in customer care; the IT manager will want to know about compatibility with existing systems and IT overhead costs. Both are concerned about ease of use and price—classic buying center interests as a result of each member's professional focus.

In searching for information, the vice president has to wander through several sections of each supplier's Web site. He has to look in the "Company" section of a Web site for information about the strengths of the supplier. He has to look through the "Products" section for a listing of features and maybe a description of specific benefits. He has to look at the "Customer Cases" section to see how other customers have deployed

the systems and to get customer references. The "Partners" section lists various software, hardware, integration, and consulting partners; but in most circumstances, he has to read between the lines in this section and the "Customer Cases" section to really understand which partners provide what pieces of the system that can best fit his situation. The IT manager probably finds a fair amount of technical information under the "Products" section of the project, but also needs to examine the "Partners" and "Customer Cases" sections to obtain a sense of what an implementation project will involve in his case.

If the site asks whether the visitor is a service executive, service manager, IT project manager, IT executive, or someone filling some other role in the buying center, then prepackaged groups of Web pages can be presented. In addition, the marketer can use a form to ask what else the visitor would like to see. A service rep can follow up with e-mail. The marketer can also collect these requests and build new pages in the site that can provide the commonly asked-for information.

a good idea to understand how the search engines try to give users the best results for their searches, and then adapt the design and programming of the marketer's site accordingly. For instance, some search engines will include image content in their results scoring if the image is provided in the jpeg format. So, if the marketer wants the search engines to recognize the product pictures he has included in his site, he will make sure the images are in jpeg.

Banner advertising also provides a means to get a message in front of prospective buyers and draws them to the marketer's website. The ad itself is a link to the website, usually to a portion of the site that is related to the offer in the ad. The problem with banner advertising is that "click-through rates"—the proportion of viewers who see the ad who actually click through to the Web site—have declined to levels where banner advertising's effectiveness is questioned. Targeting, when done carefully, can increase banner click-through rates. Too often, though, the targeting is too broad to be effective. Other means are usually required. One of the advantages of purchasing advertising on large sites or through online advertising agencies is that they usually are members of large advertising networks. Through complex analysis of data from across multiple sites, they can serve the purchased advertising to specific Web users to coincide, at least somewhat, with their interests. This is much better than the inaccuracy of segmenting audiences through print and broadcast media, but there are still many users who either are not actively involved in the buying decision process or who do not pay attention to banner ads.

A marketer can also purchase key words on search engines, usually through a bidding process. The marketer selects key words that he believes prospective customers will use when looking for the kinds of products or services he offers. When a user searches on a word or phrase that the marketer has purchased, his banner ad will display on the results page or a short ad with a link will appear in a "paid results" box. By tracking the results of click-throughs and purchases, the marketer can refine and update his list of purchased words and increase his return on investment in search engine ads.

Search engine marketing is one of the most important marketing aspects of managing a website. Prospective buyers use search engines in the early stages of the buying decision process. Since they are already in search mode, getting a targeted message in front of them at the right time can be very effective—much more effective than placing an ad in a trade magazine for which the audience is mostly not in the buying decision process.

Opt-in E-mail

E-mail has proven to be one of the most useful methods of Internet marketing communications in business-to-business marketing. When e-mail is unsolicited, it is called spam. Because the Internet and e-mail grew up as a communications medium with a strong anti-commercial culture, spam is viewed as annoying by most recipients (perhaps more so than is direct "junk mail"). E-mail is best used when an interested person gives permission—opts in—to the marketer to send e-mail messages. Once permission is obtained, e-mail messages are sent often enough to be noticeable but not so often that they are annoying. The key is to have something of interest to say each time.

E-mail can then be used to provide product notices, notices of special events, or other short messages of interest. E-mail is attractive because it is quick, inexpensive to produce, and almost costless to add people to the audience. The downside of e-mail is that it can wear thin quickly. The marketer must truly have value for the customer in mind. Otherwise, it is too easy to turn good customers into sour ex-customers.

Newsletters

Closely related to opt-in e-mail is the use of e-mail newsletters. These are specialized content news briefs, usually with links to full news stories located on a Web site. The reader signs up for a subscription, usually for free, and receives the newsletter in his e-mail mailbox periodically. Newsletters have proven to be very useful marketing tools for business-to-business marketers for several reasons. First, the content is valuable to the user—as long as the writer/editor is doing a good job of finding stories and reporting them well. Second, good newsletters usually are short enough to keep the reader's interest—they get read. Third, the newsletter is a good branding tool for the supplier. It keeps the supplier's name in front of prospective customers on a periodic basis.

Online Seminars

Just as seminars can be useful in educating prospective customers and generating sales leads from the audience, business-to-business marketers can use online seminars to great effect. The Internet communications methods we have mentioned have, as their primary objective, attracting a prospective customer to a Web site. Online seminars, webinars, though, seek to accomplish more: the establishment of a relationship with a prospective customer who is already very interested in the company's products or services. Seminars can be done in combination with a conference telephone call or can be done solely on the Web. They can involve self-paced Web presentations or elaborate combinations of broadcast video and audio delivered via the Web. The audience can range from one to thousands. The best Web seminars have relevant content that is well designed for Web delivery. The marketer has to be careful not to be too technologically adventurous. Many audience members may not have the latest software and hardware available and the company's server must be able to handle the interaction. There are now a number of companies that will provide webinars as a service for marketers. These companies provide a lot of functional capability that is relatively easy to customize for the marketer. The webinar attendees only need to access a website through their browser and login to the temporary webinar website with a prearranged login code.

Social Networking and New Media

The general-purpose online environment has changed drastically since the dotcom bust. Marketers have many new tools with the advent of blogs, pod casts, online video, social networks, and variations of these techniques. While the media available—and the media that people prefer to access—have evolved dramatically, the general rules of communication are still the same. People respond to messages; buyers seek solutions to their problems. So communications must deliver messages that are crafted to buyers going through decision processes. Marketers must understand their customers and customer segments, and craft effective messages and deliver them through appropriate media.

Having said this, the new media change the context of communications. Marketing contact with prospects and customers has come to resemble a conversation more than it looks like traditional broadcast, one-way communications.

"**Blog**" is a shortened name for Web log, which, as we've noted earlier, is a running commentary on some series of events. A blog can be simple running commentary newsletter. However, if the blog allows readers to post their own entries, the blog becomes a running conversation or even a running series of conversations. Marketers have used blogs to provide commentary on industry trends, communicate with customers about usage and service issues, maintain discussions with channel members, and conduct all sorts of other interactions with various stakeholders.[11]

A more recent development, **social networking**, is still in its early stages of usage innovation. Sites like Facebook and LinkedIn are providing marketers with a rich new medium whose uses are not yet fully appreciated or discovered. Among the more creative uses so far is the posting of video on the company's social media site, or providing a link to a YouTube video that presents product or service stories. The Ford Modeling Agency has become a leader in providing product discussions in video segments featuring models talking about fashion and style tips. These videos have become very popular among young women who share them through their own social networks or link back to their original postings on the Ford YouTube site.[12] These creative early efforts suggest that social networking may evolve into a combination of service and customer participation that we are just now beginning to glimpse.

Effective Internet Communications

As we mentioned at the beginning of this section, good online marketing requires integration of Internet communication with other forms of communication. This is not as easy to do as it sounds. Companies typically have initiated their Web and e-mail marketing by launching semi-autonomous organizational units with dedicated budgets. Due to the specialized technical nature of Web site development, the differences between interactive communication and other kinds of nonpersonal communications, and the necessity of the unit manager to follow the dictates of his own budget, many Internet or Web marketing units have a tendency to maintain their autonomy and may create messages that do not reinforce the other messages promulgated by the company.

Internet communications can be more timely than other marketing communications. It is relatively easy to change messages and to experiment with new presentations. Trade advertising, publicity events, trade show booths, and the like do not lend themselves well to fast design and extensive testing. Designs take longer, and opportunities for testing are limited, if they exist at all. There is a natural difference in outlook between the people who work in either camp. A marketing manager who has responsibility for Internet marketing, as well as other kinds of marketing, needs to recognize these differences and keep the two camps talking to each other.

PROMOTION AND THE IMPACT OF TRENDS IN BUSINESS-TO-BUSINESS MARKETS

The two general trends affecting business-to-business marketing, time compression and hyper-competition, influence both the purposes and the requirements for competent execution in promotion. Overcoming the problems that are caused relies upon recognition of these problems and adjusting, rather than on adopting new techniques intended to address the problems.

Promotion and Time Compression

The principal problem arising from time compression is the tendency to create "hype" to deal with short time horizons.[13] One source of this problem is the inability to rapidly achieve an understanding of customers. When the marketer does not have time to understand and develop appropriate communications, the temptation is to communicate in superlatives just to be sure that the offering is perceived as good enough. A second source of the problem arises from the time it takes to achieve the purposes of business-to-business nonpersonal promotion. Too often, the marketer is faced with the task of trying to establish trust and assurance of quality when the customer has little time to arrive at these states of mind. The tendency here is to try to come across as the best—again the tendency to create hype—and to create memorability by using multiple kinds of media and a high number of repetitions.

To address time-compression, marketers need to understand the limits of what can be accomplished in a short period of time. The fact that it takes time to build trust and it takes time to build a business should not be lost on the marketer or his hired agency. The problems created by the Internet companies' recent efforts to build businesses too fast should convince most marketers to consider building their own businesses for the long term. Perhaps a bit more emphasis on corporate image advertising would be useful to help set the stage for entry into new markets, but marketers should resist the temptation to rush into ridiculously misguided promotional excesses.

Promotion and Hypercompetition

As we have noted in prior chapters, hypercompetition and time compression often are related. In this case, time compression has induced marketers to increase their promotion efforts. In the recent past, the excess of investment money available to many companies created a lot of competitors with a lot of marketing money trying to obtain awareness and brand associations. All of this promotional activity created a lot of clutter—a lot of messages bombarding target audiences. This made it more difficult for marketers to get the attention of target audiences, so they responded with more repetitions and messages that got more shrill or "edgier." Many marketers found themselves with campaigns that were so "edgy" that the message and the purpose of the ads were lost in the angst or weirdness.

When hypercompetition has this result, the marketer needs to focus on purpose, benefits of the offering, the buying decision process, and the segment, that is, get back to basics. The way to compete is not by being louder, stranger, or more ubiquitous. The best way is to understand the needs and decision process of the buying center. The marketer and his agency can then create and deliver messages that address the customers' needs that are most important in ways that help them through the decision process.

THOUGHTS TO TAKE WITH YOU INTO THE NEXT CHAPTER

This chapter has discussed communicating with the market as part of a well-planned, purposeful effort. Communications, whether through personal selling or through nonpersonal promotion, begin with an understanding of stakeholders—most importantly, the buying center members, their roles in the buying decision process, and their individual motivations. The marketer must start by crafting a message that is intended to address specific kinds of people and to achieve some reaction from them. If the target audience is members of the buying center, usually the purpose is to help them progress through the decision process. Different variables in the promotion mix are best suited for different communication intentions. Just having an advertisement is not necessarily the answer, even though it may be the path of least resistance because it is what has been done before. Rather than focus on the process of promotion, this focus has been on the outcomes that serve the overall marketing plan.

In the development of promotional plans, consider questions like: What function will the promotional materials perform? How complex is the product? Does complexity prevent any brochure or advertisement from being successful? Is the promotional material consistent with the language and customs of the target audience? What combinations of promotion tools, in a fully integrated approach, are necessary to achieve the results desired?

Looking forward to Chapter 16, the role of promotion in a crisis is discussed. The fundamentals of promotion still apply, though with a sense of urgency not previously addressed. Also discussed are ethical issues that, beyond promotion, really involve the corporation as a citizen, a member of society, and a respected resource to customers. As you conclude this chapter, it is our hope that, with the foundation of the prior chapters, the ethical issues addressed will be a natural part of your approach to business-to-business marketing.

Key Terms

advertising *367*
blog *394*
direct response requests *372*
fulfillment firms *387*
guerrilla marketing *376*
jargon *371*
leave-behind materials *383*
media buy *374*
noise *372*

nonpersonal communications *369*
opt-in e-mail *393*
premium merchandise *385*
product configurator *391*
promotion mix *367*
public relations *367*
public stakeholders *376*
publics *376*
RFB *380*

RFP *380*
RFQ *380*
SEO *392*
sales promotion *367*
selective attention *372*
selective exposure *372*
selective retention *372*
server log *390*
social networking *395*

Questions for Review and Discussion

1. Compare the relative importance of the promotion mix variables in consumer markets versus business-to-business markets. Why do these differences exist?

2. When would the use of industry-specific jargon be acceptable in the communication process?

3. What is the importance of the encoding-decoding process in message accuracy? How do individuals attach meaning to messages?

4. How will the communication capabilities of the Internet impact the ability of business customers to receive feedback from customers?

5. Explain what promotion can do and what it cannot do.

6. How are the promotion mix variables interrelated? Why is it necessary to coordinate efforts between the variables?

7. What types of promotion are most appropriate at the different stages of the buying decision process?

8. What are the promotional goals most desired at each stage of the buying decision process? How well does this relate to your answer to Question 7?

9. Trade shows have usually been classified as sales promotions. The text makes the case that trade shows are excellent publicity and public relations tools. Which is it: Are trade shows sales promotion or publicity? Does it matter? Why or why not?

10. What communication purposes can be addressed in a business-to-business Web site? What purposes can be addressed by e-mail?

Endnotes

1. Based on H.M. Fattah, "A Giant's Rebirth," *Technology Marketing*, 21(6) (June 2001), pp. 44–47.

2. Regis McKenna, "Marketing Is Everything," *Harvard Business Review* (January–February, 1991).

3. Norman Govoni, Robert Eng, and Morton Galper, *Promotional Management* (Upper Saddle River, N.J.: Prentice-Hall, 1986), p. 53.

4. Ibid., p. 384.

5. Recall that the Sensacon example is a composite of the experiences of more than one company in this market. Simplifications have been made for clarity and care has been taken to prevent any direct relationship with any single market participant.

6. Incidentally, both of these trade journals went out of print after the dotcom bubble burst. The *Industry Standard* was out of business within eighteen months of the beginning of the collapse; *Business 2.0* hung on for several years, but it too closed shop in 2005.

7. Phillip Kotler, *Marketing Management*, 8th ed. (Upper Saddle River, N.J.: Prentice-Hall, 1996).

8. MarketingProfs and Forrester Research, Inc., *B-to-B Marketing in 2008: Trends in Strategies and Spending,* MarketingProfs Research Insights, 2007.

9. Ibid., p. 9.

10. Ibid., p. 9.

11. Stephen Baker and Heather Green, "Beyond Blogs," *Business Week* (June 2, 2008), pp. 44–50.

12. Freedman, David, "A Digital Makeover for the Modeling Business," *Inc. Magazine* (February 2008), pp. 82–86.

13. Lou Hoffman, "Haste Makes Hype," *Technology Marketing*, 21(6) (June 2001), p. 56.

Chapter 16

Business Ethics and Crisis Management

OVERVIEW

This chapter discusses ethics in business-to-business marketing, followed by a discussion of crisis management. The second is often necessary when there is a lack of the first.

This chapter follows the chapter about publicity and public relations as these promotion tools play a major role in crisis management. To fully understand ethical concerns in business-to-business marketing, an understanding of the many facets of these tools is necessary. Our discussions with associates and practitioners lead us to suspect an underlying sense of skepticism about business ethics. We do not agree with this; the term *business ethics* is not an oxymoron, notwithstanding highly publicized examples.

Business-to-business managers make many day-to-day decisions—some routine, some significant—that include application of an ethical standard. That ethical standard can be a compilation of many inputs. Organizations may define and hold employees to a high ethical standard, professional associations contribute policy statements about what is (and is not) ethical behavior, and individual lifestyle and beliefs weigh in with distinctive influences.

In the first part of this chapter we discuss different influences in ethical business decision making and examine the *societal marketing concept* that defines the "citizenship" of a firm. In the second part of the chapter, we discuss how, in the long-run, ethical standards improve the chances of successful crisis management and organizational as well as individual success.

TWA Flight 800 Revisited: Crisis Management and Ethical Concerns

On July 17, 1996, TWA Flight 800 took off from New York bound for Paris. Thirteen minutes after take off, the Boeing 747 exploded, plunging into Long Island Sound, killing all 230 people on board. With the crash of TWA 800 there began an unprecedented investigation into the cause of the explosion that involved TWA and its suppliers, Boeing (the aircraft manufacturer) and its suppliers, at least three government investigative bodies, and international safety advisory groups.

While airline travel is statistically safe, crashes happen. As terrible and unthinkable as any airline tragedy is, airlines must not ignore their possibility. Airlines have crisis response teams that are trained to deal with the complex personal, legal, and emotional issues surrounding such an event. They are expected to cope with such a tragedy in a professional and compassionate way. Anything less would not be acceptable.

Effective management of the crisis is not the only behind the scenes story of TWA 800. Travelers expect that whatever caused this mishap will be investigated and resolved quickly. In the United States, the National Transportation Safety Board (NTSB) has the responsibility to determine causes and recommend corrective actions to the Federal Aviation Administration (FAA). In December 1996, five months after the crash, the FAA received NTSB's initial recommendations. The NTSB found that a combination of events, not any one single factor, likely related to the center wing tank (CWT) caused the explosion aboard TWA 800. The recommendations included participation by many stakeholders:

- engineering design modifications to fuel tanks, air conditioning insulation, and wiring (which would need to be addressed by Boeing);
- upgrading of fuel quantity indicating systems (to be addressed by Boeing and Honeywell);
- changes in refueling procedures and equipment to fill the area above the fuel level in tanks with inert gas (a process called "inerting," to be addressed by various ground facilities management and crews);
- changes in fuel composition (to be addressed by petroleum refining companies); and
- changes in flight procedures (to be addressed by airlines and pilots).
- The recommendations raised several issues and before acting on them, in February 1997, the FAA took the unusual step of seeking public comment.[1,2]

The recommendation to fill the empty portions of fuel tanks with an inert gas was the most controversial and caused the most comment. While used on many military aircraft, the procedure is considered by the commercial air industry to be cumbersome and costly. By mid-1998, two years after the crash, the FAA issued directives regarding the inspection of wiring systems on existing aircraft and design changes in fuel quantity indicating systems, addressing the first two of the four concerns. Further investigation into the fuel vapor problem was ordered.

In October 1999, after more than three years of investigation and deliberation, it was revealed that Boeing knew about CWT overheating as far back as 1980. At that time, Boeing had been investigating problems with the military version of the 747. NTSB was not informed of the results of that investigation at that time, nor after the TWA 800 explosion. Ironically, key findings of the Boeing study in 1980 are similar to those eventually determined by NTSB following the TWA 800 crash—that hot runways and air-conditioning equipment can overheat fuel tanks. The Boeing study recommended that additional insulation be used to stop the heat from reaching the tanks. Boeing was somewhat embarrassed that the report did not make it to NTSB, but a Boeing official claimed that the study was about military fuel pump problems, different from those used in commercial aircraft.[3]

In March 2001, five years after TWA 800 and more than twenty years after the Boeing study for the military version of the 747, a Thai Airways Boeing 737 burst into flames on the tarmac in Bangkok, Thailand. One crew member was killed, seven others were injured. The NTSB study said that the CWT, located adjacent to the air conditioning system that had been running continuously, exploded.

On August 8, 2001, a special task force of an Aviation Rulemaking Advisory Committee (ARAC) submitted its final report to the FAA regarding fuel tank flammability. An ARAC is a committee of airline industry professionals, FAA representatives, and often, their international counterparts—many stakeholders with a global reach. The report cites the benefits of work already underway to improve fuel tank safety (safer designs, better inspections, upgraded wiring systems), estimating that these steps had already eliminated approximately 75 percent of the potential risk through 2020. Without additional regulations, the remaining 25 percent risk is likely to result in two additional fuel tank explosions over the period between 2001 and 2020. Contrary to the NTSB recommendations, the task force did not recommend inerting. In fact, the report stated that none of the additional safety alternatives produced "reasonably balanced" results—they are not cost effective.[4] (Based on projected costs of $10–12 billion each over the next fifteen years, yielding an estimated economic benefit of only $250–440 million.) Airline manufacturers, airlines, and European regulators strongly opposed any further unnecessary and expensive action.

Here are excerpts from the statement issued by acting NTSB Chairman Carol Carmody after the ARAC report was submitted:

> The . . . report clearly demonstrates the significant benefits to . . . safety . . . provided by inerting. I am disappointed that their cost-benefit analysis leads them to not recommend inerting systems. . . . I am pleased that the ARAC Executive Committee appears to share our concerns and has requested a further clarification of that analysis.
>
> The recent destruction of a Boeing 737 in Thailand shows that center fuel tank explosions continue to occur, and likely will occur again in the future. This problem must be addressed if we are to maintain the confidence of the traveling public.[5]

The end of the story? Not quite. In July 2008, after twelve years of deliberation, negotiation, and battle between stakeholders, Transportation Secretary Mary Peters announced the final rules.[6]

- Within two years of the 2008 announcement, new airliners will be required to have inerting systems that use nitrogen to prevent ignition of the hot vapors in the fuel tanks.
- Airlines will have nine years to retrofit older aircraft.
- Cargo planes and charter aircraft are not required to have the inerting systems.

Initially, Boeing strongly resisted the inerting of tanks, but toward the end of deliberations accepted the concept and has voluntarily begun installing inerting systems on new aircraft. Airbus, which also resisted, is expected to comply.

- How many ethical lapses or questions can you count?
- What is an ethical lapse? Does the definition change with circumstances?
- Is it an ethical lapse when individuals make a decision as part of a group or committee that they wouldn't make as an individual (singly responsible) person?
- Are you confident that decisions have been made that will protect your safety?
- Why did it take twelve years to act on what was recommended after only five months of investigation?
- When lives are involved, cost-benefit analysis usually relies on the belief that "it will never happen."

LEARNING OBJECTIVES

By reading this chapter, you will:

- Understand that a good ethical foundation is a good business foundation.
- Recognize that ethics are, ultimately, an individual decision.
- Understand the source of ethics, both organizational and personal.
- Develop an appreciation for how differences in personal ethical standards versus organizational standards can lead to an uncomfortable environment.
- Recognize the role of publicity and public relations in crisis management.
- Become familiar with the elements of good crisis management.

INTRODUCTION

Many students and business professionals are skeptical about the value and sincerity of business ethics. Claiming that for-profit organizations have only one overriding goal—to maximize profit—the inexperienced or uninitiated give business ethics little regard. For whatever reason, stories about "bad" business behavior attract more attention than stories about "good" business behavior. Is this because "good" behavior is common and not as newsworthy as "bad" behavior? Perhaps. Mass news media often report about a firm producing defective products and then resisting recalls, dumping hazardous wastes inappropriately, or conspiring with competitors to fix prices. Combined with reports of individuals engaged in stock fraud, swindles, and scams, it is not surprising that many people are skeptical.

Most consumers form beliefs—individualized truths—based on information from the news media, word of mouth, and personal experiences. These beliefs, or perceptions, form the public impression or **value image** of the firm much like product positioning attempts to create a product image. Once established, these "truths" can be changed only with an overwhelming amount of information, often involving personal experience. Value image, when positive, grants forgiveness in times of crisis or, when negative, will lead to a guilty verdict before trial. The importance of value image, then, cannot be measured, at least in the short term.

Value image, as described in Chapter 3, is the total of all impressions that the public will have of the firm. An individual's beliefs about a firm, situation, or occurrence are based on many inputs. The public reception a firm will receive can be impacted by the value image of that firm.

Several factors contribute to value image. The attitude of a company toward its customers, suppliers, and employees and its approach to living in the community are major elements of the reputation of the firm. Employees who treat customers well and speak highly of the firm are goodwill ambassadors. Suppliers not only take more interest in working with customers who recognize the value of the relationship but will likely make judgments about resource commitments based in part on this recognition. How the firm addresses controversial issues and problems in its markets is also a major influence. The corporate "attitude" portrayed in these circumstances can be a reflection of the philosophy or culture of the company.

ETHICAL ISSUES AND THE MARKETING CONCEPT

The marketing concept, discussed in Chapter 1, says that the successful firm, while meeting corporate goals, should be market sensitive, understand customer needs, and meet those needs in a coordinated way that provides value to the customer. In a truly market-driven firm, all employees recognize that they contribute to the marketing effort. The marketing concept fosters competition and maximizes choice in the marketplace.

Consider the example of the McDonald's switch from plastic to paper packaging, cited in Chapter 2. McDonald's switched from plastic to wax-coated paper for its products because its customers perceived paper as an environmentally friendlier packaging material. A Florida state senator asked, "For a hamburger that lasts a few minutes, why do we need a package that lasts as long as the pyramids?"[7] Was McDonald's following the marketing concept in delivering the greatest value as perceived by its market? What other choices did McDonald's have? Well, they could have implemented a customer education program about the intricacies of recycling. However, they had some experience in this area—customers at its restaurants had not done a good job of separating plastics from paper in collection containers. If the consumers, who are ultimately responsible for their actions, did not respond well to the request to keep waste material separated, what responsibility does McDonald's have? Note that McDonald's is not alone in this quandary. Many organizations face the situation where customers' actions are not as environmentally committed (or ethically, or legally, or socially committed) as its own organization, but still expect the highest standards from the organization. What place does the supplier have in imposing standards on customers that the customers would not voluntarily adopt?

THE SOCIETAL MARKETING CONCEPT

Is the marketing concept a philosophy that is compatible with the complexity of the business environment? Throughout this book, we have endorsed the marketing concept and value creation as the criteria for success for business-to-business organizations. Critics of the concept say that (1) the marketing concept is unrealistic as it imposes ethical constraints on an organization that reduces its competitiveness—other firms will see an opportunity and exploit it; or (2) the marketing concept is inappropriate as it often allows satisfying customer needs without acting in the best interests of society. With today's resource limitations, degrading environment, world hunger, and neglected (or failed) social services, the marketing concept does not go far enough. Obviously, the same critic does not hold these two views.

We believe that marketers have a responsibility, as the defining function of a modern organization, to include society's interests in decision making. Perhaps the place to start the development of a greater view of marketing is with one of the tenets of the *American Marketing Association* (AMA) *Code of Ethics* and a basic paradigm of professional ethics—*not knowingly to do harm*.[8] The AMA *Code of Ethics* says that "marketers must accept responsibility for the consequences of their activities and make every effort . . . to identify, serve and satisfy all relevant publics: customers, organizations, *and society*." [Italics added for emphasis.] This expansion of the responsibilities of the marketing function leads to the **societal marketing concept**.[9] The societal marketing concept states that, in addition to being market sensitive, understanding customer needs, and meeting organizational goals, marketers must deliver satisfaction more effectively than competitors and in a way that considers the well-being of society. Operating under the concept requires that social, ethical, and community considerations are built in, rather than added on, to every marketing plan. The goal of the societal marketing concept is quality of life.

> *Organizations operating under the **societal marketing concept** meet organizational goals by understanding customer needs and delivering customer satisfaction more effectively than competitors and in a way that considers the well-being of society—not knowingly doing harm. Firms operating under this concept have several constituencies—stockholders and investors, customers and suppliers, and employees and community.*

Critics of the societal marketing concept say that it blurs the separation of business, government, and individual responsibilities. How far should a firm be allowed to influence the quality of life of its customers, employees, and suppliers, beyond what is required to perform a narrowly defined business function? At what point does the good citizenship of the firm become advocacy for the agenda of the leaders of the firm? While much of the in-depth discussion is beyond the focus of this text, we believe that the marketplace answers many of these questions. As customers and customers' customers demand greater application of responsible and sustainable business practices, firms have little choice but to meet the standard.

Events of the 1990s serve as excellent examples of firms paying heavy prices for ignoring or denying the societal responsibility of the organization. Tobacco companies became the focus of consumers—not just smokers or former smokers—who were no longer willing to tolerate the marketing of tobacco products. Restrictions were placed on promotion of tobacco products, particularly those promotions that seemed aimed at children and teens. Local community groups placed initiatives on ballots to ban smoking from public-access facilities. As a result, many states now ban smoking altogether in enclosed facilities. The popular movement led to government action to recover health-care costs allegedly attributed to smoking. Whether you agree with these actions or not, whether you are a smoker or not, it must be recognized that tobacco companies have paid a very high price for ignoring the potential hazards of their products.

The same type of grassroots effort and application of law that led to the tobacco companies' reduced market access are often considered as tools to approach the makers of alcoholic beverages and handguns and rifles. In narrower instances, manufacturers have been forced to answer for the performance of their products through product recalls and class action damage suits. Whether baby strollers, appliances, or tires for SUVs, product recalls are ever more frequent than many years ago. We suggest that the increased number of recalls is not a sign of lower product quality but a sign of increased awareness on the part of manufacturers as to how society will hold the manufacturer responsible for the outcomes of the use (or in some cases, misuse) of its products. The organization that operates from the societal marketing concept will be proactive in ensuring the reliable and safe use of its products. We suggest that, in fact, the demands of the marketplace have led to products of greater quality, safety, and reliability for all consumers.

Societal Marketing as an Ethical Base

The societal marketing concept touches every part of the organization—recruiting, hiring, training, and retaining of personnel; contractual relationships with suppliers and service providers; and environmentally sound decisions regarding the use of natural resources. Many of these elements are visible to the marketplace, in part at least, in many organizations. The challenge—often called a dilemma—for an organization is to be at the forefront of societal marketing in every part of the firm. This level of effort starts with a well-defined and communicated mission statement that should encourage individual ownership at every level of the organization. Herein lie some problems. First, management that creates the mission statement (or its corporate culture substitute), either through ignorance or intention, may not define ethics as they are viewed at all levels of the organization (or the market, for that matter). It is a challenge to develop ethical standards for an organization that will fit contextually with the standards of the many individuals who will work together toward common goals. This creates a gap between what is perceived as ethical by different members of the organization.

Second, reward systems must in fact support ethical behavior. Management that rewards short-term results and then advocates that those goals be met "at any cost" immediately widens the gap between the individuals' view of what is ethical and what is required to succeed. Employees may have personal economic needs, such as continued employment or meeting sales quotas, which dictate behavior inconsistent with what might be considered ethical.[10] What may begin as "minor" ethical discrepancies can bloom into major causes of stress and friction among participants.

A CLASH OF ETHICAL STANDARDS

The previous section hinted at a clash between the ethical standards of the individual and the performance standards of the organization. The clash also occurs between ethical standards at different levels in the organization and among different stakeholders in the situation. Let us consider the last clash first.

Ethical Standards Among Different Stakeholders

Suppose you are the marketing manager charged with deciding the fate of certain products in the product line. The line has been expanded, and several earlier variations of the product are no longer competitive. The firm has successfully *crossed the chasm* with this product line, and the success of the product line has led to increased competition. As is its nature, competition "improves the breed" and your product is no exception. Improvements in your products have been encouraged by the desire to maintain a competitive edge—your goal has always been ownership of this market segment. Competitors have, of course, been able to use your product as a starting point and have added innovative product attributes to the mix. As the market has grown, competitors have relied on the low costs of offshore manufacturing facilities. While this has been a challenge, your product is recognized as the leader and has maintained the number one position in the segment, though not by the same lead as earlier in the product life cycle.

When your firm started large-volume production of the first-generation product (the one you are now considering eliminating), dedicated manufacturing facilities were built in a relatively rural section of the state. Because of high unemployment resulting from the decline of agricultural interests in the area, the region was more than willing to help with tax breaks, infrastructure improvements, and code variances in construction of the new manufacturing facility. The community has embraced the company, and the area has prospered compared to its previous economic climate.

Manufacturing management has informed you that the new products planned to replace the products to be discontinued must be manufactured offshore to meet cost targets. The facility built for the original product is not capable, with its existing equipment, of meeting productivity goals. Without replacement for the discontinued product, the workers will be let go and the facility idled. The alternative would be to increase the production of the old product at the facility to create a stockpile to meet customer needs then shut down the facility for six months while upgrading its equipment. You like this idea, but it will delay the introduction of the new product by four months.

Who are the stakeholders in this situation? Of course, there is the community and its workers who will be impacted, directly and indirectly, by the shutdown. Manufacturing management, who are also stakeholders, want the lowest-cost, quickest way to produce product. Marketing and sales management are not very receptive to losing four months in the market, particularly since competition is increasing. The board of directors, made up of members from inside and outside of the company, question the ability to maintain continuously improving quarterly sales and profits by "losing" four months of sales. The media in the community where the facility is located have heard of the dilemma and are being critical of the company and its facility engineers. The media are saying the company and engineers did not plan with enough flexibility in the building of the plant in the first place. Further, they are raising the issues of the company commitment to the community while workers are talking of forming a union. From their *individual* perspectives, particularly in relation to their job requirements, do any of these stakeholders appear to be acting in an unethical manner?

Ethical Standards at Different Levels in the Organization

Frontline employees should not be asked to accept ethical standards different from those embraced by executive management; and, of course, no firm's executive management would create such an ethical standard. But, as the saying goes, actions speak louder than words. The existence of a common ethical standard does not ensure that all levels of an organization regard it equally.

Behavior of individuals in organizations is best influenced by leadership rather than by control. Executive management sets the context—the example or defining paradigm—for the rest of the organization by the standards it demonstrates. It is difficult for a regional sales manager to strictly enforce written policies regarding legitimate business expense account deductions with her sales team if she knows that the vice president of the organization has had his home landscaped at company expense or has committed price-fixing or some other antitrust violation. Similarly, it will be difficult for the field seller to take seriously corporate policies related to bribery or collusion with unscrupulous buyers if she knows the firm is paying market access fees (read: bribes) to foreign officials.[11] The immediate management of the department or workgroup often defines what is acceptable in an organization, compared to what is written as acceptable. This institutionalized definition of what is acceptable moves through the organization and probably takes on different properties at different levels. Maintaining consistency throughout the organization then becomes an *individual responsibility* of managers and those they manage.

Another way that standards can mutate through levels of the organization is when executive management leads in a way that corresponds with the corporate standard but places performance demands on subordinates that may not be realistic. Individuals will work in their best economic interest. A corporate mantra of obtaining goals "at any cost" can encourage expedient but questionable practices. This scenario has often been accompanied by executive denial of any knowledge of a questionable practice occurring at lower levels in the organization. In large organizations, the CEO cannot know the details of every transaction.[12] However, goal setting without knowledge of the markets, followed by rewarding the attainment of the goals without concern for how it was done, is, at best, conveniently naïve.

Consider the situation where a member of a marketing team succeeds with a major target customer.

The team member, who we will call Jim, a field market development specialist[13] (FMD), has accomplished a very difficult task, one that means a lot to the organization. The resulting business is significant in the short term as the new business was wrestled from a major competitor, and significant in the long term as this target customer will be an excellent development partner for translation of several new opportunities. It appears Jim has been able to capitalize on the relationship he has developed with the customer. Management is ecstatic as, of course, this success contributes to its performance goals. A party is planned (marketers are really good at finding reasons to party!), not only to celebrate the new business, but also to acknowledge the contributions of Jim. The party is announced, and the corporate rumor mill has the newly anointed Jim on a prominent career path. There is, however, a cloud on the horizon.

Other members of the team are aware of the circumstances of the success. Jim may have gone beyond what other members of the team considered appropriate. The team knows that it is likely that not only may there have been questionable practices as defined by the Robinson-Patman Act (see Chapter 4), but corporate as well as their personal ethical standards have been, at best, stretched. Management is unaware of these issues.

The party takes place; Jim is rewarded with a substantial bonus, and definitely appears to have the inside track on the next headquarters marketing position, particularly as it is now obvious that management is beginning the grooming process. The method of Jim's success becomes the "unofficial" way to get ahead.

After a short period of time, management becomes aware of the details of "The Jim Method." They cannot let this stand. Not only is this serious ethical breach, it conveys a poor example and dangerous precedent to members of the organization. However, this is a very lucrative piece of business, one whose accomplishment will be noted positively by higher echelons of management.

What should be done? Any abrupt action against Jim will likely also involve the customer and place a very important business relationship in jeopardy. But this conduct cannot continue to be rewarded. What about Jim's upcoming promotion? Certainly, knowing this information, the promotion cannot happen as it would appear to reward unethical behavior. Additionally, steps must be taken to overcome the office gossip about how to get ahead.

In a low-keyed manner, Jim is sidelined, and after a few months, finds other employment opportunities.

The implications of the preceding examples are that executives and managers should be clear and consistent as to what standards apply for everyone in the organization. Also, employees need to have a good sense of what degree of ambiguity they themselves can tolerate. If the organization creates more ambiguity than they would want, they must either work to obtain more clarity or decide that they need to work for a different organization.

Ethical Standards of the Individual and Performance Standards of the Organization

Individuals develop moral and ethical standards by which they make day-to-day decisions. While there is much debate over how and where these standards originate, the actual development of a personal standard probably varies. **Natural law**, developed or **positive law**, and religious beliefs are possible sources that contribute to the formation of a personal moral or ethical standard. For some, these standards are absolute; for others, they may be flexible. Generally, ethical behavior can be said to be the degree to which others' well-being and success is accommodated in our decision making.[14] We expect this consideration from others. To manage our own ethical base, we must manage the tension between virtue and self-interest, and short- versus long-term goals, as well as recognize "**self-interest considered upon the whole**" (please see the definition box). There is an inherent assumption here that individuals can subordinate their short-term goals and immediate satisfactions to a higher end.[15]

Individuals can have acceptable levels of application of their own standards depending on the demands of the circumstances. Sometimes this flexibility is a convenience, and sometimes it may be viewed as a necessity. When the mission of an organization or the context under which a firm operates sets an ethical tone different from that which an individual accepts or believes, the individual may develop a level of anxiety or unease with her participation in the operation of the firm.[16] Note that we have said *different*; no judgment is offered at this point as to the relative *good or bad* of the individual or organizational ethical standard. As an alternative, the individual may choose to set flexible standards that allow departure from personal ethical levels in order to survive within the organization. Establishing standards based on the circumstances is often called **situational ethics**.

SITUATIONAL ETHICS   Day-to-day events provide many examples of flexible ethical standards. Often justified by "the greater good"—or maybe just convenience—situational ethics use ad-hoc standards influenced by the

Natural law is a term applied to the theory of ethics that holds that individual moral standards are derived from a higher, universal source. This is contrasted to man-made, created, or positive law standard of moral or ethical behavior. Ethical standards derived from positive law are said to be determined simply by what is legal.

Self-interest considered upon the whole is extending decision-making efforts to what is often referred to as "the greater good"—a decision-making culture that sustains principled behavior. This culture requires leadership to create it and reward to those who follow it. In business, this often becomes a balancing act—and individuals will implement their own scale to measure this balance.

How many times have you heard these justifications for less than exacting ethical behavior?

- *But everybody else does it.* This implies that statistics are a valid basis for ethical decisions.

- *This is the way we've always done it.* Either "it" was not previously significant or nobody has been caught yet. Compare this to the substantiality test cited in Chapter 4.

- *I was just following orders.* Often heard in military trials, this implies that the individual does not have the power of free choice or an internal ethical standard. Being told to do something illegal or unethical does not make it okay to do it.

- *It is considered standard practice in that market.* Often a rationalization for bribes, questionable gratuities, or other attempts to inappropriately influence a situation.

EXHIBIT 16-1 Situational Ethics, Ethical Lapse or Convenience? *Note:* Jennings discusses similar and additional phrases as early warning signs of ethical rationalization in Chapter 2 of *Business: Its Legal, Ethical, and Global Environment* (Cincinnati: South-Western College Publishing, 2000)

circumstances of the dilemma. Small ethical choices are made on a daily basis; *it is okay to speed—you're late for an important meeting.* It would be truly difficult to find anyone who could positively say she had never exceeded the speed limit. Sometimes individuals justify ethical choices with larger consequences based on some consideration of relative right or wrong; *it's OK to cheat on income taxes because everybody does it and you probably will not get caught.* Exhibit 16-1 lists some circumstances in business in which situational ethics, perhaps better called ethical lapses, occur. In all of these examples, the ethical standard is lowered to accept a situation that may lead to a short-term gain. Depending on the extent of the ethical lapse, individuals in these situations can feel conflicted and uncomfortable. With the added pressure of creating results in the organization, employment can evolve into an unsatisfactory experience.

Often a situation arises in which ethics stand in opposition to costs or convenience. For instance, after two previous errors on a customer's orders, for which the customer's purchasing manager has rebuked the sales team, the marketer's company makes a minor mistake in the next order. There is a reasonable chance that the error will not be noticed, but if it is, the purchasing manager undoubtedly will be furious. While the marketer's company will not likely lose the account, even if the mistake is found out, the customer will have so much bargaining leverage that the account may not be profitable for some time to come. The marketer is tempted to pretend she had no knowledge of the mistake, hoping that the customer does not notice the mistake, and face the consequences only if the customer does find it and complains.

In practical reality, most ethical marketers will have occasional instances in which they take the easy route—usually when the trauma of doing the absolute right thing is substantially greater than the ethical price of not doing it. Caution should be exercised if occasional instances develop into ethical rationalizations—standard ways of doing business. Some indicators are listed in Exhibit 16-1.

On the other hand, some organizations have a culture in which little decisions continuously strive toward "seeing how much can be gotten away with," and the larger ethical decisions are made based on whether the organization can win in a court of law (or even based on whether a settlement after-the-fact is likely to be within a tolerable dollar range). These are organizations for which it is difficult for an ethical person to work. It is also difficult for an ethical company to do business with such an organization, except at an arm's length. Consider some of the following situations that occur often enough that questions of ethics may not be immediately recognized.

ETHICS IN PRODUCT ANNOUNCEMENTS   Failure to meet preannounced dates for product introductions may not, at first, seem like an ethical problem. Most common in consumer markets, these delays are acceptable only when there are no large investments relying on the availability of the delayed product. Consumers may be frustrated by waiting longer than expected for the latest version of that game software, but there is seldom any financial investment by the consumer that is put at risk by the delay. However, in business-to-business markets, many firms assess penalties for late delivery. In the extreme, some firms—particularly those that rely on closely monitored inventories and continuous production methods, such as the automotive industry—may assess fines by the minute or hour whenever a supplier fails to meet a shipping commitment and shuts down an assembly facility.

A more obvious ethical dilemma is preannouncing a new product, even though you know the product will be late or underfeatured. In markets where being "first" is important, preannouncing might be done to match the timing of competitors' new products. Is it ethical to promise an offering to a customer within a certain time frame, knowing that the timing cannot be met, the real goal being to prevent the competitor from being successful (if I can't win, maybe I can keep them from winning)?

ETHICS IN PRODUCT CAPABILITY CLAIMS   It is a fundamental principle in marketing that you never promise more than you can deliver. How is this reconciled with advertising claims that are unsupportable? Again, many consumers are skeptical of *any* advertising claims. In business-to-business marketing, exaggerated or false claims just won't work. Customers will test the offering for its suitability to their needs before committing to large purchases. The most that the supplier can gain with exaggerated product claims is short term—early consideration in the decision process. When the exaggerations are discovered, the value image of the firm and the individual may be damaged and future dealings will be heavily scrutinized.

ETHICS IN OBTAINING COMPETITIVE INFORMATION   What is ethical when obtaining competitive information? While many firms zealously guard proprietary or competitive information from the marketplace, many opportunities exist for companies to obtain competitive information. Misrepresentation, taking the form of employees posing as customers of competitors or as student interns, among other circumstances, can abuse the good intentions of customer service organizations and the willingness of companies to support academic efforts. Two interesting circumstances come to mind. First, many firms will offer internships to students from local universities, ostensibly to provide a real-world experience in the student's area of study. As an intern, the student is compensated for her effort, either by earning money from the firm or credits from the school. Once she is compensated for her efforts, is the student still a student or is she an employee? What position should she take if asked to identify herself as a student working on a project while calling competitors to obtain competitive information?

The second circumstance is probably one cause for the increase in sales of paper shredders and carbonless forms in recent years. Consider this scenario:

> Newly hired into a field sales position, you complete the company's training program and are assigned to a field territory working with a senior seller for some on-the-job training. You feel really lucky because the senior seller you are working with has an outstanding reputation not only for meeting sales quotas but for having a thorough understanding of the territory and the competitive environment. This will be a great learning opportunity.
>
> After a couple of weeks in the field, the senior seller tells you to meet her at a nearby office complex in the evening—"wear old clothes." When you arrive, she asks you to

join her in some "dumpster diving"—explaining that your major competitor has offices in the complex and tosses out the carbon paper from computer output showing territory sales and targeted business activity. You participate, but are uncomfortable as you think about it later. Was this ethical?

Basically, any information available *to the public* is fair game in a competitive investigation. Any discomfort felt regarding the preceding examples should be a tip-off of an ethical lapse. In either example, the uninitiated or inexperienced person can use the situation as a pattern for future acceptable behavior, or, if uncomfortable with the circumstances, take a stand to overcome the discomfort—avoid the ethical lapse. The choice is one the individual must make.

OTHER QUESTIONABLE ETHICAL CHOICES AND OPPORTUNITIES   As you ponder your degree of discomfort with the examples you have just read, examine the following ethics dilemmas. Should you, or shouldn't you? *Would you, . . . or wouldn't you?*

- Paying bribes to foreign officials (or to government officials in the United States) by having a consultant pay the bribe and reimbursing the consultant for "miscellaneous marketing costs"
- Charging an exorbitant price for your product at a time when your product is in a temporary state of shortage
- Taking marketing allowances or promotional money even though there is little likelihood you will perform the marketing activities required to receive such bonuses
- Posing as a prospective customer to obtain competitive information
- Favoring one distributor over another; creating an unfair advantage through sales promotions and incentives *designed for one of your distributors,* knowing that your other distributor in the same territory is not likely to participate as effectively

Many of these behaviors are justified as "what's best for all stakeholders"—the "greater good" defense. The higher in an organization, the more often the greater good is offered as a defense, until, eventually, the reasoning offered is "pressure from stockholders." Read the box, "They Did What?" If asked ahead of time, do you think stockholders would have approved of these actions?

INDIVIDUAL ETHICAL BEHAVIOR

Students will often ask for advice when faced with these and similar situations, as they occur in group study projects, their careers, and life in general. The advice we usually give is that ethics are a self-realized code of behavior. Our experience is that many business students, operating from the skepticism fostered by media reports, are apprehensive of what they perceive as questionable ethics in business. We have found that the anticipated standards (or lack of standards) are actually worse than the reality. This is compounded by the fact that individual ethical standards are internally generated.

Win–Win, Win–Lose, and Zero-Sum

The need to succeed, to win, is inherent in Western culture. Peer pressure, family responsibilities, and self-centered needs contribute to a win-at-any-cost attitude. When faced with winning or losing, most people will elect to win. Built into the win–lose paradigm is the idea that, for there to be a winner, there must be a loser. Business schools go as far as teaching "zero-sum" management approaches in decision making. The concept of win–win gets lost in this shuffle.

They Did What?

Do You Think Stakeholders Would Approve?

- Microsoft predatory practices result in U.S. courts declaring it an illegal monopoly. At this writing, decision is still pending in Europe. (2001-current)
- Hewlett-Packard board members spy on each other, questioning each other's loyalty during stressful acquisition of Compaq and hiring of new CEO. (2005)
- Tyco CEO charged with tax evasion, waste of corporate assets, resulting charge of $6 billion to earnings.
- WorldCom: Fraudulent loans to CEO.
- Merrill Lynch conflict of interest settlement results in $100 million settlement, loss of half of market capitalization. (2002)

- Firestone betrays largest customer (Ford) with shipment of questionable tires; Ford tire recall costs over $3 billion.
- Enron manipulation of electric power markets, and eventual loss of entire corporate equity through accounting and finance manipulations leads to demise of Arthur Anderson, a major public accounting firm.
- Qwest Communications CEO resigns, profits restated, assets cut by 50 percent ($34 billon).

Sources: Stephen Young, *Moral Capitalism* (San Francisco: Berret-Koehler Publishers, 2003) "Living in Microsoft's Shadow," *Wall Street Journal* (July 2, 2001)

How do individuals behave when faced with these choices? Our experience is that many people will rationalize ethical standards to fit the situation. If the organization cannot win, actions are taken to ensure that the opponent(s) will not be a winner—keep the playing field level (lose-lose). This fosters individuals to suspect that others, either individuals or organizations, are playing to keep them from winning. Instead of "playing to win," the self-protective approach of "playing to not lose" becomes the operating posture.

Some More Ethical Dilemmas: What Would You Do in Each Case?

- You have started a new sales job with a successful telemarketing company. Pay is commission based. Your manager is reviewing calling tactics. She tells you to start each call by asking potential customers if they are willing to answer some market research questions. The questions are about the discretionary income and credit cards used in the household. When it is determined that the household can afford your product, the sales pitch starts; otherwise, you are instructed to hang up.
- As field marketing manager, you are about to hire a new FMD for a major territory. Of the three top applicants, the best is a woman. You know that, even though it is the twenty-first century, some of the customers in the territory prefer dealing with men.
- You are the seller at a contract provider who just landed a big job from an end user where

your product has been cospecified with a competitor's product. Closing this piece of business will put you over the top of your sales quota. The purchasing agent keeps saying things like "good sellers know how to land a big fish—they just use the right bait" while talking about a new video camera she's interested in.
- A good customer asks you for four tickets to a hockey game for himself, his wife, and another couple. You give him the tickets. The following week, he asks you for six tickets. You respond that you have only four and that you would like him and his wife to join you and your significant other at the game. He reluctantly says yes but then asks you to not mention the previous week's tickets as he was not there with his wife.

Mutually exclusive

EXHIBIT 16-2 Circumstances That Are a "Win" for A and B: Mutually Exclusive

Consider the preparation for a negotiating session. Good business practice would have participants learn as much as possible about the other party's position—strengths, weaknesses, likely negotiating strategies. Part of this analysis should include a reasonably good understanding of what the other party considers "a win." If, as shown in Exhibit 16-2, there are no circumstances in which a win for one party is also a win for the other party—each party's definition of a successful negotiation excludes the other party—then there is no chance for a "win–win" scenario. It may even be inadvisable to enter the negotiation process, as one side must lose for one side to win. If a long-term association is planned, another partner should be found, as the "loss" on one side may build resentment and a search for an opportunity to "get even."

If, as shown in Exhibit 16-3, there are circumstances in which a win for one party is also a win for the other party—the area labeled as *C* bounded by the arcs from each circle—then there is a win–win scenario that should satisfy both parties. This becomes the foundation for future efforts as well as immediate success. Neither party need succumb to a defensive "playing to not lose" posture.

Readers ask about the portions of the circles that are considered a win by each party but do not fall in the mutually inclusive area *C*. The inference is that these winning positions, *A* minus *C* and *B* minus *C*, are lost in the negotiation, the loss a result of a *compromise*. This is not the case. They could not be "lost" because they were never in consideration as a positive outcome by *both* parties. The winning opportunities represented by the areas that are not overlapped are still winning opportunities, just not immediately between these two parties.

COMPROMISE AND WIN–WIN Recall the box "Now What Did That Really Mean" from Chapter 15. When students are polled as to the meaning of the word *compromise*, the most frequent reply is *to give up*. Yet, compromise is the outcome of negotiations, area C in Exhibit 16-3, aimed at creating win–win situations that work for all involved, enabling all parties to commit to an agreed-on

Common Ground

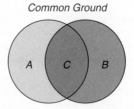

EXHIBIT 16-3 Circumstances That Are a "Win" for A and B: Common Ground

direction, goal, or *common promise*. Commitment to the common promise is important. Alliances are more likely to generate mutually beneficial outcomes when each party can depend on the other to work toward *mutual* benefits.

Markets' participants have long memories. Before entering into an alliance, each party will examine the history and reputation of the other party. Actions by individuals can reflect on the entire organization. Previous behavior by individuals that was other than mutually beneficial or raised issues of trust and co-operation may exclude the organization from the new alliance. Again, the long-term positive impact of ethical decisions and actions reflects positively on future opportunities.

ETHICAL BEHAVIOR AND VALUE NETWORKS

In Chapter 2, the concept of the value network was introduced as different combinations of capabilities merged in alliances to serve various sets of customer needs. When a marketer seeks new customers, value networks may be formed to tailor the offering to specific customer criteria. Exhibit 2-3 attempted to show graphically the intricate web possible in the creation of a multidimensional value network. When two firms participate in value networks, they are working in an alliance to serve both firms as well as a specific customer. This is not unlike the relationship shown in Exhibit 16-3. The common ground, area *C*, is the offering created to satisfy the needs of the specific customer. For another customer, Firm *A* may combine with Firm *B* again or with a third firm or create a network of many value providers.

Exhibit 16-4 shows a value network of three providers. Intertwined relationships work in alliances to create offerings for specific customers. Not all participants engage in each creation. However, participants in other networks become aware of the reputation (value image) of each firm as an ally in the network. *A*, *B*, and *D* participate in a value network to create an offering comprised of the common area, *E*. A contributor's respect for proprietary information shared in each alliance, as well as even-handed, ethical treatment of each partner improves the long-term outlook for that contributor.

The firms and individuals involved in the preceding scenario that have long-term value network opportunities are those who operate ethically as partners in previous networks. The

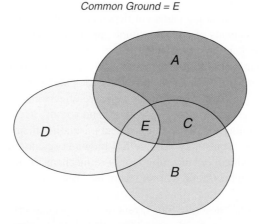

Common Ground = E

EXHIBIT 16-4 Winning Common Ground for
Three-Party Value Network

win–win scenario, then, is determined not by size, technology, or leverage but through trust and regard for all members of the team.

Ethical Behavior and Value Image

As previously discussed, the overall attitude toward an organization can be described as its value image—the sum of all impressions that have been made. An investment in value image is an investment in the *social capital* of the organization. As any capital investment, the short-term benefit may not be immediately obvious, but organizational planning has determined a need for this capitalization to be successful within the long-term goals of the organization. In the following section, crisis management is discussed. Consider social capital as one of the resources available to the organization in a crisis situation.

CRISIS MANAGEMENT

The relationship between ethics and crises is obvious in some situations; the crisis is the result, in part, of ethical choices made by the organization's executives, managers, or employees; and the social capital or value image that has been built long-term (positive or negative) will strongly influence the next steps. Sometimes a crisis may occur because someone took an ethical stance in dealing with a situation. More often, a crisis related to ethics occurs because someone in the company has addressed a situation with sub-par ethics. Many crises derive from other sources, though—technological failure, human error, unanticipated consequences of complex system elements, or really bad weather, for instance—and ethics are minimally involved in their creation.

So why should a marketer be concerned about crisis management? First, the marketer often is asked to manage the external communications with stakeholders. Even if the company has a corporate communications department, this department is often organizationally within the marketing organization of the company. Second, in a crisis, the whole company ought to be involved in dealing with it. Marketers and the sales force are charged with managing relationships with customers and channels during a crisis, just as they are during normal periods. Third, in preparing for a crisis, the marketers need to represent the needs and concerns of customers and channels as crisis plans are made.

At its core, effective crisis management depends on ethical attitudes and behavior. The two most important components of ethical attitude applied to crisis management are a willingness to take an honest look at the organization and the possible consequences of its actions and a willingness to feel compassion for those who are affected by the organization's actions. This means that an ethical company will take the effort to anticipate the negative effects of its actions just as it anticipates the positives. Some of the negative effects can be prevented or mitigated with proper safeguards, quality controls, incentives, and so on.[17] Crisis preparation can establish mechanisms for handling incidents and accidents, isolating them, and keeping them from growing into crises. Some events may become full-blown crises no matter how much preparation has been done. The ethical organization will have mechanisms in place for assisting those affected, minimizing the impacts, and learning from the crisis so that future crises can be better addressed.

Pauchant and Mitroff[18] describe four layers of crisis-related systems within an organization that must be understood and addressed *in specific order* to effectively manage crises, as listed in Exhibit 16-5. At the core are the people—particularly those in leadership roles—in the

Level one. Character of the people in the organization—willingness to take responsibility and take corrective action.

Level two. Culture existing in the organization—supports appropriate preparation and response actions.

Level three. Organizational structure—crisis management structure in which all stakeholders are represented.

Level four. Plans and mechanisms for dealing with crises—crisis management team has fully prepared plans, disseminated them, and trained people in key roles.

EXHIBIT 16-5 Layers of Pauchant and Mitroff's Crisis Management Model *Source*: Thierry C. Pauchant and Ian I. Mitroff, *Transforming the Crisis-Prone Organization: Preventing Individual, Organizational, and Environmental Tragedies* (San Francisco: Jossey-Bass, 1992).

organization and their mental and emotional capabilities for addressing crises. The next level is the culture within which the people operate. The culture must be conducive to introspective and external learning and planning to avoid and manage crises. The third level is the organizational structure. The structure must directly address crisis prevention and management if it is to be effective. The fourth level is the strategic integration of crisis management. The strategy and mechanisms pursued by the company must recognize negative impacts as possible and directly address crisis management.

Crisis Preparation

So let us assume that the organization has enlightened, open-minded management, unencumbered by neurotic defense mechanisms that prevent good crisis management. They have infused this thinking in the organizational culture (i.e., the first two levels of the crisis management model are successfully addressed). How should a company then prepare itself for crises, and what are the marketers' roles?

Four key aspects of crisis preparation are establishing effective structures for planning and handling crises, assessing the elements of the company's operations that produce risks and working to reduce these risks, planning for procedures to follow as events occur to minimize the damage and isolate the effects, and inoculation against negative public attention that will occur during a crisis.

ORGANIZATIONAL STRUCTURE FOR CRISIS MANAGEMENT An important organizational structure for crisis preparation and for handling crises when they occur is an established, ongoing crisis management team. The team has representation from inside and outside stakeholders. In an organization large enough, it may have its own full-time staff. It has the charge of assessing crisis threats, changing operations or recommending operational changes to head off crises, and establishing roles and procedures for dealing with crises when they occur. It needs to have top-level support if it is to succeed.

ASSESSING AND ADDRESSING RISKS Assessing crisis risk involves first asking the question, "What is the worst that could happen if we continue to do XX?" If the crisis management team represents the views of the major stakeholder groups, then a fair representation of potential crisis areas will emerge. For instance, the marketing executive's concerns that a new product platform will miss the market when it is introduced, causing major financial problems, will likely be represented. Concurrently, the concerns of users will also be represented. Let us say that the product

How Remote Are the Chances of the Worst Happening?

Once in a thousand?
Once in a million?
Once since the Jurassic period?

Small actions can precipitate major situations. Crisis management teams should ask what series of events and interactions might produce the worst-case scenario. This exercise helps the team to understand the negative effects of current systems and the possibility for worst-case circumstances that would otherwise be seen as unlikely. Just as in the novel *Jurassic Park*, park developers thought they had considered *every* possible *reasonable* circumstance to insure the containment of the dinosaurs, Exxon officials apparently underestimated the likelihood of a major oil spill from a tanker mishap. Only months before the *Exxon Valdez* crash, an Exxon executive suggested that such an incident was a one-in-a-million likelihood event.

Source: Thierry C. Pauchant and Ian I. Mitroff, *Transforming the Crisis-Prone Organization: Preventing Individual, Organizational, and Environmental Tragedies* (San Francisco: Jossey-Bass, 1992).

platform is a new type of programmable manufacturing equipment. Users' concerns could range from labor unrest as a result of displaced workers to injury or death caused by machinery malfunctions. If the crisis management team had included representation of only the company's internal perspectives, the users' concerns about safety might be underemphasized.

PLANNING FOR UNANTICIPATED CRISES   Thinking through potential problems is not enough, though. The nature of complexity and chaos makes it impossible to foresee all potential problems that may arise. Consequently, the crisis management team must prepare procedures for handling the unanticipated events.

Crises come in stages (Exhibit 16-6).[19]

- Early on, there is a buildup period in which early signals indicating an impending crisis usually occurs.
- The second stage depends on whether the organization has received and understood the signals. If so, the organization can go through a preparation period. If not, the crisis will be triggered by some event and will arrive on the organization's doorstep full-blown.
- If the organization has been able to prepare for but not head-off a crisis, a trigger will occur that creates an incident or accident.
- A period of intense activity and public scrutiny will ensue. The organization must address the situation with "crash management" activities. During this period, the organization's experience will be made more tolerable if good preparation has occurred.

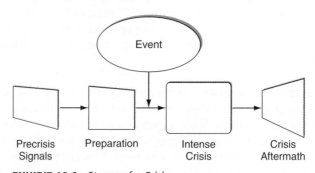

EXHIBIT 16-6   Stages of a Crisis

- Following the disposition of the crisis, a lower-intensity period occurs in which the organization and its environment and stakeholders proceed to a new normalcy, which may be very different from "doing business as usual."
- The organization may take follow-up actions and may go through a period of serious learning. In most cases, follow-up and learning *should* be done or a new crisis may be brewing soon.

INOCULATION AGAINST NEGATIVE MEDIA ATTENTION   Once a crisis occurs, the analysts working for the media will present their views on causes for the crisis, how well it is being handled, and what the future implications are likely to be. An existing relationship with the media will tend to set the context for such scrutiny. In the absence of a good relationship, media analysts may consider or even impute that unscrupulous motives are at play on the part of the company. However, if the company has established a good relationship with the media, displaying sincerity and good citizenship, this will set the context for the media analysis of the crisis. As we suggested in the discussion of branding, a good public image must be backed by substance; *the company must truly act in the public interest if the public image is to be believed.* This must continue during the crisis as well. The company must be co-operative and open to the media, providing useful, accurate, and timely information. The media will eventually see through the efforts of a company that tries to project an image of openness and sincerity, when it really does not possess these characteristics. The negative media attention that will ensue will only exacerbate the crisis—and rightly so!

Media Relations During a Crisis

When the inevitable occurs (and it has been planned for), there are standard methods for handling the public exposure that will occur. The organization acting ethically will follow a few basic rules: give the media access, tell the truth, be proactive, and stay calm.

With these principles in mind, media relations should be managed a little differently in each stage of a crisis. In the precrisis stage, the organization is still unsure what early signals mean and has a good chance of heading off a crisis if it can be identified and addressed. The organization's crisis spokesperson will not want to be proactive with the media. Rather, if a reporter asks about a potential crisis, then the spokesperson can respond that the organization is paying attention and will take actions to avoid problems.

In the preparation stage, the media may be contacted to demonstrate how the organization is preparing for certain kinds of emergencies—those caused by sudden outside forces, such as natural disasters and so on. This may have some news value and help to establish relationships with the media. Other than this, the company's preparation efforts should remain mostly private and media relations should be reactive.

When a triggering event occurs and a true crisis begins to erupt, the crisis team will need to determine whether a response is actually needed. In some cases, the company may consider not responding to accusations of wrongdoing, figuring that a response would validate the legitimacy of the accusation. However, in most cases, a quick response is better than no response. If accusations are unfounded, a quick display of overwhelming facts should quell the problem. This means that the company's spokesperson should have access to executive management to learn what the company's latest information and decisions are. It also means that the company's information-gathering mechanisms need to activate at the first sign of a problem.

Early on, the crisis team and company executives should begin deciding what messages the company will communicate. The message may change as events proceed and as new information becomes available. The crisis management team should take steps to ensure that all messages emanating from the company are consistent with the current core message coming from the crisis management team. All communications efforts need to be sensitive to the needs of the audience. If the company is running an emergency hotline, the people answering the 800-number calls should be knowledgeable and helpful and have authority to make appropriate decisions for individual callers. If callers are likely to speak different languages, company representatives who speak all the major languages that callers are likely to speak should be available. Mechanisms for doing all this should have been established as part of general crisis planning.

In many crises, the company may come under fire for its practices or ways of doing business. When appropriate, the company might ask for support (though not through coercion) from customers and partners. This may help sway public opinion and media attention. These partners may be waiting to be asked or may not want to interfere until the company has indicated a need for help.

In some circumstances, it becomes obvious that the company will not be able to "win" even though the company may be right in its position. The company may have to accept blame, apologize, and move on to the next stage. In such cases, the company may decide it is better to "lose" quickly than to get involved in a protracted public battle. It becomes difficult to make this decision, though, when the costs of "losing quickly" are not known and could potentially be catastrophic.

In the aftermath stage, the impact on the company's public image will already have been done. Any repair that needs to be done to the image of the company or the brand will take time and effort. If the relationship with the media has been fostered throughout the intense portion of the crisis, and the company has been sincere in its efforts to address stakeholders' needs and concerns, it will be easier for the company to do the image repairs necessary. As we have stressed all along, though, this means providing value for customers and behaving ethically in the company's relationships with partners and the community in general.

MINOR CRISES: PREPARATION FOR AND HANDLING OF INCIDENTS   While the high-profile crises get all the attention, they only occur infrequently. Most companies deal much more with crises that are not going to kill or seriously impair the company (at least any time soon). These are minor crises, incidents, or fast-occurring problems that merely erode confidence among the company's stakeholders and reduce the company's financial performance. Some of these incidents may be quite public, but they usually do not last long in the public eye. The effect on customers and channels may be much longer lasting, or the effects combine with other minor crises to add up to major problems for the company. These minor crises range from handling the media attention when the company announces poor performance in its most recent quarter to dealing with the public attention associated with a major lawsuit or arrest of one of the company's executives for violating trade laws. If the company has several of these accumulate, then it has long-term credibility or even viability problems. If these occur infrequently and they are handled well, then the company will face temporary embarrassment and perhaps some extra costs, but viability is never in question.

Just as with major crises, avoiding problems is preferable to having to deal with them. Early detection, diagnosis, and corrective action are important. Some nasty surprises will always occur, and they must be handled appropriately. In such instances, it is better to have policies and mechanisms in place to deal with the everyday nasty surprises than it is to address them completely in an ad hoc fashion.

What would you do?

Assume you are the marketing manager in the following circumstances. What kind of crisis planning would help you prepare for these examples of crises, both minor and major?

- An industrial accident occurs at one of your production plants. Several of your employees are severely injured. Community leaders call for safer working conditions.
- A competitor openly accuses your company of unethical behavior in obtaining competitive information. There is internal evidence that some of your marketing people have indeed gotten some sensitive information through illicit means.
- An industry trade journal reports deterioration in your company's service quality. The data reported in the article are open to interpretation, but customers are beginning to question the value of your company's offering.

Competitors are using the supposed problems as a competitive lever in their advertising and their sales presentations.

- An industrial accident occurs at the plant of one of your customers. Several of their employees are severely injured. The cause of the accident is traced back to a defective part in equipment that you sold to the customer.
- Your company is the target of a hostile takeover attempt. Your customers are concerned because the company attempting the takeover is famous for dismantling acquisitions in such a way that old relationships with customers are often torn asunder.

In each of these cases, suppose the crisis occurs despite your best preparation efforts. How might you, as the marketing manager, handle your role?

HANDLING MINOR CRISES IN A YOUNG COMPANY   If the company is doing a good job of inoculation—preparing for a major crisis—it will generally be in good shape to handle minor crises as well. Crisis plans and mechanisms will be in place. Roles will be defined and people will understand how to act.

There is one set of circumstances in which an ethical company will probably not be in a good position to handle minor crises. This is when the company is new. A young company may not have had the resources available for crisis planning. It is important, then, for the young company to retain a good public relations firm as soon as it reaches a size sufficient to be able to pay the retainer. Whether it is the same agency that handles promotion campaigns or a different one, the job is different from proactive marketing publicity. The crisis-related job for the agency should be to manage ongoing relationships with the media to begin the inoculation process we mentioned in the prior section. This is just as important for minor crises as it is for major ones.

The company should pay particular attention in the selection process to the public relations firm's track record in dealing with negative public attention. Also, the company should be certain to try to find an agency with ethical values closely aligned to its own. The company's executives do not want to be in the position of arguing with their public relations agency on what to say to the public media and how to say it in the middle of a crisis.

To facilitate clear understanding between the company and its public relations agency, as well as between the company and its management and employees, the management of the young company should set out a policy of how it deals with public adversity. This written policy should reflect the company's core values and ethics. This policy will then form the basis for the company's attitude in addressing public adversity in a major crisis, as well.

MAINTAINING VIGILANCE WHILE MARKETING ENTREPRENEURIALLY   Monitoring threats and anticipating crises would seem to contradict and undermine the entrepreneurial efforts we espoused in Chapter 9. This is a real concern. The role of crisis planning and crisis management efforts needs to be couched within an entrepreneurial context and not allowed to overwhelm it. The key to attaining balance between the two kinds of efforts is to first realize where the two coincide and then to co-ordinate the purposes of the two efforts.

The marketing organization with an entrepreneurial orientation should be willing to accept some risk of poor financial performance. Crisis management people can raise questions that can halt a marketing strategy or require substantial change when the strategy appears to create other kinds of risks, such as risks of harm to customers or other stakeholders. Entrepreneurial marketing does not mean that new ventures will be pursued when they create moderate non-financial risks for stakeholders or for the community at large.

THOUGHTS TO TAKE WITH YOU AS YOU FINISH THIS CHAPTER

In this chapter, we have presented the societal marketing concept and its relationship to business ethics and crisis management. We hope that you recognize that the societal marketing concept can significantly reduce the need for crisis management. We also hope that the material presented in this chapter demonstrates the dilemma many people face, both as professionals and as individuals in society. Ideal conditions do not exist, yet this is neither an excuse for less than ethical individual behavior nor less than an organizational commitment to ethical standards. Situational ethics (or ethics of convenience) permit a spiraling down of standards that lower the image and esteem of the people who make up the organization. Ethics are an individual choice. We hope that this chapter has given you some things to consider as you make choices in the professional world.

An ethical approach to marketing and to doing business in general also obliges the company to prepare for the crises that it cannot anticipate and avoid. The societal marketing concept requires businesses to prepare for times when they have negative impacts on society, mitigate the problems that arise, communicate with all stakeholders honestly, and to take responsibility for the company's actions and their impacts. The marketer's role in crisis management is to manage the relationship with channels and customers even during these periods of stress.

This is the last chapter in the book but what we hope will be the beginning of your continued interest in business-to-business marketing. The differences between business-to-business marketing and consumer marketing have been discussed. The creation of the total offering based on customer perceptions of need and value has been strongly advocated. Process and methods to influence business buying decisions have been described, based on the establishment of long-term relationships, partners, and value networks. Revisit these concepts after you obtain more experience in business-to-business marketing. We think you will recognize the real value of what you have learned when you apply it "in the real world."

Key Terms

natural law *407*

positive law *407*

self-interest considered upon
    the whole *407*

situational ethics *407*

societal marketing concept *403*

value image *402*

Questions for Review and Discussion

1. Discuss consumer attitudes toward business ethics. Why are so many people willing to accept business ethics as an inconsistency in terms?

2. Are ethical marketing practices more important at the business-to-business level or at the consumer level? Is there a difference?

3. Should a company respond (or "go along with") customers that want something because it is best for them, but not aligned with what may be beneficial for society?

4. Considering the nature of relationships in business-to-business marketing versus consumer marketing, are ethical lapses more likely to occur in consumer markets or in business-to-business markets?

5. Select a recent crisis faced by a prominent member of society—politician, statesman, community leader, and so on—how well was the crisis handled with regard to the principles discussed in this chapter?

6. What ethical factors can contribute to individual discomfort in a position in an organization?

7. Do all crises, big and small, involve ethics? Briefly explain.

8. Can all crises be averted with good crisis planning? Why, or why not?

9. What should an organization look for in a public relations agency to handle the company's public crises? When should the public relations agency be hired? Why?

10. Think about the emotions experienced by TWA's stakeholders (both internal and external to the organization) during the Flight 800 crisis. If you were the spokesperson for TWA, whose emotions would you be expected to address? How might you, in your role as spokesperson, address these emotions?

11. Go to the Web site for the American Marketing Association, www.ama.org, and review the AMA Code of Ethics. Consider how difficult it would be for *you* to adhere to it, in the examples described here and from your personal experience.

12. How can a business-to-business marketing organization be watching for the sources of minor crises without becoming too conservative in its strategies and actions? How can marketers stay entrepreneurial while still proactively managing crises?

Endnotes

1. Federal Aviation Administration, "Summary of FAA Actions on TWA 800/747s," *FAA News* (December 8, 1997).

2. Robert Davis, "FAA to Review Safety of Fuel Tanks," *USA Today* (December 16, 1996), www.usatoday.com.

3. Deborah Feyerick, "Boeing Delayed Handing Over Study of Fuel Tanks to TWA 800 Investigators," *CNN.com* (October 30, 1999).

4. Andy Pasztor, "Plans to Avert Fuel-Tank Explosions Tied to '96 Jet Crash Called Too Costly," *Wall Street Journal* (August 8, 2001), p. A2.

5. National Transportation Safety Board, "NTSB Advisory" (August 8, 2001), www.ntsb.gov.

6. Christopher Conkey and Andy Pasxtor, "U.S. Set to Toughen Jet Fuel-Tank Rules," *Wall Street Journal* (July 16, 2008), http://online.wsj.com/article_print/SB121616726397856251.html.

7. Moira Marx Nir, *Implications of Post-Consumer Plastic Waste* (Society of Plastics Engineers, Inc.), An article from *Plastics Engineering*, 46(9) (September 1990).

8. American Marketing Association, *AMA Code of Ethics*, http://www.ama.org/about/ama/fulleth.asp

9. Philip Kotler, *Marketing Management*, 10th ed. (Upper Saddle River, N.J.: Prentice Hall, 2000), p. 25.

10. Betsy Cummings, "Slowdown Effect: Lack of Ethics," *Sales and Marketing Management* (June 2001), p. 13.

11. The Foreign Corrupt Practices Act (FCPA), passed in 1977 makes it a crime for a U.S. corporation to bribe officials of another government to obtain favorable business decisions. However, under the FCPA, *gratuities* are permitted. The dilemma is in defining the difference.

12. Vernon R. Loucks, Jr., "A CEO Looks at Ethics," originally published in *Business Horizons* (March–April 1987), pp. 2–6.

13. FMDs and the role they play in the marketing organization are discussed in Chapter 11.

14. Stephen Young, *Moral Capitalism* (San Francisco: Berret-Koehler Publishers, 2003), p. 11.

15. Ibid, p. 17.

16. Marianne Jennings, *Business: Its Legal, Ethical, and Global Environment* (Cincinnati: South-Western College Publishing, 2000).

17. Steven Fink, *Crisis Management: Planning for the Inevitable* (New York: AMACOM, 1986).

18. Thierry C. Pauchant and Ian I. Mitroff, *Transforming the Crisis-Prone Organization: Preventing Individual, Organizational, and Environmental Tragedies* (San Francisco: Jossey-Bass, 1992).

19. Ibid.; Fink, *Crisis Management*.

CASE I

LastMile Corporation II: Choosing a Development Partner

Overview

In this hypothetical case, LastMile's CEO is faced with a decision on who to partner with for development and launch of LastMile's new product. LastMile has two offers on the table and is trying to decide how to proceed.

In this case, you will be asked to determine the best approach, given the company's situation.

LastMile's Dilemma

Stepping out from a meeting that had just ended, Tom Sherman, the president and CEO of LastMile Corporation, was reviewing the main points discussed. This was a meeting with internal LastMile directors and executives, discussing alternatives for LastMile's strategy. LastMile had two proposals on the table for strategic partnerships. One was a proposed technology licensing agreement from Midwest Technologies, Inc., a large defense contractor and advanced technology supplier to many industries. The second offer was an acquisition proposal by ANZ Investment Group, a medium-sized venture capital firm and incubator, who offered LastMile substantial funding in exchange for a significant ownership share of LastMile. The meeting had reached no conclusions but raised a number of issues pertinent to the decision the whole board of directors would have to make. Tom, who as CEO was a member of the board, was trying to make up his mind on the position he would take tomorrow when the entire board would next meet in a videoconference session.

Tom still remembers the early days of LastMile when he and seven others, working in rented cubicles in a technology incubator, had given an idea a definite shape, which resulted in what the company is today. They had come a long way since those endless hours of constant struggle. The effort paid off and the company, on its own in its own facilities for two years, was a pioneer in technology for wireless broadband access. They were very proud of their achievements.

However, Tom realized that now, in 2005, the company might do better with closer ties to a larger company with more resources and complementary technology products. The business environment is fast changing and new technologies are coming up much faster than in the earlier years. The gestation period for new technology has been rapidly cut down. The market environment was promising, with money pouring into new ventures. New companies were springing up and more and more players were entering the wireless communications industry. Being a privately held, small company, LastMile did not have the financial resources to invest enough in its future technological developments. LastMile was "at the chasm," the company unable to respond as rapidly as the market growth opportunities. The company was facing financial problems, which needed to be addressed immediately.

Industry analysts predicted that the broadband wireless communication industry would experience a growth rate in the next couple of years that would be four times the present rate. This was largely attributed to the exponential growth of the Internet and e-business. The broadband wireless communication technology is relatively inexpensive and quick to install, with a high data transmission rate, more than 2,700 times faster that the fastest dial-up modem used in personal computers. The transceiver technologies for broadband access systems are also used for wireless infrastructure connectivity in cellular networks. As the density of cellular users continues to increase, broadband wireless communications promises to be a strong growth area.

The Internet has revolutionized the way businesses communicate and exchange information, becoming a crucial factor in the success of any business. The products that LastMile Corporation manufactures will help businesses overcome problems that are encountered when trying to connect to the local switching office or Internet access point at broadband frequencies.

Midwest Technologies, Inc., provides advanced technology products and services to the automotive, aerospace, and information technology markets worldwide. Having annual sales of about $20 billion, the company employs more than 115,000 employees with primary locations in more than thirty-five countries. Founded early in the 20th century, it has been at the forefront of some of the significant technologies of the last hundred years. The mission of Midwest Technologies is to accomplish a leadership position in the automotive, aerospace, and information technology markets by serving the needs of its customers in innovative ways—by being the best in everything it does. One of the strategies that the company has adopted is to create value for its customers, through the execution of alliances, new ventures and mergers that bring an array of communication technologies to the marketplace.

Monolithic microwave integrated circuit (MMIC) is a generic technology that is used in the amplification of microwave frequencies. It is a low power consumption device, which is used in all high frequency transmission devices like cell phones. Micro Manufacturing, a fully owned subsidiary, is Midwest's telecommunications systems development and manufacturing unit. It develops and produces telecommunications equipment, including MMIC modules, for Midwest's contract customers. Midwest customers include many telecommunications service providers, such as AT&T and Comcast, who often contract to Micro to produce devices tailored to service provider's systems. Micro is both a captive supplier to Midwest for Midwest-branded products and a contract electronics component provider to other companies in telecommunications.

LastMile Corporation is a privately held company, founded in 1998 with its headquarters in Santa Clara, California. LastMile's core competency is based on its innovative efforts in transceiver systems design and integration. This expertise has been used to develop low-cost microwave transceivers based on revolutionary MMIC design. It has over a dozen patents covering the core technology in its line of products. LastMile sells its subsystems directly to telecom equipment makers like Hughes Electronics, Nokia, and Nortel Networks. They in turn, refine and sell the broadband wireless systems to the actual communication service providers. LastMile serves as a core building block vendor in the broadband wireless arena and is a crucial player in the build-out of the widely anticipated third-generation cellular networks. With the explosive growth that this industry is anticipating, the company faces competition from companies like Infineon Technologies, Raytheon and Andrew Corporation. New competitors like Telaxis Communications and MTI Technology are also vying for a slice of the broadband wireless equipment market pie. Tom was thinking about what needs to be done, so that the company will be able to ride the tide. The primary need was for cash that could be used to support the rapid growth in response to customer demand.

ANZ Investment Group provides investment to companies to realize their financial goals and objectives. Established in 1983, it has its headquarters in Torrance, California. It emphasizes quality service and long-term client relationships. In its portfolio of investment companies are several young companies with technology related to LastMile. There was the possibility that, with the cooperation of all parties, the ANZ companies together could approach the telecom equipment vendors with a fuller line of products, but these would still have to be made compatible with the products of other technology suppliers.

Since the end of December, Micro Manufacturing has been showing an active interest in LastMile and, together with Midwest's technology licensing group, had recently put forth the proposal to Tom Sherman. Micro Manufacturing is a leader in the manufacture of the kinds of transceiver modules made by LastMile, but has only a rudimentary development capability itself in this area. It is looking for an increasing involvement in the broadband telecommunications marketplace. The vice president of business development for Micro Manufacturing sees LastMile products and capabilities as a perfect fit with Micro Manufacturing's products and their future plans. Additionally, Micro capabilities as a low-cost manufacturer of electronic components could provide LastMile, as volume expands, with an efficient producer of products.

The Midwest–Micro proposal is for a licensing agreement with LastMile. Midwest Technologies has an interest in and has hinted at financial support for LastMile's technical research and development. The agreement would require LastMile to supply its technology to Micro Manufacturing. Micro Manufacturing would be able to provide this technology to its customers. At the end of the term of the license agreement, both Micro Manufacturing and LastMile could go their own way.

Some of the terms of the license concerned Tom. As Micro Manufacturing used LastMile technology as its own at customers, Micro would have an opportunity to co-develop the next-generation offering with direct customer input, using the LastMile technology to establish a beachhead in the market segment. This could provide Micro with a strong presence with customers, as it would be the defending source. The agreement also implied that LastMile would modify the technology to suit the needs of Micro Manufacturing customers, which would result in LastMile

narrowing its market to Midwest Technologies only. Tom was wondering whether this might not be too large a hurdle in LastMile's progress and development of its new technologies. If and when LastMile decided to approach the marketplace directly with next-generation technology, the licensing agreement may have created a formidable competitor.

ANZ Investment Group had proposed a direct investment option. This would provide LastMile with the much-needed cash for further development that would help the company keep competition at bay. A direct investment would give ANZ Investment Group a genuine interest in the future of LastMile Corporation. LastMile would also have total control over its products and will be free to choose which markets it would like to pursue.

Tom Sherman was leaning toward the offer from Midwest Technologies. It offered better access to the markets he wanted to address. It also would be easier to co-develop compatible products with Micro Manufacturing, thereby reducing development costs and time. His principal concern was the loss of flexibility in pursuing technology directions, particularly if the market moved away from Micro Manufacturing's architectures. He wasn't too fond of the situation once the license period was over, either. The ANZ option, on the other hand, provided money with few strings attached. Tom's concern, though, was that this option did little to improve LastMile's marketing punch, and he was not convinced that cooperation with other ANZ companies would be easy or useful. Tom was wondering whether Midwest Technologies would be willing to consider an alternative proposal.

Questions for Discussion

1. What are the other alternatives that LastMile could look at that would create a working relationship between Midwest Technologies and LastMile?

2. What are the advantages and disadvantages of these alternatives?
3. What are the objectives that LastMile would like to accomplish out of such a partnership?
4. What counter proposal(s) would you recommend? Explain.

Note: Though based on real situations, individual and company names are fictional and several simplifications have been made, in the interest of academic clarity, to product and market information. For this reason, specific situations and factors mentioned herein may not recreate the actual circumstances experienced.

CASE II

B2B E-Commerce in China: The Story of Alibaba.com

In 2008 China had the most Internet users in the world; 253 million users were online, looking for information, sending e-mail, and doing business electronically. E-business is defined as "any economic transaction where the buyer and seller come together through the electronic media of the Internet, form a contractual agreement concerning the pricing and delivery of particular goods and services, and complete the transaction through the delivery of payments and good or services as contracted." Business-to-business (B2B) e-commerce thus involves adding this new technology to the "traditional" business settings to enable companies to buy and sell online between themselves.

The emergence of B2B e-commerce is relatively new to the business world, since it was not until the mid-80s with the introduction of the first desktop operating systems that the Internet began to finally take shape. By 1990, Tim Berners-Lee developed the first World Wide Web software and as a result opened up the Internet to the growing masses of computer users. It was then just matter of time before businesses all over the world began to see the tremendous opportunity of using the World Wide Web, and rushed to start finding ways to benefit from it. By 1993, over 100 countries had an online presence, and commercial users outnumbered academic users for the first time in the history of the technology.[1]

B2B e-business, or e-commerce, rapidly became one of the most talked-about topics by leading industry experts and the latest marketing "gurus" during the period of the Internet bubble in the late 1990s.[2] So much pressure was placed on business leaders to adopt B2B e-commerce solutions that near panic often ensued in the rush to set up thousands of online marketplaces (e-marketplaces). However, when the Internet bubble finally burst, these e-marketplaces and all the money invested in them disappeared as fast as they had once appeared. This incident served to cast a dark shadow over the future of B2B e-commerce, and it has only been in the last few years that a strong resurgence in its usage has been noticed. (See "Covisint: Illustrating the Importance of Adapting to Customers' Buying Behavior," in the opening of Chapter 3.)

The rise of B2B e-commerce can be understood as a kind of third wave of e-commerce, following the first wave that consisted only of a Web site where the company offered a catalogue of its products, and a second wave where the consumer could buy those products by a link established between the Web site and the company's back-end.[3] In this third wave the company is so focused on the Internet that not only does it offer its services to its clients online, but also it does transactions with its providers online, too.

By separating the physical and information flows connected with each transaction, the Internet radically changes the ways in which corporations provide and trade goods and services with each other.[4] It is the prospect of such change that motivates companies to consider B2B, since there are several significant advantages that can be gained.

---

[1] Augusta C. Yrle, Sandra J. Hartman, and Kenneth R. Walsh, "E-business: Linking Available Services and Entrepreneurs' Needs," *Journal of Small Business and Enterprise Development*, 11(3) (2004), pp. 390–399.

[2] Alberta Efuture center, "Business to Business E-Commerce Basics", *Pan-Western E-Business Team* (2006), p. 1.

[3] Augusta et al., "E-Business: Linking Available," pp. 390–399.

[4] Steven N. Kaplan and Luis Garicano, "A Framework for Analyzing B2B E-Commerce," University of Chicago Graduate School of Business (November 2000), p. 1.

The key effect of B2B e-commerce is to change the costs (and benefits) of transacting compared to the "traditional" methods. Companies can potentially reduce or even eliminate costly tasks that slowed efficiency or used valuable resources. Another advantage of B2B e-commerce is that the Internet can provide buyers with better decision-making information about a product's characteristics (including price and availability) since this information is less expensive to obtain and much easier to find. A third advantage is that it can eventually provide better information about buyers and sellers themselves, which is vital in B2B situations when dealing with issues such as credit.

However, the most widely acclaimed merit of B2B e-commerce is that it has "levelled the playing field" for small companies to compete with larger ones despite differences in size and scope.[5] Allowing small companies global access to markets that were once only the playing ground for large multinationals has revolutionized the business landscape and radically changed the old rules of conducting business transactions.

Therefore the rise of B2B e-commerce as witnessed by the worldwide increase in the number of virtual marketplaces and more fully integrated and coordinated supply chains has given companies big and small new tools for them to remain competitive in the increasingly competitive globalized business environment.

Difficulties of B2B E-Commerce in China

The proliferation of B2B e-commerce has taken different paths in different nations. Although there is no precise breakdown of the kinds of e-commerce available in China, scattered data suggest that more than 75 percent of transactions are business to business.[6]

Yet compared to other similarly developing nations, China's B2B e-commerce activity has been ranked well below the average score in a recent survey.[7] This is partially because of difficulties concerning the technology and the political and economic environments for B2B e-commerce adoption. On the other hand, the impressive annual growth rates of B2B transactions in recent years, as well as the positive forecasts, are pointing to the fact that China is progressing on gradually working on its business, legal, and cultural barriers while upgrading its technology infrastructure.[8] Statistics from domestic Internet research and consulting company iResearch predict the e-commerce market will grow 50 percent annually, reaching revenues of 7.5 trillion yuan in 2012, up from 480.9 billion yuan in 2006.[9]

China's infrastructure for e-commerce can be characterized by "disparities" among geographic areas, demographics, industrial fields, and firm size.[10] Large cities and economically advanced coastal provinces typically enjoy much better infrastructure and many more Internet users than remote and economically poor provinces. Most Chinese firms have also poor internal management information systems that lag far behind that of their counterparts in developed countries.

Along with the poor technical infrastructure, there are many other barriers to B2B e-commerce in China. The most significant barriers include lack of security, lack of a system to monitor and guarantee buyer and

[5] T. Friedman, "The World Is Flat," Farrar, Strauss and Giroux publishing, USA (2006).

[6] The Economist Intelligence Unit Limited, "Country Commerce: Ecommerce in China" (2006), p. 124.

[7] A. Zixiang and T. Wu Ouyang, "Diffusion and Impacts of the Internet and E-Commerce in China," School of Information Studies Syracuse University, USA (February 2004), p. 4.

[8] Ibid.

[9] D. Qingfen, "E-commerce Evolution," *China Daily* (October 10, 2007).

[10] Zixiang and Wu Ouyang, "Diffusion and Impacts of the Internet," p. 4.

seller credibility, and an inefficient delivery system.[11] In addition, there is no sophisticated legal framework to facilitate e-commerce activities and to protect the interests of both vendors and consumers.

In regards to a deficient legal framework, domain names are a special area of intellectual property and they have been a particular headache to many companies operating in China. So-called cyber-squatters often acquire the rights to domain names similar to those of well-known companies and then demand fees to relinquish those rights. There is currently little legal protection in China offered to companies who find themselves victims to such practices.

Though not peculiar to China, government censorship poses more difficulties than in many other countries surveyed. Chen Yun, Mao Zedong's former economic wizard, is well known in China for his "bird cage" theory.[12] The bird cage theory posits that the economy should be allowed to fly free like a bird but only within the confines of a good strong cage. Hence China's e-commerce policy seeks to control Internet information, flow, economics, and key players with albeit varying degrees of success.

A variety of different Chinese agencies have over the years tried their hands at regulating and supervising every aspect of the country's e-commerce. The result has been greater confusion and increasing bureaucratic hassles for businesses, with the result that the development of B2B e-commerce has been curbed significantly.

Other major limitations to the adoption of B2B e-commerce, although again not specific to China, include the high start-up costs of developing or buying the technology and the relative difficulty of finding and retaining the necessary qualified people to establish and maintain these e-commerce platforms.[13]

Because of these limiting factors, only a very small number of firms have actually moved to the next step to conduct e-commerce activities via their Web sites. A recent report says that sales from online transactions in 2006 accounted for just 16.62 percent of the nation's total. The figure was even smaller in 2005, when 9.85 percent of sales were made online.[14]

What China Is Doing to Promote B2B E-Commerce

The official Chinese media had hinted in early 2001 that comprehensive rules governing the Internet would be made available soon. However, as of the date of this writing, still nothing has been officially announced. In the meantime, the State Council did issue "Proposals on Accelerating the Development of E-commerce" in March 2005. The document called for accelerating the pace of e-commerce development and examined potential regulations on electronic trading, credit management, security certification, online payment, and taxation of e-commerce.

Some isolated steps already taken by the Chinese government toward facilitating B2B e-commerce include the passage of the "Law on Electronic Signatures," which went into effect in April 2005 and improved legal support for e-commerce. The law grants electronic signatures the same legal validity as handwritten signatures and seals in business

---

[11] Ibid., p. 5.

[12] C. Trappey and A. Trappey, "Electronic Commerce in Greater China," *Industrial Management & Data Systems*, 101/5 (2001), p. 202.

[13] Kaynak Erdener, Ekrem Tatoglu, Veysel Kula, Turkey Afyon, "An Analysis of the Factors Affecting the Adoption of Electronic Commerce by SMEs Evidence from an Emerging Market", *International Marketing Review*, 22(6) (2005), pp. 623–640.

[14] D. Qingfen, "E-commerce Evolution," *China Daily* (October 10, 2007).

deals. This is vital for conducting business online. Along with the law, a market-access system to certify online signatures began operating to facilitate the country's growing online trade.

This was in addition to another important measure taken earlier in 2001 by the Chinese government that involved the creation of the China Finance Certification Authority (CFCA). The CFCA is responsible for the creation of a certification system for e-commerce and online banking, including cross-bank transactions among the twelve participating banks.

Yet despite these early measures, a 2004 survey by the China Internet Network Information Centre (CNNIC) showed that 62.4 percent of Chinese Internet users cited fears of being cheated by fraudulent Web sites as the main obstacles to online purchases.[15] This is because the Chinese government is simply unable to fully enforce many of the Internet and e-commerce regulations it has already established, and it is also unable to keep up with the rapid pace of new technological developments and the need to regulate them.

Alibaba's Strategy of Online E-commerce

A company that has now become synonymous with the Chinese B2B e-commerce industry is Alibaba. Since its humble beginnings in 1999, when it was launched by Chinese businessman Jack Ma, Alibaba.com had, in 2007, become the world's largest online B2B global trading marketplace, with 25 million registered users and 255,000 paying members in its international and Chinese domestic marketplaces.[16] Its spectacular rise over the years and the numerous challenges it has faced are a reflection of the entire Chinese B2B e-commerce industry that it has actively helped to shape.

Company History

It was in 1995, when Jack Ma, founder and CEO of Alibaba.com (Chinese: 阿里巴巴; pinyin: ā lǐ bā bā) was on a trip to the United States, he touched a computer keyboard for the first time. When some friends in Seattle showed him the Internet, he typed "China" and "beer" into Yahoo—yielding no results. Ma decided to start a company to help Chinese firms get on the Net. Returning home, he launched China Pages, an online directory of Chinese firms which was widely believed to be the country's first commercial Web site. Two years later, Jack Ma headed the first government Web site by the Chinese Ministry of Foreign Trade and Economic Cooperation. In 1999, the core team from the ministry followed Ma as he took his quest to next level by founding Alibaba.com.

The Arabian Nights–inspired name was chosen because it is meaningful to people around the world. Alibaba opens the door to doing business, enabling an interactive community of millions to meet, chat, trade, and work online. The mission is to make doing business easier.

The main feature of Alibaba.com is a B2B Web site where buyers and sellers, everything from bamboo toothpicks to farm tractors, can find each other and trade. The firm sees opportunities from linking China's small businesses into global supply chains. But Alibaba is remarkable in two respects. First, it mostly introduces not big firms but small companies ("shrimps" rather than "whales," as Ma likes to say "there are more shrimps in the ocean than whales"). Second, the shrimps are from all over the world including, crucially, the vast and largely uncharted small-business hinterland that is China. This makes Alibaba different from most U.S. e-commerce companies who mainly focus on big corporations to help the buyer to

---

[15] The Economist Intelligence Unit Limited, "Country Commerce: Ecommerce in China" (2006), p. 131.
[16] C. Splinder, "The Alibaba Story," p. 1.

save time. After several years of experience, Ma found that small- and medium-sized enterprises (SMEs) are the ones who really need e-commerce.

Based in Hangzhou in eastern China, Alibaba now has sixteen regional sales and service centers across the country, as well as corporate offices in Beijing, Hong Kong, the United States, and Europe. The company had more than 5,000 full-time employees as of December 31, 2006. Their English-language Web site alibaba.com specializes in B2B trades, especially for international buyers trying to get into contact with Chinese sellers. The Chinese-language chinese.alibaba.com focuses on B2B trades within China while www.taobao.com is a consumer-to-consumer (C2C) trade site for Chinese customers.

Yuxin Chen, a marketing professor at New York University's Stern School of Business, has commented on Alibaba's three distinct target markets and portals (Alibaba.com, Alibaba China, and TaoBao) as a further reason behind Alibaba's success. Chen sees them as an important source of synergy. "Those [small-business] sellers who use Alibaba will also use Taobao," in much the same way that small-business owners who use eBay to sell goods may also buy and sell items as consumers on eBay.[17]

Meet Jack Ma: "The Jack Who Will change the World"

If you don't have enemies in your heart, nobody is an enemy in your eyes.

—Jack Ma

Ma is probably the only Chinese Internet entrepreneur anyone in the West has heard of. Aged 43, Ma stands barely 5 feet tall, stick-figure thin, especially in his oversized suits. As a child of the Cultural Revolution, Ma was once a Mao-loving Red Guard. Along with most of his peers, he grew up thinking that the outside world was a terrible place. This view was changed only in 1985 when he first traveled abroad to Australia. The experience turned his worldview inside out, and he became a fanatical xenophile. Back in China, he listened to the Voice of America and would cycle for almost an hour, in any weather, to give free tours to foreigners in the nearby hotels. With his English skills, Ma was sent to the United States in 1995 by a Chinese company to collect money owed by an American company. That visit opened his eyes to the Internet. Ma came back to China and tried to tell his friends in Hangzhou to get aboard this amazing new invention. They thought he was mad but he went ahead and founded the first commercial Internet business in China. "I decided to try it although I knew nothing about the technology and had no people. I called myself like a blind man riding the back of a blind tiger." Today, Ma has delivered speeches at Harvard Business School and World Economic Forum. As part of the Chinese delegation to Sydney Asia-Pacific Economic Cooperation (APEC) Business Advisory Council in September 2007, Ma was described by the Australian papers:

Ma is typical of many very successful self-made Asian entrepreneurs who approach life from a very different point of view than the more hidebound Western business-people. They don't bother about defining themselves or acquiring the right skills to approach a task. They don't seek the advice of high-priced consultants or "experts" or take years formulating plans. They don't worry about pay and bonuses and complex share option deals. They just go and do it. And keep on going, riding the blind tiger like Ma, on the edge of the China boom. While Western businesses limit their operations—seeking to concentrate on

---

[17] Knowledge@Wharton, "Open Sesame? Or Could the Doors Slam Shut for Alibaba.com?" (July 27, 2005).

narrowly defined markets—self-made Asian business people often operate conglomerates, cheerfully moving into a whole range of businesses, from trading and manufacturing to property and restaurants and travel. In China today, particularly, there's a fast-moving open-mindedness and a freedom from tradition that leaps beyond the thinking of "New World" countries such as Australia and America.

The Supporters

Despite Ma's history with the Chinese government, Alibaba enjoyed no initial support from the government. When the initial funding of RMB 500,000 (approximately US$60,000) from Ma's personal savings and loans ran out, Alibaba looked for venture capital investors. The first group of investors, led by Goldman Sachs, contributed US$5 million. This was followed by Softbank's commitment of US$20 million in January 2000. MA's personal charms wooed not only capital, but admirers from the top of the corporate world. Peter Sutherland, former WTO director-general and chairman of Goldman Sachs, and Masayoshi Son, CEO of Softbank, both sit on the board of directors for Alibaba. Ma's admirers are especially important to the success to Alibaba. Softbank, the world's largest investor in cyberspace, owns stakes in Yahoo! and E*Trade as well as hundreds of other companies. Softbank's support provides Alibaba with both quality advice and credibility in the corporate world. With strong backing from the corporate world, Ma was able to attract Web stars such as John Wu, the chief designer of the Yahoo! Search Engine, as his chief technology officer.

Alibaba Today

Today **Alibaba.com Corporation** is China's leading e-commerce company, operating the world's largest online marketplaces for both international and domestic China trade, as well as China's most popular online payment

system, **AliPay**. Alibaba.com also owns and operates Yahoo! China, which it acquired in October 2005. The Web site www.china.alibaba.com is China's largest online marketplace for domestic trade among business people. With more than 25 million registered users and 255,000 paying members, Alibaba China is a trusted community of members who regularly meet, chat, search for products, and do business online. The site covers 30 industries and more than 5,000 product categories. Customers pay an annual subscription fee for membership, which entitles them to post trade offers and products online. The subscription fee also includes authentication and verification of the member's identity, which is performed by a third-party credit reporting agency.

TaoBao and eBay

TaoBao (www.taobao.com) is China' most popular C2C trading site with more than 20 million registered users. Since its founding in May of 2003, TaoBao has risen to become a leader in China's consumer e-commerce market. Compared with similar services, the Web site has the highest number of product listings and the highest penetration among China's 160 million Internet users.

Ma's greatest adversary had always been U.S.-based eBay. Watching the U.S. Internet auction company's increasing China presence in early 2003, Ma secretly moved a group of his most trusted employees into an apartment in his native Hangzhou where he had founded Alibaba in 1998. Holed up in the apartment for several months, the executives drafted plans for TaoBao.com, Alibaba's consumer auction site.

Launched in July of that year, TaoBao quickly snared market share from eBay in China. Ma had pledged not to charge TaoBao customers, and as the site had no conventional advertising, the company brought in no revenue and relied on loans and venture capital. Since 2004, TaoBao was engaged in a massive winner-takes-all battle with eBay, believing that in the long run businesses and consumers only want to deal with one market, one auction house, and one payment system.

After a year of fierce competition, eBay was forced by Alibaba's policy of offering auction services for free to change tack in China, scrapping all sellers' transaction fees. In 2005, eBay committed a further 100 million, which it announced as "a sign of an unmistakable commitment and an unstoppable determination to be number one in China." However shortly after, eBay announced in December 2006 that it would close its main online auction Web site in China and replace it with a minority-invested joint venture with Beijing-based portal and telecom service provider Tom Online. Industry analysts widely believed eBay's move reflected wider failures among foreign Internet companies to adjust quickly enough to consumer demand and challenges from local rivals, and in maintaining good relations with Beijing regulators.

Jack Ma has told local media that TaoBao.com has already taken 67 percent of the market share of online auction sites in China and has left eBay far behind. TaoBao.com has 26 million goods online and its Web pages are browsed 110 million times each month. Jack Ma aims to make the online auction site volume of TaoBao.com reach US$450 million in each quarter of 2008, and the total transaction volume of the whole year will increase to US$1.8 billion from the previous year's US$1 billion. At the same time, he estimates that the total registered users of TaoBao.com will exceed that of eBay.

Feedback from Alibaba's B2B Customers

Regardless of whether they traded consumer goods or sold second-hand paper processing machinery through the e-market, the companies polled in a recent survey viewed their membership to Alibaba as being very helpful and cost efficient.[18] These ranged from free membership to paying members who obtain a quality certification. Companies use Alibaba.com to primarily find contacts. The business transaction itself, including order taking and receiving payment, is usually handled using traditional methods. For Morgan Nylander, CEO of a micro SME in the pulp and paper industry located in Sweden, being a member of Alibaba complements their traditional ways of doing business. "For us it is a useful tool to market our products. Even if your company sells products that have a very low value it doesn't take many additional sales to recoup the initial investment."

The only problem apparently with Alibaba has been the fear that using e-markets is so easy that a company runs the risk of becoming too lazy and complacent. The reality of the business world continues to be that to do business you have to meet in person, as you can't expect customers to automatically come rushing.

Cultural Differences

The success of Alibaba over eBay is the result of deep national understanding. Online commerce was completely foreign to the Chinese culture, where buyers like to inspect the merchandise in person then haggle over the price. But the dynamic of online commerce is precisely the opposite: Buyers agree to buy something based on a picture, and the auction drives the price up. To the Chinese, the whole arrangement smelled fishy at best. Further, sellers worry about non-paying buyers, and buyers worry they would never see the goods they paid for. To tailor to such cultural requirements, TaoBao prices start high, and buyers haggle to get them down. TaoBao also offers an escrow service to ensure the buyer is happy with the goods before payment goes through; and

---

18 eMarket Services, "Feedback from Alibaba Customers" (2004).

people can buy in groups. This means friends usually get together to form group purchases. This is desirable to the sellers because of the volume, and likewise to buyers as they obtain a discount.

Innovation

Behind each of Alibaba's battles with its competitors, user-friendly innovations seemed to be key to success. Long before eBay acquired Skype, TaoBao had allowed buyers to send instant - messages to sellers. In fact, it is widely believed amongst Alibaba executives that Meg Whitman, CEO of eBay, acquired Skype after she was introduced to TaoBao during her trip to China.

Despite Google's reputation as "the innovative company," Ma believes the Chinese Internet market will change the direction and pave the way for new types of progress in the search market. "If you follow Google's way, you will always be a follower," Ma explained, "so we have to make the Yahoo! search engine more human, more interactive, something for the 1.3 billion people in China who aren't technology-oriented, who don't know how to ask the right questions to a search engine—for people who are like me."

AliPay Online Payment Solution

Completing China's e-commerce transaction chain, Alibaba operates AliPay (www.alipay.com) which enables any individuals and businesses to securely, easily, and quickly send and receive payments online. To provide AliPay, Alibaba has partnered with China's leading banks, including China Merchants Bank, China Construction Bank, Agricultural Bank of China, and the Industrial and Commercial Bank of China. AliPay now has 48 million users, compared to only 33 million credit card users in China. AliPay was born out of necessity; given the poor financial infrastructure in China, Alibaba had to leapfrog the technology in order to attract SMEs.

In October 2007, AliPay facilitated transactions in 12 foreign currencies, including U.S. dollars, Japanese yen, and euros. This means Alipay could open up China for e-commerce giants such as Amazon and global businesses lacking the scale and manpower to set up retail operations on the ground in China. As foreign companies often have trouble getting licenses to sell online in China, Alipay provides foreign companies the alternative of piggybacking on Alibaba's license rather than to acquire their own.

Alibaba Enters Strategic Cooperation with China Post

Previously, Alibaba.com Group, operator of China's largest online marketplace Alibaba.com and the country's biggest auction site TaoBao.com, just recommended on its sites several privately run express delivery companies whose networks don't cover the whole country. Traders complained about damages to and even losses of their goods during transport, for which they would only be compensated at most three times the delivery fee based on the express delivery companies' rules.

Alibaba and China Post, the postal service of the People's Republic of China, have signed a long-term strategic cooperation agreement to further develop China's e-commerce infrastructure and make it easier for Chinese consumers to shop online. Under the agreement, the two organizations will cooperate in parcel delivery and money remittance services. In the short term, China Post and Alibaba.com's online payment platform, Alipay, will launch a new economical parcel service for online purchases called "e-Youbao" and allow customers to fund their Alipay account at any of China Post's 66,000 locations across mainland China, without the need for a debit card or bank account. China Post's Green Card debit service will also become a new partner for Alipay's online payment service. China Post, one of China's most trusted brands, will enhance traders' confidence in e-commerce and they have also worked out a mechanism to offer full compensation for traders in case of commodity damage and loss during transport, further contributing to customers confidence and trust.

The organizations say the partnership will leverage China Post's unmatched geographic coverage and strong brand name with Alibaba.com's leading e-commerce platform and online community of more than 160 million businesses and consumers. China Post's Postal Savings Bank also operates China's fifth-largest depository institution after the big four banks, making it an important partner for Alipay.

China Post and Alipay have already begun to test "e-Youbao" in China. The parcel delivery service, developed specifically for online purchases, is cheaper than China Post's standard mail service. On November 1, 2006, China Post also opened its first online postal shop on TaoBao.com selling stamps and books. This agreement paves the way for further cooperation of this sort in the future. The partnership will help Alibaba to penetrate underdeveloped e-commerce regions like the rural areas using China Post's most extensive parcel delivery and money remittance network. It's the most important strategic partnership they have ever entered since the establishment of Alibaba.

Alibaba Acquired Yahoo! China

On August 11, 2005, Yahoo! announced that it would purchase a 40 percent stake in the company for US$1billion plus Yahoo!'s Chinese assets (worth about US$700M). Alibaba took charge of Yahoo! China, and Alibaba's founder Jack Ma continued to run the company. That deal was heating up the race to dominate China's fledgling online auctions industry.

That deal gave Alibaba access to Yahoo's search technology to help it fend off expected competition from Google, which was then just starting a big push into the Chinese market. In addition, it gave Alibaba the cash it needed to buy out the shares of venture-capital backers, easing pressure on the Hangzhou, China,

company to take itself public. By all accounts, Yahoo was struggling in China against the market leader in search, Baidu, and against the advances of Google.

As Yahoo! forecasts the company's revenue at about US$200 million for 2006, most of that money has been generated by Alibaba's business-to-business ventures in a bid to steal market share from eBay. Although Ma realized that search technique from Yahoo is also essential to his e-commerce strategy, he admits that the acquisition had been a pain. "For the first six months, I wanted to give the money back!" Ma was reported to have said, "but a good dish takes time to cook."

Future for Alibaba and B2B E-Commerce

A lingering question in the minds of many business experts has been whether Alibaba's business model is sustainable. Being located in the middle of the world's largest collection of factories, near hundreds of thousands of suppliers, and being able to speak the language and understand the culture are all very valuable. But, according to Wharton operations professor Ravi Aron, other companies can still come in and beat Alibaba at its own game.

The challenge for Ma, who has had to defend himself against charges that his business model is fragile, is to help his company bridge the gap from a company that was initially responsive to the B2B e-commerce's early growth needs to the now new rapidly maturing needs for higher value-added services.

As a result of this reflection, Ma hopes in the future to derive Alibaba's revenue and ultimately its profits from add-on features. Shipping, trade financing, on-site inspections, quality control services, and insurance are a few of the services that could earn money for the site. Ma also hopes to make money by offering a premium service to members and through advertising and promotions. He plans to start sharing in the revenues made by the insurers, shippers, and others who benefit from the trade generated on his site, and to charge members for online advertising and fancy services. "Alibaba has made a big step forward in how business is done in Asia," says Hong Kong–based IDC Internet analyst Matthew McGarvey. "Sites like Alibaba are injecting transparency into the trading process."

Elsewhere, however, it faces lots of competition. Ma isn't the only one targeting this enormous market. Some are trying to aggregate big buyers across industries, mostly in the United States and Europe, as Commerce One and Ariba have tried. Others are verticals for a single industry, such as e-Steel for the metals industry and Covisint for autos.

Alibaba has grander ambitions. Ma wants the site to be both global and horizontal across all products. But he may well have picked the best starting point: Asia, by some estimates, is home to about 70 percent of all the world's exporting companies. There are about 400,000 exporters in China alone and more on the way. Ma believed in the next ten years, of the top three Internet companies in the World, one will be from China—and the company has to be Alibaba.

Certainly the potential market is enormous. FORBES figures that about US$470 billion a year is spent just servicing world trade—phone bills, invoicing, sales calls, overseas travel. If Web sites like Alibaba can cut that bill by even 20 percent—and that may be conservative—there is a potential savings pool of nearly US$100 billion from which it can draw revenues as profits.

Similarly, in the consumer market, there are currently 253 million Internet users in China, exceeding the population of Internet users of United States (220 million) in July 2008. Despite the success of Alibaba, the company was not without its critics. Many doubt Alibaba's

profitability, arguing that if Alibaba was as profitable as Ma claims, it would have gone public long ago. Others argue Alibaba lacks depth, that it is nothing more than a user-friendly bulletin board, offering too many product segments and too few services.

IPO: Alibaba Aims for 1.3 Billion in Listing

Ma wants Alibaba, which is set to list its B2B business on the Hong Kong Stock Exchange, to become the world's largest Internet company and a member of the Fortune 500. On October 2007, Alibaba raised 1.33 billion HKD in an initial public offering in Hong Kong. Alibaba sold 858.9 million shares, or 17 percent of its enlarged share capital, at a price of US$12, according to its preliminary prospectus. Alibaba.com used roughly 60 percent of the proceeds from its share offering "for strategic acquisitions" and other business development initiatives. The remainder of the proceeds was used to fund organic growth and to develop new technologies. In 2009, in the midst of the global financial recession, Alibaba expanded its offering heavily in the United States.[19]

China's B2B E-Commerce Industry and Alibaba

The Chinese B2B e-commerce industry owes much to Alibaba's CEO Jack Ma. Ma, however, does not necessarily think so, since for him B2B has various formats and there are many ways to establish a big marketplace to help medium- and small-sized companies succeed and make money. So according to Jack Ma, "B2B would exist even without us, but it would likely be a B2B different from Alibaba.[20]"

How different? It is unlikely B2B e-commerce in China could have developed so rapidly from its infancy if it was not for Alibaba's

---

[19] Alibaba Group planned to increase its current workforce of 12,000 by more than 4,000.
[20] Knowledge@Wharton, "Open Sesame?"

CEO's continuous efforts to create and educate new users, and to relentlessly push the Chinese government for greater Internet reforms to spur the growth of the entire Chinese B2B industry. Hence it has been Ma's vision that has ultimately shaped the evolution of B2B in China. As Ma states: "we don't know theories, but we are the ones who came in from the bloody battlefield, and we know which way to go. It's not investors' money that will take us there, and it's not money that forces us to go. It's our mission: to help China's suppliers."[21] In fact this belief is so important to Alibaba and the company's future direction that every new employee must go through a six-month training program to learn about the company's mission, vision, and values.

There can be no doubt that Jack Ma has accomplished a lot, and many view his company as the B2B standard in China and maybe the world.[22] After all, Jack Ma can be credited with being responsible for many "firsts" in China. It was Jack Ma who was the first entrepreneur to develop e-commerce in China. He founded the first Internet commercial Web site in China, and created a B2B marketplace platform to help all small- and medium-sized enterprises in Asia and around the world. He promoted the "Trust Pass" plan on the Web site, which created the world's first online credit platform for companies.

Yet being the first has also meant that Alibaba had to always frustratingly lead the way through the uncertainties of the Chinese B2B industry, something that late-comers were glad to have been spared. However, in hindsight, obtaining a unique first-mover advantage has made the hard work well worthwhile for Alibaba and its associates.

The question remains whether the Alibaba business model is sustainable as the B2B e-commerce industry in China in particular continues to grow and mature. It is unlikely that what has worked well in the past will continue to be relevant for businesses such as Alibaba in the future, and so Jack Ma will need to look for new ways to once again shape and control the direction of the Chinese B2B industry in order to survive in the increasingly globalized business environment. Yet the fickle nature of new technology development means that the next step in the B2B evolution may not necessarily come from today's industry leader; but perhaps from the basement of a house in some distant suburban town no one has heard about.

Questions for Discussion

1. Does the "bird cage" theory when applied to China's Internet policy constitute a serious threat to the development of the B2B e-commerce industry?

2. What is the focus of Alibaba's business and what makes it so different from some U.S. e-commerce companies?

3. Would Alibaba have been as successful today without the leadership of someone like Jack Ma?

4. What are the benefits of the strategic cooperation with China Post?

5. What are the current and future benefits of the cooperation with Yahoo?

6. Is there room for Alibaba in the global race for online supremacy, and what would you do to secure the future for the company?

Appendices

1. Key Development Milestones for Alibaba

- At the end of 1998, Jack Ma and his team of 18 founders created www.alibaba.com.
- March 10, 1999, the day when team leader Jack Ma came back to Hangzhou,

---

[21] Sumie Kawakami, "China's Visionary B2B: Who Says the dot-com Era Is Over? Company Profile," Japan, Inc. (May 2003).
[22] Knowledge@Wharton, "Open Sesame?"

is considered the Web site's founding date.

- July 9, 1999, and September 9, 1999: Alibaba (China) Technology Co., Ltd established in Hong Kong and Hangzhou.
- October 1999: Goldman Sachs, the world's largest investment bank, invested US$5 million in Alibaba.
- January 2000: Alibaba was selected as an excellent Chinese business Web site by China Internet match organization committee.
- June 2000: Alibaba was honored as one of China's Yearly Best Top 100 Web sites and was chosen by Forbes Magazine as "Best of the web: B2B."
- November 2000: Alibaba was elected as most popular global B2B Web site by readers of Far Eastern Economic Review.
- December 27, 2001: Alibaba became the world's best B2B e-commerce Web site with more than 1 million registered members.
- March 10, 2002: Alibaba China promoted "TrustPass" plan, which made Alibaba the world's first online credit business community.
- December 2002: Alibaba began to make a profit.
- May 2003: The goal of 1 million RMB in daily income was realized.
- May 10, 2003: Invested 10 million RMB to launch TaoBao.com, a C2C Web site.
- October 18, 2003: AliPay was launched.
- November 28, 2003: Business real-time communication service "Ali Talk" was issued.
- December 31, 2003: Annual profit exceeded 10 million RMB.
- February 17, 2004: Alibaba.com Corporation raised US$82 million from institutional investors in the largest private equity commitment ever in the Chinese Internet sector. The funds will allow

Alibaba to continue its rapid expansion and to consolidate its position as China's largest e-commerce company.

- July 2004: Chinese online marketplace TaoBao.com received US$42 million in new funding.
- October 2004: Alibaba distinguished itself as the only import–export Web site ever to win Forbes "Best of the Web" Award, five years in a row.
- March 10 2004: Alibaba China launched its keywords bidding service.
- March 31 2004: Alibaba China launched its excess products auction service.
- March 2005: Alibaba E-business Forum began in Guangdong Province.
- October 2005: Alibaba formed a strategic partnership with Yahoo! Inc. and took over the operation of Yahoo! China.
- January 2007: Business software services company Alisoft is launched
- October 2007: Alibaba is approved for IPO

Source: C. Splinder, "The Alibaba Story."

2. The Companies

Alibaba International (www.alibaba.com) is the world's largest online B2B marketplace for global trade, and the number one destination for sourcing professionals and entrepreneurs. More than 500,000 people visit the site every day, most of them global buyers and importers looking to find and trade with sellers in China, and other major manufacturing countries. Alibaba International has more than three million registered users from over 200 countries and territories.

Alibaba China (www.china.alibaba.com) is the largest Chinese-language B2B marketplace for domestic China trade. With more than 16 million registered users, Alibaba China is a trusted online and off-line community of SMEs who regularly meet, chat, search for products, and do business.

Alisoft (www.alisoft.com) is a leading provider of easy-to-use, Web-based business software services for SMEs in China. It allows customers to access and manage their CRM, inventory, sales, finance and marketing information, and communications tools anytime they need via a simple Web site. Alisoft serves Chinese SMEs by seamlessly connecting e-commerce to their back-end business services.

Yahoo! China (www.yahoo.com.cn) is a leading Internet search engine and portal serving China's consumers and businesses. It plays a valuable role in powering e-commerce in China and is a leading advertising platform for China's SMEs. Alexa.com ranks it in the top 20 most popular global Web sites. Yahoo! China combines global technology with local know-how to give Chinese Internet users the best local search engine. In October 2005, the Alibaba Group acquired Yahoo! China and formed a long-term strategic partnership with Yahoo! Inc. Under the agreement, Alibaba owns and operates Yahoo! China, with exclusive rights to the use of the Yahoo! brand and technologies in China.

TaoBao (www.taobao.com) is the largest consumer e-commerce Web site in Asia with more than 30 million registered users. Alexa.com ranks it in the top twenty-five most popular global Web sites. Since its launch in May 2003, TaoBao has become China's leading C2C and B2C marketplace, surpassing competitors on all key metrics, including Web site traffic, active users, product listings, and transaction volume. In 2006, TaoBao's transaction volume, or gross merchandise volume (GMV), reached US$2.18 billion (RMB16.9 billion), up 110 percent from 2005.

Alipay (www.alipay.com) is China's leading online payment service by both number of users and total transaction volume. It enables individuals and businesses to securely, easily, and quickly send and receive payments online. To provide Alipay, Alibaba has partnered with all the leading banks in China, including Bank of China, China Construction Bank, Agricultural Bank of China, and the Industrial and Commercial Bank of China, as well as other financial institutions. Alipay works like an escrow service, solving the issue of settlement risk in China. As of October 2007, Alipay has more than 47 million users and daily transaction volumes exceeding US$20 million (RMB150 million), through as many as 78,000 daily transactions. More than 80,000 new users register each day. Very few companies have realized AliPay is a very big deal, as Chinese can now buy foreign products online for the first time. Current international partners include Sa Sa International Holdings, discount beauty-products seller StrawbenyNet and J Shoppers, a subsidiary of Japan mail-order company Nissen Online.

3. Chinese Auction Market Share

Other	3.6%
eBay China	29.1%
TaoBao	67.3%

4. Chinese Search Market Share

Other	12.6%
Sohu	9.2%
Google	13.2%
Yahoo China	21.1%
Baidu	43.9%

Sources: Analysis; China Internet Network Information Center.

5. Chinese Internet Giants

Baidu

Core business: Search (founded by Robin Li in 2001)

Other services: Bulletin board system (BBS), a collaborative encyclopedia, an answers service, voice search (by telephone)

China's leading search engine has only one real rival: Google. To date it has relied on its loyal base and advantage in Chinese-language and MP3 search to stay ahead of the American behemoth, though it also offers a strong forum service, Tieba. Baidu is a mainstay for online community. Online community—BBS and blogs—is such an important part of Internet in China.

Baidu is also not shy of trumpeting a nationalist tune. Baidu want to be more Chinese than anyone else on the Internet. To date they have succeeded, but the risk is that Baidu might get too complacent, which is the one thing they can not afford to do with Google on their backs.

Tencent

Core business: Instant messaging (founded by Pony Ma in Shenzhen, 1998)

Other services: Online games, communities, e-commerce, search, a product innovation platform, online video, music player, micro-blogging

Tencent is one of the best-run companies in China. Tencent understands Chinese Internet users and has moved beyond its core QQ instant messaging product—home to 273 million accounts—into blogs and online games. Almost all Chinese Internet users use QQ, and Tencent also has very powerful BBS communities. By providing a central communication platform, they've

become a part of online culture. In fact, the strength of its virtual currency, 'QQ coins,' has became so sought after it threatens to undermine the renminbi.

Tencent has capitalized on that popularity by aligning itself with major brands such as Coca-Cola, and it has just launched MIND, an online marketing solutions strategy for advertisers, media agencies, and brokers.

Sina

Core business: Portal (created after 1999 merger of SinaNet.com and Stone Rich Technology)

Other services: E-commerce, search, mobile VAS

Sina claims more than 230 million registered users and 700 million daily page views. A lot of that punch comes from the company's popular celebrity blogs. Sina has the stickiness factor because of its blogging communities but, because it is more media based, it lacks the 'cool' factor of Tencent's QQ. Sina is also perceived as less innovative than QQ or NetEase—something which contributes to high management turnover in the last four years.

In spite of that, Sina and rival Sohu are must-haves in any large-scale advertising campaign and they are dominant forces in China's Internet landscape. To Chinese online users, they've become places you go to every day as sites of habit.

Sohu

Core business: Portal (founded in 1996 by Internet pioneer Charles Zliatig)

Other services: Search, mobile VAS provider, online games, online mapping

No sooner had Sohu secured the rights as the official Web site of the 2008 Beijing Olympics, Tencent, Sina, and NetEase combined their might in a resource-sharing alliance to neuter Sohus power position. Sohu can be seen as a "lifestyle company" but suffers from a lack of clear brand positioning. Sohu is not a market leader in games, search, or blogs.

NetEase

Core business: Online games and entertainment portal (founded by Ding Lei in 1997)

Other services: Mobile VAS, search, e-commerce

With an aging stable of games, NetEase's prospects, many analysts believed, rested on the success of its new title, Tian Xia II. When that received less than enthusiastic reviews in beta testing, NetEase's stocks slumped. However, many believed NetEase will bounce back, being perceived as the definitive leaders in games but currently lacking a clarity of vision.

Tom

Core business: Wireless Internet portal (founded in 1999 as a joint venture in Hong Kong)

Other services: Short message service (SMS), Multimedia messaging service (MMS), Wireless application protocol (WAP), search, and classifieds

Tom is one of China's leading wireless Internet services and a substantial portal in its own right. It understands community and the logistics involved with selling online, but it faces tough times ahead. Many believe it would be hard for Tom to be number one or number two in search or portal. Their opportunities would be trying to beat NetEase on entertainment and to go after Alibaba on commerce and auctions. Despite Tom's intention to revive eBay, critics are skeptical of its chances as it hasn't yet demonstrated an understanding of why eBay failed in the first place.

CASE III

Dow Corning Success in China

Tom Cook, the president of Dow Corning Greater China, was overlooking his clean empty desk facing the People Square in Shanghai. He was ready to take up his new tasks in this current position. He joined Dow Corning in 1985 as a member of the Information Technology (IT) group. After working in various positions he was promoted to assume his current vice president and general manager responsibilities in 2006. In 2007 he also became the president of the Greater China region. Tom played a major role in strategy development for the innovative and highly successful XIAMETER® brand offering—a Web-based business model for large-volume users of commonly used high-quality products for customers who do not require personalized service. He was also instrumental in the transformation of Dow Corning from a product-focused supplier to a solution provider. He had a long track record within the company to make challenging work triumph. But his current task is a particularly demanding one.

In an extremely short time, Xiameter, a brand of Dow Corning, was developed and implemented in 2002. This project helped the company to address the price seekers for silicones and foster explosive growth. During the introduction of Xiameter model, Tom was in charge of improving the value proposition offering for Dow Corning. With the combined efforts of both the *Dow Corning*® and XIAMETER® brand, sales for the company nearly doubled from 2002 to 2007.

But now he is leading the Dow Corning and Xiameter Brand in a booming market like China, where the competitors are fighting fiercely and the local Chinese customers were asking for even lower prices. This was not only the dilemma of the day, but a question of survival in the global arena.

Dow Corning

Established in 1943, Dow Corning is a joint venture between The Dow Chemical Co. and Corning, Inc. (formerly Corning Glass Works), and it is equally owned by both companies. With a mission to explore the potential of silicone, Dow Corning provides performance-enhancing materials and solutions to serve the diverse needs of more than 20,000 customers worldwide with more than 7,000 products and services. With gross sales of $4.94 billion in 2007, Dow Corning is a global leader in silicones and silicon-based technology and innovation, and it provides a wide range of products to diversifying industries, from shampoos to cables, as well as in semiconductors, transportation vehicles, and electronics. (Refer to Exhibit III-1.) With half of its sales outside the United States, Dow Corning is in the process of building China's largest siloxane manufacturing facility in Zhangjiagang, China. The company was also expanding in India, Russia, Turkey, Vietnam, and Brazil.

The Birth of Xiameter Model

In the late 1990s and early this decade, Dow Corning had been facing significant external pressure. Historically, Dow Corning has been positioned as a company capable of providing the highest levels of support and value-added service to its customers with its innovative research and design. It was perceived to be a high-price supplier. However, competition in the global marketplace, rising costs of raw material, commoditization of mature products, and downward pressures on pricing converged to create a complex business environment for the industry. At the same time, the management team in Dow Corning found that they needed new ways to meet changing customer

Key Figures Note: Approximate Numbers as of December 31, 2007

2007 sales	$4.94 billion
2007 net income	$690.1 million
Employees worldwide	10,000
Manufacturing and warehouses locations worldwide	45
Number of products and services offered	7,000
Number of customers	20,000
Active patents in the United States	1,080
Active patents worldwide	4,400
Percentage of sales invested in R&D	4–5%

Industry Expertise

Automotive	Moldmaking
Aviation & Aerospace	Oil & Gas
Beauty & Personal Care	Paints & Inks
Chemical Manufacturing	Photonics
Compound Semiconductor	Plasma
Construction	Plastics
Electronics	Power & Utilities
Food & Beverage	Pulp & Paper
Healthcare	Pressure Sensitive
Household & Cleaning	Rubber Fabrication
Imaging	Solar
Industrial Lubrication	Textile, Leather, Nonwoven

EXHIBIT III-1 Dow Corning Fast Fact *Source*: Dow Corning Web site

demands and the needs of different customer segments.

"Dow Corning has spent the past five years transforming Dow Corning into a customer-centric organization," explained Gary Anderson, the former chairman, president, and chief executive officer of Dow Corning in 2002. "This introduction (Xiameter model) is the culmination of extensive research into customers' varying needs, detailed segmentation based on product lifecycles, and a complete redesign of our services to support each."[1] The effort has involved significant investments: more than $100 million in its global IT platform (SAP) in its e-business capabilities with the redesign of dowcorning.com to support this choice-based strategy.

To understand needs of each customer segment and their product life cycles, Dow Corning has also invested heavily in market research which revealed some unexpected results: a strong need in the marketplace among "price-seeker" customers who knew what products they needed and didn't want to pay for the added services that traditionally came together with Dow Corning's products. In order to stay competitive, Dow Corning came up with the new business model to serve this market segment by introducing an entirely new brand, named XIAMETER®. In 2002, Dow Corning launched the Xiameter brand and became the first in the chemical industry to introduce a product-only, Web-enabled business model. (Refer to Exhibit III-2.) Xiameter predominantly supports products in the mature stage of the life cycle and it operates almost exclusively via the Web,

---

[1] Corporate press release: DOW CORNING LAUNCHES NEW CORPORATE STRATEGY: Emphasizes Customer-Centric Approach (March 5, 2002).

When it comes to buying silicone in bulk, there are three things that matter. Quality, reliability, and price. At Xiameter, you can get them all. That's because we've simplified the entire buying process to make it easier to purchase fluids, sealants, and rubber online. By working directly with us, you eliminate the added cost of sales and technical support.

The result? High quality products at market-driven prices.

So how do you know if Xiameter is right for you? Ask yourself the following questions.

- Do you generally buy materials in large quantities?
- Can you meet your own technical service needs?
- Can you plan your material needs two to four weeks in advance?

If you answered yes to these questions, Xiameter may be right for you. Still unsure? Contact us for additional questions you may have.

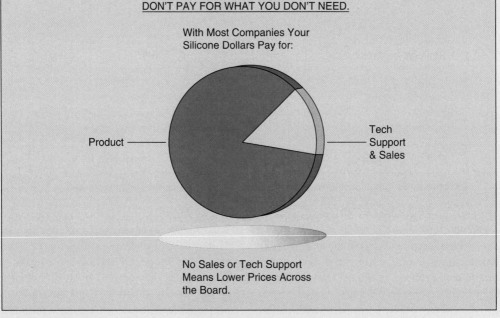

EXHIBIT III-2   Xiameter's Value Proposition   *Source:* http://www.xiameter.com/content/bxmeet/meet_us.asp

offers limited services, and requires high-volume purchases. These features allow Xiameter to offer market-driven prices for silicone materials.

Although the Xiameter brand is a separate brand and sales organization, it manufactures and sells the same high-quality products from the same manufacturing sites as the full-service (total offering) priced Dow Corning brand. The differentiation is in the market model, the levels of service and support, and the price. The

Xiameter model defines clear, straightforward business rules to ensure reliable shipping dates, confirmation of order, and inventory through its Web site:

- **Transparent, dynamic, and "real time" pricing**—Xiameter displays the pricing of four of the most commonly purchased materials on the Web site homepage. Prices are subject to change at any time.

- **Minimum orders**—Customers must purchase a minimum-order quantity. This quantity is set by the manufacturing location and is based on what is considered large volume by the marketplace. Orders could range from full truckloads to several pallets of material depending on the product.
- **Strict business rules**—Required lead time for product deliveries drives customers to plan their forecast two to four weeks in advance and follow strict business rules such as standard payment terms (standard terms of net thirty days from the date of invoice) and conditions of cancellation.

Cannibalization?

With the launch of this online business, the Xiameter model has been regarded to be a bold step both internally and externally. The biggest risk Dow Corning could have faced was the possibility that the Xiameter model would cannibalize Dow Corning's existing business. Current customers might move to the new offering because of its online convenience and competitive pricing. Fortunately, Dow Corning successfully communicated the differences between the two brands to customers and most customers valued the services offered by Dow Corning. Cannibalization has been minimal.

The two brands complement each other, and the Xiameter brand provides another choice for the customers. The model is designed for customers who already know what they need and don't require additional services or technical support. This online business addressed the needs of price-seekers who can follow straightforward business rules. From their perspective, the Xiameter brand offered a convenient way to purchase silicone materials.

At the same time, the corporate brand, Dow Corning, was further enhanced with the introduction of a wide range of solutions and services. This additional emphasis on the brand clarified its brand promise and reinforced its added value offer: expertise, technical support, and a wide range of solutions and services. Some customers purchase from both of these businesses because of different benefits provided by the two business models. (Refer to Exhibits III-3,–III-5.)

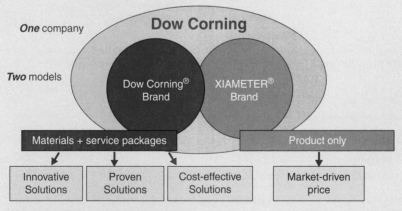

One Company: Two Business Models, With Multiple Choices

EXHIBIT III-3 Two Brands under Dow Corning *Source*: Dow Corning

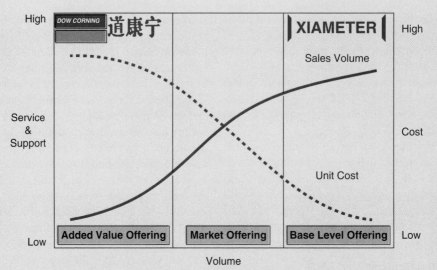

EXHIBIT III-4   Brand Differentiation between Dow Corning & Xiameter
Source: Customer Value Discovery by Ron Shulman & Phil Allen (http:www. csiforprofit.com). Applied to Dow Corning's brand position

The Xiameter model has been enormously successful for Dow Corning since it allows the company to keep competence in a high-cost market segment as well as to take a stake in the low-cost segment. Besides, Dow Corning could utilize the high-volume business to reduce costs across the whole value chain and improve productivity and profitability not just for Xiameter brand, but the Dow Corning brand as well.

Dow Corning	Xiameter
Flexible ship dates	Reliable shipping dates
Materials delivered in all sizes and quantities	Lead time requirements, average 7–20 days
Extensive services and solutions	No technical service
E-commerce services	Large volume orders
Innovative, proven & cost effective solutions	Web-enabled business
Technology and R&D	Commonly used silicones
Personal customer service	Market-driven prices
	Dedicated Traders

Dow Corning® and XIAMETER® brands share the same

- Global manufacturing sites
- High quality products
- Reliable global supply
- SAP infrastructure
- Both brands are part of Dow Corning Corporation

Dow Corning creates customer value through choice. Customers can purchase both Dow Corning® and/or XIAMETER® brands.

EXHIBIT III-5   Customer Value Proposition of the Two brands   *Source*: Dow Corning

Innovative Brand Strategy Leads to Growth

Dow Corning Corporation has experienced double-digit sales growth (Exhibit III-6) every year since it launched the two-brand strategy. The investment in the Xiameter business paid off quickly. It only took three months for Dow Corning to achieve investment payback. In its first year, Xiameter logistics costs were reduced by an estimated 60 percent when compared to the Dow Corning channel, saving approximately $3.5 million, primarily due to the elimination of warehousing costs and more efficient shipping based on larger loads.[2] The "made to order" policy, which required minimum lead times, contributes to significant reduction in inventory and frees up the company's working capital. Therefore, online sales have increased and surpassed the industry average.

Online sales for the company (both Dow Corning and Xiameter brands) grew from virtually zero in 2000 to 30 percent of sales in 2006. According to a benchmark study conducted by the American Chemistry Council, on average, U.S. chemical companies conducted 12.8 percent of their sales online in 2005. Xiameter has also supported geographic expansion. Originally offered in fifty countries, Xiameter is now available in eighty four countries, several of which were new to Dow Corning.[3]

Dow Corning's Footprint in China

Dow Corning expanded into the China market in 1973, and since then has established offices in Shanghai, Beijing, Guangzhou, Shenzhen, Chengdu, and Hong Kong, providing comprehensive products and services to its clients all over the country. Through 2007, the company

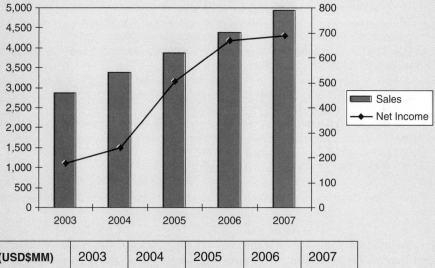

(USD$MM)	2003	2004	2005	2006	2007
Sales	2,872.5	3,372.6	3,878.7	4,391.6	4,940
Net Income	176.6	238.3	506.5	668.4	690.1

EXHIBIT III-6   Dow Corning Financial Result 2003–2007 (USDMM)   *Source*: Dow Corning Corporate finance data

---

[2] Dow Corning press release "Two-Brand Strategy Spells Success for Dow Corning" (March 7, 2007).
[3] Ibid.

Dow Corning expanded into the China market in 1973, and since then has established offices in Shanghai, Beijing, Guangzhou, Shenzhen, Chengdu, and Hong Kong, providing comprehensive products and services to its clients all over the country.

- 1973 Established Asia regional office in Hong Kong and has begun to supply silicone materials and technical services to China
- 1991 Set up office in Shanghai, started to expand their business in Mainland China, covering the eastern and central regions of China
- 1995 Dow Corning (Shanghai) Co., Ltd. was established as Dow Corning's first wholly owned enterprise, responsible for building and operating its site in Shanghai's Songjiang Industrial Zone.
- 1996 Established Dow Corning Beijing Office, which was responsible for pioneering company's sales in Northern and Northeastern China.
- 1997 Opened Songjiang site, Dow Corning's first manufacturing site in China, and provided products and services serving China's electronics, textiles, construction, personal and home care products, rubber, plastics, and other industries
- 1998 In response to Chinese Government's "Western China Development" policy, Dow Corning established its office in Chengdu, pioneering the rapid development of the central and western markets.
- 1999 Dow Corning set up Construction Analytical Lab in Songjiang site, providing service for China's construction projects. At the same time, Dow Corning expanded the plant and increased emulsion production there to meet growing demand of personal care products and the textile industry.
- 2001 Dow Corning set up its office in Guangzhou for the sales development in Southern China.
- 2002 Dow Corning China Application Center was officially established. The center has six specialized laboratories with world-class technology and equipment.
- 2003 Dow Corning China Applied Technology Center was expanded to double the technical services and development capability.
- 2004 Set up Dow Corning China Technology Information Centre which provides technical advice hotline and Web site for real-time help system for customers with convenient and efficient information technology services.
- 2006 Ground Breaking Ceremony was jointly held by Dow Corning and Wacker Chemie AG (Munich, Germany) to establish China's largest siloxane plant in Zhangjiagang
- 2007 Established strategic partnership with CEIBS
- 2008 Opened Silicone Rubber Plant in Zhangjiagang

EXHIBIT III-7 Dow Corning's Expansion and Development in China *Source*: Dow Corning Chinese Web site

has invested over $470 million in China to build and improve its infrastructure to serve customers locally (refer to Exhibit III-7). In 2006, Dow Corning and Wacker Chemie AG (Munich, Germany) announced that their manufacturing joint venture company Dow Corning (Zhangjiagang) Co, Ltd. received official approval from the Chinese government to jointly build a world-class siloxanes[4] manufacturing facility in China.

Dow Corning broke ground for an integrated silicone manufacturing site in the Jiangsu

---

[4] Siloxane is a key starting material for the production of silicones. Major silicone application industries include: construction, chemicals, cosmetics, textiles, automotive, paper, and electronics. Fumed silica is used as an active filler in silicone elastomers, as a viscosity-adjusting agent in coatings, printing inks, adhesives, unsaturated polyester resins, and plastisols or as a flow aid, for example, in the cosmetics, pharmaceutical, and food-processing industries. Source: Dow Corning.

Yangtze River Chemical Industrial Park, Zhangjiagang City, Jiangsu Province, in September 2006. Completion is expected during 2010. This integrated site includes China's largest facility to manufacture siloxane (basic silicone materials) with an investment of $600 million, as well as downstream finishing plants, which support the vigorous growth and demand for silicone materials in China and throughout Asia.[5] In April 2008, Dow Corning opened its new rubber plant in Zhangjiagang. The new 6,000 square meter building at the site manufactures high consistency rubber (HCR) and liquid silicone rubber (LSR) for a full spectrum of industrial and consumer applications.

The chemical park in Zhangjiagang provides distinct advantages, especially superb port facilities, and access to high-quality local talent. This will be the biggest integrated production site of silicones in China and is expected to produce over 200,000 tons of silicone products annually, reaching full production by 2010.[6]

"China is one of the priority markets for Dow Corning and an engine for our future growth," said Tom Cook, Dow Corning Greater China president and Asia area vice president. "We are excited about the new silicone rubber plant, which plays a strategic role in our global manufacturing network. The opening of the rubber plant underscores our continued long-term commitment to China and our confidence in the huge potential of the entire Asia region."

Dow Corning also established Dow Corning Silicone Rubber (Shanghai)—a wholly owned subsidiary in 2007 to offer an expanded range of Dow Corning-branded silicone rubber products and solutions in China. This company provides customers in China a wide range of quality silicone rubber products formulated to Dow Corning-brand quality standards. Furthermore, customers will have access to tailor-made service support from dedicated Dow Corning commercial teams committed to satisfying customer needs in a variety of vertical markets including consumer, transportation, image reproduction, and power and utility. "The introduction of Dow Corning Silicone Rubber signals the company's continuing commitment to meeting customer needs in China as they expand to new geographical markets or aspire to upgrade their product and service offerings," said Diane Kelly, Asia commercial director for Dow Corning Engineered Elastomers.[7]

Drivers for Future Growth: Differentiation and B2B E-Commerce

Differentiation—Building a Stronger China and Meeting Consumer's Demand

Dow Corning's innovative and quality products have led its way to China's major public construction projects. For example, Shanghai Oriental Arts Center features a unique façade that resembles a butterfly orchid in bloom. Dow Corning weatherproofing sealant was successfully used to protect the curtain wall façade from glass delamination. Furthermore, Beijing's new Poly Building is protected against Northern China's harsh weather with the use of two Dow Corning sealants—one for surface enhancement and one for waterproofing. A more astonishing example is that Dow Corning's silicone rubber also contributes to the robustness of power cables for China's Qingzang railway (the highest railway in the world) in harsh weather conditions. With Dow Corning's silicone rubber, which could function throughout wide temperature ranges and have long-term stability, China's Qingzang railway can keep running under snowstorms, sandstorms, and low temperatures at an average altitude of 12,000 feet.

Featuring excellent weather resistance ability, a high level of stability to extreme temperatures, good fluid resistance and water-repellency, Dow Corning's silicone rubber is

---

[5] PR Newswire. New York (April 24, 2008).
[6] Dow Corning Overview Source: Dow Corning.
[7] Dow Corning Corporate press release, Shanghai, China (February 12, 2007).

increasingly used in industries ranging from consumer electronics and construction to automobiles and power distribution. Notable is China's spending boom in the power distribution sector, providing a potentially large market for its products. The silicone rubber demand from China's electric utility sector rose more than 30 percent over the prior three years,[8] and it is expected that the demand will rise even more rapidly in the upcoming years accompanying the double digit GDP growth of China.

Besides serving public construction and enterprises, Dow Corning also found the key to the door of China's cosmetics market.[9] Dow Corning saw opportunities in the large demand that exists for cosmetics and shampoos in China's huge population. The research firm Euromonitor International forecast China's personal-care industry growth rate, including skin-care and hair-care products, to be approximately 14.6 percent in 2008. Dow Corning was working to seize the opportunity behind the trends such as using natural ingredients and

developing culturally specific products. In 2005 alone, more than sixty such products were launched across the Asia-Pacific region.[10]

B2B E-Commerce in China's Market

For small and medium enterprises, or SMEs, price has been a key criterion in their procurement system. In addition, the growing usage of the Internet for e-commerce activities among SMEs in China has also contributed to the opportunities for Xiameter. According to China's Statistics Bureau, in 2004, SMEs and other private sector companies contributed about 58 percent of China's GDP and 48 percent of China's tax revenue. According to the PRC National Development and Reform Commission, there were over 42 million SMEs and other private sector organizations in China by 2006.[11] As the Internet continues to gain acceptance in China, the number of SMEs using the Internet to conduct B2B e-commerce has also increased dramatically. (Refer to Exhibit III-8.)

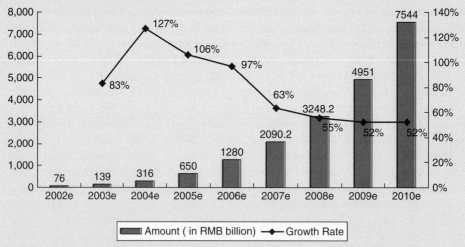

EXHIBIT III-8   China B2B E-Commerce Amount 2002–2010   *Source*: iResearch 2006

Note: Chinese B2B industry comprised nearly 95 percent of the e-commerce market. Chinese B2C and C2C comprised less than 5 percent of e-commerce market

---

[8] Shanghai Daily (April 23, 2008).
[9] China Knowledge (March 4, 2008).
[10] "White, bright outlook for Dow Corning", ShangHai Daily, by Fu Chenghao (March 4, 2008).
[11] Alibaba.com Limited Prospectus (October 2007).

By 2006, the percentage of combined Dow Corning and Xiameter sales conducted online had risen to 30 percent—significantly higher than the industry average. Dow Corning is expecting that the potential B2B online market in China will further contribute to its growth. In the current Chinese B2B online market, there are several major players: Alibaba (see the Alibaba case in this text) continued to lead the market for online B2B service and accounted for over 50 percent; Global Sources and HC360 also made improvements in online B2B business after their cooperation in June 2006, which together represented over 10 percent of the whole B2B total sales income.[12] (Refer to Exhibit III-9—HC360 was the fourth ranked, by share, in the industry.) New players continued to enter the market, such as the launch by china.com.cn of "China Suppliers," and Yaphon, which launched its TQS (that stands for total quality sourcing) service into this industry.

Dow Corning plans to continue to develop its online transaction platform, setting the market standard for e-commerce in silicone products. As a result of the somewhat "generic" nature of the B2B online paradigm, industry B2B sites must significantly differentiate services and target industry characteristics. This might be a direction for Dow Corning to focus but there are still some challenges. On top of the severe competition among current online B2B giants, Alibaba.com dominates the B2B online market and Dow Corning products are also available on Alibaba.com. How does Dow Corning differentiate itself from those B2B giants to exploit the fast-growing B2B market in China?

How to Map Out Dow Corning's B2B Marketing Strategy in China?

China, a country with a double-digit economic growth rate, seems to provide a stage for Dow Corning to pursue aggressive growth. Building up a strong brand is very critical for the success of B2B companies in this dynamic market. Even if Tom could attribute Dow Corning's recent success to the Xiameter model, however, the evolving market, especially a fast-growing market like China, would not guarantee a sustainable success if Dow Corning only maintains the status quo. Tom wondered what role the Xiameter brand would play in Dow Corning Greater China's future competitive positioning.

China market: Market share breakdown of leading Web portals of B2B services by transaction value	
Company	Market share (%)
Alibaba (Chinese)	54.30
Global Sources	8.70
Made-in-China (Chinese)	8.10
HC360 (Chinese)	3.40
EmedChina (Chinese)	2.60
MainOne (Chinese)	2.60
315.com.cn (Chinese)	2.60
Toocle (Chinese)	2.10
Others	15.60

EXHIBIT III-9   China B2B Online Service Market Share 2008
Source: Analysis International, compiled by *Digitimes* (May 2008)

---

[12] Analysis International, China B2B Market.

Questions for Discussion

The upcoming challenge for Tom Cook would include the following issues:

1. How should Dow Corning make good use of its two brands to grasp the China market to sustain its long-term growth?
2. If the target companies in China cover a broad range of industries—transportation, construction, power and utilities, electronics, personal care, textiles, solar, manufacturing—how should Dow Corning map out its brand strategies and communication activities?
3. With the expanding market for personal care in China, will this increase in sales of consumer products provide Dow Corning another growth opportunity?
4. With increasing Internet users and fast-growing online market, what could Dow Corning do to stand out among those major B2B online service providers?
5. How can Dow Corning prevent channel conflict if its products are available both in its own Xiameter site as well as in other major Chinese B2B e-commerce sites?

CASE IV

Marketing Plastic Resins: GE and BW II

Overview

Borg Warner Chemicals (BW) and General Electric Plastics (GE), prominent suppliers in the engineering plastics markets, were facing increased competition and a changing market environment. Value as viewed by customers was evolving, and sales channels and field marketing organizational structure played a major role in the way each company elected to provide products and services to its customers.

In this case, you will be asked to determine an optimal channel structure for this market.

Introduction

Consumer awareness of plastics is usually limited to the final products manufactured from the plastics. Many consumer products either are enclosed in plastic cases or contain component parts manufactured from plastics. Manufacturers whose products include plastic components or cases must either manufacture the plastic parts themselves or outsource production to a contract provider. A manufacturer that makes the components itself at its own plastic manufacturing facilities is said to have "captive facilities"—manufacturing facilities that produce plastic parts strictly for the manufacturer. When outsourced, plastic components are produced to the manufacturer's specifications by *custom injection molders*—contract providers that produce plastic parts as designed and specified by the manufacturer. As contract providers, custom molders are often independent small businesses, engaged in the manufacture of plastic components on contract to the company who will eventually incorporate the components into its own product.

The term *injection* refers to the method of manufacturing plastic parts. Most plastics are supplied in pellet form. The pellets are heated to a molten state and "injected" by a hydraulic ram into a clamshell-like mold, much in the same way cookie presses squeeze dough to make holiday cookies. The mold cools rapidly and is opened, the part is removed, the mold is closed, and another "copy" is molded immediately. Depending on part size and design, this cycle may be repeated several times a minute.

As an example of this process, consider the design and manufacture of the water reservoir for a new home coffee pot. The coffee pot manufacturer, let us say Black & Decker (B&D) in this case, decides what features the reservoir should have (should it be transparent so the water level can be seen inside it, will it look better with a glossy or satin finish, how high will the temperature get while the coffee is brewing, and so on). The engineering staff then designs the water reservoir to meet these requirements, specifying the type of plastic material needed to meet the design standards. A custom molder is contracted by B&D to mold the plastic reservoir to the requirements specified by the engineering group—including the type of plastic materials to be used in the part. The manufacturer of the coffee pot, B&D, is the customer of the molder. The molder will purchase the specified plastic raw material (usually supplied in pellets by a plastics producer) to make the reservoir. The molder is the buyer, but not the specifier of the material. From the point of view of the molder or plastics material producer, B&D would be the end user, because B&D would be the final decision maker, or specifier, of what type of plastics material would be used. B&D retains control of the design and material specifications.

Purchasing Habits

Plastic materials are generally purchased by either very large companies who have captive molding facilities (e.g., General Motors, Ford, IBM, Rubbermaid, etc.) through volume buying agreements or by smaller custom molders whose volume, as contract manufacturers, is significantly less. To take full advantage of the economies of scale, larger purchasers usually process very high volumes of just a few material types, in bulk quantities shipped in tank trucks (approximately 40,000 pounds) or railcars (approximately 250,000 pounds).

Custom molders will manufacture a variety of parts for several different customers, often from several different types of materials, making large volume purchases of any one material unlikely. Thus, they buy a larger assortment of both engineering and commodity materials (see the next section, below, for explanations of these two material categories) in smaller quantities. Smaller custom molders purchase the specified plastic materials in pellet form, packaged in 50-pound bags or 1,000-pound boxes. Quantity pricing policies exist, with higher unit prices charged for the additional handling and packaging required for smaller purchases. Plastic producers usually suggest quantity-scaled list prices from a full truckload, usually 40,000 pounds, also known as truckload (TL) pricing, down to minimum purchases of 50 to 1,000 pounds, known as less than truckload (LTL) pricing.

The Products

While there are thousands of different plastics in the marketplace, there are two basic categories of plastic materials: *commodity plastics* and *engineering plastics*. These materials are characterized as follows:

Commodity plastics: These plastics are used for consumer packaging, fast food and "throw away" items, toys, and items that generally are not required to perform any mechanical or structural functions or demonstrate any long-term durability. Commodity plastics are generally inexpensive, available from several sources, and most often known by their generic chemical names. A few of the generic names for these plastics are *polystyrene* (PS), *polypropylene* (PP), *polyethylene* (PE), and *polyester* (PET). Typical examples of products made from these materials are detergent and fabric softener bottles (PE); throwaway cups, forks, and so on (PS); and soft drink bottles (PET). The price range for commodity plastics—also known as commodity resins—is typically $0.60—$1.00 per pound. Commodity plastics, generic in nature, are considered to be in the mature phase of their product life cycle. Little brand loyalty exists—selection is by generic type, with greatest attention paid to price and availability.

Engineering plastics: These plastics are used for components that are generally required to perform one or several mechanical or structural functions and/or meet durability and safety standards imposed by independent agencies such as Underwriters Laboratories, as well as by the specifying end user or manufacturer. A few chemical names for these types of plastics are *acrylonitrile-butadiene-styrene* (ABS), *polybutylene terephthalate* (PBT), *polycarbonate* (PC), and *nylon*. Many of these products are branded by their manufacturer (such as Lexan® polycarbonate from GE, Cycolac® ABS from Borg Warner, and Zytel® Nylon from DuPont) though comparable materials are usually available from at least one other source. These materials are considered to be nearing the end of the growth stage of their product life cycle, with the exception of nylon, which is a mature product. Typical application examples are computer cases (ABS & PC, with PC used where impact resistance, color stability and appearance, or transparency are critical), automobile bumpers (PC), plastic gears and other mechanical components (nylon & PBT), kitchen appliances (ABS &

PC), and fibers (as in nylon carpets and rope). The price range for engineering resins is $1.50–$3.00 per pound.

Market History

One of the first applications of plastic materials was the result of a quest to find a substitute for ivory in billiard balls. In the late 19th century, the game had become so popular that hundreds of elephants were killed each day to obtain ivory for billiard balls. In 1866, an American named John Wesley Hyatt discovered celluloid. After some trial (and error—the early prototype billiard balls made with the material would disintegrate when hit), celluloid became the first substance molded under heat and pressure to retain its shape (and survive the game) after the pressure and heat were removed. So was born the American Cellulose Chemical Corporation (later to become part of Celanese Corporation), a fledgling plastics industry, and greater safety for elephants.[1]

Initially, modern development of commodity plastic materials grew out of the improved refinement of petroleum by-products. Approaches to the marketplace varied by company, product, and life cycle. Producers of commodity plastics, usually large chemical or petroleum companies such as Dow Chemical, Arco, Mobil, Amoco, and so on, preferred to sell in very large quantities (truckload, railcar) on a contract basis to large molders. Many of these suppliers provided very little direct sales coverage, if any, at small custom molders. Because these products were commodities, profit margins and logistical costs often did not

allow the luxury of significant sales attention to small accounts. Like many other products in the chemical industry, pricing was often based on the addition of a set margin to manufacturing costs. Price was strongly influenced by competitive supply in the market and the going rate for that particular product. Molders interested in purchasing these products in LTL quantities found that they had to pay a significant price penalty (per pound) for their low-volume purchases. Because of the lack of sales attention to these smaller customers, product information and assistance was often difficult to obtain.

The major oil and chemical companies had historically shown little interest in the engineering plastics, originally considering them small-volume niche products best handled by other companies.[2] Many of the engineering materials required additional manufacturing and processing steps to create "specialized" products. These low-volume refining operations neither suited the capabilities of the oil companies, nor were the volumes attractive to them.

Most suppliers of engineering plastics were not backward integrated in the supply chain for chemicals. Major engineering plastics suppliers were BW, GE, DuPont, Monsanto, Celanese, and Miles Chemical.[3] (Note that a few companies, notably Dow, DuPont, and Miles participated in both the engineering and commodity materials market— see Exhibit IV-1.)

With the exception of nylon (which was commercially available after World War II),

---

[1] History of Plastics, American Plastics Council, www.americanplasticscouncil.org (September 1, 2001).
[2] Ibid. U.S. production of plastics in 2000 totaled 100,093 million pounds, of which only 5,732 million pounds (5.7 percent) were injection moldable engineering plastics. In the interest of academic clarity, the American Plastics Council classifications of engineering materials has been modified with the addition of nylon and ABS, more closely reflecting market conditions at the time of this case.
[3] Miles Chemical went through many name changes through the 1980s and 2000, contributing to somewhat of an identity crisis. In 1980 Miles was known as Mobay Chemical, later as Miles Chemicals, and finally, Bayer Chemicals. For additional history, see "Makrolon: The High-Tech Material" elsewhere in this book.

Material Types	DuPont	Miles	Celanese	Monsanto	Arco	Amoco	Mobil	Dow	BW	GE
Commodity										
PS					•	•	•#2	• #1		
PP					•	• #1				
PE					•	• #2	•	• #1		
PET	•#1	•				•				
Engineering										
PBT	•	•	•#2							•#1
ABS				•#2				•	•#1	
PC		•#2						•		•#1
Nylon	•#1	•	•#2	•						

Note: A "•" indicates that the supplier has a share in that particular material market. A blank indicates that the supplier does not participate in that material market. A number following the "•" indicates the supplier's relative market position, based on sales volume, in that market such that "#2" indicates that the supplier holds the #2 market position. Only 1st or 2nd positions are shown. As an example, the table shows that Amoco is the largest supplier of polypropylene (PP), the second largest supplier of polyethylene (PE), participates in the polystyrene (PS) and PET markets (but does not hold the #1 or #2 position), and does not participate in any engineering materials markets.

EXHIBIT IV-1   Material Suppliers and Their Market Positions

engineering plastics, whose development and commercialization followed commodity products by several years, did not gain significant market presence until the mid- to late 1960s. By the end of the decade GE recognized that while these advanced materials were capable of successfully performing mechanical and structural functions, making it possible to replace more costly materials and processes (e.g., many cast metals that required a large number of machining steps, sheet steel that required corrosion protection, etc.), traditional plastics sales techniques used by commodity producers as well as the consumer perception of "cheap plastics" would hinder the successful communication of these unique benefits. A new approach was needed that more fully informed customers (designers, end users) of how to take advantage of the benefits of these materials. As a result, GE began to provide extensive services related to end-user education, plastic component design, development, and manufacturing as well as product information intended to maximize the value potential of its products. The pricing of engineering materials became based on a "value added" strategy, reflecting the premium performance of engineering materials—what they could do, rather than what they cost to produce.

By the early1970s, GE had extended the value-added sales approach through the use of field market development (FMD) personnel. FMDs, part of the GE Plastics *marketing* operation, complemented the GE field sales force by working with plastics specifiers and end users *(not molders)* to encourage the design and development of products that would rely on the properties of GE plastics. FMDs, as relationship builders, kept specifiers/end users up to date on new product developments and design techniques, generally creating goodwill and an allegiance to GE products. FMDs generally did not call on custom molders and were not responsible for any direct sales, leaving the direct sales responsibilities to the field sales team. A large customer that had its own captive molding facilities would have two GE field representatives calling on them—a field seller worked with purchasing influences, and an FMD worked with design and specifying influences in the buying centers. Smaller end users that contracted manufacturing to custom molders might develop a relationship with just the FMD. As custom molders usually were the responsibility of the field sales team, FMDs were not involved in the relationship. An organization chart is shown in Exhibit IV-2. Plastic material suppliers who relied on a sales

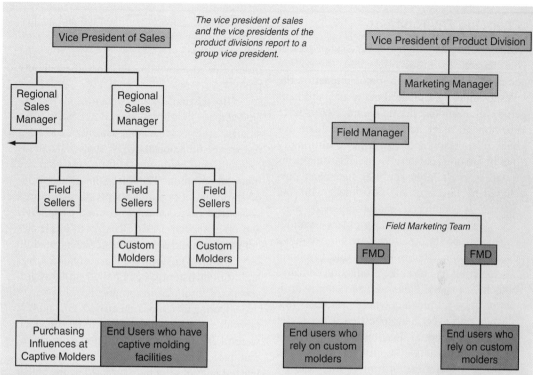

The vice president of sales and the vice presidents of the product divisions report to a group vice president.

EXHIBIT IV-2 General Electric Plastics Field Organization

force for both sales and marketing efforts initially viewed this field organization as a very expensive approach. The GE value-added pricing approach, however, allowed the FMD system to be margin supportable.

The FMD approach was very successful in the marketplace. GE gained a reputation as an aggressive innovator in the market and soon developed sales leadership in all product types they marketed. Through the FMD effort at the specifying influences, GE-branded materials were often preselected when custom molders were contracted to produce plastic parts. This success led other engineering plastics suppliers to begin to imitate the GE field structure. Borg Warner, the leading supplier of ABS, and Miles, the chief rival to GE in PC, were forced to adopt the FMD approach to the market to stay competitive, though account coverage and

resource commitment were not as broad as that provided by GE. Other engineering material suppliers such as DuPont and Celanese found it necessary to provide some kind of design assistance to specifiers, but a formal field organization rivaling FMDs was not completely developed.

Engineering materials suppliers that did not provide some type of coverage at end users and specifiers (as GE had done with the FMD system) soon found their sales efforts at molders much more difficult. Field sales personnel from GE's competitors found they were locked out of opportunities to pursue the business because designers had already specified the use of GE products. Custom molders at times also resented the GE value-added approach because it took out of their hands the choice of what manufacturer they could buy materials from.

Changing Environment

Though plastics comprise a very small part of the demand for crude oil (<5%), the energy crisis of the 1970s had a major impact on the plastics industry. Cutbacks in the availability of crude oil meant that plastic manufacturers were not able to meet demand from molders for materials. Many molders who traditionally purchased their materials in LTL quantities found that available supplies had been purchased by large-volume customers who had previously established relationships with plastics companies. Smaller molders without consistent buying patterns or high-volume demands found themselves unable to obtain raw materials and meet the production demands of their customers. This was a particularly difficult position for molders whose customers (the plastics end user) had specified a particular engineering material, leaving the molder with very little alternative supply flexibility. The customer's specification limited the molder's ability to find a second source for material.

To lessen the impact of this situation, some specifiers developed new strategies. As an example, a specification that once required the use of "Lexan 500" would be modified to require "Lexan 500 or equivalent." This modification was time consuming, as the specifier would have to certify that the equivalent products from competing sources, in this case other PC suppliers such as Dow or Miles, met the originally established standards required by the application. Where the materials were used in critical applications, where failure of the alternate material could lead to injury or other harm, specifiers would be cautious about accepting a second (though theoretically chemically identical) material. This lack of flexibility led many large-volume specifiers (e.g., Ford and GM) to develop internal standards for engineering materials. By using the internal standard, engineers specifying a material for their designs would automatically allow the use of generic or other branded materials of like kind and quality, provided they had met the internal standard. While this helped with new designs, it was of little value in alleviating the immediate supply problem.

By the end of the seventies, BW concluded that a new approach was needed to serve small- and mid-sized customers. Market research commissioned by BW showed hundreds of small- and medium-sized molders who had much in common. They used small quantities of three or more kinds of plastics, required short lead times, and had limited cash flows and other special needs. Because most plastics companies' field sales forces concentrated on large-volume customers, these smaller users had not consistently been called on by representatives from plastics producers.

During this same time period, GE and BW (as well as other engineering material suppliers) were facing increased competition. Companies that had previously ignored the engineering plastics market were now attracted by the higher margins available and the expiration of many U.S. company patents. In addition to competition from U.S. firms, foreign companies, like Mitsubishi (Japan) and Lucky (Korea), were beginning to compete in the U.S. market. Without established channels in the United States, many of these new competitors sold through brokers and independent, regional resellers.

Channel Implications

Recognizing an increased competitive threat and the need to distinguish themselves from their new competitors, BW established Plastic Service Centers (PSCs) in 1981. Plastic Service Centers was a nationwide full-service distributor catering to LTL customers whose service needs were not fully addressed by direct representation from major plastics companies. While BW continued to maintain its direct sales force for its large customers, it turned over small account responsibility to the new

PSC sales team—some of who moved from BW to be part of the new organization. In the process of developing the PSC assortment, BW approached other plastics companies whose product types did not directly compete with its own. Several of these companies agreed to use PSC as their distributor, turning over their LTL customers to the PSC team.

The establishment of PSCs was a significant competitive development in the marketing channel for plastic resins. Critics of using distribution for engineering plastic resins (notably GE) responded by saying that using distribution was an admission by plastics manufacturers that they could not handle the needs of their smaller customers. In the February 1986 edition of a then-major trade publication, *Plastics Industry News*,[4] GE and BW presented their viewpoints on the issue of using distribution versus using a direct sales force to meet the needs of plastics resin customers. Joseph Sakach, vice president and general manager of Borg Warner Chemicals Inc., and Herb Rammrath, vice president of General Electric Plastics' Plastics Sales Division, represented their companies.

In the following passage, Joseph Sakach described how BW's approach addressed customer needs:

Solid customer service had helped establish Borg Warner as an industry leader. . . . Borg Warner had the skills and the culture to assemble the kind of service package these LTL customers needed and the kind of distributorship our fellow resin producers needed.

With all this in mind, we mapped out what we wanted the PSCs to be. To processors [custom molders], we're a one-stop shop for . . . [plastic] material in producers' standard packaging [e.g., fifty pound bags], and at producers' quantity-scaled prices; we ship quickly, typically [from local inventory] within 12 hours; we give special assistance in emergencies; we eliminate the need for processors to keep large inventories; and we provide technical advice. The icing on the cake is that we provide the personal touch typical of resin-producer/large-customer relationships.

Meanwhile, resin producers themselves continue to concentrate on volume accounts that justify the high cost of sales and service calls. It was becoming a problem for us [BW], and we were confident other resin producers felt the same way. For those suppliers, PSCs provide an independent, nationwide distribution network for engineering . . . and commodity materials with a skilled sales staff.[5]

Many molders in the target segment corroborated the BW view of the market. An Oklahoma City PSC customer stated that service from the PSC was much better than that received from large plastics companies such as Monsanto and Dow, as they were only interested in the larger accounts. The PSC seemed to fill a void in customer sales and service.

The advantages of the system were not lost on some plastic resin producers who, because of the high costs involved, did not have extensive sales coverage at smaller accounts. Use of PSCs provided an opportunity to reach the smaller accounts and more effectively organize their field sales. Management at one firm noted that the market was changing and that, without some

---

[4] The trade publication was *Plastics Industry News*, which ceased publication several years ago. In this case, some individuals' names have been changed and market and product conditions have been simplified in the interest of academic clarity.

[5] From "How Borg-Warner handles less-than-truckload customers" (sic) by Joseph Sakach, from the February 1986 edition of *Plastics Industry News*.

accommodation, small volume purchasers would be increasingly ignored as competitive pressures increased. Senior management at DuPont, a producer of both commodity and engineering plastics, saw the PSCs as an opportunity to free up some field resources that could now be devoted to end-user assistance and application development efforts, better enabling them to compete with organizations that had large FMD organizations, such as GE.

An initial concern of the resin producers that would eventually sign up with the PSC to distribute their products was that the PSCs might give favorable treatment in sales and application development to the BW materials rather than the other product lines. PSCs took steps to alleviate this concern.

Sakach continues:[6]

We [PSCs] offer the same culture and experience that made Borg Warner successful, yet [PSCs also offer the] independence to ensure the PSCs credibility among other [resin] suppliers. The PSCs have been steadfast in a commitment to viewing Borg Warner as only one of their many quality suppliers [avoiding any possible claims of favoritism by other resin producers distributing their products through PSC].

We at Borg Warner think of ourselves as good business persons with foresight, imagination, and an ability to serve a dynamic marketplace. That's what the PSCs are all about. Last fall we opened our 11th PSC location built on those principles. The PSCs offer a full range of products from producers including Borg Warner Chemicals, Gulf, Arco, DuPont, . . . and Miles. . . .[7] The PSCs have more than 4000 customers, and our

projections of market potential were on the mark.

For Borg Warner, the PSCs are an important part of our service mix. For LTL customers, Borg Warner, and the PSC's other suppliers, the PSC concept is an innovative, effective, and cost-efficient way to address the former's needs in the context of a sound and profitable overall business strategy.

The suitability of using industrial distributors for engineering resins was not a universally agreed-upon idea. GE, which had grown to an industry leader through its market development efforts, didn't necessarily see the fit.

Herb Rammrath from GE Plastics comments:

General Electric Plastics has taken a hard look at distributors and recognizes the needs they are satisfying in today's marketplace. The bottom line is that we have opted to continue selling our materials through [our own] direct sales [team].

The most important reason for our decision to sell directly is our desire to help molders grow. We are investing a significant portion of our resources in the development of new applications, many of which involve a conversion from metal into plastics. As a resin supplier, we need to work closely with the companies who will handle that conversion. This is important to the industry as a whole, as there is a need to develop the molding capacity necessary to meet the demands all of us are generating for plastics. At G.E., we believe that much future capacity will come from what are now small molders. We'd like to help them grow, and we can

---

[6] Ibid.

[7] In this case, the number of participating companies has been reduced. Also, names as used may not reflect current names as a result of acquisition, merger, or other corporate exchanges.

do a much better job of that by serving them directly.

The move toward just-in-time delivery systems, plus the cost of carrying inventories, is forcing molders and resin suppliers to manage inventory differently and better. Distributors help meet that need by reducing inventory . . . of . . . molders . . . They [distributors] are, in fact, inventory-management companies, and have little to do with application development or technical service. At G.E., we believe there are several advantages in using direct sales:

- While distributors may be able to handle commodity materials effectively, they are generally not equipped to handle engineering plastics. Engineering resins are not commodities and require sales support both before and after the sale.
- Engineering plastics also require much more technical support than the typical distributor can provide.
- We have found that our customers would rather deal directly with the prime supplier than with a middleman. The reasons are obvious, but crucial—they get better overall service, better response to their needs, and faster resolution of their questions and concerns. In addition, they know that all of the resources of a company like General Electric stand behind their resin purchases.

I feel that using a distributor to handle our products is an admission that we are not able to serve customers ourselves. That's not an admission that I would like to make on behalf of G.E. Plastics. So, having decided not to use distributors, yet recognizing that they do serve some needs, we know we must manage our business to satisfy all of the needs our customers have. Among other things, we have done the following:

- We have put into place additional sales resources [more field sellers] so we can maintain our already high level of direct communication with customers, and increase our contact with the smaller molders. In short, we've increased our capability to manage higher levels of direct contact with more molders by investing in an expansion of human resources.
- We have centralized our customer service efforts [across all of our plastic product lines] to respond more quickly and effectively to customer needs. This operation . . . enables us to provide improved order handling and better inventory management, develop just-in-time inventory management, and establish electronic order entry which we expect to be a major factor in customer service. We have taken the steps necessary to meet the whole order-entry/ inventory-control challenge.
- We have established our first specialty compounding facility at our Indiana manufacturing site. This facility produces small lot quantities for both developmental and commercial use, giving us greater flexibility to meet special customer needs ["small order sizes"].

These systems we are putting into place will help provide many of the services that customers need in addition to a direct link to their material source—direct contact, instantaneous communication, and feedback. In taking this approach, we know we are bucking an industry trend. We stand virtually alone in this commitment to direct customer service. In a sense, we are "out of step" with almost everyone else, but perhaps that's what leadership is all about. We take our leadership role in this industry seriously and would relinquish that title if our service to customers were no longer second to none. We can only guarantee quality service when we provide it directly. . . .

In summary, we at G.E. Plastics are designing our business in such a way that we can service our customers—large and small, short term and long term—with the complete range of products and services they demand. We simply are not willing to compromise that objective. We call ourselves the "Strategic Supplier." We want to be a company our customers can call upon, can rely upon—directly—for all their needs.[8]

Questions for Discussion

This case presents two large, experienced, and well-reputed firms who have selected two very different approaches to market similar products. BW formed PSCs to handle smaller LTL customers not only for their own products but also for other resin manufacturers as well, while maintaining their established direct sales force for larger customers. GE, on the other hand, relied entirely on its own direct sales force.

General Question: Given all the facts at your command, what is your recommended channel structure for plastic resins? What are the alternatives?

In the development of your case analysis, it will assist you to consider the following:

1. From the information provided, describe the market environment *as viewed* by GE and BW. Are both views the same (consistent with each other) or are they different?

2. If GE and BW have the same views of the environment, why are the two approaches to the market dramatically different? If they are different, which view do you feel is more useful?

3. Consider customer needs, as viewed by GE and BW. Do they see customer needs from the same perspective?

4. Are both companies segmenting the market the same? Have they targeted the same segments? Are they interested in the same market?

5. Does selection of target markets impact channel design?

6. From what you can discern in this case, describe and compare the goals of BW and GE.
   a. How do their goals impact their channel structure?
   b. Do their goals impact how they view the market? Are their views realistic?
   c. It may be of assistance to consider how their goals and market view compare to others in the market, such as DuPont.

7. Are certain channel structures more suited to certain goals?

8. Consider the service mix BW and GE intend to provide. Relate these services to promotion strategy and marketing functions. Is the mix of services consistent with their and/or your view of customer needs?

9. What role does the FMD specialist play in the marketing organization of GE? What potential conflicts do you see in the dual field structure of GE (having both field market development personnel and field salespeople in sales territories)? Consider all viewpoints—the custom molder, the plastics end user, and the individuals serving as either FMDs or salespeople.

---

[8] From "Why GE Plastics relies on a direct sales force" (sic) by Herb Rammrath, from the February, 1986 edition of *Plastics Industry News.*

Note 1: As described in the case, extensive use has been made of articles appearing in the February 1986 issue of *Plastics Industry News*, as well as the author's personal experience and discussions with professionals in this market. When quoting from the article, bracketed comments have been added for clarity while " . . . " indicates the deletion of parts of the article not considered germane to this academic exercise. Though based on real situations, some names have been changed and several simplifications have been made, in the interest of academic clarity, to product and market Information. For this reason, specific situations and factors mentioned herein may not recreate the actual circumstances experienced.

Note 2: This case can be used as part of a "trilogy" when combined with the cases "Automotive Headlamps II" and "Makrolon: The High-Tech Material," found in this text. All three concern the same general core product but discuss how different organizations will approach the market at different times. Additional details are provided in the Instructors' Manual.

CASE V

Automotive Headlamps II: The Paradigm Shift from Standardized Glass Sealed Beams to Today's Plastic Custom Designs

Overview

This case brings together many factors:

- Strategic business unit management philosophy
- Innovation in the face of contrary "conventional wisdom"
- How innovation can be viewed differently by various stakeholders
- Customer organizational as well as product goals
- Value, as perceived by the customer, rather than the supplier.

Introduction and Company Backgrounds

For clarity, the backgrounds of the main players in this case are provided.

General Electric

The two strategic business units (SBUs) of General Electric directly involved in this case are the General Electric Plastics Division and the General Electric Lamp Division.

The General Electric Company Plastics Division (GEP) began as an internal supplier of thermoset phenolic molding compounds used in electrical components (such as vacuum tube bases and radio cabinets) and, in 1930, formed the company's first plastics department to market these plastic materials in the general market to other manufacturers of similar devices.

Plastic materials with improved physical properties were a continuously evolving need as more complex component designs demanded improved physical material properties. General Electric Research and Development Laboratories, one of the premier industry-sponsored R&D centers, maintained an ongoing materials research effort. This led GE research labs to the development of new, thermoplastic engineering plastics such as *polycarbonate* (Lexan®) in 1959, polyphenylene oxide (PPO) in 1965, and PPO alloys (Noryl®) by 1966. With these materials, GEP, then led by Jack Welch who was eventually to become GE chairman, became a significant factor in the growing plastics materials industry and a star in the GE corporate portfolio.

The General Electric Lamp Division (GEL) is an outgrowth of the very beginning of GE, dating back to the company's founding by Thomas Edison in 1878. Over the years, GEL has been at the forefront of lighting developments in almost every market: stadium lighting, aircraft and airport lighting systems, home lighting, to name a few; and in every technology—incandescent (such as standard light bulbs), fluorescent, mercury

Thermosets and Thermoplastics

Simply defined, *thermoset phenolics* are those materials that undergo a chemical change when heat is applied in the molding process and, when reheated, do not melt. These materials are capable of withstanding high heats without deforming but usually have poorer physical properties than thermoplastics.

Engineering *thermoplastics* are materials that can be melted again after the initial molding process, analogous to ice melting to water and then being cooled to ice again. Thermoplastics are easier to recycle and generally have better physical properties, making possible more complex part designs.

vapor, sodium, and others. GEL is an integrated, high-volume producer and is among the only lighting device manufacturers that make most of its own glass for its products.

The glass sealed-beam automotive headlamp, introduced in the 1930s, is one of the developments that GEL is most proud. At the time of this case, GEL was the largest supplier of "light bulbs" to the North American automotive market. The sealed-beam design had remained an industry standard from the 1930s to the date of this case. Within the GE corporate structure, GEL was a significant cash cow.

General Motors

General Motors (GM), the largest automotive company in the world, at the time of this case, held almost 60 percent of the American market. GM was built primarily through acquisition of not only smaller car companies but supplier companies and brands as well. AC Spark Plugs and Delco electrical components were among GM-owned, through acquisition, supply divisions. The GM Guide Lamp Division (GMGuide—not to be confused with GEL) produced various lamp assemblies for the interior and exterior of GM products. GMGuide was also the primary supplier of sealed-beam headlamps to GM vehicles, though they were not as integrated as GEL.[1]

Ford Motor Company

Ford Motor Company was the second largest automotive company in the world, with approximately 25 percent of the American market.[2] The growth of Ford was achieved primarily through vertical integration rather than acquisition. At one time, Ford owned and operated its own steel mills, rubber plantations, automotive glass plants (windows, windshields—not lighting), iron ore barges and mines, and paint manufacturing facilities.[3] Ford, like GM, manufactured many of its own components including lighting devices and was strongly vertically integrated in the manufacture of components made of plastics. However, Ford did not manufacture headlamps and thus was the largest customer of GEL.

Regulatory Agencies

The U.S. Department of Transportation (DOT) and its component National Highway Traffic Safety Administration (NHTSA) were responsible for maintaining safety standards for the industry. DOT performance standards regulated windshields, windows, lighting effectiveness, occupant protection devices (airbags, seatbelts), and so on, on the vehicles.

Professional Organizations

The Society of Automotive Engineers (SAE) is the professional society of automotive and transportation engineers. As the auto industry evolved, the SAE, as with many professional societies, created voluntary performance standards for many vehicle systems and devices. Many SAE-recommended performance standards became standard industry practice. DOT adapted many of these voluntary standards as regulations.

GEP Organization

GEP initially served the automotive industry from a district office in Cleveland, coincidentally the "home" of GEL. Early applications of GEP plastics included use in the production of

---

[1] At this writing, many GM captive supply divisions have been spun off into Delphi Corporation, a separate company engaged in the supply of automotive components to the automotive industry.
[2] At this writing, Toyota has passed Ford in number of worldwide vehicle sales.
[3] As with GM, many Ford captive supply divisions have been spun off into Visteon Corporation, a separate company engaged in the supply of automotive components to the automotive industry.

vehicle ignition components (distributor caps and rotors) and, as plastics materials are good insulators, the plastic parts of many other electrical devices. As the use of engineering plastics in the automotive market grew, GEP established a field office and development center in the Detroit suburb of Southfield, Michigan, in closer proximity to the concentration of automotive customers. With the establishment of the Detroit center, a local manager and a team of market development specialists were assigned responsibility for business development at the U.S. vehicle OEMs. The focus shifted from plastic sales used in traditional applications (insulators, rotors, distributor caps, etc.) to generating new business at the car companies through the development of automotive applications that incorporated the use of GE plastics. At the time of the relocation (approximately 1972), GEP annual automotive sales at the time were less than a million dollars, but destined to grow. GE Plastics was moving out of the shadow of larger GE divisions, becoming a star in the corporate portfolio.

During the 1970s the GEP product line, automotive application development efforts, applications, and sales grew rapidly. The market development efforts of the GEP team established applications in several areas of the vehicle, including engine and body electrical components, interior and exterior trim and lighting, where plastics had not been successfully used before. With its higher thermal and impact performance offsetting higher cost, Lexan polycarbonate had replaced acrylic in lenses as well as zinc and *acrylonitrile-butadiene-styrene (ABS)* in housings—in specific, demanding signal lighting applications. Tail lamp applications of Lexan polycarbonate began in the commercial truck segment and then were translated into pickup trucks and other vehicles with bumper mounted lamps—where break resistance was a major concern. Smaller, more compact signal lamps that enclosed the heat of the light bulb (park and turn, cornering, etc.) and thus

required the heat resistance properties of polycarbonate also became selective applications of Lexan.

By the late 1970s, GE's automotive marketing team, in pursuit of new applications, speculated that headlamps would also benefit from what their plastics materials could do. By this time, the quest for better fuel economy was a major factor in design and material selection decisions. Headlamps, made of glass, were very heavy when compared to other vehicle lighting applications made of plastics. Substituting Lexan polycarbonate for the glass was a natural fit. The GE team set out with a new goal: to convert headlamps to their plastics, worldwide.

The History of Forward Lighting—Headlamps

In the 1930s, prior to the development of the standardized sealed beam, cars manufactured in the United States had glass headlamps of various shapes, such as the "teardrop" design on the Lincoln Zephyr and the rounded rectangular shape on the 1939 Plymouth. The construction of these lamps was typically comprised of a glass lens, a bright surface metal reflector, and a separate incandescent bulb. The multipiece design of these lamps did not prevent sealing and corrosion problems. Over time, the performance of the headlamps deteriorated, becoming a major safety issue. The many different shapes and sizes also prevented standardization of performance and the easy availability of service and replacement parts. This became a larger issue as more people drove longer distances from their local communities.

As a result, the "sealed beam" came into use and became the standard of headlamps for many years. The term *sealed beam* was used to describe a hermetically sealed, all glass lens, and reflector unit, containing filaments in an inert gas atmosphere—similar to an incandescent light bulb. From their inception in the

Acrylic versus Polycarbonate

Acrylic, best known as Plexiglas® from Rohm & Haas Chemicals, and polycarbonate (Lexan from GE) are two of the most widely used plastic materials when optical-quality transparency is required. While both exhibit excellent optical properties, acrylic is considered to have poor impact and less high-temperature capability when compared to the polycarbonate. Products molded from polycarbonate are often considered to be "virtually unbreakable" and are able to perform in higher temperature environments.

Why not use polycarbonate all the time? Cost. Polycarbonate is 50–100 percent more expensive than acrylic. As a result, polycarbonate gets used only in the more demanding applications.

1930s until 1957, they were available in one round size: 7″ diameter, usually with two filaments to provide both low- and high-beam lighting (Exhibit V-1). Becoming standard on every car, they were readily available, low cost and easy to replace.

By the 1957 model year, styling trends of "longer, lower, wider" led to the advent of the 5¾″, four-lamp system, with two outer high/low beams and two inner high-beam units. This system was first seen on such cars as the 1957 Mercury Turnpike Cruiser and the 1958 Edsel[4]—with most other 1958 models adopting the same configuration (Exhibit V-2). By the mid-1970s, rectangular sealed-beam headlamps also became available in rectangular 4″ × 6″, four-unit systems and 5″ × 7″, two-unit systems (Exhibit V-3). Obviously, the desire for greater

EXHIBIT V-2 Typical 4 Lamp Round System

diversity in headlamp appearance was increasing; however, it was unlikely that regulatory bodies would approve additional complexity.

During most of this time, headlamps in Europe evolved differently. The sealed-beam phenomena—the requirement to seal the lamp

EXHIBIT V-1 Typical 2 Lamp Round System

EXHIBIT V-3 Typical 4 Lamp Rectangular System

---

[4] At the time of this case, GM brands included Chevrolet, Pontiac, Oldsmobile, Buick, and Cadillac. Ford brands included Ford, Mercury, Edsel, and Lincoln. The Edsel was discontinued in 1961.

from potentially damaging and/or corrosive elements—never became a major factor. Instead, headlamps continued to evolve in shapes designed to fit the vehicle design, and construction continued to evolve and improve. Typical units were comprised of a glass lens, a metal reflector, and one or more replaceable bulbs, with an industry-standardized connection at the base of the bulb. Bulbs evolved from standard incandescent to halogen-cycle units, typically exemplified by the H4 two-filament high- or low-beam design in the main headlamps, with single filament bulbs used for long-range driving, front fog, and other forward lighting applications. These designs were a "bulb within a bulb"—the halogen filament itself was fully and separately encapsulated within its own glass envelope, which was then protected within the headlamp housing. However, these designs did not meet U.S. standards, though they were considered more stylish and, with fuel economy becoming an issue, more aerodynamic. European vehicles sold in the United States required to comply with DOT standards had their designs modified to incorporate the U.S. sealed-beam units—often to the detriment of the vehicle appearance.

In the late 1970s, the domination by the conventional incandescent sealed beam in the United States was challenged by the desire for better lighting and the availability of European halogen-bulb replacement units in the aftermarket—the consumer replacement and retrofit market. As a result, OEMs developed headlamps with halogen bulbs added inside of the standard-shaped glass sealed-beam headlamps, resulting in a premium range of products, producing a whiter, brighter light (the halogen filament was encapsulated separately and sealed within the headlamp—a bulb within a bulb).

At this juncture (with the exception of headlamps), all exterior lighting on modern vehicles had evolved to all-plastic units, designed to fit the style and shape of the car, using replaceable, standard bulbs inserted from the rear of the lamp, and standard sockets and connections. Acrylic plastics were typically used for lenses, with various other plastics and metals competing for the reflector or housing and trim components.

The Situation

When GEP began to approach car companies with the idea of plastic headlamps, they encountered many objections. Some of those objections were that plastic headlamps wouldn't work because:

- compared to glass sealed-beam units, they will be unable to maintain a hermetic seal, thus causing premature filament failure (note that this was likely to be an issue only when "bulb within a bulb" was not used);
- the lens surface will be insufficiently resistant to weathering and abrasion over the life of the vehicle;
- engineering *says* they're not legal or not approved by the U.S. Department of Transportation, the NHTSA, nor are they endorsed by the SAE;
- they will cost more, and therefore offer no incentive to change;
- some car company captive manufacturing divisions (e.g., GM Guide Lamp Division) and some independent suppliers that made glass headlamps (e.g., GE)[5] had considerable investment and vested interests in conventional glass sealed-beam lamp manufacturing. Therefore, they will not be receptive to change.

At this time, GEL also suggested that, even if all of these factors could be overcome,

---

[5] GE was by far the market share leader in the supply of automotive headlamps. There were other suppliers, but up to this time these other suppliers had played a minor role.

Captive and Custom Molders

A manufacturer that makes plastics components itself at its own plastic manufacturing facilities is said to have "captive facilities"—manufacturing facilities that produce plastic parts strictly for that manufacturer. When outsourced, plastic components are produced to the manufacturer's specifications by *custom injection molders*—contract providers that produce plastic parts as designed and specified by the manufacturer.

the styled headlamp was a fad, that wouldn't be universally adopted by the industry.

Faced with these objections, a few members of the GEP marketing team felt that the project was not worth pursuing. The time spent marketing the plastic headlamp could be better spent on less complex applications (really meaning applications with easier to overcome and fewer objections). Still, the GEP Detroit team wanted to move forward and develop business in plastic headlamps, and a few people were prepared to bet their careers on it.

The Marketing Plan

Benefits

GEP marketing people began analyzing and developing ideas about the benefits of plastic headlamps to OEM's. They concluded that the primary benefits of plastics were

- the ability to create unique designs with easier optical detail reproduction than glass, allowing vehicle manufacturers to design a more modern, smooth, streamlined front end, with the headlamps integrated into the overall vehicle shape and mounted flush to adjacent surfaces.
- the plastic and halogen bulb combination could reduce the risk of fire in a rear-end collision—since the Lexan was virtually unbreakable—and even if broken, the bulb filament was separately encapsulated. Therefore the risk of fire was reduced, compared to the glass sealed-beam unit, with its incandescent filament exposed when broken.

- The Lexan lamp would be significantly lighter than a glass sealed-beam lamp, contributing to need for lower vehicle weight.

These benefits, when combined into a package, could provide a method for manufacturers to make their cars look better and different and have that advantage over their competitors, potentially reduce collision hazards, and contribute to the overall goal to produce lighter vehicles. Indeed, at this time there was a heightened concern for safety, since a spate of sensational rear-end collisions and resultant fires had occurred coincidentally. In addition to the safety aspects, GEP noted the proposed shaped-to-the-car flush designs as being more aerodynamic, and thus contributing to less drag and better fuel economy. (The new concept was quickly tagged as the *aerodynamic headlamp* at Ford, and the term was used during development and application.)

Risks

The development project was not without risks, both for customers and the GEP team. GMGuide (now part of Delphi Automotive) was the primary supplier of glass sealed-beam headlamps to GM. GMGuide was unreceptive, and its general manager typified this by stating emphatically that the company was not going to change from glass to plastic because "sand (the basic raw material in glass) will always be cheaper than oil (the raw material in plastic)." The GEP program manager also recalls being practically thrown out of a meeting by the head of GEL at GEL home offices near Cleveland. Fortunately, GEP's management at the Pittsfield, MA, headquarters backed the efforts of the GEP Detroit team and provided political support within GE for them.

Finding the Right Customer

The GEP approach to the customer then changed. Realizing that the potential customers within the customer were actually those who would value the benefits of styling differentiation, they focused on the design and styling organization of the car companies, as well as managers in product planning and marketing. In other words, attention centered on the people at the car companies who were responsible for the way a car looked and sold. The degree to which these stakeholders (marketing, styling/design, and product planning departments) within the car company buying centers could influence the other members (engineering and purchasing people) became critical. While engineering was a necessary, if sometimes reluctant ally, they did not determine vehicle content. After approaching all major car manufacturers, the GEP marketing team realized that GM was not a likely first customer because GMGuide was focused on cost, not innovation. Though some GM designers, particularly at Cadillac, had expressed interest in the plastic aerodynamic headlamp, they would not be able to take advantage of the development until GMGuide was ready to embrace the technology. The situation was different at Ford.

Ford did not manufacture its own glass headlamps, instead was purchasing most of its needs from GEL. Ford was, however, fully integrated in the manufacturing of plastic components, among those all of the other lamps on the vehicle. If headlamps were to be made of plastic, Ford could manufacture the housings itself, purchasing just the filament (bulb within a bulb) from outside sources. Additionally, Ford was known as more receptive to innovative ideas, particularly from a marketing perspective as it understood the role innovation played in a better product and image in the market. These factors combined to lead the GEP team to focus on Ford as the most likely company to innovate.

The GEP team developed a champion within the Ford organization: an open-minded, creative manager in advanced engineering— who not only "got it," but wanted to see it happen himself. Though the effort was considered to be a waste of time by some Ford personnel, particularly in regard to the previously mentioned regulatory risks, the Ford "intrapreneur" and the GEP team began a program to make the new lamp happen.

Challenging the Standard

GEP marketing people started to politely but systematically question "legal" assumptions. They made some important discoveries. Most everyone had assumed the incumbent designs to be necessary (sealed, one-piece glass). However, Sylvania, a small lamp producer, was to shortly prove that this was not the case.[6] The applicable SAE standard was in place primarily as a design guideline to describe the significant dimensions, mounting and aiming points, and so on of sealed-beam headlamps—but not outlining or determining performance.

GEP also decided to question the "legal" assumptions at the external agency level. The GEP program manager contacted a senior DOT official in Washington, D.C., and arranged

---

[6] Sylvania, a small competitor to GEL but looking for a bigger presence in automotive lighting, was attempting to enter the market with glass "sealed" beam halogen headlamps that were made of a separate lens and housing. The two separate parts were bonded and the hermetic seal was achieved with adhesive rather than the industry-standard "flame sealing" that melted the two pieces of glass together. If the adhesive system worked, Sylvania could avoid the investment in the flame-sealing process. GEL believed that, ultimately, this adhesive design would not survive neither the DOT approval process nor vehicle durability requirements.

a meeting to discuss a new, safe headlamp idea. At this meeting, the official indicated that the government's only real concern was that headlights provided the driver consistent, safe illumination over the period of its life (or that of the car) and, should one fail, replacements be widely available. In fact, they did not care about their material or shape. The GEP representative cited the safety benefits of the plastic concept. The plastic and halogen bulb combination would reduce the risk of fire in a rear-end collision—since the Lexan was virtually unbreakable and even if broken, the bulb filament was separately encapsulated. Therefore the risk of fire was reduced, compared to the glass sealed-beam unit, with its incandescent filament exposed when the glass housing was broken.

Validating the Concept

GEP decided to make some prototype plastic headlamps, test them in simulated use to see if they would work over an acceptable period of time. Since GEL was the lighting expert, and at this point, they did not want to get too far from the project (at least to maintain knowledge of what was going on), they agreed to work with GEP and Ford to develop the prototypes. All agreed that if those tests went well, then the next step would be to further prove it out with a production vehicle trial. Until then, no one had questioned the prevailing assumptions.

Prototypes were designed, fabricated, and tested. Results were favorable and reviewed with Ford as well as with the appropriate agencies. Ford decided to further validate the concept in actual field use and requested GEL to manufacture the lamps. The first polycarbonate headlamp to be used on a production U.S.-built vehicle was a two-piece injection molded version of the standard 4″ × 6″ rectangular high beam-only design—using a halogen capsule bulb as its light source. It used an injection molded lens with an ultraviolet (UV) protective coating, bonded to an injection molded, metallized, and coated reflector/housing. The vehicle application was the inboard lamp of the four-lamp rectangular system (high beam only, as part of the standard four-lamp configuration) units on the 1980 Lincoln Town Car, of which approximately 60,000 examples were produced and sold that year. Conventional glass sealed-beam units were used on the outer high/low beam pair of headlamps. This configuration provided a way to gain production use and experience and prove the durability of the plastic lamp in actual field use. (Should the new plastic lamps fail, the vehicle would still have the normal, safe use of the primary outer "high/low" sealed beam, and the inboard plastic high beam could be easily retrofitted with the standard glass lamp.) The plastic lamps were manufactured by GEL as part of a development project funded by GEP and Ford.

The test application on the Lincoln Town Car was deemed successful, paving the way for further use.

GEP hired an experienced automotive designer/stylist (they don't like to be called stylists!) from Europe, where aerodynamic headlamps, made of glass, styled to fit the car were the norm. The designer developed "before and after" illustrations of existing and potential vehicle models, graphically showing the appearance advantage of smooth, new, flush plastic designs—compared to the upright, rectangular holes in the otherwise stylish front end of most vehicles. It worked.

At about this time, GE Lamp withdrew support of the development program. To say that both Ford and GEP were disappointed would be an understatement. While Ford was proficient at the manufacture of plastic parts with some of the largest captive molding facilities in the industry, it was convinced that the development required a cooperative lamp manufacturer. Over dinner with a GEP representative, the Ford vice president of Car Engineering made the Ford position clear. Ford was going to go ahead with the aerodynamic lamp development. It preferred to partner with GE, as GE had both plastics materials and lighting expertise. However, it wouldn't refrain from finding another lighting manufacturer and/or another plastics material supplier and put them together into a team (e.g., a value network) to make the project happen. The vice president of Ford asked the GEP representative to get that message back to GE.

Analysis

This case represents a situation that is often associated with innovation. A few people within a company have a bright idea that would benefit them if accepted and implemented. However, the current industry situation is characterized by a well-established technology and committed manufacturing, combined with external, third-party government and industry standards developed around the incumbent systems.

Questions for Discussion

1. What is your assessment of the situation?
2. What are the benefits of plastic headlamps? To whom?
3. How would you overcome the objections of the GM Guide Lamp division?
4. What is the rationale behind the GEL decision to withdraw support from the development?
5. Does it make sense to innovate the offerings of a cash cow? Why?
6. How has GEL impacted the GEP relationship at Ford?
7. What approaches would you take with other potential customers?
8. How would you address and overcome the issues regarding agency approval?
9. What are the key factors likely to determine success in this application?

CASE VI
Makrolon: The High-Tech Material

People all over the world come into contact with polycarbonates every day. Ever since 1953, this plastic has built an impressive array of success in many different product Today, countless producers all over the world rely on the properties of polycarbonates. And more products and applications are constantly being added. It is impossible to imagine the future without polycarbonates. One of these polycarbonates is Bayer's Makrolon.® The 45 billion or so CDs that have been produced from Makrolon since the birth of the compact disc in 1982 up to the beginning of 2008 would create a belt about 10,800,000 kilometers long. This is roughly equivalent to twenty eight times the mean distance between the Earth and the Moon.

In 2007, Makrolon had a brand awareness of 31 percent and was absolutely the best-known polycarbonate in the marketplace in Europe. In the United States Lexan from GE Plastics had the leading position.[1] The following case study describes Bayer's ingredient branding strategy for Makrolon in Europe. We focus on the rise of Makrolon and we broach the issue of developing this strategy for the future. In the end, awareness is not everything. Does branding pay off? What are the conditions that determine the benefit Bayer can achieve with Makrolon? All these questions are germane to successful management of the Makrolon brand.

When the Bayer Corporation from Leverkusen invented the polycarbonate Makrolon® in 1953, it did not cause any particular shockwaves. Bayer patented the invention in the same year. In the early days Makrolon was primarily used as an **insulating plastic**, for example for switches and fuse boxes, but it is now recognized as a highly versatile material that can be used in many areas of life. With its high transparency, impact strength, and dimensional stability, even at high temperatures, Makrolon is versatile in the extreme. Makrolon continues to be used in electrical engineering applications but also, for instance, in headlamps and interior fittings for cars, transparent roofing for carports and swimming pools, UV protection for sports goggles and sunglasses, and packaging for reusable milk bottles and water dispensers. When Polygram, a subsidiary of Philips, made the first CD, they used Makrolon, which is now used by renowned manufacturers as a fixed component of many CDs, CD-ROMs, and DVDs. Recently it has also been adapted for blue-ray discs.

Bayer Polymers did not pursue an ingredient branding strategy until 2000, when it began marketing Makrolon as a brand in its own right and bringing it into the public eye (see Exhibit VI-1). Prior to this, it was largely unknown to consumers and only marketed to businesses as an application chemical.

Bayer has had little difficulty in finding ingredient branding partners to use and process

made of

EXHIBIT VI-1 Makrolon Trademark/Logo

[1] On May 27, 2007 General Electric (USA) sold GE Plastics to Saudi Basic Industries Corp. (SABIC) for $11.6 billion. In 2006, the Pittsfield, MA-based business employed 10,300 people and generated $6.6 billion in sales and $675 million in profits in that year. In 2002 they had started a branding campaign which improved Lexan's reputation outside the Americas.

the product, given that Makrolon has had a good reputation in the plastics processing industry. The strategy aims to make the consumer aware that both the manufacturer of the end product and the company that makes the most elementary component of the product stand for **flawless quality** and that the customer can trust this product.

But being a processor of Makrolon does not necessarily mean that the end product meets the same quality standards or reflects Bayer's level of prestige. The polycarbonate could be simply an ingredient, which cannot compensate for a manufacturer's poor reputation or the inferior quality of other ingredients used in the manufacturing process. To protect the reputation of Bayer and Makrolon and make sure it is not damaged by quality issues of this kind, Bayer tests all products that are destined to carry the Makrolon label.

Bayer also uses brand usage agreements to ensure the required level of quality and assumes the right to take samples during production to offer end consumers assurance of consistently high quality. But Bayer does not only consider a company's products when choosing its ingredient branding partners; it also scrutinises the company and its image as a whole. When it comes to ingredient branding the Leverkusen firm wants to know exactly with whom they are associating in the public eye and who is allowed to use the **Bayer cross** for their own marketing purposes. This process aims to avoid associating the company with partners engaged in "price wars"; a close association with the end product could potentially damage the image of Makrolon.

Becoming an ingredient branding partner is a coveted position amongst companies that process Makrolon. As a result, Bayer is signing brand usage agreements with more and more firms. At the present time, cycling, skiing, and sports goggles from UVEX Sports

GmbH & Co. KG, CD-ROMs and DVD-ROMs from MMore International BV, and ampoules for a needle-free injection system from Rösch AG all carry the Makrolon seal of quality.

But the **ingredient branding family** also includes CDs and DVDs from other manufacturers (regionally separated), protective floor mats, water dispensers, flexible solar modules, and many other products. What Bayer and its partners are both aiming to achieve is to differentiate themselves from the competition and competing products by means of the branding strategy. It is important to highlight the advantages of Makrolon and transfer this positive image to the end product with the help of brand name. This differentiation gives the ingredient a **unique selling proposition,** or USP, and encourages the end customer to give preference to products with the Makrolon logo or even keep a lookout for this particular product when looking to make a purchase. The potential customer then may ask for a product manufactured with Makrolon.

But the pull effect cannot be achieved simply by adding the Makrolon quality seal to product, packaging, and advertising material. Quality and credibility must also be conveyed to the consumer, who must be able to build up a familiarity with the Makrolon brand. Bayer's ingredient branding partners label their products and brochures all over Europe with the words "Made of Makrolon®" and the Bayer umbrella brand (branded house). The partners explain the advantages of this special polycarbonate and why customers should choose products with this ingredient in print advertisements, brochures, catalogues, on their Web sites, and at trade fairs. To initiate the **pull effect**, Bayer uses advertising campaigns to appeal directly to (potential) end consumers and in 2000 it began targeting individual audiences with appropriate motifs, giving the brand the right emotional associations for the particular segment. Bayer used PR in the print media and on television to convey its messages. The "fastest" and most conspicuous advertising medium was the intercity locomotives operated by Deutsche Bahn. Bayer was the first company to use intercity locomotives as advertising space.

The Makrolon brand was given five different motifs, which were partially oriented toward Bayer's partners UVEX, Legoland, and MMore. These locomotives proved extremely popular with railway fans, and a dedicated Web site set up by Bayer attracted **huge numbers of hits**. Model railway maker **Märklin** currently stocks a model of the locomotive featuring partner MMore, which is delivered with a computer mouse made of Makrolon.® This is another example of Bayer seeking to demonstrate the versatility of its plastic, and by partnering with Märklin, it aims to highlight the fact that the polycarbonate is used in many models from the Göppingen toy manufacturer.

The ingredient branding partnership between Bayer Makrolon and its customers is balanced because of its interdependence. The principle is based on synergies, that is, each partner integrates the other and refers to the partnership in their advertising, brochures, catalogues, Web sites, and other publications. This does not result in advertising cost allowances or similar benefits and concessions for either side.

As a relative newcomer to ingredient branding, Bayer is still in the early stages of establishing its high-tech plastic Makrolon as a brand with the user. Establishing a brand that has hitherto been completely unknown to consumers is an extremely difficult task and often incurs considerable advertising costs. So Bayer exploited its well-known name and **reputation** and incorporated the Bayer cross into the Makrolon logo. This had the effect of making consumers associate the plastic from the outset with the Bayer Corporation, which already represents tradition and quality and has proven it with brands such as Aspirin. The positive image of the company can thus be transferred to the new Bayer brand. Demonstrating the link between the two brands cuts down on costs for introductory and ongoing advertising, partly because Makrolon benefits indirectly from product advertising for other Bayer products.

Background on Bayer AG

The History

The general partnership "Friedr. Bayer et comp." was founded on August 1, 1863, in Barmen—now a district of the city of Wuppertal—by dye salesman Friedrich Bayer (1825–1880) and master dyer Johann Friedrich Weskott (1821–1876). The object of the company was the manufacture and sale of synthetic dyestuffs. Between 1881 and 1913, Bayer developed into a chemical company with international operations. Although dyestuffs remained the company's largest division, new fields of business were joining the fold.

Of primary importance for Bayer's continuing development was the establishment of a major research capability by Carl Duisberg (1861–1935). A scientific laboratory was built in Wuppertal-Elberfeld—which was also the company's headquarters from 1878 until 1912—that set new standards in industrial research. Bayer's research efforts gave rise to numerous intermediates, dyes and pharmaceuticals, including the "drug of the century," Aspirin, which was developed by Felix Hoffmann and launched onto the market in 1899.

World War I interrupted Bayer's dazzling development. The company was largely cut off from its major export markets, and sales of dyes and pharmaceuticals dropped accordingly. Bayer was increasingly integrated into the war economy and began to produce war materials, including explosives and chemical weapons. In 1917, during the war, Bayer launched its third production site in Dormagen.

A community of interests had already existed between Bayer, BASF, and Agfa since 1905. In order to regain access to the vital export markets, these and other companies of the German tar dyes industry joined together to the IG Farben AG in a larger community of interests in 1915–1916 on the initiative of Carl Duisberg. After World War II in November 1945, the Allied Forces confiscated the operations of IG Farber AG and placed all its sites under the control of Allied officers. The company was to be dissolved and its assets made available for war reparations. Yet the British permitted Ulrich Haberland (1900–1961), who had been in charge of the Lower Rhine consortium since 1943, to remain in his position. Soon they allowed production to resume as well, as the chemical industry's products were essential to supply the population. In the years that followed, Haberland worked to build up a new and competitive company in the successful Bayer tradition. The Allied military governments had initially planned to break up the IG Farber AG into as many small companies as possible. Yet these companies would hardly have been able to survive on the world market or even in Germany itself. The Allies finally came to this realization as well, and thus—on the basis of Allied law—twelve new thoroughly competitive companies were created in the Federal Republic of Germany. Thus in 1946, while still under Allied control, Bayer began to re-establish its sales activities abroad. By the 1950s, the company was allowed to acquire foreign affiliates as well. At first the United States and Latin America were the focus of these activities.

The reconstruction of Bayer was closely linked with the Wirtschaftswunder ("economic miracle"), in the Federal Republic of Germany. As a result of World War II, Bayer for the second time had lost its foreign assets, including its valuable patents. It was clearly vital to rebuild Bayer's foreign business. Farbenfabriken Bayer AG was newly established on December 19, 1951. The Leverkusen, Dormagen, Elberfeld, and Uerdingen sites were allocated to the new company, and in 1952 Bayer also received as a subsidiary the newly established Agfa "joint stock company for photo fabrication," but lost their foreign subsidiaries.

The first mild recession in the Federal Republic of Germany occurred in 1966, but it was the oil crisis of 1973–1974 that ended the "economic miracle" once and for all. By the time Herbert Grünewald succeeded Kurt Hansen as Management Board chairman of the Bayer AG following the 1974 Annual Stockholders' Meeting, the global economy was undergoing a radical transformation. Within just a few months, prices for chemical raw materials based on oil had risen astronomically. Makrolon too was affected by these developments. The crisis reached its apex in the early 1980s as a severe global recession set in.

The 1990s saw another major structural transformation, with Bayer, like other companies, facing the challenge of globalization. In the wake of the radical political changes that took place in Germany and Eastern Europe after 1989, the company increased its focus on these promising markets. As early as 1992, Bayer broke ground on a new site in Bitterfeld in eastern Germany, where production of Aspirin began in 1994. The importance of North America to the Bayer Group continued to increase. In Canada Bayer acquired Toronto-based Polysar Rubber Corporation in 1990—the most significant acquisition in the company's history up to that point. The transaction made Bayer the world's biggest supplier of raw materials for the rubber industry.

Under the leadership of Dr. Manfred Schneider, Bayer acquired the North American self-medication (over-the-counter drugs) business of Sterling Winthrop in 1994—a milestone in the company's history, as the purchase also allowed the company to regain the rights to the "Bayer" company name in the United States. For the first time in seventy five years, Bayer could operate in the United States under its own name and with the Bayer Cross as its corporate logo.[2] In 1995 U.S.-based Miles, Inc., was renamed Bayer Corporation, and Makrolon could also use the Bayer Cross in their logo.

To better equip itself for the challenges of the future, Bayer set up a third pharmaceutical research center, this time in Japan, in addition to the locations in Europe (Wuppertal) and North America (West Haven, Connecticut). In 1995 the research center of Japanese pharmaceutical subsidiary Bayer Yakuhin Ltd. was dedicated at Kansai Science City near Kyoto. This marked the basic completion of Bayer's Europe–North America–Japan "pharmaceutical research triad." In the years that followed, these operations were supplemented by alliances with numerous innovative biotechnology companies.

In 2001, Bayer acquired Aventis Crop Science for €7.25 billion, making it a world leader in crop protection. In December of the same year, the company's management announces planned to establish independent operating groups. One year later Bayer CropScience AG was launched as the first legally independent Bayer subgroup. In 2003, the subgroups Bayer Chemicals AG and Bayer HealthCare AG and the service company Bayer Technology Services GmbH gained legal independence as part of the reorganization of the Bayer Group. The subgroup Bayer MaterialScience AG (which produces Makrolon) and the service companies Bayer Business Services GmbH and Bayer Industry Services GmbH & Co. OHG followed.

In 2005, Bayer completed the acquisition of the Roche consumer health business, advancing to become one of the world's top three suppliers of nonprescription medicines in the same year. Lanxess AG was spun off from the Bayer Group. This company now continues Bayer's chemicals business and parts of its polymers business.

In January 2005, an Extraordinary Stockholders' Meeting of Bayer Schering Pharma AG resolved to effect a "squeeze-out" of the remaining minority stockholders. Bayer Schering Pharma AG, headquartered in Berlin, now operates together with Bayer's existing pharmaceuticals business as a division of the Bayer HealthCare subgroup. Bayer is now one of the global leading enterprises with core competencies in the fields of health care, nutrition, and high-tech materials.

Organization

Bayer AG defines common values, goals, and strategies for the entire group. The three subgroups (HealthCare, CorpScience, Material Science) and three service companies (Business Services, Technology Services, Industry Services) operate independently, led by the management holding company. The Corporate Centre supports the Group Management Board in its task of strategic leadership (see Exhibit VI-2). The revenues of each business unit at the revenues of the whole Bayer Group is shown in Exhibit VI-3.

Bayer MaterialScience AG

Bayer MaterialScience is a renowned supplier of high-performance materials, such as polycarbonates and polyurethanes, and innovative system solutions, such as coatings, for a wide range of everyday uses. Products holding leading positions on the world market account for a large

---

[2] Prior to this time, Bayer had competed with GE in the United States through a subsidiary, Mobay Chemical. Mobay used the brand name "Merlon" for its polycarbonate.

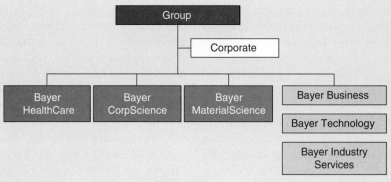

EXHIBIT VI-2   Bayer Group Organization

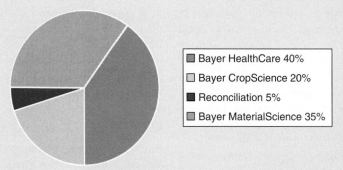

EXHIBIT VI-3   Revenues Per Business Unit of the Bayer AG 2007

proportion of its sales.[3] The business unit of Bayer MaterialScience holds five subdivisions. Collectively, the subdivisions provide the basis for Bayer MaterialScience's operations. They develop and manufacture products within their focus. The subdivisions are

- **Coatings, Adhesives, Sealants (BU CAS)**
  This business unit is responsible for the development and production of a broad range of raw materials for coatings, adhesives, and sealants.
- **Polycarbonates (BU PCS)**
  Makrolon polycarbonate is a classic among Bayer MaterialScience's products.
- **Polyurethanes (BU PUR)**
  Polyurethanes are one of the major materials used in the manufacturer of foams

for padding, furniture, and so on, and also of many durable industrial and commercial coatings.

- **Thermoplastic Polyurethanes (BU TPU)**
  Thermoplastic polyurethanes have become simply indispensable. They make sure, for example that your car functions properly.
- **Inorganic Basic Chemicals (IBC)**
  IBC is responsible for worldwide chlorine supplies at Bayer MaterialScience.

Background on Makrolon

Today's Makrolon production reaches an everyday use of more than 500 tons and a capacity of more than 740,000 tons in four existing subsidiaries. Bayer MaterialScience is increasing its market share based on high investments

---

[3] The financial key data for the whole Bayer Group and its subdivisions are attached in the Exhibits VI.5 and VI.6.

and focusing on China in the future.[4] With an expected growth of more than 8 percent per annum in polycarbonates Bayer chose China with Shanghai as location to strengthen its competitor advantage. Bayer MaterialScience is investing more than 720M € up to 1.1 billions from 2006 to 2012 in projects including polycarbonates. Makrolon has been crowned with success and is used by different segments, ranging from roofing, surface coating, and medical technology to car windows. Because of the great success and diversity Bayer has had with Makrolon they opted for the marketing tool "ingredient branding." The key to Bayer Makrolon's new ingredient

brandings concept was the requirement that the component was used for high-class care products labelled with the Makrolon logo. Within consumer's faith in the core product and the qualitative ingredient, the new instrument of "ingredient branding" puts both the product and the component in an excellent competitive position by creating and communicating added value.

The locations for the Makrolon production are organized globally. There are seven production places: Newark and Baytown in the United States; Uerdingen, Antwerp, and Filago in Europe; and Caojing and Map Ta Phut in Asia (see Exhibit VI-4).

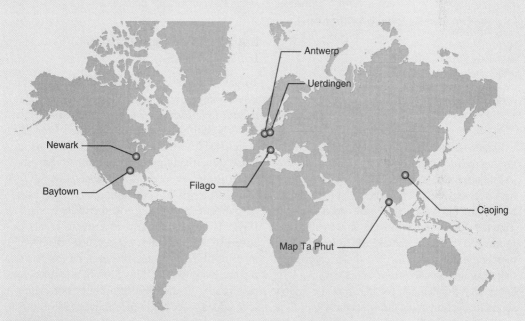

EXHIBIT VI-4 Local Production of Makrolon

---

[4] As noted, Bayer also benefited from the sale of its largest competitor, the Plastics Group of General Electric. Until the sale to Saudi Industries Corp., GE had been a very strong competitor, dominating the U.S. market with its Lexan® Polycarbonate. In the 1970s, GE considered a consumer branding effort for its Lexan Polycarbonate, including filming of commercials (A Bull in a Lexan Shop) and tagline development (Lexan—A Good Name to Stand On), and logo. Deemed too expensive at the time, the full implementation of the project was abandoned, with a minor effort to tag products with the new logo (an elephant standing on a circus stand of Lexan). For greater understanding of how these companies competed, particularly in the arena for development of new applications of polycarbonate, see the case "Marketing Plastic Resins; BW and GE," elsewhere in this book.

The Market for Polycarbonate

Polycarbonates (PC) were first prepared by Einhorn in 1898 and extensively researched until 1930 when they were discarded. Research was then started in the mid-1950s by General Electric and in 1958 the polycarbonate popularity expanded to a global community. Today, approximately 75 percent of the polycarbonate market is held by Bayer and GE Plastics, now acquired by Saudi Basic Industries (SABIC).[5]

Hollow sunlight panels are semistructural, corrugated (much like cardboard) panels that take advantage of the clarity and toughness of polycarbonate. They are often used instead of glass for greenhouses and other similar structures, as they are virtually unbreakable. Bayer pioneered this application in the 1970s in Europe, bringing the application to the United States by the early 1980s. GE entered the market in the middle of the decade, but this application has remained a major application for Bayer.

Experts predict that the demand of computers and home appliances will continue to grow in the next few years, and the demand for PC from this sector will increase at an annual rate of 10–12 percent. For the railway, highway, airport, and urban construction sectors, it is expected that they will also have a strong demand for hollow sunlight panels. In the past few years, enterprises located in the Yangtze River Delta (YRD) and Pearl River Delta (PRD) regions that use PC to manufacture panels greatly outperformed those enterprises that produce panels from other resins. It is anticipated the demand for PC from the hollow sunlight panels manufacturing sector will grow at an annual rate of 12–15 percent. Moreover, experts forecast that PC-based blend alloy composite material suppliers will become one of the largest consumers for PC, as the automotive industry has a great demand for their product.[6] The main competitors in the marketplace for Bayer MaterialScience polycarbonate are

- SABIC (GE Plastics Lexan®)
- Dow (Calibre®)
- Teijin
- Mitsubishi Chemical Group
- Idemitsu
- Sam Yang
- Chi Mei
- Formosa
- Policarbonatos do Brasil

Bayer's Branding Strategy for Makrolon

To get in touch with consumers and retailers, Bayer started with ingredient branding campaigns to inform end users about Makrolon. Bayer's multistage marketing differs from the "Intel-Inside" strategy. Whereas Intel is using brand advertising and cooperation advertising, Bayer is almost solely using cooperation advertising. In terms of cooperation marketing both partners are advertising together. Interestingly, Bayer is not paying any advertising grants to advertise with partners. Cooperation advertising in terms of Bayer means that each partner has to finance his own part. This form of a partnership results in a "win-win" situation of both sides, with added value for both without sharing costs.

---

[5] General Electric sold its plastics division to Saudi Basic Industries, Saudi Arabia's largest industrial firm, for $11 Billion. General Electric's plastics unit reached $6.6 billion in revenue in 2006. The division had struggled to meet aggressive margin and share goals amid inflation in natural gas and raw materials like benzene, and profits at the unit fell about 22 percent, to $674 million 2006 from $867 million in 2005. The sale has always been controversial, but it is not unusual for GE to leave markets when the major offerings reach the mature stage. (Such as phenolic plastics, consumer electronics, television, small appliances, etc.)

[6] By the late 1970s, the competition between GE and Bayer was a global battle. The 1985 European Ford Sierra and some Fiats were the first to use Polycarbonate blended with polyesters for energy-absorbing bumpers. In 1986, the U.S. Ford Taurus and Mercury Sable used the PC blend for bumpers. These blended derivatives of PC were developed specifically for these applications by GE Plastics.

Bayer is furthermore expecting good reputation with high quality and good image of the end product. With signing license contracts the partner has to agree with pre-product tests before labelling the ingredient on the core product, the allowance of samples taken by Bayer to secure the quality.[7] The Makrolon logo is labelled on the core product or packages. The integration of Bayer Makrolon logo is further extended to exhibitions, advertising campaigns, events, and sponsoring activities.

With Bayer's ingredient branding campaign of cooperation advertising from 2001, Bayer targeted the selected end user groups for products such as CD/DVD, sunglasses, and medical products. Bayer and its partners were pushing the message to consumers to call attention to Makrolon, the labelled polycarbonate, and create the pull effect. Bayer and its partners communicated the new branded ingredient in magazines, journals, and popular magazines. The campaign was launched in Germany, Great Britain, Spain, and other countries.

In collateral materials, the chosen partners educated the end user of the ingredient through advertising campaigns, flyers, Web sites, and exhibitions. The integration of advertising and public relation pushes the message to more consumers' minds. Today Makrolon is a well-known brand to many end users in most of the world, with consumers in the United States still lagging behind. For Bayer Material Science, brand management became an important part not only for B2B customers but also for addressing end users. Makrolon created a competitive advantage through communication with the end user, and it showed that ingredient branding can properly improve the brand value of polycarbonate.

Bayer's aim is to communicate Makrolon's benefit to the end user. This could lead the end users to be more willing to pay more for the products labelled with the Makrolon ingredient as well as demand the ingredient in core products.

The communication process usually starts with partner campaigns, using the Bayer cross and "made of Makrolon." The communication process also includes "point of sale" marketing activities. In addition public relations is helping to inform the target customers. End user surveys help to define consumer wants and needs. Building partnerships and the resulting "win-win" situation is an important step in implementing an ingredient branding strategy. The "win-win" situation can occur through reduction of prices for the core product manufacturer or support in advertising campaigns.

The different partnership campaigns made the ingredient as well as the core product known. Advertisements on intercity train locomotives had been a communicator in pushing the messages and they strengthen Makrolon's profile.[8] By applying this seal of quality, branding partners like MMore, HiSpace, and DataTrack convey the message that the material used for their recordable CDs and DVDs guarantees optimum storage quality and security. Through CDs, automotive headlights,[9] eyeglass lenses, helmets, household appliances, and water bottles almost everybody comes into contact with Makrolon at least once a day. Makrolon is about to become a well-known brand, like Aspirin,® the other big Bayer brand.

To accompany the labelling of their products, the partners also use ads, flyers, Web sites, and exhibition stands to draw attention to

---

[7] Horizont 2002, Zeitschrift für Marketing, Frankfurt, S. 26.

[8] Ironically, by the 1970s, one of the major U.S. applications for polycarbonate was in commuter train windows, primarily for safety reasons. Though initially more expensive, the lower replacement frequency and added passenger safety overcame the initial costs. Today, polycarbonate glazing (windows) are the standard in all passenger rail applications.

[9] See "Automotive Headlamps II: The Paradigm Shift from Standardized Glass Beams to Today's Plastic Custom Designs" elsewhere in this book.

OEM	End Product Brand	Product Categories
RS Office	Rollsafe, Roll-o-Grip u.a.	Flor cover mats
BNL Eurolens	BNL Eurolens	Eye glasses
Euro Digital Disc Manufacturing	Data Track	CDs
MMORE	MMORE	CDs/DVDs
Tera Media Corporation	Nashua	CDs/DVDs
Videolar	EMTEC/Nipponic	CDs/DVDs
Luceplan	Constanza	Design-lamps
Salman Plastik	Salblend, Salflex	Electronic
Spirit of Golf	Laser Line Tee	Golf equipment
Matsuzaki Industry Co. Ltd.	Maruem	Suitcases
G+B Pronova	Holo Pro	Holographische Projektionsscheiben
Geomag SA	Geomag	Magnet-Toys
Societe Bourgeois	Galaxy	Optical Lenses
Alurunner GmbH	Alurunner	sleigh
Sunovation	Sunovation	Solar modules
UVEX	UVEX	Sports equipment
Goldwell Enterprises Inc.	Goldwell	Water bottle
Watertek	Watertek	Water bottle
Capsnap Europe	Capsnap	Water bottle
Portola Packaging Inc.	Portola, Garafón	Water bottle

EXHIBIT VI-5 OEMs Using Makrolon for Their End Product

Makrolon.® Other co-branding partners include water bottle producers Capsnap in Austria and Watertek in Turkey, and Makroform GmbH, a member of the Bayer Group whose products include polycarbonate sheeting for high-quality roofing.

Exhibit VI-5 shows selected OEMs which use Makrolon in their end product. All these companies further show the ingredient by using the Makrolon brand on their final product. For additional information regarding Bayer Group's earning see Exhibit VI-6.

The Example UVEX

UVEX was one of the early participants in the ingredient branding activities of Makrolon. Since the company was founded in 1926, UVEX has always focused on its mission "Protecting People" at work, sport, and leisure activities and Makrolon was the perfect material to help to achieve this mission. UVEX WINTER HOLDING comprises four international subsidiaries under one roof:

- UVEX SECURITY, for protection at work: eyewear, helmets, gloves, hearing protection, foot, and workwear.
- UVEX SPORTS, for sport and leisure: helmets for skiing, cycling, and motorcycling; sunglasses and goggles for skiing, cycling, motorcycling, and protective clothing and boots for motorcyclists.
- ALPINA, for sport, leisure, and the optical trade: ski and cycle helmets, ski goggles, cycle and sports sunglasses, optical frames, and sunglasses.
- FILTRAL, Fashion sunglasses and reading glasses.

Bayer's partner for the ingredient branding strategy is UVEX SPORTS. This business unit offers products for motor sports, cycling, and skiing that are sold in specialist shops throughout the world. As well as distributing to all major world markets, the company has subsidiaries in Switzerland, Austria, the Netherlands, the United States, and Japan.

UVEX SPORTS is known as a professional supplier of protective equipment in international top-class sports. Far-reaching sponsorship activities in bobsledding, luge, snowboarding, and both downhill and cross-country skiing increase the company's market presence and significance. Top professionals such as ski jumpers Janne Ahonen, Sigurd Pettersen, and Kazujoshi Funaki; racing skiers such as Michaela Dorfmeister, Renate Götschl, Sonja Nef, Fritz Strobl, Andi Schifferer, and Sammi Uotila; luger Georg Hackl and bobsledder Christoph Langen; and many more represent the UVEX winter sports team.

Makrolon can be transparent or opaque, is resistant to impact and weathering, and withstands high and low temperatures. These attributes linked to the Makrolon brand are major aspects for high-quality sport products. The partnership between these two brands embodies similar or complementary attributes to the end user.

UVEX product portfolio is an excellent example. UVEX offers products in which Makrolon can be used to build flexible eyewear frames, breathable coated textiles, transparent shells for ski shoes, transparent high impact resistant cases for bindings, and lightweight and attractive surfaces for skis and snowboards as possible applications.

Bayer and UVEX have created a promotion campaign together. Both companies communicate the brands not only on the

Bayer Group Key Data		
	2005 (in € million)	**2006** (in € million)
Bayer Group		
Net sales	24,701	28,956
EBITDA[i]	4,122	4,675
EBITDA before special items	4,602	5,584
EBIT[ii]	2,514	2,762
EBIT before special items	3,047	3,479
Income before income taxes	1,912	1,98
Net income	1,597	1,683
Earnings per share (€)[iii]	2,19	2,22
Gross cash flow[iv]	3,114	3,913
Net cash flow[v]	3,227	3,928
Capital expenditures	1,21	1,739
Research and development expenses	1,729	2,297
Dividend per Bayer AG share (€)	0,95	1
Bayer HealthCare		
Net external sales	7,996	11,724
EBITDA[1]	1,28	1,947
EBITDA before special items	1,487	2,613
EBIT[2]	923	1,313

EXHIBIT VI-6   Bayer Group Key Data

Bayer Group Key Data

	2005 (in € million)	2006 (in € million)
EBIT before special items	1,177	1,715
Gross cash flow[4]	923	1,72
Net cash flow[5]	1,087	1,526
Capital expenditures	225	576
Bayer CropScience		
Net external sales	5,896	5,7
EBITDA[1]	1,284	1,166
EBITDA before special items	1,273	1,204
EBIT[2]	690	584
EBIT before special items	685	641
Gross cash flow[4]	964	900
Net cash flow[5]	904	898
Capital expenditures	201	197
Bayer MaterialScience		
Net external sales	9,446	10,161
EBITDA[1]	1,721	1,499
EBITDA before special items	1,764	1,677
EBIT[2]	1,25	992
EBIT before special items	1,293	1,21
Gross cash flow[4]	1,254	1,166
Net cash flow[5]	1,337	1,281
Capital expenditures	642	753

EXHIBIT VI-6   (continued)

[1] EBITDA = EBIT plus amortization of intangible assets and depreciation of property, plant, and equipment. EBITDA, EBITDA before special items, and EBITDA margin are not defined in the International Financial Reporting Standards and should therefore be regarded only as supplementary information. The company considers underlying EBITDA to be a more suitable indicator of operating performance since it is not affected by depreciation, amortization, write-downs/write-backs, or special items. The company also believes that this indicator gives readers a clearer picture of the results of operations and ensures greater comparability of data over time. The underlying EBITDA margin is calculated by dividing underlying EBITDA by sales.

[2] EBIT as shown in the income statement.

[3] Earnings per share as defined in IAS 33 = net income divided by the average number of shares.

[4] Gross cash flow = income after taxes from continuing operations plus income taxes, plus/minus non-operating result, minus income taxes paid, plus depreciation, amortization and write-downs, minus write-backs, plus/minus changes in pension provisions, minus gains/plus losses on retirements of noncurrent assets, plus noncash effects of the remeasurement of acquired assets. The change in pension provisions includes the elimination of non-cash components of the operating result. It also contains benefit payments during the year.

[5] Net cash flow = cash flow from operating activities according to IAS 7.

products but also in sports events or in image brochures. Both companies perform together in fairs and shows, illustrating the use of the raw material polycarbonate. They also use these events to show other possible applications for Makrolon. However, the UVEX sport products are made for high-performance sportsmen. These products symbolize the high-performance standards that bring the consumer closer to the ingredient Makrolon thereby enabling both companies to achieve a win-win situation.

Questions for Discussion

1. What was the original motivation behind Bayer's decision to launch the Makrolon ingredient branding concept?
2. What factors were responsible for the success and failure of the efforts?
3. What was the brand promise and how was it materialized?
4. How did they manage the ingredient branding concept and what other options does the management have?

CASE VII

SENSACON Corporation[1]: High Technology Evolves to High Volume

Amanda Nguyen and Dan DelMonaco were sitting in the **Bella Mia Restaurant & Bar** on First Street in downtown San Jose, California. Together with Tom Foster, their third partner and co-founder of SENSACON, they reminisced about how they got to this point, why they separated, and what did it mean to their joint company. The past years had been a very traumatic period for SENSACON. Its markets were changing—the transition beyond visionary adopters was occurring and the founding partners had to make tough choices for the company and themselves.

Six years prior they had each worked for different companies in the sensors and controls industry. They met at a four-day Sensors Expo trade conference at the San Jose Convention Center in a plenary session about "the future of micro-robots." Each of the three professionals saw a unique opportunity, not in micro-robots, but in the enabling technology known as silicon micromachining. Their friendship began at the conference and they recognized their common interests and business outlook. At the time, Amanda was a product development manager with General Controls (GC), a well-known and established electrical controls company; Dan was "Chief Technology Evangelist" of

Ameritrol, an electronics company that catered to OEM applications of electronic control modules; and Tom, a financial professional, was enjoying six months of sanity-checking vacation enabled by financial gains from the acquisition, by a large conglomerate, of a small start-up company where he had been one of the first employees. Amanda and Dan were anxious to move ahead, with little patience for the "bureaucracy" of their current employers, and Tom was interested in his next business-building opportunity. They made a natural team.

Silicon micromachining is an extension of the technology that makes integrated circuits, extended to three dimensions. This process is used to manufacture many types of microstructures, referred to in the industry as micromachined electromechanical systems—MEMS.[2]

Within four months, the TDA team (Tom, Dan and Amanda –TaDa!), as they called themselves, had relocated to Silicon Valley to begin the ground roots development of their new start-up, SENSACON Corporation. They believed that each member of the team brought a needed expertise to the venture. Tom, with his experience with some of the financial aspects of start-up

---

[1] This case study is a compilation of the experiences of several companies as they progress through organization and product life cycles. Simplifications have been made for academic clarity, and care has been taken to prevent any direct relationship with any single market participant. Much of this case has been used as a continuous example through the text. Portions have been repeated and/or edited here. Students can find additional discussions and issues in Chapters 8, 11, 13, and 15.

[2] Microelectromechanical systems (MEMS) (also written as micro-electro-mechanical, or MicroElectroMechanical) is the technology of the very small, and merges at the nano-scale into nanoelectromechanical systems (NEMS) and nano-technology. MEMS are also referred to as micromachines (in Japan), or Micro Systems Technology—MST (in Europe). MEMS are separate and distinct from the hypothetical vision of molecular nanotechnology or molecular electronics. MEMS are made up of components between 1 and 100 micrometers in size (i.e., 0.001–0.1 mm) and MEMS devices generally range in size from 20 micrometers (20 millionths of a meter) to a millimeter. They usually consist of a central unit that processes data, the microprocessor and several components that interact with the outside such as microsensors. At these size scales, the standard constructs of classical physics do not always hold true. Due to MEMS' large surface area to volume ratio, surface effects such as electrostatics and wetting dominate volume effects such as inertia or thermal mass. See also Jean-Baptiste Waldner (2008), *Nanocomputers and Swarm Intelligence* (London: ISTE John Wiley & Sons), p. 205, ISBN 1847040020.

companies, became CEO/CFO of the new company. Dan was the technologist—his doctorate in microelectronics and his custom design experience led to his position as Chief Technology Officer (CTO), and Amanda became the Chief Product and Production Development Officer (CPPO). Suitable staff were hired to create a functional organization.

Branding and Positioning the New Company

Shortly after becoming established, it became apparent to the TDA team that the company competency was in the application of very precise micromachining technology to critical measurement applications. However, large customers were not likely to trust this capability without some tangible evidence. While they were fortunate enough to have attracted early funding, they knew that they would not be able to take on existing large players in the silicon electronics market. TDA elected to carve out their niche as the leading-edge technology leader in silicon micromachining. The goal was in place—how could this be carried out? How does a company without any current customers, products, or volume manufacturing capability convince the market that it has special expertise?

TDA soon recognized that they had little expertise in the communication area. They hired a marketing and public relations consultant to assess the competitive environment and recommend a positioning strategy for the company. At the same time this was to happen, Tom would work to strengthen the financial support for the new organization while Dan would focus on leading-edge sensor technology. Amanda would put together the capability to make "more than one of" any new products.

The new marketing consultant provided his recommendations to TDA. Basically, the TDA team learned that strong brands take time to build unless special circumstances prevail. A start-up or young company without a brand

reputation has little opportunity to become successful in markets dominated by others—SENSACON would always be playing by someone else's rules. Without special circumstances, the company must expend considerable effort to build a strong reputation. In established markets in which young companies compete against companies with strong brands, young companies are at a disadvantage because they have no brand recognition or reputation. In other markets, principally early markets in which there are no established competitors, a young company can build market ownership and brand reputation quickly. Consequently, from an early point in time, the young company needs to think about whether and how it should build its brand. In general, unless a company is going to be a low-cost, low-price supplier, a strong brand reputation will translate into competitive advantage. This fits well with the goal of becoming known as the technology leader in the market—but not large markets in head-to-head competition with established firms.

Following the recommendations of the consultant, the TDA team and a select set of technical employees were supported in active membership in all related professional societies. This support included both financial incentives and time commitments; the active membership became part of the job description for these individuals. Soon, SENSACON representatives were chairing technical committees and conferences. This was only the start. Technical papers were written for presentation at conferences focusing on SENSACON technology and its potential in the marketplace. Hypothetical examples of high-volume applications of the technology were demonstrated at associated trade shows. A delicate balance was necessary between revealing proprietary information and presenting technically enlightening information. Through the relationships of the PR consultant, SENSACON was able to get mentioned as an up-and-coming organization by editors of trade journals and magazines.

Technical papers authored by SENSACON employees were accepted for publication in peer-reviewed professional journals. As momentum developed, SENSACON experts were asked to contribute signed articles about pressure sensor developments to trade journals in that market segment. In reprint form, the signed articles were used as leave-behind sales support items. After approximately two years, SENSACON was the technology icon in the pressure sensor industry.

The Business Development Strategy

SENSACON engineers and developers spent these two years developing new products in collaboration with customers. To support the business needs of the firm, management focused on low-volume but technically complex markets. In these markets, SENSACON could prove the technology without investing in high-volume manufacturing. Initially, the market was comprised primarily of visionaries; typical applications were in self-contained underwater breathing apparatus (SCUBA) equipment and healthcare devices. Both market segments were ideal targets for SENSACON as market demand and SENSACON manufacturing capabilities (high variable costs, no economies of scale, quality, and accuracy of greater value that low cost) were well matched.

In the product development stage and the introductory stage of the product life cycle, the SENSACON staff of technology-savvy "customer engineers" worked closely with customers. The creation of the pressure sensor was dominated by the specific customer needs of the visionary market. Product changes were mostly incremental, as the customers in this market segment were interested in the performance of the sensor and were willing to design their products to accommodate the SENSACON product. The customers' low-volume products provided an excellent proving ground for the SENSACON technology.

Customers acquiesced to time delays and initial delivery problems; investors anxious to see positive cash flow at SENSACON expressed the only sense of urgency.

SENSACON Corporation had successfully developed a growing market for the micromachined pressure sensor and began to deliver on the profitability promises that management made to investors. By avoiding large-scale manufacturing, fixed costs were kept relatively low throughout the introductory period. Sensors were etched and assembled without much automation. The labor force was increased or reduced as needed through the use of an agency that provided skilled temporary assembly workers. Users of the sensors were technology-oriented themselves, and volumes were such that the inconsistencies that resulted from hand assembly could be adjusted in the users' operations. SENSACON's production volume developed to approximately 5,000 units per month as the sensors became widely accepted in SCUBA diving equipment used to measure pressure underwater and in medical devices used to measure blood pressure. Additional high-value customers in chemical process control and environmental monitoring developed confidence in the product.

New Market Development

The marketing and PR consultant retained by the TDA team advised them that SENSACON business was growing to the point where they should invest in a strong internal marketing organization. SENSACON must develop markets to avoid becoming a one-product company. A business development effort that will reach the first pragmatist market segment that can serve as a beachhead for crossing the chasm would soon be necessary, and shortly after that, a market development effort to translate those business successes to other segments would be required. As SENSACON becomes comfortable with the capabilities of its offering, so will potential users.

Shortly after receiving the consultant's advice, SENSACON began development of a missionary sales effort to reach out to new customers where the success of SENSACON technology could be translated to new business. At about this time, vehicle rollover problems, mostly attributed to Firestone tires on Ford Sport Utility Vehicles, were major headlines. The battle between the two corporate giants, long regarded as inseparable, was creating waves throughout the industry. Among those waves was an inquiry by the Department of Transportation. Regardless of whether the tires or the vehicles or the owners were eventually determined to be at fault (or a combination of factors), industry pundits were asking for a system to warn the (maintenance inattentive) driver of low tire pressure. Manufacturers of SUVs had to find sources with the capabilities to solve the tire pressure monitor problem. These capabilities had to be not only in technology, but also in the ability to support the SUV unit volume requirements and to work with the culture of a mass production-oriented customer—not something for which high-technology companies are known. SUV manufacturers had to believe that SENSACON was capable of meeting the standard.

Among other factors, SENSACON management used publicity and corporate positioning to establish its positioning in the market. SENSACON pitched its technology to SUV manufacturers demonstrating that the technology satisfied the need of a low tire pressure warning to the vehicle driver. SENSACON, along with other companies who proposed solutions to the pressure monitoring problem, had to go through a series of demonstrations and trials to prove the effectiveness of the product design. SENSACON had found its "beachhead" pragmatist segment. The TDA team believed that once the manufacturing and quality problems associated with manufacturing in quantity were addressed, SENSACON could realize rapid increases in sales, as did the other competing manufacturers.

The SENSACON breakthrough came when the sensor was selected for use in an automatic tire pressure monitor. Two vehicle manufacturers specified systems for all of the SUVs they produced. The combined volume of the two companies was forecast to reach over three million vehicles. With four sensors on each vehicle, the sensor volume would be over 12 million units. SENSACON had been selected to supply approximately 50 percent of this volume. The remaining volume was divided up among three competitors. SENSACON *monthly* sales volume at the start of tire monitor production would exceed the most recent *annual* volumes experienced by the company and was expected to reach an annual rate of approximately six million units. Initial shipments were to begin in four months. SENSACON employees and investors were ecstatic.

To be sure, the SUV manufacturers did not select SENSACON automatically. Competitors were entering the sensor market as the potential profitability was a very attractive lure. SENSACON executives were aggressive in the price to the SUV manufacturers as they wanted to establish a leadership position in this new market segment. Recognizing the newly arrived competition, SENSACON had started development of the next-generation offering, SensorSUV. The aggressive price to the manufacturers did not concern SENSACON as it was believed that the experience curve combined with economies of scale in manufacturing would create the necessary low-cost position to enable profits at the aggressive price.

One of Many Changes

Tom, Dan, and Amanda remembered a joint meeting that had taken place about four years ago in the middle of the decision making process for the large automotive customer. They were discussing the company's major turning point. They were at the chasm. Several corporate and personal upheavals were on the horizon. The TDA team had just left the first meeting of a task force created to solve a major problem.

About three days after the new business was announced, manufacturing management attempted to scale up production of the existing sensor. In anticipation of a production tryout, additional space had been leased and temporary workers were added to the regular workforce. Unfortunately, even with added automated etching, manufacturing and machining for the brass enclosure, and increased facilities and labor, the tryout could not meet anywhere near the volumes hoped for. In addition, the part-to-part variability of the sensors was outside of the SUV manufacturers' specification. While SEN-SACON technology was up to the challenge, manufacturing was not. This was among the issues addressed by the task force of key SENSACON personnel.

It soon became obvious that the sensor would have to undergo a complete redesign to enable high-volume manufacturing. The necessary changes in the sensor included redesign of the sensor itself for automated handling and insertion into the enclosure; redesign of the enclosure and investigation of new materials, like plastics, to replace the brass enclosure; new manufacturing expertise in high-volume plastic molding and assembly; and new high-volume, production-capable sealing techniques to protect the sensor core from the harsh vehicle environment.

The TDA team discussed strategy to solve this new set of problems. They recognized that both a long-term and a short-term strategy were necessary to satisfy immediate customer needs and develop the organization to handle such situations in a more routine fashion.

SENSACON management began the search for a qualified independent contract manufacturer. Hoping to eventually develop its own capabilities later in the contract period, immediate time pressures from customers did not allow SENSACON the luxury of developing its own high-volume manufacturing facility.

Concurrent with the revelation that a significant product redesign was necessary, SENSACON was overwhelmed with inquiries from its new customers. Contract and procurement provisions, supply chain requirements, as well as a significantly more complex and larger buying center had exceeded SENSACON organizational capabilities. The staff that served a small number of healthcare and SCUBA equipment manufacturers was unable to serve the new customer base.

Manufacturing development, significant product redesign for volume manufacturing, and support for significantly larger and more complex customer buying centers became necessities of the transition. The small staff that had been successful in creating value for technophiles and visionaries—moving R&D invention to market innovation—was overwhelmed by the volume of new customer inquiries and application requirements. Additional marketing resources were added to interface with customer demands in all phases—supply chain organization and development, customer education in the proper application of the sensor, and so on—all required development and coordination. SENSACON needed to learn a new way of doing business.

Partners with Different Goals

SENSACON was going to get big—bureaucratic, diverse, decentralized. The impact of the new business would impact not only manufacturing and product design but also the culture of SENSACON. Once a small specialty product company, SENSACON now had to redesign itself organizationally. Crossing into the growth stage can be traumatic.

Tom, Dan, and Amanda were not in agreement on the possible solutions to the problems. Tom was interested in moving on to his next entrepreneurial effort, and Dan wanted to pursue the next generation of micro-machining technology. Only Amanda and the SENSACON marketing team were excited by the new direction. TDA recognized that at least the "T" of their team was likely to move on.

"Under New Management"

Two years ago, while SENSACON made the transition to the growth stage of the PLC, senior management made many changes. While Tom remained a director of the company, a search firm was hired to find a new CEO with high-volume business experience. Eventually, Allen Chen, formerly with Motorola, a large automotive electronics supplier, became CEO of SENSACON. Concurrently, the process began to make the customer relationship routine and to establish SENSACON as the standard in its market. A decentralized management approach was required.

Innovating the Need—Not the Technology

One of Allen Chen's first initiatives was to shift SENSACON from a technology-driven company to a market-driven company. Allen recognized that as SensorSUV matured and became known throughout the customer base, less application development would be necessary on the part of SENSACON. However, users of SensorSUV would begin to look to the next generation of *their* product and how it could be enhanced. This enhancement could lead to a need for a next-generation sensor. This next-generation product, if it was to be truly new, might require new technology, style, and materials and/or would have different performance requirements. By serving the need and not the product, the SensorSUV brand could become known as a solution rather than a component part.

Allen also realized that as long as SENSACON was known as a technology company, technology innovation would be necessary, though not sufficient, for success. The argument that SENSACON was focused on high technology was a dangerous position. If the customer believed that he or she was "just buying parts" rather than "specifying a solution" the business would be vulnerable to a "me-too" organization that could focus on manufacturing efficiencies, distribution economies, and alternative cost (read "lower") positions with purchasing departments.

Allen wanted SensorSUV to be a standard in the industry. Through the development process with customer engineering staffs, customer laboratories as well as an independent investigatory body selected by the customer verified the performance of SensorSUV. Based on samples performance data supplied by SENSACON, the customer's laboratories developed a standard, based on the accepted performance of the sensors as previously approved. Once this standard specification was completed and accepted, copycat products would be required to meet it. This standard is "owned" by the first manufacturer—SENSACON. Any "me-too" manufacturer will always be faced with the question, "Does your sensor do everything that SensorSUV does?"

New Channels

Allen also immediately expanded the field market development team and approached the SUV manufacturers with application designs for all vehicles, not just SUVs, and also approached other vehicle manufacturers. The process began of translating this new business success to additional opportunities. Customers were soon found that were interested in the development of hand-held tire pressure sensors for car owners and heavy-duty models for tire shops.

SENSACON would soon find it necessary to develop a new marketing channel for the product as dealers and tire repair shops adapted to the new vehicle feature and needed service and replacement parts—and the training to use them.

Translation to the automotive aftermarket to reach vehicle owners that wanted to upgrade older vehicles was also anticipated.

An additional channel was to be developed—another level of decentralization. Eventually, the SENSACON total offering included the training and deployment of service personnel at the consumer level. As competition entered the aftermarket, a consumer positioning effort was deployed to attract customers to the "real" tire pressure system. Though the core product did not change (other than those changes that made it possible to mass-produce it), the marketing organization, at each transition through the adopter categories, evolved to meet different customer needs and opportunities.

Allen Chen's Challenge to His Staff

SENSACON has invested in new technology to create the next-generation sensor. The new technology gives SensorSUV a faster response time and greater resistance to shock and vibration, both features in which the market has expressed interest. This new distinction is primarily the result of the incorporation of a new component into SensorSUV. While the technology of the component is not, by itself, new, it is the first time it has been used in the sensor market and SENSACON has modified the component somewhat. The challenge: Should SENSACON manufacture this "new" component itself or purchase it from an outside source?

Defending the Market Position

SensorSUV is a profitable item, thus there will be imitators, either copycats trying to be the low-cost producer or modifiers trying to slightly move the technology envelope—at least enough to meet all the properties of SensorSUV while enhancing their own product's attractiveness. Allen's next challenge to his staff is, "What are your ideas on how to defend our brand and grow the company significantly and what future challenges face SENSACON?" These questions were new challenges for the company, but not unfamiliar for companies who had moved through the TALC.

INDEX